Praise for *Dubrovnik*

'Detailed, scholarly and eminently readable, *Dubrovnik* is a triumph of book production. This is a splendid volume.' *Literary Review*

'There are few introductions to the city's past available to general readers ... Harris's splendid study meets this need admirably.' *TLS*

'Learned, fluently written and lavishly illustrated.' *The Sunday Telegraph*

'A fascinating and scholarly account ... a learned and well-written labour of love.' *The Daily Telegraph*

'Harris tells the whole story more faithfully than any previous English historian has done. A triumph, indeed, to set beside those of the great journalists.' Michael Foot, *Tribune*

'Harris offers up an intense look at a curious world. Truly fascinating.' *Good Book Guide*

'Unravelling the complex history of Dubrovnik takes skills of a high order, and Robin Harris has these.' Professor Norman Stone

'Splendid ... the book about Dubrovnik we have all been waiting for.' Dr Noel Malcolm

'Robin Harris has written a splendid and discerning history of Croatia's Adriatic pearl.' Professor Ivo Banac, Yale University

Territory of the Ragusan Republic

ROBIN HARRIS

DUBROVNIK

A HISTORY

SAQI

British Library Cataloguing-in-Publication Data
A catalogue record for this book is available from the British Library

ISBN 0-86356-959-5
EAN 9-780863-569593

First published in hardback in 2003 by Saqi Books, London
This edition published in 2006

SAQI
26 Westbourne Grove
London W2 5RH
www.saqibooks.com

Contents

Illustrations

Acknowledgments

The history of the Ragusan Republic can be told in considerable detail because it is so well documented in the Dubrovnik Archives, which contain some 7,000 volumes of documents and about 100,000 *separata*. As the eighteenth-century French consul there, André-Alexandre Le Maire, noted with pardonable exaggeration: 'The archives of the town are perhaps those of all Europe which are the best conserved and which go back furthest.'[1]

Indeed, so extensive is the information that they contain that those archives also provide insights into the history of other states – such as medieval Serbia – whose traces would otherwise be largely lacking.

In the preparation of this study I made only limited direct use of that manuscript material. Many of the key documents have already been published in the series listed in the bibliography. Those manuscript documents to which reference is made in the text were chosen mainly for illustrative purposes or to elaborate in more detail a point contained in secondary sources. In any case, what this book seeks to do is something different from the various excellent monographs on which it draws. Its purpose is to bring together the conclusions of the best available scholarship, most of which are inaccessible to those unable to read Serbian or Croatian, and then to provide a clear, critical and readable synthesis. The reader must judge for himself whether that has actually been accomplished.

To the extent that it has, much of the credit should go a number of individuals and institutions without whose help the task would have proved quite impossible. In London I benefited from the resources of the British Library and the Library of the School of Slavonic and East European Studies. In Zagreb I was helped by the staff of the spanking new National and University Library (*Nacionalna i sveučilišna knjižnica*). In Dubrovnik I received invaluable advice and assistance both at the State Archives (*Državni arhiv*) from its (now former) director Ivan Mustać, from Ante Šoljić, from Ivana Lazarević and from their colleagues. At the Dubrovnik Institute for Historical Science of the Croatian Academy of Arts and

Sciences (*Zavod za povijesne znanosti hrvatske akademije znanosti i umjetnosti*), I was offered advice and assistance by the director Nenad Vekarić and his colleague Stjepan Ćosić. Pater Mijo Horvat allowed me to consult the work of Crijević (Cerva) in the Dominican friary's library – the latter's must, dust and bullet-indented shutters reminding the researcher of things old and new. Fra Marijo Šikić made available the work of Matijašević (Mattei) stored in the Franciscans' library – still disabled by damage incurred during the fighting a decade ago.

My time in Dubrovnik was made infinitely more agreeable by the generous hospitality of Andrija Kojaković and of Marija Kojaković and by the kindness of many others. I also benefited from discussions with Pave Brailo, Slavica Stojan and the director of the City Museum, Mišo Đuraš, who helped me obtain material for illustrations used in this book. (Others appear thanks to the co-operation of the State Archives.)

Perhaps the single greatest difficulty in writing such a book as this in the time available after (quite unconnectedly) trying to earn a living is that, no matter how fascinating the subject matter, one can risk losing heart. Among those who ensured by their interest that this did not happen I would mention Ivo Banac, Jadranka Beresford-Peirse, Chris Cviić, Miroslav Kovačić, Norman Stone and Mike Shaw. And Nile Gardiner generously gave of his time in preparing the final text.

Two people, though, had a special role. Branko Franolić enthused, advised and guided me along the way: without him I would not have reached my goal. I am also enormously grateful to Noel Malcolm who read the manuscript, offered many helpful suggestions and provided – as he does for all those writing on these subjects – a gold standard against which to measure achievement.

Finally, I am delighted to acknowledge the help of the Croatian Ministry of Culture; INA; The Lukšić Group and Karlovačka pivovara; and Vartex Textiles Ltd. in ensuring that this book appears in such good shape.

A Note on Names

Both personal and place names in Dubrovnik and elsewhere in Southeast Europe are subject to many variants reflecting political change and cultural mixture. The great families of Dubrovnik had both Italian and Croatian variants of their names. Scholars have chosen one or the other form or even the Latin version that most often appears in official documents. All these options are equally valid, and none is absolutely so. I have used the Slavic form throughout, simply because that is the one most commonly found in the historiography.[1] No other significance is implied. The most important Italian/Slavic alternatives are as follows:[2]

Basilio – Basiljević
Bobali – Bobaljević
Bona – Bunić
Bonda, Bionda – Bundić
Bucchia – Buća
Caboga – Kaboga, Kabužić
Cerva – Crijević
Ghetaldi – Getaldić
Giorgi – Đordić, Đurđević
Gondola – Gundulić
Gozze – Gučetić
Gradi – Gradić
Luccari – Lukarević
Menze – Menčetić
Palmotta – Palmotić
Pozza – Pucić
Ragnina – Ranjina
Resti – Rastić, Restić
Sorgo – Sorkočević
Stay – Stojković
Zamagna – Zamanja, Zamanjić

For Christian names I have tried to use the appropriate Dubrovnik variant, e.g. Frano (Francis) rather than Frane (as in Split) or Franjo (as in the North).

Place names are generally given in their modern form – thus, for example, Durrës, not Durazzo (Slavic: Drač). I use, however, Constantinople rather than Istanbul, Adrianople rather than Edirne and Salonika rather than Solun, because to do otherwise – however strictly logical – smacks of anachronism. In other cases – as with Duklja, Zeta, Montenegro – the name alters in line with what is known of current usage. Throughout the book I use Ragusa and (more frequently) Dubrovnik alternately and without distinction, since both names are equally applicable to the settlement/town/city/community/state/ Republic which is the object of this study. But there being no elegant English equivalent of *Dubrovčani*, I describe the inhabitants as 'Ragusans' (though naturally only until 1808). Similarly, I use *Konavljani* for the inhabitants of Konavle, *Kotorani* for the inhabitants of Kotor and *Pelješčani* for those who dwelt on the Pelješac peninsula.

Otherwise, my aim has been accuracy without pedantry. Thus I have used English equivalents or spellings of the names of rulers. I have generally, though not without exception, used Slavic equivalents of Turkish terms applying to the Balkans, e.g. *harač* for the tribute paid to the Sultan.

Finally, where it was necessary to insert a Croatian noun in its plural form in the text I have generally (as in English) added an 's' – thus *knez*s not *knezovi*: such a solution seemed preferable on the grounds that this is a book written, in the first instance at least, for English-speaking readers.

A Note on Pronunciation

Croatian and Serbian are spoken very much as they are written, and each letter is pronounced. But English speakers should note the following:

c – is pronounced *ts* as in 'its'
č – is pronounced *ch* as in 'chatter'
ć – is pronounced similarly, but more like *ty* as in 'future'
đ – is pronounced *j*, but harder (as in 'D'ye ken John Peel?')
h – is pronounced *ch* as in 'loch'
j – is pronounced *y* as in 'yet'
š – is pronounced *sh* as in 'shape'
ž – is pronounced *s* as in 'pleasure'.

A Note on Citations

Yugoslav historiography developed something of an obsession with numbering of series and sub-series: I have sought to simplify these a little, and so only the main series numbers are given. With a few exceptions – notably Serbian, Yugoslav and Croatian 'national' publishers' major series and some American university publishers – the names of publishers are not generally noted, only places and dates of publication.

The following abbreviations have been used throughout:

Anali – *Anali zavoda za povijesne znanosti hrvatske akademije znanosti i umjetnosti u Dubrovniku* (and other earlier equivalents).
DAD – *Državni arhiv Dubrovnika* (i.e. the Dubrovnik State Archives).
Dubrovnik – *Dubrovnik, časopis za književnost i znanost* (publisher: *Matica hrvatska*, Dubrovnik).
HAZU – *Hrvatska akademija znanosti i umjetnosti.*
JAZU – *Jugoslavenska akademija znanosti i umjetnosti.*
PSHK – *Pet stoljeća hrvatske književnosti* (publisher: *Matica hrvatska*, Zagreb).
Rad – *Rad JAZU, filologički-historički i filosofički razredi.*
SAN – *Srpska akademija nauke.*
SKA – *Srpska kraljevska akademija.*
SPH – *Stari pisci hrvatski* (publisher: JAZU, Zagreb).

Subject to these qualifications, the first mention of any work in a reference contains the full title. If there is reference to only one work by an author, subsequent references are made by means of the *op. cit.* formula. If there are several such works, a shortened version of the title is given. Cyrillic titles are transliterated into Roman. Translations into English are my own, unless otherwise stated.

Preface

'I can't bear Dubrovnik... I find it a unique experiment on the part of the Slav, unique in its nature and unique in its success, and I do not like it. It reminds me of the worst of England.'[1]

Rebecca West's prejudice against Dubrovnik – unlike some of her other prejudices – has, thankfully, not rubbed off on her fellow countrymen. Until the 1991–1992 crisis the British, like thousands of other foreign visitors, flocked each year to the city. At the time of writing, with what I later optimistically but confidently term 'The Last Siege' a quite distant memory, the visitors are back again. Unfortunately neither they, nor the general reader, nor indeed scholars, as yet have access to a modern, well-sourced and readable account in English of the history of the Ragusan Republic whose cultural traces all but Dame Rebecca regard with fascination. It has been my aim to fill that gap.[2]

Dubrovnik's history is, in any case, less well appreciated than it deserves. One partial explanation for this was given in 1766 by Le Maire, a distinctly unsympathetic observer:

> The little Republic of Ragusa is rather little known. It has experienced, like other states, the alternatives of good and bad fortune; but since its most brilliant periods have never permitted it to play a certain role among the other nations, it has not sufficiently excited the curiosity of historians or politicians to obtain a distinguished place in the annals of the world.[3]

There is, however, another perspective on Dubrovnik's past, as expressed by that enthusiastic Ragusophile Italian Francesco Maria Appendini, who wrote, in 1802, in his episodic literary history:

> A long series of wars, of feats of arms, of leagues, of treaties and of other striking events – this is what is usually required to arouse the enthusiasm of the historian and to charm the reader. But a history that instead of presenting scenes of desolation and horror embraces the acts of a nation which not by force, that easy resource of great empires, but rather by the most subtle policy, has known how to maintain its freedom over many centuries despite the most dangerous circumstances – such a history can be all the more interesting for both writer and reader in that it more fully displays the admirable powers of the human spirit. Such is the history of the Republic of Ragusa.[4]

In actual fact, neither Le Maire nor Appendini fully appreciated Dubrovnik's historical significance. Ragusa was, of course tiny. But it had a recognisable social, economic, religious, cultural and political identity over some six centuries.[5] That in itself makes the story of the place distinctive. In its heyday, moreover, the Republic had an impact far beyond that which its size or power would have normally warranted. This importance stemmed from Dubrovnik's strategic significance at the intersection between the Mediterranean basin and the Balkans, between Christendom and Islam, and between West and East. It reflected the little Republic's maritime prowess and great commercial wealth. It was magnified by the Ragusans' sophisticated and astute international diplomacy. Finally, it was manifested in a rich cultural achievement of unique value for Croatia, for the wider Slavic world and – at times – for Europe as a whole.

ONE

Ragusan Roots and Riddles: The Origins of Ragusa/Dubrovnik

Natural Advantages

The precise circumstances of Ragusa/Dubrovnik's foundation will, it seems safe to predict, continue to be the subject of almost disproportionate scholarly debate involving not just distinguished historians but eminent archeologists and linguists. The subject has always had a burning importance, not least for the inhabitants of Dubrovnik itself who, over the centuries and uninhibited by excessive scruple, devised a number of reassuring myths to reinforce their ancient but tiny city-state's legitimacy.

Why, though, might the first inhabitants have chosen to settle in Dubrovnik? After all, the whole Dalmatian coastal stretch enjoys the benefits of a typical Mediterranean climate, conducive to the cultivation of olives, vines and citrus fruit. There are long months of productive fishing, though mariners have always feared the destructive violence of the cold northeast wind – the *bura.* Unlike the western (Italian) coast of the Adriatic, the eastern (Dalmatian) is endowed with sheltered bays and harbours, while the mountains, though they make access inland more difficult, offer valuable navigation points. Unlike the people of the hinterland, those who live along the Dalmatian coastal strip have always enjoyed easy communications with each other's settlements and manageable ones with the rest of the Mediterranean world. Whereas inland the rugged mountains and thick forests marked off one rural community from another and induced a certain isolationism and backwardness that would come to be synonymous with the term 'Balkan', the Dalmatian communities were more open and sophisticated. They were also richer. And from this point of view the mountains, which hindered access to the less civilised hinterland, had an added benefit: they constituted a useful barrier against at least casual raiders from the interior, lured by the prospect of easy pickings along the more developed coast.

Dubrovnik, however, had particular natural and other advantages which marked it out from the rest of coastal Dalmatia. Most important from the very beginning must have been its harbour. This faced southeast, and so escaped the unwelcome force of the *bura*. But the harbour was also sheltered in large measure from the southeast wind (known locally as *šilok*) by the island of Lokrum, which acted too as a kind of breakwater against the incoming swell. Similarly, while the southwest wind (or *lebić*) often sent waves thundering against the western part of the town, the cliffs and, later, walls of Dubrovnik afforded good protection for ships riding in the harbour. In Greek, Roman and early medieval times – before the invention of rudders and primitive compasses – ships travelled whenever possible during spring and summer and, unless in the direst emergency, during the hours of daylight. Along the eastern Adriatic coast in these seasons the prevailing wind was the northwesterly *maestral* which would usually blow quite steadily from mid-morning till sunset. For ships using sail and oars to make their way up the coast, for example from the Greek settlement of Budva to that on Korčula, Dubrovnik would have served as an ideal, secure haven – all the more so since in ancient times it was usual to pull ships ashore, and Dubrovnik's harbour had (in those days) to the west a sandy bank against which to do so. A further benefit was that in these early times there were sources of drinkable water to the east of the harbour: many centuries later, as the sea level rose and the land sank, the water in these wells became brackish and other water had, particularly in summer, to be brought by ships from the springs of Mlini some four nautical miles down the coast.[1]

Dubrovnik had other benefits as well. It is the only one of the Dalmatian towns that looks straight out onto the Adriatic. This enabled those within to gain early warning of approaching danger.[2] Moreover, while Dubrovnik's harbour offered by far the best protection, there were also more or less satisfactory alternatives for ships unable to reach it by nightfall or because of adverse conditions. Thus for ships seeking shelter along the coast there were the possibilities offered by the bay of Župa, the bay of Zaton and the Channel of Koločep, which lies between the 'Elaphite Islands', as the older Pliny termed them (that is Šipan, Lopud and Koločep), and the shore. There was also, at a pinch, the nearby inlet of Rijeka Dubrovačka, though it was unpleasantly open to both *bura* and *maestral*.

The mouth of the Neretva river, further up the coast, provided another haven. But above all, it was from the earliest times – when travel by boat was so much swifter and easier than travel overland – the easiest access point to the interior and had indeed been the site of the flourishing Roman trading centre of Narona (Vid, near modern Metković). Not surprisingly, once Dubrovnik began to develop as a trading centre, the Neretva estuary quickly fell under Ragusan influence.[3]

Situated towards the southeastern end of the Adriatic, with prevailing winds and currents operating in its favour, Dubrovnik must from the earliest times have enjoyed a modest coastal trade with its Dalmatian neighbours. But once the size of its ships and the experience of its mariners grew, it was also well-situated to exploit the valuable East-West link with Italy – Ancona (which became for many Ragusans a home from home, and where a Ragusan colony flourished up until the nineteenth century) and the grain-rich lands of Apulia.[4] Looking further ahead, however, it was Dubrovnik's development of the Balkan trade which, in association with its commercial fleet, would be the basis of the Republic's economic success: so the fact of the town's proximity to ancient roads into the hinterland, via Župa and Konavle to the southeast and Slano to the northwest, should also be mentioned when listing Dubrovnik's natural advantages. These were the routes by which the Ragusans would exploit the mineral wealth of Serbia and Bosnia. And later it would be by way of the *dubrovački drum* – the famous Dubrovnik Road – that the Ragusans would establish their fraught but fruitful relationship with the Ottoman Empire.

But this, of course, is to anticipate by many centuries. What sort of people were the inhabitants of Dalmatia from among whom, in uncertain combinations, under obscure circumstances and with a contentious chronology, the little settlement at Ragusa would emerge?

Ragusan Prehistory – Epidaurum

The Eastern Adriatic was already populated at the start of Neolithic times, and the near surrounds of Dubrovnik – and perhaps the cliff site of Ragusa itself – were inhabited in the Bronze and Iron Ages.[5] But the precise movements or even identity of the peoples who populated Dalmatia in these early times are extremely obscure. The Illyrians are regarded as the oldest historically established people in the region, but who they really were – and what ultimately happened to them – is less clear.[6] One tribe called the 'Histri' occupied what is modern Istria, to which they gave their name. A second tribe called the 'Liburni', who may or may not have been ethnically Illyrian, lived along the Croatian littoral as far as the River Krka. A third tribe, the 'Delmati', who gave their name to Dalmatia, inhabited the Dalmatian coast as far as the River Cetina and inland to the territories (in what is modern Bosnia) of Livanjsko Polje, Duvanjsko Polje and Glamočko Polje.[7]

The Celts appeared in the Balkans in the fourth century BC and lived with or integrated among the Illyrian population they found. But the earlier (fifth/sixth century) Greek colonisation of much of the eastern Adriatic left a more abiding impression. Under the leadership and protection of the city of Syracuse, there grew up the Dorian colony of Issa on the island of Vis, which itself spawned other Greek towns on the neighbouring islands and coastal region.

Interestingly, in view of so much subsequent myth-making down the centuries, and in spite of its sharing a name with a famous classical Greek city, it is clear that Dalmatian Epidaurum – later known as *Ragusa Vecchia* ('Old Ragusa'), the modern Cavtat situated some miles down the coast from modern Dubrovnik – was not a Greek settlement.[8] In fact, Epidaurum does not even figure in accounts of those Roman-Illyrian Wars which convulsed the region beginning in 230–229, continuing in 220–219 and 167 BC and only coming to a bloody close with a Roman victory in 9 AD.[9] From then on, Dalmatia was subject to strong social, cultural and political influence from Rome, which would have decisive consequences for its future. In particular, the new rulers settled colonists and built up towns as centres for them. Epidaurum was one of these centres.

The place is first mentioned in 47 BC, when Pompey's legate, Marcus Octavius, attacked it because it was held by a garrison loyal to Caesar. Epidaurum was besieged by land and sea but got word to Caesar, who sent an army to relieve it. Marcus Octavius's fleet and army, however, withdrew before the relief force arrived.[10] Epidaurum was described as a 'colony' by Pliny the Elder (who died in 79), but when it formally became one is unknown. Probably, it received that designation at the same time as Narona and Salona (modern Solin, a suburb of Split) under Augustus.[11] The name 'Epidaurum' deserves some explanation, because the – false – assumption that it was Greek had such a strong bearing on the myths subsequently attached to it and to Dubrovnik.[12] It seems, in fact, to be a Latinised Illyrian expression, perhaps meaning 'behind the forest'. The place was probably first established as an Illyrian fishing village, or perhaps as a fortified place useful for pirates, and then was seized and developed by the resourceful Romans for their own purposes.

In any case, it quickly became an important stop on the Roman road which stretched north to Narona, Salona, Jadera (Zadar), Senia (Senj), Tergeste (Trieste) and finally Rome itself. To the south the road led to Resinium (Risan), Butua (Budva), Ulcinium (Ulcinj) and through modern Albania to Solun (Thessalonika). The link with Narona, which flourished mightily at this time, was particularly important.[13] Of Epidaurum's buildings and monuments hardly anything survives: a few inscriptions are the most important remaining evidence of the life once lived there.[14] For centuries, though, there remained other, more impressive visible reminders. The Ragusan historian and man of letters Junije Rastić (Giunio Resti), writing in the early eighteenth century, noted that the magnificence of ancient Epidaurum could be judged by the evidence of twenty miles of ruined aqueduct – some underground, some spanning arches – on which could be read Latin inscriptions. The aqueduct, as he rightly observed, gave its name to the district of Konavle (from *canales*). He also remarked on the number of vases and medals, and on the tomb of a certain Dolabella, a Roman pro-consul.[15]

In fact, given reasonably settled political conditions, Epidaurum was naturally well situated to thrive. It was built on a peninsula, protected from the elements by the three little islands of Mrkan, Bobara and Supetar, and on the land-side from attack by the walls and fortifications of Spilan. It boasted two small, sheltered harbours, one on each side of the peninsula, allowing ships to moor in whichever gave better protection against the wind that happened to be blowing.[16]

The Destruction of Epidaurum

There are two historical conundrums bearing on the origins of Dubrovnik, neither of which can be definitively solved. The first relates to the circumstances of Epidaurum's destruction, the second to the relationship between Epidaurum and Ragusa. Fortunately, the most appropriate starting point for consideration of both is a well-known passage in the Emperor Constantine Porphyrogenitus's *De Administrando Imperio* – a kind of manual on statesmanship drawn up, on the basis of extensive documentation, for the benefit of his son – which remains the single best source available to historians seeking answers to the Ragusan riddle. It runs:

> The city of Ragusa is not called Ragusa in the tongue of the Romans, but, because it stands on cliffs, it is called in Roman speech 'the cliff, lau'; whence they are called 'Lausaioi', i.e. 'those who have their seat on the cliff'. But vulgar usage, which frequently corrupts names by altering their letters, has changed the denomination and called them Rausaioi. These same Rausaioi used of old to possess the city that is called Pitauru; and since, when the other cities were captured by the Slavs that were in the province, this city too was captured, and some were slaughtered and others taken prisoner, those who were able to escape and reach safety settled in the almost precipitous spot where the city now is; they built it small to begin with, and afterwards enlarged its wall until the city reached its present size, owing to their gradual spreading out and increase in population. Among those who migrated to Ragusa are: Gregory, Arsaphius, Victorinus, Vitalius, Valentine the archdeacon, Valentine the father of Stephen the *protospatharius*. From their migration from Salona [*sic*], it is 500 [*sic*?] years till this day, which is the 7th indiction, the year 6457. In this same city lies St Pancratius, in the Church of St Stephen, which is in the middle of this same city.[17]

Historians have disputed the significance of this passage, and since the controversies bear directly on Dubrovnik's early history they cannot be ignored. Some details of the Emperor's account are fairly clearly wrong. 'Salona' is an error for 'Pitauru', which itself is evidently Epidaurum. Since Constantine wrote in the mid-tenth century, and since the destruction of Epidaurum is usually placed in the early seventh century and associated with the destruction of Salona, it is widely believed that '500 years' is similarly an error for 300 – except, at least, by those who argue that it was not barbarian invaders but an earlier catastrophic earthquake and tidal wave that destroyed the city.[18]

According to Constantine Porphyrogenitus here, it was the Slavs who destroyed Epidaurum, though elsewhere he says that it was the (Turkic) Avars who conquered Salona and Dalmatia and settled down there.[19] In fact, it seems likely that the Emperor drew no very clear distinction between the two peoples. Did the Croats and Serbs form part of the original (undifferentiated) 'Slavic' mass incursions? Or did they constitute a distinct second wave of aggressive migration, probably in the 620s, of peoples from somewhere north of the Carpathian mountains? Modern scholarship inclines to the second of these hypotheses.[20] But it also stresses that we cannot regard the disputable origins of the Croats and Serbs as the last word about their early identity. For certainly in the case of the Croats who settled in Dalmatia, that identity was deeply influenced, probably from an early date, by the Romanised inhabitants among whom they had come.[21]

This latter perception is also relevant to an appreciation of Constantine Porphyrogenitus's account of the destruction of Epidaurum and the foundation of Ragusa. What the Emperor described as occurring suddenly and catastrophically was in all probability one particularly dramatic episode in a more protracted series of events.

Perhaps the greatest impact of the decline of the late Roman Empire was on the towns. The Roman Balkan towns in the interior completely disappeared, with the exception of some modest continuity of settlement in places like Jovia Botivo (Ludbreg) and Aquae Iassae (Varaždinske Toplice) in modern Croatia. Circumstances were only slightly less difficult for Roman towns on the Dalmatian coast. The once-great emporium of Narona decayed as communications became more uncertain, and it was soon almost deserted. Salona – the administrative capital of its province – was simply too big to survive as the imperial provincial administration itself crumbled. The 'fall' of these towns may have been the result as much of economic decay and social decline as feats of arms. Equally important, archeological research in recent times has shown continuity of settlement on their sites. Even though the secular and religious authorities transferred (according to tradition, in 614) with most of the population from Salona to rebuild the community amidst the remains of the Emperor Diocletian's palace in modern Split, it is now clear that Salona itself remained inhabited. Indeed, after their first plundering raids, it is likely that the Slavic invaders established some kind of understanding with the Empire. Certain tribes established their own territories. But alongside them much of the original Romanised population remained. A *modus vivendi* between the two is evidenced by the large number of Christian place names of late antique origin which are preserved outside those areas that remained under the Empire's direct control. A similar conclusion can be drawn from the survival of Christian churches during this period within the as-yet pagan Slavic territories.[22]

The Slavic Myth of Ragusa's Foundation

The relevance of this to the beginnings of Dubrovnik is confirmed, albeit in a confused manner, by the Ragusan and Dalmatian Chronicles.[23] These manage to combine with varying degrees of unease two accounts of the foundation of

Ragusa: one based on Constantine Porphyrogenitus and another which is entirely mythical, though also historically revealing if only because of its illumination of the mentalities of those who constructed it.

This second – what might be termed 'Slavic' – account of Dubrovnik's foundation begins with a certain Radoslav the White, King of Bosnia, who in 458 was overthrown by his son, Berislav (Časlav, according to the chronicle of the Priest of Dioclea). Radoslav initially fled to Albania and then sailed with his loyal barons across to Apulia and journeyed on to Rome. There he was given command of the Roman city guard. He married a noble Roman lady and had three sons by her, one of whom, Stefan the White, succeeded his father as guard commander. He in turn had a son called Radoslav the White. In 524 King Berislav died without a successor. So ambassadors from Bosnia were sent to Radoslav to ask him to return as their king. Radoslav accordingly left Rome with his men and sailed from Ancona to Ragusa where he was greeted by a great gathering of Bosnians. He was advised to build a castle over against the sea for his protection in which he could place the treasure and holy relics he had brought with him from Rome. This he accordingly did in the place called *Chastel Lave*. Such is the account given by the Anonymous Ragusan chronicler. The Priest of Dioclea's version adds various details – about the fate of the treacherous Časlav (who was mutilated and drowned), about Radoslav's reasons for leaving Rome (quarrels with his family's enemies) and about his later departure to Trebinje and exploits there.

The other Ragusan chronicles supply further elements. Nikola Ranjina, who repeats Constantine Porphyrogenitus's account of the destruction of Epidaurum, interestingly links it with a somewhat longer and slightly different account of Radoslav the White's arrival on the Adriatic coast (which he specifically places at Gruž). Among those who awaited the hero were apparently the people and bishop of Epidaurum.

The story of the Slavic foundation is, of course, historically specious and consists of imagined events placed in a later political context – that of the early medieval Balkans. But the need to ensure Slavic involvement, represented by Radoslav and his barons, shows how from an early stage Ragusa's identity was confessedly inclusive of a strong Slavic element. Yet equally this was an identity which was determinedly something more than Slavic: the hero Radoslav has, after all, proved himself by defending the Eternal City, and he is of Roman as well as Slavic stock. The wisdom of Rome is thus called upon to bring order to the barbarian chaos of the Balkans. It is easy to see why this idea appealed to successive generations of sophisticated, Roman Catholic

Ragusans as they played their inspired game for survival confronted with wayward, violent, semi-barbarian Slavic neighbours.

The Slavic myth did, though, also reflect a more tangible reality – the presence of a Slav settlement on the lower slopes of Mount Srd from a very early date. This is also evident in the early use of an alternative Slavic name for Ragusa – 'Dubrovnik'. The first known use of the word *Dubrovčani* for the inhabitants of Ragusa is to be found in a charter of 1189 from *Ban* Kulin, ruler of Bosnia; the first known use of 'Dubrovnik' occurs in a charter of 1215 from the ruler of Serbia, Stefan Nemanja. But both the eleventh century verse-chronicler known as Miletius and the Priest of Dioclea state what subsequent linguists have accepted – namely, that the reference is to the forest of oak trees (Slavic: *dubrava*) which once covered the mountain of Brgat, or Srđ as it was subsequently known. Mount Brgat (a name which would later come simply to refer to a particular village on the site) was called in Latin *Vergatum*, which comes from *virgetum*, a wood of saplings.[24]

The Site and Construction of Dubrovnik

The Ragusan chroniclers also let slip some assertions, however, which imply greater continuity than either their accounts of the flight of the inhabitants of Epidaurum or of the arrival of Radoslav and his barons suggest. They speak, for example, of how the Epidaurans initially sought refuge in fortified places, which are differently named but which have been plausibly located at Spilan and Gradac, before finally settling in Ragusa.[25] This is very much in line with what archeological research shows of the use to which these two sites were put. The remains of buildings from the second century suggest that together with Ragusa they already had a strategic significance for the Roman control of the area. When Epidaurum became economically weaker, less populated and more exposed, it is easy to imagine the inhabitants seeking refuge – temporary at first, later permanent – in each of three little fortified settlements. The final decision in favour of Dubrovnik may simply have reflected its combination of security with opportunities for fishing, and it was probably gradual rather than the result of any sudden administrative decision.

Certainly, archeological research in recent years has supported the theory of gradual development by emphasising the continuity of settlement in Ragusa. The chronology of the evidence is as follows:

- A find of bronze jewellery in Iron Age graves on Lokrum (probably fifth-sixth century BC)
- Finds of Illyrian and Hellenistic money on the sites of today's Dubrovnik cathedral and *Bunićeva poljana* (third-second century BC)
- Remains of a wall between the fortresses of Our Saviour (*Sveti Spasitelj*) and St Stephen (*Sveti Stjepan*), variously dated between first century BC and the fifth-seventh centuries AD
- Fragment of a gravestone, found in Pustijerna, in commemoration of a member of the Roman Eighth Volunteer Cohort, which was stationed in Dalmatia from the start of the first to the end of the third century
- A granite column, part of a now-disappeared late antique basilica, and twelve stone catapult balls
- The latest archeological finds on the site of the cathedral and *Bunićeva poljana*: remains of a late antique castle (probably sixth century) and of a Byzantine basilica (seventh-eighth century).[26]

So great is the evidence of continuous settlement on the site of Dubrovnik, in fact, that for one scholar at least, on the basis of discoveries made in the course of excavation under Dubrovnik's Cathedral and elsewhere, 'there is no point in linking the histories of these two settlements – Epidaurum and Ragusium'.[27] This, though, seems unnecessarily dismissive of the traditions relayed in the chronicles, and perhaps overly confident of archeological technique as a fail-safe source of historical illumination.[28]

Certainly, however, there is enough evidence to suggest that the defining features of the oldest settlement date from the sixth century: as noted above, in the Pustijerna district, remains of the early Christian era (fifth and sixth centuries) have been discovered. It has, therefore, been suggested that Ragusa was constructed by the Byzantines in their struggle with the Ostrogoths (on what was doubtless an earlier Illyrian site), as one of the fortified centres erected from Durrës to the western shores of Istria, designed both to control the shipping route and to provide a place of refuge for the local population in case of attack.[29] In any case, Ragusa was evidently a place of some importance well before the likely date of Epidaurum's destruction.

The original site of Ragusa was clearly on the south-facing cliffs above the Adriatic in the place referred to as *Castellum* or *Chastel Lave*, but how did it acquire its name? Some scholars have followed Constantine Porphyrogenitus in deriving it from the Greek root *lau*, meaning cliff. The term thus became a toponym, reflected later in '*Labes*', the early name for the town's oldest district, in '*Labusedum*' used in papal letters referring to the town itself and finally (with replacement of 'l' with 'r') in the form 'Ragusa'.[30] Others, however, suggest that 'Ragusa' is derived from an Illyrian root and always referred to the whole of the area on which the settlement began and expanded, while *lau*, *lava* or *labes* just referred to the cliff.[31]

By whatever name it was called, this southern cliff-top was always the most easily defensible place. Long after the original Castellum had been pulled down to make way for the Benedictine convent of St Mary's (*Sveta Marija*) which rose in its place, this spot remained the heart of the *sexterium* '*od Kaštela*' (or *Kaštio*), the oldest of the administrative districts of Dubrovnik to which it gave its name. Kaštio, though, only covered a small part of what would be included within the walls of Dubrovnik. Later the settlement spread out to form the *sexterium* of St Peter (named after the church of St Peter the Great, *Sveti Petar Veliki*) and then into the easternmost area of what today is called the Old Town, the third *sexterium* of Pustijerna.

It used to be thought, in the days when the line of today's Placa was believed to trace that of a marshy stream which allegedly divided the 'island' of Ragusa proper from the land at the foot of Mount Srđ, that Pustijerna was only settled in the eighth and ninth centuries and the rest of Dubrovnik a good deal later.[32] But this view must now be revised. A proper understanding of the change in sea level, combined with evidence from probes put down into ground in the wake of the 1979 earthquake, confirms that the centre of the town was not uninhabitable marsh at this time but eminently inhabitable dry land. It was probably first used for agriculture – hence its ancient name of *campus* – and then for building. This process doubtless long preceded the area's inclusion within the walls.[33]

Life in Early Dubrovnik

Originally built (and perhaps rebuilt) with primarily military purposes in mind, Dubrovnik's development as a civilian settlement was probably sharply accelerated in the early seventh century with the flight of many or all the people of Epidaurum *via* Spilan and Gradac to find a more secure refuge. This early Dubrovnik was under Byzantine authority. Constantine Porphyrogenitus judiciously recalls as much when he mentions 'Valentine the father of Stephen the *protospatharius*' (that is, a Byzantine patrician official). The settlement was within the political-territorial unit of Dalmatia, which was first governed from Zadar by a Byzantine pro-consul and then in the ninth century when, as part of the Empire's reorganisation, Dalmatia was made an Imperial 'theme' by a *strategos*. There is no evidence about Dubrovnik's internal administration in these early centuries. By 1023, however, a *praeses* was in charge of its affairs, and by 1052 this official was called a *prior*, as in the other Dalmatian towns.

Also from the very first we know that Dubrovnik would have been Christian, as Epidaurum had been – probably from at least the mid-fourth century (when St Hilarion was apparently greeted by the Epidaurans). A Christian burial ground discovered at Slano shows that the area around Dubrovnik had been converted by the fifth century. There was probably a bishop of Epidaurum by then; certainly, one was present at the first Dalmatian church synod held in Salona in 530. The bishopric was transferred to Dubrovnik under obscure circumstances but probably, as tradition and the Ragusan historians suggest, on the fall of Epidaurum.[34] (Dubrovnik's claims to be the seat of an archbishopric were to be the subject of later hot dispute, but not its inheritance of the see of Epidaurum).[35]

The Ragusan chronicles dwell upon the marvellous relics which were kept in the town. Radoslav the White was said to have brought with him those of Saints Petronilla, Domicella, Nereus, Archileus, Pancratius and two pieces of the Holy Cross, all of which were placed in silver reliquaries. Within the precincts of the Castellum he is said to have built a church dedicated to Saints Sergius and Bacchus, and to have established outside the walls a church dedicated to St Stephen (*Sveti Stjepan*).[36] In truth, these relics probably only reached Dubrovnik much later. But the strength of the tradition is itself significant of the pride taken in the town's early distinction as a centre of Christian piety. (In later years the cult of Ragusa's patron saint, St Blaise [*Sveti Vlaho, San Biagio*] dwarfed those of the other traditional intercessors.)[37]

The ethnic and cultural make-up of early Dubrovnik and the relationship between Roman/Latin and Slavic elements within it have provoked much controversy. The information from the chronicles is of limited help. The names of Constantine Porphyrogenitus's six key figures who originally migrated from Epidaurum are, as one would expect, Romano-Greek. The Ragusan chronicles give (slightly different) lists of the noble families of Ragusa with their alleged places of origin – Epidaurum, Rome, other Italian cities, Germany, Albania, Kotor, the territories of the Vlachs, Slavs and so on.[38] For the year 743 the Anonymous chronicler signals, in his confusing way, political upheavals which sent more refugees fleeing to Dubrovnik – 'Morlachs' (or Vlachs) from above the Neretva who brought with them their cattle, which they were allowed to pasture on Mount Srđ.[39] For the following year he records in a still more mysterious passage that an assembly was held and a 'division' made among all the people of Ragusa into three social classes –

nobles (*gentilhomeni*), common people (*populi*) and servants or slaves (*servidori*). Among the groups participating were 'Bosnian' families, each household with its own patron saint, and rich Vlachs who owned gold, silver and cattle.[40]

In spite of all these outside elements, Ragusa can only properly be understood for the first centuries of its existence as essentially a post-Roman community, having far more in common with the little proto-urban communities on Italian soil than with the life of the Balkan hinterland. Ragusan territories were divided like theirs into the *civitas* (city) and *districtus* or *distretto* (surrounding district). The latter was itself divided between the mainland Astarea (sometimes called *terra firma* or *hereditas*) and the Islands (*insulae*). Astarea stretched from Epidaurum/Cavtat (derived from the Latin *civitas*, i.e. city) to the bay of Zaton. The whole territory had, in fact, been settled long before the arrival of the Slavs. The inflow of Slavic settlement, when it came, was from the northwest and was accordingly strongest near Zaton. But these settlers lived under Ragusan administration and their property rights were governed by Roman law. Generally, the ethnic mix in early Astarea is shown by the interweaving of Roman and Slavic place names, while other areas of the mainland like Primorje and Konavle, which would eventually fall under Ragusan control, were much more heavily Slavicised.

Also under Dubrovnik's authority from the earliest times were the three principal islands of Koločep, Lopud and Šipan, the smallest inhabited islands of Mrkan, Supetar, Daksa, Lokrum, Sveti Andrija (St Andrew) and Jakljan (all given by the Ragusan community to ecclesiastical foundations) and the other tiny deserted islands of Bobara, Grebeni and Rudo.[41] Of the Elaphite Islands, Constantine Porphyrogenitus's generalisation seems to hold true: '... After the said Slavs had settled down, they took possession of all the surrounding territory of Dalmatia; but the cities of the Romani took to cultivating the islands and living off them.'[42] The archeological and toponymic evidence from Koločep, Lopud and Šipan shows that Slavicisation proceeded only very gradually as this earlier Romanised population died out.[43]

The picture which the sources – narrative, archeological and linguistic – present of Dubrovnik in the early ninth century, 200 years or so after the 'fall of Epidaurum' (with the qualifications which must be made to that expression), is therefore of a modest but growing community, heavily shaped by Roman culture, Byzantine administrative habits and Christianity. As its location emphasises, and as the slow expansion inland of Ragusa from its original craggy nucleus confirms, security was the first consideration. This and its direct access to the sea, with the fishing and local trade which went with it, would have attracted many; upheavals and conflicts in the hinterland doubtless drove more to seek shelter within its originally primitive defences. Either through the intermediary of the Byzantine authorities or possibly of the Church, the Ragusans were able to establish good relations with the Slavs, who appeared first as barbarian raiders but who quickly settled to farm the land. Roman, Slavic and Vlach communities co-existed, with the Romanised population dominating the town itself and its near surrounds, the Slavs increasingly changing the ethnic balance in their favour in the more distant territories under Ragusan control and a shifting population of Vlachs taking advantage of the relatively settled conditions around Ragusa to pasture their livestock on the slopes of Brgat. And all the while Ragusa, in search of legitimacy and prestige, fiercely clung to its claim to be the successor of Epidaurum, inheriting its episcopal status and the rich myths which fertile imagination would bestow on that modest Augustan colony.

1. Bull of Pope Benedict VIII in favour of Archbishop Vitalis, the oldest original document in the Dubrovnik archives and the first confirmation of the Ragusan archbishopric (1022)

2. Trade agreement between Dubrovnik and Pisa (1169)

3. Charter in favour of Dubrovnik granted by Ban Kulin of Bosnia (1189)

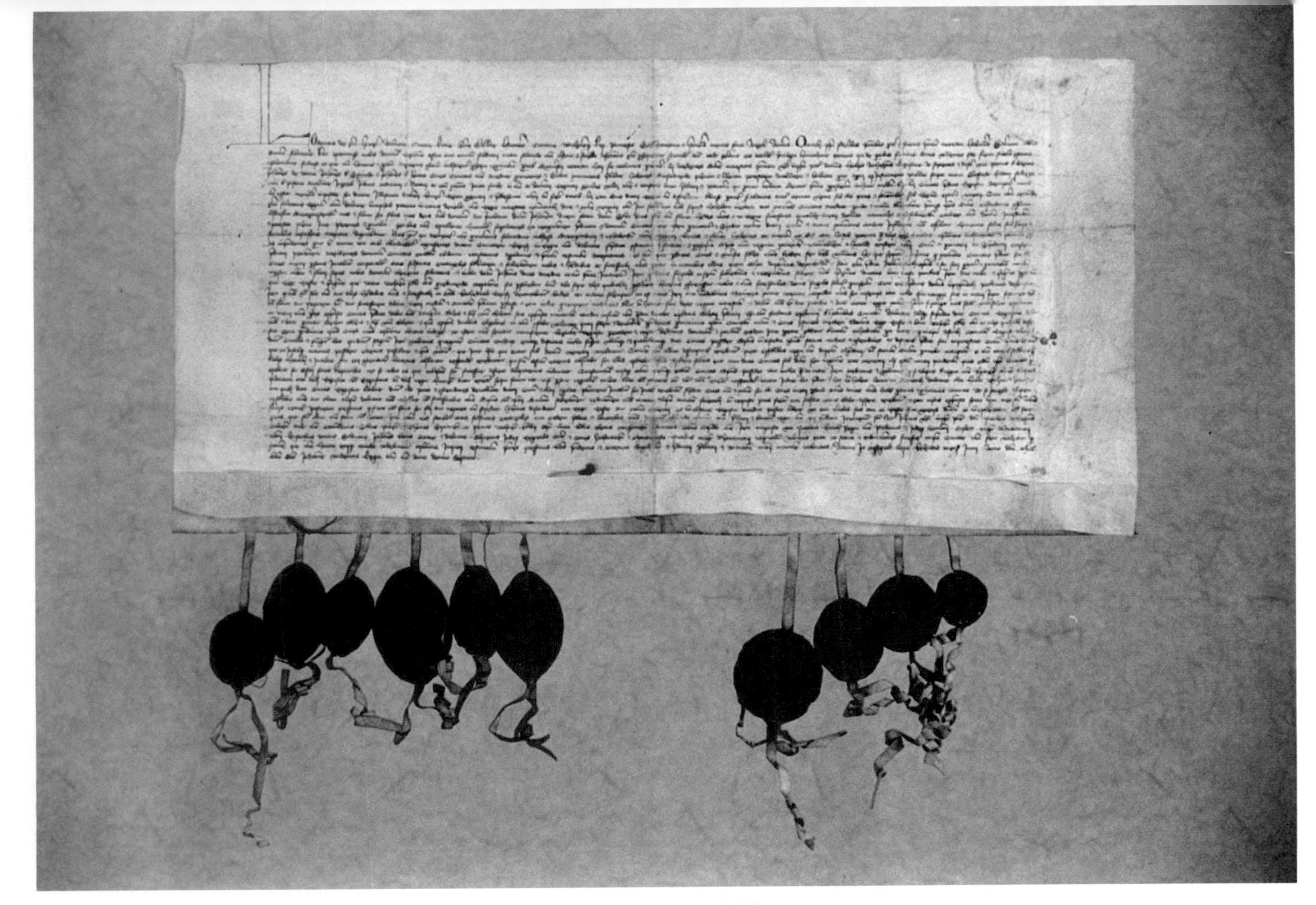

4. Charter in favour of Dubrovnik's autonomy granted by King Louis I of Hungary (1358)

5. Charter in favour of Dubrovnik granted by the Bosnian King Tvrtko I (1367)

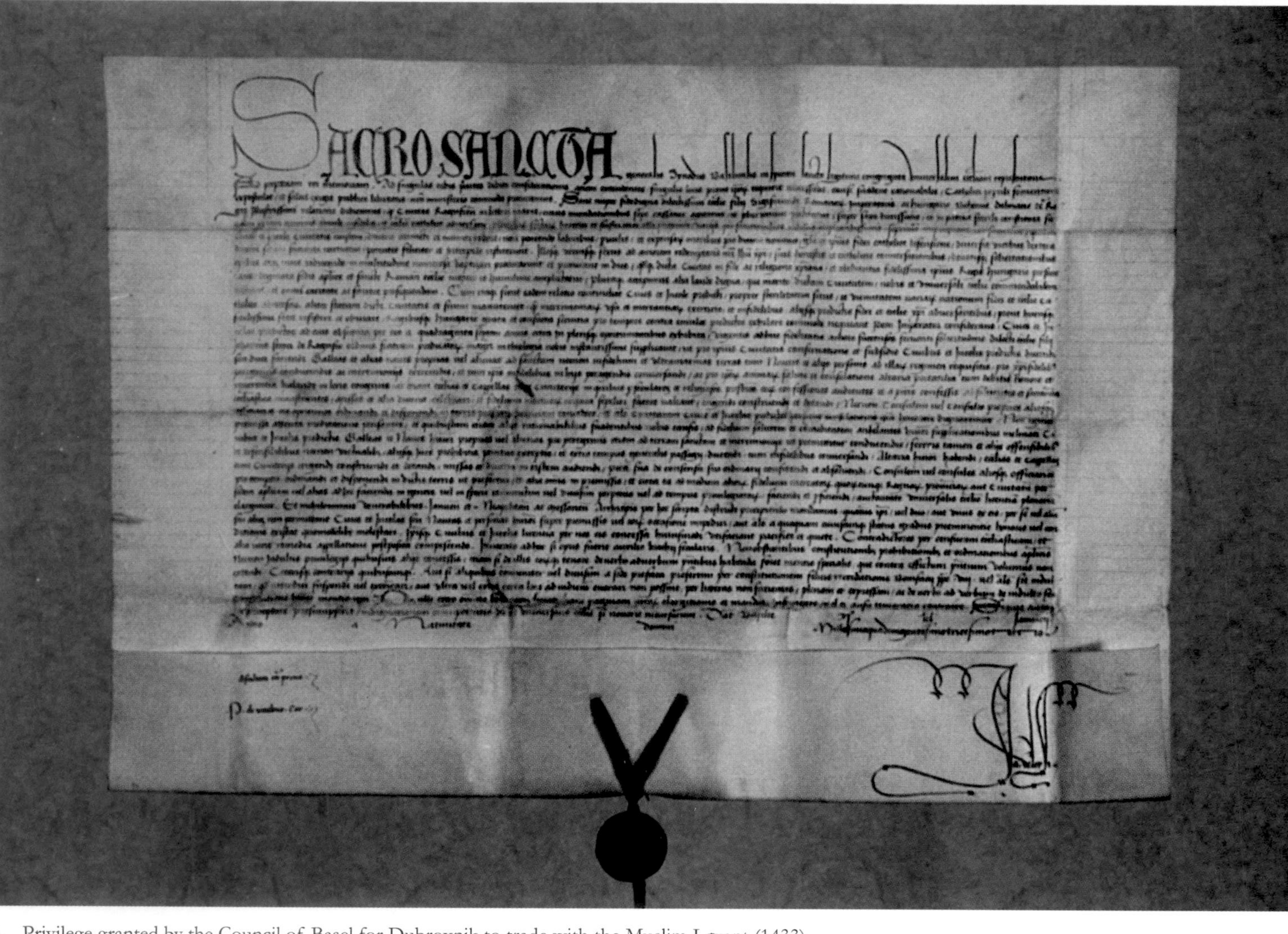

SACROSANCTA

6. Privilege granted by the Council of Basel for Dubrovnik to trade with the Muslim Levant (1433)

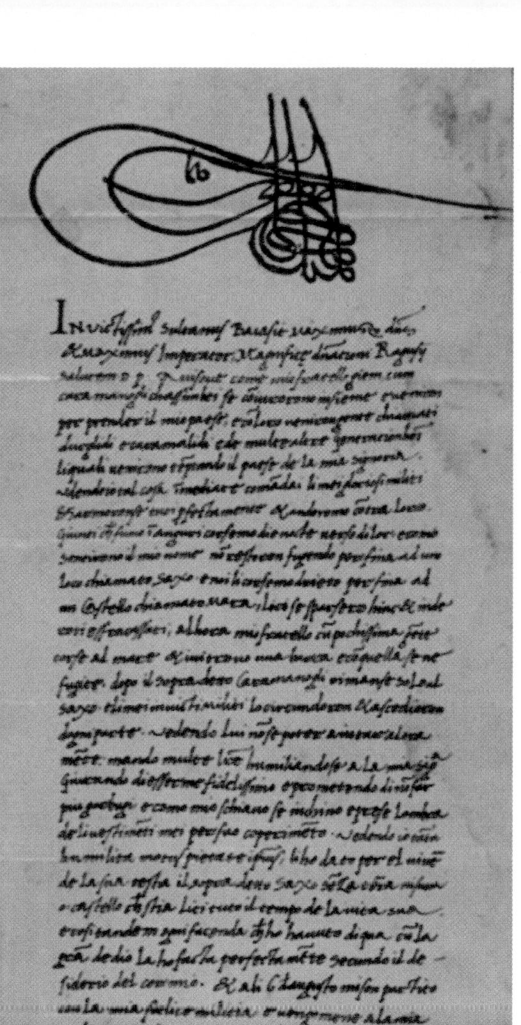

Invictissimus Sultanus Baiasit maximus Rex [illegible]
et Maximus Imperator. Magnifici domini Ragusii
salutem [illegible]. [illegible] come mio fratello [illegible]
cum [illegible] se acconciorono insieme [illegible]
per prendere il mio paese, et [illegible] chiamati
[illegible] et Caramanlida e de molti altri [illegible]
liquali venivono [illegible] il paese de la mia signoria
vedendo io tal cosa [illegible] comandai li mei [illegible] militi
[illegible] et andorono contra loro
[illegible] de loro et come
sentirono il mio nome non [illegible] fugendo per fina ad uno
loco chiamato Saxo e noi li [illegible] per fina ad
un Castello chiamato [illegible], loco [illegible]
[illegible], allora mio fratello con pochissima gente
[illegible] al mare et [illegible] una barca et con quella se ne
fugiete. dopo il sopradetto Caramanogli rimanse solo al
Saxo [illegible] lo circumdorono et assediorono
[illegible] parte. vedendo lui non se poter [illegible]
mente mando molte lettere humiliandose a la mia signoria
[illegible] fidelissimo et prometendo di [illegible]
[illegible] et come mio schiavo se [illegible]
de li [illegible] per suo [illegible] vedendo io tanta
humilita [illegible] li ho dato per el nome
de la sua testa il sopradetto Saxo [illegible]
castello [illegible] tutto il tempo de la vita sua
[illegible] ho hauto [illegible] con la
gratia de dio la ho facta perfectamente secondo il de-
siderio del core mio. Et ali 6 d'augusto [illegible]
con la mia felice militia et [illegible] a la mia
sedia a Constantinopoli. ma del mio fratello [illegible]
per mare non habiamo hauto ancora nova nisuna dove
sia andato. niente dimeno [illegible] chel tempo [illegible]
ali loci de Christiani. ma io me confido [illegible]
lo saperete dove sara. et cosi come lo saperete avisarete
il mio fidelissimo [illegible] Sangiacbei [illegible]
me avisa subito dove se trova [illegible] facendo cosi
[illegible] fina al fine havete [illegible]
fidelmente a la felice memoria de mio padre, cosi anche
[illegible] a me [illegible] molto
[illegible] comandate li subditi [illegible] per tutto il [illegible] paese che
facino bona et diligente guardia [illegible] mio fratello non passasse
[illegible] et si pur [illegible] prendere
[illegible] la anima de mio padre et mia
[illegible] generosamente
et per piu chiara fede de le [illegible] ne ha [illegible] il
mio fidelissimo schiavo [illegible] Dat. [illegible]
die [illegible] augusti anno D. MCCCCLXXXII

Nos Haermoni [illegible]
[illegible] Turci [illegible]
[illegible] Baiasit [illegible] maximi Secretarius

7. Ferman addressed to Dubrovnik by the Ottoman Sultan Bayezid II seeking the Republic's cooperation against his fugitive brother Ðem (1482)

1679. Al Mar.o Gozze. 1808/8

Il Prencipe S. P. O | il Vis.r M. Q | VV. Cl.e T. V | Venetiani A. B. | Bassà di Bosna L. S.

Punto fermo. D. Nulle per confonder la Cifra E. G. H.

Adrianopoli	100
Adrianatico	101
Imperator	102
Italia	103
Contado di Canal	104
Primorie	105
Narenta	106
C. Novo	107
Sarraio	108
Puglia	109
Rè di Spagna	110
V. Rè di Napoli	111
Gente di Dal.a	112
Dalmatia	113
Zara	114
Spalatro	115
Galere	116
Fuste	117
Stato di Rag.a	118
Fortificationi	119

Da qui si scriverà
A Senor Mosè Abenun.
Belgradi

Da Sarraio si scriverà qui.
Al Sig.re Matteo Roberti
Ancona Ancona

Segno che vi sia la Cifra.
Belgradi
Ancona

8. An Example of Dubrovnik's Code, employed in secret diplomatic transactions (1679)

TWO

Distant Friends and Hostile Neighbours: Dubrovnik Under Byzantine Protection (c. 800–1205)

The Eastern Adriatic in the Ninth, Tenth and Eleventh Centuries

The ninth century in the lands of the Eastern Adriatic was dominated by interlocking power struggles, which provided a turbulent background for the early establishment of Dubrovnik as an effectively self-governing commune and a modest commercial power under Byzantine protection. Such protection was sorely needed – not least from the Arabs (called 'Saracens') of Tunis and Algiers, who began a systematic occupation of Mediterranean bases in the ninth century. In the 820s they seized Crete and various Sicilian towns from Byzantium, and their destruction of Brindisi in 837/8 ominously signalled their entry into the Adriatic. Osor (on the island of Cres) was burnt down in 841. An Arab fleet shattered the Venetian opposition and then returned to seize Budva, Rosa and Kotor. The following year the Saracens were again in the Adriatic.[1]

It was thus only a matter of time before Dubrovnik was singled out for Saracen attack. Legend, as recorded in the anonymous Ragusan chronicle, has it that a Frank, Orlando (based on the hero Roland) had helped the Ragusans drive off the Saracens in 783 after the latter had earlier destroyed (whatever remained at the site of) Epidaurum.[2] Dubrovnik was for perhaps a second time subjected to a fifteen-month siege by the Saracens in 866. The Ragusans sent envoys to Constantinople for help, and the new Emperor Basil I despatched a large fleet to relieve the town. When the Saracens heard of its imminent arrival, however, they lifted the siege and sailed away.[3] The effect was to secure the Ragusans (and indeed the neighbouring Slavs) in their allegiance to Byzantium, the value of whose protection had thus been amply demonstrated.[4]

Dubrovnik's recurrent problem was that the Byzantine Emperor was a somewhat unreliable protector. Consequently, the Ragusans had to reach their own arrangements with their neighbours in order to preserve their security. Byzantium was happy to enable that, as long as its ultimate sovereignty was still recognised. Basil I (867–886) therefore decreed that the Dalmatian towns should henceforth give to the neighbouring Slavic rulers the financial tribute they had previously paid to the Byzantine *strategos*. In the case of Dubrovnik, this involved the payment of 36 *numizmata* each to the rulers of Hum (the future Hercegovina) and Trabunija (the territory attached to Trebinje).[5] By contrast, any failure by Dubrovnik to make provision to ward off threats from the hinterland when Byzantium was weak could be disastrous. Thus, at the end of the tenth century, the Macedonian-Bulgarian Tsar Samuilo (974–1014) ravaged the Dalmatian coast as far as Zadar and burnt Dubrovnik as he passed.[6] After Samuilo's death, a Byzantine counter-offensive restored the Empire's control in the region. But in the meantime had occurred a development of much greater long-term significance for Dalmatia in general and Dubrovnik in particular: the first assertion of Venetian imperial ambitions.

Venice's origins had – in everything but scale – obvious parallels with those of its tiny Ragusan counterpart. Like Dubrovnik, it had maintained a continuity with Roman tradition; it, too, had been a refuge for those fleeing from invaders; its lagoons had served something of the same protective role as Ragusa's cliff-top; of necessity, its inhabitants had from the first exploited maritime trade; and it had accordingly developed a navy which was valuable militarily to it and to others. But of course, Venice's wealth, population and reach were always greater than Dubrovnik's, and this disparity only increased as in the tenth century it skilfully maintained the friendship of both the Byzantine and German Empires, widened its autonomy and developed its commerce. That trade was most threatened in the middle Adriatic by the Croat pirates living at the mouth of the Neretva, who had killed one Doge in battle, defeated other Venetian expeditions and forced on the Serenissima the humiliation of paying them tribute for half a century.[7] Under Doge Pietro II Orseolo (991–1002), Venice sought to deal decisively with the Neretvan Croats and to exploit political conditions so as to project its power along the Dalmatian coast.

In 992, in exchange for Venice's help in protecting Byzantine possessions in southern Italy and Byzantine shipping, Venice received significant trading privileges within the Empire. Whatever Byzantium may have intended, Venice interpreted this as a right to take action to provide for security of navigation in the Adriatic as a whole, and indeed to do so in the most aggressive fashion.

The precise details are obscure; but perhaps with the authority of the Byzantine Emperor, quite probably at the request of the Dalmatian towns, and in either 998 or 1000, Doge Pietro II Orseolo set out with a fleet and army down the Dalmatian coast. He occupied the towns and islands one by one – Osor (on the island of Cres), Zadar (where there awaited him to make their submission representatives from the islands of Krk and Rab), Biograd, Trogir and Split. Sufficiently impressed to make concessions, even the Neretvan Croats agreed no longer to demand their tribute. The Venetians had, though, to fight to overcome the tenacious resistance of the inhabitants of the islands of Korčula and Lastovo. Near the little island of Majsan, off Korčula, a delegation from Dubrovnik headed by its archbishop met the Doge. Exactly what occurred then was hotly disputed in later years. Venetian writers claimed that Dubrovnik made a formal submission to Venice; the Ragusan historians denied any such thing.[8] It seems likely, though, that Venice did indeed demand Dubrovnik's submission – as it had that of the other Dalmatian towns – and highly improbable that the Ragusans could have resisted such a demand.

The Venetian Doge proclaimed himself Duke of Dalmatia, *Dux Dalmatiae,* and ended payment of tribute to the Croats. But Venice was not yet powerful enough to command obedience from faraway Dubrovnik once its fleet had sailed into the distance.[9]

This first assertion of lordship over Dubrovnik by Venice would, however, come to be seen by future generations of Ragusans in the light of their centuries-long struggle with the Serenissima to keep themselves out of its clutches. That may explain the account in the oldest, anonymous chronicle of earlier alleged struggles by Dubrovnik against Venetian plots and violence.

The chronicler, followed by many later accounts, tells in particular how in 971 a great army of Venetians arrived at Dubrovnik, allegedly *en route* to the Levant, but in reality intent on seizing the town. The priest in charge of St Stephen's (*Sveti Stjepan*), a certain Don Stoico, on entering his church at midnight, had found it full of soldiers under the command of a captain with a long, white beard who turned out to be St Blaise. The saint told him that he and his men had been fighting hard to keep the town safe against the Venetians who planned to seize it. Don Stoico immediately rushed to inform the town authorities, who made prompt provision against the Venetians; the latter, seeing their plan was foiled, then sailed away.[10]

These events do not seem likely to have occurred at this time, so long before Doge Pietro II Orseolo's expedition. But a strong local tradition does link the Ragusan cult of St Blaise to this occasion and to this date. Certainly, the cult in Dubrovnik began very early: a church dedicated to the saint was built in the late ninth century.[11]

After the Doge's departure, Dubrovnik was in any case soon back under Byzantine authority and in 1023 Ragusan documents were being dated according to the Byzantine style. Indeed, the presence in Dubrovnik in 1042 of a Byzantine *strategos* – who was outwitted and captured in that year by the Slavic prince of Duklja (also called Zeta, the modern Montenegro) – suggests that the town may have temporarily become the site of a separate Byzantine 'theme' (military/administrative region).[12]

But now another major force made itself felt in Dalmatia, challenging Byzantine control. Norman soldiers had been serving in southern Italy for profit since early in the eleventh century. In 1071 fell Bari, the last Imperial possession in southern mainland Italy.[13] The Normans were also active against the Byzantine Empire in Dalmatia. In 1074 they briefly seized control of Split, Trogir, Biograd, Zadar and Nin. Dubrovnik also now fell under Norman influence.[14]

The Normans, like the Saracens before them, were not, however decisive long-term players in the great power game in Dalmatia. The most important geopolitical change of the twelfth century in the eastern Adriatic was the shift of dominance from Byzantium to Venice.

Although Venice's main preoccupation was with northern and central Dalmatia, this did not preclude its attempting to reassert control over Dubrovnik. In 1125 the Venetian Doge, in a manner that prefigured the events of 1205, used a fleet and army returning from the Levant to seize Byzantine-held Dalmatian towns, including Dubrovnik.[15] Accordingly, Venetian counts ruled there for some twenty years until the resentful Ragusans threw them out.[16]

Venice again occupied Dubrovnik in 1171. Having destroyed the town's towers and walls and appointed a count, the Venetians sailed away. And their control again proved ephemeral. When what was left of the Venetian fleet stopped in on its way home, humiliated and plague-ridden from a failed expedition in the Aegean, it simply collected the count and departed. Dubrovnik temporarily placed itself under the protection of the Normans, later returning once more to Byzantine allegiance.[17]

The death of the great Byzantine Emperor Manuel Comnenus (1143–1180) exposed the fragility of Byzantine power and, as the Empire slipped into decline once more, a new period of danger accordingly opened up for Dubrovnik. In particular, the Ragusans were soon put to the test in their dealings with Serbia (Raška). The appearance of the Nemanjić dynasty in Raška in the late 1160s, with the accession of a certain Tihomir – soon overthrown by his brother Stefan Nemanja – is one of the turning points in the history of the Balkans, and Dubrovnik could not but be affected. One of Nemanja's brothers, Miroslav, also gained control of Hum, and Duklja was conquered by Nemanja himself in the 1180s.[18]

Precisely when Nemanja and Dubrovnik first clashed is unclear. But it seems to have been Ragusan support for the islanders of Korčula and Vis, when they were attacked by Nemanja's brother Stracimir, that was the occasion for serious hostilities. In 1185 Nemanja himself besieged the town and breached its defences, seizing documents relating to the metropolitan claims of the archbishop of Dubrovnik – which suggests that the latter's conflict with the see of Bar (Antivari) – now under the Orthodox Nemanja's influence – should be seen as a contributing factor to the war itself.[19]

In this crisis, Dubrovnik turned to the Normans for protection, and it was accordingly in the 'court' of King William II at Dubrovnik that a peace treaty between the Ragusans on one hand and Nemanja and his brother Miroslav on the other was drawn up. By this Nemanja recognised Dubrovnik's rights to its traditional territories – its *hereditas* or Astarea; each side agreed to forgo claims for damage done to property; Dubrovnik promised not to try to take Korčula and Vis, on which the Nemanjići still clearly had their sights; the Ragusans might without hindrance trade, cultivate the land, cut wood and generally go about their business in the lands of the Nemanja brothers, especially in the port of Drijeva at the mouth of the Neretva; similarly, the Serbs could go about their affairs freely in Dubrovnik.[20] The terms of the treaty provide an insight into the degree of contact which the Ragusans clearly enjoyed with the hinterland and *vice versa*. But this contact, however mutually beneficial in the longer term, was also a contributory factor to the tension between the town and the neighbouring Slavs.[21]

That is surely what lies behind both the confirmation by the Serbian rulers of Dubrovnik's rights on the fringes of Astarea, and the subsequent use of the Slavic institution known as *stanak* to resolve disputes. This *stanak* consisted of a process of judgement and mediation between representatives of both sides appointed to resolve issues relating to property rights: a *stanak* was held, for instance, in 1193 between Stefan Nemanja's men and those of Dubrovnik because of a dispute over some land belonging to the Church of St Martin (*Sveti Martin*) in Šumet. (The procedures relating to the institution of the *stanak* would be enshrined in the great Dubrovnik Statute [*Liber Statutorum*] drawn up in 1272.)[22]

Dubrovnik used Norman overlordship to protect it from the Serbs and Venetians between 1186 and 1192, then returned to Byzantine authority as the Norman kingdom began to weaken. Under the terms of the re-established relationship, it was agreed that Byzantium would send a governor to protect the town; the Ragusans must not in future renounce Byzantine sovereignty or assist foreign rulers; they would provide refuge for the Emperor's army and take his part if he fought against Venice and Zadar; as a sign of subjection, the traditional *laudes* would be sung three times a year (at Christmas, on St Blaise's Feast Day – 3 February – and at Easter) in the Emperor's honour. In exchange, the Ragusans were promised the right to trade freely throughout Byzantium and Bulgaria.

In practice, things seem to have continued very much as before, and the Ragusans chose their count from their own ranks, rather than receiving one from Constantinople. Byzantium was too weak to enforce its authority – indeed, far more worrying for Dubrovnik was the perception that it was too feeble to offer much protection either.[23]

Trade Relations

Throughout this period the Ragusans were engaged in establishing and reinforcing commercial ties with other urban trading communities.[24] These agreements, in the absence of other quantitative information, also, of course, illustrate the scope of early Ragusa's maritime trade. The first such commercial treaty mentioned (but not preserved) is one with the town of Molfetta in Apulia in 1148, which exempted each other's citizens from paying specified dues levied on foreigners, their merchandise and ships. In 1169, Dubrovnik negotiated an important trade agreement with Pisa. Apart from exemption from commercial dues, the Pisans undertook to protect Dubrovnik's goods, and not just in Pisa but elsewhere too. Since the Pisans sailed from Syria to Gibraltar and had their own representatives in the most significant ports, this last provision was of considerable significance. Dubrovnik also early on established close relations with the towns of the papal states – Fano and Ancona in 1169 and Ravenna in 1188.

Nor were the other towns of the eastern Adriatic neglected. In 1181 Dubrovnik signed a commercial treaty with Kotor. The Ragusans were also active in Istrian ports. In 1188 a trade agreement was renewed with Rovinj, and in 1194 an agreement to resolve some outstanding issues was made with its neighbour Poreč. In fact, the negotiation of commercial treaties between

Dubrovnik and its counterparts continued right up to the Venetian extinction of its independence in 1205.

Disputes between individual merchants of different towns, which could escalate through the practice of taking reprisals against third parties, were only one threat to trade. At least as dangerous for merchants sailing along the eastern Adriatic, particularly anywhere near the mouth of the Neretva River, was the threat of piracy – which the Venetians still railed against in vain. The piratical people of Omiš, the Kačić clan, were the most notorious; but in 1190 the Ragusans bought them off with a tribute in exchange for the right to safe navigation.

By the end of the twelfth century Dubrovnik had, therefore, more or less satisfactorily stabilised its relations both with near neighbours and with more distant regional powers. And not only Serbia but Bosnia, which had emerged as an effectively autonomous entity, was opened up to Ragusan traders. *Ban* (the title, of mysterious origin but distinctively Croat, meaning ruler) Kulin ruled Bosnia in the 1180s, a time of some prosperity, and in 1189 agreed a treaty, written in both Latin and Slavic, with Dubrovnik. By this agreement Kulin permitted Dubrovnik's merchants to trade in his lands without paying any dues, except what they gave as voluntary tribute, and each side pledged eternal friendship.[25]

Institutions of Government

The treaty which was agreed by *Ban* Kulin and Dubrovnik was made in the name of the Ragusan count (or *knez*) – called Krvaš – with a list of named Ragusan dignitaries. Exactly how long a Ragusan count served is unknown; certainly Krvaš held the post from 1186 to 1190 and again in 1192. The names of other Ragusan counts have been recorded.[26] Counts were also, as has been noted, sometimes sent from Venice in the years when Dubrovnik was under that republic's control.

A vicar – also known as *ban* – served as the count's assistant and substitute. The count had his council, which was in embryo the organ that would develop into the later Ragusan Small Council. He also held his own court, first mentioned in 1186. He presided over all important discussions, particularly those relating to relations with foreign powers. Mentioned too are 'judges', alongside whom would sit 'consuls' who must be present at the pronouncement of judgement. When important decrees were being considered, 'wise men' (*sapientes*) would be called upon to assist.

In fact, to the limited extent that the workings of the early administration of Dubrovnik can be glimpsed, it is notable that consultation was one of its distinctive features. The basic consultative institution was a gathering consisting (in theory at least) of all the population – clergy and laymen, nobles and commoners. This assembly met regularly in order to decide the most important items of public business. Indeed, it continued to function in order to ratify laws until the end of the fourteenth century, though after the break with Venice it had much less importance.

Alongside that popular assembly a more limited council soon grew up, consisting of the count, sometimes the archbishop, and the nobility – the latter appearing first as a specific group in 1023. In 1190, this council is described as having 60 members, who then swore to keep the peace agreed with Miroslav, *Knez* of Hum. Probably by then the council, rather than the full popular assembly, was already the effective forum of government. By its authority monasteries were founded; it spoke for the town on border disputes; it gave legal validity to issues of ownership and, as in the case of *Knez* Miroslav, it ratified treaties.[27]

Ragusa itself was at this time referred to as a 'community' (*communitas*) or 'city' (*civitas*). In fact, it bore in its public features many of the marks of a 'commune', as that term was understood in contemporary Italy.[28] The creation of a class of 'law-worthy men', sharing power and governing by permanent institutions a city-state with control of its surrounding *distretto*, and developing autonomous relations with other such communities, all set against a self-consciously propagated cultural background drawn from classical antecedents: this seems a model which describes twelfth century Ragusa quite satisfactorily. Indeed, even the characteristic fragility of Italy's communal institutions, in the face of the ambitions of a would-be tyrant manipulating his power to subvert the legal order, would also – if only briefly – afflict Ragusa in the early years of the thirteenth century. One of the unsung contributions of subsequent Venetian rule was to cure Dubrovnik of this potentially fatal affliction and imbue the governing class with a suspicion of the politics of self-promotion that exceeded that of even their Venetian mentors – themselves regarded throughout Italy as the supreme practitioners of concord and stability.[29]

The Archbishopric of Dubrovnik

It is rather easier to trace the development of Dubrovnik's early religious than its political life – though, not least through the role of the archbishop, the two were intimately linked.[30] The sources disagree about when the see of Dubrovnik itself was raised to metropolitan status. The Ragusans, ever-conscious of the importance of historical pedigree, were keen to claim that this happened very early indeed, alleging that the pallium had been sent to a Dubrovnik (arch-)bishop as early as 743. But this was almost certainly wishful thinking, since a mere bishop of Dubrovnik was present at synods in Split in the 920s.

In fact, the original creation of the Ragusan metropolitanate seems to have been the result of several different impulses. One of these was the pressure of practicalities at a time when travel was so dangerous. In 998 a further synod was summoned in Split and the bishops of Upper Dalmatia – that is Kotor, Bar, Ulcinj and Svač – took ship together and were all drowned at sea. As a result, these towns now asked for a new archbishopric to be founded closer at hand. The pope apparently agreed, making Dubrovnik its seat, with Bar, Kotor, Svač and Ulcinj as its suffragans.[31]

On the other hand, it is highly unlikely that the authority of the archbishop of Split would have been successfully challenged in this fashion if politics had not played a decisive role. The institution of the Ragusan archbishopric was, in fact, a response to the conditions created by the establishment of Tsar Samuilo's rule in the region. Dubrovnik was at this time subject to his control, and the place represented a much more reliable focus for the ecclesiastical loyalties of the Tsar's Catholic subjects than faraway Split. For his part, the pope of the day – Gregory V (996–999) – was equally anxious to co-operate and oblige Samuilo's wishes. The original Bull erecting the archbishopric has been lost. But the first preserved original document in the Dubrovnik archives – a Bull of Benedict VIII (1012–1024), dated 27 September 1022 – which refers to a Ragusan archbishop, also refers back to a previous Bull of a certain Pope 'Gregory' (clearly Gregory V) organising the affairs of the archdiocese. It can thus be stated with some confidence that the archbishopric of Dubrovnik was first erected between 996 and 999.[32] So it was that when, in 998 or 1000, Dubrovnik sent a delegation to meet the Venetian Doge on his triumphant military expedition along the Dalmatian islands, Dubrovnik's own archbishop was at its head.[33]

The fortunes of Dubrovnik's metropolitanate remained highly dependent on political circumstances. After the collapse of Samuilo's empire following his death and the reassertion of Byzantine authority, the Ragusan archbishopric lost much of its earlier significance. Some twenty years later, the ruler of Duklja, Stefan Vojislav, anxious to assert independence from Byzantium, began to exert strong pressure to have the bishopric of Bar removed from

Dubrovnik's jurisdiction. Other Ragusan suffragans similarly asserted themselves and in these chaotic circumstances in the 1050s the archbishops of Split seem to have persuaded Rome to abolish the Ragusan archbishopric altogether. Dubrovnik itself fought hard to restore the see's metropolitan status. But this was made even more difficult by the ambition of the Dukljan rulers to gain for their bishopric and town of Bar the same privilege. Efforts which might have gone into lobbying for Dubrovnik had thus to be directed to lobbying against Bar. Still worse, the Ragusans were unsuccessful. The anti-pope Clement III (1080–1100) in 1089 made Bar an archbishopric, though Dubrovnik was spared the final indignity since neither it nor Ston was placed under Bar's authority.

Dubrovnik spent the following decades pressing for the annulment of this decision. But again it was the shifting balance of political influence which was decisive. While Dubrovnik was growing steadily wealthier and stronger, Duklja was weakening. At last, on 28 September 1120, Calixtus II (1119–1124) restored the Ragusan archbishopric. The struggle now focused on Dubrovnik's ambition to ensure that the new archbishop's authority was exerted over his bishoprics in the face of the influence of Bar and Split.[34]

The Ragusans were remorseless, seeking and when necessary (like their opponents) forging the required documentation for their claims. In 1142 Pope Innocent II confirmed Dubrovnik's authority over its rebellious suffragans. In 1154, Pope Anastasius IV sent to Dubrovnik a legate *a latere* who obligingly excommunicated the recalcitrant bishops of Drivast, Ulcinj and Kotor.[35] Dubrovnik then obtained confirmation of its claims from Popes Adrian IV in 1158 and Alexander III in 1167.

In fact, the Ragusans appeared to be on course for unqualified victory. But then, on a visit to Zadar in March 1177, Pope Alexander III (1159–1181) bestowed the pallium upon the (arch)bishop of Bar and placed the bishoprics of Upper Dalmatia under his authority. This was a disaster for Dubrovnik, and it turned out to be a decisive one. The emergence of a strong state of Serbia under the Nemanjić family at the end of the twelfth century and the subsequent imposition of Orthodoxy over much of the region meant that Rome would never fundamentally reconsider its decision. Sandwiched between Split on the one hand and Orthodoxy on the other, Dubrovnik's archbishops would be left to rule over the faithful of the Ragusan state.

Dubrovnik's metropolitan authority was, however, for a time at least more acceptable in Bosnia. The Ragusans' close commercial relations with *Ban* Kulin had their counterpart in ecclesiastical ties. As metropolitan for the see of Bosnia, the Dubrovnik archbishop appears to have been a tolerant, indeed compliant authority. The bishops of Bosnia were local clerics, locally chosen, using the Slavonic liturgy, having it seems been unaffected by successive decrees intended to impose Roman practice. For example, in about 1189 the archbishop of Ragusa is recorded as having consecrated a certain Radigost as Bosnian bishop. And, 'not being literate in Latin or anything other than Slavic, when he made his oath of fealty and allegiance to his metropolitan, he did it in the Slavic language.'[36]

These rather liberal arrangements, though, were unsatisfactory both to the Hungarian-Croatian kings, intent on asserting control over Bosnia, and to the archbishops of Split, who had their own reasons to try to wrest sees from their Ragusan counterparts. In 1192 the King of Hungary persuaded the pope to remove Bosnia from Dubrovnik's metropolitanate and transfer it to Split – though in practice the Bosnians continued to look to their old authority. To the general charge of lax administration levelled against the archbishop of Dubrovnik were more dangerously added, between 1199 and 1202, accusations that *Ban* Kulin was giving refuge to heretics in his dominions. At a Bosnian Church Council in 1203, attended by an archdeacon from Dubrovnik rather than any representative from Split, reforms were promulgated which temporarily averted the danger of outside ecclesiastical or military intervention.[37]

By contrast with the obscure and – if the Hungarians were to be believed – doctrinally suspect circumstances of the Church in Bosnia, the Ragusan archbishop presided in Dubrovnik itself over a strongly and exclusively Catholic city-state. As regards its ecclesiastical administration, it was highly centralised, there being no other parishes than that based on the Cathedral, its archbishop and chapter. The archbishop himself was usually elected by the cathedral canons of Dubrovnik, often from among distinguished foreigners deemed able to advance the Ragusan church's interests; for example, one of the most doughty defenders of Dubrovnik's rights against Bar was the Venetian-born Tribunio, who ruled as archbishop between 1153 and 1189.[38] In fact, of the twelfth century Ragusan archbishops only one hailed from Dubrovnik – archbishop Bernardo, who proved in Ragusan eyes the least satisfactory of all.[39]

Venice Takes Control

By the beginning of the thirteenth century Ragusa had, therefore, emerged as a successful commercial community. It had established links with both its neighbouring states and more distant towns. It had its own civic institutions and its own archbishop – even if the scope of his metropolitanate was somewhat depleted. This achievement was a tribute not just to Ragusan resourcefulness but also to the fact that Imperial Byzantium had over the centuries – perhaps largely inadvertently – served tiny Dubrovnik's interests very well. When it was in the ascendant, Byzantium had been a generally benevolent but conveniently distant protector. The decisive decline in its influence after 1180 had already caused Dubrovnik problems in dealing with a rejuvenated Serbia, which harboured ambitions to control the Adriatic towns. But it was Byzantium's sudden collapse at the hands of the Venetian-financed knights of the Fourth Crusade which was fatal for Dubrovnik's early prospects of effective independence.

The background to the Fourth Crusade consisted of a potent mix of high- and low-mindedness. The pope, Innocent III, had sought a new Crusade in which the combined strength of Western and Eastern Christendom should be brought to bear against the Infidel. The crusaders themselves, though, were imbued with a rankling Western resentment against Byzantium. They were also motivated by the immediate requirement to obtain effective passage – which they felt should on this occasion mean maritime passage – to the Holy Land. Venice for its part, under its blind, aged, crafty Doge, Enrico Dandolo, wanted to punish Byzantium for its past obduracy, exclude rivals from trade and secure a dominant position in the Levant; its unmatched naval capability gave it a unique opportunity that it now exploited ruthlessly.

Accordingly, in 1202, in exchange for agreeing to transport the crusaders and to postpone demands for payment of the impossibly large sum originally promised to them by the naive organisers of the Crusade – and without the knowledge of the pope – the Venetians persuaded the knights to seize Zadar for them from Hungary. The city was duly taken that November, the crusaders and Venetians spending the winter there. The following year the Venetian navy transported the crusaders to Constantinople where, after the failure of negotiations and various upheavals within the city, they finally seized and plundered it. Venetian sea-power had been crucial to the siege's success and the Venetians had still not been paid: so they demanded and obtained recompense. This took the form of a three-eighths share of Byzantium's territories. A further aspect of the deal was that Venice's Tommaso Morosini was made Patriarch of Constantinople. On his way back with the Venetian fleet from Constantinople in 1205, it was this new Patriarch who secured the submission of Dubrovnik to Venetian rule.[40]

Doubtless Venice would have seized Dubrovnik in any case, once it was offered such a promising opportunity. But a rift in the Ragusan governing group made the task much easier. Perhaps in response to the disorderly conditions in the region at the time and the end of even nominal Byzantine overlordship, the then-count of Dubrovnik, Damjan Juda, began to act the tyrant. It seems to have been an affair very similar to those in which the *podestà* of numerous Italian city republics were prompted to overthrow their communal institutions. Rich and temporarily popular, Juda did not give up his office after six months as custom then required, but held on to power for two years. He also intimidated his opponents by introducing soldiers into the city. So his son-in-law, a wealthy merchant with friends in Venice, organised a conspiracy against him among the leading Ragusan nobles and persuaded them to give him the authority to invite the Venetians to Dubrovnik in order to overthrow their count. The Venetian Patriarch of Constantinople then tricked Juda onto his ship and took him prisoner, whereupon the latter in despair at his predicament committed suicide by beating his head against the ship's hull. A Venetian count was appointed to take his place.[41] A new era in Dubrovnik's turbulent history had begun.

THREE

The Serenissima's Subjects: Dubrovnik Under Venetian Rule (1205–1358)

Coming to Terms with Venice

The Ragusans in later years would have little that was pleasant to say about Venice, and their reflections upon the century and a half they spent under Venetian rule were no less jaundiced. Viewed more objectively, however, the balance looks different. For each obstacle that Venice placed in Dubrovnik's way it also provided, if only in its own interests, corresponding advantages; and when the Serenissima did reluctantly abandon its former subjects and future competitors to their own devices, Ragusa was more capable of successfully maintaining an autonomous existence than it would have been without those long years of irksome Venetian tutelage.

Each of the first two Venetian counts of Dubrovnik served for two years. But their successor, Giovanni Dandolo, then served continuously until 1230, and under him the Ragusans started to chafe. A sign of this was that in April 1226, Venice required Dubrovnik to send twenty named hostages drawn from its most distinguished families before the Feast of Saints Peter and Paul (29 June). But no hostages arrived. So in October Venice renewed the demand, now increasing the number.[1] Then in 1231 Giovanni Dandolo returned to Venice (probably having been expelled), and in his absence Dubrovnik resumed effective charge of its affairs, appointing as vice-count (*potknez*) one of its own nobles, Andrija Dobrana. Dobrana, during his short spell of control, concentrated on negotiating trade agreements with Italian towns, notably Rimini, Ferrara and Fano. But splits and dissensions flared up so badly among the Ragusan nobility that it was agreed to ask for a new count to be sent from Venice.[2]

The terms imposed by Venice on Dubrovnik in 1232 usefully summarise the main aspects of the relationship between the two, as well as pointing significantly to the future. Some of the requirements were simply designed to ensure Venice's continuing political hold. Three times a year *laudes* in honour of the Doge and Patriarch would be sung in Dubrovnik's cathedral. All Ragusans of thirteen years of age and over must take an oath of loyalty to the Doge, and to each new count every ten years. If the Doge came to Dubrovnik he must be received with due honour. If he wished to stay in the archbishop's palace the Ragusans must make it available or, if he chose to reside somewhere else, they must find him another suitable house. Similarly, the Doge's envoys must be properly received and accommodated. Every All Saints Day (1 November) Dubrovnik would send to the Doge personally 12 *hyperperi* and 100 *hyperperi* to the Venetian Republic; on the same day, the Venetian count in Ragusa would be paid 400 *hyperperi*.[3] Each year, twelve hostages drawn from illustrious Ragusan noble families would be chosen, six of whom would stay in Venice for half the period, to be exchanged for the others for the following six months. Dubrovnik would henceforth choose its archbishop from among Venetian clerics and, as long as the pope agreed, he would be subject to the Venetian Patriarch of Grado.

The new terms also regulated military relations. Whenever the Venetians sent a war fleet into the Adriatic in the zone north of the Durrës-Brindisi line, Dubrovnik must provide proportionate armed assistance. If a Venetian fleet of thirty ships and more was involved, this proportion was specified as one thirtieth. Venetian preoccupation with the threat of piracy – and Venice's well-founded suspicion that the Ragusans were not beyond striking mutually advantageous deals with pirate chiefs – is shown by the provision whereby Dubrovnik must not receive the notorious Kačići and the men of Omiš or other pirates in the town. If the Venetians sent their galleys against these pirates, Dubrovnik must also send a ship with 50 well-armed soldiers.

But the most significant provisions were those relating to trade. On goods brought to Venice from 'Romania' (that is to say, the lands of the defunct Byzantine Empire) the Ragusans were to pay dues of 5 per cent by value. On goods from the kingdom of Sicily they would pay 2.5 per cent and on goods from 'beyond the Sea' (Egypt, Tunisia, the Barbary Coast) 20 per cent. The Ragusans could send in total four merchant ships a year to Venice, each with a capacity of 70 *miliara* : over and above that, a flat rate of 20 per cent was payable.[4] But the most important provision was that on goods from 'Slavonia' (that is to say, Serbia, Bosnia, Croatia and Dalmatia) the Ragusans need pay no customs dues at all. In peacetime the Ragusans would be allowed to trade freely from the Gulf of Corinth westwards, but when and where Venetians were forbidden to trade the Ragusans could not trade either. In Venice itself the Ragusans were not permitted to do business directly with foreigners.[5]

These conditions, on which Dubrovnik once more acknowledged rule by Venice, are revealing of the latter's intentions during the whole period up to 1358, and to some extent beyond. Venice was not a classic imperial power. It showed no desire to send Venetian nobles or soldiers to Dubrovnik, beyond the count and his company. It was unconcerned with altering Dubrovnik's sense of identity or its institutions, though it had an effect on both. Its interests were commercial and, only insofar as successful commerce required, military. As for the military value of Dubrovnik, this is fairly obvious: it was a crucial staging post on the way from the Adriatic to the Levant with which, after the Fourth Crusade, Venetian fortunes were so closely linked; Dubrovnik was also the only Dalmatian sea-power which might help Venice repress the piracy that flourished along that coast.

Whatever the Ragusans in their frustration may have felt, Venice had no desire – at least while it remained in control – to throttle Ragusan trade. Dubrovnik was after all not just a competitor, it was an offshoot of the Venetian Republic, and it would be less valuable and more vulnerable if it were neglected. In fact, what Venice wished to achieve throughout the Adriatic was to enforce the 'staple rights' which all medieval towns tried in a more modest way and with more limited scope to impose: this required that all trade in the surrounding area take place at the staple town where dues and taxes were payable. Although Venetian 'lordship of the Gulf' had its own special, splendid ritual – the 'marriage' of the Adriatic to the Venetian Doge symbolised by a golden ring cast into the sea – it was only an ambitious application of staple rights.

In practice, the requirement that all trade take place in the Venetian Rialto market was evaded, particularly by the towns of the middle and lower Adriatic. For example, Venice never succeeded in bringing Ancona fully within the system and effectively came to accept that.[6]

A similar attitude was taken by the Venetians towards Dubrovnik. The Serenissima did not, as the terms of 1232 illustrate, seek to impose a closed and exclusive staple system, which would anyway have been un-enforceable. But it did lay down certain specific prohibitions – notably, those against trading with foreigners in Venice and against sending more than four shiploads of goods a year. In a later period the trade in salt and grain would also be subject to close control.

The most important concession made by Venice at this time was, of course, the provision whereby the Ragusans need pay no dues on goods imported from the Slavic hinterland – a reversal of the earlier position.[7] There is no reason to think that the change resulted from either wise statesmanship on behalf of the Venetians or even a strong demand on behalf of the Ragusans: it probably represented a simple recognition of the difficulty of enforcing the original provision. In any case, with so many more lucrative and less perilous opportunities for gain, the Venetians were doubtless happy to abandon the Slavic hinterland, with its unpredictable princes, barbarous peasants and incomprehensible language, to the Ragusans. Be that as it may, the decision had far-reaching consequences.

By checking the expansion of Dubrovnik's maritime commerce and forcing it to look towards the overland trade with the interior, Venice helped assure Dubrovnik's future survival. It was the fund of knowledge and connections that the Ragusans built up in the Slavic hinterland that would allow them to fit so well into the plans of any power that dominated the Balkans – even, in future centuries, an Islamic superpower. Dubrovnik had also, as it were, the benefit of breathing with two lungs: when either maritime conditions on the one hand or the circumstances of the overland trade on the other proved especially difficult, it could turn elsewhere for sustenance until the difficulties passed. The commercial and political uniqueness of Dubrovnik at its zenith was thus that it was firmly ensconced in both the Balkan and the Mediterranean worlds.

This, of course, is to anticipate. For most of the thirteenth century Ragusan resentment against Venetian lordship manifested itself in a series of disputes and revolts. After the final return to Venice of Count Giovanni Dandolo there was a time when Dubrovnik was ruled instead by two *potknezs*: certainly, in 1235, when it made agreements with Rimini and Ravenna, Dubrovnik was not recognising Venetian suzerainty. The following year, however, the Ragusans sent envoys to make their submission once more to Venice, which was agreed on very similar terms to those of 1232, and a new Venetian count was sent. In 1251 Dubrovnik rebelled once more, returning to Venetian allegiance the following year. Again in 1266 the Venetian count was expelled after he had decreed the exile of some Ragusans, and Dubrovnik had to despatch an embassy to Venice to excuse its actions and receive another count. Disputes between the town and its Venetian counts continued over what the latter claimed was due to them, as did Dubrovnik's attempts to escape or minimise the military demands made by Venice itself.[8]

Conflicts with Serbia

Venice's main value to Dubrovnik lay in the protection it offered – above all, against the Serb rulers who frequently threatened the town. The Venetians rarely involved themselves directly. But the Serbs must have recognised that in the last resort Venice would never allow Dubrovnik's existence or prosperity to be imperiled. The two main points of dispute continued to be the territorial limits and cultivation of the Ragusan Astarea and issues of ecclesiastical jurisdiction.

Dubrovnik found itself at war with successive Serb rulers during the thirteenth century. Of these, Stefan Uroš I (1243–1276) was probably the ablest and certainly the most assertive. He could also draw upon the resources which the rapid development of Serbia's mineral wealth provided. Uroš's two main external imperatives were to assert Serb control over Hum and to resist pressure from Hungary, to which his disagreements with Dubrovnik were peripheral. But naturally the Ragusans did not see matters in this light and disliked him even more heartily than his predecessors.[9]

The old points of contention – both territorial and ecclesiastical – continued to rankle, and finally war broke out in 1252. Uroš's army attacked the town, a specific Serb war aim being to prevent Dubrovnik's building new walls to enclose the most recently settled area, the suburb of St Blaise (later called *Garište*). The Ragusans sought to resolve the dispute by diplomacy. Dubrovnik's envoys had secret instructions to stir up as much dissension as possible at the Serbian court if Uroš proved obdurate – which he did. The failure of their mission led to renewed conflict, this time centred on territory disputed between Ragusans and Slavs in the fertile area of Župa Dubrovačka, where each side engaged in mutually destructive raids on the other's property.

Dubrovnik had more to lose in this kind of skirmishing – if only because it could make more profitable use of peace – and so sought to bring to bear outside pressures. Doubtless with the support of Venice, the Ragusans accordingly negotiated a full military alliance with the Tsar of Bulgaria. The treaty's practical results were a disappointment to Dubrovnik, but its terms are revealing of the scale of Ragusan self-confidence and ambitions. Formally at least, it was a treaty between equals which somewhat improbably envisaged Ragusan forces seizing Serb-held towns and fortresses and handing them over to Bulgaria. Dubrovnik's longer-term economic concerns were expressed in the provisions for its merchants to trade freely through the lands of the Bulgarian Tsar and for maintenance of its monopoly of salt sales between the rivers Bojana and Neretva.[10]

Faced with the threat not just of Bulgarian intervention but of trouble in Hum, whose ruler Dubrovnik had also drawn into its diplomatic web, and doubtless fearful of pressing too hard an enemy enjoying Venice's protection, Uroš made peace in 1254. The new agreement sought once more to regulate the territorial issue, guaranteeing the Serbian king his rights over the contested fields and vineyards but allowing the Ragusans, with his special permission, to farm land not presently under cultivation. War, however, broke out again in 1265. Apparently, Uroš sought at this time to have Dubrovnik recognise his rather than Venice's suzerainty, but in spite of the conflict between Venice and Dubrovnik in 1266 about the latter's expulsion of its Venetian count, the offer was decisively refused. The next peace treaty (in 1268) instituted the tribute called St Demetrius's Revenue (*Svetodimitarski dohodak*), whereby the Ragusans undertook to pay the Serbian king 2,000 *hyperperi* a year.[11] It thus placed on a systematic basis the payment by Dubrovnik of substantial bribes in order to be left in peace by the Serbian rulers.

In 1275, however, there was yet another war with Uroš in which the Serb army plundered the houses and wrecked the vineyards outside Dubrovnik and tried unsuccessfully to take the town itself. On this occasion, the Venetian count proved more useful, leading a Ragusan army to victory over the Serbs in one engagement. Venice's direct involvement induced the king to agree a new peace.

In 1276 Uroš was overthrown by his son Stefan Dragutin (1276–1282), with whom Dubrovnik maintained good relations until he too was pushed aside by his brother Stefan Uroš II Milutin in 1282. During Milutin's long reign (1282–1321) there was one war with Dubrovnik (in 1301), as usual provoked by territorial disputes, but relations were clearly a good deal better than with his father.[12]

Ecclesiastical Conflict

This chronicle of an apparently endless and almost indistinguishable succession of wars and peace treaties reveals one aspect of Ragusa's relations with Serbia. But that relationship was also conducted at other levels, one of the most important of which, as has been mentioned, was ecclesiastical.

The Serb population had become increasingly Orthodox as Catholic influence had waned. The Catholic bishop of Hum, whose see was in theory based in Ston, had left to live on the Ragusan island of Lokrum in the early thirteenth century. The ruler of Hum proposed instead that Dubrovnik send one of its own clerics to his lands, though he demanded 200 *hyperperi* in exchange. Whether for financial or other reasons, Dubrovnik refused. Similarly the Catholic bishop of Trebinje was forced by Uroš to abandon his see. He too later moved to Lokrum, where he became abbot of the monastery and also a canon of the Ragusan chapter. In 1275 he was appointed by the pope to be Archbishop of Dubrovnik.[13] Future Catholic bishops of Trebinje, finding conditions impossible in their nominal see, adopted the practice of taking refuge on the little island of Mrkan, where from 1296 there stood a Benedictine monastery. Finally, in 1456, the bishop definitively settled in Dubrovnik – leaving Mrkan to continue to be used as a quarantine station – and was duly compensated with a house and garden in the city.[14]

The Serb rulers also remained determined to support the claims of the bishopric/archbishopric of Bar against Dubrovnik, so as to maximise their influence over Zeta. Moreover, as time passed, the population became ever more hostile to Dubrovnik's claims. In 1247, during a vacancy at Bar, an envoy from the Dubrovnik archbishop arrived to proclaim the latter's rights. He was shouted down, and when he adduced the authority of the pope the people cried: 'What is the pope? Our lord, King Uroš, is our pope!'[15]

The archbishop of Dubrovnik's authority was also under pressure in Bosnia. The earlier challenge represented by Split for control of the Bosnian archbishopric had been overcome, principally through local refusal to acknowledge Rome's decision in Split's favour. But in the 1220s the papacy, at Hungarian prompting, again began to take a close interest in Bosnian doctrinal deviations.

How, when and whence heresy came to Bosnia is obscure. Also unclear is the relationship between Bosnia's heresy and its schism, that is, between the (probably quite small) number of educated people who had fallen into dualist error and the (much more significant) schismatic Church of Bosnia, which had its own structure and hierarchy.[16] The kings of Hungary had a strong interest in promoting Rome's wish to root out heresy, because they sought to reassert control over the effectively independent *ban*s of Bosnia and religious zeal provided a convenient justification for doing so. The resulting Bosnian 'crusade' of 1235–36 was initially quite successful. Even Dubrovnik, whose archbishop had nothing to do with the enterprise, decided to suspend its relations with the Bosnian ruler, *Ban* Ninoslav. Friendly contacts between the *ban* and the Ragusans soon resumed, however, for the attempt to impose Catholic orthodoxy on Bosnia by means of Hungarian soldiers and Dominican friars was shattered when the Tatars invaded Hungary.

From now on, form and substance in Bosnia's ecclesiastical affairs were almost entirely divorced. The pope pressed ahead between 1246 and 1252 with transferring the Bosnian bishopric from the archbishopric of Dubrovnik to the Hungarian archbishopric of Kalocsa. But the bishop of Bosnia was in any case never able to administer his see and simply resided at Djakovo in Slavonia, while in Bosnia itself a schismatic Bosnian church was now firmly established. Such Catholic influence as was brought to bear continued to come from Dubrovnik and later from the Franciscans.[17]

Territorial Expansion

Philip de Diversis, Dubrovnik's Tuscan schoolmaster, would later write that 'while almost all other peoples strive by war, by force, by the sword, by arms and by deception to increase their dominions, that community of Dubrovnik has expanded its territory peacefully and in a friendly fashion.'[18] This was, in actual fact, something of an oversimplification: in particular, it underrated Dubrovnik's single-minded ruthlessness in achieving its territorial objectives by any combination of means available. But it is fair to say that the Ragusans proved particularly skilled in finding opportunities to advance their interests in highly unpromising circumstances.

Those circumstances were rarely less favourable than during the reign of the Serbian King Stefan Uroš I. Yet it was now, some time before 1272 (the date of the great Dubrovnik Statute), that Dubrovnik acquired the island of Lastovo. The place had had a violent and unsettled early history. At the end of the tenth century, when it was under the suzerainty of the Croatian kings, it sheltered a nest of pirates who resisted fiercely the Venetian force launched against them by Doge Pietro II Orseolo. Lastovo's history is then obscure.[19]

In 1240 Dubrovnik sought to employ the authority of Venice in order to acquire Lastovo, along with the islands of Mljet and Korčula. On this occasion, the Ragusans failed. Some authorities claim that Lastovo was finally sold to Dubrovnik by King Uroš. But the introduction to the Lastovo Statute clearly states:

> Be it noted that *when the men of Lastovo gave themselves and the island of Lastovo to the commune of the city of Ragusa*... the commune of Ragusa swore to maintain them in all their ancient customs which they have among themselves...

In fact, it seems likely that Dubrovnik merely purchased from the Serbian king any rights he claimed as ruler of (part of) Hum, while the main transaction was that by which the Dubrovnik government offered its protection to the men of Lastovo, who under certain specified terms agreed to accept Ragusan rule.[20]

The island which Dubrovnik thus acquired, lying some 90 miles to the west, was always the least accessible of its possessions. With a surface area of 3,860 hectares, it was hilly and heavily wooded and had one important harbour, at Ubli on its western shore. It was fertile, but there was a lack of fresh water, and in the absence of natural springs the inhabitants had to rely heavily on cisterns to catch the rain. The islanders were largely peasant property-holders and fishermen, stubbornly attached to their rights and customs. The chronicler Razzi regarded them as tough and courageous, and, to judge from the number of priests (on which he also remarked) and the number of churches, which can still be seen, exceptionally devout.[21] Jakov Lukarević, writing somewhat later, enthused like Razzi about the island's rich soil that produced such excellent wines, oil and fruit. He even likened its vegetation to that of Madeira. Lastovo's waters, full of fish, also produced red, white and black coral, on which a prosperous little industry was based for centuries.[22]

The Venetian count (and in later times the Ragusan Rector) appointed his own representative – a count or *knez*, or *potknez*, or *vicarius* – to rule the island, including its offshore islets and reefs from Sušac to the Vrhovnjaci. This agent was obliged each year to bring from Lastovo to the count in Dubrovnik live hawks, dead rabbits, and suitable women to serve in his household. The count of Lastovo was entitled to levy a tithe of corn and wine and other profits for his own benefit. Over time, the demands of the Dubrovnik count increased: he insisted on his own share of corn, wine, fines and the profits from the tiny islands off Lastovo on which sheep were found temporary grazing. The Lastovo count, in order to meet these demands, correspondingly increased the burdens on the islanders, who in 1308 appealed to the Doge in Venice for relief. The Doge abolished all the existing dues and taxes and instituted instead a remuneration of cash and hawks to go from Lastovo to the count of Dubrovnik, whose own count on Lastovo would henceforth receive a salary. The profits of justice and other profits would all remain with the community of Lastovo. The Ragusan Great Council confirmed these arrangements in 1313 and the men of Lastovo similarly gave their consent.[23]

Ragusan attempts to use Venetian power in order to gain control over the islands of Korčula and Mljet also continued after 1240. The family of the Venetian count of Dubrovnik, Marsilio Zorzi, had in the previous century acquired an hereditary claim to Korčula which he managed to assert successfully after his appointment to Dubrovnik in 1254. He accordingly ruled Korčula for several years as its count. The Zorzi family were still established on Korčula in 1358, when the ties between Dubrovnik and Venice were definitively cut; but the family's claims had not, it seems, benefited the Ragusans, who continued to plot (albeit unsuccessfully) in the next century to bring the island within the scope of their Republic.

Mljet was a very different case. In practice, it was firmly under the lordship of its Benedictine abbey, which was naturally more likely to look to Catholic Dubrovnik than to the island's notional secular overlords, the Orthodox Serb rulers of Hum.[24] Dubrovnik continued to try to have its own control more clearly established over the island, which was also formally within the Ragusan archdiocese. Finally, in 1301, on the occasion of war with the Serbian King Stefan Uroš II Milutin (1282–1321), the Great Council of Dubrovnik authorised the seizure of Mljet and appointed a count to rule it.[25]

Although not as distant as Lastovo, Mljet was still far enough from Dubrovnik not to be extensively colonised by Dubrovnik's noble families. It was, however, greatly loved by the Ragusans, who were making bequests to its abbey from the late thirteenth century and who came, as did both other Catholics and Orthodox from much further away, to pray before the holy treasures possessed by its abbey, particularly the famous painting of the *Gospa od jezera* ('Our Lady of the Lake').[26] For Serafino Razzi it was the island's claim to be Melita (otherwise believed by bible scholars to be Malta) – the place where, according to Chapter 28 of the Acts of the Apostles, St Paul was shipwrecked and later bitten by a viper – that was most exciting.[27] Jakov Lukarević, who also mentions the famous Madonna, described the island as mountainous and difficult for arable farming, but excellent for viticulture – Razzi, too, admired its powerful red wines. It produced plentiful fruit, livestock and wood. Its potential for iron ore was, however, underdeveloped because the inhabitants preferred the life of fishermen.[28] It fell to Dubrovnik to regulate the affairs of Mljet when, in 1345, the island's peasantry rose in revolt against the monastery's feudal exactions. The archbishop of Dubrovnik, Ilija Saraka, mediated, and the resulting agreement was enshrined in the Statute of Mljet which firmly ensconced the community within the Ragusan state. The peasants were given full title to the land they had been working in exchange for 300 *hyperperi* a year and a chicken from each household on St Blaise's day.[29]

The most important Ragusan territorial acquisition was, however, that of the Pelješac Peninsula (also known as *Stonski rat*, 'Ston Point'). This was the first occasion when Dubrovnik fully demonstrated what would be regarded as its almost legendary diplomatic virtuosity, by dabbling in other powers' conflicts to advance its interests. After the death of the Serbian king Stefan Uroš II Milutin in 1321, a civil war had broken out and with it a weakening of Serbian central control over the state's outlying regions, among them Hum. Different noble families struggled to assert themselves there, and of these the Branivojevići came out on top. Most important from Dubrovnik's point of view, the Branivojevići had control over Pelješac. The family quickly proved unruly neighbours, preying on Dubrovnik's merchants. The new Serbian ruler Stefan Uroš III Dečanski (1321–1331) was unwilling or unable to check their activities, and so both the other local nobles of Hum and the Ragusans – who doubtless already had other ends in view – called upon the *ban* of Bosnia, Stjepan Kotromanić, to intervene.[30]

Dubrovnik now agreed a full-scale military alliance with Kotromanić against the Branivojević family, proceeded to wage an effective campaign against them, and even captured one of the Branivojević brothers. The Bosnian and Ragusan forces were completely successful. But it was the Pelješac peninsula, along with a strip of land from Trebinje across Popovo Polje and the coast (Primorje) up to Ston, which most interested Dubrovnik. This territory remained in the hands of the Serbian king. So it was on the latter, rather than on the Bosnian *ban*, that the Ragusans now primarily focused their diplomatic attentions.[31]

Luckily, in King Stefan Uroš IV Dušan (1331–1355; Tsar after 1346) Dubrovnik found someone with whom it could deal. Dušan's interest lay in expansion towards the south, rather than in drawn-out conflicts over Pelješac. Dubrovnik also made good use of its friends at the Serbian ruler's court, whom it generously rewarded. Dušan accordingly agreed to yield to Dubrovnik his rights to Pelješac, to the strategically important little island of Posrednica lying off the mouth of the Neretva, and to Primorje, all in exchange for a cash payment of 8,000 *hyperperi* and an annual tribute of 500 Venetian ducats.

The Bosnian *ban*, though, proved less accommodating. He yielded to Dubrovnik the rights he claimed over Pelješac (which he did not in practice hold) in exchange for an annual tribute of 500 ducats. But he refused to relinquish his rights to Posrednica and the coast from the Neretva to the Dubrovnik Astarea (which he did actually hold). This presented Dubrovnik with a vexing problem: it would have to try to defend and settle the Pelješac peninsula without having overland access to it.

Nor was this the end of the matter as regards Dušan, for in 1334 he quarrelled with the Ragusans over the non-payment of his 8,000 *hyperperi* and seems also to have had second thoughts about the conditions under which he was prepared to see Dubrovnik administer Pelješac. In the agreement which settled the dispute the Ragusans had to pledge that they would not harbour the

Serbian king's subjects and would allow his official to seek them out if they arrived on the peninsula; they promised to allow Serbian Orthodox priests to continue to serve the Pelješac churches; and they undertook to prevent the region's inhabitants serving in Ragusan armies, if Dubrovnik was at war with Serbia. Whether Dubrovnik honoured the first and third of these conditions is unclear: but it certainly never abandoned its intention of Catholicising the peninsula, as events subsequently showed.[32]

Dubrovnik had not acquired Pelješac by agreement with the inhabitants (as it had in the case of Lastovo), but rather by purchase from the territory's feudal lords. Consequently, unlike with Lastovo, it did not feel bound to respect the wishes and interests of the existing inhabitants. Indeed, it assumed from the first that the local population could not be trusted. The population were either Orthodox (that is, 'schismatics') or members of the shadowy Bosnian Church (that is, 'heretics'), for neither of whom the Ragusans had the slightest sympathy. As the anonymous Ragusan chronicler dismissively noted, the men of Ston and Pelješac 'did not believe in God or the saints, but in dreams, fortune-tellers and enchanters.'[33] The district was, moreover, extremely exposed and difficult of access. Although fertile – it would produce some of the region's finest wines – and productive – the salt pans at Ston would become an important source of state revenue – it would not for many years be sufficiently secure to attract a satisfactory immigration from Dubrovnik. For all these reasons a forceful strategy was required.

The government consequently decided upon full-scale colonisation according to an elaborate but effective system intended to ensure both a fair allocation (according to the prevailing social criteria) of land, and speedy settlement of it. In 1333 Dubrovnik, therefore, divided up the farmland of the peninsula (excluding Ston) into thirty units called 'tens', each of which broke down into ten 'parts', each of which was itself subdivided into four 'quarters'. The parts were then allocated by lot to Ragusan noble families. For each of these parts the landowner must pay two ducats a year to the state to be used for the peninsula's fortification and defence. That decision was somewhat modified later in the same year: an eighth of the territory was now formally allotted to the non-noble citizens of Dubrovnik, though in practice they seem to have received somewhat less. Nothing, however, was given to the existing inhabitants, who were merely expected to contribute their labour as demanded. Three nobles were, therefore, appointed to divide up the peasants of Pelješac among the new Ragusan landlords, so that they could be called upon to perform all the work required. The new owners were forbidden to alienate their land for the next ten years. They were also discouraged from bequeathing it to the church. A special cadastral register was drawn up containing the decrees relevant to the settlement of the peninsula, listing the owners of the different plots of land and precisely describing the latters' location.

In practice, the work of allocating land went more slowly than the government envisaged. The commissioners responsible concentrated on the most vulnerable territories first – the land around Ston and that on the north-western part of the peninsula. A revolt by the local peasantry in 1335, which resulted in Dubrovnik's conceding that the inhabitants should not be expelled from their homes by their new landlords, also retarded progress. Furthermore, the landlords themselves were often reluctant to go and cultivate the property they had been granted and had to be threatened with punishment when they failed to do so. Only in 1344 was the remainder of Pelješac allocated, and still further revisions were made in the 1390s. In other words, it took some 60 years for the full process to be completed. But, that said, it represented a very considerable – if hardly very humane – achievement, which not only provided the continuing basis for control over the peninsula and the increasingly important Ston but also a model for the later similar treatment of Primorje (acquired in 1399) and Konavle (acquired in 1419 and 1427).[34]

Shifting Allegiance: the End of Venetian Suzerainty

The good relations which Dubrovnik enjoyed with the Serbian Tsar Dušan seem to have been valued on both sides. Whereas in its dealings with his predecessors Dubrovnik found it necessary from time to time to rely on the support of its Venetian suzerain, it now felt able to conduct an independent diplomacy whose success was amply demonstrated by the acquisition of Pelješac. It is possible that the greatest of the Nemanjić rulers was also temperamentally better able to appreciate the wealth and sophistication of the Ragusan state. His first visit to Dubrovnik had been made in May 1331, shortly before he ousted his father Dečanski. He was received with great hospitality and valuable gifts and seems to have stayed in the Count's Palace (the *Knežev dvor*). In 1346 Dušan had himself crowned Tsar in Skopje. Naturally, Ragusan envoys were present at the occasion.

In 1350 the Dubrovnik government, learning that Dušan – who had been waging war against Bosnia – would be in their vicinity, invited him once more to visit the town. Detailed preparations were made to deal with this distinguished visitor. Dušan was asked to limit his escort to 100 men, but that still required a special effort to make adequate provision. Ragusan nobles were chosen to organise food for the tsar's men and horses, and a special tax was levied on the landowners of Pelješac and Ston to pay for the presents he would be given. Two ships were despatched to bring Dušan, his wife and young son from Cavtat to Dubrovnik's harbour. The royal party disembarked on 13 November, walking across a small bridge specially erected to bring them to the *Knežev dvor.*[35] The Serbian tsar, oblivious it seems to the finer differences between the Catholic and Orthodox Churches, made generous donations to the church of St Stephen (his martyred namesake), to the new church of St Blaise (whose miracles during the Black Death had still further reinforced his cult in Dubrovnik) and to the nuns of St Clare. The tsarina also made votive gifts of her pearls and jewellery, and at her request the Clares were granted by the government of Dubrovnik revenues from taxes levied on fish and from other dues. Before they left, the imperial couple were given bales of woollen cloth to deck out their courtiers at home. Dušan's visit only lasted three days, but it made a great impression, reflected in the Ragusan chroniclers' subsequent awestruck accounts. He was, (as Ranjina puts it), '... a pious and great warrior'.[36]

Dušan's political achievement proved fragile, and after his death the Serbian state soon began to decay. But Dubrovnik used its good relations with the new ruler, Tsar Stefan Uroš V (1355–1371), whom it had entertained so lavishly as a boy, to persuade him in April 1357 to grant what his father had always refused – the territory stretching from Ljuta in Župa to Petrovo Selo above Rijeka Dubrovačka. This was the land which lay on the frontier of Astarea rising up to the first high ridge, and it had been a constant source of friction between Ragusan farmers and their Serb neighbours.[37]

As on Pelješac, the business of division and settlement in Župa was carried out with great thoroughness. A commission of ten nobles, none of whom owned property there, was appointed by the Ragusan Great Council in 1362 to 'examine, confirm and define'. Local witnesses were interrogated about the precise assets involved. Then in 1366 began the actual dividing up the territory into 'tens'. The process of allocation was still continuing three years later.[38]

This acquisition in Župa had represented the last territorial concession Dubrovnik would be able to gain from the rulers of Serbia, and in this sense it marked the end of an era. Even more so, however, did the events which were now taking place along the Dalmatian coastline, where Venice and Hungary were locked in a struggle that was approaching its climax.

The rivalry between the two powers had its origins in the early twelfth century and it had continued with alternating shifts of advantage ever since. The key to the conflict was Zadar, which rebelled repeatedly against Venetian rule. A particularly virulent revolt broke out in 1345 and the Hungarian king, Louis I of Anjou, sent troops to the city to support it. But Zadar could not hold out, and after a long siege Venice regained control, destroyed its sea-walls and imposed a harsh regime on the inhabitants. Having become embroiled in the affairs of Naples, Louis accepted an eight-year peace with Venice in 1348. But it was only a matter of time before the conflict was renewed.[39]

Initially, the Ragusans were not much affected by the rivalry between Venice and Hungary. Dubrovnik was, of course, committed to provide military assistance to its Venetian suzerain; but it was a past master at resistance by procrastination and argument. For example, in March 1324, when instructed by the Venetian Doge to provide two fully equipped galleys to join the Venetian fleet in its campaign against the Emperor of Byzantium, the Ragusan Senate decided to reply that this could be done, but Venice must pay: they would, of course, have met the cost if they could have afforded it, '... but God knows that the Ragusan Commune is in such poverty that it cannot afford to arm those ships at its own expense'.[40] In August 1345 the Ragusan Great Council took rather more seriously a Venetian demand to despatch an armed galley and crew to join the siege of Zadar.[41] Further demands from Venice, now at war with Genoa but fearful of Hungary, were made, debated and probably accepted by Dubrovnik in 1350. By 1355 Dubrovnik, however, again felt able to be obstructive. In spite of Venetian demands and the pleas of the Venetian count, Dubrovnik claimed that Venice had not in fact armed at its own expense the thirty galleys required to trigger Dubrovnik's contribution. (This latest Venetian military activity was prompted by awareness of the likelihood of renewed fighting with Louis of Anjou, now that the earlier eight-year peace had expired.)

Apart from its grumbling about the Serenissima's military demands, Dubrovnik had not shown any recent signs of wishing to liberate itself from Venetian suzerainty. But as it looked ever more likely that Venice would face a crushing defeat at the hands of Hungary, the Ragusan patriciate began to examine how best to advance its own and Dubrovnik's interests. In 1356, with the (in fact premature) news that war had resumed, a party in Dubrovnik's Great Council urged the pursuit of a more assertive policy towards Venice. They wanted the Venetians to concede to Dubrovnik the right to choose its own count and to accord greater economic privileges to Ragusan merchants, placing them on an equal footing with those of Venice.

Venice's military position rapidly deteriorated with the renewal of full-scale hostilities in 1357, as the Dalmatian towns fell one by one into Hungarian hands.[42] In Dubrovnik the anti-Venice party's demands now became still more strident. Indeed, some nobles over-reached themselves, going too far for their more cautious colleagues. One of their number, Mato Menčetić Mencijev, was in October exiled by a majority of the Great Council to the island of Hvar for a year and a day and deprived of his right to sit in the Council or hold office for two subsequent years, for making a speech attacking the Venetian count. The need for caution was doubtless reinforced by the arrival of two Venetian special commissioners. They were well received and their suggestions as to how to improve the defences of Ston were accepted. At the end of December Dubrovnik renewed its oath of fealty to the Doge and even expressed regret at the loss of Zadar. In January 1358 Venice was desperate enough to grant Dubrovnik what it had always previously refused, namely all the civic and commercial rights enjoyed by its own citizens.[43]

But by now Dubrovnik had glimpsed the prospect of far greater autonomy under a different protector. So at the start of February 1358, while the Venetian count was still *in situ*, it was decided to send an embassy to King Louis. The precise circumstances of the departure of the last Venetian count, Marco Superanzio, from Dubrovnik are unclear. The Ragusan chroniclers suggest that he was sent off in a friendly fashion – though he certainly left in a hurry because the Ragusans had to send his belongings on after him. The strategy, it seems, was to distinguish Dubrovnik in Venetian eyes from the other 'proud and rustic' Dalmatians who had rudely ejected Venice's representatives: indeed, in order to reinforce that distinction, which the Ragusans hoped might yield future commercial benefits, the bold decision was taken to send an envoy to Venice to minimise the rift.[44] But for all the diplomatic niceties the days of Venetian rule were over.

FOUR

A Kind of Independence: Dubrovnik's Autonomous Development Under Hungarian Suzerainty (1358–c. 1433)[1]

Dubrovnik and Louis I of Hungary

Ragusan diplomatic finesse, first evident in the manoeuvrings preceding Dubrovnik's acquisition of Ston and Pelješac in 1333, was applied still more effectively in the negotiations with King Louis at the Hungarian royal court in Višegrad in 1358–59. It was all the more notable because the hand which the city's government and diplomats had to play was not obviously strong, while that of the Hungarian king after his crushing victory over Venice could hardly have been stronger. By the Peace of Zadar of 18 February 1358, Venice renounced in Hungary's favour all its claims to Dalmatia from the Kvarner down to Durrës, specifying by name each of the Dalmatian islands, territories and towns – including Dubrovnik. The formal position from the Hungarian viewpoint was quite simple: the 'Kingdom of Dalmatia' had now at last been restored by conquest to the Crown of St Stephen. But there the clarity ended; for 'Dalmatia' was a term of varying and ambiguous political and geographical significance. Dubrovnik was in a general sense clearly part of it, and indeed had long been so considered.[2] More specifically, it had been a part of Venetian-controlled Dalmatia for a century and a half. By contrast, it had never been within Hungarian-controlled Dalmatia at all. And so unlike the other Dalmatian towns, it had never been riven by struggles between pro-Hungarian and pro-Venetian factions: the unity and cohesiveness of its patriciate was, in fact, distinctly un-Dalmatian.

It is on the face of it surprising, therefore, that Dubrovnik accepted so easily the Hungarian claim to it as part of the newly conquered Dalmatia. It seems likely, however, that what mattered to the Ragusans at this stage was reality not theory, and that realism suggested giving an immediate warm welcome to the assertion of Hungarian claims. Dubrovnik always needed outside protection and was always ultimately prepared to swallow its pride and pay real or symbolic tribute to one or other great power in order to obtain it. Moreover, the easiest power to deal with was – as it had been with Byzantium in the past and was with Hungary now – one both sufficiently distant and sufficiently different not be always intervening in Ragusan business. This was particularly the case for Dubrovnik in its present state of development, that is, as a rapidly growing commercial power but a relatively weak military one. Louis I of Hungary was thus in all respects likely to prove a more satisfactory lord than the Doge of Venice.

Yet acceptance of Hungarian suzerainty did not, in Ragusan eyes, preclude seeking to secure maximum autonomy, indeed so great a degree of self-determination as to approximate to the modern concept of 'independence'. The other Dalmatian towns quickly found themselves ruled by Hungarian-appointed counts supported by pro-Hungarian factions of nobles. Such a fate would not at all be to Dubrovnik's liking. The diplomatic challenge, therefore, was to achieve both effective self-government and Hungarian protection, which in turn meant interpreting the settlement of the Peace of Zadar differently in regard to Dubrovnik than in the cases of all the other Dalmatian urban and island communities.

For a full two months the Ragusan Great Council debated the precise position which Dubrovnik should adopt in the forthcoming discussions at the Hungarian royal court. In the instructions finally given to its ambassadors, agreed in the Great Council on 11 April 1358, Dubrovnik authorised them to recognise the Hungarian king as its lord and offer him tribute and military support but also seek the widest autonomy as regards administration and internal security and the right to collect all its revenues for the city's own use. The embassy was to seek confirmation of Dubrovnik's existing territory – particularly mentioning the islands of Mljet and Lastovo (the latter having shown some unwelcome signs of wanting to extricate itself from Ragusan control). The ambassadors should also seek to obtain Primorje – specified as the coast from Kurilo (today's Petrovo Selo) to Ston – which Dubrovnik had briefly acquired from Tsar Dušan but then quickly lost. Cunningly playing upon the king's presumed ignorance of local history and geography, the ambassadors were also to claim Cavtat and then if asked what precisely that claim entailed they were to answer that it embraced Konavle, the *župa* ('county') of Dračevica (on Boka Kotorska) and even Trebinje – all of which, argued Dubrovnik, had been attached to ancient Epidaurum, of which their little state was the proud successor. Finally, the envoys were to urge that Dubrovnik's rule be extended to the islands of Korčula, Hvar and Brač – over none of which it had, of course, any legitimate claim whatsoever.[3]

The embassy entrusted with negotiating for this ambitious programme was a distinguished and impressive one, as befitted the circumstances. Its most senior member was the Ragusan archbishop, Ilija Saraka, whose prestige and experience had been acquired in Dubrovnik's past diplomatic dealings with the papal Curia. His four fellow ambassadors were equally seasoned negotiators. An escort of 50 accompanied them, including a chancellor, priest, book-keeper and numerous servants. The ambassadors themselves were commanded by the Ragusan government to appear before the king looking their best; they were to be dressed in new purple outfits and wear velvet cloaks edged with ermine. On their arrival at Višegrad they would present the king, queen and courtiers with expensive and attractive gifts, including five hawks and various sweetmeats. And so as to ensure that in the substantive negotiations they should follow their instructions to the letter, they were threatened by the Ragusan government with death if they exceeded their authority.[4]

The negotiations at Višegrad were friendly and productive. It seems that Louis raised no objection either to treating with Dubrovnik separately or to envisaging a diminution of the rights previously enjoyed by Venice over the city's affairs. Perhaps this was a case of realism on his part too: for the practical difficulty of ruling Dubrovnik from as far away as Hungary, especially since there was no local pro-Hungarian faction on which to call in emergencies, must have been obvious. In any case, the king's goodwill towards Dubrovnik had already been won by another distinguished Ragusan diplomat, Marin Gučetić, with whom Louis had had earlier dealings.[5]

The work of the Ragusan ambassadors was not, however, immediately accomplished, and they seem to have become anxious about the reception they might receive should they return to Dubrovnik with their tasks still incomplete. Most of the main difficulties had been resolved by the time Louis issued his first charter of 26 May; but there were several still-unresolved issues. That document is particularly revealing since it enumerates not only the points agreed but those on which the king had made offers that the ambassadors claimed they lacked the authority to accept. The next day a second charter was issued whose contents demonstrate that each side had made some further concessions; but, fearful of the wrath of their touchy compatriots in Dubrovnik, the ambassadors still insisted that all must be confirmed separately by the Ragusan government. Accordingly, on 3 June the king commissioned Petar, Bishop of Bosnia, to go to Dubrovnik, taking with him the two charters.

There, on 18 July, the Ragusan Great Council duly accepted the terms offered by the king.

The first document (of 26 May) began by spelling out the duties accepted by the Ragusans. They were to pledge allegiance to the king and his successors. They would pay him a yearly tribute of 500 ducats and in their cathedral the traditional *laudes* would be chanted in his honour as their sovereign lord. His flag and coat of arms would fly on their land and their ships. If the king (or his son or nephew) should come to Dubrovnik he must be properly received and entertained. If he raised at his expense a war fleet of thirty or more galleys, or if he raised an army from the Dalmatian towns including ten or more galleys, Dubrovnik must provide one galley. Then the king set out his own duties towards the city. He undertook to defend Dubrovnik against the king of Serbia, the *ban* of Bosnia and anyone else. As overlord of Bosnia, he granted them Primorje (though in fact it was not in Louis's control and so they did not yet actually acquire possession of it). He generally confirmed their possessions and rights and customs. He allocated between his and Dubrovnik's judges jurisdiction in any future disputes between Hungarians and Ragusans. Finally, he permitted Dubrovnik to trade with Serbia or Venice, even if Hungary was at the time at war with them.

All these terms had been agreed by the time of drawing up the first charter and remained unchanged in the second. But the king had also made some other demands. He had wanted the oath of allegiance be to him and his successors *forever*. He had specified that if he had to defend the Ragusans against Serbia or Bosnia they should pay to him rather than to the rulers of those states the traditional tributes of 2,500 and 500 *hyperperi* respectively for lands which had earlier been acquired from them. He demanded that if a Dalmatian town or subject rebelled against him, Dubrovnik must assist with one galley, and that it should generally regard his friends and enemies as its friends and enemies. Most importantly, however, he insisted that Dubrovnik receive as its count the man appointed by the king from among the ranks of his own trusted people.

The Ragusans were, after some discussion, prepared to accept most of these requirements – though they insisted that the galley sent at their expense in time of rebellion serve only for three months. But on the question of the appointment of the count they held their ground. Here it was the king who made the concession. He was now persuaded to grant that the count be chosen *by the Ragusans themselves* from among the faithful subjects of the king, and that he would simply confirm their choice. The new count would enjoy the rights of his Venetian predecessors, but now both the Senate and (a significant change) the count's Small Council would be elected by Dubrovnik's Great Council – that is, by the Ragusan patriciate.[6]

Marin Gučetić and another Ragusan, Lovro Vukasović, had remained at the Hungarian court (to which they already in practice belonged), and it seems to have been due to their efforts that a final royal concession on the matter of the count was made. On 3 January 1359 the king granted the Ragusans the right to choose anyone they liked as count, without need of royal confirmation of the appointment, as long as the man was neither a Venetian nor any other enemy of the king.[7]

In the years after 1358 Dubrovnik had for the first time to face up to the full implications of *de facto* independence. The Hungarian king was a benevolent but distant force, still chiefly preoccupied with preventing any revival of the threat posed by his Venetian enemies. For Dubrovnik, however, the main determinant of local political conditions was the continuing decline of the Serbian state and the struggle between various Slavic princes to exploit the opportunities which this offered. Vojislav Vojinović, lord of Trebinje and Konavle, was one of these unruly neighbours: between 1358 and his death in 1363 he and Dubrovnik fought a series of wars for possession of Pelješac and Ston, which he claimed as lord of Hum – a title bestowed on him by the Serbian ruler, Stefan Uroš V. Astarea was extensively pillaged, but Vojinović's army was kept away from the city itself. When it found it could not defeat him militarily, Dubrovnik paid him off, though as the Ragusans explained in a letter to the *ban* of Bosnia in 1359 it was done 'with great sorrow and not a little resentment'.[8] After his death, his widow ruled for a short while before being driven out by Vojinović's nephew Nikola Altomanović, lord of Rudnik.

The Ragusans quickly developed a quite special hatred for Altomanović, who pillaged and burnt their land. As they put it in a request for help from King Louis:

> Of all the lords of Serbia, although they are all insincere and malicious, [Altomanović] is the worst, the most brutal and the most treacherous.[9]

With the subsequent destruction of Altomanović, it was the ruler of Bosnia who became Dubrovnik's most powerful neighbour. *Ban* (later King) Tvrtko I (1353–1391) of Bosnia and Dubrovnik for most of the time maintained quite good relations, cemented by mutual economic interests, and the Bosnian ruler visited the city himself in 1367. Bosnia became even more important as a focus for Ragusan diplomatic activity after Tvrtko conquered Trebinje and Konavle, and in 1377 had himself crowned King 'by the grace of God' of Serbia and

Bosnia. The following year he visited Primorje and then entered Ragusan territory where he and Dubrovnik negotiated a treaty, later confirmed in the Bosnian royal court. By this, Dubrovnik agreed to pay him the symbolically important tribute of the Revenue of St Demetrius (*Svetodimitarski dohodak*), which was taken as implying recognition of Bosnian rule over Trebinje and Konavle. The Ragusans for their part were assured of the right to trade (while paying the proper customs dues) throughout Tvrtko's lands.[10]

As was demonstrated by the immediate sending of an embassy after the end of Venetian rule, Dubrovnik did not underestimate the importance of its future relations with its earlier ruler.[11] Venice's convoys continued regularly to stop for supplies at Dubrovnik on their way to the Levant, and although the Venetians rigidly refused to carry Ragusan goods on these ships they brought useful information and some business to their old subjects.[12]

In 1378, however, Dubrovnik was drawn into the War of Chioggia. The city was, of course, necessarily involved in a formal sense when the original dispute between Venice and Genoa over possession of the Aegean island of Tenedos erupted into a full-scale war in which Dubrovnik's sovereign lord, Louis of Hungary, supported the Genoese. It was natural too that the Genoese fleet would wish to use Dubrovnik and other Dalmatian ports loyal to Hungary as bases for its operations in the Adriatic. But in fact the Ragusans seem rather to have relished the opportunity of wounding a commercial rival, at least when events were moving in the direction willed by the Hungarian-Genoese alliance, which they did through most of the conflict. Even more important, the Ragusans could use the cover of the hostilities to try to gain influence over Kotor, which they regarded with envious resentment.[13]

But Dubrovnik soon began to sense that Venice was far from beaten. The Ragusans now sought to reduce their direct involvement with the Genoese, who – Dubrovnik complained – had also failed to hand over a fair share of the booty acquired at a maritime engagement off Pula. When Kotor finally recognised Hungarian sovereignty, this even prevented Dubrovnik's having an excuse to destroy its salt pans. So, as it turned out, the Peace of Turin of August 1381, which ended the war, brought the Ragusans none of the hoped-for benefits.[14]

The succession of threats to its security in these years had, on the other hand, required the Ragusans to adopt elaborate and expensive measures to defend their city and territory. Unpredictable dangers facing faraway Ston and Pelješac required special foresight: thus the government of Dubrovnik had an arrangement whereby through a prearranged signal – of smoke by day, fire by night – the count of Ston would summon military help from the count of the islands.[15] The fortifications of Ston were also steadily strengthened. During the War of Chioggia it was Mali Ston that received most attention, because of its vulnerability to Venetian seaborne attack: the local nobility was told to stay and defend it or face fines of 1,000 *hyperperi*.[16] But Dubrovnik itself was also vigorously reinforced. After the departure of the last Venetian count there had been a general review of security and all openings in the walls, except the four city gates, were sealed. In 1366 precise numbers and dispositions of the city guard were decreed by the Great Council: 81 men were to mount guard in twenty-nine specified positions. On the outbreak of the War of Chioggia, churches and houses near the walls were torn down, men employed on the construction of the church of St Blaise were diverted to work on the fortifications, and others were sought from Astarea and the islands to dig out the city ditch in front of the Pile Gate.[17]

Dangers and Opportunities of the Hungarian Civil War

Louis of Anjou had been a successful monarch in the medieval mould, and his achievement fragmented after his death on 16 September 1382 for the characteristically medieval cause of a lack of male heirs. Louis's daughter, Maria, betrothed to Sigismund of Luxemburg, son of Charles IV, King of Bohemia and Emperor of Germany, succeeded to the Hungarian throne. Her mother, Elisabeth, acted as regent while Elisabeth's associate Nicholas Garai wielded most of the real power. These arrangements were, however, opposed by significant groups of nobles. One of these factions offered the crown of Hungary to Charles of Naples, the closest male relative of the dead king Louis. This action marked the beginning of a period of widespread disorder.

A bloody and complicated war broke out between the rival contenders – Sigismund of Luxemburg, who had married Louis's daughter Maria, and in the other camp Charles of Naples and later his son Ladislas. The Bosnian king Tvrtko seized the opportunity of this struggle to break free of Hungarian suzerainty altogether and then under cover of support for the House of Naples grabbed a swathe of Dalmatia. On Tvrtko's death in 1391 the Bosnian magnate Hrvoje Vukčić Hrvatinić emerged as the strongest figure, and he and his brother Vuk were appointed joint *bans* of Croatia and Dalmatia by Ladislas.[18]

Dubrovnik's attitude to these events, which it followed closely, was opportunistic, though hardly more so than that of the other parties involved. Its objectives amid the violence and confusion of Sigismund's long and dismal reign (1387–1437) were to defend its existing possessions, acquire whatever further territory it thought would be commercially or strategically valuable, and seize every occasion to expand its trade and increase its revenues. To achieve all this it struck up alliances with whichever of its neighbours seemed most useful, though at the same time it generally honoured its obligations to the Hungarian crown.

After Louis's death, Dubrovnik duly swore allegiance to the two Hungarian queens and engaged their support in the city's opposition to Tvrtko's attempts to build up his town of Novi (the future Herceg-Novi) as an alternative market for salt and wine.[19] The Ragusans also recognised and stayed loyal to Sigismund after his coronation in 1387. But none of this prevented their establishing equally good relations with the most important regional potentate, Hrvoje Vukčić Hrvatinić.

Duke Hrvoje's friendship was extremely useful for Dubrovnik, if rather less so for Hrvoje. It was he who persuaded the Bosnian king Stjepan Ostoja (1398–1404 and 1409–1418), to grant to Dubrovnik the lands of Primorje, which at last permitted the Ragusans uninterrupted access by land between the Astarea and Pelješac. Stjepan Ostoja's charter of 15 January 1399 was the fruit of many months of hard bargaining. Dubrovnik avoided having to pay a continuing tribute for the lands acquired. Instead, it simply rewarded Ostoja and Hrvoje with membership of the Ragusan nobility, houses in the city worth 1,500 ducats and property in Primorje itself.[20]

Dubrovnik entered into possession of the newly acquired 27,735 hectares of what were called the 'new territories' *(terre nuove)* in February and wasted no time in parcelling them out. Five Ragusan nobles were appointed as *partitores* to organise the territory according to the system of 'tens', 'parts' and 'quarters' applied to the colonisation of Ston, Pelješac and the margins of Župa Dubrovačka. In the final allocation of Primorje, the Ragusan patriciate acquired 221 of the 290 'parts', the non-noble citizens of Dubrovnik 66.5 'parts' and Ostoja and Hrvoje the remainder. The existing population received nothing.[21]

Ostoja came to have second thoughts about these arrangements and went to war with Dubrovnik in 1403 and 1404. But the Ragusans crucially managed to turn Hrvoje against Ostoja, and the latter was duly overthrown. The vulnerable new Bosnian king now confirmed Dubrovnik in possession of its freshly acquired territory and was duly rewarded in the traditional fashion by incorporation into the Ragusan nobility and the grant of a house in the city.[22]

Attempts to Acquire Korčula, Hvar and Brač

According to the chronicler Ranjina, when King Stjepan Ostoja gave Primorje to Dubrovnik he also offered the city other territories, but the Ragusans refused because they did not feel able to defend them.[23] Whether or not such an offer was actually made, Ranjina probably faithfully reflects Dubrovnik's thinking at the time. The city's expansionism was always strictly calculating. It had every reason to know how difficult it was to hold on to exposed territory and how many well-armed enemies it could expect to face when doing so. Islands, however, were more easily defensible, as well as specially attractive to a commercial maritime state. So it was natural that the Ragusans should look covetously upon the three most important South Dalmatian islands that still eluded their control – Korčula, Hvar and Brač. Of these, Korčula was the real potential prize.

The Korčulans and Ragusans had become near-neighbours once Dubrovnik acquired Pelješac in 1333. Both had also, of course, been ruled by Venice till 1358. The narrow channel between Korčula and Pelješac was no bar to regular social and economic contacts between two similar populations. The island and peninsula were also linked until 1541 by ecclesiastical jurisdiction; for the old Catholic bishop based in Ston had moved his see to Korčula at the start of the fourteenth century, as Pelješac became more heavily Orthodox. The Korčulans even shared Ragusan veneration for St Blaise, symbolised in the island's church popularly called by that name. A more tangible connection lay in the large shipments of Korčulan stone and in the numerous Korčulan stonemasons who came to Dubrovnik, drawn by the demands of the city's programme of public and private, secular and ecclesiastical building in the late fourteenth and fifteenth centuries. A more awkward similarity between the two communities, on the other hand, was Korčula's strong tradition of jealously guarded autonomy, as Dubrovnik was about to find to its cost.[24]

In 1403 Ladislas of Naples came to Zadar and there made Hrvoje Vukčić Hrvatinić his chief representative in Dalmatia, granting him possession of Split and the islands of Korčula, Hvar and Brač. Without much regard for their friendship with Hrvoje, the Ragusans now saw their chance and seized it. They sent galleys first to Korčula, then to Hvar, then to Brač, with instructions to the inhabitants that they should return to the allegiance of Sigismund, their natural lord, and hand over their ships to Dubrovnik's safekeeping. But the manoeuvre seems to have failed.[25]

A better opportunity soon presented itself. Ladislas's fortunes began to worsen after he left Dalmatia once more for Italy. Then, in a gesture with fateful consequences for the future history of Croatia, he sold in July 1409 what his supporters still held in Dalmatia and abandoned the rest of his rights – all in favour of Venice. One after another, the Dalmatian towns accepted Venetian rule. In anticipation of Ladislas's action, Duke Hrvoje submitted to Sigismund and for a time continued to rule what remained of his Dalmatian possessions on his former enemy's behalf. But in 1413 Sigismund denounced Hrvoje as a traitor and stripped him of his lands, while Hrvoje for his part turned to the Ottoman Turks for help.[26]

In 1409 Dubrovnik had proved both its commitment to Sigismund's cause and its continued interest in Korčula by despatching ships against Ladislas's fleet after the latter had attacked the island. Duke Hrvoje's shift of allegiance had frustrated its hopes temporarily, but his disgrace now seemed to open the way to fulfilment of its ambitions. Accordingly, in June 1413 Dubrovnik persuaded Sigismund to grant it possession of the three islands.[27]

But Dubrovnik faced strong resistance from the islanders, especially in Korčula.[28] In fact, during the three years of nominal Ragusan rule over the island, there operated two parallel governments – a count sent by Dubrovnik and a Korčulan Great Council consisting of the local nobility. The count was tolerated, his name even appearing on island government documents, but the local Great Council bypassed him on all important matters. Dubrovnik's early optimism had been misplaced. In August 1413 it had given its envoys detailed instructions as to the financial terms on which it would seek to acquire the three islands in perpetuity. But all this diplomatic activity proved fruitless. Finally, in September 1416, Sigismund simply removed the islands from Dubrovnik and granted them to one of his courtiers. By then the realities of local obstructionism had in any case already proved more than a match for Dubrovnik's best efforts at effective government. The three islands were destined to remain for ever outside the Ragusan Republic.[29]

The Acquisition and Settlement of Konavle

In fact, Dubrovnik had already fastened its gaze on a more attainable, though still highly problematic objective – the acquisition of Konavle. It had a powerful sentimental reason to do so because of the connection between that fertile but exposed territory and Cavtat, the site of Ragusa's own birth-place.[30] The economic connection, though, was real enough too. Dubrovnik's farmers had long been making private agreements with the inhabitants to pasture sheep and cultivate corn in Konavle. The territory was almost as fertile as – and much more extensive than – Župa Dubrovačka, though it also included karst, mountains and forest. It comprised five districts: Cavtat and neighbouring Obod, the agricultural lands of Konavle proper, Donja Gora (the western part of the region, along the coast from Cavtat to Molunat), Planine (the wild, virtually uninhabited, mountain area) and Vitaljina (adjoining Boka Kotorska). The inhabitants by the early fifteenth century were an ethnic and religious mix, Catholic and Orthodox Slavs and a shifting population of Vlach shepherds, none of whom had any particular sympathy for Dubrovnik. The main stronghold was the powerful fortress of Soko: other fortifications existed at the settlements of Cavtat and Molunat. A *knez* traditionally ruled on behalf of the feudal lord of the day from Ljuta. In fact, apart from the remains of the ancient aqueduct and the fragmentary ruins of Epidaurum there was little to suggest that the region had any affinity with the neighbouring city-state which was preparing to lay hold of it. Such was the scale of the challenge.[31]

It was, however, taken up with alacrity by Dubrovnik as soon as the death of the Bosnia's King Tvrtko I opened the prospect of a weak central authority lacking the will to hold onto Konavle. The Ragusans quickly despatched an embassy to the brothers Radić and Beljak Sanković who held Konavle at the time and surreptitiously bought it from them for an annual tribute of 1,000 *hyperperi*. But the barons of Bosnia were outraged and utterly refused to accept this alienation of Bosnian land. The Sankovići were driven from Konavle and Dubrovnik was left frustrated.[32]

The Ragusans persisted. Having failed to make any headway at the Bosnian court, they transferred their attentions to Dubrovnik's own sovereign and Bosnia's principal enemy, Sigismund. Dubrovnik constantly badgered him to concede in its favour his rights to both Konavle and Dračevica. For a decade Ragusan diplomats sought to exploit every opportunity to bend Sigismund to their will. They told him, for example, what a danger Konavle in the wrong hands posed to him: this was a none-too-subtle reference to Duke Sandalj Hranić, who held the eastern half of that territory, and to Pavle Radenović who controlled the western half – both of whom stood in the way of the fulfilment of Dubrovnik's ambitions. But it must in due course have become clear that the best the Ragusans could hope from Sigismund was his good offices as mediator, and that the substantial negotiation would have to be with the real controllers of Konavle. This was the route Dubrovnik finally adopted.

Initially, Sandalj Hranić was unresponsive, but his attitude changed when he found – like so many before and after – that he had to look to Dubrovnik as a place of refuge. As Philip de Diversis put it, thinking perhaps of this very event:

> Perhaps someone will ask why do these [Bosnian] lords sell [Dubrovnik] their lands? I will answer him: from love and from the great and constant favour which the Ragusan patriciate in every circumstance shows towards them... for in case some mishap befalls them, and the security of Dubrovnik is not involved, that town is their most peaceful and secure haven, their most reliable refuge... I have heard that this is how the saying arose among the Slavs: 'When the hare chased by the hunters goes to a safe place, it goes to Dubrovnik.'[33]

Held responsible by the Pavlovići, that is the sons of Pavle Radenović, for the latter's death, Sandalj was all but driven by them from his lands. In fact, his fortunes later improved. But he was now in a much more co-operative state of mind to deal with Dubrovnik about Konavle.

So it was that in January 1419 envoys from Sandalj Hranić and Petar Pavlović came to Dubrovnik to negotiate. The Republic offered the former's representative its classic rewards – membership of the Ragusan nobility and a house in the city – and the latter's a more direct bribe of 500 ducats, if they brought their respective masters to accept Dubrovnik's terms. Duke Sandalj was successfully persuaded, but Petar Pavlović was not. After some deliberation, the Ragusan Senate agreed to go ahead, hoping to obtain later Pavlović's half of Konavle – the more important one in fact, since it included Cavtat and Obod. By its treaty with Sandalj Hranić, Dubrovnik confirmed him, his brothers and his nephew (the future Herceg, Stjepan Vukčić Kosača) as members of its nobility, gave them a house in the city, granted them an estate in Župa worth 3,000 *hyperperi* and promised a yearly tribute of 500 *hyperperi*. Most important, however, was the large cash payment which Dubrovnik undertook to make to Duke Sandalj of 12,000 ducats (36,000 *hyperperi*). Half of this would be paid immediately. The other half would for the present remain on deposit in Dubrovnik, earning 5 per cent interest until the Ragusans actually gained possession of the territory.[34]

This, however, was to prove a hazardous enterprise. Once the documents had been exchanged with Sandalj, a commission of five Ragusan nobles was despatched to Konavle with a formal statement of the 'graces and immunities' which the Dubrovnik government was prepared to grant to the inhabitants. The terms broadly reflected the policy adopted towards the other newly acquired territories – that is, they should be fully and quickly integrated into the Ragusan system, which meant expropriating the local nobility, dividing up the local peasantry and colonising the whole area with Ragusan landlords. But some concessions were also made at the beginning, probably in order to avoid an economically damaging exodus of the available workforce. So the inhabitants were freed from the Bosnian ducat-per-hearth tax they had paid to Sandalj, and serfs were freed from compulsory unpaid work for five years. Konavle's feudal lords – the nobility – were forbidden to raise any dues from their peasants after St Luke's Day (18 October) that year, because all Konavle's land henceforth belonged to the state of Dubrovnik. The inhabitants could keep their law (which promise was kept) and their faith (which was essentially not) and, generally, they would enjoy the rights enjoyed by the other ordinary inhabitants of the Ragusan state.

Not surprisingly, these terms were strongly resisted by a group of leading Konavle nobles, and the Dubrovnik government despatched soldiers and armed ships to try to bring the rebels to heel. More effectively, they also called on Sandalj Hranić to intervene. He did so, and a compromise was agreed that temporarily suspended Dubrovnik's possession of the territory.

During this interval Dubrovnik turned its attention to the lord of the other half of Konavle, Petar Pavlović. The Ragusans had just managed to win him over to accepting in principle the sale of his half of Konavle when he was inconveniently killed by Sandalj and a force of Ottoman Turks. Nothing daunted, Dubrovnik now sought from Duke Sandalj the cession of the part of Konavle which he had seized from the late Petar. It succeeded. Accordingly, in a document of 30 May 1420, Sandalj Hranić claimed that he had acquired Petar Pavlović's part of Konavle as a gift from the Ottoman Sultan Mehmed I and gave it to Dubrovnik. In exchange, the Republic agreed similar terms to those for Duke Sandalj's own part – that is, a further house and estate, a 500-*hyperperi* annual tribute and a cash payment of 30,000 *hyperperi*.

Dubrovnik again sent in its agents to take control of Konavle, but again it was frustrated by resistance – this time fomented from outside by the late Petar's brother Radoslav. In response, Dubrovnik employed various stratagems, including the summoning of a *zbor* (local assembly), the despatch of troops and once more the influence of Sandalj Hranić, who managed to force Radoslav Pavlović to enter into negotiations in 1423. Dubrovnik used this lull in hostilities to begin the division and allocation of land in what had been Duke Sandalj's half of Konavle. But it also kept up the pressure on Radoslav Pavlović, bribing his father-in-law and leading nobles of his household to make him more acquiescent. Turkish attacks in 1426, also helped Dubrovnik's cause by making Radoslav desperate to raise money to build a fortress from which to resist the onslaught. So it was that on 31 December 1426 and on terms very similar to those earlier agreed with Duke Sandalj,

Radoslav Pavlović ceded the territory to Dubrovnik. The Ragusans began to divide it up and allocate it the following year.[35]

Though neither of the two divisions of Konavle (1423 and 1427) passed off smoothly, both revealed the intelligence, resourcefulness and ruthlessness of Ragusan policy. The arrival of a commission accompanied by the new Ragusan count to divide up eastern Konavle in early 1423 was met by a fresh revolt, and the Ragusan officials had promptly to flee back to the safety of Župa. The Senate sent a force of 400 men to restore order; a pardon was offered to those who submitted; prices ranging from 300 to 500 *hyperperi* were placed on the heads of the recalcitrant ringleaders. A *zbor* was then summoned and an agreement reached with the remaining Konavle nobles, which secured them at least something. As a special concession, 66 local noble families, though deprived of any rights over what had been farmed by their tenants, were allowed to keep a modest amount of the land which they had cultivated themselves. This seems to have satisfied the most powerful families. They were probably wise to accept the terms, for when it came to the later division of western Konavle, Cavtat and Obod in 1427 the Dubrovnik government made no such compromise: the local nobility there were simply all expelled.

The basic system of division in Konavle was (as elsewhere) by 'tens', 'parts' and 'quarters'. Obod and the fertile valley of Lug were excluded from this system: being particularly desirable, they were divided according to a system of *gionte* (that is, 'additions') added on to the other 'tens'. Also treated separately was the uninhabited Planine district, which was only really suitable for pasturing livestock. The rest of the land was divided up into 75 'tens'. Two of these were given to the new Franciscan friary and church of St Blaise. The three 'tens' which comprised Cavtat were specially reserved for the Ragusan state. The different Bosnian lords to whom Dubrovnik was indebted received something amounting in all to just over two 'tens'. Of the remaining 68 'tens', the nobility of Dubrovnik received 58 and the more important Dubrovnik citizens, ten.

This division, as elsewhere, only accounted for the land deemed fit for cultivation. Other land was held in common, and no individual or community could prevent another using it or the rivers which, with the mills along them, were throughout Ragusan territory the exclusive property of the state.

Dubrovnik, as a very urban community, had little natural sympathy with the migratory transhumant Vlach shepherds who for centuries had been accustomed to come and go in Konavle. It initially forbade them to enter the territory at all. But by 1430 the prohibition had been eased. And when Planine was finally itself shared out in 1442 the Vlachs were allowed to come and settle there as long as they paid compensation for any damage done to crops.

The question of Konavle's security – like that of Ston and Pelješac a century earlier – was seen by Dubrovnik as inextricably bound up with the population's religion, Orthodoxy (the faith of a large part of the population) never being considered as compatible with loyalty to the Ragusan state. At the outset, while its control over Konavle was shaky, the Ragusan government was prepared to make some compromises. Thus it upheld, for example, an earlier gift by Duke Sandalj to the Orthodox priest of Sveti Đurađ (Saint George) and then recognised his son as a member of the local nobility, rewarding him with land. The Popović family became a distinguished house among the Catholic Konavljan gentry and are remembered in the name of the modern settlement of Popovići.[36] With all of Konavle in Ragusan hands, the process of Catholicisation quickened. A Franciscan church staffed by Franciscan friars from Rijeka Dubrovačka and Bosnia was endowed with the land first at Sveti Đurađ, later at Sveti Martin (today's Pridvorje). The Dubrovnik government did not persecute the Orthodox, but it did pressure them. So in 1435, at the urging of a Franciscan missionary, an Orthodox priest was moved out of his house on Franciscan land at Sveti Đurađ, but allowed – like others – to remain in Konavle. By the mid-fifteenth century the process of religious assimilation and unification was largely complete.[37]

Dubrovnik's promulgation of measures to settle Konavle by no means guaranteed peaceful possession of it. In 1430 Radoslav Pavlović – now a vassal of the Ottoman Sultan – sought the return of his share of the territory, complaining that Dubrovnik had been fortifying Cavtat and that it had not paid him interest on the 6,000 ducats he had deposited with them. A three-year war of destructive plundering by both sides ensued.[38]

The war between Dubrovnik and Radoslav Pavlović for possession of Konavle was of more than passing significance; indeed, it signalled for Dubrovnik another historic turning point. Years of persistent diplomacy, opportune bribery and judicious use of force had won for the Ragusans what was to prove the final extension of their dominions. Between now and the fall of the Republic in 1808 there were only marginal changes to Dubrovnik's frontiers, and they involved territorial losses, not gains.[39] But already by the time of the Konavle War of 1430–1433 it was apparent that the decisive element in all future quarrels about territory in the vicinity of Dubrovnik would be the intentions of the Ottoman Sultan and his officials. It was this perception that now led Dubrovnik towards a shift, first of attention and later of formal allegiance, from Hungary to the Ottoman Empire.

FIVE

Eastern Approaches: Dubrovnik Within the Ottoman Empire (c. 1396–1526)

Early Contacts with the Ottoman Empire

As the power of the Ottoman Empire increased in the Balkans during the late fourteenth and early fifteenth centuries, Dubrovnik had every reason to be alarmed. It was not simply that the successful political and trading relationships it had built up in Serbia and Bosnia were threatened. So was Dubrovnik's very existence. And the reasons for this were bound up with the Ottoman state's nature and history.

One of the principal reasons why the early Ottoman emirate had outgrown its neighbours was its rulers' single-minded commitment to the ideal and practice of *gaza* or Holy War. In this, religious zeal and material benefit went nicely together, for the infidel could be plundered at will whereas permissible action against other Muslims was strictly limited. The early Ottoman state in northwest Anatolia bordered Byzantium and was thus well-placed to flourish at the expense of its neighbours and competitors. The Ottoman rulers soon came to show considerable tolerance towards the Orthodox Church and population; but in the early years they viewed Catholicism in a different light as a threat to their rule. None of this boded well for relations with vulnerable, Catholic Dubrovnik, which would have to establish a unique understanding with the Porte if it was to survive.[1]

Unfortunately for the Ragusans, the resistance offered to Ottoman advances by Dubrovnik's more powerful neighbours was ineffective. Weak central authority and divisions between competing lords in Serbia meant that the Turks gained early, devastating successes in their struggle to penetrate, influence and ultimately control the Slavic Balkans. At the battle of Marica in

1371 a Serb army was crushed and Serb lords soon started to become tributaries to the Ottoman Sultan. In the early years, Turkish penetration of the Balkans was undertaken by plundering, free-ranging bands. But it began to take on a clearer shape under Sultan Murad I (1386–1389), and in the mid-1380s Turkish armies started raiding the lands of Prince Lazar of Serbia (1371–1389). Lazar's refusal to accept Ottoman suzerainty decided the Sultan to punish him. Although Murad himself was murdered just before or during the battle of Kosovo, the death in the fighting of Prince Lazar and his army's heavy losses meant that the outcome must be reckoned another serious defeat for the Serbs.[2] Serbia was now riven by competing factions. Lazar's widow Milica considered fleeing with her young son, Stefan Lazarević, to Dubrovnik, but instead accepted the terms of the new Sultan, Bayezid I (1389–1402).[3]

Dubrovnik, whose merchants were present in all the major Serb trading centres, observed these events with mounting apprehension. Ragusan territory was first directly threatened by the Ottoman advance in 1386, when Turkish forces broke through to the Neretva river and refugees from Hum poured across the frontier seeking safety in Ston and Pelješac. The Dubrovnik government provided food for the fleeing Slavs but let only a limited number through, suspicious that many were really economic migrants whom it had tried to keep out in previous years. Yet the pressure proved unstoppable. In 1395 the Ragusan authorities even debated whether to round up indigent immigrant Slavs in Dubrovnik and ship them all to Apulia, though the proposal was finally rejected.[4]

The following year was one of still greater crisis for Christendom, when a mainly Franco-Hungarian army was destroyed by the Turks at Nikopolis. King Sigismund had to flee for his life, travelling down the Danube across the Black Sea and arriving in Dubrovnik on 21 December, escorted by four Venetian galleys. Whatever their private fears about the future, the Ragusans received him with much ceremony and at considerable expense.[5]

Dubrovnik was, in fact, already in negotiations with the Ottoman authorities. Precisely when the first contacts were made is unclear, but it was evidently some time before the spring of 1396. That June a messenger brought to the town a safe-conduct (*litteram securitatis*) from the Sultan. But the catastrophic Ottoman defeat at Ankara in July 1402 at the hands of Tamerlaine's army of Tatars and Mongols postponed by several decades Turkish dominance in the Balkans – and thus postponed Dubrovnik's need to come to terms with it.

Sultan Bayezid himself was captured by Tamerlaine's force and a little later died in captivity, precipitating a civil war between his sons. These years gave the remaining Slavic rulers a last – as it turned out temporary – opportunity to assert themselves. In particular, the Serb ruler (now calling himself Despot) Stefan Lazarević, having intervened actively in the Ottoman civil war, threw off Turkish suzerainty. This suited Dubrovnik very well. Its business in Serbia now developed to its zenith as Ragusan merchants supplied Serbian mining centres with food and luxuries and brought out of Serbia silver, lead, gold, wax, skins and dairy produce, while farming Serbian customs dues.[6]

In fact, it was really Dubrovnik's problems with Radoslav Pavlović, touched on earlier, that again brought home to Dubrovnik its need for some outside power to help it defend its interests against what Diversis described as Bosnian lords prone to violence through 'ill-will, arrogance, stupidity, or greed', being always 'more subject to impulse than reason'.[7] Hungary was clearly no longer capable of providing this protection. Worse still, Dubrovnik's neighbours showed no scruple in turning to the Turks in order to achieve superiority in their own mutual conflicts. Soon both Dubrovnik's friends and enemies were tributaries of the Turks, and the city's opportunities for successful military or diplomatic action without first squaring the Porte narrowed alarmingly.

Dubrovnik struggled long and hard to escape the political logic of the new situation. When in 1430 it approached Sandalj Hranić for assistance against Radoslav Pavlović, Sandalj advised the city not to take military action without first sending an embassy to the Sultan. But Dubrovnik feared that if it did so it might be asked for tribute. So instead the Ragusans approached the *sandžak-beg* (governor) of Skopje. But they then learned that Radoslav had sent his own envoys to the Sultan to put his case for Konavle. This news worsened their quandary. They still sought to avoid a direct formal approach to the Porte, preferring to send a Ragusan from their colony at Novo Brdo to accompany an embassy from Sigismund. But by now the Sultan had learned of their reluctance and wrote to Dubrovnik criticising them and informing them that he would judge the matter of Konavle himself. In August a Turkish official arrived to hear the case: he inspected the documents proffered by Dubrovnik and ruled in its favour, but also urged the city to send an embassy to the Sultan. He promised, though, that Dubrovnik would not be asked to pay the tribute – *harač* – which symbolised acceptance of the Sultan as sovereign.

In actual fact, the Senate had already decided on a direct approach. On 13 September the first known Ragusan envoys to the Porte, Petar Lukarević and Đuro Gučetić – predecessors of the long line of special ambassadors called *poklisari* – left for Turkey bearing costly gifts, going via the Turk's vassal Duke Sandalj, who sent one of his own men to accompany them. The envoys had been given an ambitious brief. They were not only to justify Dubrovnik's stance on Konavle but also to seek a charter guaranteeing the city's trading rights and to offer 20,000 ducats for a share of Radoslav Pavlović's other lands. A Turkish official accompanied by a Hungarian envoy was sent by the Porte in January 1431 to make more enquiries in Konavle. These proved satisfactory from Dubrovnik's viewpoint and the territory was accordingly restored to it, though no decision was made on the Ragusans' further demand for the huge sum of 60,000 ducats of reparations.

All this time Dubrovnik's envoys were still negotiating with the Porte on the matter of Dubrovnik's trading privileges. But their persistence bore fruit. On 6 December 1430, Dubrovnik obtained from the Sultan a document giving Ragusan merchants the right to trade freely by land and sea throughout the Ottoman Empire and to pay only those dues ordained by law. This notable achievement was more important than Dubrovnik's failure to achieve its other objective of despoiling and punishing Radoslav Pavlović. The grant of privileges which it obtained, though framed in general terms, regularised Dubrovnik's commercial relations with the Porte without accepting any new political or financial obligations. Securing it had been costly in bribes and sweeteners – as the Ragusans complained subsequently to the Bosnian king, Tvrtko II: 'Your Highness knows well and is acquainted with the Turkish nature: they do everything for money, and he who gives more wins.' But this was a game which wealthy little Dubrovnik was well-equipped to play.[8]

Dubrovnik Begins to Pay the Harač

For all its attractions, the settlement that Dubrovnik reached with the Porte in 1430 was never likely to prove more than a transitional one. This was so for both practical and theoretical reasons. For its part Dubrovnik, though it still viewed with distaste the prospect of becoming a permanent tributary to the Sultan, had reasons for wanting a more solid understanding with the Porte. This was because the general goodwill of a particular Sultan was unlikely to be sufficient to keep the often wayward, brutal and avaricious Ottoman officials in check. Only arrangements which were clear, specific and had a firm basis in Ottoman law could do that. But these practical considerations were linked to a thorny doctrinal question: how could Dubrovnik remain both an autonomous, mercantile, Catholic-Christian state and yet be accommodated within the Ottoman Empire's view of its mission and identity?

Any solution to that problem would inevitably need religious sanction. On the side of Christendom there were useful precedents from which the

Ragusans had already benefited. For example, in 1373 Dubrovnik had received permission from Pope Gregory IX to trade *ad partes Saracenorum*. The Ragusans had thus been allowed by Rome to send two merchant ships a year to the Levant, though trade in certain 'prohibited' items (deemed useful for the Muslim war effort) was forbidden. By 1427 when Dubrovnik approached Pope Martin V for permission to trade with the Turks, however, the stakes were much higher: the Ragusan Balkan trade through Turkish-controlled territory was increasingly valuable, but against this the Christian powers were also ever more apprehensive of the Turkish advance and so reluctant to assist it in any way. Dubrovnik's pleas were, therefore, unsuccessful. A further approach in 1429 also failed.

In March 1433 Dubrovnik sought the intervention of Sigismund, who was then in Italy, impatient and increasingly impoverished, waiting for Pope Eugenius IV to open the gates of Rome and crown him Emperor. The Ragusans eased Sigismund's problems by paying him 4,000 ducats – eight years' tribute. But before he could resolve Dubrovnik's problem, the (now-crowned) Emperor had to hurry off to the Council of Basel. There in December Sigismund – assisted by the eloquence of the learned Ragusan Dominican Ivan Stay – persuaded the Council to grant the permission Dubrovnik sought, which would be the model for privileges endorsed by subsequent popes.[9]

The Council of Basel allowed Dubrovnik to carry goods (excluding arms, food and other specified items) to Muslim lands, have dealings with Muslims, to transport pilgrims to the Holy Land, erect churches, cemeteries and have mass said in Ragusan colonies and enjoy all other such rights earlier granted to other Christian states.[10] These provisions, subsequently confirmed by successive popes, were of course meant to be exceptional, recognising the reality of Dubrovnik's position, and implicitly too the cost to Christendom if this beleaguered bastion of Christianity were lost. They were not intended to open the way for Dubrovnik to become a tributary, let alone a subject, of the Ottoman Sultan, nor free the Republic from its obligations to its feudal lord the King of Hungary or its spiritual lord the Pope. But this solemn recognition of Dubrovnik's special situation – at once part of Christian Europe but also exempt from many of the obligations that required – was to be the basis for grudging Western tolerance as the Ragusans now moved much further towards acceptance of the Sultan's authority.

The doctrinal obstacles to accommodation with Dubrovnik on the side of the Ottoman Empire were also overcome – in this case by adapting traditional concepts to take account of the large material benefits that Ragusan collaboration could bring to the Porte. Muslim theory traditionally divided the world into two. On one side was the Muslim state itself, the *Dar al-Islam* (the 'House of Islam'); ranged against it on the other was the *Dar al-Harb* (the 'House of War'). The former was ruled by the Caliph (who, since Selim I took the title, was the Ottoman Sultan) and governed by Islamic law, *the shari'a*, administered by a *kadi* or judge. The inhabitants of all non-Muslim lands, called *harbis,* were to be invited to embrace Islam: if they did not, war must be waged against them until they submitted to the Caliph's authority. But (Orthodox) Christians, Jews and other non-Muslims living within the *Dar al-Islam* would be treated differently: they were permitted to practise their religions and keep their property upon condition of paying the poll-tax (*cizye*) and the land-tax (*kharaj*; Slavic: *harač*), though they were forbidden to bear arms, ride horses or otherwise act the equal of Muslims. These non-Muslim subjects of the Sultan living in his dominions were known as *dhimmis*, derived from the Turkish word meaning 'responsibility', because in exchange for payment of their taxes the Muslim state accepted the responsibility to protect them.

As the Ottoman state became a great power it started to find this rigid distinction unsatisfactory and a third, less precise, theoretical entity emerged – the *Dar al-'Ahd* or *Dar al-Sulh*. Into this category fell those states and peoples which were prepared to pay the *harač* but not to accept mere *dhimmi* status. With them a specific treaty framed in the form of a solemn promise by the Sultan (*'ahd* or *sulh*) would specify the amount of the tribute (also called *harač*) and the terms of the relationship. The practical consequences of this grant – or *'ahd-name* – varied. At different times both Venice and Austria paid tribute to the Sultan, but they were powerful enough to enforce their own understanding of what it implied. In Dubrovnik's case, however, the sovereignty claimed by the Sultan and symbolised by the payment of the *harač* was a closer reflection of reality.

Although it is impossible to avoid the expressions entirely, concepts such as 'treaty' or 'charter' or 'rights' had no real significance in Ottoman eyes. All property, power and people were the Sultan's; his officials, from the humblest messenger (*çavuş*; Slavic: *čavuš*) to the Grand Vizier, were his slaves; his *ferman*s and *berat*s were personal orders accompanied by promises bestowing favours, which the Sultan's officials and other subjects must obey but which the Sultan himself could alter or rescind at will. The *harač* payments from Dubrovnik and elsewhere were of substantial financial importance to the Ottoman treasury. But they were no less significant by virtue of the subordination they implied – just as, on a lesser scale, the payments made by Dubrovnik to influential

Ottoman officials were valued by the recipients not merely as attractive bribes but as signs of submission. This was the system into which Dubrovnik was about to enter – one which was flexible enough to accommodate Ragusan distinctiveness but where the authorities would not feel inhibited about taking away everything that had been bestowed should that seem advantageous.[11]

The moment for further engagement between Dubrovnik and the Porte was fast approaching. In the 1430s the Turks stepped up their attacks on Serbia. The Serb Despot, Đurađ Branković, erected the fortress of Smederevo to resist them, but little by little Serbian territory was occupied and in 1439 Smederevo itself fell. Now only Zeta (starting to be called Montenegro) and the town of Novo Brdo held out. These were perilous times for Dubrovnik too, whose citizens were to be found all over Serbia, not least in Novo Brdo, which was the site of a flourishing Ragusan colony. In fact, Dubrovnik now demonstrated remarkable *sangfroid*. It told its people in Novo Brdo to resist the Turkish attacks, which they did till the town fell in June 1441. Dubrovnik also provided Sigismund with information about Turkish military movements and forwarded the Emperor's letters to the anti-Ottoman rebels in Albania. Still more provocatively, Dubrovnik gave help and shelter to the Despot as he struggled to retain what remained of his lands. Finally, when he was forced to leave Montenegro, the Ragusans resisted Turkish demands to hand him over and instead supplied him with a ship to escape to Hungary.[12]

In September 1440, even before the fall of Novo Brdo and the Despot's departure, a Turkish official arrived in Dubrovnik with instructions from Sultan Murad II (1421–1451) commanding that the Republic should send an embassy bearing the *harač* which, it was claimed, the Ragusans had paid to the Sultan's father Mehmed I (1413–1421). After lengthy debate, Dubrovnik despatched the embassy, but in place of tribute it was entrusted with a detailed (and not entirely honest) set of explanations justifying recent Ragusan behaviour. In answer to the demand for payment of the *harač*, the envoys were to say that Dubrovnik as a free city had never paid it to the Sultan's father (which was true). If the Sultan should draw attention to the fact that Dubrovnik paid tribute to the king of Hungary, they were to explain that this tribute was in fact owed by all Christian states to the pope, but that the latter had made it over to the rulers of Hungary (which was completely untrue). If mention was made of the tributes Dubrovnik paid to Bosnian lords, the envoys would say that these were mere payments made for lands sold to the city (which was true, from the Ragusan viewpoint at least). If the Sultan complained about the assistance given to the Despot, the envoys would minimise its significance but go on to explain that on Dubrovnik's willingness to uphold its reputation as a place of refuge for princes who were driven from their domains depended its continued ability to trade with its neighbours (which contained some truth, though it hardly reflected present realities). If they were faced with complaints that Ragusans in Serbia were fighting for the Sultan's enemies, that is for the Serbian resistance, the envoys should say that these Ragusans had merely been trapped in the besieged towns and could not get out. (In fact, the Ragusan merchants seem to have defended towns like Novo Brdo with vigour.)

These instructions, while revealing Dubrovnik's virtuosity in devising diplomatic argumentation, were also over-optimistic, as was quickly apparent. As soon as the envoys revealed to the Sultan that they had not brought the *harač* they were threatened and driven from his presence. In various parts of the Empire, Ragusan merchants were now imprisoned and their goods seized. Dubrovnik was also anxious about the intentions of the city's unreliable neighbours – both vassals of the Sultan – Radoslav Pavlović and Stjepan Vukčić Kosača (who had succeeded his uncle Sandalj Hranić on the latter's death in 1435). Dubrovnik did not, however, immediately yield to Turkish pressure. Instead, it instructed its envoys to tell the Ottoman Viziers that if it agreed to pay the *harač* this would encourage other neighbouring rulers to demand tribute and that would drain Dubrovnik's wealth and depress the trade it conducted in Ottoman territory, which so greatly benefited the Turks.

It was the *pasha* of Rumelia who suggested the compromise which resolved the deadlock. He suggested that Dubrovnik find some financial way other than the *harač* of satisfying the Sultan. The government accepted this suggestion. The *pasha* proposed, through Dubrovnik's envoy, that by way of homage rather than *harač* they agree to send an annual gift of 1,000 or 1,500 ducats. The government itself hoped to give at most 600 ducats, in cloth or silver plate rather than money. When the embassy arrived that November at the Sultan's court, however, it was met by a demand for an annual tribute of 10,000 ducats, later reduced to 5,000. This convinced the envoys of the imprudence of trying to offer the modest sum mentioned in their commission. Instead, they offered annual gifts to the *pasha* and the Viziers of 100 ducats each. This broke the ice and as a sign of goodwill a number of Ragusan merchants were now released from prison.

Finally, an agreement was reached on 2 February 1442. Its substance is contained in two documents written in Cyrillic. Dubrovnik's is much shorter – unsurprisingly, since the Ragusans were anxious to minimise the awful significance for their Republic (a term perhaps first self-consciously used in the course of these negotiations) of what was being undertaken. Dubrovnik pledged to be 'true to the great lord Sultan Murad' and to send him annually an embassy bearing a gift in silver dishes worth 1,000 ducats.[13]

The Sultan's document is much longer and spells out in detail the terms of his relations with Dubrovnik. It starts with a long Muslim oath in which he swears to fulfil his undertakings. The Sultan will respect the freedoms of the 'free city' of Dubrovnik, which is permitted to govern itself, its property and its citizens according to its own laws. He will ensure that his men and those who pay the *harač* do likewise. None of his officials except his ambassadors will come to Dubrovnik. Dubrovnik's merchants are to trade without hindrance by land and sea throughout the Sultan's dominions, paying only a custom of 2 per cent on goods that are sold and nothing on unsold goods. The Sultan also regulates jurisdiction: in disputes between Muslims and Ragusans the *kadi* will judge; in disputes between Ragusans, it will be Dubrovnik's court.[14] There are to be no reprisals taken against Ragusans generally for the misdeeds of any individual. The property of Ragusans dying within the frontiers of the Empire will revert to Dubrovnik, not the Sultan or any of his people. If the Sultan wages war, the Ragusans can still continue to trade.[15]

The exact terms of this arrangement would vary significantly over the years and so would the way in which they were executed. But the basis of the relationship was now established. However Dubrovnik liked to describe the tribute to be sent, the truth is that in 1442 the Republic first agreed to pay the *harač*. In return the Sultan granted the Ragusans maximum autonomy, effectively approximating to independence, but he regarded them as his subjects and it was in that capacity that he promised to protect them. It was the combination of this pledge of protection with a highly favourable rate of customs dues levied on Ragusan goods that transformed the prospects for Dubrovnik's trade. In future years, the 2 per cent rate would be challenged, but the principle that Dubrovnik's merchants paid a lower rate than those of any other non-Muslim state was usually upheld. The agreement thus opened the way for Dubrovnik's merchants to continue and even strengthen – albeit with much transitional disruption as a result of war – the hold on the Balkan trade which they had achieved under the Slavic rulers of Serbia and Bosnia. And once the whole region was brought under the orderly control of the Sultan, that trade rapidly increased, benefiting from secure conditions and lack of internal frontiers.

It is intriguing to speculate how far the Porte had calculated the potential advantages of the arrangement.[16] In retrospect at least, they must have been clear. The Empire needed the revenues from a flourishing Balkan trade in order to fight its wars, pay its officials and reward its friends. But now and for most of the next two centuries it lacked the inclination, the skills or the people to conduct that trade itself. It was especially convenient to have the Ragusan mercantile class fulfil this role because Dubrovnik was small and vulnerable and presented no threat – unlike Venice, which the Empire quickly came to see as its principal enemy.

These benefits to the Ottoman Empire may, though, have taken time to affect the way in which the Porte regarded Dubrovnik. Certainly, that is true of how Dubrovnik regarded the Porte. For while Dubrovnik was negotiating its way towards a stable relationship with the Sultan, it was also desperately hoping that the Christian powers would come together successfully to drive the Turks out of the Balkans altogether. Its envoys encouraged the new king of Hungary, Vladislav I (1440–1444), to prepare an army, and it passed on to him information about Turkish dispositions. One major obstacle to a successful campaign was overcome with the official union between the Orthodox and Catholic Churches agreed at the Council of Florence in 1439. When in early 1442 Eugenius IV received a request for help from the Byzantine Emperor John VIII (1425–1448), the pope pressed ever more forcefully for a great crusade against the Turks. The exiled Serb Despot, Đurađ Branković, was another strong proponent of action which he hoped might return his lands to him. He, King Vladislav and the Hungarian nobleman John Hunyadi were the leaders of the large force which moved into Serbia and Bulgaria in 1443. It achieved some early victories, which in turn encouraged an anti-Ottoman revolt in Albania under the leadership of George Castriot, known as Skanderbeg.

Dubrovnik was delighted by these developments. Large sums raised through the grant of indulgences in the city testified to popular enthusiasm for the project, and the news of early victories was celebrated by solemn processions of thanksgiving. Dubrovnik even agreed to contribute to the Christian fleet, though it also sought from Vladislav as a reward some of the fruits of (what seemed) imminent victory in the shape of the strategically and commercially valuable towns of Valona (Vlora) and Kanina in Albania.

Now, however, the position began to deteriorate. The impetus of the crusade was lost as winter closed in. The following spring, the Sultan managed to win over the Despot by offering him the return of his lands and twenty-four towns in Serbia. To the pope's annoyance King Vladislav agreed in the summer of 1444 a ten-year truce with the Sultan. The Hungarian king's initial error was compounded by the further error of then – at the pope's urging – breaking the agreement. The plan was that the Christian fleet, to which Dubrovnik had contributed its two galleys and a hired supply ship, would sail to the Bosphorus and prevent the Sultan's bringing his army into Europe to confront the crusaders. But the stratagem failed. Murad II's forces crossed without difficulty and the heavily outnumbered Christian army was crushed at Varna on 10 November 1444. King Vladislav was among those killed. Hungarian power was shattered and all prospects for retaking the Balkans disappeared. The future of Constantinople was also bleak. Most important for Dubrovnik, the way was open, as and when the Turks should wish to take it, to Bosnia, Croatia and indeed Hungary.[17]

It took several anxious months before Dubrovnik learned the full details of the catastrophe that had occurred at Varna.[18] The Republic now had to face the unpleasant consequences of its support for the crusade. The only consolation was that its friend, Đurađ Branković, whom the Ragusans had earlier succoured and sheltered, was now both a neighbour and, still more important, one who enjoyed the Sultan's favour. The urgent priority for Dubrovnik was to use the Despot as the means of re-establishing relations with the Porte. In this it was again remarkably successful – so much so, in fact, that it improved, for a time at least, on the agreement of 1442.

Again, Dubrovnik was initially wary of establishing direct contact with the Porte. Instead, in February 1447, it decided to send a Ragusan citizen as part of an embassy from the Despot to the Sultan. The mission was successful. In August, Dubrovnik self-confidently distributed to Turkish officials copies of the privileges it had received from the Sultan. There was soon more good news. In October the Ragusans learned that the Grand Vizier had refused leave to Stjepan Vukčić Kosača to attack Dubrovnik, because 'the Sultan on the Despot's undertaking had agreed with us a good peace and sworn to respect it.' The new *'ahd-name* was actually an improvement on that of 1442 in that there was no requirement for a regular *harač*, just a one-off payment of 1,500 ducats.

Dubrovnik and the Herceg

As earlier with Radoslav Pavlović, Dubrovnik's conflict with Stjepan Vukčić Kosača revealed how diplomatic virtuosity alone was insufficient to preserve the city's security and interests. These needed a measure of active intervention by the Porte. And that in turn meant that the Republic had to engage itself more closely with the Sultan and his officials than it would otherwise have wished.

Stjepan Vukčić Kosača posed a greater problem than had any of Dubrovnik's earlier Slavic neighbours and enemies. This was probably not mainly the result of their enemy's character – though Ragusan sources drip vitriol whenever Stjepan Vukčić is mentioned.[19] It is also unclear to what extent he deliberately pursued a novel policy of state-building, trying (as has been suggested) to 'break free' of Ragusan economic domination. The main driving force for his attempts to make his town of Novi a major trading emporium was probably simply the desire to raise money to pay off and fight encroaching Ottoman forces.[20] The Herceg's title (meaning 'duke'), which he assumed as 'Herceg of Hum and Primorje' in 1448 and 'Herceg of St Sava' in 1449, has left its mark on today's Hercegovina. But it was not necessarily indicative of an ambition to achieve anything more than local dominance; it was, after all, actually confirmed by the Turks.[21] The fleeting but real importance of the Herceg was rather the result of the conjuncture of circumstances which prevailed in the Slavic Balkans at a time when Ottoman influence was already decisive in preventing any other outside power dominating the region – but not as yet directed towards overthrowing rulers prepared to pay *harač* and submit to the Sultan's demands.

Dubrovnik's relations with Stjepan Vukčić Kosača were initially good. In 1436, he gave shelter in one of his castles to two Ragusan caravans ambushed by the Turks, for which Dubrovnik expressed its appreciation. But there was always potential for difficulty. An ambitious ruler like Stjepan Vukčić might be tempted to retake Konavle, which his uncle had sold, if he could gain the permission of his Turkish masters to do so. Furthermore, needing money for his wars and defences he was likely to chafe at the restrictions which the Ragusans were determined to place on access to the 12,000 ducats of his late uncle Sandalj's legacy held on deposit in Dubrovnik. In fact, the Kosača legacy was to bring the Republic no end of trouble.

In any case, Dubrovnik was inevitably involved for reasons of geography in Stjepan Vukčić's plans and problems. In his warfare with Radoslav Pavlović, Stjepan Vukčić's men pursued their enemies onto Ragusan territory. Then, as the Turks attacked the Bosnian King Tvrtko II in 1438 and 1439, people from Stjepan Vukčić's lands fled in terror to Dubrovnik, which had to cope with them.

From about this time, Dubrovnik became very suspicious of its neighbour. The most serious causes of friction now were the fiscal and trading arrangements in Drijeva at the mouth of the Neretva. At the end of Duke Sandalj's rule, Dubrovnik had taken the farm of the customs levied at Drijeva, where its merchants already controlled most of the trade including all of the trade in salt. The custom itself – and thus the farm – was shared out between the lords of the area, with a half going to Sandalj (and so later to Stjepan Vukčić) and a quarter each to Radoslav Pavlović and the Radivojević brothers. The farm was specified in the contract as not being payable when war disrupted trade, and so made the custom valueless. This provision was an initial source of difficulty, because Dubrovnik and Stjepan Vukčić disagreed about whether it applied as a result of recent conflict in Bosnia. Eventually, Dubrovnik gave way. But Stjepan Vukčić then complained about the behaviour of the Ragusan customs collectors, and Ragusan merchants for their part complained about his treatment of them. For all these difficulties, Drijeva was still a valuable source of income, so Dubrovnik was even more angry and alarmed when it heard that Stjepan Vukčić was negotiating with Venice to exchange the place for Venetian-controlled Kotor. Nothing in fact came of this proposal, though Stjepan Vukčić and Venice improved their already good relations. And bad relations persisted between him and Dubrovnik, also because of Drijeva.

Drijeva's problems soon multiplied. In 1448 it was attacked and burnt by the Turks. The following year the Herceg suddenly ordered all the remaining inhabitants of Drijeva to leave and go to a local fortified centre. This provoked indignant protests from the Ragusan merchants to Dubrovnik and from Dubrovnik to the Herceg. The latter's subsequent attempts to administer Drijeva directly were unsuccessful. But in any case, the Herceg's (and so Dubrovnik's) attention was by now mainly focused not on Drijeva and the Neretva but on Herceg-Novi and Boka Kotorska.[22]

In seeking to establish Herceg-Novi in the *župa* of Dračevica as a major mercantile and manufacturing centre, the Herceg was following in the footsteps of the Bosnian king Tvrtko I. Like Tvrtko, the Herceg intended to break to his own advantage the grip which Dubrovnik had obtained over the sale of salt, and to a lesser extent other commodities; but he was also more ambitious. Tvrtko's efforts, though they annoyed Dubrovnik, had had no lasting consequences, because in 1382 he recovered control over the lower Neretva and so the old arrangements at Drijeva – where the Ragusans and the king shared the profits – could be restored. Between then and the Herceg's project, Novi had sunk back to being a pleasant wintering resort for local rulers.[23]

That now changed. The Herceg reactivated the Novi salt pans and created a salt market, thus breaching the convention whereby salt was sold between the rivers Neretva and Bojana in just four places – at Drijeva, Dubrovnik, Kotor and (on the Bojana) Sveti Srđ. That traditional arrangement effectively consecrated the Ragusan salt monopoly, for the Ragusans controlled the trade at Drijeva and, of course, Dubrovnik; Kotor (which the Ragusans frequently bullied and intimidated) was not of great significance; and Sveti Srđ too was only a local market. So in practice the inhabitants of the Bosnian and Serb hinterlands generally bought Ragusan salt. The new Herceg-Novi market threatened that. The Herceg demanded that his subjects, and indeed anyone on his territory, use his and not Ragusan salt. In 1449 he went further. Not just salt but wine, oil, grain and iron were now to be found on sale in Herceg-Novi. The Herceg set up a textile mill and workshop for armour and metal goods. He attracted craftsmen by giving them loans and – to the fury of both Dubrovnik and Kotor – he offered immunity from debt for citizens from these two cities if they agreed to come and work in his new centre. Kotor protested to Venice, which ineffectively intervened with the Herceg. Dubrovnik protested too to anyone who would listen – the Hungarians, the king of Bosnia, the Despot, the pope. Dubrovnik eventually decided to impose the only measure it knew would hurt: in July 1450 it forbade all trade with the Herceg's lands. Ill-tempered and futile negotiations then dragged on between the two sides between November 1450 and July 1451.[24]

While the Herceg sought and eventually obtained permission from the Sultan to attack Dubrovnik, the Ragusans also prepared for the seemingly inevitable war – in fact, as it turned out, the last war they would fight till the fall of the Republic. Stjepan Vukčić began the conflict with two important advantages. First, he was an Ottoman vassal, paid the *harač* and had received the Sultan's approval for his action. By contrast, Dubrovnik, in spite of its early friendly contacts with the Porte, was a tributary of the king of Hungary who at this time was at war with the Sultan. Still more important, the Herceg was militarily much the stronger.

Dubrovnik took all the measures it could to protect its territory. Reinforcements were sent into Konavle and concentrated in the fortress of Soko. The garrison in the fortress of Tumba (Brgat) on Mount Srđ, the main obstacle to an attack on Dubrovnik itself, was strengthened. Armed ships were sent to patrol along the coast. Mercenaries were hired in Italy and brought to the city. But Konavle was, in truth, for all practical purposes indefensible, and the Herceg had no great difficulty in seizing it and then concentrating on plundering and burning Župa Dubrovačka. Finally, he attacked Tumba and soundly defeated the Ragusan army which tried to defend it.

From this position of strength the Herceg renewed and increased his demands. He insisted on payment to him of Duke Sandalj's 12,000 ducats on deposit in the city and other sums he claimed to have spent on Dubrovnik's behalf in intervening with the Sultan when the latter was angry about their sheltering the Despot. In the meantime the Herceg's forces destroyed the walls of Cavtat, which Dubrovnik had already evacuated.

Dubrovnik was more successful against the Herceg in its diplomatic action. In order to construct an alliance capable of shifting the balance in their favour, the Ragusans mediated a peace between the Despot and Stjepan Tomaš, King of Bosnia (1443–1461). Both then agreed to attack the Herceg in co-operation with Dubrovnik, whose territorial goals were, as in its earlier struggles, the seizure (and then purchase from the Sultan) of Trebinje and other lands, this time also including Dračevica and Herceg-Novi. Dubrovnik played too on the fact of the Herceg's adherence to the schismatic Bosnian Church to obtain from the pope letters excommunicating anyone who helped him, which might make the Venetians less willing to involve themselves.

The Ragusan Republic's greatest diplomatic success in 1451, however, lay in its exploitation of divisions in the Herceg's household. A Sienese girl brought, it seems, to the Herceg's court to be betrothed to his son Vladislav, had found her way into the Herceg's own bed. The scandalised Vladislav and one of the leading Hum nobles, Ivaniš Vlatković, now entered into a conspiracy with Dubrovnik against the Herceg.

For the present, however, none of these developments compensated for Dubrovnik's military weakness. The Herceg's soldiers plundered and ravaged the Ragusan *distretto* and fired their cannons at the city. In September 1451 the Republic vented its anger and frustration by publicly sentencing the Herceg – who was, of course, an honorary member of its nobility with property in the city (including the palace known as 'Hercegovina') – to death and confiscation. In the Slavic and Italian languages and to the sound of trumpets, Ragusan heralds proclaimed that anyone who killed the Herceg would be rewarded with 15,000 gold ducats, an annual pension of 300 ducats, a house worth 2,000 ducats and membership of the Ragusan nobility. Placing such a large sum on the Herceg's head was something more than a formal gesture, and it may have been one reason why he prudently decided to withdraw from the neighbourhood.

Dubrovnik's old friend the Despot had been having more success in interesting the Porte in the proposal to strip the Herceg of his lands, for its share of which the Republic was willing to pay 50,000 ducats. This may have partly compensated for yet another military defeat when Ragusan forces tried to retake Župa Dubrovačka. It was only, however, when the new Sultan Mehmed II, on 24 November 1451, agreed a three year peace with Hungary that Dubrovnik could deal with the Porte without the shadow of its relationship with the Sultan's enemy inhibiting its efforts. Dubrovnik was now included in the peace and the Sultan ordered the Herceg to return all he had seized.[25]

Dubrovnik's respite on this occasion was, though, short-lived. At the start of 1452 hostilities broke out once more and the Herceg quickly re-occupied Konavle. Dubrovnik, for its part, persisted with attempts to persuade its allies to embark on serious military engagements against the enemy; so the Ragusans were highly displeased when Vladislav broke his engagement with them and made peace with his father. It may have been news of the fall of Constantinople at the end of May 1453 which concentrated minds and convinced both Dubrovnik and the Herceg that the time had come to abandon hostilities; for it must have been clear that the pressure from the Turks on the Balkans would now resume with a vengeance.

Eventually, in 1454, peace was agreed on the basis of Dubrovnik's continued possession of Konavle but of its both abandoning claims for compensation for war damage and, a still bitterer pill, implicitly accepting the competition posed by Herceg-Novi. The Senate was minded to continue its action against those Ragusan citizens who had treacherously abandoned Dubrovnik for Herceg-Novi, but the Herceg successfully intervened on their behalf. The place continued as a market for salt and – till 1465 at any rate – a manufacturing centre for textiles.[26]

Dubrovnik and Mehmed II, the Conqueror

During the last years of the reign of Sultan Murad II, Dubrovnik had continued to hope for some relief from Hungary even after the disaster of Varna. But once Mehmed II embarked on a systematic conquest of the Balkans it became more dangerous for Dubrovnik to allow its natural sympathies and traditional loyalties to influence its behaviour. After the fall of Constantinople, the Sultan claimed to be the legitimate ruler of all the former territories of the Byzantine Empire and spent the next quarter-century putting that claim into effect through war. The Porte's earlier *ad hoc* dealings with the rulers of the Balkans, witnessed in Dubrovnik's case by the falling into abeyance for some years of the *harač* payments, were replaced by a new, remorseless programme of annexing all the states and territories in the Balkan peninsula south of the Danube.[27]

In 1455 the Turks marched into Serbia, seizing most of it, including Novo Brdo. The old Despot, Đurađ Branković, died the following year and was succeeded by his son Lazar, who was allowed for the present to remain in nominal authority while the Sultan concentrated his attention on Hungary. Dubrovnik, for its part, was preoccupied with other complications. A friar had come to the town to preach the crusade and raise money for it, but both the pope and the Hungarians wanted the proceeds and placed Dubrovnik in the invidious position of deciding between the two – while hoping to keep the whole enterprise secret from the Turks.

In March 1458 there were public celebrations in the city on the occasion of the accession of the new Hungarian king, Matthias Corvinus (1458–1490). But at the same time the Ragusan government was engaged in the delicate task of preparing an embassy to the Sultan. Its envoys were charged with asking for a new *'ahd-name* confirming their commercial and other privileges. The ambassadors were allowed to offer up to 600 ducats a year to be sent to the Porte every three years. But this turned out to be unrealistic. The envoys had to return home, obtain new instructions and then offer a year's tribute of 1,500 ducats, with various other large sums to be distributed to influential Ottoman officials. This time the negotiations were successful. The envoys were received in Skopje by the Sultan and gave him 1,500 ducats as *harač*, gaining from him in exchange confirmation of Dubrovnik's privileges.[28]

Dubrovnik's success in negotiating its way back under Turkish protection was in marked contrast to events elsewhere in the Balkans. In June 1459, with the seizure of Smederevo by the Turks, Serbia ceased to exist, while Turkish armies were already attacking Bosnia. In the same year, the Bosnian king Stjepan Tomaš desperately agreed to suppress the Bosnian Church and return his lands to Catholicism. But this measure was too late to provide the opportunity for a serious Western attempt to rescue Bosnia from its rapidly approaching fate. Indeed, the effect may have been to undermine popular resistance to the Turks and Islam among sympathisers with the old Bosnian Church. Stjepan Tomaš died in 1461. His successor, Stjepan Tomašević (1461–1463) boldly accepted his crown from the pope and then refused to pay the *harač*. In 1463 the Sultan responded. Turkish troops conquered Bosnia in a matter of weeks and Bosnia's last king was beheaded at the Sultan's orders in Jajce.[29]

In these very dangerous conditions, Dubrovnik pursued a twofold approach, shifting between one and the other as circumstances required. In the first place, though never regardless of risk, it did what it could to encourage resistance to the Turks and to assist their victims. But secondly, the Republic applied all its diplomatic skill to ensuring that there was no break in its relations with the Porte, initially resisting but ultimately retreating before the

Sultan's demands. As time went by, and as the fortunes of Christendom and its defenders declined, Dubrovnik had increasingly to turn its attention from West to East.

It must have taken some courage to continue to support Skanderbeg. But Dubrovnik received the Albanian rebel leader and supplied him and his men with food and money when they were on their way to Apulia in August 1461, and again on their return the following year. And although the Republic prudently refused the Bosnian king's hopeless request for soldiers in April 1463, it did send envoys to Hungary and the pope to alert them to the imminent collapse of Bosnia.

The Ragusans even helped their old enemy, the Herceg, as he fell on hard times. When Stjepan Vukčić found his territories under Ottoman attack, Dubrovnik offered a ship and an escort to take him to safety on their territory. In fact, he succeeded in restoring temporary control over some of his lands, inviting the Hungarians into those places he felt unable to defend, notably the fortress of Počitelj on the Neretva. Although fearful of the consequences, Dubrovnik supplied the Hungarian garrison there with money, food and ammunition and even provided builders under the direction of the Ragusan city engineer, Paskoje Miličević, to construct a bridge and strengthen the fortifications. (After Počitelj fell to the Turks in 1471, the Ragusans similarly helped provision the Hungarian-held fortress of Koš (modern Opuzen) in the mouth of the river Neretva, until that in turn finally fell in 1490.)

In 1465 Turkish forces had returned to seize more of Hercegovina. The following March, the Herceg visited Dubrovnik to deposit his wealth there before departing to die in Herceg-Novi in May. And yet again the Kosača inheritance was destined to cause Dubrovnik difficulties.

The Herceg had given extensive territories to his eldest son, Vladislav, after the two were reconciled. But these were then seized by the Turks. To his younger son, Vlatko, however, he left the bulk of his inheritance along with the title of Herceg. The two sons then quarrelled about their rights, while Dubrovnik held back from making any payments until Vladislav finally disappeared to Slavonia. But this did not resolve the matter, for Vlatko's remaining fortified centres were defended by Hungarian troops and Hungary now demanded payment out of the Kosača legacy. This placed Dubrovnik once again in an awkward position. Despairing of any other means of self-preservation, Herceg Vlatko now turned definitively to the Porte. The Sultan took up Vlatko's and his younger brother Stjepan's case for payment of the remaining Kosača legacy, upon which Dubrovnik prudently and speedily complied. But the bad blood remained, and the Kosača brothers apparently contributed to Dubrovnik's difficulties with the Sultan by encouraging him to demand increased *harač* payments. Vlatko lost Herceg-Novi in 1481 and died in 1489; but Stjepan was to figure more importantly in Dubrovnik's dealings with the Porte. He must in fact have understood Dubrovnik well, for as a child he had been brought by the Herceg to Dubrovnik to be raised as a Ragusan noble, though his father had later been forced to take him away and send him as a hostage to the Sultan's court. There he converted to Islam, becoming Ahmed-*pasha* Hercegović, and subsequently rose to a position of great influence, serving more than once as Grand Vizier.[30]

If Dubrovnik's attempts discreetly to assist the enemies of the Turks yielded little practical benefit – and the entanglement with the Herceg and his family actually increased the Republic's problems – its diplomatic dealings with the Sultan were more successful, though at a heavy financial cost. Dubrovnik's territorial integrity and its privileges were upheld, but from 1469 Dubrovnik's *harač* was raised from 1,500 to 5,000 ducats a year. Then in 1471, when Herceg Vlatko was busily agitating against Dubrovnik for his own reasons, the Sultan demanded – and Dubrovnik had to concede – a *harač* of 9,000 ducats for that year and 10,000 in future years.[31]

At the end of 1476 there was a further crisis when the Turks opened a customs post on Mount Srđ above Dubrovnik and began to levy a new customs due of 5 per cent on all imports and exports from Dubrovnik's merchants, and 4 per cent from Turkish subjects. This, in fact, constituted a far more dangerous threat to the Republic's livelihood than increases in the *harač*. Dubrovnik had, of course, hitherto paid only a 2 per cent custom on goods sold and had enjoyed exemption from all other levies. If that position were to be undermined so would Dubrovnik's trading advantages within the Empire. The Republic responded with vigour, forbidding overland trade with the Ottoman territories. Eventually, Dubrovnik's envoys agreed with the Sultan that the Republic would pay over and above the 10,000 ducats of *harač* a further 2,500 ducats in lieu of this extra import/export tax or *đumruk* (Turkish: *gümrük*).[32]

Ottoman financial pressure, backed up with threats and plundering by Turkish troops, continued to mount till the end of Mehmed the Conqueror's reign. The Sultan, in May 1480, only reissued confirmations of Dubrovnik's privileges in exchange for an increase of 2,500 ducats in the *harač*, which would have represented a tenfold increase in annual payment (that is, in *harač* and *đumruk* together) in just twelve years. In fact, this final increase never occurred, for Mehmed died in 1481 before it could be put into effect and his less aggressive successor Bayezid II (1481–1512) reduced the annual payment once more to 12,500 ducats.[33]

Even without the extra increase which Mehmed II had proposed, the *harač* was now a substantial burden, and on top of it must be added the various large bribes – some customary, some exceptional – which the Ragusan envoys had to distribute on their visits to Constantinople. Dubrovnik thus paid a very high price for the Sultan's protection; but when compared both with the fate of its neighbours and with the great wealth which was soon to flow from the Ragusan merchants' unique position in the Empire, it was worthwhile. What Mehmed the Conqueror's real long-term intentions had been towards Dubrovnik are unclear. He was not, it seems, temperamentally hostile to the Ragusan identity, and certainly not a bigot, but rather a cultured man with an appreciation of Western art that stretched to inviting the Venetian painter Gentile Bellini to paint the frescoes of his palace and even his portrait. Yet towards the Ragusans he certainly showed a ruthlessness that led them to conclude that he intended to destroy their city.

From this time arose two traditions, relayed in the Ragusan chronicles. According to one account (recorded by the anonymous chronicler), in 1463 the Sultan reached the river Sutjeska, a tributary of the Drina, intending to march on towards Dubrovnik. However, he was three times thrown from his horse and so, taking this for an evil omen, decided not to continue. This 'great miracle' (as the chronicler describes it) was attributed to the intercession of St Blaise and the public prayers and processions of the people of Dubrovnik.[34] Rastić prefers an account which illustrates the *sang froid* of the Ragusan patriciate rather than the piety of the Ragusan populace. According to this chronicler, the aged Senator Šimun Bunić advised his colleagues to answer the Sultan's demand that the Republic cede to him all of the Ragusan *distretto* with a counter-threat – namely, that if he persisted they would turn their city over to the Hungarians.[35] But whatever Mehmed II's motives, Dubrovnik would not face similar pressure from the Porte for another century.

Consolidation of Relations with the Porte

In fact, during this whole period relations between the Ottoman Empire and Dubrovnik were developing at a level other than that of public diplomacy. Individual Ragusans established contacts with the Turks which, both for better and worse, had an important impact on the Ragusan Republic. Ragusans who farmed Ottoman taxes acquired invaluable insights into the way business was

In xpi noie
Amen. Millesi
mo cccc°xxxij.
Indicne. x. deze
naro.
A laude e reue
rencia gloria ⁊
honore de leterno
dio padre e figlio
lo e spūsancto li q̃
li in una substãtia
e deita remane en re
gna etnalmẽte. E de
la gloriosa e intem
rata uergene ma
madonna scā Ma
ria. E de tutti li spi
riti celestiali li qua
li canta ctinuamẽt
nel conspetto dello

9. Illuminated opening page of the register of the Confraternity of St Anthony (*Antunini*) (about 1445, possibly by Lovro Dobričević)

10 & 11. Illuminated opening pages of the register of the Confraternity of St Lazarus (*Lazarini*) (1531, possibly by Pietro di Giovanni)

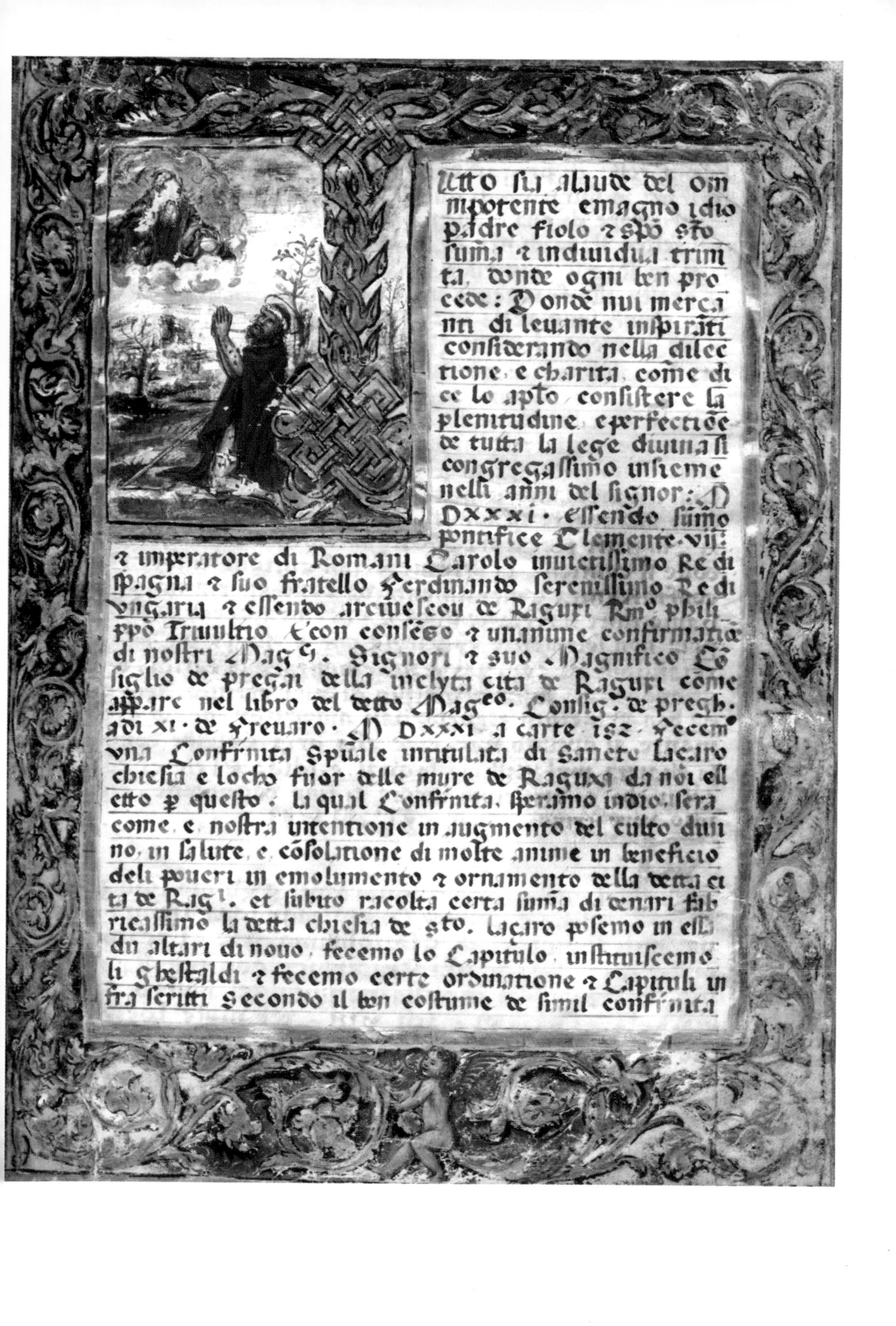

utto su aliude del om
nipotente e magno idio
padre fiolo & spu sto
suma & indiuidua trini
ta, donde ogni ben pro
cede: Donde nui merca
nti di leuante inspirati
considerando nella dilec
tione, e charita, come di
ce lo apto, consistere la
plenitudine, e perfectione
de tutta la lege diuina si
congregassimo insieme
nelli anni del signor: M
DXXXI. essendo sumo
pontifice Clemente. vii.
& imperatore di Romani Carolo inuictissimo Re di
Spagna & suo fratello Ferdinando serenissimo Re di
Vngaria & essendo arciuescou de Raguxi Rmo. phili
ppo Triuultio & con consenso & unanime confirmatione
di nostri Mag.ci Signori & suo Magnifico Con
siglio de pregai della inclyta cita de Raguxi come
appare nel libro del detto Mag.co Consig. de pregh.
adi xi. de Freuaro. M DXXXI a carte 152. fecem
una Confraternita Spirituale intitulata di Sancto Lazaro
chiesia e locho fuor delle mure de Raguxi da noi ell
etto per questo. la qual Confraternita, speramo in dio, sera
come, e nostra intentione in augmento del culto diui
no, in salute, e consolatione di molte anime in beneficio
deli poueri in emolumento & ornamento della detta ci
ta de Rag.a et subito racolta certa summa di denari fab
ricassimo la detta chiesia de Sto. Lazaro posemo in essa
du altari di nouo, fecemo lo Capitulo, instituissemo
li Ghestaldi & fecemo certe ordinatione & Capituli in
fra scritti secondo il bon costume de simil confraternita

بسم الله الرحمن الرحيم ولا حول ولا قوة إلا بالله العلي العظيم

جمادى الأولى عام أربعة وتسعين ومائة وألف 1194 الموافق لعاشر مائة

عام ثمانين وسبعمائة وألف 1780

12. Charter in favour of Dubrovnik granted by the Sultan of Morocco (1780)

13. The Rector's Palace

14. Atrium of the Rector's Palace

15. The Sponza Palace (or *Dogana*)

16. Atrium of the Sponza Palace

17. The Cathedral

conducted within the Empire, and they could certainly make large profits. But they also ran the risk, faced with unpredictable Turkish officials and uncertain political conditions, of finding themselves saddled with huge debts. In such circumstances, the Porte required the Ragusan state to pay whatever was owed. An example of such profitable but perilous relations is provided by the career of the Ragusan patrician Jakov Bunić. Bunić was, as well as a tax farmer, a confidant of the Sultan, a Turkish spy and, in 1465, an Ottoman ambassador to Venice. But in obscure circumstances in 1471 he was claimed by Ottoman officials to have embezzled the enormous sum of 55,000 ducats. The Porte demanded that he be handed over and his property sold. In this case, the dispute was quickly settled and Bunić successfully resumed his career in the Ottoman state service.[36]

The reigns of the Sultans Bayezid II and Selim I (1512–1520) and the early years of Suleyman I the Magnificent (1520–1566) saw first the restoration and then the further aggressive expansion of the Ottoman Empire, which now reached its zenith. Dubrovnik observed, and its chroniclers recorded, all these events closely, not least the power struggles at the turbulent Ottoman court. But after the fall of Bosnia, and as the Turks controlled greater areas of Croatia and Hungary, the Ragusans were no longer on the front line of hostilities: they had moved wholly into the Ottoman sphere of influence and adeptly managed their relations with successive Sultans so as to take maximum advantage of that fact.

After the death of Mehmed II, the Empire was engulfed in a civil war from which the old Sultan's eldest son, Bayezid emerged triumphant. But he was still faced by an exiled pretender to the throne, his brother Đem, who was supported with varying degrees of enthusiasm by the Western powers.[37] Partly because of this danger, and partly because of the need to restore the weakened central authority, Bayezid pursued a peaceful approach until Đem's death in 1495. This was a period of great economic advance, which created the conditions for the later conquests of Selim and Suleyman.[38]

Dubrovnik gained from Bayezid's peace, but it also benefited from the subsequent war he fought against the Venetians (1499–1503). There were, it is true, discomforts and dangers as a result of both sides raiding and retaliating along the Dalmatian and Istrian coasts. A development which would have greater repercussions for Dubrovnik in later years was the growth of raids by *hajduks* – rebels against the Ottoman authorities – directed at Ragusan merchants, regarded as fair game for robbery. The war also provided an excuse for the Venetians to destroy the Ragusan salt pans at the mouth of the Neretva and to seize Ragusan ships and their cargoes. But such unpleasant incidents were more than compensated for by a large increase in Ragusan trade as direct commercial relations between the Porte and the Serenissima were broken off and contacts between East and West were perforce channelled through neutral Dubrovnik. The number of registered Ragusan credit transactions and trading ventures accordingly multiplied in the years of war and tailed off as it ended.[39]

Dubrovnik had no reason to lament the early reverses suffered by its Venetian rivals. But its sympathies were probably more evenly divided when Venice managed to persuade the pope, the Hungarians, France and Spain to join a Christian League against the Ottoman Empire. In any case, Dubrovnik provided information about each side's movements and intentions to the other, trying to ingratiate itself to the maximum extent by stressing the risks it was taking. Thus the Ragusans begged the Porte to keep silent about the contents of their letters '... because of the great danger in which we find ourselves from all the Christians'.[40]

In 1512 Selim overthrew his father with the aid of a revolt of the Janissaries, eliminated his brothers as potential rivals and then embarked upon successful military campaigns against Persia, Syria and Egypt. The new Sultan also prepared for military action against the West, assembling a fleet in conditions of maximum secrecy – though not secret enough to escape the attentions of Dubrovnik, which wrote to the pope:

> From our people who arrive from Constantinople, Gallipoli and Anatolia, we know that the Sultan in many places of the Empire is building a great number of galleys which he is fitting out in the newly-built Constantinople Arsenal. So far he has already collected 120 galleys...[41]

In the last years of Selim's reign Dubrovnik again felt itself under pressure, though it is difficult to know how much of the problem was the result of the Sultan's own policy or of the exactions and possibly the ignorance of his officials. In 1518 the custom levied on Ragusan merchandise sold in Pera and Constantinople was raised to 5 per cent at the instigation of the *emin* of Pera, who alleged that Ragusan merchants had been passing other foreigners' goods off as their own, so cheating the Porte. The area in which the new higher customs due applied continued to widen to include even the immediate hinterland of Dubrovnik, and the Turkish *emin* based at Ploče started to levy it as well. Dubrovnik managed to persuade the Sultan to make some concessions: the customs would be levied at 5 per cent in Pera and Constantinople and 4 per cent in Edirne and Gallipoli, but elsewhere return to 2 per cent. Beyond that he would not budge.[42]

The early death of Selim and the accession of Suleyman in 1520 allowed the Ragusans to reopen the question of their customs dues before the levy of the new rates had become too deeply entrenched. The Sultan was already regarded as well-disposed towards Dubrovnik. Still more important, he had an interest in simplifying the dues he levied on Ragusan trade, if only because the greater the complication the greater the opportunities for local extortion, and so the less predictable the income to fill the Sultan's war-chests. Suleyman therefore received favourably the suggestion, which seems to have come from Dubrovnik via the Rumelian *defterdar* (registrar), that a separate 'Dubrovnik Custom', levied as a one-off annual payment, be instituted. It, too, would be called the *đumruk* (*gümrük*). The approach was similar to that adopted under Mehmed the Conqueror after 1476, when customs dues over and above the traditional 2 per cent levied on Ragusans were consolidated into a 2,500-ducat payment, also called *đumruk*: but it was now proposed that the whole of the Ragusan customs payments to the Porte be so transformed. It was to be designated in Ottoman official parlance as *mukata'a*, that is, a separate earmarked public revenue farmed by a *mültezim*. But in this case the customs farmer would be a Ragusan nominated by the Dubrovnik government.

This offered the Republic a number of important advantages. First, it meant that Dubrovnik would now effectively tax its own merchants on their commercial dealings in the Empire, simply handing over the agreed sum to the Porte. Secondly, Dubrovnik would benefit from no longer having so many dealings with the frequently troublesome Turkish *emin* based at Ploče, who from now on would levy a 5 per cent custom only on Turkish subjects, nothing on Ragusans. Thirdly, the canny Ragusans might hope to exploit the uncertain grasp of Ottoman officials in public (as opposed to private) finances to strike an advantageous bargain – which is what they now proceeded to do.

It took time and much diplomatic effort to bring these plans to fruition and the Ragusans were careful in choosing the occasions on which to put their case. The Sultan publicly received Dubrovnik's envoys in December 1521 and granted most of their requests, including that for the proposed 'Dubrovnik Custom' whose detailed negotiation, however, he entrusted to the Rumelian *defterdar*.

By now Suleyman had set off on a campaign against the Hungarians. Dubrovnik accordingly sent its envoys after him. For thirty-five days in circumstances of famine and plague they remained in the Sultan's camp before Belgrade. But they were well rewarded, because they were among the first to congratulate him and exploit his high spirits when the city fell. The designated customs farmer – Nikola Petrov from the island of Šipan, a city official whose father was a *dragoman* (interpreter) experienced in the ways of the Ottoman Empire – had been instructed by Dubrovnik to accept the three-year farm of the Custom for 8,000 ducats. The government had also decided to offer over and above the usual gifts, a total of 8,631 ducats and 10 *grossi*, of which 3,000 ducats and fine cloth worth 481 ducats and 10 *grossi* went to the Grand Vizier.

The envoys despatched to the Sultan had been entrusted with a number of tasks of which the arrangement of the terms of the Custom farm was only the most important. They were also to obtain confirmation of Dubrovnik's privileges, removal of the unco-operative *emin* at Ploče, resolution of problems in the trade with Egypt and Syria, and diminution of the current 12,500-ducat *harač*. They failed in the last of these. They were also unable to have the arrangement for the 'Dubrovnik Custom' extended to Anatolia as well as Rumelia. But in all other respects they were successful.

Most significant were the arrangements for the farm of the Custom. These effectively confirmed Dubrovnik's near-monopoly of the Balkan trade. Moreover, the *defterdar* seems, for whatever reason, to have allowed the Ragusans to obtain that position on astonishingly good terms. He substantially underrated the trade's value, which continued to grow while the sum paid to the Porte by Dubrovnik did not. He also miscalculated the exchange rate. Dubrovnik's offer of 8,000 ducats should have been worth 424,000 Turkish aspers, but he accepted it at 300,000 aspers. And again future exchange rate developments would work against the Porte.[43]

With this remarkable diplomatic triumph, Dubrovnik established itself firmly within the new framework created by Ottoman success, just as it prepared to move decisively out of the old one based upon fealty to Hungary. On 29 August 1526, at the battle of Mohacs, the Turks gained an overwhelming victory over their Christian opponents. The young King Louis II of Hungary was killed in the fighting, and the Hungarian nobility now divided between supporters of the claims of Ferdinand of Habsburg and the Hungarian nobleman Janos Zapolyai. Dubrovnik, however, took only a distant interest. Its gaze was now firmly focused not on Buda, but on Constantinople.[44]

SIX

War, Diplomacy and Chaos: Dubrovnik Between the Habsburgs, Venice and the Porte (1526–1667)

Habsburg Entanglements

The break, after the battle of Mohacs in 1526, between Dubrovnik and its old suzerain, Hungary, was decisive but not clean. Naturally, there was no prospect of the Ottoman-backed candidate for the Crown of St Stephen, Janos Zapolyai, demanding tribute from the Republic, for the Sultan regarded Dubrovnik as now within his own, not Hungary's, sphere of influence. But Zapolyai's rival Ferdinand of Habsburg for long remained unwilling to abandon his claims to Ragusan allegiance. In fact, he repeatedly demanded the traditional tribute, and his exasperation steadily grew at Dubrovnik's polite but firm resistance.[1] For its part, Dubrovnik instructed its ambassadors to the Habsburg court to remind the insistent prince

> … [of] the calamity [that is, the Plague] which we have suffered for so many years past and which we still suffer, [that] our city is situated in a stony, sterile and arid place from which we cannot maintain sustenance for two months for our subjects and inhabitants [not to mention the need to pay] for the conservation of liberty and Christianity… a very large tribute to the Great Lord Turk.

In order to make this hard-luck story more convincing, the Ragusan ambassadors were told to recount it with tears in their eyes. And so as to create a still more favourable impression, and although they brought no tribute, they were to distribute suitably generous sweeteners to the royal court.[2]

But in fact Dubrovnik's importance to the Habsburgs went far beyond the sums foregone with the ending of the tribute. The city was a vital source of information, and agents there supplied whatever was lacking in the intelligence which the Ragusan Senate itself found it prudent to transmit. Dubrovnik was generally prepared to overlook such espionage; but it was much more sensitive when its own citizens were caught actively spying for the Habsburgs, because that involved great risks. Hence the lengthy dispute with Ferdinand over the Bučinčić brothers, members of a Ragusan patrician family in the Habsburgs' service.

The Dubrovnik government had already had occasion to seize one of Miho Bučinčić's letters because of its compromising contents, when in 1532 it discovered that he was still secretly passing on information to his masters about the Turks' military activities. Miho was promptly arrested and sentenced to a year's imprisonment with loss in perpetuity of all offices and privileges in the Republic. Ferdinand protested and demanded the sentence be reversed, but in any case Bučinčić escaped from jail and fled. He was joined in exile by his brother Pavao who, after serving a term as Dubrovnik's administrator of the sale of salt on the Neretva, made off with the profits.

The Bučinčić brothers in 1536 seem to have involved Ferdinand, or at least one of his officers, in a plot to attack and occupy Ston. But the plan was discovered and, meeting in secret session, the Ragusan Senate proclaimed the Bučinčići traitors and seized their property. The dispute dragged on, with the brothers on Ferdinand's authority taking reprisals against Dubrovnik, and their offspring then continuing the feud, which was only resolved twenty years later.[3]

The way in which the quarrel developed prefigured a future pattern by which Habsburg ambitions and a mixture of murky private ambitions and resentments placed Dubrovnik in jeopardy. To many, the Republic's territory appeared the obvious base from which to launch a counterattack against Turkish domination of the Balkans. Equally, though, the Ragusan government was determined that this should not happen. As Counter-Reformation zeal increased after the Council of Trent (1545–1563), and as the Ottoman Empire weakened, the risk of such Western intervention in Dubrovnik's affairs increased[4].

With Ferdinand's brother, the Emperor Charles V (1519–1558) – heir both to Ferdinand II of Aragon (1479–1526), ruler of Spain, and to the Holy Roman Emperor Maximilian I of Habsburg (1493–1519) – Dubrovnik enjoyed a much better relationship. Dubrovnik had, for many years, had friendly dealings with the House of Aragon.[5] Ferdinand II had ruled Catalonia and Sicily, both of which were commercially important to Dubrovnik. Ragusan trading interests were still more closely dependent on unimpeded contacts with the ports and territories of the kingdom of Naples. The latter was first under the control of one branch of the house of Aragon, then fell briefly (and in Ragusan eyes unsatisfactorily) under the French, before being definitively conquered by Ferdinand II's armies in 1504. From then on, the Spanish were directly concerned with political and commercial affairs in the Adriatic, and so even more than previously with Dubrovnik.

When Charles succeeded his grandfather as King of Spain and of the Aragonese dominions in Italy the relationship with Dubrovnik acquired a new importance and intensity. The Emperor was happy to confirm Ragusan privileges to trade with his subjects and – after a certain amount of recrimination and confusion – to settle a long-running dispute between Dubrovnik and some indignant and importunate Biscayan merchants. There was, however, a price to be paid by Dubrovnik for its entanglement in Charles's affairs: that of risking the Sultan's displeasure.

Charles was in constant need of ships to transport and supply his armies, and sea-power was crucial to his struggle with the Ottoman Empire around the shores of the Mediterranean. Indeed, the military engagements of these years often resembled a kind of duel fought at sea between two admirals and their fleets. On one side was the corsair captain Barbarossa, who in 1518 had been appointed by the Sultan as supreme commander of the Ottoman navy; on the other was the Genoese Andrea Doria, whose discontents Charles had used to win him over from the Emperor's rival Francis I of France.[6] Although Doria was personally sympathetic to Dubrovnik, he had no compunction when the need arose about forcing Ragusan ships to join his fleets. So at the same time as its envoys sought Charles V's assistance in resolving commercial disputes, Dubrovnik also secretly gave the strictest orders to its captains in Spanish harbours not to join – nor let their ships be commandeered into – Spanish fleets. When Dubrovnik later learned of Charles V's preparations for an attack on Tunis, as well as judiciously informing the Porte it sent orders to Ragusan sailors in Naples that none of them must join the expedition. On occasion, the Republic simply ordered its ships not to sail outside the Adriatic at all.

But it proved almost impossible to guard against Ragusan ships being commandeered if the Spanish were intent on it, and so the Republic sought to minimise the resultant dangers. In January 1533 the Ragusan Senate laid down that if one of the Republic's ships were seized and the captain could not have it released, he was to leave it in the care of a skeleton crew of at most four sailors and to make off with the rest, taking with him the telltale Ragusan flag of St Blaise. Thus if the vessel were later captured by the Turks, they might not discover its true ownership. Anyone infringing this instruction was to be fined. The orders were promptly relayed to Ragusan captains in Italian ports.[7]

Dubrovnik was equally firm – and probably more successful – in resisting similar demands from the Porte. When the Sultan's ambassador arrived in the city, bound for Venice in November 1536, he was fêted, regaled and invited into a secret session of the Senate; but when he told them that the Sultan wanted the loan of 50 ships, suitably manned and equipped, Dubrovnik immediately refused, and the refusal was accepted.[8]

Dubrovnik's government was probably serious enough in its repeated injunctions to its shipowners, captains and sailors to steer clear of the Spanish fleets. It had, after all, every reason to keep the Turks persuaded of its strict neutrality. But Ragusan ships did, in fact, regularly take part in Spanish expeditions. At the battle of Lepanto on 7 October 1571, a Ragusan contingent was present. Dubrovnik's ambassador in Rome boasted to the pope that thirty-three Ragusan ships had been part of the Christian fleet's reserve, though in fact they appear to have been used just for transporting provisions.[9]

Some Ragusan captains, however, ignored Dubrovnik's orders altogether and attached themselves more or less permanently to the Spanish. The Ohmučević family from Slano, for example, prospered mightily by this means. The relationship was an embarrassment for Dubrovnik in its dealings both with the English and the Turks. The English ambassador in Constantinople, Sir William Harborne, in 1587 accused Dubrovnik of sending its ships to join the Spanish, the Porte's sworn enemy. The Ragusan ambassador Orsat Crijević replied, however, that the ships in question had simply been taken by force and that Dubrovnik had no alliance with Spain. Dubrovnik also instructed its merchants in England to rebut these claims.[10] But that must have been a difficult task, since three Ragusan ships had indeed taken part in the 1588 Spanish Armada against England, sharing that fleet's misfortunes. One of these Ragusan vessels was smashed against the Irish cliffs, another was burnt to prevent its falling into enemy hands and a third was treacherously blown up by Scottish boarders as it rode off the Isle of Mull.[11]

Both the English and French representatives in Constantinople kept up a campaign of vilification against Dubrovnik for its involvement with the Spanish enemies of the Ottoman Empire. In 1592 they jointly presented an accusatory petition, claiming that Dubrovnik was building twelve ships on its territory for the Spanish king, that corn which Dubrovnik had received Ottoman permission to export was in fact going to the Spanish, and that the Ragusans had persuaded a Spanish embassy to turn back before reaching

Constantinople. The Ragusans vigorously and successfully rebutted the charges. But, as in the case of the Armada, Dubrovnik's diplomatic skills were stretched to explain the undoubted cases of Ragusan participation in Spanish fleets.

The Ohmučević family's squadron of ships known as the 'Twelve Apostles' was the most notorious and embarrassing. Three were seized by the Turks in 1594, and Dubrovnik had to explain that Petar Ohmučević was a dissatisfied Ragusan who had cut off all links with his native Dubrovnik and now served the king of Spain. The Ohmučević squadron was also engaged in Spain's attempts in the 1590s to raise Ireland against English rule. The ships met various unfortunate ends, but members of the family and other Ragusans continued in Spanish service.[12] Moreover, it continued to be common knowledge that Dubrovnik regarded the fortunes of Spain as closely linked to its own, and equally common knowledge why. As the French agent in Dubrovnik reported to his government in 1611:

> Their [the Ragusans'] wealth which is all at Naples, the hatred they bear towards the Muslim religion and the bad treatment they receive from Venice, make them very affectionate towards Spain.[13]

Relations with the Porte

Although Dubrovnik rarely stopped grumbling and worrying about the Turks – often with good reason – its fortunes from the second quarter of the sixteenth century onwards were inextricably linked with and heavily dependent upon those of the Ottoman Empire. The Ragusans had acquired a sure instinct for accommodating the whims and wishes of the Sultan and his officials. Dubrovnik certainly did not overlook the opportunity, for example, to win favour by sending its *poklisari* with gifts to Constantinople in 1530 to celebrate the circumcision of Suleyman the Magnificent's three sons.[14] By about this time the custom had become established of Dubrovnik's appointing the Grand Vizier, the most powerful figure in the Empire after the Sultan, as its special protector. The Ragusans could thus address the newly appointed Grand Vizier, Mehmed-*pasha* Sokolović, as 'our patron and our dear and special friend', a role for which he, like the other Grand Viziers, was generously rewarded.[15] The succession of Ottoman officials hailing from Bosnian and Serb families also offered Dubrovnik opportunities for a closer understanding with the Porte. Several of these clearly enjoyed the opportunity to speak the language of their birth – like Murad-*pasha* who sat down beside the Ragusan *poklisari* saying: 'We are neighbours, my friends; let's speak the same language!' Similarly, Mustafa-*pasha*, Vizier of the Sultan's *divan* (council), whose family came from Mostar, told the Ragusans not to be afraid, for '... I am your friend and from your neighbourhood'. Bostanđija Mehmed-*aga*, born in Zvornik, went even further:

> I am proud and pleased that I am speaking to you in this language. So, when you are in audience with His Highness [the Sultan], don't speak in the Italian language but in that Bosnian language, because every time the Great Lord asks which is this language in which the envoys speak in audience we answer, 'Lord, this is our Bosnian language.'[16]

But in any case Dubrovnik had long since adapted to the linguistic requirements of negotiation with Turkish speakers. Just as it had previously created a special 'Slavic Chancery' to cope with the business of negotiation with neighbouring Slavic rulers, so in the sixteenth century a new 'Turkish Chancery' was established to receive Turkish letters and translate them into Croatian or Italian.[17] Its officials received a modest payment from the state treasury, about whose niggardliness they often complained. Most important, however, were the *dragomans*, interpreters specially trained for the conduct of Dubrovnik's negotiations with the Porte. A future *dragoman* was educated from youth for the task. He began his studies in Dubrovnik – a Turkish *hodža* (Turkish: *hoca*, priest) was often brought to the city to act as tutor – and then the apprentice was sent to one of the great Ottoman cities like Salonika (Solun), Adrianople (Edirne), Smyrna (Izmir), Alexandria or even Constantinople, for two or three years to complete his training. He would later act as assistant to a serving *dragoman* or perhaps return to work in the Dubrovnik Turkish Chancery before undertaking minor missions and, finally, the supreme responsibility of accompanying the *poklisari* to Constantinople. There he would attend all their meetings with Turkish officials and the Sultan, interpreting as necessary. An experienced *dragoman* would also build up a range of personal contacts with the Porte which often allowed him to make a substantive contribution to the diplomatic mission.[18]

In dealing with the Porte, experience, which acquired the form of tradition, prescription and even ritual, was just as important as Dubrovnik's famed guile and sinuosity in making the most of the relationship. From the fifteenth century, the nature of the formal gift made to a new Sultan had been established: a bowl, jug and twelve plates of the finest silver, worth 200 ducats.[19] In their approach to the Sultan the *poklisari* were urged by their government to adopt the grovelling demeanour expected when dealing with Eastern potentates, kissing his cloak, begging his favour, offering gifts.[20] With the Sultan's officials a mixture of stubbornness and flattery was more appropriate, but presents of various kinds oiled the wheels of justice: fine cloth, sweetmeats, coffee and spices – purchased in Constantinople. Cash, of course, was also indispensable. The Ragusan ambassadors often complained to the government that the predetermined value of the gifts for these officials was too low, but the Republic was always careful not to allow inflation of official demands to raise the price of future services. After 1580, when the *pashaluk* (province) of Bosnia was created – alongside the existing *pashaluk*s of Buda and Rumelia – Dubrovnik became part of it. From then on the flow of bribes and envoys was directed more towards the seat of the new *pashaluk*, Banja Luka, and less towards the neighbouring *sandžak* of Hercegovina. But Constantinople remained the principal focus of Ragusan diplomatic attention.[21]

The annual mission of the two *poklisari* to Constantinople had by the early eighteenth century adopted such an established style that a detailed description of its conduct was written into Dubrovnik's official book of Ceremonial (*Cerimoniale*), though the procedures certainly reflected practice of a much earlier date.[22] Before the *poklisari* left on their mission, they entered the Rector's Palace and appeared before the Rector and the Small Council. Here the Rector, clad in his scarlet toga, gave a speech in which he exhorted the embassy to serve the Republic's interests faithfully, to which the ambassadors responded by taking an oath to serve the public and not their private interests. The Senate's official instructions were now delivered to them and they went outside to form a procession in front of the Palace. Dressed in 'Hungarian style' (that is, as was traditional when the *harač* was first paid by Dubrovnik), the *poklisari* had a second – public – audience with the Rector and the members of the Small Council, who sat on the upper row of stone benches at the entrance to the Palace.

After this, the mounted procession filed off towards the Ploče Gate. At its head were two Ottoman Janissaries, dressed in green with distinctive headgear, who saluted the Rector in Turkish fashion, with head bowed and right arm across the chest. Their presence was a demonstration that the *poklisari,* as they travelled through the Ottoman Empire, were on the Sultan's business and enjoyed his protection. Next in line came a force of Ragusan mercenary soldiers, dressed in red. In their wake followed the *dragoman*s and a few young men learning that profession. In the middle of the procession were the two *poklisari*, the elder on the right, followed by four more soldiers, a chaplain and a barber-surgeon. At the end came the servants, the first two carrying the standards of the Republic. On that first day the party only travelled to the Ploče suburb where it lodged. Here the *poklisari* received the *harač* which they were to take to the Sultan, presents for him and the Turkish officials, and the secret instructions – which were always the important ones – as to what they were to achieve and how.

The *poklisari* were not only the most important of the Ragusan Republic's diplomatic agents, they were also entrusted with special judicial powers to exercise in the course of their long mission. The route was fixed by tradition in the fifteenth century and it took them through the Ragusan trading colonies of Novi Pazar, Prokuplje, Priština, Sofia and Plovdiv, where they were to pronounce upon disputes which the colonies' own institutions and leaders had not been able to resolve. This meant that the journey to Constantinople often took more than the thirty or forty days otherwise required. During their nearly-four-month stay in Constantinople the *poklisari* resided at Phanar, whereas other foreign ambassadors lodged at Pera because the Ragusans were not, in Ottoman eyes, representatives of a sovereign power but of an autonomous entity within the Empire. They were now to seek from the Sultan not only a quittance for receipt of the *harač* but also other specific favours, the most important of which was usually the permission to export 'prohibited' goods, notably corn, from the Empire. But there were often thornier diplomatic questions to resolve as well, and the *poklisari* would report back to and receive instructions from Dubrovnik as the negotiations evolved, sometimes using code.[23]

The wars between the Ottoman Empire and the West in the sixteenth and seventeenth centuries placed the relationship between Dubrovnik and the Porte under strain in several respects, as will be described. But the incident which perhaps best illustrates both the difficulties and the possibilities is that which concerns the legally preposterous but practically dangerous claims of an Ottoman high official called Ine Han.

The heirs of Ahmed-*pasha* Hercegović (Stjepan Vukčić Kosača's Muslim-convert son) were supposed to be paid a modest annual sum from Dubrovnik for certain rights in Konavle and other property on Ragusan territory.[24] In 1582 they complained to the Porte that they had not received this for the previous nine years, and Dubrovnik undertook to look into the matter. The death of the last Kosača heir soon afterwards meant that these and any other claims fell to the Porte, which was the occasion for a new manoeuvre. The second Vizier, Ibrahim-*pasha*, had already clashed with Dubrovnik when he had unsuccessfully sought to build a tower on Ragusan territory, ostensibly to strengthen the Empire's defences against attacks from *uskok* raiders.[25] He now took up the Hercegović case and claimed that Dubrovnik had cheated the heirs of Ahmed-*pasha* not just out of their property but also out of their legitimate rights to Ston, Primorje, Gruž, Župa Dubrovačka and Konavle. At the end of October 1588, in what Dubrovnik rightly regarded as an ominous development, Ibrahim-*pasha* ordered a Turkish official to cross the Ragusan frontier and begin to draw up a register of Ragusan households.

Before this ploy could go further Ibrahim-*pasha* was in fact dismissed, but in early 1589 a certain Ine Han, the *nazor* (inspector) of Belgrade, took up the claim with still more determination. Ine Han claimed that Dubrovnik should be paying 1,000 ducats annually for these named territories which properly belonged to the Kosača heirs, proposed that a separate *sandžak* be created for them and asked to be appointed its governor or *sandžak-beg*. Furthermore, he stated that Dubrovnik should hand over 150,000 ducats for what it owed since the death of Ahmed-*pasha* Hercegović. The Grand Vizier enthusiastically fell in with this opportunity for extortion and before Dubrovnik could take any effective action on the matter the Sultan's Chancery had issued orders in Ine Han's favour, creating out of Dubrovnik's territories the '*sandžak* of Konavle'. In early 1590, Ine Han began preparations to take possession of the *sandžak*.

Dubrovnik now brought to bear all its resources. At the Sultan's court it mobilised its special friends, like Skender-*aga* who was chamberlain of the Sultan's daughter and whose family came from Lopud, Rabbi Abiathur, a Jewish doctor who treated the chief *defterdar* and whose brother was also a doctor in Dubrovnik; and another Ragusan doctor who was treating the Bosnian *pasha*. By various stratagems it also won over several of the Viziers and the *begler-beg*s of Rumelia and Buda and some influential *kadi*s. But in order to allow this accumulation of influence to prevail, Dubrovnik had to hold firm against Ine Han when he arrived on its territory.

The would-be *sandžak-beg* of Konavle soon showed his unwillingness to compromise by throwing into prison the Ragusan envoys who came to meet him at Zupci. So when Ine Han started to cross Konavle towards the Turkish port of Herceg-Novi, Dubrovnik lined the road with 300 soldiers – whom the disingenuous Ragusans later described, when making their excuses to the Porte, as a guard of honour. Ine Han vented his frustration by threatening to beat the captive Ragusan envoys morning and night till Dubrovnik paid him his money and yielded him his *sandžak*.

But Ragusan influence was now starting to prevail. Ine Han was summoned back to Constantinople and instructed to pursue his claims in an orderly manner before an Ottoman court. In December 1590 his case was heard in the presence of six Ragusan envoys and the following April it was resolved in Dubrovnik's favour. Ine Han was despatched to a different and distant posting and died three years later. The Ragusans had triumphed, though at the cost of an expenditure of 10,000 pieces of gold judiciously distributed in Constantinople.[26]

Thus Dubrovnik strove and so flourished. But its symbiotic relationship with the Ottoman Empire meant that its fortunes faltered as the Empire's problems worsened in the later sixteenth century. The international situation grew more difficult. The Turks could no longer look to France as a makeweight against their Habsburg rivals after the Peace of Cateau-Cambrésis (1559) ended the French struggle with Spain for dominance in Italy. The Ottoman withdrawal from the siege of Malta (1565) and Suleyman's last faltering Hungarian campaign (1566) were early indicators of decline. Of great symbolic – and some practical – significance in the story of Ottoman decline was the defeat of the Turkish fleet at Lepanto (1571). By Catholic Christendom it was celebrated with the institution of the Feast of Our Lady of Victory (later of the Rosary); Muslim commentators, for their part, saw Lepanto as a manifestation of divine judgement on Ottoman decadence and impiety. Meanwhile, a succession of incompetent Sultans presided over an interconnected social and economic crisis in the Ottoman Empire, worsened by the pressures of war.[27] None of this meant that either the Empire or Dubrovnik was doomed to imminent destruction. But time began running against them both.

Holy Wars

Viewed from one perspective, that of the Counter-Reformation and the idealists and adventurers who fought under its banners, the sixteenth and seventeenth centuries were dominated by a more or less continuous Holy War against the Ottoman infidel. There was a small, though influential, group of Ragusans who saw the world in this way too.[28] But for the most part the governing elite of Dubrovnik did not, and dared not, accept this interpretation of events and sought by all possible means to maintain the Republic's neutrality and thus its prosperity and security.

Even before the first of the major sixteenth century wars between Christendom and the Ottoman Empire, the War of the Holy League (1538–1540), Dubrovnik had become a hive of foreign agents and informers. The chief Ragusan representative of Spanish influence in the city was the distinguished patrician Marin Zamanja. He had been sent as the Republic's envoy to Charles V at the end of 1533, where he not only accomplished his diplomatic task but won the Emperor's favour to become Charles's servant, confidant and informer and a knight of the Spanish Order of St James. Marin Zamanja's sympathies and activities were so well known that a herald from the Sultan was sent to denounce him by name as a 'Spanish' spy. Dubrovnik rejected the accusation, explaining that Zamanja was no Spaniard but a Ragusan noble whose family had lived in Dubrovnik for six centuries. The Ragusan government tried discreetly, however, to have Charles V stop making use of Zamanja's services – though in vain.[29]

Working against Marin Zamanja and anxious to obtain every possible advantage for his patron was the chief agent of the French government, the Milanese-born archbishop of Dubrovnik Filippo Trivulzio. In pursuit of the interests of France, which under Francis I was secretly negotiating with the Ottoman Empire, the archbishop was entrusted with doing whatever he could to inform the Porte about its actual and potential enemies' movements. In July 1537, a ship carrying letters from Venice for the count of Kotor to be relayed to the Venetian *bailo* (ambassador) in Constantinople stopped to shelter in Slano and, being unable to continue because of the weather, the captain decided to send the Venetian despatches overland to Kotor by messenger. Trivulzio learned of this from a Ragusan noble, Petar Pucić, and arranged to have one of his agents rob the messenger while he was staying the night at an inn in Konavle. The letters, which were in code, were brought to Trivulzio who in turn sent them on to the French ambassador to the Porte. The Frenchman not only deciphered and read them but told the Turkish *pasha* of Valona, where he was staying, what they contained. Dubrovnik, meanwhile, learned of what had happened and immediately sent a messenger to retrieve the letters, which the government now transmitted to the count of Kotor. The government apologised profusely to Venice and, in spite of the intervention of the Porte, severely punished Pucić. Venice responded by seizing Ragusan ships carrying grain for the city.[30]

In fact, in this Venice was motivated by more than revenge. Turkish troops had besieged Corfu in September, and the Venetians were now reluctantly making preparations to enter an alliance of Christian powers against the Ottoman Empire. They also had every intention of ensuring that neutral Dubrovnik did not benefit at their Republic's expense. The Venetian government, therefore, ordered the seizure of all Ragusan ships heading for Turkish harbours and, from its base on Korčula, a Venetian fleet enforced a strict blockade on Dubrovnik, provoking Ragusan protests.[31]

Venice now exerted strong pressure in Rome to have Dubrovnik join the Holy League, which a succession of Ragusan envoys vigorously and successfully resisted with the understanding of the Vatican. But the pope's personal goodwill had little effect on the activities of the nominally papal – but in practice, Venetian – fleet sailing the waters of the Adriatic. On its way to the Levant in the summer of 1538 the fleet occupied Lopud, plundered the town and took many of the islanders hostage, before sailing away. The Ragusans protested to the pope that even the Turks behaved in a better fashion. Dubrovnik and Ston, both short of food for even their own inhabitants because of the blockade, were flooded with refugees from *uskok* attacks; and the best that the Ragusan government could suggest to the peasants of Pelješac was that they should send their families and belongings up into the hills and then prepare to defend their homes.[32]

A new and still more dangerous phase of the conflict was marked by the fall of Herceg-Novi in the autumn of 1538 to Andrea Doria and the Christian fleet. On learning the news, Dubrovnik sent a message of condolence to the Turks, while at the same time agreeing to lend 10,000 ducats to the financially hard-pressed Christian admiral. Doria had already more than deserved this favour because (so he told the Ragusans) he and the governor of Naples, Ferdinando Gonzaga, had blocked the Venetian proposal that their force be directed against Dubrovnik rather than Herceg-Novi. In any case, in July 1539 Barbarossa retook Herceg-Novi for the Turks, which was doubtless a relief for Dubrovnik; the Ragusans sent him their congratulations and a present of 1,000 ducats. But Barbarossa was incapable of protecting them from Venice, whose fleet continued to blockade the city, which was soon facing starvation. Finally, in February 1540, one of Dubrovnik's ships loaded with grain managed to slip through the cordon. Only when the Venetians sought a separate peace with the Porte could the Turks insist that the blockade of Dubrovnik be lifted and its ships and cargoes restored.[33]

Although war between the Turks and Spanish continued to rage in the western Mediterranean, Dubrovnik now enjoyed almost three decades of relative peace. Venice, too, was anxious to stay out of the conflict. But confronted in March 1569 with a Turkish demand to hand over to the Empire the prized Venetian colony of Cyprus, Venice found itself again forced to take up arms and the 'War of Cyprus' (1570–1573) began.

Dubrovnik initially benefited from the early Turkish successes: as the Turkish armies conquered Cyprus, Ragusan merchants moved in behind them. Still more important was the flood of trade and traders into Dubrovnik itself as soon as war broke out and commercial communication between the

Ottoman Empire and the West via Venetian outlets ended. Although the benefits to Dubrovnik of this situation may have been exaggerated – not least by the Venetians – they were clearly real.[34] But so were the dangers, notably from Venice. On learning of the imminent conflict, and bearing in mind Venice's earlier tactics, Dubrovnik immediately instructed Frano Gundulić, who was living in Rome, to seek the pope's protection for the Republic.

Gundulić was ideally suited to the task. A highly educated patriot, he was, still more importantly, a pious Catholic, enjoying close relations with senior Vatican dignitaries including two successive popes, Pius V (1566–1572) and Gregory XIII (1572–1585).[35] As soon as he received his commission from the Republic, Gundulić sought an audience with Pius V, who promised his support. That proved all too necessary. The Venetian ambassador to the Holy See sought by every means to force Dubrovnik into the anti-Ottoman alliance, going so far in May 1570 as to suggest that the allies occupy Dubrovnik to prevent its falling into Turkish hands. The pope refused to countenance this. And of course the argument was specious, since the Turks had no interest in seizing the city. The Spanish king, Philip II, was generally prepared to follow papal direction in these matters, and in any case had inherited from his predecessor a favourable view of Dubrovnik; but in order to make doubly sure, the Republic despatched Ivan Cvjetković, a Ragusan captain in the service of the Don John of Austria (the future victor of Lepanto), to see Philip in person. The perilous journey led Cvjetković via Naples, Rome (where he received further advice from Frano Gundulić), Antibes and Barcelona to Madrid, where he was able to reinforce Philip's sympathy for Dubrovnik's situation.

In Rome the parties were now discussing the terms of the new Holy League. The papal and Spanish representatives urged that Dubrovnik be offered an explicit undertaking of special protection, at which the Venetian envoy quite lost control of himself and said that that 'snake' Dubrovnik would become impossible if it was accorded any such thing. The Venetians tried to win over the Spanish to their viewpoint, but in vain, for Philip continued to insist that the wording proposed by the pope be adopted. So it was that a special clause in the agreement to form the Holy League was inserted according to which Dubrovnik with its territory and property must not be damaged by the allies nor suffer any loss, unless for some just cause appearing so to the pope or his successors.

This diplomatic triumph did not, however, tempt Frano Gundulić or the Ragusan Senate into complacency. In Rome Gundulić continued to remind the pope and his advisers of the importance of the little Republic in the Christian scheme of things, while also defending its reputation from other quarters. Don

John of Austria was highly suspicious of Dubrovnik's dealings with the Turks, not least when a Ragusan ship he had arrested in Messina turned out to have been carrying 7,000 cannonballs, probably for onward transmission to the Ottoman Empire; Gundulić was sent to Naples to have the ship released.[36] Dubrovnik repaid the favours it received from Vatican and Spanish benevolence with a flow of despatches to Rome containing information about the Ottoman Empire's fortunes: as a safeguard against embarrassment these were signed with fictitious names.[37]

Unfortunately, subtle diplomacy availed little against the *uskok*s. (The name '*uskok*' derives from the Croatian verb *uskočiti* – 'to jump into'). These resistance fighters against the Turks – originally drawn from refugees, supplemented by adventurers, living off plunder and based in the great coastal fortress of Senj – were regarded by Dubrovnik with fear and loathing. Unlike those other anti-Ottoman irregulars, the *hajduk*s, with whom they were often confused and with whose personnel they undoubtedly overlapped, the *uskok*s had a continuing organisation and political existence.[38] Accordingly, Dubrovnik initially hoped to establish negotiated agreements with the *uskok* leaders in Senj to restrict their depredations against Ragusan territory and property. But as the sixteenth century wore on it became clear that such secret deals were ineffective; and, of course, if they should come to light they would also prove severely embarrassing in Dubrovnik's relations with the Ottoman Empire.

The Venetians too had reason to dislike the *uskok*s: indeed, at the end of the century Venice fought the Habsburgs, the *uskok*s' protectors and occasional paymasters, because of the Serenissima's fury at *uskok* attacks on its Dalmatian territories. But until then Venice's attitude was that since the *uskok*s could not be curbed they could at least be used in the struggle against the Turks – and incidentally for the punishment and humiliation of Dubrovnik. That was particularly the case in the War of Cyprus. So it was that in 1570 '*uskok*' raiders launched some thirty attacks on Ragusan territory, making off with livestock, victuals and hostages for ransom.

What such raids entailed is revealed by a dossier drawn up as a result of investigations carried out by two Ragusan commissioners, Marin Bunić and Sebastijan Menčetić, in the presence of Giuliano di Giacomo, the Venetian consul. It shows that under the all-embracing title of '*uskok*s' the Ragusans lumped together piratical raiders from different islands and ports the length of Dalmatia, who were not obviously under the command of the *uskok* leaders of Senj. Among the most hated and dangerous were the men of Boka Kotorska, particularly Perast; but others from Hvar, Korčula and elsewhere participated in the attacks as well. In the spring of 1570 Mljet was probably the raiders' principal focus. Two of their vessels broke through the chain blocking off the island's 'lake' from the open sea and imposed their demands on the monks, sailing away with the monastery's best wine, oil and livestock. They also landed and raided at other spots around Mljet where, as one witness put it (in a favourite expression), 'they behaved worse than the Turks'.[39]

Naturally, anyone at sea with a valuable cargo was also regarded as fair game. One of the Dubrovnik Dominican fathers told the commissioners that he had been at Trsteno loading a bark with wine for the friary when men from Perast, Korčula and 'other *uskok*s, subjects of Venice' appeared. They took everything, lamented the friar, so that '... of forty-five bottles of wine, not one full bottle was left'; and they shouted insults at him into the bargain.[40] Similarly, the owner of a Ragusan brigantine was attacked by three armed barks of 'malefactors and assassins' from Perast – he was able to name a number of them. They descended when he was at the port of Žuljana, on Pelješac, loading his vessel with wine for the government of Dubrovnik. They beat him and two others of the crew and went away with a rich haul consisting not just of wine but of four light cannons, 63 cannonballs, gunpowder, other firearms and weaponry, money, sails, row-locks, nails, flags, clothes, ship's biscuits, lard, flour and other supplies.[41] Nor was Dubrovnik's modest battle-fleet liable to be of much effect against such people. When its frigate was sent to the waters off Korčula it was promptly attacked by six barks of '*uskok*s' from Perast and Kotor. The Ragusan captain had to sail his vessel right into the port of Korčula where he and his crew leapt ashore and fled to take refuge with the Venetian count. Nor did the raiders show the latter much respect either.[42]

Probably the most difficult and dangerous predicament was faced by the inhabitants of Konavle. The villagers of Vitaljina and Molunat in particular were all too close to predators from Boka Kotorska, who came overland and by sea, stealing their livestock and victuals.[43] And though the principal town of the area – Cavtat – was better protected, it too was vulnerable. Moreover, because it held attractions for both pro- and anti-Turkish raiders, neither of whom respected Ragusan territory or property, it became in 1570 the centre of a dispute which entailed special risks for the Republic. By what was claimed to be an oversight, but what clearly looked to the Venetians and the '*uskok*s' a matter of connivance, a Turkish force was allowed into Cavtat where three '*uskok*' vessels had sought shelter. One vessel crewed by men from Paštrovići made off; but the other two – manned by men from Perast – engaged in a fierce battle with the Turks, while the local inhabitants went in fear of their lives. The Ragusan captain of Cavtat ignominiously fled, but was later persuaded to return. When he remonstrated with the Turks about their behaviour towards the inhabitants they replied (as he later reported) that

> ... if it was allowed for the men of Perast to abuse... the men and make them slaves in this place, which is said to be Ragusan territory, we are allowed to do the same.

For their part, the Venetians and their unruly allies clearly suspected that the captain of Cavtat and the Ragusan authorities had deliberately contrived the ambush, well knowing Dubrovnik's hatred for its violent neighbours. In the light of subsequent events, perhaps they were right.[44]

In 1571 the attacks from both *uskok*s and those, like the men of Perast, who had become all but indistiguishable from them, became still more intense. The government of Dubrovnik now seems to have planned the death of the most famous *uskok* of the day, Juraj Daničić. In July 1571 Daničić and a body of *uskok*s plundered Primorje and then Vitaljina, returning through Župa Dubrovačka to Brgat, where they robbed a merchant's caravan. On the way across the Šumet hills to their ships moored in Rijeka Dubrovačka they were intercepted by the Ragusan army. Dubrovnik's and the *uskok*s' accounts then differ: but it seems that the Ragusans lured Daničić into their hands under cover of a safe-conduct and then killed him and a number of others, while allowing the rest of the leaderless *uskok*s to sail away. Daničić's sons later waged a bitter campaign against Dubrovnik in revenge for its treachery. It was, as the *uskok*s explained to the Rector of Trogir, when threatening him with similar treatment, really a matter of honour. The dispute was only resolved with great difficulty by papal intervention.[45] Indeed, the incident provoked an international scandal, for the *uskok*s were regarded by Christian opinion as crusaders and Daničić as a hero. Dubrovnik publicly protested its innocence, drawing up an exculpatory memorandum signed by the French and Venetian agents in Dubrovnik. But at the same time the Ragusans secretly related and indeed exaggerated the incident to the Porte as evidence of the Republic's loyalty to the Ottoman Empire and hostility to its enemies.[46]

The end of the War of Cyprus saw the accession of a new weak Sultan, Murad III (1574–1595), and while senior officials peculated and jostled for power the Empire fell into ever deeper crisis. Then in 1593 the humiliating rout of a raiding Turkish army at Sisak in Croatia precipitated the (first) 'Long War' between the Austrians and the Turks (1593–1606). News of the defeat was greeted with spontaneous enthusiasm in the streets of Dubrovnik, while the Ragusan government expressed its official regrets to the Porte.[47]

In fact, Dubrovnik already had a great deal to regret in its recent dealings with the Ottoman Empire. In 1590 occurred perhaps the single greatest commercial blow the Republic ever suffered, when the Venetians opened up Split as an alternative *entrepôt* to Dubrovnik and gained the Sultan's agreement to channel Turkish trade through this excellently situated port. From now until 1645 – when Split's prosperity fell victim to a new war (the 'War of Crete') between Venice and the Ottoman Empire – Dubrovnik's diplomacy struggled in vain to reverse the decision.[48]

Dubrovnik's value in the eyes of the Porte had in any case somewhat diminished. In increasingly hazardous conditions it was unable to perform as effectively as in earlier years its role as a secure link with European commerce. Nor could it prevent its territory being used by anti-Turkish fighters. And though after 1613 the *uskoks* avoided the waters round Dubrovnik, raids by other *hajduk* bands continued. Also important in fuelling Ottoman suspicions in the late sixteenth and early early seventeenth centuries was the fact that Dubrovnik was at the centre of a web of anti-Turkish intrigue, whose threads stretched across the Balkans and beyond.

The 'Long War' saw stirrings of Christian revolt against the Turks in many parts of the Ottoman Empire, including Dalmatia, which the papacy and the Habsburgs did what they could to encourage.[49] Turkish military reverses encouraged the Slavs of Hercegovina to seek help from the West. In January 1604, an assembly of Orthodox priests and other Hercegovinian local leaders resolved to offer their submission to Austria. They nominated Fra Dominik Andrijašević, Hercegovinian by birth but resident in Dubrovnik, to conclude an alliance in Vienna – a duty he performed when on the diplomatic business of the Ragusan Republic (with or without the government's knowledge is unclear).[50]

The end of the Long War and the temporary withdrawal of the Habsburgs from direct participation in the Balkan struggle against the Turks only made political conditions more chaotic and complicated for Dubrovnik. Moreover, the adventurers who now adopted the principal roles were less predictable and more irresponsible and posed a greater threat to the Republic's jealously guarded neutrality and security.[51]

The Climax of the Struggle with Venice

The first half of the seventeenth century also marked the climax of Dubrovnik's long struggle with Venice. The Venetians had, of course, lost no opportunity during the late fifteenth and sixteenth centuries to plot against Ragusan interests and autonomy. But Venice's determination now to press its claims of lordship over its 'Gulf' was all the greater because tinged with desperation, as elsewhere Venetian trade retreated before French, English and Dutch competition. In truth, Venice's real interests were more likely to be served by exploiting Split's possibilities than by seeking to diminish those of Dubrovnik, but the temptation to try to hurt and humiliate its rival over even trivial matters proved irresistible.

Venice took its claims of lordship of the Gulf so far as to assert not only a monopoly over the trade which was conducted across it but even sovereign rights over the islands which lay within it. This was what prompted Venetian mischief-making over Dubrovnik's island of Lastovo.

For a number of years the Dubrovnik government had been gradually chipping away at Lastovo's limited autonomy. In November 1601 the Ragusan Senate passed two apparently innocuous decrees altering the remuneration paid by the islanders to the count appointed by Dubrovnik, and requiring the construction of two new prisons (one for men and one for women) at the islanders' expense. The community of Lastovo initially resisted, and then under pressure accepted these measures, but they seem to have constituted the occasion for a conspiracy that the Venetians subsequently sought to exploit. In May 1602, 50 of the island's more distinguished inhabitants – under the leadership of three priests – resolved to throw off Ragusan rule. They told the Dalmatian *Provveditore* that they were willing to submit Lastovo to Venice. But he reflected on the offer too long, and by the time he arrived to occupy the island on Venice's behalf he found that Dubrovnik had landed its own army; the *Provveditore* accordingly sailed away and Venice awaited further developments.

In the meantime, Dubrovnik dealt ruthlessly with the rebels. Ragusan judges imposed the death penalty *in absentia* on those who had fled. Other rebels who had been imprudent enough to remain were rounded up and taken to the mainland. Two of the three clerical ringleaders (the other had got away), with another Franciscan friar involved in the conspiracy, were sentenced to be strangled under cover of darkness and buried in the church of St Luke near the Ploče Gate. Rome was indignant about this gross breach of clerical rights and it took Dubrovnik's best diplomatic efforts to repair the damage.

Yet nor had the rebellion been properly extinguished. Once Dubrovnik scaled down its military presence on Lastovo it broke out again, in January 1603. Dubrovnik now sent a new force which retook Lastovo castle. But this time Venice had learned the dangers of procrastination. The Venetian captain of the Gulf suddenly arrived with 2,000 men and forced the Ragusans to abandon Lastovo, which Venice occupied until June 1606. Dubrovnik waged a fierce diplomatic battle to regain its island, but only when the 'Long War' came to an end and the Porte was free to impose a solution on Venice did it succeed in having Lastovo restored. The Venetians withdrew, only insisting that there be a general amnesty – which Dubrovnik agreed and then ignored, throwing eighteen of the ringleaders of the revolt into the city jail.[52]

The little Ragusan Republic found it difficult to challenge the overweening assertion of Venetian claims in the Adriatic, but others were better able to do so. The *uskok*s fought – though they eventually lost – the struggle; the Austrians would fight – and ultimately win – on behalf of Trieste. In the meantime, between 1616 and 1620, the Spanish viceroy of Naples, the duke of Osuna, repeatedly challenged Venetian maritime dominance with his formidable navy. The fact that Dubrovnik's ships were to be found serving in these fleets, and that the Ragusans openly regarded Osuna as a scourge of their mutual enemies, was the occasion of protests and retaliatory action by Venice. In 1617, for instance, the Serenissima ordered that Dubrovnik's ships carrying corn from southern Italy be intercepted and that any sailors captured should be forced to serve as oarsmen on Venetian galleys.[53]

Venice's spite and resentment at this time are reflected in the orders given to the commander of its fleet and the polyglot force it carried that August:

> Damage the Ragusans from the sea and permit the Croatian and Dutch troops to do every sort of harm on the land, particularly on Pelješac, at Ston, on Lopud and in the harbour of Gruž, where the most distinguished men of the city go for recreation. If for security it is necessary to stay some time in Gruž, do them as much harm as possible as regards their victuals with the excuse that they are necessary for our soldiers. Allow the soldiers to destroy their vineyards and do harm to all their possessions; let them completely destroy the mills at Rijeka; smash and cut off the aqueducts which are on the hill above the city. You will, it goes without saying, give orders that churches be spared and that the honour of women be respected. All this must be done without your [the Venetian commander] being present, because this deception is in the interest of the state... [But] spare from these attacks the men of Lastovo, who in the past showed themselves very loyal to us.[54]

In these miserable circumstances, the Ragusans complained to the Porte and found considerable sympathy in Constantinople. Dubrovnik's ambassador there, Marko Basiljević, argued the Republic's case in front of the Grand Vizier and his *divan*, while the Venetian *bailo* defended his own government's action. The *bailo* claimed that Venice had only been defending Turkish interests, thus alluding to Dubrovnik's collaboration with Osuna's fleet which had seized Turkish merchandise. In order to bring home Ragusan links with the hated Neapolitan viceroy, the *bailo* even improbably alleged that the Ragusans were secretly planning to move to Italy. The Porte, though, sided with Dubrovnik; the Venetians had to lift their blockade; and in the autumn of 1618 the Sultan publicly proclaimed that Dubrovnik was a vassal of the Ottoman Empire and ordered Venice strictly to refrain from any hostile action against it.[55]

The Venetians, however, though temporarily willing to appease the Porte, had no intention of reducing the pressure on Dubrovnik to accept the widest interpretation of Venice's lordship of the Gulf. In the 1620s Venice began to insist that Ragusan ships sailing the Adriatic should, unless bound for a Venetian harbour, pay a special customs due. In 1629 the Serenissima decreed that Ragusan ships could only carry corn if it was destined for Dubrovnik or Venice, otherwise they and their cargoes would be seized. Similarly, Venice forbade the transport of any salt other than Venetian and impounded whatever they found in Ragusan ships. The Venetians claimed the right to decide on fishing rights within Ragusan waters. They interfered in other disputes as well. The men of Perast (a traditional nest of piracy in Boka Kotorska) landed on the little island of Molunat, the possession of the bishop of Mrkan-Trebinje who lived in Dubrovnik, and harvested and sailed off with the produce. Rights on the other tiny island of Sušac, which was traditionally regarded as an adjunct of neighbouring Lastovo, were also disputed by the inhabitants of Korčula, Vis and Hvar who fished and pastured their animals there. Dubrovnik and Lastovo resisted this. Venice claimed the authority to settle all these matters.

More serious for Dubrovnik's security, however, was the Venetians' attempt to lay claim to the island of Lokrum, which, if successful, would have placed the city's harbour and commerce at their mercy. There was an initial incident in July 1630, when Venetian warships attacked a Ragusan armed escort ship accompanying another ship taking the wife of the Rector of Dubrovnik and some of her friends on a day's outing to Lokrum. The Venetians, acting on the theory that only Venetian ships could go armed in its Gulf, drove the Ragusan escort ship ashore and robbed it, then spent the night on Lokrum before sailing away. It was clear that the Ragusans' resolve was being tested, and Dubrovnik fired its cannons to show its determination.

Then in May 1631 Venice invented a new excuse to assert its claims: the Venetian *Provveditore* in Zadar complained that Dubrovnik had established a *lazzaretto* (quarantine installation), without Venice's permission, on Lokrum – which he insisted on calling Venice's island of 'St Mark'.[56] In June five Venetian fleets temporarily seized Lokrum and destroyed the installation, but left when they came under fire from Dubrovnik's cannons. Dubrovnik protested to the viceroy of Naples, informed the Spanish and even won the support of Cardinal Richelieu of France. But as usual it was Ottoman pressure to which the Venetians responded and which forced them to come to an agreement with the tenacious Ragusan special envoy sent to Venice, Miho Sorkočević.

After negotiations lasting some four months, in September 1635 Venice finally accepted that Ragusan ships that sailed the Adriatic need pay only a nominal customs due, so confirming in principle but hardly in practice the Serenissima's authority over its Gulf. Venice also recognised Dubrovnik's rights over Lokrum, Molunat and Sušac. It refused to pay any reparations for the damage it had inflicted and, most galling to Miho Sorkočević, it also refused – in the Doge's official act which encapsulated the settlement – to address Dubrovnik as a Republic, only referring to the 'Count, Council and Community of the Town of Ragusa'. But in truth the agreement was highly satisfactory to Dubrovnik, which had always been more interested in substance than form.[57]

For another decade Venice's Dalmatian possessions flourished. But in 1645 the Sultan authorised a Turkish invasion of Crete, which from 1204 had been under Venetian control, so precipitating the 'War of Crete' (1645–1669). And second only to the loss of Crete itself was the damage to Venetian interests when its flourishing *entrepôt* of Split was effectively closed down and Ottoman trade with the West was channelled – as before 1590 – through Dubrovnik. This certainly helped Dubrovnik's economy, though whether it made up for the general breakdown of order and communications that had such a devastating impact on trade in the Balkans is more doubtful.

The outbreak of war was a signal to the *hajduks* based in Makarska, Omiš and Krajina to launch attacks on Ragusan territory, property and personnel. In the spring of 1647 Dubrovnik's islands were targeted. Then in early June a band of *hajduks* under their *harambaša* (commander) actually assembled in Gruž, intending to prey on Turkish caravans, but were driven off with casualties by Dubrovnik's mercenaries. In revenge, the *hajduks* returned to ravage Pelješac, seizing livestock, wine, cash and hostages.

The fall of the great fortress of Klis, overlooking Split, to anti-Turkish fighters in March 1648 was a boost to *hajduk* and a blow to Turkish morale. The raids on Ragusan territory accordingly intensified in 1649 and 1650 and

Dubrovnik had to hand out muskets to the peasants of Ston to defend themselves. Meanwhile, attacks against the other flank of the Republic were launched from Boka Kotorska, which had attracted a growing population of robbers and adventurers living nominally under Venetian sovereignty. The men of Perast were, as has been noted, among the worst offenders: Dubrovnik complained to Venice that these people behaved worse than Barbary pirates, but they continued their depredations. A final twist to the violence and disorder came when Ottoman-controlled Herceg-Novi fell under the control of brigands originally employed to protect Turkish caravans in Hercegovina, but who found it more rewarding to raid Ragusan villages on the excuse that Dubrovnik allowed its land to be used by the enemies of the Sultan. And to add to the Republic's misery it was also during these years ravaged by the plague.[58] In fact, Dubrovnik was already in a perilous predicament, when in the spring of 1667 a natural catastrophe on a quite different scale suddenly threatened the Republic with extinction.[59]

Nor was Dubrovnik's image such as to inspire much international sympathy for its travails. One of a group of Frenchmen who visited Dubrovnik in January 1658 noted that the inhabitants were known as 'the Ragusans of the *sette bandiere* (seven flags)' because they gave tribute to seven foreign rulers. And he provided the following cynical assessment of their motives:

> The Turks they fear; the Venetians they hate; the Spaniards they love, because they are useful; the French they suffer because of their fame; and foreigners they spy on very much.[60]

It was unenviable reputation.

SEVEN

Governing Passion: The Institutions of Government and the Challenges They Faced (c. 1272–1667)

The Law

The political community which the Venetians left behind in Dubrovnik was one already firmly founded on law. On 29 May 1272 was promulgated in the public square by Count Marco Giustiniani the codification of Dubrovnik's laws, the *Liber Statutorum*, popularly known as the Statute of Dubrovnik.[1] It consists now of eight books; but the final two, relating respectively to maritime affairs and miscellaneous matters, were almost certainly added later.

The Statute was the most nearly comprehensive collection of Dubrovnik's laws ever achieved. But it does not represent the first attempt at codification, let alone the first laws. A number of earlier legal ordinances have been preserved: for example, that which on 3 February 1190 instituted the 'franchise of St Blaise', and that which on 13 April 1235 regulated dowries.[2] Something more ambitious was attempted in the time of Count Giovanni Tiepolo (1237–1238), who sought to codify Ragusan criminal law. It seems likely that Count Giovanni was influenced by the example of his uncle, Doge Giacomo Tiepolo, who presided over the drawing up of the Venetian Statute. The Ragusan criminal code which resulted from Count Giovanni's initiative remained in force even after the promulgation of the Dubrovnik Statute of 1272, and it seems to have exercised a strong influence over the criminal provisions contained in the customs of both Lastovo and Korčula. From the Statute's explanatory preamble it is also clear that there were other (unsatisfactory) collections of Ragusan laws before 1272:

> ... The statutes of Ragusa previously edited by different counts and at different times were dispersed in several books; between them there were some discrepancies; they were in certain things superfluous, and in many there were not a few defects. [Consequently, they] are obscure and even confused, so that from many of them arguments and different opinions arise between judges.[3]

The thirteenth century was the high point of medieval jurisprudence, influencing the practices of governments and not merely the life of universities. But in the case of Dubrovnik, as of other early political communities, law was understood as having force before its codification or even its written form. The Dubrovnik Statute does not refer directly – as, for example, does the early Croatian Statute of Vinodol (1288) – to oral traditions, but the presumption of a pre-existing law based upon custom is still evident. Sometimes a particular provision in the Dubrovnik Statute is described simply as 'ancient custom' (*antiqua consuetudo*); sometimes there is a stipulation that a judge should act 'according to ancient custom', without specifying that custom's contents. Not, however, that custom was deemed all-powerful: it could be and was reformed when necessary – so on occasion action of a certain kind is prescribed, 'custom notwithstanding'. The way this might work out in practice is suggested by the terms of the oaths taken by Ragusan judges, who swore on taking office to judge without fraud and according to the custom of the *civitas* of Ragusa if they knew it, and if they did not, to judge honestly and according to good conscience.[4]

Custom was particularly important when it came to relationships with Dubrovnik's neighbours, which had achieved a stable basis as much through the habitual solution of disputes as through formal treaties. The (already mentioned) institution of the *stanak*, by which territorial and property disputes were settled by judges appointed by each side, is an example. When there arose a problem between the men of Dubrovnik and those of Šibenik, Trogir or Split which could not be resolved by the two communities, a *stanak* would be called 'according to the ancient custom', the parties going to the isthmus at Ston where the court was held.[5] Such custom, though it could on occasion be changed, was highly prized, and even the count might run up against strong opposition if he sought to override it. This is illustrated by the practice relating to the payment of a prescribed sum of money, called *vražda*, levied as punishment when a Ragusan killed a Serb or *vice versa*.[6] In 1308, when the Venetian count tried to exact the death penalty instead, he was opposed by the Ragusan community – though he successfully appealed to the Doge. A later count, however, seeking better relations with the Serbian ruler on the basis of limited legal reciprocity, thought it best to reinstate the system.[7]

Yet, while custom remained important, the Dubrovnik Statute did mark a new era in which written authority and recorded precedent exercised ever greater influence. In 1277 the Dubrovnik Customs Statute (*Liber Statutorum Doane*) was drawn up.[8] Then at the end of that year Dubrovnik's first known notary, a priest called Master Tomazinus, began work in the town.[9] He probably also acted as clerk to the Ragusan Councils, though the first preserved book of consolidated Council minutes – misleadingly known as the *Libri Reformationum* – only begins in 1301. The Council decisions which were subsequently deemed to have a more than ephemeral significance were from this time also inscribed in a separate volume, called the *Liber Omnium Reformationum*. Its contents were officially confirmed on 10 May 1335, but were later supplemented by other Council decisions till as late as 1410.[10] When the last Venetian count left Dubrovnik in 1358 a new volume was begun, which because of the colour of its cover came to be known as the Green Book (*Liber Viridis*) and which contained laws up to 1460. In that year was begun a successor, the Yellow Book (*Liber Croceus*), some of whose versions end in the sixteenth century and others in the seventeenth, while one reaches 1806 – almost to the end of the Republic. Other important collections are the Ston Statute (*Statuta Stagni*), consisting of provisions relating to Ston and Pelješac, the Customs Statute (mentioned earlier), the Customs of Lastovo (1310) and of Mljet (1345), a Book of the Great Custom (*Capitolare della dogana grande*, 1413) and the much later Ragusan Maritime Statute (*Regolamenti della repubblica di Ragusa, per la navigazione nazionale*, 1745).

There was no separate Ragusan law school. But Dubrovnik was fortunate in having as one of its most public-spirited citizens the famous sixteenth century lawyer, Frano Gundulić, who organised, indexed, and commented upon this amorphous body of legal documentation and so provided Ragusan judges and lawyers with the means of applying it.[11]

Early Institutions

The Dubrovnik Statute and its successor volumes describe a city-state governed through political institutions heavily modelled on those of Venice. This remained so throughout the life of the Ragusan Republic and there is no evidence that its ever-practical patricians felt any need to disown Venetian institutional – however fiercely they combated Venetian political – influence.[12]

At the time of the promulgation of the Statute of 1272, of the early minutes of the Ragusan Councils, and of the *Liber Omnium Reformationum*, the formal arrangements still reflected the underlying realities of power.

The Venetian count of Dubrovnik, as the representative of the Doge, enjoyed a unique social and economic status. He was, for example, assured of a special allowance of salt for himself and his household, at a time when salt was a highly prized and state-controlled commodity. He received special dues whenever livestock was slaughtered in the town abattoir. The millers of Dubrovnik had to mill his and his household's grain without charge. He received a share of any large catch brought home by Dubrovnik's fishing boats. He, himself, had the exclusive right to fish in Rijeka Dubrovačka during the fortnight before Christmas. People bringing loads of pine logs to Dubrovnik by land or sea were bound to give him one. Anyone who bought slaves in Dubrovnik paid him a fixed due per head, unless the slave were a midget or child. Probably most financially important was the requirement that captains of ships coming from Apulia, Sicily, the Marches of Ancona and the Romagna must pay the count a *hyperperus* for the due called *arboraticum*, levied on vessels entering Dubrovnik's harbour. (In 1313 it was resolved that the count should not receive *arboraticum* from ships arriving from other places). The archbishop, who clearly appears from the Statute as the other leading figure of Venetian Dubrovnik, also benefited by custom from privileges similar to those of the count, as did, in a more modest fashion, the abbot of Lokrum.[13]

For his part, the count had corresponding economic and social obligations. At Christmas the sailors of Dubrovnik customarily arrived at his castle, bearing a log of wood which would be placed on the fire amid much merriment and the singing of the traditional carols: they then received from the count two *hyperperi* and their fill of wine. So too, the captain and crew of the first Ragusan ship to enter the harbour on Christmas or Easter day received a *hyperperus* 'by ancient custom'. On New Year's Eve it was the fishermen and the master craftsmen of Dubrovnik who turned up to receive their 'customary' bounty from the count.[14]

All these arrangements reflected the fact that, until the end of Venetian rule over Dubrovnik, the Venetian-appointed count was formally regarded as the supreme political authority in the town. Behind the theoretical facade, however, reality was shifting. The count's power waned inexorably in the course of the thirteenth century, and his position had become largely ceremonial by the time of the last crisis.

Assisted by a *socius* (literally, 'companion') from Venice, the count ruled through his Small Council, which was at once an advisory, executive and legislative body – though some kind of wider consent from the community was also required in certain solemn and important matters. In the early years, it was the count himself who appointed the Small Council and then, jointly with that Council, appointed the other organs of government. The latter included the Great Council and the body called the *Consilium Rogatorum*, which would later – after its Venetian equivalent – be termed the Senate. Initially, both the Great Council and the Senate had a tentative and spasmodic existence, being overshadowed by the Small Council. In fact, the Great Council only began to emerge as a force in its own right during the Venetian count's absence in 1235, when two local Ragusan deputy counts (*potknezs*) were in charge. The restored Venetian authority seems from now on to have accepted the Great Council as a permanent institution, and from 1252 the Senate also became a permanent fixture.

Equally significant was the erosion of the count's control over his own Small Council. From 1293 it became accepted custom that the members of the Small Council would be appointed from the ranks of certain distinguished noble families, thus greatly limiting the count's freedom of manoeuvre and opportunities for patronage. The Small Council's authority also waned in proportion as that of the Great Council grew.[15]

Contributing to the greater political importance of Dubrovnik's communal institutions and their assertiveness was the fact that the count and his Small Council so often had to rely upon Ragusan nobles to perform important tasks. In April 1324, for example, two nobles were appointed to go through Astarea and two to the islands to draw up a list of oarsmen for Dubrovnik's galleys.[16] Still more significant was the increasing use of commissions of noble 'wise men' (*sapientes*) appointed to handle delicate political questions or cope with pressing dangers. In July 1345, for instance, five wise men were chosen to propose modifications to and provide for execution of the statutes relating to the import of wine to Dubrovnik.[17] In January 1351, ten wise men were again appointed to work with the count and the Small Council on the arming of the Ragusan war galley.[18] Nobles were also regularly – and almost exclusively – appointed to perform diplomatic missions to the Slavic rulers of the hinterland.[19] These diplomats too were in some cases subject to the orders of wise men.[20] When the crucial embassy was sent to the king of Hungary in 1358 its instructions were drawn by a special commission of fifteen noble wise men.[21]

Nobles were not in fact always enthusiastic about carrying out their public duties. In November 1344 the Great Council resolved that those chosen as ambassadors to Bosnia could not excuse themselves by any device, under pain of fines of 100 *hyperperi*.[22] When, in November 1347, one ambassador returned from a delicate mission from that state without permission, he was thrown into prison and then exiled for three months to Ston, in order to set an example.[23]

This tendency to unreliability was also reflected in the numbers turning up to the Great Council, which varied considerably. For example, in September 1312, at the session where the main officials, judges and members of the Small Council were elected, there were 190 nobles present in the Great Council.[24] But only 108 nobles turned up in January 1323 to a session of the Great Council, called to authorise a special payment from the state treasury for expenditure on the city walls.[25] Numbers were, of course, heavily depleted by the Black Death, and in May 1348 the minimum age for membership was therefore reduced from twenty to eighteen years. Yet even on the solemn occasion in February 1358, when the new constitutional arrangements to cope with the ending of Venetian rule were proclaimed, only 130 councillors were present.[26] By then, the membership of the Great Council had become clearly established. It was limited to the adult male members of Dubrovnik's noble families; indeed, membership came to constitute a proof of Ragusan nobility.[27]

The oligarchical features of Ragusan government became, over time, steadily more pronounced. This appears as part of a general trend in late medieval Europe's urban communities. The underlying causes were probably economic – namely, the emergence of a class of self-confident mercantile families whose wealth was such that their corporate interests and those of their political community almost completely coincided.[28] But the process of restricting membership of the Ragusan Great Council – and thus membership of the other organs of government, since they were chosen from it – was evidently most heavily influenced by the Venetian example.

In Venice the change in the rules for admission to the Great Council seems to have been mainly prompted by the need to cope with factional squabbles. In 1297 the previous limit on the size of the Council was removed. But as a counterpart to this, it was decided that those who were already Councillors, or had been so at some stage during the last four years, were to be members of the new Great Council as long as they received the approval of twelve of the members of the powerful Council of Forty (a body somewhat similar to Dubrovnik's Senate). Other candidates for the Great Council could at this date still be proposed, but the institutional obstacles to their entry were progressively raised until it was finally declared that in order to be a member of the Great Council a man must first show that he had an ancestor who had held high office in the state. In this way membership of Venice's Great Council became hereditary. The 'closing' (*serrata*) of the Venetian political system was thus complete.[29]

The closing of the ranks of the Ragusan Great Council took slightly longer and, unlike Venice, in Dubrovnik's case divisions within the patriciate do not seem to have been a factor. The first significant step was taken in 1321, when it was formally accepted that all adult (twenty-one-year-old) noblemen had the right to be members of the Great Council.[30] This did not, of course, resolve the notionally more tricky problem of which Ragusan families were actually 'noble'. But custom had probably already satisfactorily established that, for it is notable how little – now or later – is to be heard of disputed claims to nobility. Certain demeaning activities were also regarded as incompatible with 'living nobly'. Thus in the Small Council on 12 May 1332 it was decreed that:

> No member of the Great Council or anyone whose father or grandfather was of the Great Council may butcher animals, or stand at the bench where meat is sold to receive money for it, from now till the end of July next, under pain of a fine of 10 *hyperperi* for each infraction.

More importantly, on the same day another decision was made by the Small Council:

> Four men must be chosen to write down and put in writing [*sic*] all those who at present are members of the Great Council, *and others who seem to them to be worthy of the Great Council* [emphasis added], and to collect money from those who today were not in the Small Council.[31]

The wording seems to admit the possibility of a future revision of the assessment of those who were noble. But the actual effect was to establish once and for all the membership of Dubrovnik's patriciate. There was a very practical reason for doing so at this juncture, because the Ragusan government was preparing to parcel out the Pelješac peninsula for colonisation, with the lion's share going to the nobility. Only later would the final measures be taken to establish the patriciate as an almost entirely closed caste, by banning entry by marriage. However, these early developments meant that by the time the last Venetian count hurriedly packed his bags, the Ragusan state was already equipped with a well-defined ruling elite.[32]

The Constitution and Offices of the Republic

It was only, though, with the ending of Venetian rule and the inauguration of *de facto* independence under the kings of Hungary-Croatia that the full expression of Dubrovnik's aristocratic republicanism was possible.[33] There was no doubt in the minds of the governing patriciate that a new order had been established. Significantly, one of the early decisions of the Geat Council (26 October 1358) was to call in all copies of the Statute Books of Dubrovnik, which were to be presented within five days so that they could be revised to replace mention of the Venetian Doge and count by that of the count of Ragusa.[34]

Initially, it was decided to choose three 'Rectors' (as the Ragusan counts began to be called), who were to serve for two months and exercise the powers of the old Venetian count, ruling through the Small Council. But their authority was circumscribed by two new provisions: first, if just one judge or councillor were absent from the Small Council nothing could be decided without reference to the Great Council; and second, it henceforth fell to the Great Council, not to the Rectors and Small Council, to appoint Ragusan ambassadors. (In fact this last, along with many other powers relating to the conduct of foreign policy, increasingly gravitated to the Senate). The Rectors were to serve in succession week by week in the Rector's Palace. At the end of 1358 the procedure was somewhat simplified, so that each of the Rectors now served for one month. A little later still, the system of regularly electing a different Rector to serve each month was preferred.[35] All these arrangements had one overriding purpose – the limitation and dispersal of executive power, so that real authority remained with the patriciate as a whole. In the preferred Ragusan scheme of things the Rector was to be a revered but entirely ceremonial figurehead. Paradoxically, this was an extreme manifestation of the characteristically Venetian impulse, which the Ragusans had inherited, of guarding at all costs against personal domination.

Prompted by the same concern for its corporate liberties, Dubrovnik was deeply suspicious of even its most effective and patriotic citizens, if their loyalties risked being diverted to a focal point outside the Ragusan state. Thus Marin Gučetić, who in 1358 used his best efforts to influence Louis of Hungary in Dubrovnik's favour, had to bear a stream of complaints from his compatriots who clearly thought that he was getting above himself. Dubrovnik's formal prohibition of any of its citizens receiving honours and lands from foreign rulers was aimed in the first instance at Gučetić.[36] But it reflected a wider anxiety, and one which sharpened when the Republic found itself perilously perched on the border between Christendom and Islam. Thus the government solemnly decreed that anyone accepting privileges from the Turks would be executed as a traitor.[37]

In the course of the late middle ages the Ragusan Republic became ever more conscious of its dignity. This was shown, for example, by the history of its seal. Dubrovnik had had its own great seal to lend solemn authority to public and international agreements from at least 1235: the first reasonably well-preserved example is to be found on an agreement with Kotor of 1279. The seal bore the inscription '*SIGILLUM COMUNIS RAGUSII*' and portrayed St Blaise in front of the city gates; above each of two towers on either side of the saint are the letters 'S' and 'B' (*Sanctus Blasius*). Dubrovnik also had from at least the late fourteenth century a small seal, applied to administrative documents like summonses to court, as well as seals used by important officials like the counts and captains of its territories. But now, perhaps in response to the quasi-regal pretensions of Herceg Stjepan, Dubrovnik sought and obtained from the king of Hungary the right to use red wax for its great seal as a symbol of sovereignty, and a new seal matrix was made.[38]

The less powerful Dubrovnik's suzerain was, the greater the readiness of the Ragusan patriciate to seek from him ceremonial emhancements of the status of the Republic. So apart from the use of red wax, Dubrovnik obtained other privileges from the weak king Ladislas V 'Posthumous' (1444–1457) and his conveniently distant successor Matthias Corvinus. Dubrovnik's Rectors were thus allowed to call themselves 'arch-Rectors' of the Empire.[39] Dubrovnik was also permitted to incorporate in its crest the Hungarian royal coat of arms, under a phoenix wearing a gold crown, alongside the image of its traditional protector, St Blaise.[40] In time, the Dubrovnik coat of arms developed into a shield surmounted by a gold crown, resting upon a crossed sword and sceptre. Within the shield was depicted a green field traversed by four rivers of silver. In later years, after the collapse of Hungary, when the Ragusans ceased to raise the Hungarian standard on their walls, the field became red and the rivers azure, and these colours – red and azure – became established as those of the Ragusan Republic. The white banner portraying St Blaise – sometimes with 'S.B.' and sometimes the word '*LIBERTAS*' – remained the Ragusan maritime commercial flag.[41] The war flag, also borne aloft at the time of the celebrations on St Blaise's Feast Day, was red with an imprint of the Saint. And '*Viva San Biagio*!' ('Long Live St Blaise!') remained the battle-cry of the soldiers of the Republic.[42] As further symbols of sovereignty, Dubrovnik was also permitted to mint gold coins or silver florins bearing the arms of the Republic, and the Rector could have a drawn sword – signifying the power to do justice – carried before him in procession.[43]

Dubrovnik was proud of its aristocratic republican constitution. Foreigners admired it too, and no one more than Philip de Diversis, who dedicated the third section of his treatise to the subject. Diversis had no hesitation in calling Dubrovnik a 'republic', and as a Tuscan humanist who spent most of his life in Venice he presumably knew precisely what he meant. According to Diversis, although Dubrovnik paid tribute (in his day) to the king of Hungary, it was not a monarchy but rather a republic – that is, 'the rule of free and equal men who alternate in power so that they are at one time in charge, and at another subjects.'[44]

This republican system, together with Dubrovnik's effective independence (whatever its status in Hungarian or, later, Ottoman eyes), was what lay behind the great baroque Ragusan poet Ivan (Djivo) Gundulić's conviction that Dubrovnik, unlike the rest of Dalmatia, was 'free'. In Gundulić's pastoral play, *Dubravka*, life in the charmed grove (Dubrovnik) is praised by its inhabitants in these terms:

> Oh beautiful, dear, sweet Freedom,
> The gift in which the god above hath given us all blessings,
> Oh true cause of all our glory,
> Only adornment of this Grove...

And though (as the moral of the play emphasises) greed for material riches can jeopardise freedom, the latter also brings with it harmonious prosperity:

> United people, peaceful villages,
> Full fields, fruitful trees,
> Swarming bees, unharried flocks.[45]

Within this system, as Diversis stressed, and as Ivan Gundulić would enthusuastically accept, political authority was vested in the patriciate, so that 'those merchants who bear the title of nobles exercise all power in the city'. They did this through the Great Council, which, to continue quoting Diversis:

> ... represents, if one can speak metaphorically, the source from which proceed large and small streams, or the tree on which are to be found thick and thin branches, because from that Council proceed all the other main city administrative institutions – they flow from it and depend on it.[46]

More than a century and a half later, Jakov Lukarević came to a similar conclusion in the course of his own very full description of the 'Form of the Aristocratic Government of the Republic of Ragusa', in which he asserts that it is 'upon this base [the Great Council] [that]... the Republic is founded.'[47]

That said, as Lukarević goes on to emphasise, the Rector was still the 'head of our government'. He held the keys of the city gates and of its fortifications, kept the password required to enter them, and had charge of the Republic's seals. He alone had the authority to summon the Senate and the Great Council, and proposed their order of business. He wore a special red toga and wig, a style based on the Venetian model. He had his own apartment in the Rector's Palace and only left it on certain prescribed occasions during his month in office. Then he would be accompanied in solemn procession, preceded by twenty-four heralds (called *zduri)* who were dressed in red, and accompanied by his secretaries and other officials. If he were ill or (as Ragusan convention insisted) had to exclude himself because his own or his family's personal affairs gave him a private interest in some public decision, the oldest member of the Small Council would take his place.

Even the procedure to be followed in the case of his death was carefully laid down. The late Rector's mortal remains were to be interred with considerable ceremony. The body was clad in black, wearing the ring of office, gold chain, gold spurs and ceremonial dagger that were kept in the Cathedral treasury. It was borne on the shoulders of ten appointed nobles to the Cathedral for a solemn funeral mass, where the ring of office was given to the new acting Rector. The shops were closed and the city gates kept shut. From midnight before the burial, the bell of the Great Council tolled continuously till the body was finally laid in its grave.[48]

The Ragusan Rector had already to be a Senator. Having served his month of office, he could not be re-elected for two years. Though his power, outside the Small Council at any rate, was negligible, he had moral influence and the Rectorship was highly valued as the supreme mark of honour in the Republic. The most distinguished Ragusan nobles who enjoyed sufficient longevity might hope to be Rector on a number of occasions.[49]

In due course, the Rector and his Small Council lost various functions. In 1448 a Civil Court and in 1459 a Criminal Court were established to take on most of their judicial responsibilities. A Ragusan noble acted as vicar to the Rector. He carried out the Rector's (now minor) judicial functions and was responsible for conserving the collection of Slavic documents in the archives, kept in the Cathedral treasury. The members of the Small Council had long been drawn as a mark of honour from the oldest patrician families. This

Council received ambassadors and other distinguished visitors, read despatches from Ragusans abroad, gave leave for appeals in civil matters, issued safe-conducts to debtors, and appointed trustees and guardians for widows and orphans. It also discussed other matters of public interest, though only in a preliminary fashion before reporting to the Senate. The youngest member of the Small Council acted as a kind of Foreign Minister, though again the Senate was ultimately responsible for the Republic's foreign policy.[50]

By the fifteenth century, the Senate – also known as the 'Fathers' (*Senato de' Padri*) or the 'Council of those Asked' [i.e. by the Rector to attend] (*Consiglio di Pregati*) – had become the most powerful institution of the Republic. It had been enlarged over the years, partly because in the fifteenth century there was a substantial increase in the total number of Ragusan patricians.[51] By Lukarević's time it had grown again, and now (at the start of the seventeenth century) included the Rector, the eleven members of the Small Council, the five *provveditori* (see below), the twelve judges of the Criminal and Civil courts, the three supervisors of the Wool Guild and the members of the College of Twenty-Nine (also see below). The Senate was, in theory, elected annually by the Great Council. But the most senior and experienced Senators were often re-elected, so its membership was more stable than theory suggests. Consequently, it acquired great prestige and authority. The Senate conducted more and more of the important business of the Republic, and had to meet four times a week in order to do so. It was a court and heard civil cases involving 150 ducats and more. No appeal was possible from its decisions. It could review capital sentences and grant pardons. It also nominated to the bishoprics of Trebinje and Ston. But it was its wider – indeed almost all-encompassing – political functions which placed it squarely at the centre of government. It imposed taxes and dues, audited accounts, regulated trade, supervised security and acted against those who threatened order. It had by the sixteenth century taken to itself all the main foreign policy functions, appointing and instructing ambassadors and judging their conduct.[52]

The Senate's decisions on the most sensitive matters were recorded separately in the series known as *Secreta Rogatorum* and often destroyed, and so its secret motives are often obscure. Indeed, a culture of secrecy was regarded as essential to effective government. Thus the government forbade ordinary citizens' gathering to discuss senitive political matters, particularly anything regarding relations with the Turks. This applied still more strictly to noble councillors, who were instructed not to reveal who had said what, or how people had voted, in the course of council business.[53]

The abiding intention of the authorities was to give the impression, for the benefit of both foreigners and the lower orders, that the government was united and monolithic. But this was, naturally, not always the case. Consequently, strict measures were taken to prevent caballing. In 1394 a law was passed against plotting to secure the election of particular candidates for office. The enormous sum of 1,000 *hyperperi* was to be levied on the ringleaders. In 1470 oversight of the voting procedures in the Councils was entrusted to the officers known as *proveveditori*. If the latter discovered instances of the 'abominable crime' (*abominabile delictum*) of electoral malpractice, the miscreants would be imprisoned and lose their offices and privileges for five years or – in the worst cases – for life. Precisely how effective these prohibitions were it is hard to know. It is clear that at times the Senate was a focus for serious struggles in which personalities, foreign influences and religious sympathies all played a part. On the other hand, it does also seem that patrician politics in Dubrovnik was good deal less affected by factionalism than in Venice.[54]

For all the Senate's practical political dominance, it was, though, as Lukarević observed, within the Great Council that sovereignty (to the extent that the term is appropriate) resided. In Diversis's time the minimum age for entry of young male patricians to the Council was eighteen. Later, however, with the growth in patrician numbers, it was possible to return to the old system of admission at the age of twenty. It was also now specified that no patrician councillor should hold office unless he could read or write.[55]

From 1440 the names of those admitted to the Great Council were written every year into the book called the *Specchio* ('Mirror'). The motives of the Ragusan Chancellor of the day in beginning the practice were severely utilitarian – to 'avoid disputes and uncertainty over offices'.[56] Accordingly, the offices of the Republic were listed in alphabetical order and before each were written down the rules applying to its selection and conduct. But the most practically important – and the most historically valuable – information consists of the lists of all the members of the Great Council till the end of the century.[57]

By Lukarević's day there were some 250 of these Councillors, of whom between 100 and 200 generally turned up to meetings. But at the Council's solemn session on 1 December all had to attend, and their names were read out to ensure that they did so: they were fined if found to be absent.[58] In fact, though, it is remarkable how little absenteeism there was. Only rarely could nothing be decided because the prescribed quorum was lacking. One can only conclude that the great majority of Ragusan patricians, at least for most of the life of the Republic, took their responsibilities extremely seriously. Nor, indeed, is this surprising, because in Dubrovnik political institutions served a real purpose whereas in the Venetian-controlled Dalmatian cities, where absenteeism was a problem, those institutions had been largely drained of significance.[59]

The Ragusan patriciate applied different methods of election for different offices.[60] Until the mid-eighteenth century the most important offices of the Ragusan state were chosen by the (somewhat misleadingly titled) process called *electio*.[61] This involved not direct election but rather selection through voting by 'chambers' (*camare*). In early times, those who were to make the nominations actually withdrew to separate rooms, whereas later they just sat apart on different benches – hence the name. The process was complicated and it could be lengthy: in July 1478, for example, there had to be twelve attempts before a Rector was chosen, and in October 1553 eleven attempts.

Initially modelled on Venetian practice, the procedure's theoretical basis was that office should follow the man, not the other way round. But of course the Ragusans, like the Venetians, were also sufficiently practical to realise that those with responsibility for their Republic's well-being had to command the support of a sufficient proportion of the ruling class. The problem of reconciling elevated theory with low politics was resolved by dividing the process of election into two distinct parts, nomination and approval, and by combining choice by lot with choice by votes.[62]

On the eve of the elections, the Small Council examined the list of Great Council members, the *Specchio*, to decide who should be summoned. Then on the day itself the bell of the Council was rung three times, half an hour before the time for assembly, in order to summon the Councillors. Once the Ragusan Great Council members had taken their places along eight benches in the Chamber in order of age the Rector, surrounded by members of the Small Council and facing the five *provveditori*, stood up and announced the offices to which election was due.[63] On the most solemn occasion, the meeting in December, the Rector also began by urging the Councillors (according to an established formula) to perform their duties honourably. Then each of the Councillors took the prescribed oath, one by one laying his hand upon the relevant page of the Dubrovnik Statute. (In the eighteenth century this procedure was also adopted in the Council meetings of March and November.)

The Republic's Chancellors then went down each side of the hall and gave to each Councillor a ball which was thrown into an urn, and the Councillor's name called out. Then balls were added for the Rector, the members of the Small Council, the state advocates and the Chancellors. Finally, all the balls were taken out of the urn and counted. This was to prove how many people were present. No one could subsequently enter or leave the hall without the approval of the Rector and the Small Council.

The actual business of election (by *electio* in 'chambers') now began. One of the Chancellors brought a leather bag full of silver cards marked with Roman numerals, each card representing a particular place in the Council hall. The cards were then drawn. Those Councillors found to be sitting in the designated places went and sat on two benches apart. These Councillors then came forward, one by one, and each placed his hand into an urn containing six gold balls mixed up with a number of black (or silver) balls. Only those who drew out a gold ball had the right to nominate for an office. They formed the first nominating chamber. The procedure was undertaken a second time to create a second nominating chamber. (The members of the Small Council constituted a third chamber). Then within each chamber the name of one Councillor was drawn by lot: he it was who actually made the nomination of a particular candidate to the office in question.[64] The full Council would then vote on the three nominated candidates.

As soon as a Councillor heard his name called, he and all his close relatives left the hall to wait outside. Each Councillor remaining in the hall was now given a little ball made of linen, specially designed to be inaudible when it fell. He then approached an urn which bore the arms of Dubrovnik, and which was divided into two parts. He dropped his linen ballot into the first (red) section if he approved a candidate and into the second (green) section if he rejected him. After the voting, the ballots were poured out and counted and if none of the candidates was found to have obtained more than half the votes of the whole Great Council the process began anew.

The other means of election – *scrutinium*, direct election by the Council – applied principally to offices outside the city. The logic of this seems to have been that offices in the central government of the Republic were more politically contentious and so the premium was on ensuring the minimum of intrigue; but those further afield were less desirable and so the priority was to have competent people fill them. As with election through chambers, complex and ingenious measures were undertaken to minimise dissension. Under this system each Councillor had the right to nominate a candidate, but in conditions of (relative) secrecy. The Chancellor would approach each Council member, starting at a different place in the hall for different offices. He had with him a tape, joined at the ends and wound round a baton. He wrote on to the tape the name each Councillor whispered to him. This procedure ensured that no one knew who had nominated whom. It also meant that no nominating

Councillor knew for sure whether his candidate had any other support. When all had made their choice, the Chancellor read out the names of those candidates who had received more than five nominations and the Council cast its votes.[65]

Care was taken to minimise family influence both in election for office and in its conduct. For example, if it turned out that two members of the same family had been chosen to sit on a particular committee of officers, unless it was the Senate or the College of Twenty-Nine, the decision was declared invalid. All such provisions were designed to guard against private interests being placed above the public – that ethos of Ragusan politics which was summed up in the words inscribed over the entrance to the hall of the Great Council, *Obliti privatorum, publica curate* ('Forget private matters, look after public ones'). At the same time, as Lukarević notes at the end of his description of the procedure, 'with such an arrangement for sharing out honours, there is to be found hardly any illustrious noble citizen who can complain that he is not properly esteemed'.[66]

The actual importance of offices varied over time. In fact, the emergence of new offices and the semi-redundancy of others was proof of the practical as well as honorific purpose of the system and thus of the Republic's political vitality. Two of the bodies whose members also had the distinction of sitting as members of the Senate provide instructive examples. The five *provveditori* had developed from the earlier institution of the two 'advocates fiscal' (*avvocati fiscali*), whose function it was to introduce criminal and civil cases before the Senate. But in 1473, as Lukarević notes disapprovingly, two unsatisfactory young men were chosen who conducted affairs so badly that the institution was abolished and the *provveditori* created instead. The latters' responsibilities were extremely broad, since they supervised the actions of all officers and public institutions so as to ensure that they were not 'against reason': only the decisions of the Senate and the Great Council could not be appealed to them. The *provveditori* held office for a year and could succeed immediately to the Rectorate, whereas other officers had to wait two years before they were eligible for that post.[67]

The second such instance is that which led to the creation of the College of Twenty-Nine. As already observed, the Senate emerged in the fifteenth century as the most powerful organ of government, and as part of this process of accumulating power it had in 1440 acquired the role of supreme court of appeal in civil matters. But the amount of business this involved soon proved excessive and so a new body – of first twenty and later twenty-nine nobles – was set up, which heard appeals in matters of 150 ducats or less.[68]

The tendency for new magistracies to evolve in order to take on and then develop the functions of old ones was no less evident in other quarters. Thus the three officers responsible for supervising corn supplies (*massari*) were downgraded in favour of the staff of the optimistically entitled 'Office of Abundance' (*l'uffizio dell' abbondanza*) instituted by the Senate. The officers supervising the sale of salt (*salinari*) were in due course placed under the control of others (*soprasalinari*), also appointed by the Senate. The four 'chamberlains' (*camarlenghi*) over the years ceded most of their financial responsibilities to the five 'Treasurers of St Mary' (*tesorieri di Santa Maria*), whose task it was both to safeguard the Republic's cash and title deeds in the Cathedral Treasury and to invest inheritances left to the state at interest in Italian banks for the benefit of the town hospices and those in need.[69]

Some of these Ragusan magistracies were directly based on Venetian equivalents. So the three Proctors of St Mary (*procuratori di Santa Maria*), who were appointed for life to supervise the income and expenditure and provide for the needs of the Cathedral and of the poor, seem to be based on the model of the Venetian Proctors of St Mark. The six Ragusan nobles called 'Lords of the Night' (*signori della notte*), designated by the Great Council to keep the town orderly and secure after dark, had counterparts of the same name in Venice. Dubrovnik's three state advocates also probably derived from a Venetian model. So almost certainly did the five Ragusan *giustizieri*, who oversaw weights and measures.[70]

There was, in fact, a profusion of offices. It has been estimated that in the fifteenth century the administrative apparatus of the Republic consisted of about 160 officials. Probably the number continued to increase. There existed a traditional path from one to another, a true *cursus honorum* – which indeed the Ragusans called it, after the Roman original. But it is evidence, once more, of the practical wisdom of those responsible for operating the system that the actual official career paths of young nobles differed substantially, with some specialising in legal, some financial and some quasi-military functions.[71]

The seniority of magistracies was generally reflected in the age required of any candidate to fill them: so, for example, the Rector and the *provveditori* had to be 50, the night guards and those who guarded the fortresses between thirty and 50, and the members of the College of Twenty-Nine must be thirty years of age. Some offices were specially reserved for young nobles at the lower rungs of the ladder of promotion. In this category fell the six *lavoratori* who were responsible for the administration of public works – paving streets and squares, repairing architecture and altering the course of roads leading into the countryside. A similar duty, reserved for three young nobles, was that of supervision of the community's water: these *uffiziali all'acque* were responsible for the upkeep of the aqueduct, the removal of obstacles to the flow of water and the oversight of mills and fountains. Generally, the Ragusan Republic, while venerating the wisdom of age, avoided obsession with it. Thus in contrast to the gerontocratic tendencies of Venice, whose Doges at this time averaged 72 years of age on their election, Dubrovnik allowed its seventy-year-olds to escape fines if they failed to turn up to meetings of the Great Council.[72]

With very few exceptions, the offices of the Republic were filled by nobles. This was not only a way of giving them something useful and reasonably profitable to do. It was also an expression of the aristocratic republican concept summed up by Diversis as 'the rule of free and equal men who alternate in power'.

There were, though, also certain offices which for one reason or another were considered the preserve of non-nobles. Priests, for example, filled the posts of chancellors to the counts of Ston. Some consular posts in later years were fulfilled by commoners for want of suitable or willing patricians. Other tasks were traditionally performed by foreigners. Italians and Jews – almost never Ragusans – filled the role of the city's doctors. But the most important non-noble and indeed non-Ragusan officers were the secretaries or Chancellors of the government of the Republic. Diversis had a particular interest in their role because they, like him and the city's schoolmasters, were generally Italians. There were six of these secretaries. The two most senior acted as clerks to the governing councils as well as serving as notaries, drawing up wills and title deeds. Two more were clerks to the courts and prepared other public documents such as summonses. A fifth secretary was attached to the officers responsible for keeping the city accounts. A sixth, who could also on occasion be Italian but was usually a Slav, was responsible for the Slavic Chancery and drafted (not always correctly) documents in Slavonic language and Cyrillic script encapsulating Dubrovnik's agreements with its neighbours.[73]

Local Government

Those aspiring to move up in the political world were not, however, limited to the public offices functioning within the city: the *distretto*, the new territories and the islands had also to be administered. Each year (in some cases every six months) appointments were made to the countships of Ston and Pelješac, Primorje, Župa and Konavle. The islands of Lastovo, Mljet and Šipan, Lopud and Koločep (the last four sometimes separately, sometimes combined) also had counts. There were captains at Mali Ston, the fortress above Veliki Ston on mount Podvizd, sometimes Trstenica (the area around modern Orebići, in the western part of Pelješac), Cavtat and the fortress of Soko in Konavle. These officials between them had also a considerable number of assistants, many of whom might be commoners or clerics. Generally, the counts and captains furthest away from Dubrovnik had the greatest authority, so the count of Ston was probably the most powerful and the counts in Astarea most subject to central oversight.[74]

In Župa Dubrovačka in the thirteenth century, when the district was still dangerous, a count had his seat at the fortified centre of Tumba (today's Brgat Gornji). But as Dubrovnik's territory expanded and as its immediate surrounds became more peaceful and secure, the need for a separate count of Župa diminished. Indeed, from 1367 counts were not appointed at all and reliance was placed instead upon two separate *potknezs* for Župa with Šumet and for Rijeka Dubrovačka with Zaton. This system prevailed until the second half of the sixteenth century when, because of the government's concern about the level of crime in the district, a count of Župa was once again appointed.

This count had his seat initially at Mandaljena, later at Čibača Donja. Like the other regional counts, he had his own chancellor, appointed by Dubrovnik. Also like his fellow counts, he relied upon a local structure of self-government to assist him in his duties. The new count of Župa would therefore, soon after his appointment, summon a *zbor*. This was attended by representatives from each of the eight *kaznačine* – the local units for taxation and administration – of Župa.[75] For each of these units, a *kaznac* would now be appointed whose responsibility it would be to keep order in his district. Other local officials selected at the *zbor* were the overseers of weights and measures, prices and public hygiene, the count's messengers and the locally recruited guards who would assist the *barabanti* and other soldiers sent from Dubrovnik. These local guards were also to man the border and ensure that no one with an infectious disease was permitted to enter the Republic. The other major function of the *zbor* was to hear proclaimed in Croatian the legislation which was in force. The local laws were known as *kapituli* and these in Župa, as elsewhere, covered an extraordinary range of prohibited and punishable actions.[76] But relevant decrees from the central government were also proclaimed at these assemblies. *Zbor*s could be called for other pressing purposes too. They retained in Župa, as elsewhere, their vitality and importance till the end of the Republic.[77]

The workings of administration on the island of Lopud illustrate how local and central factors interplayed in an area not as remote as Ston or Lastovo but more distant from Dubrovnik than Župa Dubrovačka. Lopud was sufficiently distinctive to have its own coat of arms, a crowned serpent devouring a naked child. One legend traced this crest to the Visconti family, said to have founded a chapel on the island; the other legend referred to a miracle, by which the son of a visiting noble was saved from out of a dragon's gullet after invocation of the Blessed Virgin. The self-confidence epitomised by the coat of arms was echoed in local institutions. The principal church of the island at the cove of Šunj was also the centre of the most important of the island's four confraternities, that of Our Lady of Šunj (*Gospa od Šunja*). This confraternity was so influential – and rich, for it also owned a number of houses on the island – that it was virtually synonymous with Lopud's popular assembly and itself undertook a number of administrative and judicial functions.

The count of Lopud was chosen annually on 1 March by the government of Dubrovnik and served as the main administrator and judge of the island. Every year, before he arrived, an inventory was done of the modest contents of the count's palace, which was then signed by the incoming count. In early May he summoned a *zbor* at which he confirmed the decrees of his predecessor and announced new ones. As in Župa Dubrovačka, different local officials were now chosen to oversee weights and measures, to supervise public health and – in this case – to guard the island against pirates. In Lopud such *zbor*s were held regularly every six months, or whenever events required.

The count of Lopud was also usually count of the island of Koločep, and so was expected to visit it every ten days or so, hold a *zbor* when necessary and appoint local officials. Understandably, therefore, he needed a deputy (*potknez*). He also had a chancellor: the latter, appointed by Dubrovnik, was expected to perform not only his own administrative functions but also to spy on the count himself, telling the central government whenever he left his residence. In this way, Lopud was kept secure, its inhabitants (as far as can be judged) content, and the central government well-informed.[78]

Unlike Župa Dubrovačka or the Elaphite Islands, there was never any questioning of the need to have a full-time, resident count of Ston and Pelješac. In the early years after its acquisition, Ston's count was appointed for a six-month term. He was accompanied by four servants and three horses, the cost of which he was expected to pay out of his salary of 200 *hyperperi*. He also had a chancellor (a priest) whose salary was met by Dubrovnik. The count was expected to work particularly closely with the captain of Trstenica: once a month the two officials met to discuss security in the area.[79] In 1349 the Great Council revised the terms of the Ston count's commission. Henceforth he was to be appointed for a year and have ten servants and six horses. There was now also to be a separate captain who would preside over the stretch of the shore of Pelješac which faced the River Neretva.[80] In order to prevent corruption, the count was forbidden to receive any presents from the local inhabitants. Neither he nor his household were to conduct business there and there was a specific prohibition against his running a tavern.[81]

The count of Ston's three principal duties were to keep Ston and the Pelješac peninsula secure, to ensure the smooth working of the valuable salt pans, and to enforce Dubrovnik's laws regulating the import of wine.[82] The peninsula was extremely vulnerable to outside attack – not from across the isthmus, where the powerful defences of Ston created a solid bulwark against the hinterland, but rather from the sea.[83] The peasants of the area were expected to contribute to its defence. They were required to have their own swords and shields, and their masters were instructed to ensure that they did.[84]

The government of Dubrovnik was always quite ruthless in ensuring that order was maintained in Pelješac and miscreants there could expect the harshest treatment if they were caught.[85] Once a month, the count of Ston was expected to travel throughout Pelješac inquiring into crimes and misdeeds and administering justice. His judicial functions were carried out in conjunction with two judges, whom he was required to appoint from among the worthier inhabitants of the place. In civil matters this court was to judge 'according to their [i.e. the area's] customs' and in criminal matters according to decrees laid down by the government of Dubrovnik. The latter reserved for its own courts jurisdiction over the most heinous offences like murder, arson and treason. Below the count's court at village level there was, as elsewhere in the Republic, a system of local administration and justice – in this case one presumably inherited from the peninsula's previous Slavic rulers. The towns of Pelješac were each to elect one of their inhabitants as *gestaldus*, with responsibility for executing the count's orders and for judging minor civil cases.[86]

After Dubrovnik's acquisition of Konavle between 1419 and 1427, that region took over from Ston and Pelješac as the Republic's most exposed territory. Its government was therefore a risky and perilous responsibility. The count of Konavle had his modest *dvor*, first at Ljuta, then at nearby Sveti Martin (now Pridvorje), where a more substantial building was erected for him. In the course of the seventeenth century it was expanded and fortified.[87] Pridvorje was a distant and lonely posting, so the counts of Konavle preferred to spend their days in Cavtat – for which they could be fined if caught. The count was chosen by the Ragusan Great Council, and usually served a six-month term for which he was paid 500, though later only 300, *hyperperi.* (From 1636 the counts of Konavle were, however, appointed for a year.) Like the count of Ston, the Konavle count had a chancellor. The count was similarly expected to pay out of his salary the wages and expenses of his household. Its members were chosen by him in the first instance but had to be confirmed by the government. If possible, these *familiares* were to come from Dubrovnik or its immediate surrounds and they could not remain in the service of successive counts: this was presumably to prevent their becoming too involved in the region and so correspondingly detached from the central government in Dubrovnik. In Konavle the count's deputies – *potknezs* or *vojvodas* – had a particularly important role. They were appointed to serve for a year, but could be confirmed for a further year by the Great Council. Initially, like the *familiares,* they were to come from Dubrovnik or its *distretto*, and under no circumstances from Konavle, though this provision was relaxed in time. These *potknezs* were mainly responsible for the suppression of crime and disorder. From 1435 each had his official house and prescribed territory, so that they began to function a little like local counts in their own right. At the main stronghold in the territory, the fortress of Soko, a Ragusan noble served as captain along with eight soldiers recuited from Dubrovnik or from the islands. Soko was a still more dismal posting than Pridvorje. For reasons of security its garrison was effectively sealed off from the outside world. The humanist writer Ilija Crijević was severely punished when captain of Soko for bringing a woman into the fortress. In his unfinished poem, *De Epidauro*, he described the bleak view from his eyrie over the forbidding surrounding landscape.[88]

Geographical, social and legal circumstances made governing the island of Mljet a distinctive challenge for Dubrovnik. By far the most important landlord was the abbey, so the Ragusan government was particularly keen to ensure that the abbot was a sympathetic and reliable figure.[89] Moreover, Mljet was not only quite distant – some forty kilometres – it also had its own statute, entrenched customs and administrative traditions. Initially, Mljet was ruled directly from Dubrovnik, but in 1410 it was placed under the authority of the count of the (Elaphite) Islands, whose seat was Šipan. Within two months of his appointment, the count was to travel to Mljet and choose two judges from among the local worthies, then with them he was to name the other local officials in accordance with the local customs. This process was doubtless accelerated once Mlet gained its own count in 1493. From 1500 a count was constantly resident on the island and in 1554 a *dvor* was built for him at Babino Polje.

As elsewhere within the Republic, the local *zbor* on Mljet played an important role. Judges and other local officials were selected at it. Here the *kapituli* were solemnly read out each year to the community – proscribing mannual work on Holy Days, regulating where livestock could be pastured and how wine must be measured, and enjoining children to show respect to their parents or face punishment by the count. Special attention was to be paid in this exposed island to the movements of ships, both foreign and Ragusan, and the *kapituli* threatened any guards who were not at their posts by sunset with twenty-five strokes of the lash.[90]

The count of Lastovo, like the count of Mljet, had a crucial role in keeping his (still more distant) island secure for the Republic. Similarly, like the count of Mljet, he was appointed by the Dubrovnik government but ruled in co-operation with the community of Lastovo – and specifically with two judges drawn from its number – according to the laws, customs and privileges contained in the island's Statute. Again like his counterpart in Mljet, he was quite cut off from his peers, since Ragusan patricians (like all outsiders) were unable to own land on either island.[91]

Despite, or perhaps because of, these limitations, the Ragusan rulers of Lastovo were clearly determined to replicate as far as possible, though necessarily in miniature, the Dubrovnik system of government. So Lastovo had its own fourteenth century *knežev dvor* (pulled down in the nineteenth century), with a surrounding wall and garden and a pergola which the local population had to cover with twigs to keep out the sun from those who strolled beneath it. The Lastovo count used a silver signet ring bearing the seal of St Blaise to authorise public documents. There was a clerk in the Lastovo chancery who kept the archives and confirmed wills and other deeds. Lastovo had (like Dubrovnik) its own *fondik* (grain warehouse) and (also like Dubrovnik) its own pillar of shame (*berlina*), at which offenders were bound as punishment for a variety of offences. From 1659 Lastovo even had its own school and schoolteacher. The Lastovo revolts in the early seventeenth century betokened both the islanders' sensitivity if they considered their rights infringed and their ability to cause trouble when Venice was seeking to maximise its control in the Adriatic. But the Dubrovnik government seems generally to have governed these touchy people warily and reasonably well.[92]

Order and Disorder

Although Ragusan writers might extoll the 'liberty' of Dubrovnik, it was order that alone allowed 'free', that is, aristocratic republican, institutions to flourish. Indeed, Ivan Gundulić implicitly recognised the point when he had one of his characters contrast the charmed Ragusan 'grove' with Venetian Dalmatia, where:

> … the home is not secure for the father
> To guard his daughter from the evil force of the hell-bent lecher.[93]

The Dubrovnik Statute, its successor volumes and the governing councils' decisions all repeatedly concentrated on the need to punish and deter crime, particularly those offences which threatened social order and public security. Punishments were carefully graduated: people committing homicide (unless in self-defence) were banished and their goods confiscated; those found guilty of wounding were fined, or lost a limb if they could not pay; those who stole were fined according to the value of what was stolen and the number of times they had previously offended – with whipping, branding, and loss of limbs and eyes decreed if they were unable to pay. People who committed robberies in the street were still more harshly punished: anyone committing a street robbery of goods worth more than 10 *hyperperi,* and who was unable to pay his fine, was hanged. Rapists were fined 50 *hyperperi*; if they could not pay, they lost both eyes – though the Statute added the cynical proviso that if the woman raped decided to marry the rapist, the punishment was remitted. Forging documents was severely punished by the loss of one's right hand. Stealing grapes from vineyards could involve a fine or, if it was not paid, a whipping. Blasphemers might be punished by public humiliation.[94]

Respect for the officers of the state who came to execute its warrants and instructions was instilled by doubling the fine levied in the case of striking any other citizen.[95] This was not, though, necessarily effective. In 1345, for example, the herald Marko was sent by the count to summon a certain Djono Dersić to appear before the committal court. When Marko and an assistant arrived at Dersić's house they found him having lunch with his son who, however, denied that his father was present at all, tore up the count's letter of summons and drove off the officers, brandishing his sword.[96]

Not surprisingly, in such circumstances the government tried to keep control over the carrying of swords and other weapons. It was one of the responsibilities of the night guard to enforce the rule that no one could carry weapons in the city; only the guards themselves and the Rector's household were exempted from this provision. These guards patrolled the streets with their assistants and were expected to suppress any disorder. They could enter the homes of malefactors to arrest them, and if they happened to kill a fugitive in the course of their duties they would not be punished. No one, citizen or foreigner, was to go about at night after the 'third bell' had sounded without a bright lantern.[97]

The streets of Dubrovnik even in the daytime could be rumbustious. No less an admirer of almost all things Ragusan than Philip de Diversis complained that the people of Dubrovnik were very ill-mannered and constantly bumped into one in the street, so that Ragusan ladies would prudently send a servant to walk ahead of them.[98]

By night Dubrovnik was still more prone to crime. It was a time when daring thefts could occur. In August 1441 a wealthy Ragusan dyer returned home to find that during his overnight absence from the city money, gold rings, silver chains and – most suspiciously – some letters of credit had been stolen from his strongbox.[99] The following month another Ragusan had his house burgled while he slept. His strongbox was carried off and with it valuable silver plate, rings, armour and clothing.[100] When dusk fell acts of violence were also more easily concealed. In September 1537 a woman made a complaint against a certain 'Jerko X' (his surname unknown) who one evening broke in and badly beat her old, blind husband before dragging her into the street by her hair; three witnesses backed up her story.[101] It was certainly imprudent of another Ragusan earlier that same year to go out searching after midnight for a missing servant girl. He asked information from a woman he met in the dark, winding, vaulted streets of Pustijerna, and quickly found himself set upon by a group of assailants.[102]

Among the main perpetrators of violence were young nobles, the victims anyone who got in their way. Serafino Razzi disapprovingly relates how gangs of young nobles would attack non-nobles in public places where the latter feared to respond in kind; the commoners would then have their revenge on their noble tormentors later out of sight.[103]

But probably still more frequent were quarrels between nobles that stemmed from patrician pride. Such a case occurred in February 1538, at the time of Dubrovnik's evening *passeggiata*. Nikola Buća encountered Bernardo Bunić and looked at him (in Nikola's words) 'politely, as one gentleman looks at another'. But Bernardo said: 'Why are you looking at me?' Nikola replied, 'I am looking at you because I have eyes to look at other people on equal terms.' Upon which Bernardo hit him and was preparing to hit him again when Nikola fled. Nikola Buća then lodged a complaint against his attacker's 'audacity and insolence', summoning members of the Gradić and Crijević families as witnesses.[104]

Frequently, young bucks falling afoul of the law in their early years went on to lead respectable lives thereafter. Such misbehaviour was indeed something of a convention among the patrician families, and the government did not generally punish it too harshly. On the other hand, sometimes the crimes these young nobles committed were so serious that the path back to respectability became blocked, and this might even lead to seditious conspiracy. The cases of two Ragusan poets provide convenient examples of each of these two outcomes.

Savko Bobaljević, a member of a distinguished patrician family, grew up with a strong sense of family honour. So when the sixteen-year-old Savko learned that another noble, Paladin Djono Crijević, had publicly insulted his father and pulled his beard, he attacked his father's assailant with his sword and cut off his nose. Savko was thrown into the Dubrovnik jail, while both families received strict instructions not to proceed with the feud. But they seem to have taken little notice. Eventually, his father paid an 800-ducat fine and Savko left Dubrovnik. After three years of exile he returned home in 1550 and was quickly in prison for a further offence. In 1552 he was involved in a dagger fight with another noble. In 1554 he was part of a brawl over a prostitute. Six months later, he engaged in a quarrel with one of the chancellors of Dubrovnik, Lorenzo Gigante, and was sentenced to a term of imprisonment in one of the damp subterranean jails on the eastern side of the Rector's Palace. But he broke out and fled to Italy, where he spent his time writing poetry and in other activities which resulted in his catching the syphilis that finally killed him. Needing money, he returned to the Republic and took up a series of offices at Ston. There he led a quiet life writing, going for walks, saying his prayers, playing cards and occasionally visiting Dubrovnik where he was a leading member of a literary academy meeting in the Sponza Palace. He died in 1585, and his friends wrote verses lamenting his passing.[105]

The life of a second poet, Stijepo Đurđević, illustrates a different scenario – one in which disorder led in a kind of continuum to treason. Stijepo, like Savko, was of ancient patrician stock and, similarly, was a riotous and violent youth. At carnival time in 1596, Stijepo Đurđević and a companion broke into an artisan's house by night and attacked the owner. Two years later Stijepo attacked a gardener in the middle of Placa. One summer evening in 1600, having taken umbrage at being mistaken for someone else by a group of shopkeepers, he attacked them with his sword. In 1601 a deaf tailor was his victim. Eventually he killed someone, though leniency born of patrician solidarity and a convenient lack of evidence allowed him to escape punishment. In 1610, however, Stijepo became involved in a conspiracy in which his equally unruly brother was one of the main participants and which, however frivolously the Đurđević brothers regarded it, was linked to the wider struggle between Counter-Reformation Europe and the Ottoman Empire.[106]

Plots and Plotters

As has been observed, Dubrovnik's geographical, religious and political circumstances made it during the sixteenth and seventeenth centuries a focus for spies and military adventurers. But the Ragusan government had acquired experience in dealing with conspirators much earlier. A plot to overthrow the state in 1400 is described in detail by the early chroniclers. Collective memories were still sufficiently sensitive for Serafino Razzi, writing in the late sixteenth century, discreetly to omit the names of those involved because two were members of the still extant and highly respected Zamanja family.[107] It seems that a small but powerful group of nobles and their followers, the latter drawn from among the lower orders of Dubrovnik and from the Vlachs, had plotted with shadowy Bosnian lords (probably including the Bosnian king Ostoja, with whom Dubrovnik was at loggerheads) to seize the city, using the fact that plague had emptied the place and disrupted its policing. Their motive was described (in the heavily biased sources) as the traditional one of seeking a tyranny, while their co-plotters from outside the city simply aimed at its despoliation. Certainly, there is no evidence of a discernible political programme.

Nor, clearly, was the plot particularly well organised: it was discovered by the hero of the hour, Nikola Marinov Gučetić, who rose from his sickbed to alert the government to what was planned. In spite of the city authorities' interception of a letter from other plotters in Bosnia, the details remained murky. But the noble ringleaders were rounded up and executed, and their bodies put on display around Orlando's Column before being buried in bricked-over graves in Dubrovnik's Franciscan church. Large numbers of their humbler followers – Vlachs, farmers and butchers – were also executed. The conspiracy was unearthed on the Feast of the Forty Martyrs (9 March). Accordingly, the government declared it an annual day of civic rejoicing, marked by a solemn procession led by the Rector, Senators and clergy.[108]

A second plot, which like that of 1400 was particularly heinous because it involved the proposal to bring foreigners into the Republic, was discovered in June 1525. A merchant living in Ston had apparently plotted with certain Slavic Hercegovinians to hand over Ston to the Turkish *sandžak-beg*. In the light of later attempts by the Christian powers to seize the place, the Ottoman objective was perhaps simply to take pre-emptive action to prevent its falling into the hands of their enemies. Or the conspiracy may have been a freelance initiative by the neighbouring Turkish governor and various troublemakers. The captain of Trstenica learned of what was planned and the Dubrovnik government sent an armed ship to arrest the merchant and take him back for interrogation, where he died under torture. The plan was thus foiled.[109]

The attempt by the Bučinčić brothers to involve Ferdinand of Habsburg in a plot to seize Ston in 1536, already discussed, opened up a new era. From now on the principal threat to Dubrovnik's security came from one or other of the Christian powers; and from the mid-sixteenth century the wider Counter-Reformation religious and political programme also sharpened Ragusan internal factional tension.

Such was the background to the misdeeds of Marin Andrijev Bobaljević. He was part of a group of Ragusan nobles opposed to another faction led by the lawyer and Counter-Reformation enthusiast, Frano Gundulić. The young Bobaljević had in 1576 been one of a band of patrician youths who murdered an elderly noble, for which they were later pardoned. In 1589 Marin returned from exile in Italy and, furious at a slur made by Gundulić on his morals, stabbed him to death in the church of the Holy Cross in Gruž. Marin prudently fled, but in 1590 he was back in Dubrovnik in the company of a gang of nobles, who intimidated his opponents until the Senate plucked up courage to send him back into exile. He then remained in Italy, befriended by the duke of Urbino, and became the patron of Mavro Orbini, author of the famous proto-Pan-Slavic work, *Il Regno degli Slavi* ('The Kingdom of the Slavs').[110] Although Marin Andrijev Bobaljević performed useful diplomatic services for Dubrovnik, his pleas to be allowed home were refused and he died in Italy.[111]

The greatest threat to Dubrovnik's security, however, was what became known as 'the Great Conspiracy' into which the previously mentioned poet and rowdy, Stijepo Đurđević, was drawn in 1610. It was a time when the Slavs of Hercegovina were hopeful of overthrowing Ottoman rule and when, in the absence of direct Habsburg leadership, the initiative fell to princelings like Charles Emmanuel I, Duke of Savoy, and then his son-in-law the duke of Mantua. The latter's agent in Dubrovnik, Imberto Saluzzo, energetically recruited a number of nobles and adventurers to the cause, but the project's main supporter was Marin Rastić, head of a powerful patrician faction. A complication was added, however, when Marin's nephews were banished from Dubrovnik and fled to join him, after having beaten to death a Ragusan commoner who had complained to the Senate of their molesting his wife. They were pardoned after a year. But the Senate's attention had been drawn all too closely to the Rastić faction's activities, and when one of Marin's letters was intercepted, he himself fled.

The plotting, though, continued, both in Dubrovnik's territories and in Mantua. The conspirators persuaded Count Maurice of Nassau, the *stadtholder* of Holland, to provide a man-of-war full of arms and ammunition destined for the Hercegovinian rebels; the force on board the ship was to seize Ston as a base for operations against the Turks. Marin Rastić's brother, the bishop of Ston, was also plausibly suspected of involvement. In the event, the presence of a Venetian fleet scared off the Dutch vessel. Meanwhile, the Ragusan government summoned the bishop of Ston to Dubrovnik to answer for his conduct, and arrested Jakov Rastić and Jakov Đurđević.

The ensuing trial dangerously split the governing patriciate. From September to early November 1611 the city was in the grip of almost continuous tumult. The accused were put to torture and dozens of witnesses examined. There were armed clashes in the streets between rival groups and on one occasion swords were even drawn in the Senate. The scandal worsened when, in February 1612, under cover of a fierce storm but probably with the connivance of the Rector, the prisoners Jakov Rastić and Jakov Đurđević escaped. A full inquiry was launched, and in April other members of the Rastić and Đurđević families were sentenced to exile for their part in the escape: among these was Stijepo Đurđević. Marin Rastić, at the head of a force of *uskok*s, attempted a further unsuccessful assault on Ston that May. By then, however, the duke of Mantua, the prime mover of the conspiracy, was dead, opinion in Dubrovnik's patriciate had shifted against the Rastić faction and the Venetians seem to have agreed to remove the Rastići and Đurđevići from nearby Korčula.

The exiled Stijepo Đurđević proceeded to Naples, where his family's money was invested. Four years later he was allowed to return to Dubrovnik. He and his brother Jakov had depleted their inheritance, so Stijepo decided to marry a rich wife. But he died some time after 1632 without an heir, his brother having predeceased him. Stijepo Đurđević's turbulent career epitomises the challenge which the governing patriciate of Ragusa faced from its own unruly members, especially when supported and manipulated by outside interests.[112]

EIGHT

Merchant Venturing: Economic Development (c. 1272–1667)

I. Overland Trade with the Balkan Interior

Early Contacts

By its policy of discriminating against Ragusan maritime trade, Dubrovnik's Venetian overlords forced it to develop its economic contacts with the Balkan hinterland. But those contacts had already long been in existence. As early as 1189 – as we have seen – *Ban* Kulin, the ruler of Bosnia, concluded a treaty with Dubrovnik which regulated the terms on which Ragusans could trade in his dominions.[1]

But Dubrovnik's first contacts with the immediate hinterland were mainly connected with agriculture, for from a very early date Ragusan farmers had been pressing outwards onto territory over which Slavic lords jealously claimed ownership. A tribute called *mogoriš* was thus paid to the Serb ruler of Hum for Ragusan cultivation of Slavic lands at Rijeka Dubrovačka, Zaton and Poljice. Another *mogoriš* was paid to the Serbs as rulers of Trebinje for Ragusan farming of Župa Dubrovačka and Šumet. These dues should probably be understood both as rent and as protection money; at any rate, in the 1330s Dubrovnik refused to pay the Hum *mogoriš* to the *ban* of Bosnia when Ragusan property was damaged by disorder on its frontiers. More significant, and apparently serving as a *quid pro quo* for the right to trade within the Serbian king's dominions, was the already mentioned *Svetodimitarski dohodak* (St Demetrius's Revenue): it was fixed at 2,000 *hyperperi*. Like the *mogoriš*, this due later passed into the hands of the kings of Bosnia and then lapsed after the Ottoman conquest of the Balkans.[2]

The Salt Trade

Territorial disputes between Dubrovnik and the rulers of the Slavic hinterland were, as has also been noted, a regular source of conflict, often provoking military clashes and interrupting trade.[3] But each side had pressing reasons for compromise. In particular, the people of the hinterland looked to Dubrovnik to provide them with salt. The only alternative supply in the interior was the salt springs of Tuzla in northern Bosnia. Otherwise, rock salt from Hungary and Wallachia competed with sea salt imported from the Black Sea, the Aegean and the Adriatic. But the Adriatic was the single most important source, and Dubrovnik tried with considerable success to exert a tight grip on it.

Dubrovnik's own salt was first produced at Gruž and Slano and on the islands of Šipan and Mljet, but from the time of its acquisition of the Pelješac peninsula the most important centre of domestic production was at Ston.[4] The rights to operate the Ston salt works were initially auctioned off to the highest bidder for a five-year period. The entrepreneurs had full charge of the plant and equipment and enjoyed the right to export the salt to wherever they wanted.[5] Later, however, the government undertook the running of the works itself. Production would continue from May to September, and the inhabitants of Pelješac and Primorje were obliged (though also paid) to provide their labour.

Dubrovnik's future role as quasi-monopolistic supplier of salt to the hinterland was originally achieved in grudging co-operation with the Serb rulers. The latter initially tried to maintain their own monopoly, but when this proved impossible they insisted on levying a due equivalent to half the profits made from sales to their subjects by Ragusan merchants. From the 1360s that arrangement too ended, but the Ragusan grip on salt sales remained.[6]

Dubrovnik's ambition to control the whole supply of the salt used in the interior prompted it, in particular, to seek dominance for its merchants in Drijeva (otherwise known, as today, as Gabela) at the mouth of the Neretva.[7] To Drijeva came salt from all over the Adriatic, and indeed beyond. But the Ragusan merchant community there, strongly supported by the Ragusan government, was generally successful in ensuring that imports and exports alike were under its management and worked to its benefit. Dubrovnik's violent action against Kotor and later against the Herceg, when the latter wished to establish Herceg-Novi as an alternative market for salt (and other goods), has already been mentioned.[8]

As in other respects, the arrival in the Balkans of Ottoman armies and officials altered the basis on which the Ragusans carried on their salt trade.

Dubrovnik could not henceforth expect to exert pressure on its rivals by bullying, only by making it worthwhile for the Turks to allow it to enjoy its quasi-monopoly. In 1482 the Turks seized Herceg-Novi and initially themselves sought to develop it as an independent emporium, as the Herceg had previously done. But, doubtless discovering that such an enterprise was beyond them, they concluded three years later an agreement which effectively handed the Herceg-Novi salt market over to Ragusan management. Only local or Ragusan salt was to be supplied there; the price was fixed by the Ottoman authorities; and the income was to be divided equally between Dubrovnik and the Turks. The same model was broadly applied to other salt markets. Of these, the most important was by far and away Drijeva, which the Turks conquered in 1493. And with its better access to the developing Bosnian interior, it quickly surpassed Herceg-Novi.

Dubrovnik managed to retain its dominance at Drijeva, though not without some Venetian competition. Drijeva in the middle ages served something of the same purpose as Narona in late Roman times, that of a bustling emporium on the geographically and economically pivotal Neretva delta. It was built round a spacious, often flooded, marketplace, with its own customs office, warehouses, shops and churches, and was home to a permanent and usually flourishing Ragusan colony. Smaller vessels unloaded their wares directly for sale in its markets, while larger ships with more important cargoes lay at anchor off the little island of Posrednica.[9] The Turkish authorities were always prepared to be extremely accommodating to Ragusan demands there. In 1559, arguing the high costs of transport, Dubrovnik obtained a revision of the arrangement for dividing the profits from salt: henceforth the split would be two-thirds/one-third in its favour. In 1574 the price was raised on condition of Dubrovnik's guaranteeing always to keep Drijeva supplied with salt. Foreigners were only permitted to sell salt there when no Ragusan salt was on hand. In later years, when the Turkish currency was devalued by inflation, Dubrovnik obtained a further rise in the salt price.[10] For all this consideration, however, the Ragusans never acquired a true monopoly in the Ottoman Balkans. Smuggling was always a problem. Moreover, in the seventeenth century Venice launched a direct attack on Dubrovnik's salt trade, insisting on its own monopoly. For its part, Dubrovnik fought back, and in 1640 obtained from the Sultan a *ferman* granting Ragusans the exclusive right to sell salt on the Neretva.[11]

Precious and other Metals

If salt was the single most important import which Dubrovnik provided for the Balkan interior in the first centuries of commercial contact, precious metals were undoubtedly the most important export. Both gold and silver had been obtained from the Balkans in Roman times. But in the thirteenth, fourteenth and early fifteenth centuries Serbian and Bosnian mines and their ore acquired an international reputation. Copper, iron, mercury, lapis lazuli and antimony were also obtained and exported. Iron ore, too, was mined and smelted for local use. But the most important minerals extracted in this period were silver and lead. Lead, which was a byproduct from Balkan argentiferous ore, was important to Dubrovnik, principally because of its use for the roofs of the city's many churches. Silver, though, was in a league of its own, because of the demand for it from all over Italy and beyond.

The number of silver mines grew steadily between the mid-thirteenth and mid-fifteenth centuries. Just two mines are known to have been operating in Serbia at the beginning of the period. There were five at the start of the fourteenth century, and seven by the start of the fifteenth. There was then a rapid growth, particularly in Bosnia, so that on the eve of the Ottoman conquest some thirty mines were active. Their importance was all the greater because of the modest total volume of silver produced in Europe, the supply of which was further restricted in the mid-fifteenth century as the Hussite wars paralysed Central European production.

The most important Balkan mine was undoubtedly that at Novo Brdo in Serbia, first noted as functioning in 1333. It was famous for its auriferous silver, *glama* or 'white silver', as it was called. It was Srebrenica, however – long disputed between Serbia and Bosnia – that produced silver of the highest quality. After these in importance came Rudnik in Serbia and then, some way behind, Fojnica and other Bosnian centres. Srebrenica also produced lead, though that from Olovo in Bosnia was preferred because it was softer and more malleable.[12] Copper was obtained in Rudnik in Serbia and from various places in Bosnia. Iron ore was obtained at Busovača in Serbia.

Crucial to the development of the mining industry was the influx of settlers – known variously as *sasi* (Saxons) or *purgari* (burghers) – from Hungary. Whether intially fleeing from the Tatars or specifically invited by the Serbian king Stefan Uroš I (1243–1276), the *sasi* are mentioned for the first time in Serbia in 1254. In spite of their influence, to which toponymical evidence bears witness, the *sasi* were probably not in fact very numerous. But they brought with them technical expertise which effectively recreated the Balkan mining industry. They had learned the value of well-placed drainage and ventilation shafts. They knew how to heat and then abruptly cool veins of ore, so that it split up into manageable blocks. They had mastered the techniques of harnessing the flow of streams and rivers in order first to crush the ore and then to smelt it in furnaces heated by water-driven bellows.

Next to that of the *sasi* the largest role in Serbian and Bosnian mining was taken by the Ragusans. The latter, however, did not (like the *sasi*) act as mining engineers, nor (like the indigenous Slavs) as ordinary miners, but rather as mine owners and investors. Traditionally, ownership of a mine was divided into 64 shares, and wealthy Ragusan merchants often purchased some or all of these. Other Ragusans also lived around the mining communities, working in other capacities such as goldsmiths, masters of mints and shopkeepers. For example, at the start of the fifteenth century, Ragusans were present in Novo Brdo both as mine owners and wholesale traders. On occasion, Ragusans even acted as counts, in charge of the security of these settlements; such, for instance, was the case of the commoner Latinica family from Dubrovnik, which provided counts for Srebrenica – where some 500 Ragusans altogether could be found.

When it first emerged from smelting, the metal was still in a very impure state: the final stages of production would take place later. Silver and lead in blocks, gold in ingots, copper in plates, would be loaded onto horses – sometimes 300 at a time – whose task it was to bring them back to Dubrovnik in caravan. These packhorses were usually driven by Vlachs known as *ponosnici*, and their valuable loads were guarded by other Vlachs armed with swords, daggers and crossbows. Runners regularly connected the Ragusans at the mining centres with Dubrovnik, passing on information and so allowing investors to follow the fortunes of their investments.

The routes which these caravans took were well established. There were two roads between the Adriatic and the mining and commercial centres of Serbia. The first was called by the Ragusans the 'Way of Bosnia' and the second the 'Way of Zeta' (or 'Zenta'). The Way of Bosnia went either from Dubrovnik or from the mouth of the Neretva; the Way of Zeta from one of the ports on the coast between Kotor and Durrës.[13]

Balkan silver was – by the standards of the day – copious. Calculations of annual production, based on patchy evidence, vary widely. But an average of twelve tons a year for the first half of the fifteenth century seems likely – bearing in mind that Novo Brdo and Srebrenica at their peak were producing, respectively, nine and five or six tons. Much of this silver was initially turned into silver currency – the *grosso* minted in very large quantities in the Serbian kingdom. Bosnia also began to issue its own coinage under King Stjepan

Kotromanić (1322–1353).[14] The rulers of Serbia and Bosnia understandably wanted first call on their own silver. Thus the Serbian Despot Stefan Lazarević tried to block the export of silver so as to direct it to his mints: this provoked a series of disputes with Dubrovnik. Similarly, the fifteenth-century kings of Bosnia insisted that the export of silver was only permissible with a royal warrant.[15] But, of course, Dubrovnik had its own requirements for silver, both for its mint and its goldsmiths.[16]

Obstructive as the rulers of Serbia and Bosnia sometimes proved, silver continued to flow into Dubrovnik and then on to the West. It was the Ottoman Empire which, as an act of policy, brought the business to an abrupt end by prohibiting silver exports altogether; there was a certain amount of smuggling, but henceforth only lead was legally exported. The Turks then delivered a second blow to the profitability of the mines by imposing an artificially low price for silver. It was these decisions rather than damage sustained in the process of conquest that led to the decline of Serbian and Bosnian mining – a decline which would become terminal from the late sixteenth century, when large quantities of bullion from the New World posed unsustainable competition to the weakened Balkan mining industry.[17]

Other Merchandise

Precious metals were only the most important of the raw materials from the Balkan interior which in the middle ages found their way to the coast. Ragusan merchants from at least the fourteenth century were also bringing back loads of skins – both hides (of cattle, buffalo, goats and sheep) to be made into leather, and pelts from wild animals that served to adorn clothes and hats. Most were despatched, in both raw and processed states, to Italy. Another bulk import from Serbia and Bosnia to Dubrovnik was beeswax. It was not only used for the candles which lit Ragusan churches, homes and workshops, but by the early fifteenth century was the basis of a flourishing export trade – again to Italy.[18]

A Balkan export to Dubrovnik which has received close attention from scholars is slaves. The trade was already flourishing by the end of the thirteenth century. The majority of slaves seem to have been Bosnians – deemed fair game because of the dark rumours of Bosnian heresy – and the most prized were women, suitable to act as domestic servants. There were also, however, Greeks, Tatars and even African slaves to be found in the city.[19] The trade was carefully regulated. All those who brought slaves to Dubrovnik had to pay a due of four *grossi* per head. Ragusan slave-traders were to declare the number of slaves they had to the Ragusan customs officers within three days of their arrival. The export of slaves from Dubrovnik was also taxed at a rate of one *hyperperus* per head.[20] Most of the exported slaves went to Italy, though others reached Marseilles and Majorca.[21]

On 27 January 1416 the government of Dubrovnik forbade slave trading on its own territory and anywhere along the coast from Budva to Split. Although the text of the decree makes clear that moral arguments were of importance in the decision, it is equally evident that what prompted the move were complaints by neighbouring Bosnian lords, angered by the selling of their subjects into slavery. The decree of 1416 did not forbid the ownership of slaves nor, indeed, commerce in them outside the proscribed geographical limits. In 1418 new prohibitions had to be issued, occasioned by the raids of Catalan and Sicilian pirates who seized people in the vicinity of Dubrovnik and took them away into servitude.

With the Ottoman conquest it was Christians, not infidels or heretics, who were most at risk of slavery, and Dubrovnik's attitude accordingly became more severe. Any Ragusan selling someone as a slave would now be imprisoned. If the slave was freed within a month, the slave-trader would merely lose both eyes; if the slave remained in servitude, the man who had sold him would be hanged. The trade by now had anyway dwindled, though the sale of Christian slaves to the Turks still occurred on occasion.[22]

The Turkish prohibition of all silver exports from the Balkans, resulting in the collapse of most of the old trading centres in Bosnia and Serbia, prompted the ever-adaptable Ragusans to become more deeply involved in other areas. Ragusan merchants concentrated their efforts on new markets like those in Sarajevo and Banja Luka. They also used the privileged position which Dubrovnik consolidated under Suleyman the Magnificent to acquire an effective monopoly in the export of hides, leather, wool and wax to Italy. Dubrovnik, too, became a very important intermediary for Italian goods supplied to the Ottoman Empire. The merchants of Ancona and Florence, as well as the Ragusans, shipped woollen cloth – English 'kerseys' and finer Italian weaves – along the caravan routes from Dubrovnik to Adrianople and Constantinople. This was supplemented by the production of Dubrovnik's own textile industry.[23]

A new challenge emerged when Sarajevo developed as a commercial centre in its own right, with its own merchant class. These Muslim merchants began, with those of Goražde and Olovo and enjoying Ottoman official protection, to compete with the merchants of Dubrovnik. So, increasingly did the Adriatic Jews, particularly after the opening of Split.[24]

Ragusan merchants then responded by shifting the focus of their business away from Bosnia to southern Serbia and Bulgaria. The volume of trade with these areas grew almost continuously from the early sixteenth to the mid-seventeenth century, when it reached its peak. It was then weakened by the general collapse in Dubrovnik after the 1667 earthquake and had effectively ended twenty years later. The trade involved the most traditional products of the Balkan interior – skins and wool – brought to Dubrovnik by caravans of packhorses. It was necessarily a high-volume because a relatively low-value business. The packhorses were heavily loaded, each carrying up to 180 kilogrammes, so sturdy beasts were much in demand. Experienced (usually Vlach) guides, known as *kiridžije,* were required to see the caravan along its often dangerous route, menaced not just by the terrain and the elements but also by *hajduk*s and other robbers. The trade itself was organised by (usually Hercegovinian) go-betweens called *kramari*. These people, working out of the towns of southern Serbia, were responsible for purchasing the merchandise and hiring the guides and packhorses on behalf of Ragusan merchants. Many of the caravans were huge and must have presented an extraordinary spectacle. For example, at the end of December 1590 one Ragusan merchant alone sent from Sofia 10,500 buffalo and cow hides; the following June he despatched a similar number. A large caravan might consist of well over 1,000 horses and be accompanied by over 200 men.[25]

Ragusan Colonies and Settlements in the Balkans

The Ragusans were so successful in adapting to changing political and economic conditions in the Balkans because they had acquired such long experience of life there. Their communities had been profitably co-existing with the Slavs and other groups for at least two centuries before the Ottoman conquest, and despite the upheavals of that time soon began to do so again under Turkish control.

The Ragusans had long enjoyed their own special privileges. Under the early Slavic rulers mixed juries of Saxons and Ragusans, for example, were appointed to judge in disputes between members of the two communities, while internal Ragusan conflicts were resolved by a Ragusan consul and two Ragusan judges chosen from among patrician families.[26] Under the Ottoman Empire, it became one of the regular duties of Dubrovnik's diplomats to establish with incoming Sultans the precise, privileged status of Ragusans living and working on Turkish soil. So, for example, Dubrovnik obtained from the new Sultan Selim II (1566–1574) provisions requiring that Turks pay their debts to Ragusans, that Ragusans in Skopje and elsewhere not be evicted from shops they rented, that all Ragusans and the children they had from Turkish wives be subject to Dubrovnik not to the Sultan, that Ragusans be permitted to own property securely as long as they paid the proper dues, and that Ragusans who fled Dubrovnik to Turkish territory so as to escape debt or punishment be returned.[27]

There were well-organised and judicially recognised Ragusan communities in trading centres through much of the Balkans from at least the late fourteenth century. These communities were governed by 'consuls': for example, there were consuls in Novo Brdo in 1370, Srebrenica in 1376 and Drijeva in 1381. In 1387 the Dubrovnik government decided that from now on the consuls of the Ragusan mercantile communities in the Balkans would be appointed by Dubrovnik's Rector and Small Council from among Ragusan merchants living there, preferably from among the patricians. Alongside the consul were appointed two judges, also preferably patricians. These officers were sent copies of appropriate legal regulations by the Small Council and were expected to judge according to them. There was a book in which judgements were recorded locally, and they were also registered in the Dubrovnik Chancery. Appeals could be made to the Ragusan courts.[28]

This basic organisational structure remained in place after the Ottoman conquest. But the collapse of a number of the earlier centres, the rise of others and above all the new relationship with the Empire brought some changes. Although there were other important Ragusan mercantile communites, by the sixteenth century there were only five – Novi Pazar, Prokuplje, Priština, Sofia and Plovdiv – which were officially designated as 'colonies' (*kolone*). These five centres were the most commercially important in the Balkan interior. The colony was still a well-defined unit integrated into the Ragusan legal system, and it now had its own *skup* or assembly of local merchants alongside the consul and judges, but its privileges depended upon and were spelt out in Ottoman grants. The colonies would be visited, usually annually, by the Ragusan *poklisari*, who would deal with matters too serious or contentious to be handled locally.[29]

II. Maritime Trade

Of course, the overland trade with the Balkans cannot ultimately be disentangled from the maritime trade with Europe. It was, after all, Dubrovnik's skilful exploitation of its role as a link between East and West

18. The Dubrovnik Franciscans' Cloister

Following pages
19. Depiction of Dubrovnik inserted into the *Liber Viridis* (Laws of Dubrovnik 1358–1460: the picture itself is later)

20. Petar Sorkočević's Villa on Lapad

21. Paolo Veneziano's painted crucifix (1340s)

22. Matko Junčić: Blessed Virgin with Saints (1452)

23. Lovro Dobričević: The Baptism of Christ (1448)

24. Mihajlo Hamzić: The Baptism of Christ (1508)

25. Detail of Lovro Dobričević's Virgin and Child (1465)

that was the foundation of its commercial prowess. The value of what its merchants procured from the Slavs and Turks was greatly enhanced by Dubrovnik's ability to despatch the merchandise efficiently and swiftly from its own port and in its own ships. Initially, however, Dubrovnik's main concern was for the import by sea of supplies for its own requirements – in particular, corn.

Grain

The supply of corn to the city's and *distretto*'s population had always been a major headache for the Ragusan government because of the lack of suitable agricultural land. The first extant records of the Ragusan Small and Great Councils at the beginning of the fourteenth century bear witness to this preoccupation. Corn was obtained at public expense either by reliable government agents (called 'syndics'), or by Ragusan or foreign merchants from southern Italy or the Levant. It could only be sold at the town corn warehouse (*fondik*). Its weight was carefully recorded before and after milling. It was distributed at fixed prices, often separately to the urban population and to those of the islands. On occasion, a further distribution was made to Slavs who would gather at the gates.[30]

In the fourteenth century the overall annual consumption of grain in Dubrovnik was perhaps 20,000 *staria.*[31] Diversis estimated that by the 1430s more than 70,000 *staria* were required to feed the inhabitants of the city and *distretto.*[32] Jakov Lukarević noted that the figure by his day was over 80,000 *staria.* He also described the system of providing for the shortfall. The Ragusan government would obtain grain from Turkish dominions in the Levant and supplement this in times of dearth with grain from Italy. And besides this, 'the government [had] made very fine grain stores under ground to hold the grain.'[33] These *rupe* (literally 'holes') were originally situated beneath the monasteries of St Andrew and St Mark. But in 1541 it was decided to build nearby the huge structure of dry wells, hewn from the rock, which alone now bears the name of *Rupe* – and to which Lukarević doubtless refers. It was the work of an architect from Apulia and was only completed in 1590. In the cellar beneath the building some 1,500 tonnes of grain could be stored.[34]

Dubrovnik had long been accustomed to obtaining its corn from Apulia and Sicily; its close relations with the rulers of those regions were in large part a result of that requirement. But the wars which followed the direct involvement of the Spanish in the region threatened this supply.[35] The Ragusan chroniclers were proud of the successful efforts the government made to overcome the problem. For example, the anonymous chronicler records that in 1503 there was a great dearth of corn as rival armies in Italy bought it up. Dubrovnik's usual Apulian source dried up, so it sent to get more from Sicily. Two ships loaded with grain arrived back on 9 March (the Feast of the Forty Martyrs) to replenish the city granaries. But as soon as the news got out, there also arrived people from Bar, Budva, Kotor, the Dalmatian islands and, indeed, the whole of Dalmatia up to Zadar – even people from Italy and Turkey – to beg for corn.[36]

In such circumstances, it was both important for Dubrovnik's own needs, and also good business, to supplement Italian corn with that from the Ottoman Empire. (In principle, there was a strict prohibition imposed by the Porte on resale of its grain by the Ragusans to other Christian powers: but naturally every load of grain from Turkish territory meant that another load could be sold by the Ragusans once their own granaries were supplied). Dubrovnik accordingly sought and obtained annual permission to buy corn in Albania and Greece, as it had before the Ottoman conquest, even in years when there was a general prohibition against export. In principle, this grain would come from the Sultan's estates, but if there was insufficient it could be obtained elsewhere – in spite of the fact that the local population on occasion rioted against fulfilment of the permits which the Sultan's *ferman*s had given.[37]

A detailed study of the trade in corn in the second half of the sixteenth century – a period characterised by sharp alternations between copious supply and extreme dearth – shows that Dubrovnik managed its affairs with considerable success. Although it enforced a system of maximum and at times even minimum prices, these were set at levels which moderated rather than blithely ignored market forces. As a result of its prudent provisions, the variations in prices in Dubrovnik were less sharp, and so less worrisome, than in Venice.[38]

Shipments of corn were crucial to Dubrovnik's survival; but other equally bulky cargoes – raw materials like hides exported to the West and manufactured goods like cloth carried to the East – were the basis of its initial maritime success. And on that foundation a wider carrying trade was later developed by Dubrovnik's shipowners. The common factor, of course, was Ragusan seamanship, which was reflected in the skilful design of Dubrovnik's ships, in the efficiency of its captains and crews, and in the preoccupation of the Ragusan state and society with maritime matters.

Shipping

The regulations governing Dubrovnik's shipping had already been laid down in the seventh book of the Dubrovnik Statute of 1272, and they were later supplemented. Some of these requirements were extremely detailed, not to say meddlesome. It was specified precisely what equipment ships of different sizes must carry, down to the number of hemp ropes, sails and anchors. More obviously practical was the order forbidding a ship's captain and crew to abandon a vessel or sell it without the owner's or his representative's permission. Such irresponsibility was, it seems, a reality. In 1511 a special ordinance was promulgated by the government because of scandals arising from the flight of whole crews from their vessels midway through a voyage. A prison sentence was henceforth to be added to the fine levied on those guilty of such abuses. Thefts on board were also punished severely.[39]

Another aspect of Ragusan maritime organisation which already existed at the time of the drawing up of Book Seven of the Dubrovnik Statute, and which remained a traditional feature, was the ordering of the duties and remuneration of the crew on each voyage. A sailor could make a voyage *ad marinariciam*, that is, at an agreed wage; he could sail *ad partem*, receiving part of the profits of the voyage; or he could go as part of a specially formed, temporary trading company – an arrangement known as *entega*. In this last case, he and his fellow crew members were rewarded with a share of the proceeds of the voyage, the other two shares going to the shipowner and to the businessman who had provided the money to buy the cargo. Crew members were also allowed to supplement their wages with the sale of some of their own property, known as *paraspodia*, carried on board. The oversight of these arrangements as well as the supervision of the cargo and its sale at the port or ports to be visited called for something more than seamanship, and so the law of Dubrovnik laid down that each vessel of 600 *modia* capacity or over must carry on board a clerk who was to log all the relevant information.[40]

The framework for Dubrovnik's maritime development had therefore been provided very early. But it was only after the end of Venetian rule that the Ragusan Republic was able fully to develop its maritime potential. So in the fifteenth century its fleet was extensively rebuilt and enlarged, and in the sixteenth century it reached its peak tonnage. The Ragusan merchant fleet's capacity grew steadily in the first half of the sixteenth century. The number of large ships also grew. At its zenith in the 1560s and 1570s there were 180 ships with a total capacity of 35,000 *carri*. (The Italian measure of a *carro* was equivalent to just under 20 hectolitres of grain). The smallest of these ships (up to 30 *carri*) was known as a *sagitta, grippo* or sometimes *marsiliana.* They were fast vessels with a long tradition of use in the region for fishing, carrying passengers and – in the hands of the *uskoks* – war. They varied in size as in nomenclature, and were equipped with both sails and oars. 'Caravels' were somewhat larger. Larger still were the ships known as 'brigantines'. Vessels of over 100 *carri* were variously called 'galleons', *navae*, 'bertons' or more generally 'caracks'. These huge ships would have three or four masts, two or three decks, raised forecastle and still higher poop-deck, and might carry up to thirty cannons.[41] Crew numbers also generally increased in size in the course of the sixteenth century.

At its peak the Ragusan merchant fleet was probably equal in tonnage to that of Venice. The Ragusans invested huge sums in their shipping, which constituted at this time the most important element in their economy. It has been estimated that the total worth of Dubrovnik's merchant navy in the 1570s was some 700,000 ducats. Only towards the end of the sixteenth century is there evidence that the capacity of the fleet had begun to decline, particularly as regards ships of medium tonnage.[42]

This decline, which accelerated in the seventeenth century, was the result of wider economic and political developments over which Dubrovnik had no control. The first of these – the decline of the Ottoman state, which began to be apparent under the successors of Suleyman the Magnificent – has already been mentioned. This gradually reduced the value of the Balkan trade, as internal conditions deteriorated, at a time when competition to Ragusan merchants was also increasing.

The second large adverse change which affected the whole Mediterranean world, though its impact has sometimes been predated and exaggerated, was the shift in commercial dominance to the European powers of the North and West. In spite of intermittent crises, the Mediterranean world flourished during most of the sixteenth century, but this very prosperity attracted Atlantic shipping whose owners and promoters were anxious to exploit it. French, English and Dutch shipping became ever more active in the Mediterranean, particularly in the last quarter of the century. None of this may have been immediately decisive for the fortunes of the region, but it certainly put the existing Mediterranean maritime powers like Venice and Dubrovnik on the defensive.[43]

It is important to distinguish two aspects of Dubrovnik's decline as a maritime commercial power. The more important aspect in the longer term was the Republic's *relative* decline, that is its decreasing economic and thus ultimately political importance as a power in an increasingly commercially integrated early modern Europe. So, for example, although the absolute size of the Ragusan commercial fleet was not very different in the later from the earlier sixteenth century, in relative terms its size had fallen from a half to a sixth that of the Dutch fleet over the period.[44] The acceleration of economic progress elsewhere is the principal explanation of the Ragusan Republic's relegation by the time of its fall in 1808 to the status of a cultivated, prosperous but also provincial and politically unimportant backwater.

But there was also in the seventeenth century an important and measurable *absolute* decline in the Republic's maritime trade, which, given the financial importance of the merchant fleet, certainly reflected a more general weakening of Dubrovnik's economic position. It was not just the result of prevailing economic trends, but also of piracy and disorder. Dubrovnik now, as in previous centuries, sought to guard against the dangers by sending its ships in convoy. But even Venice, which had the military capacity to afford its merchant ships much better protection, could not guarantee their safety at such a time.

The sharpest decline in the numbers of Ragusan merchant ships occurred in the second decade of the seventeenth century. (The Venetian fleet also suffered catastrophic decline at this time.) Later, although the number of Ragusan ships stayed the same, their size and so total capacity fell still further. The 1667 earthquake, for all its destruction and accompanying tidal wave, appears to have had remarkably little impact on the Ragusan merchant fleet. But it was not until the 1730s that the decline came to an end.[45]

Maritime Finance and Insurance

The activity of the Ragusan merchant fleet was supported by a well-developed financial system and promoted by a range of public institutions and interventions. Although some ships were owned by a single man, it was more usual for ownership, profit and risk to be spread. The traditional division of shared ownership in Dubrovnik was by means of 'karats' (*karati*), each of which represented a share of 1/24.[46] Ownership of the cargo might also be divided, with rich merchants advancing loans to cover a part share of whatever was to be purchased and resold.[47]

The same objective was served by the maritime insurance business which grew up alongside the expansion of the fleet and which reached its greatest sophistication in the sixteenth century. Both ships and cargoes – and shares of ships and cargoes – could be insured. The first stage was for the owner to register the details at the Dubrovnik state Chancery. He would specify in his statement the nature of the cargo, the destination, the name of the ship and other details. The second stage was for other insurers to approach the Chancery and offer money to cover the risk at a rate of interest reflecting the circumstances of the day, the destination envisaged, the reliability of the captain and so on. Thus for a voyage across the Adriatic to Italy, the rate might be 2 or 3 per cent, but to London, 12 per cent. Unless the cargo was government-owned or -organised, the insurance would not usually cover the whole value of ship and cargo. The rewards were often large and so accordingly was the number of would-be insurers, who in Dubrovnik (unlike Venice) were private individuals rather than companies. Members of the great noble families of Dubrovnik – the Gučetić, Sorkočević, Bunić, Pucić and Gradić families in particular – were heavily involved. So were a large number of wealthy commoners.[48]

The Consular Service

The size and spread of Dubrovnik's maritime trade required that the government appoint agents known as 'consuls' to supervise and protect Ragusan ships and merchants in the ports they frequented. These officials accordingly started to multiply in Italy after the end of Venetian rule in 1358, and their numbers increased in the fifteenth century. At the century's end there were twenty-two Ragusan consuls in different Mediterranean ports. The growing importance of Spain in the sixteenth century saw more consuls sent to the western Mediterranean. Partly for political and partly for geographical reasons, Naples emerged as the most important consular seat. The number of consulates in the West (or 'Ponent') later declined along with Ragusan trade in the seventeenth century: from forty-four in the mid-sixteenth century, the number fell to twenty-eight in the early seventeenth.[49]

The Ragusans had been coming to the Levant in general and to Alexandria in particular throughout the fifteenth century. But they only made a formal trade agreement with the Egyptian Sultan in 1510. In 1519 the new Ottoman rulers of Egypt confirmed the provision. France, however, which enjoyed the Sultan's special favour because of its long-standing hostility to the Turks' Spanish enemies, managed to secure uniquely favourable treatment. Initially, by the Franco-Turkish treaty of 1536 the ships of Western mercantile states were merely permitted to avail themselves of French protection and fly French colours when trading in the Levant. But France was determined to extend this permission into an obligation. So in 1566, the ships of all Christian states except Venice were required to place themselves under the protection of the

French consul. Dubrovnik resisted this provision with some success, though making use of French protection when it was useful to do so. In 1575 Dubrovnik even made detailed new provisions for its Alexandrian consulate: henceforth the consul must be a patrician of at least thirty years of age and would be appointed to serve for a four-year term. Ultimately, though, French influence proved too strong. After the death of the Ragusan consul in Alexandria in 1578, no successor was appointed.[50]

Like other Ragusan institutions, the consular service was notable for its practical flexibility. Its basic purpose was to serve as an extension of the central government. Thus its members acted as judges in minor matters; notaries in the registration and issue of documents; substitute tax collectors by allowing the government to know what it was owed in maritime dues; and spies through the despatch of information on political events. With their provision of protection and hospitality, not to mention cemeteries and chapels, they also offered a home-from-home for the homesick. Usually the consuls were Ragusans, but sometimes foreigners were used, some of whom stayed in office for many years – even passing on the post to other family members.[51]

Generally speaking, the number and location of consuls is a good indicator of the scale and scope of Ragusan commerce. But that relationship changed in later years. Thus the decline in numbers of Ragusan consuls was reversed after 1667 as a matter of deliberate policy to assert Dubrovnik's influence after the catastrophe of the earthquake. But in the Ponent consuls lost many of their judicial powers to the home government and their political role to other permanent or semi-permanent agents, whose role more closely approximated that of modern ambassadors.[52]

Quarantine

The inhabitants of the ports visited by Ragusan ships naturally welcomed their trade, but were extremely wary about importing their diseases. It was a favoured device of the Venetians to discredit their rival by spreading rumours about Dubrovnik's failure to de-contaminate its Balkan cargoes. For example, in 1623 the Venetian government instructed its consul in Ancona to make allegations of just this sort.[53] Such slanders in turn provided a strong incentive for the Ragusan government further to develop its quarantine procedures.

The early history of Dubrovnik's quarantine is better considered as part of the city's sophisticated public health provisions.[54] Suffice it to say here that the first quarantine law of Dubrovnik of 1377 was a delayed reaction to the horrors of the Black Death of 1348 and to subsequent epidemics. It was a compromise between the requirements of trade and those of public health, applying a *cordon sanitaire* without entirely disrupting business. All those coming from places where epidemics raged were to be placed in isolation just outside Cavtat (for overland traffic) and on the island of Mrkan (for maritime traffic). In 1397 disused buildings on the island of Mljet were converted into what was probably the first quarantine detention station or *lazzaretto* in Europe.

In spite of the provisions of 1377, Dubrovnik was again affected by plague in 1391 and 1397. These outbreaks prompted the government to adopt still tighter controls. Special officials were appointed to watch the frontiers, certify the papers of those arriving on Ragusan territory, organise quarantine and punish anyone who infringed the regulations. It was not just merchants but merchandise that were subject to scrutiny: while corn and new cloth could be imported without impediment, clothes which had been worn were to be aired and fumigated. In all this Dubrovnik was ahead of any state of its day – even Venice.[55]

In the early fifteenth century further *lazzaretti* were built on the islands of Supetar and Bobara. In 1430 the main quarantine station was transferred to the headland of Danče, still isolated and outside the walls but more convenient for those coming from land or sea than the islands down the coast. The move to Danče also allowed the island of Mrkan finally to be returned to the Dubrovnik-dwelling bishop of Trebinje-Mrkan who owned it. In 1496 the Danče quarantine station was expanded into a self-contained complex of permanent buildings, makeshift huts, cistern, graveyard and church of Our Lady of Danče. It functioned throughout the sixteenth century. The island of Lokrum – still more convenient for ships, though inconvenient for overland imports – was chosen as the site for a new larger *lazzaretto* in 1534. But the building work on Lokrum proceeded slowly and its final completion was further postponed for fear that the Venetians might occupy the place and use it to attack or blockade Dubrovnik. This danger and the inconvenience for the overland trade, as well as the need to create a still more impressive structure to demonstrate the seriousness of its quarantine controls, probably combined to prompt the Ragusan government to decide in February 1590 to build the impressive *Lazzaretti* complex which still stands at Ploče.

The plans for the new *Lazzaretti* were frequently changed and only finally agreed in August 1627. In fact, the quarantine centre was never entirely completed. But its construction memorably demonstrated Dubrovnik's determination at this low point of its commercial fortunes, when it was under intense pressure from Split, to assert its claims as the dominant port in the Eastern Adriatic. It certainly left the Turkish travel writer Evliya Çelebi suitably impressed when he visited it in 1664. He described the *Lazzaretti* as comfortable for those staying in the adjacent accommodation, though they could expect to be pumped for information by the staff. The complex was sealed and guarded by night. Not just goods but livestock could be kept there. Travellers, their horses and their merchandise would arrive outside the town by the side of the *Lazzaretti* at the place known as Tabor (meaning 'camp'). There, through a latticed partition-wall, money could be paid to those coming from Dubrovnik in exchange for food and other things without risking contagion. The whole system worked well, however much Venice grumbled, and the proof is that epidemics, like that which struck Turkey in 1647, were henceforth almost unknown in Dubrovnik.[56]

Trade with England

Dubrovnik's trade with England in the sixteenth century provides an excellent example of Ragusan mercantile methods, as well as being of economic importance in its own right. Ragusans came to English ports in the fourteenth and fifteenth centuries, though probably only as crew members of Venetian merchantmen. But the labour-intensive, oar-driven galleys were, by the end of this period, already giving way to more efficiently rigged large sailing ships, which needed fewer crew and so had more space for cargo. So from the early sixteenth century the Venetian 'Flanders galleys', which used to stop in England to buy wool, made far fewer voyages. Dubrovnik seems to have used this opportunity to break into the English trade. Doing business with Dubrovnik also suited English economic interests better because, unlike the Venetians, Ragusan merchants were generally more interested in buying finished woollen cloth rather than just wool. By 1515 the Ragusans had acquired a strong position in the English market, and between then and the middle of the century they were probably exporting more English cloth to the Eastern Mediterranean than all the Italian merchants together.

Ragusan ships would arrive in England at Southampton or Margate – the former near the heart of textile production in Hampshire and with the benefit of its double tide, the latter with its deep harbour and convenient proximity to London. They carried wine from Crete, soap for use in the textile industry, olive oil, wax, currants, oriental carpets, cotton and costly Italian fabrics. The Ragusan ships were then reloaded with 'broadcloths' and 'straits', but above all with the prized 'kerseys', to be made into garments for well-to-do people in the Balkans. They also carried away tin, lead, pewter vessels, tanned hides and some wool for Italian cloth manufacturers.

These Ragusan caracks were of a size never seen before in English ports and created sufficient impression for onlookers to coin the English word 'Argosy' (a corruption of 'Ragusa') to describe any huge sailing ship. A Ragusan ship of this sort would have a capacity of between 600 and 800 tonnes, but it only needed a crew of between 60 and 80 compared with a Venetian Flanders galley's crew of 200.

The trade was intense and extremely valuable, but in the 1540s it was dramatically cut short by international politics. The long sea-route from Dubrovnik to England could only function profitably in conditions of reasonable security. But a combination of war between England and France in the Channel, North African piracy in the Western Mediterranean and fighting between the Spaniards and Turks off Dalmatia made it impossible. Insurance rates accordingly soared. Attempts to shift much of the commerce overland via Antwerp or Hamburg were only partially successful. Moreover, this change deprived the Ragusans of the profits their ships had earned in the carrying trade. By the mid-sixteenth century the previously important Ragusan colony in London had greatly dwindled.[57]

This was not, however, the last contact that Dubrovnik had with England. Dubrovnik might have hoped that the accession to the throne of the Catholic Queen Mary (1555–1558), which marked the end of the formal *casus belli* between England and the Catholic European powers, would have worked in its favour. But the new monarch proved no less subject to protectionist pressure from English merchants and consequently blocked exports to the old emporium at Antwerp, implementing an earlier law of Richard III forbidding 'Italians' to export English cloth via Flanders. The authorities also apparently applied this provision to Dubrovnik. The Ragusans protested vigorously that Dubrovnik was not in Italy, indeed that it was separated from Italy by the Adriatic and adjoined Dalmatia and Hungary; moreover, they added, Dubrovnik's language was as different from Italian as was English. But the protests were in vain. Mary in any case then died, and was succeeded by the still more obstructive (and Protestant) Elizabeth I (1559–1603).[58]

War, Commerce and the Challenge from Split

The commercial life of Dubrovnik in its heyday focused on its activity as a port: only in the years of decline did it rest mainly on a Ragusan carrying trade that often bypassed the city entirely.[59] The amount of trade channelled through Dubrovnik depended at any one time on the resolution of a paradox: for while Dubrovnik, like any other port, needed secure conditions for commerce to flourish, it also benefited mightily through its neutrality in general conditions of war. In the longer term, of course, endemic disorder resulting from war would do more harm than any sudden bursts of affluence did good. Moreover, the temptation to maximise its wartime monopoly position led Dubrovnik to exploit it excessively and so helped promote external competition.

During the Turkish-Venetian war of 1499–1503 Dubrovnik had to withstand the enmity of Venice, which destroyed the Ragusan salt pans at the mouth of the Neretva, and attacks by both Venetians and Turks on its shipping. But it is clear from the numbers of loans made in order to buy merchandise and of partnerships to trade that over the period of the war there was a sharp increase in Ragusan business.[60] By the time of the First War of the Holy League of 1538–1540, Dubrovnik had stabilised its favourable trading arrangements with the Ottoman Empire and so was in a still better position to prosper from neutrality. Again, Venice acted against Ragusan shipping and sought to enforce a strict blockade on Dubrovnik. But Ragusan customs dues levied on imports record a modest increase for the war years.[61]

Ragusan diplomacy during the Second War of the Holy League or War of Cyprus (1569–1573) was still more effective in maintaining the Republic's neutrality, and the economic benefits were accordingly greater. At this time, merchants of all varieties flooded into the city – Italians from Venice, Ancona, Bari, Florence and Genoa and Spaniards, Frenchmen, Turks and Jews – accompanied, it seems, by a number of undesirables. The Ragusan government struggled to maintain order, but did not overlook the opportunity to increase its revenues. In July 1571 the government sharply increased the customs dues it levied on foreigners' merchandise from 5 to 9 per cent. This provoked strong protests and, as the Venetian envoy reported to his government, caused a great deal of resentment against the Ragusans. Goods began to pile up at the Dubrovnik customs house – the *Dogana* or Sponza – as foreign merchants refused pay their dues, and the authorities now threatened to confiscate and sell the merchandise. The Venetian envoy reported that Dubrovnik's sizeable Jewish community was particularly strident in its objections and had sought the protection of the Porte. Dubrovnik responded by drawing up a list of Jews with a view to expelling those not legitimately engaged in trade and finance. But under Turkish pressure it had to back down. In the short run the city's revenues increased markedly, though only some of this reflected the increase in business channeled through the town: more resulted from the higher dues levied.[62]

The dispute between Dubrovnik and its Jews and the abiding resentment of foreign merchants who felt they had been exploited – acutely observed by the no less resentful Venetian government – would soon have unpleasant consequences. Jewish merchants in the Adriatic ports were already strong competitors to the Ragusans. They enjoyed the special protection of the Ottoman Empire, and the Ottoman Albanian port of Valona, in particular, had a large and successful Jewish community involved in trade, textiles and money-lending. Large numbers of Jews also went to exploit opportunities in other Adriatic towns and – after seeking their fortunes in Dubrovnik during the War of Cyprus and then becoming resentful at their treatment – some decided to settle in Split, under Venetian rule. One of these, Daniel Rodriguez, in 1573 proposed to Venice the development of Split as an alternative *entrepôt* to Dubrovnik, benefiting from lower customs dues than Jewish and other merchants had recently had to tolerate there. The proposal was strongly supported by the Turkish *sandžak-beg* of Klis. It was repeated in 1577 and again between 1580 and 1582. The Venetians dithered and the Ottoman Empire's Jews therefore approached Dubrovnik and managed to negotiate a privileged regime for their trade. But Venice was ultimately prevailed upon to go ahead with Rodriguez's plan.

Accordingly, on 20 June 1590 Split was made a kind of free port. Venice exempted from all customs dues bulk merchandise shipped from the Ottoman Empire to the Venetian Rialto market via Split, and cut by half the customs payable on smaller quantities. Important concessions were made at the same time to all Jews from East or West who wished to settle in Venice's Dalmatian towns: the Jews were henceforth exempt from taxes, allowed to buy and sell whatever they wished and permitted to live outside the ghetto. These concessions were particularly important – and commercially well-judged – because the Jews of Ancona had in 1555 and 1556 been subject to persecution and forced to leave and because the Jews of Dubrovnik had in 1587 been made subject to new restrictions. The impact of these measures was dramatic, as imports from the Balkan hinterland – wax, hides, leather, mohair, silk – flowed through Split rather than Dubrovnik.[63]

Split had two important advantages over Dubrovnik. First, being under Venetian rule, the merchandise reaching it was more likely to be securely shipped on to Italy under the protection of Venetian military warships. Secondly, it was better placed geographically to exploit the growing markets of Sarajevo and Banja Luka. Local Turkish officials divided into those with an interest in promoting Split and those anxious to maintain the traditional link with Dubrovnik.

The Ragusans engaged all their diplomatic influence with the Porte in trying to regain Dubrovnik's quasi-monopoly position. But economic logic told in

Split's favour. Its growth was phenomenal. In 1619, for example, the Venetian count of Split recorded that even the cellars of Diocletian's palace were used as warehouses and that goods were being stored in the city's fortress.[64] During the 1620s the traffic through the now famous *scala* (emporium) grew even faster. Plague in 1630, which effectively cut Venice off entirely from the Ottoman Empire, dealt a severe blow to Split's fortunes.[65] But it was only the outbreak of a new war in 1645 between the Ottoman Empire and Venice – the War of Crete – that finally came to Dubrovnik's rescue by precipitating the abrupt ending of the Balkan trade through Split.

Venice bitterly resented the way in which Dubrovnik now benefited from Split's loss and did what it could to damage Ragusan commerce. In the 1660s, even while war with the Ottoman Empire continued, Venice sought to persuade Turkish officials to have Split reopened, or at least a substitute outlet found. Makarska at one stage appeared a possibility, but then Gabela (Drijeva) began to look more promising. Negotiations dragged on, with Dubrovnik doing all it could to frustrate them, until the 1667 earthquake threw all previous calculations into confusion.[66]

III. The Ragusan Urban Economy

Dubrovnik's Coinage

Both Dubrovnik's external trade and its urban economy required a sound currency. The reputation enjoyed by Ragusan money, as well as the extent of Ragusan trade, is confirmed by the number and distribution of finds of Ragusan coins throughout the Balkan region. The fourteenth-century rulers of Bosnia went so far as to model their coinage on Dubrovnik's. And both they and the rulers of Serbia allowed Ragusan money to circulate freely and at its face value.[67]

The modest beginnings of Dubrovnik's currency are obscure. Private individuals were probably issuing their own copper coins in the town in the later thirteenth century. But a Ragusan state mint was already at work by 1301. Dubrovnik's special political and economic status found symbolic expression in that, unlike the currency issued by other Dalmatian towns under Venetian rule, Ragusan coins bore no mention of Venice and no impression of the Venetian lion.[68]

The gold coin used in Dubrovnik was – and remained long after the Serenissima's rule had ended – the internationally renowned Venetian ducat.

And when the ducat effectively ceased to circulate in ordinary business exchange, it became – like the Byzantine *hyperperus* before it – a standard unit of account. Dubrovnik itself minted only copper and silver coinage. The *follarus*, *minca* or *mjed* was a small copper coin, thirty of which were decreed to be worth one silver *grosso*. The *grosso* or *dinar* was always the basic silver coin of the Republic, though it came in different varieties: in the course of the Republic's monetary history, there were issued altogether fifteen denominations of silver coin. Between the late fourteenth and the first half of the seventeenth century there was, for example, a half-*grosso* or *poludinar*. A *grosso* of much diminished silver content, accordingly known as a *grossetto* or *dinarić*, was also minted between 1626 and 1761. By contrast, when the Republic wanted to make its currency attractive to foreign merchants it issued more valuable silver coins – the *artiluk* (1627 to 1701), the *scudo* and half-*scudo* (1708–1750), and two varieties of *talir* (imitating the Austrian *thaler* – 1725–1743 and 1743–1779).[69]

Dubrovnik's *grosso* was, by the standards of the day, a reasonably sound currency. But over time its value more or less steadily diminished. There were a number of contributory reasons for this. It was partly the result of a general reduction in the value of silver as against gold. A connected factor was the 'price revolution', which resulted from the import of huge quantities of bullion from the New World in the sixteenth century, and from which no one escaped – not even those who acquired the bullion. But the process was also the inevitable outcome of a fairly steady reduction in the silver content of the Ragusan *grosso* over the history of the Republic. Even during the fourteenth century, the work of Dubrovnik's mint was sometimes interrupted by shortages of Balkan silver. After the Ottoman conquest, silver was still more difficult to obtain. So the authorities increasingly sought to acquire foreign silver coins which they could melt down and mint as *grossi*. They were not always successful. It is, though, worth noting that the value of the Turkish currency – the silver asper – to which, of course, much of Dubrovnik's business was linked, declined still more.[70]

In the first two centuries of its existence the Dubrovnik mint seems to have been peripatetic, moving as convenience required between one state building and another. But in 1520 it found its permanent home in the customs house, the *Dogana* or Sponza, and the following year was accordingly placed under the direct control of the officials of the Great Custom. The craftsmen who actually constructed the dies, purified the silver and produced the coin were highly skilled goldsmiths. In overall charge of the mint, and responsible to the state for its honest and efficient operation, was a committee of Ragusan Senators.[71]

Finance

Almost as important for commerce as a credible currency was the supply of sufficient credit. It seems probable that from an early date promissory notes were in circulation within Dubrovnik. Credit was soon subject to government regulation. A law of 1275 required that all credit arrangements for sums higher than 10 *hyperperi* be recorded within eight days in a document drawn up by a notary. These notarial registers were the property of the state. (Abroad, such loans were registered by Ragusan consuls.)

Loans could, of course, be necessary for a wide variety of purposes. The business of outright money-lending was only publicly acknowledged to be undertaken by Jews. More frequent – indeed central to the way in which the Ragusan merchant did business – was the advance of loans secured upon merchandise such as wool, cloth, other cargoes or even ships. There need in such cases be no explicit mention of interest – embarrassing in a Catholic state where usury was prohibited by Church law. The gain would be concealed in the profit from the sale of the merchandise for whose purchase the loan had been made. By contrast, penal rates of interest in cases of late re-payment were permitted – and acknowledged.[72]

Payments of interest by and to the Ragusan state were also acknowledged. It was well known, for instance, that over many years Slavic lords had entrusted their money to Dubrovnik for profit as well as for security. Indeed, as has already been noted, the Kosača fortune, invested in Dubrovnik, brought with it no end of complications.[73] The Ragusan government also raised loans from its citizens, which it would repay at 10 or 12 per cent interest.[74] Money was often bequeathed to the Republic by pious, public-spirited individuals for the care of widows and orphans. It was entrusted to the officials known as the Treasurers of St Mary's, who were then responsible for investing it. In Jakov Lukarević's day at least, it was customary for Dubrovnik to deposit it in Rome, Genoa and Naples at 7 per cent interest.[75] There was also a group of private *rentiers*. For most of the life of the Republic – insofar as the records reveal – their favoured place to invest their funds was Naples, followed by Rome, with the banks of Venice, Genoa and Sicily at different times also figuring large. The prime consideration seems to have been security rather than rates of interest: hence the preference given to the politically friendly centres of Naples and Rome.[76]

Later, under the inspiration of that ardent Ragusan patriot Stjepan Gradić, Dubrovnik established a *Monte di Pietà*, a kind of state savings bank. It was known as the *Monte di San Biagio*. But the Ragusan Republic never developed a state credit institution to reduce the cost of the public debt along the lines established in Italy.[77]

Craft Confraternities

Dubrovnik's economy was primarily founded upon trade rather than industry. Accordingly, the crafts which flourished in the city were ones which added to the worth of Dubrovnik's merchandise and supplied the needs of its mercantile elite. As elsewhere in medieval Europe, they were organised into guilds or confraternities. These bodies had a range of functions, acting as a framework for standards, training and discipline. On occasion, as Diversis noted, they even served a military function: if immediate danger threatened, the members of the craft guilds would assemble to guard the city gates.[78]

The early craft confraternities of Dubrovnik began with the basic objectives of all confraternities, that is the promotion of the spiritual and practical welfare of their members and their families. Only in the late fourteenth century did they increasingly acquire their 'professional' characteristics. Nor did the latter ever entirely prevail. Thus there was no sharp division between the confraternities based on crafts and those which remained based on religious association. And even the craft confraternities often had members who were nobles or women and who had no professional association with the craft.[79]

The Ragusan craft confraternities were less rigidly organised and less integrated into the state than in some German and Italian towns. There was no official policy of limiting entry into the confraternity, and within it apprentices often enjoyed full membership. An apprentice would enter a master's service by a written agreement registered by a notary. For his part, the master would usually provide lodging, food and clothing but no wages. At the end of the apprenticeship – which could last for anything between two months and twelve years – the apprentice received the tools for his trade. The craftsmen of Dubrovnik cannot be said to have formed a single social or economic class: some were very rich while others, particularly those in the woollen cloth business, were very poor.[80]

The crafts and industries which flourished in the longer term were those which fitted most easily into Dubrovnik's social and commercial life. That was obviously the case, for example, with the butchers: there was a butchers' confraternity from the fourteenth century, and in view of the town's concern for the regulation of the trade on grounds of hygiene it would be surprising if it had not existed earlier.[81] There is mention of separate confraternities of stonemasons, smiths and cobblers from the fourteenth century and confraternities of tailors and of barber-surgeons (the two professions in medieval times being regarded as one) from the fifteenth. There also existed from the fifteenth century a confraternity of shopkeepers under the patronage of St Luke. It began by incorporating within it the sellers of oil, cheese, salt, fish and other food, and later sellers of shoes, rugs, leather, wool and linen.[82]

Goldsmiths

One of the most important and prestigious crafts of Dubrovnik was that of the gold- (and silver-) smiths.[83] Dubrovnik enjoyed from medieval to early modern times an unchallenged reputation in the Eastern Adriatic region for fine work in gold and especially silver. These goldsmiths plied their craft for the government (in the mint), for ecclesiastical institutions, for Ragusans and for foreigners. They worked in Romanesque, Renaissance and Baroque but, above all – and by the apparent preference of their customers – in Gothic styles. They made coins, a limited number of medals, numerous liturgical objects, votive plaques and reliquaries, cutlery, cups and bowls, and – especially from the seventeenth century onwards – large quantities of jewellery.[84]

The goldsmiths had their own confraternity (under the protection of St Mark) in the early fourteenth century, which was re-founded in the early fifteenth century and united with allied precious metal-working crafts in the early sixteenth century. Like the other guilds, one of the principal functions of the goldsmiths' confraternity was to provide a framework for training. Into its ranks between the thirteenth and sixteenth centuries entered apprentices hailing not just from Dubrovnik, but also from Bosnia, Hercegovina, the Montenegrin coast, Serbia and Albania.[85]

Because of the value of the goldsmiths' product, and always keenly aware of the need to protect Dubrovnik's reputation, the authorities from a very early date exercised close control over quality. In 1277 the government forbade goldsmiths to use silver of purity inferior to the 'sterling' standard, a prohibition which was repeated on numerous occasions. It appears from a provision of 1352 that this standard in Dubrovnik was established as fifteen ounces of fine silver to one ounce of copper. As a guarantee that the requirements had been met, an impression of the head of St Blaise was stamped as a hallmark onto all gold- and silverware produced in the Republic. In order to supervise more easily the goldsmiths' activities, they were in 1386 ordered to establish their workshops in the same street, henceforth known as *Ruga aurificium*, *Slatarska ulica* or *Strada degli oresi* (i.e. 'Goldsmith Street'). The provision was repeated in 1459; only the senior goldsmith, whose role it was to supervise the measurement of gold and silver, was allowed to have his workshop on Placa. But after the 1667 earthquake, which devastated their traditional quarter, the goldsmiths set up shops in other streets as well.[86]

The great age of Dubrovnik's goldsmiths lasted from the fourteenth to the mid-sixteenth centuries, after which there was a slow decline in quality and creativity. Sadly, little of the Dubrovnik goldsmiths' work remains. This was mainly the result of the long-standing habit of melting down and re-using silver from items that had ceased to appeal to fashionable taste. Other contributory factors to the loss were the destruction wrought by the great earthquake and the dispersal of treasure after the fall of the Republic. But both the magnificent mid-fifteenth century silver and gilt statue of St Blaise, rescued from the fire which destroyed that church in the eighteenth century, and the fine contemporary medallions designed by Pavao Dubrovčanin (Paulus de Ragusa), depicting Alfonso V of Naples and his general Federigo Montefeltro, bear witness to the technical and artistic quality of the Dubrovnik goldsmiths' achievement.[87]

Construction and Shipbuilding

As Dubrovnik grew wealthier, the crafts involved in construction also soon began to flourish. From the fourteenth century onwards there was an intense and all but continuous programme of building work – the strengthening of fortifications, the rebuilding of patrician palaces, the erection and embellishment of public buildings and churches – which attracted master builders as well as humbler labourers into Dubrovnik from the other Adriatic towns and still further afield.[88] With other craftsmen like goldsmiths and painters (whose work is more appropriately described later), these architects and builders were employed in the process of turning Dubrovnik into a city that matched, even according to the discriminating judgement of Italians like Diversis and a succession of other European visitors, the splendours of the finest cities of the day.[89]

Even more important for the Ragusan Republic than the construction of buildings, however, was the construction of ships, on which the government expended continuous effort. Shipbuilding was accorded such attention because it was seen as integral to the success of Dubrovnik as a maritime commercial power. Until the end of the fifteenth century, the main shipyard faced onto the city harbour, but it became too cramped, and as a result Ragusan ships were built in other, smaller yards on Lopud and Šipan and at Cavtat, Slano, Zaton and elsewhere. The government sometimes even had to permit Ragusan vessels to be constructed outside the Republic's frontiers altogether, on Korčula. But it did so with reluctance.

In 1525 the main Dubrovnik shipyard (known as *škver*) was officially transferred to Gruž, where there was plenty of room to expand and in whose spacious, deep harbour large ships increasingly often moored. The *škver* was 480 feet long and 180 feet wide. Anyone wanting to build a ship outside the *škver* needed special permission to do so. In 1569, when large numbers of shipwrights were threatened with unemployment, a tax was imposed on owners building in foreign yards. This was rescinded when conditions improved, but other similar financial penalties were again imposed in 1589 and 1591. In the seventeenth century, when the government was desperate to revive shipbuilding as a means of boosting Ragusan maritime commerce, it wavered between allowing the hard-pressed shipowners to build outside Gruž and fining them if they did so. Naturally, neither course of action sufficed to revive an industry whose fortunes were dependent on maritime trade when the latter was in steep decline.

The *škver* was a typically Ragusan compromise – a combination of public control and private enterprise. The Republic provided the land on which the yard stood and a state-appointed Admiral oversaw its operation and preserved order among the workmen. But the shipwrights themselves were independent artisans and agreed their own contracts with the shipowners on whose vessels they worked. There were probably about 100 shipwrights working on the Republic's territory in the sixteenth century, most at Gruž but also a substantial number on Lopud. They were divided into two crafts – carpenters and caulkers (called *calaphati*) – though they shared a single confraternity. Wood for shipbuilding came from the Croatian littoral, Albania and Italy; pitch, from Albania; and metal fittings from Ragusan or Italian smithies. The skills of the shipwrights were, though, native to Dubrovnik, and just a small number of the artisans at the yard hailed from outside the Republic. Only for the building of its small number of warships did the Republic look to Italian master shipbuilders.

The Ragusan shipbuilders enjoyed a formidable reputation. One Italian commentator in 1607 considered the Ragusans 'the best and perhaps the most skilful' builders of large ships: only the Portugese were their superiors. Another in 1614 echoed the sentiment, concluding that for the construction of *navae* and galleons 'the craftsman of Dubrovnik, Portugal and England' were most highly esteemed.[90]

The Woollen Cloth Industry

Dubrovnik's textiles industry was the object of even greater state attention than shipbuilding, though there was never as much to show for it. The Ragusans had, of course, long been trading profitably in other people's cloth – buying it in England, Flanders or Italy and supplying it to Balkan customers. There was also a modest indigenous cloth industry in Dubrovnik, producing rough woollen cloth (called *raša*) made from Bosnian wool for the citizens' own needs. The government was dissatisfied with the standard of this cloth and decided on action to improve it. Although the state still left the production to private enterprise, it began to support it with loans and to promulgate new standards, and at the end of the fourteenth century instituted formal 'crafts' to be responsible for overseeing the industry – there was, for example, an *ars saponarie* for the washing of wool, an *ars tinctorie* for dyeing and an *ars fustanorum* for weaving.[91]

The ability to ship into Dubrovnik large quantities of fine Spanish wool transformed the potential market, which might now include those in Dubrovnik or elsewhere in the Balkans who wanted good quality garments without wanting to pay what was demanded for English or Italian cloth. It was soon recognised, however, that Dubrovnik did not have among its own citizens anyone with the necessary expertise for large-scale production of high-quality woollen cloth. Accordingly, in 1398, a dyer from Augsburg was lured to the city. He was given a house for his dyeing factory and other equipment for preparing the cloth. Foreigners who brought cloth to him for dyeing were granted exemption from customs dues.

It was, however, the arrival of Paulo Cornello and his half-brother Pietro Pantella from Piacenza which transformed the industry. Cornello was promised a fully equipped factory for the production of cloth as long as he worked exclusively for the state and did not buy in foreign cloth. He was also given a loan of 2,000 ducats to buy wool and all the privileges attached to Ragusan citizenship. It was a ten-year agreement during which time he would pay no taxes on wool or anything else he needed. But Cornello died in 1417, and it was left to his half-brother to carry out the project – the loan being increased to 5,000 ducats, repayable after ten years.

Pietro Pantella was not the only foreigner to benefit from state incentives to produce or treat cloth, but he was by far the most successful and – as the accounts of the Ragusan historians testify – the most famous.[92] Pantella's main factory was built at Pile, though there were several smaller establishments. The Pile factory had three floors. On the ground floor the wool was washed and dyed. On the first floor it was spun into yarn and woven into cloth. On the second floor it was stretched and dried. Pantella's factory also washed and dyed wool for other craftsmen and merchants. It was a large employer of both master craftsmen and unskilled labour drawn from the Dubrovnik hinterland. In 1430 Pantella duly repaid his loan to the state and became a full citizen of Dubrovnik, but he also ceased production. Instead, he concentrated on trading opportunities, buying finished cloths from individual Ragausan weavers and selling them on. He also invested heavily in shipping, becoming owner or part-owner of some fourteen vessels which carried salt, oil, fish, building materials, wool, dyes and grain. He bought commercial property in the city – a pharmacy and another shop. He died, an adopted Ragusan of great distinction, in 1464.[93]

It was the processes for treating the cloth that were potentially most profitable and in which the Ragusan government as a result took greatest interest, though whether this interest was advantageous for the industry is more open to question. In 1435, fearing the effect of competition from private dyeing works on the state works, the government ordered that cloth producers must have at least half their cloth dyed in the state works or be fined. In 1442 private dyeing works were formally banned, though after intense opposition they were allowed to continue at Rijeka Dubrovačka and Gruž. In 1451, when the state-owned washeries were under-utilised, the government decided to levy a special tax on wool not washed in them. External circumstances were also a problem. So in 1463 all cloth workshops outside the city walls were destroyed for reasons of security at this time of crisis. In fact, the cloth industry recovered from this blow. But by 1481 the government was once more anxiously discussing ways to reverse decline. It was the same story in 1499 and 1504. The government reaction to setbacks was to involve itself ever more closely and to impose more controls. To judge by the anonymous Ragusan chronicle, it was an attitude which found echoes in popular feeling. Thus in 1510, the chronicler records, the wool craft fell into difficulties because 'dishonest' people had produced cloth of poor quality which resulted in Ragusan cloth falling in price and precipitated a general economic collapse.[94]

The Ragusan government continued to complain about the state of the industry and to find ingenious though ineffective ways of promoting it. In 1530, for example, the Ragusan Great Council forbade the production of hats from (high-quality) white or coloured wool. In the future they had to be made of coarse leftover fabric so that the best wool could be better used. State officials even prowled around on feast days confiscating any offensively decorative headgear that happened to be worn. In 1537 another blow to the ailing cloth industry was delivered by the forced destruction of all the factories outside the city walls because of fresh threats to Dubrovnik's security.[95]

For at least a century before this the industry had taken on increasingly corporatist aspects. In 1416 the Great Council had decided on the appointment of three officials to oversee the wool craft and in 1432 their extensive duties were laid down in considerable detail. The officials were to go three days each week to the place appointed and give judgement in cases of infraction of the rules relating to cloth production. A clerk and two assistants were appointed. This was the beginning of the 'Chamber' of the wool craft. The work and number of officials were increased by a decree of 1459, which marked the beginning of the so-called 'New Chamber' that later formed a separate and more powerful body. Its numbers were further increased in 1470. The government was determined to ensure respect for these officials whose tasks it regarded as of the greatest importance. So in 1530 it was decreed that the members of both Chambers would henceforth automatically become members of the Senate. The Wool Chambers seem to have adopted most of the functions of ensuring high quality and good order in the craft which would otherwise have fallen to the relevant confraternity; though the government appointed the *gestaldus* (or 'head') and judges of a wool craft confraternity in 1429, nothing more is heard of it. Only after the first collapse of the industry in 1481 did the different crafts involved – combers, carders, weavers, hatters and so on – obtain their own confraternities, and these remained quite closely regulated by the state.[96]

The reason for the long-term failure of the Ragusan wool industry in retrospect appears simple: whereas shipbuilding was both integral to Dubrovnik's successful shipping industry and drew upon traditional Ragusan skills, the making of cloth did neither. It was an artificially developed business, existing in the shadows of state intervention. It was also excessively vulnerable to uncontrollable external factors – both local crises requiring the destruction of Dubrovnik's cloth factories and international crises, like the great Catalonian revolt of 1463, which threatened the supply of good imported wool.[97]

Ragusan Consumption – Corn and Wine

In spite of its overwhelming social, economic, cultural and of course political importance within the Ragusan Republic, the city of Dubrovnik was also dependent on the surrounding countryside, the more distant territories of Konavle and Pelješac, and the islands. From these areas came workers for its crafts and industries. But they also provided it with such agricultural products as did not need to be imported from outside the Republic.

Diversis gives a lively description of what was for sale in Dubrovnik's markets, shops and streets: wine, bread and oil; meat (in the meat market); vegetables, fruit and flowers (brought in every morning by peasants in their baskets); and firewood (piled high on the backs of sellers, whom Diversis likened to camels).[98] It was, however, the first two of these products – bread and wine – that most preoccupied the Ragusan government.

The shortage of homegrown grain and the means employed to supplement it have already been described. The territory of the Republic was generally much better suited to viticulture than cereals, and the authorities engaged in a vigorous, continual and only partly successful strategy of trying to ensure that vineyards did not displace cornfields. The government initially sought to reserve for cereal production all cultivable land in the territories which were acquired in the fourteenth and fifteenth centuries. On Pelješac viticulture was initially prohibited, but later a limited permission was given. Vineyards quickly established themselves, and by the first half of the fifteenth century covered 300 hectares with private gardens (also largely given over to vines) another 100.

The prohibition against vine growing was more rigorously maintained along the Slano coastline. Householders there could only commit 400 square metres around their homes to vines; anything in excess of that would be ripped up by commissioners appointed for the purpose. In this area, perhaps a tenth of the land was devoted to vine growing, with 700 hectares left for cereals. In Konavle, where the same broad approach was followed, vineyards and gardens were allowed to cover some 350 hectares, leaving about 1,900 for grain.[99]

From the fourteenth century at least, Dubrovnik was an important centre for the production, consumption and, indeed, export of wine. (It also imported some rarer, foreign wines.)[100] As with the production, supply and sale of corn, the Ragusan government took an intense interest in every stage of the wine trade. Indeed, the government even decreed the date on which the grape harvest could begin and appointed officials to ensure that there was no premature picking. The state itself owned some of the taverns in which wine was sold; others were the property of religious houses and private citizens. Their prices were regulated, as were their hours of opening. A duty was levied on the wine sold there, which – when farmed – provided a useful sum for the state treasury.[101]

The vineyard owners of the Astarea – most of whom rented out their property to tenants – enjoyed the valuable privilege whereby wine from the islands and other territories was altogether excluded from the city. (Exemptions were only made for the religious orders or in times of dearth.)

The government was thus especially preoccupied with the prevention of smuggling.

Once the initial prohibition against viticulture had been eased, it was from the excellent wines of Pelješac that the main challenge to the Astarean local monopoly came. This was reflected in the obligations placed on the count of Ston, other officials and the surrounding population. The inhabitants of Broce (a village near Ston) were responsible for searching any ships they thought might be carrying wine for export. Anyone resisting them would be fined 500 *hyperperi*. Three special 'captains' were also paid by the Republic to patrol the coastline in armed ships. Only the count of Ston or another senior official could license the export of wine from Pelješac to the mouth of the Neretva and the Croatian Krajina, that is outside the Republic's frontiers. Copies of all such permits must subsequently be presented by the officials on their return to Dubrovnik.[102] As always in such matters, ultimate responsibility rested with the central government of Dubrovnik.

NINE

Ragusan Society: Dubrovnik's Social Structure and *Mores* (c. 1300–c. 1667)

I. The Political and Commercial Classes

Nobles and Citizens

Jakov Lukarević had no doubt that the Ragusan Republic was ruled by what he called an 'aristocratic government'.[1] But did Dubrovnik's ruling class really qualify as an aristocracy? In fact, Philip de Diversis had asked this very question and answered it, at least to his own satisfaction, more than a century and a half earlier:

> Perhaps somebody will wonder why I called the patricians [of Dubrovnik] merchants, since nobility is contrary to trade? I would like such a person to know that because of the infertility of the region of Dubrovnik and the large number of inhabitants, there were such small incomes that no one with his family could live off his property unless he was a good deal wealthier than the rest. So they took to trade, and fathers bring up their sons in commerce just as soon as they grow their fingernails, to use a Greek expression.

To be sure, Diversis voiced some doubts about the money-grabbing mentality which this decidedly materialistic approach to nobility generated:

> It seems, if I dare say so, that [Ragusan] nobles believe and consider that happiness consists of wealth, and virtue in its acquisition and easy accumulation.[2]

By contrast, the intense disapproval which the Ragusan noble class showed towards socially mixed marriages was lauded by the snobbish Diversis as an excellent custom.[3]

Most of the Ragusan patriciate enthusiastically traced their origins to distant times. Like their equivalents in Venice and Split, some claimed descent from the Trojans as well as the Romans. Different chroniclers give slightly different lists of about 150 noble houses, most of which at the earliest period of writing (the fifteenth century) were already extinct. Several patrician houses found in these chronicles their family histories intertwined with Dubrovnik's own: thus the Gradić family claimed to be descended from Vuk Grade, a Bosnian who helpfully betrayed a strategically important tower to the Ragusans in the eleventh century; and the Sorkočević family was portrayed (probably accurately) as having joined the ranks of the Ragusan nobility as a reward for supplying the town with badly needed grain in the thirteenth century – though the Sorkočevićs also claimed at different times to be of both Roman and Epidauran stock. Epidaurum was, in fact, credited by the chroniclers with providing some 10 per cent of Dubrovnik's nobility. Others claimed origins in Italy, Dalmatia, Zahumlje, Bosnia, Hercegovina, Albania, Serbia, Hungary, Istria, Greece and (even more improbably) Spain, England, France and Germany. The tendency to invent fanciful, distinguished ancestry, which had already been present from the time of the Ragusan commune, received a new impulse when the aristocratic Ragusan Republic fully emerged in the fifteenth century. This interest in historical and so political legitimacy was doubtless also nourished by the acquisition of Konavle and Cavtat (the old Epidaurum).[4]

In fact, the Ragusan nobility only emerges from such quasi-legendary obscurity in the early fourteenth century. In 1312 it probably numbered about 300 adult male members. Already, a number of great families clearly predominated. Together these patrician houses (*casate* or *casade*) – the Menčetići, Bodačići, Binčulići, Sorkočevići, Đurđevići, Držići, Gučetići, Krusići, Ranjine, Petranje and Gundulići – comprised between 130 and 180 men.[5] Between the start of the fourteenth and the end of the fifteenth centuries the number of noble families declined – from about 90 at the beginning of the period to about half that at the end. By contrast, the number of individual nobles grew rapidly. This increased birthrate is probably to be explained as the result of a natural recovery after the plague-ridden fourteenth century; at the same time, the surviving families, by inheriting the substantial fortunes of nobles who had perished, could afford to increase in size. The result was certainly dramatic. Thus in 1423, 203 (adult) nobles sat as members of the great Council: by 1442 the number had risen to over 280. It was still 278 in 1510.[6] The increase in the number of patricians was greatly welcomed.[7] Ragusan institutions were accordingly adapted to the new situation. Thus in 1424 the Senate was increased to forty-five, with thirty as a quorum. In 1455 the age limit for entry to the Great Council was raised, as before the Black Death, to twenty – something that was warmly welcomed by the patriciate in the conviction that 'it is a well known fact that every republic is the better governed insofar as its governors are mature and more adorned with virtue.' In 1477 the Senate was further increased to 51 members, with a quorum of thirty-five.[8]

Political influence continued to follow fertility. Assessed according to the number of important offices they held, seven large noble families figured among the most politically influential group in both the fourteenth and fifteenth centuries – the Gučetići, Gundulići, Bunići, Sorkočevići, Đurđevići, Menčetići and Crijevići. These can thus be considered the core of the late medieval Ragusan patriciate.[9]

Dubrovnik was not, of course, alone in being ruled by a patriciate. The other large Dalmatian towns also generated their own principally mercantile nobilities, with which the Ragusan patricians evinced a strong social and occasionally political solidarity. This was evident in March 1462, when it was decreed that if any Ragusan noble married the daughter of a Ragusan non-noble he and his heirs would lose their nobility. An exception was specifically made, however, for marriages to the daughters of nobles from some other 'maritime' (that is, Dalmatian) town.[10] Such arrangements were also, it seems, important to Dubrovnik's Dalmatian counterparts. So in March 1499 it was decreed that in order to keep good relations with the other maritime towns, any Ragusan noble intending to wed the daughter of a maritime patrician family must possess 800 ducats of real estate in Dubrovnik or its *distretto*.[11] The Ragusan patricians were even on occasion willing to intervene on behalf of other Dalmatian patriciates – for example, in June 1398, when a popular rebellion in Split overthrew and expelled the patrician oligarchy, Dubrovnik backed the patricians even though the rebels were acting in the name of Dubrovnik's own liege-lord, King Sigismund.[12]

But strong as the links between the Ragusan and other Dalmatian patrician families evidently were, both contemporaries and later historians have been more impressed by the differences. The Ragusan patriciate was from an early date significantly richer and larger than the other Dalmatian patriciates, and this was doubtless an important factor in preserving Dubrovnik's political autonomy. The Ragusan noble families had in effect created a socio-political virtuous circle: for while their own strength and prosperity helped secure the city's interests, the resultant security allowed the nobles to become still stronger and more prosperous.

The contrast between the fortunes of the Ragusan and the other Dalmatian patriciates continued to be strikingly evident in Dubrovnik's mid-sixteenth century heyday. At that time, Zadar had seventeen patrician noble households, Trogir ten and Split sixteen, but Dubrovnik thirty. Moreover, the Ragusan patricians were clearly much richer. In 1553 an Italian observer found the nobles of Zadar, Šibenik, Trogir, Split and Kotor to be poor, often extremely so, but the Ragusans quite the opposite. In Dubrovnik he encountered 'many individuals and families who have 100,000 ducats and more of income'. Indeed, he concluded that there was 'an infinite quantity of money in Dubrovnik...'[13]

Although by the end of the Republic many in the nobility had indeed become impoverished, it is important not to predate this development.[14] For most of Dubrovnik's history, and certainly at its zenith, the Ragusan patriciate proved extremely adept at sustaining and increasing its wealth. So between 1594 and 1623 – that is, at a time when the first signs of decay had already appeared – patricians still provided about half of all the investment channelled into Dubrovnik's five Balkan colonies.[15]

However closely they associated with the other Dalmatian patricians, the Ragusans did not behave like them in politics; perhaps because of their prosperity, their collective self-confidence was such that they never felt compelled to do so. By contrast, elsewhere in Dalmatia there were bitter disputes between the nobility and the citizens. On Hvar a bloody struggle broke out in 1510 and lasted for four years, encouraging disobedience to Venetian rule elsewhere in Dalmatia. Trogir and Šibenik were also riven with social unrest.[16]

The problems of Split were even more ruinous. In Split, in contrast with Dubrovnik, the 'closing' of the Great Council to commoners in 1334 initiated a series of bitter disputes in which, once the city came under Venetian rule in 1420, the Serenissima itself became involved. The Venetian counts were inclined to promote the interests of the wealthy commoner families (as in Dubrovnik, called 'citizens') against those of the nobility, partly perhaps because of a genuine sense of equity but also in order to divide and rule. The observation of the Venetian count Marco Barbarigo on the situation in Split in July 1568 is worth recording, because it precisely describes what Dubrovnik happily avoided:

> Between the men of Split there exists that hatred which prevails in most of the Dalmatian towns. This hatred comes from the fact that the nobles have their own council in which they choose public representatives every three months. These nobles are poor, as far as their fortunes go; but puffed up with empty ambition they envy the citizens, who because of their crafts and trade live much more comfortably... On the other side these [citizens], since they are not allowed to meet and choose some officials, cannot with a peaceful spirit tolerate the privileges which the nobles have on the basis of the old law of this city.[17]

The closure of the Ragusan nobility to all but a few foreign entrants for some two centuries – and the closure of its polity to non-aristocrats for almost five – did not have the effect of stirring up any similar resentment among the non-noble inhabitants. After a time, the very impossibility of a commoner joining the patriciate's ranks probably made for a certain acquiescence and so stability. (It is thus perhaps significant that the closure of the Ragusan Great Council to commoners was more complete than in places like Kotor and Šibenik, or indeed than Venice.) In any case, in Dubrovnik the tasks of government were, as has been noted, not particularly well-rewarded and often dangerous. Even the ordinary burden of political decision-making within the Ragusan system, particularly for senior patricians, was inconveniently heavy. It has been calculated that in the second half of the fifteenth century the Great Council annually met 80 times, the Senate 160 times and the Small Council more than 200 times. So a noble who was a Senator could annually expect to attend 250, and if also a member of the Small Council, 450 sessions. Such duties left little time for business or leisure. Non-nobles might, therefore, well prefer to ignore politics and content themselves with making money alongside the patricians and enjoying a similarly comfortable, cultivated lifestyle. Significantly, it was with the admission of new families into the patriciate in the seventeenth century that the seeds of the future factional conflicts were sown. Once the old barrier had been breached dissent began – though even then it was limited to the ranks of the patriciate, not to the excluded citizenry.[18]

The only known attempt to overthrow the Ragusan nobility's monopoly on power in favour of the rest of the citizens cannot be taken very seriously – though because of the distinguished identity of its originator it sometimes has been. In the spring of 1566 the man who would subsequently be seen as Dubrovnik's greatest literary genius, Marin Držić – then in Florence – wrote to Duke Cosimo I de' Medici proposing a Florentine protectorate over Dubrovnik. In order to justify this project, he levelled a series of tendentious complaints against the Ragusan patriciate. The patricians, claimed Držić, were stingy in their expenditure on diplomatic missions. They were foolish to forbid Dubrovnik's ships to sail the Western Mediterranean (in fear of seizure by the Spanish for engagement in the anti-Ottoman struggle). They paid insufficient attention to the upkeep of Dubrovnik's merchant fleet. They neglected the Republic's defences. They had banished Franciscans of irreproachable morals from Dubrovnik. And all these shortcomings stemmed, the poet argued, from rule by a clique of 'twenty monsters, unarmed, mad and incapable of anything'. Držić's plan (if such a hare-brained scheme can be so dignified) was that, after a papal excommunication of Dubrovnik's government had been obtained (or forged) so as to justify the attack, Duke Cosimo's soldiers would infiltrate the Republic in small groups and then, at a given moment, effect a *coup*. Power would henceforth be shared, under the duke's overall authority, between Ragusan nobles and the wealthier citizens. Not surprisingly, Cosimo de' Medici never seems to have responded to this proposal, and Držić himself died in Venice the following year.[19]

The disadvantage of the caste-like nature of the Ragusan patriciate was not, truth to tell, that it provoked internal political opposition, but rather that it resulted in a steady and ultimately disastrous shrinkage in numbers.[20] This numerical decline only became acute after the losses incurred as a result of the 1667 earthquake. But the trend was already evident well before then. From the middle of the sixteenth century to its end the numbers of nobles entering the Great Council each year fell sharply from an average of 123 to 77. The process continued, and as a consequence the total number of Great Council members declined from 376 in 1600 to 177 in 1650.[21] Just as in the fifteenth century when the patriciate was expanding, so in the seventeenth century as it contracted, the institutions of the Republic were adapted to the change. Thus in January 1639 the quorum for the Great Council was reduced to thirty.[22] In April that year the minimum age for entry to the Senate was reduced from thirty to twenty-five.[23] Finally, a revolutionary decision was made by 52 to 51 votes in the Great Council on 26 March 1662. It was then agreed that if any of the noble houses should become extinct ('Which God Forbid!'), a family drawn from Dubrovnik's 'honoured citizens' or from among foreign nobility could be accepted into the patriciate, by votes of a majority of the Small and Great Councils and of the Senate. Such a family must be of legitimate birth; its daughters and sisters must be unmarried; and its brothers should not have divided up their property – in other words, it must be in a position to make the maximum social and financial contribution to the interests of the Ragusan patriciate.[24]

The milestones of patrician decline came and went in depressing succession. In November 1663 the quorum of the Great Council was reduced by ten.[25] In January 1664 was passed a law – which would only take effect, and then in modified fashion, after the earthquake – that a citizen who donated 10,000 gold pieces to the Republic and was acceptable to its three councils could be admitted to the patriciate. But no more than ten families were permitted to enter at one time.[26] January 1665 once more saw the reduction of the age for entry to the Great Council from twenty to eighteen.[27] In April 1666 the patriciate was actually faced, on the extinction of the Lukarević family, with the need to make provision for the entry of new members into its ranks.[28] On 3 November that year in what looks very like a gesture of despair – and one that would never actually take effect – the Great Council effectively abandoned the system of a closed patriciate. By forty-eight votes to forty-two, the Council decreed three changes. First, it ended the prohibition of marriage between nobles related in the third degree of consanguinity. Secondly, nobles were now to be allowed to marry noble ladies from the non-maritime towns. Thirdly, and most fundamentally, Ragusan nobles might henceforth marry the daughters of distinguished citizens (*persone honorate e civilli*) of Dubrovnik, whose fathers had not done manual work, 'unless it will be decided by another order'.[29]

The structure and fortunes of the Ragusan patriciate have been more closely studied than those of the class of wealthy Ragusan commoners, referred to, at least from the sixteenth century, simply as 'citizens' (or, on occasion, the *popolo grosso)*. Limitations on their marriage strategies and exclusion from politics set these families apart from the patricians; but they remained their neighbours, for though branches of the same noble family might choose, understandably enough, to live nearby to one another, the nobility as such did not reside in a separate quarter of the city. This itself doubtless reflected the fact that Ragusan patricians never felt socially or physically threatened – in contrast to their equivalents in Dalmatia and Italy.[30]

The *popolo grosso* seem to have behaved very like their noble counterparts. Thus they developed important interests in shipping and finance; they built fine town- and delightful country houses; they endowed churches and chapels; they even adopted coats of arms, though these lacked the legal, heraldic significance of those of the nobility.

Ragusan commoners also joined confraternities, and the richest citizens became associated with two of these in particular. The senior were the *Antunini*. The confraternity register (*matrikula*, *matricola*), describes the background to the official foundation in 1432. An earlier confraternity of the Holy Spirit and the Holy Saviour had been founded in 1348. It consisted both of members of the greatest Ragusan noble families – Gundulići, Gučctići, Ranjine – and also of people of obviously modest status: there are, for example, several tailors listed among the 'brothers' and many others with the awkwardly transliterated Slavic names that in Dubrovnik betokened lowly origins.[31] By 1431 this confraternity had become somewhat moribund and so it was decided to incorporate it with another confraternity – that of St Peter and St Anthony Abbot. The *gestaldi* and brothers of the confraternities unanimously agreed the merger. The following year the new confraternity's institution was solemnly proclaimed as being performed before God and the Heavenly Host under the protection of St Peter and St Blaise, during the reign of pope Eugenius IV, and in the presence of the Rector, Paskoje Rastić, and his Small Council. Like the other religious confraternities of Dubrovnik, the main functions of the *Antunini* were to promote the practice of piety and charity.[32]

But, equally, it is clear that from the very start of its existence the body had a quasi-public status. This was reinforced not just by the Rector's presence at its foundation but also by the fact that members of Dubrovnik's greatest noble families and the senior Chancellor of the Republic enrolled as brothers. There is, however, a significant gap in the register at the end of this distinguished roll-call before the names appear of what might be described as the 'ordinary' brothers, whose Slavic names and occasional nicknames betoken their plebeian origin. (Later they were separately listed as '*populani*'). While the great figures of the state – the archbishop, other senior clerics, the most distinguished patricians – continue to appear on the register, the non-nobles soon overwhelmingly predominate. These men, about whom all too little is known, were in fact the wealthiest citizen merchants of the Republic. Their subscriptions, donations and bequests allowed the confraternity to acquire property which it rented it out. Its various treasures were stored in the sacristy of the Dubrovnik Franciscans. It was doubtless a reflection of the governing patriciate's estimate of the importance of these people for Dubrovnik's prosperity and stability that the authorities always followed closely the *Antunini*'s affairs. In the last period of the Republic this attention was manifested by the imposition by the Senate, in 1778, of a plan of reform to improve the way in which the confraternity worked. To the very end of the Republic's existence, membership of the *Antunini* was used as a reward for those who made special contributions to the public good.[33]

Then in 1531 the *Lazarini* were formed, very much along the lines of the *Antunini*. The confraternity's register records that in that year on 11 February the 'merchants of the Levant, inspired by love and charity' gathered together to institute the new body and that the decision was confirmed by the Ragusan Great Council.[34] The objectives of the confraternity were described as the 'increase in worship, in consolation of many souls, in the benefit of the poor, in emolument and ornament of the said city of Ragusa'. Two new altars were to be placed in the church of St Lazarus on Ploče, which was to be the seat of the confraternity.[35] There was an obvious appropriateness in this. The medieval cult of St Lazarus is, in fact, based on a pious confusion between the poor beggar of the parable (Luke 16:19–31) and the Lord's friend, the brother of Martha and Mary of Bethany. Thus Lazarus is portrayed in the opening illumination of the *matrikula* covered in angry red sores. The church itself was situated close to the city's leper colony, where doubtless such afflictions were a daily sight. It was also close to Tabor, where caravans from the Ottoman Empire arrived, and where in due course the Republic's quarantine station would be built. The choice of the cult of St Lazarus, therefore, ideally reflected the twin themes of charity towards those in need and trade with the East which defined the new confraternity.[36]

Like the *Antunini*, the *Lazarini* were from the outset regarded as an institution of special public importance. The Senate solemnly confirmed the new fraternity's privileges which in 1536 were set out in a formal statute. The archbishop of Dubrovnik and the bishop of Mrkan were among the glittering male and female noble founding figures. But the bulk of the *Lazarini* were wealthy merchants from citizen families involved with the Levant trade, leaving those trading with the Ponent in the *Antunini*. The government of the Republic continued to take a close interest in both.[37]

Merchant Lives

Perhaps the most important unifying force between nobles and members of the class of rich citizens in Dubrovnik was a common commitment to and heavy involvement in business, above all in overseas trade. Nobles had, as Diversis pointed out, no inhibitions about the pursuit of filthy lucre. This is equally well demonstrated by the career of that distinguished patrician diplomat and friend of the Emperor Charles V, Marin Zamanja. As a young man, Marin Zamanja voyaged extensively abroad on business. Later he and his father-in-law, Stijepo Gradić, invested heavily in a copper foundry on the left bank of Rijeka Dubrovačka; it was run by the city engineer and architect, Paskoje Miličević. Nor was Marin a mere sleeping partner, for it was his special task to buy copper ore in Bosnia and Serbia. Miličević's operation closed in 1513, but Marin Zamanja continued to retain an interest in another Ragusan copper foundry worked by some masters from Bergamo. Moreover, between diplomatic missions he traded on his own account in copper, cloth and grain.[38]

Good breeding was, of course, no more in Dubrovnik than elsewhere a guarantee of good judgement. Some Ragusan nobles' business ventures landed them in severe difficulties. Such, for example – and quite spectacularly – was the case of Frano Lukarević. Frano went into business in Florence with his brother-in-law Luka Sorkočević, a scion of an even more distinguished patrician house. Their firm collapsed, precipitating a long and bitter feud between the two families. Luka later went into business once more, this time with his brother, but again went bankrupt. Nine years later, having fallen into disgrace – this time for his spying – he died in exile in Naples.[39]

The most successful citizen merchants were no less wealthy, and perhaps barely less influential, than their patrician equivalents. The Skočibuha family was certainly the supreme example. The brothers Antun and Stijepo Sagroević – as the family was then known – had flourished as ship-owning sea captains in Suđurađ on Šipan in the early sixteenth century. Stijepo's three sons were also sea captains, and the second of these, Tomo, acquired the *sobriquet* 'Skočibuha'.[40] Following the tradition common to the maritime families of the Republic, Tomo spent his youth at sea, first serving under another captain, then later with his own command. He married another captain's daughter and then settled down to run his shipping business and manage his property. The latter was, indeed, extensive and Tomo substantially improved it – both on the islands (Šipan and Koločep), inland (at Brgat), and most notably in the Pustijerna district of Dubrovnik, where in 1550–1551 he built a fine palace that still stands.[41]

Tomo Skočibuha had three sons, who also went to sea – Stijepo, Rusko and Vice, the last of whom would be the outstanding merchant magnate of his day. The young Vice was serving aboard his brother Rusko's vessel when it was attacked by Algerian pirates. Rusko and ten sailors died in the struggle, and though the ship was saved Vice's nerves were, it seems, shattered by this traumatic experience. He henceforth renounced command of any of the family ships – itself a move so outlandish that it had to be confirmed by twelve distinguished inhabitants of Dubrovnik specially appointed to hear his reasons. Vice's father Tomo died in 1559, leaving large bequests to Ragusan churches, including the Dominicans in whose Dubrovnik church he was buried. Vice now took full control of the family business. He was a well-educated man. He wrote good Italian, and gave ample proof of his cultivated taste in the construction and embellishment of his houses. But above all and always, he was a shrewd and successful businessman. He traded in Italy and throughout the Balkans. He owned *karati* in seventeen different ships, which probably yielded him 6,000 ducats annually. He never lost a grip on his affairs. He kept his own account books. Not even his family escaped Vice Skočibuha's scrutiny: a fortnight before his death, on 26 December 1588, he noted in his account book that his sister owed him 10 ducats.[42]

Another citizen in much the same mould, though one who posthumously acquired a rather different kind of fame, was Vice Skočibuha's contemporary, Miho Pracat. The Pracat family, too, seem to have originated in Šipan, but they had moved to neighbouring Lopud by the time Miho was born there, in about 1522. Even more than Šipan, Lopud was at this time a centre of maritime expertise and wealth. Its enterprising captain-shipowners invested great sums in their own and other vessels. In the sixteenth century they may even have owned a quarter of the Ragusan merchant fleet.[43] In line with tradition, Miho first sailed as clerk in his uncle's ship before commanding his own. After his father's death in 1559 he came ashore to manage his shipping and banking businesses. Miho Pracat employed his huge wealth in building houses on Lopud and on the outskirts of Dubrovnik, at Gruž and at Tri Crkve (today's Boninovo); he owned fifteen properties in all. He was a deeply pious man who, both alive and posthumously, made outstandingly generous provision for churches and for works of mercy. He assisted with the construction of the beautiful little church on the headland of Danče that served the quarantine station just outside the walls of Dubrovnik. He provided for the two churches dedicated to Our Lady on Lopud. He supported the Dubrovnik Franciscans. He also gave money to be used for the ransom of Christians abducted into slavery by the Turks.

After making several wills, Miho Pracat finally died on 20 July 1607. Eventually, after the death of his remaining relations, the whole of his vast wealth went to good causes under the supervision of the Ragusan authorities. The Senate debated long about how to give posthumous recognition to such charity. There was much soul-searching, for the austere, republican spirit of Dubrovnik militated against exalting any individual above his peers. Traditionally only saints or mythical creatures, not ordinary human beings, were commemorated in Ragusan plastic art. As a result of such hesitation, combined perhaps with an equally traditional Ragusan stinginess, an early decision to erect a monument to Miho Pracat in the Franciscan Church was never in fact executed. Only in 1633, long after the death of all members of the Pracat family, was it finally decided to erect a bronze statue of Miho in the courtyard of the Rector's Palace. The project was completed by an Italian sculptor four years later and placed where it now stands, a unique (if artistically undistinguished) tribute to Dubrovnik's model citizen.[44]

Trade was so deeply ingrained into Ragusan society that it was perhaps only natural that a Ragusan should have developed a theory for it. Beno Kotruljević (Benedetto Cotrugli) is most famous for giving, in his 'On Trade and the Perfect Merchant' (*Della Mercatura et del Mercante perfetto*), the first known description of double entry book-keeping. But Kotruljević's treatise contains much else that depicts the life of the Ragusan merchant of his day. Beno himself was born at the beginning of the fifteenth century in Dubrovnik, his family having arrived in the town some 70 years earlier from Kotor. He lamented that he had been compelled at an early stage to abandon his formal studies in order to enter business. But his humanistic training left its mark. He could, he proudly notes at the outset, have written in Latin, though in practice he chose Italian because other merchants would find it easier to understand. Finding himself intellectually dissatisfied with the way in which the business of the merchant was conducted, and convinced that there were rules proper to this 'art' as to any other, he decided to write them down in the treatise that he completed in 1458.[45]

The mercantile life which Beno Kotruljević describes doubtless reflects that lived in Italy as much as in Dubrovnik. Yet there seems something typically Ragusan about the orderly mentality which the work at every turn reveals. Dawdling, for example, is frowned upon 'because for a merchant losing time is the same as losing money'.[46] Debts must be carefully noted down and collected on time, and the author describes in detail the account books and how they should be kept, adding:

> I warn and encourage any merchant that he should be pleased to know well how to keep his books in order, and whoever does not know should have himself taught, or get a sufficient and experienced young man as a book-keeper. Otherwise your trading will be chaotic and a Babylonian confusion – from which preserve yourself for the sake of your honour and your wealth.[47]

Kotruljević advises that merchants should not in their dealings look to the advice of others, but rather trust their own judgement. But such judgement must be applied according to one's resources. So the author divides merchants into three groups. A rich merchant should spread his investments, so as to offset losses in one venture with profits in another. The man with a medium amount of capital is better advised to make the most of it by keeping it all together, though smaller short-term ventures may sometimes be advisable. Someone who has only a little money is better off undertaking to work for a time for another merchant.[48]

Kotruljević also describes the values and lifestyle proper to the ideal merchant. Such a man will be diligent in carrying out his religious duties and upright in his morality. He will always dress modestly. Darker colours are to be preferred. Scarlet is only for weak women, doctors and office-holders. Silk on overcoats and tassels on shoes are excessive, though tasteful hats are acceptable in order to avoid catching cold.[49]

The merchant's house should be situated conveniently close to the port. It must have an entrance which is sufficiently striking to impress those who judge by appearances. The front room will serve as an office where business can be transacted. There should be a spacious, well-lit dining room, a modestly furnished bedroom, a room for the merchant's family and adjoining accommodation for servants. In the cellars will be kept wine and firewood; also below ground, there will be space for stables and warehouses. Above ground, grain is to be stored. The merchant is also advised to have a little study-library, set apart from the rest of the house, where he can read quietly – for (says Kotruljević, the frustrated man of letters) 'this is a glorious and praiseworthy exercise'. The merchant should, besides the town house where he conducts business, also keep two homes in the country. One of these is to serve as a farm from which the household's need for victuals can be met. The other is to serve for leisure, a cool place of retreat for the family and somewhere for the merchant to relax – though not so often as to take him too much away from his business. Within the merchant's household, he must be truly master, sometimes even putting on a salutary appearance of anger that he does not feel, inspiring respect, somewhat aloof, always alert to possible mischief, ever the last to bed and the first to rise.[50]

The Ragusans formed mercantile colonies in different Mediterranean ports, as Kotruljević's own career, ending up in Naples (in fact as the Neapolitan king's chief minister), itself illustrates. But the most geographically distant Ragusan colony was surely that which flourished in sixteenth century London, to which allusion has already been made.[51] The Ragusans of London were there for strictly business purposes. Even those who stayed many years cannot truly be said to have settled. They did not bring their families; nor did they marry English wives, though they sometimes had English mistresses and sired the occasional bastard. As aliens, they did not own their houses, though the properties they leased could be quite substantial.[52]

Most of the Ragusans in London were solid and respectable businessmen, and some prospered mightily. Nikola Nalješković, for example, one of the *Antunini*, established his business in London in 1537, buying and shipping kerseys. By 1540 he had become well established in his Lombard Street premises and from then till his final departure for Dubrovnik in 1566 he was among London's richest businessmen. Another substantial Ragusan figure in the City was Nikola Gučetić. Gučetić, too, traded in kerseys, and by 1570 about a quarter of that trade ran through his hands. He was also a banker and dealt in maritime insurance. Unmarried, living in Tower Ward, he was the richest alien in the London of his day and left nearly 30,000 pounds sterling. Unfortunately, in his old age Nikola Gučetić seems to have paid insufficient regard to the sort of advice offered by Kotruljević: after his death his accounts were found to be in considerable disorder, and from this tragedy flowed. Gučetić's executor, Nikola Menčetić, faced an impossible struggle to satisfy both the old man's heirs and the English Exchequer (which took exception to the deceased's Catholic religious bequests). Menčetić was eventually accused of embezzlement, fled the country, and finally died in a Venetian jail.

This episode was not typical of the Ragusan colony in London. But there was always a sprinkling of adventurers and miscreants. For instance, the Brailo brothers, who by 1512 had already acquired a somewhat shaky business reputation, fell foul of the English ecclesiastical authorities They were only released from their London jail at the instance of the Cardinal Campeggio. Still more murky, though not it seems the fault of Ragusans, were the events surrounding the murder of the young Jerko Đurđević on a boating trip on the Thames one summer night in 1533: robbery was apparently the motive.[53]

The Jewish Community

A significant and distinctive, if at times uneasy, role in the mercantile life of Dubrovnik was played by its Jewish community. The first Jews arriving in the town probably originally came from Provence via southern Italy. Certainly, Jewish traders (dealing mainly in salt and coral), money-lenders and doctors lived and worked in Dubrovnik in the fourteenth century. A backhanded compliment to their prominence at this time was the fact that they were blamed by some Ragusans for the onset of the Black Death.[54]

There later grew up a modestly successful diaspora of Jews in the East Mediterranean region, notably in Albania, Malta and Crete. In Dubrovnik, though, the numbers declined, particularly in the later fifteenth century.

All this changed, however, with the mass expulsions of Jews from Spain in 1492 and Portugal in 1498. Many Jewish expellees used Ragusan ships to escape. (They were sometimes robbed on board – an abuse which the Ragusan government took action to prevent.) These migrants were assured of a warm welcome by the Porte, and perhaps as many as 100,000 Jews and *Marranos* (Jewish converts to Christianity) entered the Empire at this time.[55]

Those Jews who, having disembarked at Dubrovnik, decided to stay there and try to make a living found themselves accommodated by a city that was commercially advanced and fast expanding, but one where primitive prejudices lingered. Such is doubtless the background to an ugly incident which occurred in 1502. That year ten Jews were interrogated in connection with what was said to be a Jewish ritual murder of an old Ragusan woman. Two of the Jews died under torture; four more were later burnt alive; another, a Jewish doctor called Master Moses, was executed by night, for fear that the Turks would demand he be handed over to the Sultan.[56] In spite of this, other Jews chose to continue to live in the city, for the Senate debated in 1510 and again in 1514 whether to expel them. In 1515 it actually resolved to do so. But if this decree was ever in fact enforced it was soon a dead letter, for numbers of Jews appeared once more in Dubrovnik in the 1530s, drawn to the city by large opportunities for profit offered by the current wartime conditions.

Testimony to the significance which Jews had now acquired in Ragusan economic life is provided by the Ragusan government's decision to set up a ghetto. In 1538, because of the dangers of the time, the government renewed permission for Jews to reside within the city walls. Later that year, specific houses were set aside in which they were to live and finally, by a decree of 22 April 1540 all Jews were formally required to live in this ghetto. It consisted of four adjoining houses, below each of which were two warehouses – though the Jewish community could only use six of these, since the other two warehouses were kept at the government's disposal. The street – today's *Žudioska ulica* – was walled off at each end and a gate was built leading onto Placa. This gate was closed at night and the Jews were then forbidden on pain of a fine to go out into the city. The Jewish population grew during the century and in 1589 the ghetto had to be extended: henceforth there was both a 'new' and an 'old' ghetto. Eight hundred gold *škuda*s were levied annually from the Jews for the rent of these ghetto properties, but a number of Jews continued (illegally) to live outside the ghetto.[57]

For most of its existence, the Jewish community under the Ragusan Republic enjoyed at least a fragile tolerance. There was no generalised persecution. Although Jews could not, until the middle of the eighteenth century, become 'citizens' of the Republic, they had long enjoyed the more or less equivalent status of 'inhabitants'. Jews could not individually buy real estate, but in 1652 they were permitted collectively to purchase land for a cemetery at Ploče. (In the course of the eighteenth century, Jews also came to hold property through Catholic Ragusan nominees.) After the 1667 earthquake, when Dubrovnik desperately needed the support of all its remaining wealthy inhabitants, the Jewish community of the ghetto was placed on a more formal institutional footing. By 1699 there had been created a *Schola Hebreorum*, organised very much along the lines of the other Ragusan fraternities, with its own officials (*gestaldi*) and statute. From an early date the ghetto contained its own synagogue: the building, which still functions in *Žudioska* and is claimed as one of the oldest in Europe, was given a fine Baroque interior in 1652. The Jewish ghetto was the only non-Catholic place of worship ever permitted on the territory of the Republic.

The Jews were better treated in Dubrovnik than in most of Christian Europe. But one should not sentimentalise. The Ragusan Republic was a very Catholic state, and the spirit of the Counter-Reformation was always wary of Judaism. At the start of the seventeenth century the philosopher Nikola Gučetić delivered several lectures in Dubrovnik Cathedral on the errors of the Jewish faith, though it is fair to add that he referred to the Jews themselves as his 'beloved brothers'. In 1606 the Ragusan diocesan synod demanded rigorous enforcement of the existing regime of separation between Jews and Christians. But the government was neither overly disposed to follow ecclesiastical dictates, nor inclined to inconvenience such prosperous inhabitants. In any case, Dubrovnik was well aware that the Ottoman Sultan regarded himself as protector of the Jews and this limited whatever measures the Ragusan government might otherwise have been tempted to adopt. Sometimes, though, there continued to occur outbreaks of persecution. In 1622 – in a case which had echoes of that of 1502 – a Jew was accused of involvement in the ritual slaying of a little girl in Pile. He was tried and sentenced to twenty years imprisonment, but was allowed to go into exile after two years and eight months' incarceration. In the course of the trial the Jews were all locked in the ghetto, most probably for their own safety.[58]

The characters of the Jewish businessmen who lived and worked in Dubrovnik are generally indecipherable. Those of the Jewish doctors, of whom a substantial number over the years practised in Dubrovnik, are hardly less so. Amatus Lusitanus, a learned Portugese Jewish physician, was certainly the most famous. He seems to have arrived in Dubrovnik in 1557 or 1558 and engaged in private practice, since approval from the archbishop was required if he was to be employed by the Republic. An opening for such a position arose when one of Dubrovnik's four Italian resident doctors returned to Italy. But the archbishop now proved difficult, and Amatus Lusitanus grew tired of waiting and eventually left for Salonika.

What the Jews really thought of their Ragusan hosts is difficult to judge. But that they were not without admiration or affection for Dubrovnik is suggested by the sentiments of the distinguished Portugese Jewish poet, Didachus Pyrrhus (otherwise, Isaiah Cohen). Didachus lived in Dubrovnik for many years until his death in 1599 and greatly appreciated the city and its inhabitants, as his verse shows:

> *Si tranquilla meae sedes optanda senectae,*
> *Ante alias urbes sola Rhacusa placet.*

> If I had to choose a quiet resting place for my old age,
> Dubrovnik alone, before all other towns, delights.[59]

II. Social Conditions

Families and Households

Poets like Didachus Pyrrhus and other indigenous literary figures waxed enthusiastic about what it was like to live in Dubrovnik, but naturally it was the concrete conditions of family life that primarily mattered to most Ragusans. The Ragusan family, like any other, has to be considered as both a social and a legal entity. Family life was heavily influenced by custom, but it was also lived within the framework of ecclesiastical canon law and of the secular laws established by the Ragusan Republic.

Although the nature and balance of influences on the family law of Dubrovnik have been the subject of some dispute, it now seems clear that the predominant features were Roman, with some significant local modifications – a situation not very different, in fact, to that prevailing elsewhere in the Mediterranean world.[60] In Roman law it was the *paterfamilias*, the head of the family, who unquestionably dominated its affairs. Although there were somewhat greater limits on the powers of the head of a Ragusan family, his powers remained formidable. For example, when a son married, his wife's dowry was brought and handed over to the father, who could then administer it for his own use, while the son and his spouse continued to live under the father's roof.[61] The (male) head of the family's authority was most evident, however, in relation to his wife. In the Dalmatian towns the old Roman law of equality of the sexes, according to which each was able to exercise control over his (or her) property, made way for male dominance. This, again, was particularly important as regards the dowry. Although in theory the wife's property, she had little real control of it. True, she had to give her consent if the dowry was to be alienated. But this was largely a formality.[62]

On the other hand, it is simplistic to regard the Ragusan family as consisting of a juridical forum for a kind of (unfair) battle of the sexes. In reality, family life was more complicated, not least because family structures were more complex. The simple family model – one couple with children – was only characteristic of the poorest Ragusans, such as manumitted slaves, former servants and the poorest craftsmen. Both custom and basic economics ensured that most families were complex, with different generations of adults and sometimes children living together under the same roof (or at least in the same close community). So, for example, a merchant would want to assume control not just of his wife's but his daughter-in-law's dowry in order to accumulate more capital for trade. Farmers would have the same incentive, with the added consideration that the more male family members available the greater the amount of land that could be economically cultivated.[63] There were negative considerations too. Particularly where real estate was concerned, the division of family property into ever smaller units could spell disaster – the decline of substantial farmers to mere free peasants, or free peasants to serfdom, or loss of one's livelihood altogether.

In order to cope with such problems, legally binding associations of father and son or brother and brother would be formed.[64] But no less important was the role of custom. In Konavle, for example, the practice grew up at a very early date of avoiding the division of family lands by ensuring that the eldest son inherited everything, while the other brothers could only stay living in the family home as long as they remained unmarried. Similarly, although the practice was forbidden by canon law, the *Konavljani* encouraged marriage by a widow of her late husband's brother. The aim was both economic and humane: it ensured that no new person came to place a burden on the household and that the children of the previous marriage were properly cared for. Such customs, aimed at preserving the integrity of the family estates at all costs, were particularly rigorously practised by the so-called 'Great Houses' (*Velike kuće*), the gentry families of the district.[65]

Marriage in the Ragusan Republic was thus certainly not something to be undertaken lightly, especially by patricians. This is made very clear by Philip de

Diversis's detailed account of the whole involved procedure. The process of 'courtship' between two extremely young people was carried out by an intermediary, so that the indignity of personal rejection was avoided and, doubtless, the precise terms of the arrangement coolly calculated. After several years in which the betrothed hardly saw one another, the bans were published in the Cathedral a week before the wedding on 'wedding yeast day' (so-called because this was when the yeast was prepared for the wedding cake). On the same occasion an intended patrician bridegroom would send gifts to most of the nobility and to state officials; a second set of presents had in the past been sent too – delicacies like jellied pork and roast chicken, with bottles of wine – though by Diversis's time this custom had fallen into abeyance among all but the very rich. On the wedding day itself the bridegroom went in procession, accompanied by friends, relations and musicians, to collect the bride, on whose finger was placed a ring and on whose head a silver and gold filigree crown. She was then accompanied by two older female relations, one of whom carried her train. After the wedding in the Cathedral, the bride was escorted to her new husband's house, where traditionally she was given honey, butter and a candle to take to her room; as she entered she would kick over a saucer of milk and water (though by Diversis's day this was frowned upon as a pagan custom). Nor was there just one wedding feast, for a week later a second banquet was given by the wife's relations at which she was expected to tell them about her new life.[66]

Faced with such an elaborate and expensive prospect, it is hardly surprising that both sides of the new family intended to obtain the best possible financial terms. These were influenced by two factors which the Ragusan patriciate accordingly did its best to influence – namely, the general level of dowries and the size of the pool from which eligible spouses could be drawn.

Indeed, the dowry's importance to the economic and social life of Dubrovnik meant that dowries and the associated wedding expenses were closely regulated from a very early date. In 1235, almost forty years before the Dubrovnik Statute, an *Ordo de Dotibus et Nuptiis* was therefore enacted. This ordinance prescribed a maximum dowry of 200 *hyperperi* and 10 ounces of gold; it also laid down that the wedding festivities must not last longer than a day. In 1272 the maximum dowry for a noble's daughter was doubled to 400 *hyperperi* and for daughters of non-nobles to 150 *hyperperi*. But these limits were regularly breached. In the fourteenth century, after the Black Death depleted the ranks of noble daughters and so increased the available capital, dowry sums spiralled. It became not unusual for them to consist of several thousand *hyperperi*, as well as expensive jewellery. The government intervened with repeated prohibitions against excess. In 1423 it promulgated a limit on dowries of 2,300 *hyperperi* (1,600 in cash and 700 in clothes and ornaments).[67] In 1446 it raised the limit to 2,600 *hyperperi* (1,600 in cash and 1,000 for clothes and ornaments).[68] Only in the mid-fifteenth century did the level of dowries stabilise and, judging from the new lower limit of 1,900 *hyperperi* set in 1460, start to fall.[69] But the authorities continued to bemoan the problem. In June 1504 the Ragusan government was still worrying: 'Seeing and considering that human cupidity is so much increased that every day people contract matrimony only in search of money, and the last concern of young people who get engaged is about the origin, goodness, customs and other parts that they should look for in the young woman', the patriciate resolved to seek a special decree from Rome supporting the current Ragusan limits on dowries.[70]

The government's determination to limit the strain on the pockets of the fathers of brides was understandable for wider demographic reasons too. If marriage became too costly there would be too few weddings and so too few young Ragusans to increase the Republic's prosperity and promote its interests. Indeed, the government was willing to make an exception to its laws designed to maintain the habitation and security of outlying districts in order to assist. Nobles were thus allowed to alienate their property in Primorje and Pelješac so as to pay for dowries.[71]

This collective concern of the Ragusan patriciate for the birthrate undoubtedly mirrored that of the great majority of individual patricians, and indeed wealthy non-patricians. Only by producing sufficient (preferably male) offspring could the line be continued and the family firm or estate supplied with those required to manage and enhance it. The ideal combination from an economic point of view was marriage between a man old enough to have accumulated some capital and a girl young enough to bear many children. Beno Kotruljević thus considered that the ideal marriage was between a man of twenty-eight and a girl of sixteen.[72] According to Philip de Diversis, most noblemen married girls of fifteen or sixteen, after betrothals of between two and five years.[73] In 1458 it was decreed that no Ragusan man might marry a Ragusan (or any other) woman until he was twenty and she fourteen. Infraction would cost the miscreant bridegroom six months in prison or 500 *hyperperi* and similar punishment for the bride's father, guardian or brother. Suitors were also instructed to tell the bride's father of their intentions six months in advance, so that he could assemble the requisite dowry and clothes.[74] This, though, proved unrealistically rigorous, and two years later the age limits for marriage were dropped again for the man to thirteen and the girl to twelve.[75]

The desire for offspring was a fundamental social imperative. Many noblemen would remarry and, if necessary, go on to make a third marriage.[76] In fact, such was the competition for suitable marriages that the government sought to impose some discipline and decorum. In 1429 the authorities found it necessary to act against 'criminal men of bad condition' contriving secret marriages without the parents' knowledge, which were 'against good customs and [were] a great danger to the city'.[77]

A serious complicating factor in the pursuit of marriage strategies was, of course, the need, if one were of noble stock, to find a spouse from one's own class. The available pool of spouses was strictly limited. This was particularly so after 1462, when Ragusan nobles were formally prohibited from marrying commoners. The pressures were even greater by the later sixteenth and early seventeenth century, when the number of nobles was in evident decline. The result was intermarriage and a consequent concern with the canonical limits on consanguineous unions.

From the start of the sixteenth century, the Ragusan Great Council prohibited marriages within the third 'degree' of consanguinity (for example, between third cousins). The Council of Trent (1545–1563) went further by ordering that marriages could only be joined in the third or fourth degree with special dispensation from Rome. In 1566 Dubrovnik accordingly empowered the bishop of Ston to seek from the pope special permission for the Ragusan nobility to contract marriages within the third and fourth degrees, noting that because of the reduced number of nobles 'almost all of us are joined in the third or fourth degree of consanguinity and affinity'. The mission was presumably unsuccessful, since the number of consanguineous unions fell sharply. But in 1666, on the eve of the great earthquake, the Great Council returned to the issue, declaring void the 1535 decree against marriages within the third degree of consanguinity.[78]

Both social realities and the law which reinforced them ensured that life in Dubrovnik was lived in a man's world. Naturally, the principal task of most Ragusan women was the timeless one of organising the households in which they lived. But some wealthy women engaged in business. The law of Dubrovnik allowed this, though it also limited the credit they could borrow to five *hyperperi*. This did not prevent some women making large investments, buying and selling property or renting out land for cultivation.[79] Widows were freer to dabble in such matters than married women who, as has been noted, had most of their wealth tied up in dowries which were under their husbands' effective control. Thus Nikoleta, daughter of Klement Gučetić, brought a substantial dowry of 3,000 *hyperperi* to her marriage with Jakov Sorkočević.

When he fell ill she became his agent and, after his death his executor and heir. Her enjoyment of this considerable fortune was, however, interrupted when she was accused by the government of Dubrovnik of falsifying her late husband's will. Imprisoned and then sent into exile for five years, she returned in 1396 to continue the management of her substantial properties and died one of the wealthiest women in Dubrovnik. A contemporary, Filipa Menčetić, had a less colourful but equally successful career. The daughter of a very wealthy *Kotoranin*, she married Marin Menčetić, who predeceased her, as did their son Toma. Filipa was regularly to be found engaged in putting her fortune to good use in various business ventures.[80]

But these two careers were, it has to be said, exceptional. Moreover, Nikoleta Sorkočević's troubles suggest that the freedom to act as an equal in the rough and tumble world of Ragusan life was for a woman a mixed blessing. In any case, not even widows enjoyed real equality with men. A widow could only inherit a life interest in her late husband's property.[81] The government of the Republic maintained a paternalistic scrutiny of widows' financial decisions. In January 1458, for example, 'because it is to be seen from experience that widows in their liberty often make acts which dispossess them of their possessions', it was decreed that strict limits should placed on their ability to alienate their property.[82]

Glimpses of Dubrovnik's women are few and, with just a few exceptions, stereotypical. They clearly had an excellent reputation for piety. Diversis notes that the Ragusan ladies were extremely devout and regularly went to confession.[83] According to Jakov Lukarević, the ladies of Dubrovnik dressed modestly and the young girls never appeared in public.[84] There was, in any case, no excuse for improper male flirtatiousness, because a Ragusan noble woman's marital status was clearly distinguishable by the fact that patrician wives wore earrings (called by the Slavic word *obozi* and attached not directly to the ear lobe but on a thin silver chain, called *kličak*); their non-noble counterparts simply wore a ring.[85]

Ragusan poets usually employed stylised epithets and similes to describe the charms of the women of their Republic, and consequently these are not in fact very revealing.[86] Foreign observers might reasonably be expected to give a more objective assessment, though naturally opinions and tastes differed. Pietro Casola, a canon of Milan, on a pilgrimage to the Holy Land, arrived in Dubrovnik in 1494. Canon Casola remarked in his notes on Ragusan women's peculiar costume which he though was extremely respectable, with swathes of cloth covering them from throat to toe. Although there were pretty women wearing plenty of jewellery to be seen in the city on feast days, these, he observed, as a general rule stayed demurely in their homes.[87] A French diplomat who arrived in Dubrovnik in 1573 found the Ragusan ladies very pious and modest, not receiving visitors and never dressing in silk except on their wedding days.[88] Another visiting Frenchman, in January 1658, similarly remarked on the Ragusan women's distinctive dress, but he considered that it made them look extremely ugly because they were covered in so much cloth. These well-wrapped ladies were, not surprisingly perhaps, usually taken around the city in litters.[89] Indeed, their skirts were so wide that when two of them met on foot in one of Dubrovnik's narrow streets there was no room for one to pass the other.[90]

There was no practical need for girls in Dubrovnik to receive much formal education beyond what was required to make them eligible spouses. But there were evidently exceptions, because some patrician women are known to have been active participants in Dubrovnik's intellectual life – for example, the wife and female friends of the Ragusan philosopher Nikola Gučetić, who are portrayed in two of his treatises (on Beauty and Love) as engaged in cultured discourse about aesthetics at Nikola's villa in Trsteno.[91] Of these ladies, most is known about Cvijeta Zuzorić. Cvijeta was clearly something of a bluestocking, able to hold her own in the most cultivated intellectual company. But she was also, it seems, the greatest Ragusan beauty of her day. Her family had moved from the upper Neretva valley to settle in Dubrovnik in about 1400. Her father was a successful merchant who, like many others, went to live in the Ragusan colony in Ancona in order to better supervise his Italian business ventures. The whole family received an excellent education there and in due course Cvijeta married a Florentine patrician merchant. She and her new husband returned to live in Dubrovnik, and Cvijeta now quickly distinguished herself both by her brains and looks. Nikola Gučetić described her loveliness as such that not even the most skilled artist could depict. The poet Dinko Zlatarić was similarly entranced and dedicated poetry to her. Cvijeta may herself have been a poetess, though none of her verse survives. In 1577 her husband's business went bankrupt, and after various humiliations the couple left Dubrovnik forever in 1583. Her beauty's reputation was undiminished by these trials, however, and in Italy the famous poet Torquato Tasso dedicated poems to her. She died at the great age of 96, but the reputation of this ideal of Ragusan femininity lived on till the end of the Republic, and indeed beyond.[92]

Cvijeta Zuzorić was, though, hardly a typical representative of Ragusan womanhood. It was generally understood that a Ragusan lady's place was fairly and squarely in the home. But equally, running a Ragusan household – often comprising several generations and even in-laws under the same roof – was a formidable undertaking. Consequently, few patrician or indeed well-to-do non-patrician Ragusan households could have functioned without their staff. In the early middle ages these would have mainly consisted of slaves. The Dubrovnik Statute of 1272 contains detailed provisions relating to the institution of slavery. A man was not permitted to beat another's slave, but he could recapture and then beat one of his own. It was envisaged that a slave could sell himself back into serfdom, which implies the possibility of an element of choice in the decision to abandon one's liberty. Slaves who had been emancipated could still be called upon by their former masters to perform a range of services and could be beaten if they refused to perform them.[93] Alongside the domestic slaves worked free servants, and as time went by the latter predominated. Servants were paid a wage, owned property and even made investments of their savings. They would be engaged for a fixed period. During this time they were bound to their masters and the Ragusan criminal law reinforced the obligation. For instance, on 7 December 1359 the Great Council decreed that servants who ran away from their service would be fined five *hyperperi* and that any new master receiving a runaway would be subject to the same penalty.[94] Public proclamations against named servants who had fled their masters' service were regularly issued by the authorities.[95] Most Ragusan domestic servants were, naturally enough, women. At the end of their period of service they could expect to receive a dowry, which might include a modest cottage. This tradition continued to the very end of the Republic.[96]

Health and Welfare

Whatever their social standing, all Ragusans shared a common interest in the health of the community. Philip de Diversis thought that the climate of Dubrovnik was extremely healthy. Especially beneficial was the strong, bracing northeast wind, the *bura*, which helped ensure that plagues were less frequent and less severe than elsewhere. It was not unusual, according to the enthusiastic Diversis, to encounter in the streets of Dubrovnik rosy-faced, physically fit people of up to 90 or even 100 years old.[97] (Leaving aside Diversis's exaggerations, it does seem the case that the inhabitants of Dubrovnik lived longer on average than, for example, those of Gradec [Zagreb] and Križevci in northern Croatia.)[98] But perhaps even more important than atmospheric advantages in achieving the Ragusan population's health and longevity were the intelligent measures taken by the government. These were, indeed, among the most advanced of the age.

The medieval Ragusans had, necessarily, a much less clear conception of the nature and causes of disease than their modern equivalents.[99] It is therefore unhistorical to view the various provisions which had an impact on the suppression of illness as aspects of a single policy. That does not, though, detract from the undoubted importance of Dubrovnik's public hygiene measures, which also reveal a clear and rigorous attitude to what constituted the public good. The 1272 Statute, for example, required that windows should not be built out over the sewerage channels into which waste water drained from lavatories and kitchens (both situated by custom in Dubrovnik on the top floor).[100] The revision of 1296 insisted on the provision of sewers three palms (78.8 cm.) wide between adjacent houses.[101] These channels (known in Dubrovnik as *klončine*) drained into closed septic tanks. At some point before the end of the fourteenth century, waste water also began to be drained straight into the sea. Rainwater forming unhealthy puddles in the city streets became less of a problem as the latter were gradually paved. The process was expensive and laborious, so it was also piecemeal. Only in 1407 did the Great Council decide on the eventual paving of all the city's streets with stone or brick.[102]

These streets had also, of course, to be systematically cleaned if the benefits of paving were to felt. After some spontaneous private efforts, the authorities finally appointed in 1415 a staff of four street cleaners at a cost of 60 *hyperperi* a year. It was decreed that each Saturday shopkeepers and householders must clean the street in front of their premises. Saturday was also the occasion when Ragusans were supposed to take all their rubbish out of the city. The main rubbish dumps were at Pile (today's Brsalje) and Ploče (near the church of St Luke).[103]

Dubrovnik's attitude towards the health of its population was extraordinarily enlightened. The authorities appear always to have accepted (though there is no evidence that the thought was ever explicitly articulated) that free medical attention was the right of anyone living on Ragusan territory. From a very early date Dubrovnik had its own city doctor. Between 1280 – when the first doctor (a Jew) is mentioned – and the fall of the Republic, the names of some 230 doctors are recorded. The majority of these came from somewhere in Italy. But there were also Jews, Spaniards, Greeks, Germans and French, as well as a number of Slavs, though few native Ragusans. Physicians fell in medieval times into two categories – 'doctors' who were versed in medication intended to cure internal ailments, and those barber-surgeons who tended wounds and performed surgery. Doctors in Dubrovnik were usually taken on for a year and then if the government was satisfied with their performance the contract would be renewed. Good doctors were much in demand. For example, in 1345 a syndic from Dubrovnik was appointed to go to Venice and try to lure its doctor, Master Niccolino, to the city. If this ploy failed, the syndic was to go as far as Florence to find an alternative.[104] Such doctors were well paid. In the fifteenth century a surgeon might receive 60 and a doctor 1,200 *hyperperi*. The condition for accepting this salary was that the doctor was obliged to treat all who came to him, whether from the city or the *distretto*, and do so without charge. Indeed, if he was later discovered to have accepted payment, the doctor would automatically forfeit his state salary.[105] Physicians could also play a useful role in diplomacy, and Dubrovnik was careful to lend its doctors to those neighbouring rulers whom it wished to please.[106]

As part of its arrangements for universal health care, Dubrovnik was also keen to ensure that one or more pharmacists always operated in the city. Pharmacists appear regularly there from the early fourteenth century. Generous terms were offered in order to attract them from Italy and elsewhere: for example, in 1379 it was decided to find a pharmacist to enter the Ragusan state service on a two-year contract. He would be paid an annual salary of 60 *hyperperi*, have his travel costs defrayed and receive a house and suitable shop from which to trade. Among the oldest pharmacies in Dubrovnik were those operating from the Franciscan friary on Placa and from the city's main hospital/almshouse. But by the mid-sixteenth century there were no fewer than seven chemists in business in the city. They were all subject to official inspection of their medicines by Dubrovnik's doctors and surgeons.[107]

The most serious pestilence to strike Dubrovnik was undoubtedly the plague known as the Black Death. Plague had struck the city before: for example, in 1292 there was an epidemic which lasted two years, whose deadly effects were multiplied by famine.[108] No one was prepared, however, for pestilence on the scale which struck Dubrovnik, like the rest of Europe, in 1348. The disease was evident in Dalmatia in December 1347. It took a horrifying toll in Split, Zadar and Šibenik, then spread to the islands, including Šipan. On 19 January 1348 the Ragusan Great Council debated how to deal with the threat and decided to gather together physicians and medicines, but fatally refused to endorse a proposal to prevent the entry of anyone from Šipan into the city. The plague was soon afterwards raging within the walls of Dubrovnik. By March the town cemetery could not cope with the number of corpses.[109] The chronicler Ranjina gives a detailed and clinically credible account. The plague, which classically took both the bubonic and pulmonary forms, lasted for three years. So great was the terror the disease inspired that there was a risk that the city would be completely depopulated. The Great Council ordered that all who had fled must return or face a heavy fine. Although the number of deaths cannot be calculated with any exactitude – the chroniclers' accounts are both contradictory and exaggerated – it seems likely that at least a third of the population died.[110]

The Black Death left no aspect of Ragusan life untouched. It stimulated, as been observed, the institution of a system of quarantine. It also had a profound spiritual effect.[111] It resulted in a reshaping of the government of the Republic: the Great Council was forced to lower the age of admission of young nobles to its ranks from twenty to eighteen.[112] As elsewhere in Europe, the sharp reduction in the population also had important social and economic consequences. Thus the government looked more favourably upon immigration: Ragusan citizenship was accordingly granted to people coming from other Dalmatian ports and from the Slavic hinterland.[113] But in spite of this influx the labour shortage led to pressure for higher wages, which the Ragusan government did what it could to resist. Thus in January 1351 the Great Council decreed that workers in the vineyards of Astarea receive no more that 40 *follari* a day and those on the islands no more than 45 *follari*. Officials were appointed to see that this regulation was put into effect.[114]

In any case, epidemics continued to strike the Republic. In 1361 the plague returned to last for a year, killing among others the archbishop of Dubrovnik, Ilija Saraka. It was back again in 1363, 1372 and 1374. In spite of the institution of a system of quarantine from 1377, the fifteenth century saw serious outbreaks in 1415, 1422 and 1464 (which lasted for three years). In 1526 the city was left all but deserted, guarded by soldiers and some ships off-shore, in the face of a renewed epidemic which raged for twenty months. It struck again in 1540.[115]

By the time of Diversis, who himself witnessed what turned out to be a fairly minor outbreak, Dubrovnik had developed an elaborate and quite effective system of coping with the plague.[116] This was codified in a decree of issued on 17 March 1439. If two or three cases of plague were suspected, the state officials known as *cazamorti* were at once to inform the Small Council. The town doctors were then to inspect the bodies, and if they confirmed that these were indeed plague victims the Senate was also to be told. The city's safety during this time of vulnerability to outside attack was to be maintained by an armed ship lying offshore and by a special guard of five nobles on land. The expenses of maintaining the state of alert and of all the other measures required to isolate and care for those affected were to be met by the levy of special dues raised on the sale of meat and by a forced loan.[117]

Plague (of various sorts) was not, however, the only serious health problem which the Ragusan authorities had to face. Leprosy is first mentioned in 1272 and there was a flow of pious bequests to help care for the sufferers. From an early date a lepers' house was situated at the church of St Michael *de Cresta* beyond the Ploče gate, on the lower slopes of Mount Srđ. A new house was built for them in 1430. But the city's expansion made this inconvenient, and from 1463 they were moved eastwards, closer to the sea. The lepers were placed under the charge of one of their number who acted as their 'captain' and as their official link with the authorities and with the outside world. The main difficulty was to keep them together and under proper control. They were not, in practice, very strictly separated from the rest of the population, and many seem to have wandered around on their own.[118]

It is likely that the most serious long-term danger to the population's health, though, was malaria. Ston was notoriously badly affected by it and the disease was also a problem in Rijeka Dubrovačka. Judging from the causes of death noted in the oldest extant Ragusan parish register (1637–1647), the worst killer was malaria ('fever'), and some way behind that 'flux'. Together these accounted for 66 per cent of male and 72 per cent of female deaths, whose cause is mentioned. Particularly severe attacks of fever and flux occurred in 1503, 1506, 1517 and 1540; the fever of 1517 lasted three years.[119] In fact, only in modern times was the scourge eliminated.

Not just the sick, but the poor, the very young and the very old, had a call on the resources of the Ragusan state, whose Catholic Christian ethos reinforced both collective concern for good order and individual charitable impulses. Bequests for the poor occur in Ragusan wills from the late thirteenth century. But it was in 1347, on the eve of the Black Death, that it was decided to appoint a committee of nobles to establish a suitable place for a hospice (or 'hospital') for the poor. It was originally planned to erect the building near the church of St Nicholas, where some wooden houses had once stood. But the place was later judged unsuitable. The terrible visitation of the Plague was doubtless responsible for the delay which then occurred. The hospice was finally set up on the southern side of the convent of St Clare in 1356, and the building work was completed soon thereafter. Usually known as the Great Hospice (*Hospitale Magnum*) to differentiate it from others maintained by religious foundations, it did not care for the sick – only the poor, and in practice, it seems, only poor women. (Presumably men were considered able to look after themselves.) Another hospice for the city's poor people was maintained by agreement with the Benedictine abbot and monastery on Lokrum.[120]

Children, like the elderly, could in ordinary circumstances be expected to be cared for by their own families. But where this was impossible, as in the case of orphans and foundlings, the Ragusan state again came to the rescue. The scale of this problem might have been greater had Ragusan fathers acted less responsibly towards their bastards. Ragusan merchants often had sexual relations with girls in Bosnia, Serbia and elsewhere during their long absences from Dubrovnik. The offspring of these unions were generally recognised by the fathers and grew up in their families alongside the legitimate children. The law limited the amount of the family inheritance which could be left to them, but it was customary for noble fathers to give a modest dowry – 100 or 200 *hyperperi* – to their illegitimate daughters. The Ragusan government demonstrated a similar willingness not to exclude bastards from the benefits of citizenship. For example, in the division of the newly acquired territory of Primorje between the nobles of Dubrovnik in 1399, provision was also made for noble bastards. Such attitudes, it should be noted, were not the rule in Dalmatia. Thus in Zadar there were many fewer bequests to illegitimate children and in Budva the law required that they be expelled altogether from the town. Of course, it is possible that the very lack of stigma attached in Dubrovnik to the extramarital sexual liaisons which produced illegitimacy may also have had the effect of increasing its incidence.[121]

But in any case, Dubrovnik addressed the problem of orphans and foundlings (which were likely to be illegitimate) in a practical and compassionate fashion. The inspiration of the decision made on 9 February 1432 by the Great Council to found the city orphanage was explicitly Christian. The orphanage was set up:

> … considering what an abomination and inhumanity it is to cast out little human beings who, because of poverty or for some other reason, are thrown out around the city like brute beasts without knowledge of their parents, for which reason they often die without the sacrament of baptism, or come to some other ill – and for reverence for Jesus.[122]

The orphanage, which was one of the first in Europe, was situated in a house opposite the Franciscan friary on Placa. Two special wheel-like devices were placed on each side of the building. These would be used so that a baby could be placed inside them at any time of the day or night and one turn of the wheel would see it taken safely inside. The Ragusan authorities showed considerable sensitivity by forbidding anyone to question or search a person bringing a baby to the orphanage, on pain of imprisonment. One or two women were to live in and run the place. Public officials were to be told of all new arrivals so as to ensure that they should be speedily baptised, if they had not yet already been so. They were also to try to find a wet-nurse somewhere in the *distretto* who would be paid to feed and look after the child. The orphans, who were to wear a white uniform, could stay in the orphanage until the age of five, when they would be put up for adoption. The institution was supported by alms and, when necessary, from public funds levied from the wool-craft. Any surplus money was to be used to provide for dowries for the little girls when they came of age. If a foundling's father or mother later appeared and swore that the child was theirs, they would receive it back but also have to pay the cost of its upkeep while it had been cared for by the state.[123]

Despite Dubrovnik's interest in ensuring that physicians were available to give free treatment to those needing it, the general assumption was that this treatment would be provided in a doctor's house or that of his patient. Doubtless because of the risk of mutual infection, there was no attempt in medieval times to bring different kinds of sick people together for treatment. But on 26 February 1540 the Ragusan Senate resolved to found a hospital (in the modern sense). It took over the property of the old poorhouse; the elderly women living there were provided with other accommodation. Suitable adaptations were made to the building, by now known as the Domus Christi ('House of God'). The requisite number of beds for hospital patients were installed; doctors, nurses and a chaplain were appointed. Old people with incurable illnesses were no longer admitted, because the emphasis was henceforth to be on cure rather than simply care. One aspect of the old poorhouse that did continue, however, was the Catholic Christian character of the institution. Thus, as soon as a Christian was admitted, he was required to make his confession – though, typical of the relatively tolerant spirit of Dubrovnik, if the patient was of another faith he was allowed just to live according to his own religious precepts.[124]

Rural Life

In the city of Dubrovnik itself, most of the population were directly or indirectly dependent for their livelihoods on industry and the commerce which helped sustain it.[125] But in the countryside surrounding Dubrovnik industrial activity also left its mark. The suburbs of Pile and Ploče were, as has been noted, the sites of factories.[126] Nearby Župa Dubrovačka was an economically mixed zone, with its lime kilns, stone quarry (at Brgat) and state-owned tile factory (at Kupari).[127] It was also agriculturally rich, with good soil and a favourable climate for vegetables, fruit, some livestock and above all, vines. Ensuring that the vineyards of Župa were properly cultivated was a matter of clear public interest: in 1465 the count of Župa was entrusted by the government with the task of punishing the 'great malice and laziness' of the labourers there with fifteen days' imprisonment if they failed to work properly.[128]

As a rule, the further away from the city of Dubrovnik, the more important was agriculture as a source of livelihoods.[129] The social, economic and legal status of those who worked on the land differed sharply, both as between districts and as between periods. In Astarea, from the earliest times, the workforce consisted of a mixture of immigrant Slavs and indigenous labourers. A special category of vineyard workers (*sapatores* or 'diggers') also emerged. The law of Dubrovnik regulated farm labourers' conditions of employment, but life was still extremely hard. Work was from dawn to dusk. Workers would reside in the countryside during the week, only returning to their homes in the city on Saturday night. The government appointed for each area of Astarea trumpeters whose job it was every morning to summon the labourers to work. Officials were also appointed to ensure that the state-imposed maximum wage rates in the vineyard were not exceeded, though, as has been noted, such control became more of a problem after the Black Death. These labourers were the poorest class of agricultural worker. But alongside them there grew up tenant farmer-labourers known as *polovnici* (from *pola*, Croatian for a 'half'). By the beginning of the fifteenth century these had probably taken over from paid labourers as the main workforce.

The first known example of a contract establishing such an agreement dates from 1262, when the abbot of the monastery of All Saints, Pavergen Malamacić, rented out for cultivation a church vineyard and other land at Obuljen to a peasant called Desen. The property was made over to Desen for his own lifetime and the lifetimes of his sons and grandsons. He was obliged to dig the vineyard three times a year, planting 600 vines on it, and in exchange to give the abbot and his successors half of all the fruits of cultivation. As rent for other land outside the vineyard he was to pay in kind 'according to the custom of Dubrovnik'. On All Saints Day Desen was also to give the abbot a quantity of corn and wine.

This model for cultivation was replicated elsewhere, though with many variations. For example, sometimes the tenant would receive two-thirds of the produce and the landlord one third with a money rent. Sometimes a house and garden for the tenant's use were included (though this was particularly associated with agreements amounting to serfdom). Sometimes the tenant undertook to share out the work and the produce with someone else. Such agreements did not require the consent of the landlord. Indeed, *polovnici* could sell their rights to the *polovica* and often did so. According to the laws and customs of Dubrovnik, the landlord was not able to dispossess the tenant unless the latter had failed to cultivate the land properly – and even in this case the testimony of witnesses was first required.[130]

The period during which the *polovnici* were the principal means of cultivation of Dubrovnik's agricultural land was, therefore, one in which a free peasantry enjoyed in legal if not always economic terms a rather satisfactory position compared with most of its equivalents elsewhere in Europe. This situation began to change with the advent of serfdom. Although slaves had, of course, been accepted as a source of labour (principally domestic service) from very early times, serfs as such had not. There was indeed no special word in use in Dubrovnik to describe them. This reflects the fact that serfdom was neither recognised by Ragusan public law nor promoted by the Ragusan state. Rather, it was established by private agreement. Indeed, Dubrovnik's serfdom was, at least until the seventeenth and eighteenth centuries, hardly recognisable as serfdom at all. In the Ragusan Republic, unlike most of the rest of Europe, serfdom did not imply that a man was subject to the justice of his lord rather than the justice of the state. Nor did it imply that he was bound to the land – though for certain incidental reasons he actually might turn out to be. Rather, Ragusan serfdom's defining feature was simply that a man was obliged, by his own or his predecessor's agreement, to serve his lord in perpetuity.

Serfdom appears in Astarea from the mid-fourteenth century. Whether it was the result of economic forces (a shortage of available labour, resulting in extra pressure by landlords on the poorer free peasants) or whether it was connected with the acquisition of the 'new' territories where the government behaved with considerable callousness to the existing free peasants, is unclear. In any case, there arose from about this time increasing numbers of agreements between landlords and tenants by which the lord's own land (known as the *carina*) was to be cultivated by servile work for so many days a year. In the fifteenth century this obligation involved just a few days' annual work, though by the end of the Ragusan Republic it had grown to up to four months. A serf would typically agree before a notary to become in perpetuity the lord's 'man', though the precise degree of servitude this implied might differ. In exchange he might expect to receive a house and a garden to cultivate for himself.[131]

The conditions of the agricultural population of the Ragusan Republic were much affected, at least in the fourteenth and fifteenth centuries, by the circumstances under which particular territories had been obtained. This was, for example, notably the case in Pelješac. Here the remaining free peasant smallholders became tenants of the Ragusan nobility. The government's worries about the security of the peninsula led to its placing tight restrictions on the movements of the peasantry. This was also doubtless what led the government, unusually, to draw up a model formula for the shares of crops to be made over to the landlord. Great efforts were made to bring more peasants to populate and work the area.[132] Under such conditions, it is not surprising that landlords sought to make agreements with the available peasants in order to bind them tightly to their estates. Equally, these same economic and social conditions ensured that most peasants were able to negotiate something more to their advantage. Thus of 153 agreements relating to the cultivation of land in Pelješac between 1333 and 1399, only twenty-three are ones which can be said to create a relationship of serfdom.[133] Around Ston, as in other settlements of military significance, free peasants were settled.[134]

Social conditions in poor, stony, exposed Primorje were not dissimilar from those of Pelješac. Here, too, the formerly free peasants generally lost their property. The unique exception was the village of Lisac, where the agricultural land was divided up for the benefit of the local peasantry, whose direct landlord became and remained the government of the Republic. The men of Lisac paid a unique tribute in kind known as the 'quarter' (*četvrtina*) to the state from what they produced. Primorje as a whole remained for many years a desolate and dangerous district. The inhabitants were, until 1428, even forbidden from building stone houses or using tiles for their roofs, presumably for fear that any solid structure could easily be seized by pirates and other enemies of the Republic and used as bases from which to attack neighbouring Dubrovnik.[135]

Cultivation of land by means of *polovicu* and by mutual agreements to create some kind of serfdom spread throughout all the newly acquired lands – Pelješac, Primorje and Konavle. The same was true of Koločep, Lopud and Šipan where, however, there was a slower growth of serfdom than in Astarea and where there remained a wide mix of tenures.[136] It seems probable that life for most people on the islands was generally better than on the mainland. The experience of Mljet certainly suggests this. There the status of agricultural workers was definitively resolved by an agreement of 24 September 1345, negotiated by the good offices of Archbishop Ilija Saraka and embodied with other provisions in the Statute of Mljet. By this pact, the abbot freed the inhabitants (*universitas*) of the island from all servile obligations to the abbey in exchange for an annual payment. The peasants of Mljet and the abbey (also the independent Vladimirović family) divided up the land between them. But the abbey kept the surrounding reefs (on which sheep could be pastured). The peasants of Mljet were thus confirmed in their status as free smallholders. They jealously preserved this position by insisting that no outsider could acquire land on the island and that any land that came up for sale should be offered first to family members. Although in other respects the community of Mljet saw its privileges somewhat whittled away in the fifteenth century by the Dubrovnik government, these basic social and economic relationships obtained till the end of the Republic.[137]

As in defence of its prized local autonomy, so with that of its inhabitants' social and economic status, Lastovo was at least as resolute as Mljet. One part of the land was held by the community which auctioned some of it – including the reefs – for rent in lots. (The money thus received paid the count's salary, among other things.) The rest of this common land was used for pasture and timber. Some of it was owned by the church, but most was the property of peasant smallholders. Similar provisions to those of Mljet applied to prevent the acquisition of Lastovan land by outsiders. As a result of these safeguards, there remained till the fall of the Republic no serfdom on Lastovo.[138]

Undoubtedly, one of the factors which militated against the imposition of serfdom or, indeed, of large-scale patrician landlordism, on the islands was distance. But another was probably the alternative opportunities for earning a living from the sea. Dubrovnik was so dependent upon its shipping and on the recruitment of reliable crews that its authorities could never insist on its peasant workforce remaining totally bound to the soil. Indeed, on Šipan, Lopud and along the shore of Pelješac, communities grew wealthy and their members acquired new status through their indispensable maritime expertise.

Even where the opportunities for employment and advancement through long- or short-haul maritime trade were limited, fishermen could hope to earn a living without tilling the landlord's soil. The Adriatic, then as now, contained great quantities of excellent fish. For some people, like the poet Petar Hektorović from Hvar, who in the mid-sixteenth century wrote a philosophical dialogue set against the background of a successful fishing trip, fishing was essentially an enjoyable sport.[139] But for professional fishermen it was an intensely serious business. Access to the best fishing grounds was regulated according to an elaborate ritual, at least to judge from the practice at Trpanj on Pelješac. There a priest would be paid by the fishermen of the village to say a special mass of blessing. Then lots would be drawn by little children wearing gold rings and holding bags of relics. The winning lots ensured exclusive access to the best locations.[140]

The most potentially profitable fishing was probably for coral, at least while the natural supplies held out. The first known mention of coral fishing in the waters off Dubrovnik is from 1390, when the coral fishermen of Lastovo were confirmed in their exemption from the Ragusan due known as *arboraticum*. But the business had clearly flourished long before that. Apart from Lastovo, the main sources of coral around Dubrovnik were off Boka Kotorska, along the coast of Konavle, around Koločep and to the north of the little island of Sveti Andrija. As these sources became exhausted, Ragusan ships increasingly often sailed to the Levant to find new ones, but by the mid-eighteenth century the coral business seems to have ended. In any case, its exploitation was, in later years at least, increasingly frowned upon because it was thought (probably wrongly) that the methods used had driven off the sardine shoals from the area – by then also very commercially important.[141]

The variety of activities which comprised rural life had more in common with each other, and with the more hectic urban life of Dubrovnik, than is at first apparent. A network of economic links connected even (relatively) distant outposts of the Republic with the centre. Thus wealth generated in Dubrovnik was invested by Ragusan patricians in property in the *distretto*. Meanwhile, a stream of inhabitants of poorer, distant districts like Konavle sought work in the city. And at the same time the ships which brought riches to the great Ragusan merchant families were both built and manned by the sons of sea-faring families from the islands. At least by the time of its sixteenth century economic zenith, the different parts of the Ragusan Republic had become welded into a single unit in which common material interests were reinforced by a single legal system and a common culture. These in turn were underpinned by a common religious tradition.[142]

TEN

Religious Life: Ecclesiastical Organisation and Spirituality in Dubrovnik (c. 1190–1808)

A well-informed observer, writing in 1815 a memorandum intended to acquaint Dubrovnik's new Austrian rulers with the essentials of life under the old Republic, noted that 'the religion of the Ragusans was from all time that of the Roman Catholic [Church]'.[1] Catholicism is, by its nature, a public as well as a private religion. But this was bound to be particularly so in Dubrovnik. The Ragusan Republic's claim for special consideration by the papacy and the Western powers rested, in the last resort, upon its position as an outpost of Catholicism in a region dominated by infidel Muslims and schismatic Orthodox. Any hope of restoring the sway of Catholic Christianity in the Balkans was understood by the West to be dependent on Catholicism's maintaining its precarious foothold in Dubrovnik. As in its struggles with Venice, this perception was shrewdly and repeatedly exploited by Ragusan diplomacy. But the notion of the Republic as a Catholic state was not just a piece of political opportunism: Catholicism also forged a vital and invigorating cultural link with Western Europe, a bridge across which the ideas and mindsets of the Renaissance, the Counter-Reformation and the Baroque period crossed to this little island of Slavdom. Indeed, without exaggeration it can be said to have provided the core of Dubrovnik's self-definition. True, against those parts of Dalmatia which were under the rule of Venice, it was to the concept of 'liberty' (meaning primarily independence) that Ragusan patriots and poets turned. But against the Turks and the Serbian population of the hinterland it was a jealously exclusive Catholicism that provided an ideological as much as a religious identity for the numerically weak and militarily vulnerable inhabitants. Naturally, this in turn meant that religious institutions in Dubrovnik had a special political significance.

The Archbishops of Dubrovnik

The first and by far the most important of those institutions was, of course, the archbishopric. Beyond the Ragusan state's frontiers, the archbishop of Dubrovnik's authority waxed and, rather more frequently, waned.[2] Within Dubrovnik itself, however, the archbishop had no clerical equal. The historic prestige of his office found most splendid practical expression in his Cathedral. A metropolitan basilica was, it seems, erected once Dubrovnik became the seat of an archbishop at the end of the tenth century. It was a Byzantine-style structure of over 30 metres long and 16 metres wide, with three naves and three apses and (added some time after 1054) extensive frescoes.[3] The exact circumstances in which this basilica were built are obscure and, though surrounded by an intriguing mixture of myth and history, those of its Romanesque successor's construction are barely less so.

The Ragusan chronicles and later Ragusan documents, supported by English sources, record that the Anglo-Norman king Richard the Lionheart came to Dubrovnik in the autumn of 1192. The vessel on which he was returning from the Holy Land was, apparently, caught in a severe storm. Praying for deliverance, he vowed to erect a church wherever he and his shipmates eventually found shelter. In fact, they came ashore at Lokrum. Learning that such a distinguished visitor had arrived on their territory, the leading men of Dubrovnik crossed to greet the king and urged him to come to their town, which he gladly consented to do. Richard then decided that instead of fulfilling his vow by building a church on Lokrum he would do so in Dubrovnik itself and accordingly gave the (impossibly large) sum of 100,000 ducats to build the town's new Cathedral. The role of Lokrum in the king's escape from drowning was, however, commemorated by the abbot of that island's monastery celebrating high mass each year on the Feast of Candlemas (2 February) wearing an episcopal mitre and carrying a crozier.

The archbishop of the day was a Ragusan called Bernardo, who struck up what turned out to be a useful friendship with the king. Several years after Richard's departure, Bernardo had to flee from the wrath of the citizens, possibly incurred because of his failure to prevent the loss of most of Dubrovnik's suffragan sees to the newly elevated archbishopric of Bar. Bernardo found a warm welcome in England and was made Bishop of Carlisle in the reign of King Richard's successor, John.

In spite of the internal contradictions of the different accounts, it seems likely that they do record a real visit by the English king to Dubrovnik. But they certainly exaggerate the scale of his contribution to the building of the cathedral, which must have been largely structurally complete by the time of his arrival. From archeological evidence it is now clear that the main phase of the cathedral's construction can be dated between 1131 (when one archbishop was buried in the old Byzantine basilica) and 1157 (when the epitaph of another was carved on the outer wall of the new Romanesque structure). Perhaps Richard contributed to the new church's long-continuing embellishment. At any rate, the connection was proudly related by Ragusans down the centuries to any visitor who would listen. Equally important in keeping the memory of these quasi-historical events alive was the vigorous dispute which preoccupied successive Ragusan archbishops and secular authorities about the abbot of Lokrum's privilege of celebrating mass on Candlemas with mitre and crozier. The government of Dubrovnik fought in Rome for the abbot's rights and seems to have had the better of the struggle.[4]

The new cathedral was somewhat larger than the basilica it replaced. Its style was heavily influenced by the cathedrals of Apulia. It was the first Romanesque basilica erected in the Eastern Adriatic and it, in turn, had a profound influence upon the ecclesiastical architecture of the whole region. It was undoubtedly a magnificent edifice. It covered an area of some 500 square metres. It was also unusually lofty. About a century after the main structure was completed an upper gallery was added around which people could walk, inside and out.[5]

The form of the Romanesque cathedral can be perceived from depictions of Dubrovnik before the 1667 earthquake.[6] But no one has given a fuller or more evocative description than Philip de Diversis:[7]

> The walls are not built of stone extracted from the ground but, if I may use the general expression, from living rock carved with the greatest care and polished with the greatest attention…
>
> Vaults in the form of an arcade rise halfway up walls in which are carved the faces of different animals. The roof is of lead. The church has three doors. At the great or main door for the most part enter and leave noble ladies, brides and bridegrooms and continual processions. At the second door, which is on one side and a little smaller, for the most part enter and leave the lord archbishop, some of the canons, and elderly noble ladies who listen just inside this door to the services. The church has a main aisle and side aisles, which are divided from the main one by large, stout pillars. The women sit in these side aisles. The main aisle is divided into two parts – one which was in the past called the Holy of Holies but nowadays the Choir, and a second which is laid out for the congregation who stand and pray and

> listen to the word of God. In this latter part are placed the seat of the lord count [the Rector] and benches for other men. In the choir are arranged places for the canons and priests, though sometimes some of the laymen, especially nobles, listen to the divine office there.
>
> At the summit rises the high altar, covered by a beautiful ciborium on four pillars and adorned with a gorgeous altar-piece or icon of silver. Beside the altar is to be found the stone throne on which the lord archbishop sits when he hears or celebrates mass.
>
> ... The whole church is paved with living rock of different colours. On the walls of both side aisles are to be seen figures and stories from the Old and New Testaments. All the windows, both great and small, are made of stained glass depicting the saints... On pillars above the side aisles are built vaults, above one of which is constructed a chapel. This is not so much beautiful as full of holiness, because in it are kept the relics of many saints encased in silver – and, in the first place, the completely white swaddling clothes in which Our Lord Jesus was wrapped when the prophet Simeon took him in his arms... These most holy swaddling clothes are in a crystal tabernacle... Among the other holy relics held and carefully kept there are both arms of St Blaise... On the basis of all this I could say that the chief and metropolitan church is the most magnificent and most beautiful of all.[8]

From a Tuscan – even one writing to please his Ragusan patrons – this was praise indeed.

The high point of the archbishop of Dubrovnik's authority was probably reached under Ilija Saraka, the distinguished ecclesiastical diplomat who helped negotiate the Republic's autonomous status at the time of its transfer of allegiance from Venice to Hungary.[9] A strong tradition held that on his deathbed, stricken by the plague in 1361, Saraka warned the Ragusans never to permit an archbishop to wield the kind of power that he had, for fear that one of his successors might make himself a tyrant. The Ragusan authorities consequently decided that never again would a native of their Republic be allowed to become archbishop.[10] The decision was given formal expression in a decree of 29 August 1409, which also forbade any Ragusan even seeking the position.[11] (Only, in fact, in the eighteenth century did Ragusans again become archbishops of Dubrovnik.)[12] The refusal over the intervening centuries to appoint Ragusans to the archbishopric may have been politically astute in that it ensured that the post was always held by people with no power base in the city, but it hardly made for effective pastoral care. A long line of foreign –

usually Italian – archbishops did little to enhance the archiepiscopal reputation or to promote clerical discipline.

The archbishop of Dubrovnik from late medieval times was more preoccupied with problems of obstruction from the secular power than from his suffragans. Of these, the bishop of Trebinje-Mrkan can hardly be considered a bishop at all in the pastoral sense. He had no effective control over his see, which was mainly populated by Serbian Orthodox, and, as already noted, from the fifteenth century he lived in the security of Dubrovnik. The strategically significant bishopric of Ston was much more important, but it rarely impinged on the attention of Dubrovnik's often absentee archbishops. The Catholic bishop of Ston had been forced to leave his diocese and settle in Korčula in 1300. Ever since the Ragusans acquired Ston and Pelješac in 1333, the Dubrovnik government had wanted its own bishop there. In the meantime, it ensured that the local population refused to pay tithes to the absentee bishop – indeed, the Republic never allowed tithes to be paid on Ragusan soil. There ensued a long struggle between the bishop and the government, with the former pressing for his tithes and the latter pressing Rome to create a new bishopric. Since the Ragusan state had been the main promoter of the Catholicisation of the region, it had a double claim to have its petition granted. Successive Cardinal Protectors of the Republic advanced its arguments. The main sticking point was undoubtedly Venetian influence, since it was convenient for Dubrovnik's rival to have ecclesiastical jurisdiction over Ragusan territory claimed by a prelate residing on a Venetian-controlled island. Eventually in 1541, Paul III acceded to the Ragusan Republic's wishes. Dubrovnik was granted not only the right of nomination to the new see, exercised by the Senate; the Ragusans were also allowed to collect tithes there. The Ragusan government was permitted to appoint a vicar, confirmed by the archbishop of Dubrovnik, when the see was vacant. Most of the bishops of Ston were religious, predominantly Dominicans. They were very much creatures of the Ragusan government, rather than obedient suffragans of the Ragusan archbishop. The new bishop of Korčula was also nominally a suffragan of the Ragusan metropolitan, but he too was effectively subject to the secular – in this case Venetian – power.[13]

The sharpest thorn in the archbishop of Dubrovnik's side was, on occasion, his own Cathedral chapter. The chapter appears in fully developed form at the start of the twelfth century. Over the years its size and constitution varied, but it remained a powerful body acting under the authority of its three main dignitaries – archdeacon, archpresbyter and *primicerius*. The chapter's autonomy was, naturally, much increased by the fact that Dubrovnik's archbishops were foreigners and not infrequently absentees.[14]

By a decree of 23 November 1442 only Ragusan nobles could become canons of Dubrovnik.[15] Although on the face of it this approach might seem contrary to that applied to the archbishopric, its purpose was essentially the same. The Ragusan government intended that whereas the archbishop himself should be as nearly a cipher as possible, the chapter which (usually) nominated him and which (effectively) controlled the affairs of the Ragusan church should be deeply rooted in local society and so subject to local influence. In any case, deprived by their own self-denying ordinance of the opportunity to promote their sons to become Ragusan archbishops, the patricians of Dubrovnik were doubtless determined to keep patronage over the chapter for themselves.

At the end of the fifteenth century, the Ragusan government went so far as to seek itself to choose the archbishop. But it was soon thrown on the defensive. Indeed, in the sixteenth century several appointments were made by the pope without any local consultation at all. The government reacted by prohibiting any close contact between the archbishop and the patriciate. It also vigorously supported the chapter and the religious orders in their frequent quarrels with him.

These conflicts became more bitter as the Counter-Reformation movement took hold. The Ragusan secular authorities were in fact enthusiastic, after their own fashion, about the programme of reform that was set in motion by the Council of Trent. But they regarded themselves, not the pope's commissioners, let alone the foreign archbishops of Dubrovnik, as the proper channels for it. They disliked intensely any ecclesiastical interference in the running of their state. For reasons of commercial and political prudence they were also extremely wary of the anti-Ottoman agenda which some of the reformers espoused.

The government itself, though, insisted upon an improvement by the Dubrovnik canons in the pastoral care they offered. (Since there was for centuries but one 'parish' in Dubrovnik, based on the Cathedral, the chapter had an unusually important role.) Despairing of altering the ways of the canons themselves, the government in 1496 set aside 400 *hyperperi* from the profits of church lands to pay twelve chaplains who were to perform the religious duties of the canons. The latter were most displeased but were forced to acquiesce by a combination of threats of exile and confiscation from the government, which finally gained the support of the pope.[16]

Dubrovnik was not much affected by that other driving force for the Catholic Counter-Reformation, the need to resist Protestantism. Cosmopolitan intellectuals were the most likely to succumb. The Naljesković family – the philosopher Nikola and his brothers – were quite clearly sympathisers. A student returning to Dubrovnik from Germany was apparently affected by the irregular ideas with which he made contact and was duly investigated, though he escaped punishment.[17] It is not altogether clear that the Ragusan secular or ecclesiastical authorities knew or cared much about the heretical doctrines themselves. But then accusations of Protestantism were probably mainly useful in Dubrovnik as a means of discrediting one's opponents.[18]

The real or imagined threat of Protestantism also provided a further occasion for the Ragusan government to assert its right to take the lead in safeguarding the faith on the territory of the Republic. Thus it took the initiative in setting up in 1530 a Ragusan 'Inquisition', consisting of two Dominicans of patrician lineage. Further commissions aimed at investigating suspected Lutherans were appointed in 1545 and 1549. But in 1550 the pope firmly refused permission for the secular authorities to proceed against the suspects, and it was henceforth left to the church authorities to do whatever was thought to be required.[19]

The archbishops frequently found themselves unhappily involved in clashes with the Ragusan government. It took a rare degree of tact and strength of character to ride through these difficulties – qualities which few of those appointed seem to have shown. The one unforgivable archiepiscopal sin in the eyes of the secular authorities was to meddle in foreign policy against the interests of the Republic. The worst example by far was that, already discussed, of the Milanese-born archbishop Trivulzio.[20] The black legend about him lived on. It was guilelessly repeated by Serafino Razzi, who noted that his death was a mercy for Dubrovnik. When the archbishop was hit over the head by a deranged Ragusan Franciscan, some people – says Razzi – thought that it was a deserved punishment for his wicked life.[21] Echoing the same tradition two centuries later, Saro Crijević notes of Trivulzio that he was learned, pious, industrious and improved the archbishop's palace. But the patriotic Ragusan historian could not refrain from adding that Trivulzio had sent letters to Suleyman the Magnificent congratulating him on his conquests and had been rewarded a pension paid in silver, but that the archbishop had died before he could receive it.[22]

The outstanding exception to the otherwise variously inadequate archbishops of Dubrovnik was Ludovico Beccadelli. Cardinal Giovanni Angelo de' Medici had been a grand absentee archbishop of Dubrovnik for a decade after his appointment in 1545, and he firmly intended that he should be succeeded by another absentee Italian, Sebastiano Portico. But Dubrovnik vigorously resisted and even sent a delegation to tell the would-be archbishop that his presence was unwelcome. Instead, the Ragusans, attracted by his reputation as a man of culture and piety, wanted the Bolognese-born humanist and diplomat Beccadelli. The appointment was duly made in accordance with their wishes and, after a highly unsettling thirty-seven-day crossing of the Adriatic, Beccadelli arrived in Dubrovnik on 9 December 1555. It was not an easy post to fill, but in time he made or imported friends and proved a conscientious and reforming archbishop.[23] Three years after his arrival he could write to an Italian correspondent:

> I am in a land that is foreign to Italy, in language very foreign, but in customs not much different from our own. I live in it gladly and many things render it dear to me.

As he prepared to return home in June 1560 he conveyed his sorrow in a Latin ode and an Italian sonnet. He referred to himself as Archbishop of Dubrovnik till his death and kept up a regular correspondence with his many Ragusan friends, asking for news about the Republic's affairs, sending them books and furniture and receiving the occasional cask of prized Ragusan *malvazija* wine.[24]

Beccadelli's personality was clearly well suited to dealing with the frequently fractious Ragusans. He was described as above average height, with a serious demeanour but cheerful disposition, affable in conversation and careful of his appearance. In short, he looked the part.[25] He played a distinguished role at the Council of Trent. In Dubrovnik he was responsible for implementing the pastoral thinking of the Council's reforms by dividing up his diocese into parishes – twelve within the walls and two outside them. This fundamental re-arrangement of the old unitary Ragusan church was duly approved by the Senate.[26]

Beccadelli must, however, bear the responsibility for choosing an unsuitable successor in the Calabrian Benedictine Crisostomo Calvino. According to Razzi, Beccadelli liked Calvino's conversation. The Ragusan authorities clearly liked him too, since they had earlier sought to have him as their archbishop and had settled instead for his promotion to head of the Mljet Congregation. (See below.) Calvino served in that role for fifteen years before his friend Beccadelli prevailed upon Rome to have him appointed Archbishop, in 1564.[27] Unfortunately, what had appeared Calvino's winning modesty soon turned out to be timidity. In him Beccadelli's tact was replaced by compliance with prevailing pressures, which in a Dubrovnik buffeted by the forces of the Counter-Reformation and of resistance to it was a recipe for disorder. A visiting Augustinian preacher from Siena, Cristoforo degli Amaroli, recruited by the otherwise discriminating Frano Gundulić in Rome, outraged a large number of clerics in Dubrovnik by appearing to argue for an Erastian, not to say heretical, view of the supremacy of secular over spiritual authority. In particular, this provoked the denunciations of the powerful head of the Dubrovnik Chapter, Archdeacon Marin Kaboga. Naturally, the government of Dubrovnik had no interest in becoming involved: after all, Amaroli's doctrines suited their view of the proper order of things in the Republic. But in the end, Amaroli's critics grew so vociferous that he returned to Rome and denounced the alleged abuses to be found in the Ragusan church with such vigour that a special Apostolic Visitor was appointed to inquire into matters. Archbishop Calvino was altogether bypassed by these upheavals. According to Razzi, it was said in Dubrovnik that they didn't have an archbishop at all.[28]

The Visitor appointed, Giovanni Francesco Sormano, Bishop of Montefeltro, drew up a report for Rome which constituted a scorching indictment of the church of Dubrovnik. Calvino himself was condemned not just for maladministration but also for dubious theological views. In particular – and ironically, given the events that precipitated the furore – Calvino was culpable for not resisting incursions by the secular power. The priests were poor, ignorant and did not carry out their duties. The Chapter was also strongly criticised. The canons were, said Sormano, ignoramuses, sloppy in celebrating the liturgy, idle and quarrelsome. The Visitor's severest strictures were, though, reserved for Archdeacon Kaboga. He was accused of intrigue, immorality and greed. He could not, allegedly, even manage to recite the Office. He did not keep canonical residence. He falsified the chapter accounts. He came armed into church. He published immoral poems. The lack of any kind of balance in the report suggests that, for whatever reason, its author was strongly biased; or perhaps he was ignorant and misled. Kaboga was, for the most part at least, unjustly accused. He was an educated man with strong views. His poetry, of which Sormano complained, was of the kind beloved of zealous clerics, pillorying his fellow patricians' moral shortcomings. And when he eventually went to Rome to clear his name, he was indeed vindicated.[29]

The humiliated and now senile archbishop Calvino died in 1575. His successor, the Luccan Vincenzo Portico, was a very different character, though perhaps even less suitable to cope with the prevailing conditions in Dubrovnik. The fact that his brother, Sebastiano, had previously been rejected by the authorities when suggested as Archbishop perhaps continued to rankle. In any case, according to Razzi, who was resident in Dubrovnik between 1587 and 1589 and should therefore have known, Portico was showy, proud, passionate and a poor judge of character[30]. The fact that he was an enthusiast for crusading ventures against the Ottoman Empire hardly endeared him to most of the patriciate either. Nor did the ferment around Kaboga and his views abate. Indeed, the archdeacon was thrown into prison and his clerical supporters punished, before Kaboga finally departed for Rome to clear his name.

The Ragusan patriciate was itself at this time sharply split over the right attitude to take to the Ottoman Empire and to the demands of the Counter-Reformation reformers. So the government might not have taken too close an interest in these disorders had not Portico overstepped the line in other respects. The authorities learned that their archbishop had apparently encouraged the highly damaging rumour that Dubrovnik's quarantine procedures were insufficient. And then Portico clashed with the government on the vexed question of the boundaries of secular and ecclesiastic jurisdiction in the matter of the will of a rich citizen whose estate the archbishop seized. The Senate reacted brutally by sending its officers to break into the archbishop's palace and intimidate Portico in his bedchamber. The tactic worked. Vincenzo Portico fled to Rome, and in 1579 resigned his archbishopric.

The Ragusan government defended its actions in Rome quite effectively through its envoy, the leading patrician Jeronim Kaboga. But Portico's successor, a young reformer named Girolamo Matteucci, soon also became involved in conflicts of jurisdiction with the Ragusan authorities. Initially, there was an incident concerning a cleric in minor orders who had violently obstructed the count of Šipan's guards in the execution of their duties. When the cleric was imprisoned, the archbishop responded by excommunicating the count. This seems to have prompted a campaign of petty persecution by the Senate. The archbishop had already annoyed the Senators by making some minor alterations to the internal layout of the cathedral. The Senators now complained that the archbishop's *prie-dieu* obstructed their view of the high altar, and had it moved and later taken out of the church altogether. The breaking point was reached, however, over the case of a priest who, because of a quarrel, murdered the count of Ston. The Senate asked leave from the bishop of Ston to try him. At first the bishop complied, but he then thought better of it and refused. Complaining that he had been placed under duress, he fled Dubrovnik while the priest also fled the Republic's jurisdiction. The Senate promptly sent its officers to break into the episcopal palace in Ston and seize the bishop's papers. When Archbishop Matteuci publicly denounced the Senators and demanded that they seek absolution, they met in a secret session and passed a resolution requiring him to leave the Republic within three days. Having made a public protest to the assembled clerics of his diocese, the archbishop departed and denounced the government in Rome, claiming that it was dominated by a powerful clique – that is, the faction led by Jeronim Kaboga – determined to rule the church just as it ruled the state.

The pope now appointed the bishop of Korčula to go to Dubrovnik to investigate. The result was a highly critical report of the conduct of the Ragusan authorities. The focus of the quarrel then moved back to Rome. Frano Gundulić was sent to put the Republic's case to the Curia, which he managed to do with considerable success, winning papal agreement that the secular authorities should have jurisdiction in a range of issues concerning clerical property and personnel. But the by-now rancorous Kaboga group was irreconcilable, accusing Gundulić of deceit and even forgery. Two years later, in February 1588, the Senate sent Jeronim Kaboga himself to Rome, though this time the mission was a failure. In 1589, in the ensuing bitterness and under circumstances already described, Frano Gundulić was murdered in the church of the Holy Cross at Gruž.[31]

The Religious Orders

The religious orders always played a specially active role in Dubrovnik's spiritual life. Benedictine monks, and then nuns, established themselves in the Southern Adriatic region from the ninth century. (There were, in fact, from very early times, more nuns than monks in Dubrovnik.) The Benedictine nuns were established in five – and possibly more – houses within the town. The area around Dubrovnik also had the advantage of including numbers of small islands conducive to monastic recollection in conditions of relative security. Thus within the territory of the Ragusan state were to be found Benedictine men's monasteries on Mrkan, Sveti Petar, Sveti Andrija, Šipan, Mljet and Lokrum.

Of these, the monastery of St Mary on Lokrum was the oldest. Before the 'black monks' settled there, the island had been the site of a community of hermits living according to the Rule of St Basil. The new Benedictine house was dependent on the monastery at Tremiti, off Termoli. But the secular authorities of Dubrovnik took a particularly close interest in St Mary of Lokrum. This was justified by the claim that the town itself established the original religious community. But the most important consideration was the obvious strategic importance of the place. Each year the government appointed an advocate and three proctors to administer the financial affairs of the monastery. The latter were quite complex, because the Lokrum monks received over the years endowments from all kinds of local and even distant dignitaries. As a result, the monastery found itself with lands in Župa, Šumet, Cavtat, Čibača, Konavle, Gruž, Zaton, Rijeka Dubrovačka, Slano, Ston and on the islands of Koločep, Jakljan, Lopud, Šipan and Mljet. The abbot had a residence in the city of Dubrovnik and residential and commercial property in Venice. Out of these revenues the monastery of Lokrum ran an almshouse for the city's poor until the fifteenth century, when the number of monks on Lokrum sharply declined. For most of the history of the Republic the abbot of Lokrum was regarded as the most important prelate after the archbishop. These abbots were, however, usually absentees who took little interest in the monastery. In the sixteenth century Lokrum was raided by both Turks and *uskoks* and in the seventeenth century it was badly damaged by the Great Earthquake. Eventually, in 1798, it was abolished by the pope at the insistence of the Ragusan government, which needed to raise money by selling monastic property so as to pay a forced loan to the French.[32]

Apart from the monastery of St Mary's on Lokrum, there were independent Benedictine houses with mitre-wearing abbots at the head of them just outside the city at Višnjica (St James's), on Šipan (St Michael's), and on Mljet (St Mary's). Mljet was the most important of these and became more significant than Lokrum once the project for the 'Congregation of Mljet' came to be debated by the secular and ecclesiastical authorities. In the fourteenth century the monastery on Mljet passed into the hands of the black monks. Even after the agreement of 1345, which regulated the affairs of the island in the interests of the free peasantry, the monastery remained by far the largest landholder.[33] The abbot was also the ordinary for the island and had visitation rights over all its churches, as well as the main church where pilgrims flocked to pray before the icon of 'Our Lady of the Lake'.

The decadent state of the Benedictine houses of the Ragusan Republic prompted successive popes in the fifteenth century to propose their incorporation within a separate congregation as a prelude to reform. But this was frustrated when the monastery of Lokrum passed under the authority of Padua. The project was later revived with the enthusiastic support of the government of Dubrovnik. In 1526 the government summoned four monks of Ragusan stock from the great Benedictine mother-house of Monte Cassino. The following year, on the death of the abbots of the monasteries at Višnjica and on Sveti Andrija, Mavro Vetranović, the abbot of Mljet (and the Republic's most distinguished ecclesiastical poet), received authority from the archbishop of Dubrovnik to take over administration of the other two – now quite empty – abbeys. This decision was confirmed later by the pope, who also ordered that on the death or resignation of the abbot of the monastery on Šipan it, too, should come under Vetranović's authority. When Vetranović resigned his post, Jeronim Benessa became the new canonical head of this Congregation of monasteries, to be in turn succeeded by the unfortunate future archbishop Crisostomo Calvino.

Both the papacy and the archbishop of Dubrovnik, the reformist Ludovico Beccadelli, took a close interest in the attempts to recruit more monks. Some progress was made. But the monasteries were severely damaged by the Great Earthquake of 1667 and numbers again dwindled. In the late seventeenth and eighteenth centuries the Benedictine Congregation based on Monte Cassino tried with the support of the Dubrovnik archbishops to have the Congregation of Mljet abolished. But the Ragusan government strongly and successfully resisted this proposal. In fact, the Congregation lasted as long as the Republic itself, being dissolved, along with all religious houses, by order of General Marmont on 31 May 1808.[34]

The mendicant orders – the Dominicans and Franciscans – were also early arrivals in Dubrovnik and soon played an even larger role in Ragusan religious life than had the Benedictines. A venerable but probably baseless tradition recorded that St Francis himself came to Dubrovnik in 1223 on his way to Egypt, and that he was well-received by the government and provided with what he needed to carry on to the Levant.[35] In fact, although individual Franciscans came and went, it was the Dominicans who first established themselves, in 1225. Their church and friary were built on the eastern side of the town in the course of the thirteenth, fourteenth and fifteenth centuries. Only in the fifteenth century, however, was the complex brought within the city walls, by the latter's extension.[36]

The Franciscan friars also originally established themselves outside the town – near the little church of St Thomas on Pile – in about 1235. But in 1317, when Dubrovnik was at war with the Serbian King Stefan Uroš II Milutin, the government ordered the Franciscan church and friary to be pulled down and rebuilt within the walls, so as to prevent the building being used as a vantage point by the Serb army. Papal support was sought and received to this effect, though it seems likely that the church was not in fact destroyed now because a similar decree had to be issued the following century. The Franciscans did, however, re-establish themselves within the town. Their church and friary were built where they now stand, towards the end of Placa near the Pile Gate. Financial help from the government and donations from individual Ragusans supported the project. Work on it had begun by March 1319, and the church was already in use by 1345; but Ragusans were still making bequests contributing to its completion in the 1350s. The masterpiece of the friary was the cloister, mainly the work of a Slav craftsman from Bar, Mihoje Brajkov. It was only completed after his death during the Black Death in 1348.[37]

The chroniclers were extremely proud of Dubrovnik's Franciscan friary. Diversis's enthusiasm was boundless:

> It has a beautiful and spacious *dormitorium* adorned with a large garden. A cistern with a fountain is there and above the lower parts of the cloister are tastefully designed arcades. In the middle of the cloister, in the little garden where bay and orange trees are to be found, they grow their vegetables. The church has a large sacristy and a marvellous high altar with an icon or silver altarpiece of great value. One ascends to the altar by stone steps. Both above and below it, the choir is magnificent... Many side-altars and a beautiful bell tower, with suitable bells, embellish this church. Its floors are paved with tomb stones.[38]

The Franciscans were particularly important to the life of Dubrovnik. Franciscan friars from the Bosnian vicariate, founded to maintain and where possible advance Catholic Christianity in the face of the Ottoman advance through the Balkans, were settled with the support of the Ragusan authorities on Dubrovnik's newly acquired territories. These Franciscan friars, based in houses at Ston, Rožat, Slano and Pridvorje (in Konavle), pursued a vigorous apostolate, aimed at converting the Orthodox inhabitants to Catholicism.[39]

The Ragusan government was always zealous in its attempts to promote the highest moral and spiritual standards among the friars. In 1432, according to Ranjina, the government expelled all those Franciscan friars who were conventuals and turned their houses over to the (more rigorous) observants.[40] The conventuals were allowed, though, to continue to exercise the function of confessors to the Franciscan convent of St Clare. But in 1518 the government succeeded in having this privilege stripped from them as well, employing papal authority as a means of overcoming the vigorous resistance of the nuns. The latter were given a taste of Ragusan intolerance of obstruction when they found themselves imprisoned *incommunicado* in their convent and alloted meagre rations of bread and water till they submitted.[41]

No less important than religious enthusiasm as a motivation for Dubrovnik's policies towards the religious orders was, however, *raison d'état*. It was important to the Ragusan patriciate that control over and preferment to the monasteries, convents and friaries within the Republic's borders were in reliable hands. Thus the government worked steadily to have Dubrovnik's Dominican houses separated from the rest of the Dominican Dalmatian province. It finally succeeded in 1486, when the Dominican friaries in Dubrovnik and Gruž and on Lopud were organised in a special Ragusan congregation, where they remained until after the fall of the Republic.[42] In 1500 it also succeeded in having the Dubrovnik Franciscans separated from the province of Venetian-dominated Dalmatia – which was politically useful for Dubrovnik but, as Razzi observes, not at all beneficial for the other friaries of Dalmatia which were used to relying for sustenance on the wealthy Ragusans.[43]

Generally speaking, the Republic was keen to keep foreigners out of its religious houses. Thus in 1393 the abbess of the convent of St Clare was forbidden to receive foreign nuns on pain of loss of the house's revenues and other punishments.[44] In 1422 the prohibition was formally extended to the city's other monasteries and convents.[45] Dubrovnik had at this time seven convents of nuns, five of them Benedictine houses, one Dominican and another of Poor Clares. This last, the convent of St Clare, was particularly important to the patriciate because only girls of noble birth could be admitted to it. Consequently, the government was keen to keep down the cost of the 'dowries' which were customarily donated when a novice was admitted. So in 1426 the Ragusan authorities decreed that henceforth only clothes, a bed and some books could be given, not money.[46]

Although it meddled in their affairs, the Ragusan government was also generous towards the orders. By the early fourteenth century the authorities had adopted the practice of giving regular alms to the Franciscans and Dominicans. The purpose of these good works was clearly spelt out in the minutes of the Small Council for 1322 – 'so that God may keep the city (*civitas*) of Ragusa in a good and peaceful state, and that it may be defended from molestations and injuries'.[47] In Diversis's time, the Franciscans and Dominicans would preach on alternate days in Lent and receive presents of fish for doing so. Each of the orders received at Easter a sum equivalent to the cost of a friar's habit. Friars who wished to study in Italian universities could expect bursaries from the government to cover the cost of books and clothes.[48]

The arrival of the Jesuits marked a turning point in Dubrovnik's religious life, and one which also came to have considerable political significance. The patricians of Dubrovnik first sought to have Jesuits sent to preach in their city during the lifetime of St Ignatius, and that enthusiastic reformer Archbishop

Ludovico Beccadelli tried to have a Jesuit college founded there. These initial schemes came to nothing. But in 1560 the famous Jesuit Nicolas Bobadilla came to stay in the monastery of St James at Višnjica, and the following year he was joined by another father.

There now followed a long and complex series of negotiations, agreements and misunderstandings between the Ragusan government and successive Jesuit generals. These all stemmed from an ambiguity in the Republic's view of the Jesuit order and its mission. Although, as has already been noted, there were different factions within the Ragusan Senate, the prevailing lay opinion was that the standards of the Ragusan clergy badly needed reforming and that the high educational and cultural standards with which the Jesuits were associated could only benefit Ragusan youth. Thus on both these grounds Dubrovnik wanted a substantial Jesuit presence and indeed a fully-fledged Jesuit *collegium*. On the other hand, most of the governing class was highly distrustful of the imprudently anti-Ottoman policies associated with the Counter-Reformation in general and the Jesuits in particular. The Society's fidelity to Rome and rigorous refusal to compromise with the secular authorities made it particularly difficult for Dubrovnik to handle.

So, although Bobadilla himself created an excellent impression on the Ragusans, the Jesuits withdrew.[49] They were back again in 1575, probably summoned in order to try to reform the clergy in the wake of Sormano's damning report of the previous year. In 1583 the Senate voted to ask the Jesuits to set up a college in Dubrovnik, but the necessary money was not actually raised. In 1585 the Jesuit mission was terminated by the general, apparently because of political opposition, though the Society was soon operating once more.[50]

A new mission arrived in 1604, to be received coldly by the Ragusan Senate, which objected to the fact that the fathers had been summoned by the Ragusan archbishop, not themselves who were (they emphasised) Dubrovnik's true 'rulers in temporal and spiritual matters'. The Jesuits were not, though, subsequently obstructed in their energetic catechesis. This work was particularly effective since among their number was the former papal diplomat, the Split-born Alexandar Komulović, who preached in Croatian.[51] Welcome as Komulović's presence doubtless was to the Ragusan faithful, it was considerably less so to many Ragusan patricians. Born in Split and educated in the 'Illyrian' college of St Jerome in Rome, the new arrival was one of the leading proponents of a grand pan-Slavic strategy to drive the Turks out of Europe. He had spent years in Russia and Poland vigorously though vainly pursuing this project before being entrusted by Clement VIII with reopening the Jesuit station in Dubrovnik.[52]

Komulović died in 1608, and the mission was suspended. It was then re-founded by a group of Jesuits who included a worthy successor – another gifted linguist and zealous Counter-Reformation idealist – Bartol Kašić. Kašić hailed from the Dalmatian island of Pag and so, like Komulović, he spoke the Croatian variant known as *čakavski* (or čakavian). The Counter-Reformation papacy was acutely aware of the linguistic obstacles to the re-conversion of the southern Slavs from Islam and (schismatic) Orthodoxy to Catholicism, with its Latin liturgy and culture. It was therefore deemed important to choose a Slavic language which was widely and easily comprehensible in the areas concerned One of the most linguistically significant events of the time was Kašić's decision, after initially choosing his native *čakavski*, to settle on the *štokavski* (or štokavian) variant spoken in Dubrovnik into which to translate the key documents of the faith for use in Bosnia, Hercegovina and Serbia.[53]

Kašić kept a written account of his time in Dubrovnik.[54] It reveals an extraordinarily active and highly successful ministry by the Dubrovnik Jesuits. But from the beginning, Kašić had to cope with opposition from some of the leading patricians. The Rector had at their first meeting objected to the fact that the mission had been sent by the Jesuit's general without any specific request from the Senate. The argument about who was to pay for the desired *collegium* surfaced again and Kašić angrily, though as it turned out temporarily, left Dubrovnik. Some of his enemies among the nobility apparently tried to ensure that he was not among the mission when it resumed, but they were unsuccessful. Kašić survived a rough and dangerous voyage to return to the city in 1620, and became superior of the mission in 1623.

Whatever the authorities thought about this prodigious intellectual, the faithful certainly appreciated him greatly. He was a very popular preacher, particularly with the nuns and devout ladies of Dubrovnik. He managed to persuade the young women of the city to go and confess in church and attend mass on Sundays, neither of which they had been used to doing because of their well-known modesty and dislike of being seen in public. He distributed books which he had written, such as his translation of St Robert Bellarmine's *Catechism* and a manual on meditation. Kašić also preached and administered the sacraments on Koločep and Lopud – where, however, his mission had to be hurriedly curtailed because of a rumoured attack by pirates. He visited Šipan and Slano and sailed down to dangerous and disorderly Perast. At mass he would read out the gospel in Croatian so that it could be more easily understood. He also taught in the school which the Jesuits ran. But the much discussed *collegium* had still not been founded by the time he left Dubrovnik in 1633.[55] A dispute with the authorities arose in 1636 when the Jesuits tried to acquire through a Ragusan merchant some property adjoining their house, which they wanted to enlarge. One patrician apparently declaimed in front of the fathers that the Republic had never been so insulted – not by Turks, heretics or Jews – as it had by the Jesuits. Two years later the Jesuits left Dubrovnik, not to return until 1658.[56]

Popular Religion

Foreigners were pleasantly impressed by Ragusan piety. The Tuscan Diversis noted that many Ragusans of both sexes attended daily mass and were much more generous in almsgiving to their priests than were Italians.[57] Canon Pietro Casola from Milan, who came to Dubrovnik on his way to the Holy Land in 1494 was also struck by the devotion of the population and their generosity to the church, particularly to the Franciscans. He noted that devotion to St Blaise was evidenced by the large number of Ragusans who bore the saint's Christian name.[58] Serafino Razzi had experienced Ragusan piety as prior of Vasto on the Italian Adriatic coast a decade before he actually came to Dubrovnik. He went aboard a large Ragusan merchant ship and was much struck by the religious devotion and good disposition of its 140 crew, particularly of the ship's boys who publicly recited the *Pater Noster*, *Ave Maria* and *Salve Regina* before supper.[59] On finally seeing the city he was greatly impressed by the number of churches of all sizes that the Ragusans managed to maintain: he counted forty-seven within the walls.[60]

When the Jesuits arrived they again found a devout lay population, which flocked to hear them preach. Bartol Kašić records how he gave conferences, commenting on the gospel in Croatian to the women of Dubrovnik three times a week. He would also preach during Lent at one of the women's monasteries. He coped with confessional queues that kept him occupied on the eve of major feasts till late in the evening. He and his colleagues introduced the adoration of the Blessed Sacrament known as the Forty Hours after which they communicated no fewer than 2,600 people.[61]

Long before the Jesuits came to Dubrovnik, Ragusan popular and indeed official devotion had come to centre on the figure of St Blaise (*Sveti Vlaho*). Although the cult of the saint – an Armenian bishop martyred in the early fourth century – spread throughout Europe in the eighth century, the date and circumstances of its arrival in Dubrovnik are obscure. The first Ragusan church dedicated to St Blaise was probably built in the late tenth century. It was close to the watchtower erected at that time at Pile and was later incorporated into the women's monastery of St Clare.[62] Apparently in 1026, a fragment of the skull of StBlaise was brought to the town and then procured for a large sum of money. This would have provided an impetus for devotion.[63] Probably at about this time – the eleventh or twelfth centuries – were made the fine reliquaries for the saint's head and arm, still stored in the Cathedral treasury.

Significant of the cult as well, of course, as of Dubrovnik's growing commercial importance, was the institution on the Saint's feast day (3 February) of the annual Franchise of St Blaise. This was founded upon a solemn promise by the government that any debtor or criminal, Ragusan or foreign, could come to Dubrovnik during the period of a week – three days before the Feast and three days after it – and remain immune from arrest or other proceedings against him. The Franchise thus offered an opportunity for debtors to seek arrangements with their creditors and for exiled criminals to seek remission of their punishments. It was later supplemented by a further Franchise associated with the cult. On 5 July 1346, a relic of the arm of St Blaise was brought to Dubrovnik and a solemn feast was proclaimed to honour it. In 1453 a new Franchise, along the lines of that focused upon 3 February, was declared for 5 July.[64]

As a result of the legend associating him with the miraculous cure of a boy with a fishbone lodged in his gullet, St Blaise has come to be associated with cures of ailments affecting the throat. But in Dubrovnik it was the catastrophe of the Black Death that magnified his role as the city's patron. This is clear from the chronicles, which connect the decision to build a new church in the saint's honour with gratitude for St Blaise's effective intercession.[65] Indeed, in February 1349, just a month after pestilence arrived in Dubrovnik, the Great Council unanimously decided to authorise the count and the Small Council to build a church dedicated to St Blaise 'who is the head and protector of the city of Ragusa'. It was to be constructed next to the public square in front of the palace of the Great Council. The government also decided to recompense the Ragusan citizen – a certain Tomo – who had two years earlier brought to the town the relic of St Blaise's arm, with remission of all his taxes (except the main customs due), and extend the privilege to the third generation.[66]

In fact, the building of the church of St Blaise was not only prompted by the plague; it was also materially assisted by it. Large numbers of Ragusans died intestate or with wills irregular and incomplete. In many cases heirs and executors were also dead. It was decided that some of the revenues from this property which accordingly reverted to the state should go towards the new church for masses for the dead.[67]

The church of St Blaise was to become the second church in Dubrovnik, after the cathedral. Its situation – close to the centre of government and beside the main square – made it a landmark and centre of social intercourse. Beside it was constructed a loggia (called *luža* in Dubrovnik) in which the nobility would meet, gossip and sometimes play dice or chess. Diversis lauded the church's location and contents and was no less enthusiastic about the *luža* – noting particularly how the latter's beams and walls were encrusted with impressions of the coats of arms of French, English and German knights who visited Dubrovnik on their way to the Holy Land.[68]

The Feast of St Blaise was (and still is) the most important feast day in Dubrovnik, involving the city's political and religious authorities and the whole populace, joined by passing foreigners. Indeed, it was curious outsiders – Diversis in the fifteenth, Razzi in the sixteenth and Appendini in the early nineteenth centuries – who provided the fullest descriptions of the elaborate and stylised celebrations.[69]

A triduum (three days) of eulogies preached in honour of St Blaise preceded the Feast itself. On the vigil of the Feast (which is also the evening of Candlemas, 2 February) there was a military parade followed by solemn vespers attended by the Rector at the cathedral. Offerings were also made in the church by the various guilds and fraternities. The dawn of the Feast itself was greeted by the pealing of Dubrovnik's church bells, the firing of cannons and the beating of drums. Awakened by this din, the citizens assembled in front of the Rector's palace at nine o'clock. There the Rector himself, the Senators and other dignitaries took their places outside on seats. Twelve baking women, bearing standards surmounted by flasks of oil and wine and by cakes and wreaths of vegetables, and carrying on their heads baskets of loaves laced with olive sprigs as symbols of peace and plenty, then appeared and performed a dance. Traditional *laudes* were later declaimed in honour of St Blaise, and there was a colourful, noisy military display. This was succeeded by the main religious procession, in which all the clergy and nobility were obliged to participate, carrying candles in honour of the saint's relics, and then by solemn high mass in the cathedral. The afternoon was given over to singing, dancing and war games of various sorts. In Diversis's day this was when the young Ragusans played the game known as *alka* (nowadays traditionally associated with Sinj). It was a contest in which mounted competitors sought to thread their lances though silver rings hanging on a rope.[70] By Appendini's time (the last years of the Republic) the occasion had become a highly alcoholic and somewhat dangerous event, when Ragusans young and old fired off their handguns with little regard for the consequences.[71]

The cult of St Blaise always had a political as well as a religious significance. Public events took place under the gaze of images of the saint, and his title of '*Gonfaloniere*, Protector and Governor' of Dubrovnik was naturally invoked on such solemn occasions as the foundation of the *Lazarini*.[72] In the official prayer for Dubrovnik, included by Razzi at the end of his *Storia di Ragusa*, the Almighty, 'builder and custodian of the Heavenly City of Jerusalem', is urged to watch over Dubrovnik through the merits and intercession of Our Lady and St Blaise 'your martyr' and all the saints.[73] When the *poklisari* left the Rector's Palace to begin their exacting and often dangerous mission to Constantinople, the whole cavalcade would bow towards the church of St Blaise. Then as the riders reached the Sponza Palace, and before leaving by the Ploče Gate, they would all turn to their right to bow once more to the church. They would pray for the help of God and St Blaise in carrying out their tasks, and the Rector and the members of the Small Council would do the same.[74]

Within Dubrovnik itself the priest of the church of St Blaise was heavily engaged in celebrating 'official' masses in the nearby Rector's Palace. But far beyond the city itself, wherever indeed Ragusan political control was extended, churches dedicated to St Blaise were established. Thus there were ten churches of St Blaise within the Republic by the early fifteenth century. The saint's spiritual prestige was used to reinforce the state's political authority, above all in the most exposed, frontier regions. So the Franciscan church built in Ston in 1345 is the church of St Blaise, as is that built in Pridvorje in 1429. The cult was a probably conscious response to that of St Mark, patron saint of Venice. It was able to achieve its full flourishing in Dubrovnik because unlike the cults of patron saints of the Venetian cities – St Chrysogonus (Sveti Krševan) in Zadar, St Domnius (Sveti Dujam) in Split, and St Tryphon (Sveti Tripun) in Kotor – it was not thrust into the shadows by Venice's holy patron.[75]

The Ragusan cult of the Three Martyrs of Kotor was apparently developed as a response to the Orthodoxy of neighbouring Serb princes.[76] According to the tradition, the three martyrs – Petar, Andrija and Lovro Sagurović – were Catholics living in Kotor in the twelfth or thirteenth centuries. (Accounts differed.) Having been put to death by the local Orthodox inhabitants, their bodies were buried in an unfrequented spot on the coast between Kotor and Novi. Eight years later a devout woman had a vision of their fate and brought it to the attention of the Venetian *Provveditore* at Kotor. But he refused to lend her tale any credence, so she told the authorities at Dubrovnik. They did believe her and a ship was sent by night to the place she described, where a light from heaven pinpointed the grave. The Ragusans brought back the holy relics to Dubrovnik and placed them in the cathedral. They rewarded the woman with a house and annuity for life.[77]

The appeal of the cult of the Martyrs of Kotor, like that of St Blaise, was heightened as a result of the Black Death. It was decided in 1363 to build a separate church in the Martyrs' honour, though the work went slowly and was still in progress in 1399. The church was situated off Placa. In 1419 it was given a bell tower and three bells. It was destroyed in the 1667 earthquake, though it was slowly rebuilt between 1677 and 1702. But it eventually fell into decay and was pulled down in 1801.[78] Devotion to the Martyrs persisted at least until the end of the Republic. When news arrived in Dubrovnik, under siege in 1806 by Russians and Montenegrins, that relief by the French was at hand, the citizens cried out 'Long Live St Blaise!' and 'Long Live the Three *Kotorani*!'[79]

The public devotional life of Dubrovnik was heavily influenced by the need to honour the saints who had proved the value of their intercession against disasters, both natural and manmade. Thus, as already noted, the Feast of the Forty Martyrs (9 March) was celebrated by a public procession to give thanks for deliverance from the great conspiracy of 1400.[80] In 1416 it was decreed that because of the assistance of Saints Peter and Paul in times of plague their feast day (29 June) would henceforth be celebrated by the Rector and the Small Council attending the church of St Peter the Great to hear mass.[81] In 1437 a decision was made similarly to honour St John the Baptist, also for assistance in time of pestilence.[82] Other feast days set aside for public devotion were introduced to Dubrovnik through outside influences. The feast of the Immaculate Conception was thus introduced in 1413.[83] The Ragusans, like the rest of the late medieval church, celebrated Corpus Christi with special pomp and devotion in a fashion strictly prescribed by law. All patricians were bound to attend or be fined unless they secured special permission to be absent.[84] Dubrovnik's devotional life was also influenced by its consciousness of belonging to a wider Dalmatian community. Thus in 1445 it was decided to celebrate with due solemnity the feast of St Jerome 'like the other Dalmatians of whose nation he was' (*sic*).[85]

Different saints and churches were associated with different favours. Diversis notes that those planning long journeys would traditionally call in to say their prayers at the church of St Blaise in Gruž before setting off. The same author also remarks that miraculous cures for epilepsy were traditionally associated with the church of St Stephen, which contained the holy relics of St Petronella, St Domicilla and other saints.[86] Devotion could degenerate into superstition. Bartol Kašić records, for example, how he was asked by the inhabitants of Slano to bless a stream which they thought was bewitched because those who drank from it developed fever.[87] Astrology, too, had widespread appeal. When the Black Death struck Dubrovnik, some people thought that it was the result of a conjunction of Mars, Jupiter and Saturn.[88] Nor was it only the unlettered who believed in the stars. The learned poet-monk Mavro Vetranović was firmly convinced of the beneficent effects of the moon on human affairs, which he lauded in his poem *Pjesanca mjesecu* ('Poem to the Moon').[89] Miraculous portents were perceived and analysed and may have encouraged the gullible and the mischievous to cause trouble. On 17 January 1510 a fiery apparition in the shape of a huge cross appeared in the sky over Dubrovnik. At the same time a crucifix began to bleed on the island of Hvar and was led in procession amid scenes of hysterical weeping. The following year the islanders rose in revolt.[90]

Popular piety in Dubrovnik might on occasion be naive but it was also practical. It is clear, as noted earlier, that the impulse towards the creation of the town orphanage was overwhelmingly Christian. So was that for the bequests for the poor, lepers, widows and the ransoming of captives. The most systematic form of devotional and charitable activity was, however, that of the confraternities. (The confraternities of St Anthony and St Lazarus, which in a number of respects occupy a place apart, have already been discussed.)

Although even the craft guilds retained some spiritual and charitable features, there was a large number of exclusively religious confraternities. These were based on particular churches, though over the centuries they might move from one to another. From the thirteenth and fourteenth centuries there existed the confraternity of St Andrew (founded in 1266 by the Benedictines), that of the Rosary (founded probably in the thirteenth century by the Dominicans), that of St Michael *in arboribus* (founded by the men of Gruž in 1290 in the church whose pine-shaded graveyard would become the town cemetery) and that of St Mary in Rožat (founded in 1321). The fifteenth century saw more confraternities functioning on Lopud, at Sustjepan near Gruž and at Mokošica overlooking Rijeka Dubrovačka. In the following century, the confraternity of St Rock was founded in honour of that saint in response to the plague of 1526, and in 1542 the Senate authorised that public money be spent on building a small church where the confraternity could meet.

The purposes as revealed by the rules of these confraternities were very similar. The objectives were to encourage religious devotion, provide sustenance for those in trouble, preserve social order and, more generally, enjoy mutual companionship. The statute of St Mary in Rožat, for example, prescribed that a *gestaldus* with three 'judges' and two 'deacons' be elected annually to control the confraternity's affairs. The *gestaldus* was obliged to give a banquet on All Saints Day (1 November) to which all members were invited. Each member must bring a quart of good wine to the event or be fined. The members had to work in the vineyard belonging to the confraternity and also to contribute four *grossi* annually which went towards the upkeep of the church, masses for the dead and alms for the poor. The statute of the confraternity of St Michael *in arboribus* had similar provisions. It laid down that any member who refused the *gestaldus*'s instruction to bring back to Dubrovnik another member who fell sick anywhere within the area stretching from Molunat to Pelješac must pay a fine of six *grossi*. A fine of one *grosso* would be levied from anyone refusing an order to bring back another member's body.[91]

It is clear from their provisions that most of those who joined the purely religious and charitable confraternities were people of modest means. But, of course, the craft confraternities and – even more so – the *Antunini* and *Lazarini*, contained extremely well-to-do people, who practised their devotion and charity within these bodies. The merchant of Kotruljević's treatise is extremely devout. And even if this was an ideal, the thoughts of Jakov Lukarević on the subject are revealing. This hard-headed merchant and experienced diplomat considered it one of the glories of the Ragusan Republic that the government had devoted so much effort and money to encasing its holy relics in gold and silver, embellishing the cathedral and restoring the churches of the *distretto*.[92] He also recorded with pride that wherever Ragusan merchants went they built Catholic churches and brought Catholic priests to celebrate mass in regions where the faith had otherwise almost entirely disappeared.[93]

Catholicism provided the basis of the Republic's political identity, and when churchmen got in the way of state interests they were likely to be unceremoniously ignored, upbraided or severely punished. But it is equally true that the Catholic identity of the Republic was a spiritual and not merely a political reality.

ELEVEN

Cultural Life: Literature, Scholarship, Painting and Music (c. 1358–c. 1667)

I. Writing and Writers

Education

The mentality of the poets and playwrights, painters and patrons, musicians and audiences who comprised Ragusan society can only, in the first place at least, be understood in the light of that society's education. A basic education was, of course, important to all those who took an active part in the commerce upon which Dubrovnik's success and, indeed, survival depended. But from an early date it is clear that the Ragusan patriciate were interested in their sons' acquiring something broader and deeper than that. Thus, as early as the fourteenth century, the Ragusan government was recruiting Italian tutors to educate the children of Dubrovnik.

The influence of current Italian thinking and attitudes probably increased when, in the first half of the fifteenth century, a school was opened to be run by an Italian rector and other masters. The Tuscan Diversis was the first rector, and it was he who managed to convince a reluctant Senate to set aside a separate building. The school was arranged on two floors. Older pupils were accommodated on the ground floor, but the business of teaching Ragusan boys of varying ages was conducted on the first floor – where the clamour of Vlachs and other traders was less of a nuisance.[1] The school developed from providing an elementary to a more advanced level of tuition, and some of the masters – including Ilija Crijević, rector from 1510 to 1520 – were in due course Italian-educated Ragusans.[2] Latin was the main language used at the school, though probably some Italian was too.

The humanist scholars who taught in Dubrovnik, naturally, retained their friendships with Italians elsewhere. These links also resulted in a flow of Italian books to Dubrovnik, which – whether because of the conservatism of the Ragusan patriciate or because of more straightforward economic considerations – for centuries had no printing press. At the time that the first Ragusan poets were writing, the rector of the Dubrovnik school was Daniele Clario, from Parma. He was a friend of the famous Venetian printer Aldo Manuzio. Clario, who in 1505 became Chancellor of the Republic and may even have taken Ragusan citizenship, was sent books by Manuzio to sell to interested Ragusans. Indeed, a regular supply of Venetian-printed works found its way over the years to Dubrovnik. The arrival in 1555 of Lodovico Beccadelli as Ragusan archbishop introduced a new wave of Italian Renaissance cultivation and connections.[3]

Members of the religious orders in Dubrovnik both provided and themselves received education; moreover, the libraries they developed were storehouses of erudition. As Diversis notes, the government of Dubrovnik often awarded bursaries to those Franciscan and Dominican friars who were deemed by their superiors intelligent enough to benefit from study at European universities.[4] A distinguished case in point was the famous theologian and esteemed ecclesiastical diplomat Ivan Stay, born in Dubrovnik in the early 1390s. Stay entered the Dominicans and spent some years studying in Dubrovnik before being despatched in 1414 to Padua University with his expenses paid out of Ragusan state funds. In view of his future services to the Republic, it was a good investment.[5] Indeed, many of Dubrovnik's writers, scholars and other intellectuals would over the centuries be helped by the Ragusan state in this fashion and repay their patrons accordingly.

The Dominicans of Dubrovnik who initially educated Stay benefited from a rich library. By the end of the middle ages it contained more than 1,000 volumes. But it was the quality and variety, not just the quantity, of the works housed along its twenty-two shelves that have impressed later scholars. Alongside works on language, literature and theology, there was to be found a substantial collection of volumes covering the natural sciences – mathematics, geography and astronomy.[6]

The Franciscan house in Dubrovnik, too, was a centre for theological and philosophical study for friars in the region: in the seventeenth century it became a *studium generale* at which professors from other provinces came to lecture. The Franciscans were justifiably proud of their library. The government similarly understood the value of the collection. In 1440 the Rector wrote to the Franciscan guardian asking him to mount an inquiry to ascertain what had happened to valuable books which had gone missing. The donation of private collections greatly expanded the original core of the friars' liturgical, theological and devotional material. For example, at the beginning of the sixteenth century the bishop of Mrkan and Trebinje, Đuro Kružić, donated several hundred volumes to each of the Franciscan and Dominican libraries. The Franciscan collection was, however, almost completely destroyed by the fire which raged in the wake of the 1667 earthquake. According to the former librarian, who still wept as he recalled the tragedy years afterwards, 7,500 books were lost in the blaze.[7]

It was, however, the Jesuits who revolutionised the standards of teaching and the level of education in Dubrovnik, as elsewhere. From the time of the first Jesuit mission to the city in 1560 there had been discussion about setting up a Ragusan *collegium*, and from as early as 1583 the Ragusan Senate was, in principle, in favour of such a move. It is easy to understand why it was attractive to the patriciate. The Jesuits enjoyed an unchallenged reputation for their teaching methods, and it was clearly in the interests of Ragusan patricians to ensure that their sons benefited. However, as has been noted earlier, the proposal to found a *collegium* became inextricably tangled up with other political considerations, and the Jesuit presence itself in Dubrovnik was neither continuous nor uncontroversial. This does not, though, seem to have prevented the Jesuits themselves from teaching. A modest humanistic school run by the fathers and catering for Ragusan youth was certainly functioning from 1619 or 1620. In 1622 this school had 70 or more pupils, of whom 50 were sons of the nobility.

Wrangles between the order and the Republic over finance continued to delay the establishment of a fully-fledged *collegium*. Eventually, the bequest of a Ragusan Jesuit, Marin Gundulić – who died on 30 November 1647 in his sister's house in Dubrovnik after a terrible sea crossing – paved the way for the foundation. Negotiations with the Jesuit General dragged on until a combination of the good offices of Stjepan Gradić in Rome and the presence of a new (Ragusan-born) superior in Dubrovnik, Orsat Ranjina, won the necessary permissions. Land and property were duly acquired, and in 1662 under another Ragusan superior, Frano Gundulić, the building work actually began in earnest. But not for long. Five years later the Great Earthquake destroyed the new structure before it had been nearly completed. Building recommenced in 1670, with the Emperor Leopold I contributing 800 florins. The construction of the college was finally finished in the 1690s. A fine baroque church dedicated to St Ignatius and built according to the designs of Andrea Pozzo slowly rose beside it: the work took place over a period of some twenty-five years. Then in 1765, the magnificent steps connecting the church and college with the square below were added.[8]

The Jesuits have been credited (though credit is perhaps not the appropriate word) with influencing Ragusan literature and thinking in the directions of the Counter-Reformation and away from the Renaissance. But in truth only with the beginning of records of the work of the *collegium* is it possible to determine which Ragusan *literati* were educated by Jesuits. Most important, however, is that the presence of the order – catechising and preaching as well as teaching – integrated Dubrovnik still more fully into current modes of European thinking and behaviour, in sharp contrast to the Republic's neighbours from the hinterland.

Language

The cultural life of Dubrovnik, viewed in the round, was indeed that of a distinctive but integral part of the Mediterranean world. This important truth was so evident to contemporaries that they barely bothered to remark upon it. It is only subsequent political and ideological debates that have confused the issue. There is thus, for example, no evidence that Ragusans felt that their general use of Croatian apparent in everyday speech from the late thirteenth century, and increasingly so in literary works from the mid-fifteenth century, marked out an alternative cultural direction. As the greatest Dalmatian Renaissance literary figure, Marko Marulić from Split, noted of his epic based on the biblical story of Judith (*Istorija svete udovice Judit u versih harvacki složena*, completed in 1501), it was written in Croatian for those who 'were not learned in Latin books'.[9]

It is impossible to trace with any certainty the precise balance between Slavic and Latin-Romance languages in Dubrovnik at particular times. Latin was used in official documents, changing to Italian (to judge from the decrees contained in the *Liber Viridis*) in the 1420s.[10] But Diversis notes that in his day there was still in use in the debating chamber and the courts what was known as Old Ragusan. It contained elements of Italian and Croatian and was probably a survival of Dalmatian Latin, a distinct Romance language spoken in urban centres on the Dalmatian and Albanian coast for many centuries after the end of the Roman Empire.[11]

Elsewhere in Dalmatia by the late eleventh and twelfth centuries, the common people were certainly using Croatian. In Dubrovnik also, by the 1280s there were Slavic toponyms, some of which – like the street called Prijeko (meaning 'across') – have survived to the present day. Other clues suggest that at about this time the use of Croatian in everyday parlance may have increased. In 1284 a merchant accused of ignoring an order to appear before the Ragusan count claimed that he had only read (and presumably understood) the Croatian translation of the summons, which had arrived too late to allow him to respond. In 1285, during a riot by the side of the town harbour, the crowd were said to have shouted to some popular fugitives from the authorities, '*Podhi sbogo*!' ('Go with God!'). In the fourteenth century there was a large, regular influx of Slavs from the hinterland into Dubrovnik to work as servants and workmen: this must have given a new impulse towards linguistic Slavicisation.[12]

What is less clear is the impact which such trends had upon the language used by the well-educated and well-born. Some intellectuals, like the Latinist and poet Ilija Crijević (1463–1520; he was known in humanist circles as Aelius Lampridius Cervinus), deplored the widespread use of Croatian by his contemporaries in place of the Old Ragusan used by their predecessors. A generation later a Venetian visitor noted that while the Ragusan womenfolk did indeed use Croatian, Ragusan men used Italian as well.[13] The impression that Ragusan women, being in general less educated, predominantly used Croatian is confirmed by the experience of the Jesuit Bartol Kašić in the 1620s. Kašić was specifically asked by the devout ladies who frequented the church of All Saints (known in Dubrovnik as the Domino) to deliver his commentaries on the Gospel in Croatian.[14]

It is, though, important to remember that the Slavonic/Croatian spoken and written in Dubrovnik – and what was written did not necessarily mirror what was spoken – continued to evolve. The problem is that the stages of that evolution are only patchily recorded. The development of a Slavic literary language depended fundamentally upon the evolution of Church Slavonic through the medium of 'Glagolitic' – that is, the script which, it is now believed, was originally brought by the followers of St Methodius to Croatia at the end of the ninth century – into a Croatian vernacular.[15]

Moreover, from the earliest stages this evolution took place in different dialects and sub-dialects. As already noted, of the dialects both čakavian and štokavian were present along the Dalmatian shore, with štokavian predominating inland. This picture is complicated by the existence of two sub-dialects, ikavian and ijekavian. (There also existed ekavian, the basis of modern Serbian).[16] Because of its shifting population – the result of both immigration and commerce – all sorts of languages, dialects and accents could doubtless be heard in the bustling streets of Dubrovnik. But it is clear that the basic Croatian spoken was štokavian, though with a čakavian substratum. The literary language of Dubrovnik, on the other hand, was not so clear-cut. Ragusan štokavian writers were influenced by čakavians from elsewhere in Dalmatia. Poets adapted their vocabulary to the subject they were addressing and, still more important, to the rhymes they needed. There was a change between the sixteenth century and the seventeenth century away from the čakavian and ikavian to štokavian and ijekavian forms. But more important than these linguistic technicalities is what they signified, namely the development of a sophisticated and adaptable Koine.[17] Part of the end result was that 'the best of Croat literary accomplishments rivalled the best products of contemporary European imagination'.[18]

The Place of Ragusan Literature

The literature of Dubrovnik had a decisive impact on the evolution of Croatian as a literary language. This was in large measure because of the decision of Ljudevit Gaj (1809–1872) and the Illyrianists in the 1830s to choose the language of Ivan Gundulić and his fellow Ragusan successors and imitators as the standard for linguistic unification. But that decision itself partly reflected the prestige which Ragusan literature had already acquired a good deal earlier throughout Croatia.[19]

Dubrovnik's literary output was, for the size of the population, extraordinarily large. But much of it has been lost or survives in truncated form. This was, doubtless, partly because a good deal of the love poetry written in the style of Petrarch (Francesco Petrarcha: 1304–1374) and the formalised, rhetorical letters which Renaissance Ragusans used to delight in exchanging were intended for friends and fellow *literati* rather than for a wider audience. It was equally the consequence of the fact that Dubrovnik had, until its last years as a Republic, no printing press and that although wealthy patrons, and sometimes the government itself, might subscribe to have volumes published in Italy, most had to survive (or often not survive) in manuscript copies. Indeed, in the sixteenth century only twelve books by Ragusans were published, of which just five were secular rather than devotional works. Thus, for example, three of the six volumes of poems known to have been written by the highly productive Benedictine monk Mavro Vetranović have been lost. Most of the plays of Dubrovnik's only playwright of genius, Marin Držić, have disappeared or exist as mere titles or fragments. Other literary figures of the time, who were highly esteemed by their contemporaries, appear now as simply names, since their work has perished. Such, for example, is the case of Ivan Gučetić (1451–1502), who is said to have written in Latin, Greek and Croatian and who was praised to the skies by his Ragusan and Italian contemporaries, but whose extant work consists of just one Latin epigram.[20]

Although little Dubrovnik would acquire a unique literary prestige, the background to its authors' achievements can only be understood by looking at wider cultural trends in Dalmatia. The originality of Dalmatian Renaissance literature, from the point of view of literary criticism, lies in its combination of idioms and styles derived largely from Latin/Mediterranean models with a quite different Slavic linguistic morphology and social and political colour. Its most significant starting point is not Dubrovnik but Split, where in 1450 Marko Marulić was born the son of a patrician lawyer, whose profession the young Marko followed. Marulić was past 50 when he began to publish his literary works. His own writings and the accounts of him by contemporaries reveal a man of broad culture, large historical sense and deep piety. Marulić won Europe-wide fame with his *De institutione bene vivendi per exempla sanctorum*, published in 1506. It was enormously popular. In the sixteenth and seventeenth centuries thirty-six editions of it were published in six languages; it was one of the few volumes taken by St Francis Xavier to Goa on his missionary journeys. Though principally a Latinist, Marulić turned to Croatian for his most explicitly political works, intended to rouse Christendom to the defence of his fellow Croats and of his beloved Split. His *Molitva suprotiva Turkom* ('Prayer against the Turks') was a supplication for action, not a sigh of resignation. His (already mentioned) *Judita*, with its powerful description of the decapitation of the pagan general Holophernes and the rout of his army, had a similar message.[21]

Renaissance Poets

The first two notable Ragusan writers, Šiško Menčetić and Djore Držić, could not on the face of it have been more different than Marulić. Menčetić was born in Dubrovnik in 1457, Držić in 1461. Both were obviously and unashamedly influenced by Petrarch, of whom they must indeed be considered imitators. 'The Petrarchists,' it has been said, 'took from Petrarch everything except his genius.'[22] Moreover, other, more artificial and less genuinely poetic influences from Italy were also at work.[23] Thus overwrought phrases – rapidly becoming clichés – of unrequited love are the stuff of both Šiško Menčetić's and Djore Držić's verse. The former's poem 'Your Hair' runs:

> When you let down your hair, O beautiful maiden,
> Such glory won't be seen in the blossoming rose.

And it seems to me that whoever looks at you
Either envies you or dies of desire.[24]

The two Ragusan poets were not, it seems, much alike in character. Šiško Menčetić (of a distinguished patrician family) spent his youth in regular, rowdy brushes with the law, while Djore Držić, a commoner, avoided a criminal record, had a good education, wrote in Latin as well as Croatian, and rather late in life was ordained a priest.[25] Though their subject matter was similar, their vocabulary was somewhat different: more čakavian has been detected in Držić. Apart from Petrarchan (and other Italian) influences, the most historically significant element that their verse has in common is the use of a double-rhyming, dodecasyllabic line – the traditional line of popular Croatian (and Serbian) verse. Indeed, the earliest line of Croatian verse recorded in Dubrovnik, written by one of the town clerks in the margin of the Customs Statute of Dubrovnik, already bears the form:

Sada sam ostavljen srid morske pučine
Valovi močno, bjen daž' dojde s visine

Now I am left amid the ocean,
The waves soak me, while the rain pours down furiously from the skies.

The poems of Šiško Menčetić and Djore Držić have largely been preserved because they were included in a collection (*zbornik*) drawn up by their Ragusan contemporary, Nikša Ranjina (1494–1582). Ranjina's *zbornik* – the original is lost – contained 820 poems, many of them anonymous, and testifies to the amount of poetry which Dubrovnik's literary figures, talented and not so talented, were producing.[26] Djore Držić died in 1501 before the full flowering of Dubrovnik literature, but Šiško Menčetić, who succumbed to the plague of 1527, lived long enough to witness it.

In this the pivotal figure was Mavro Vetranović (called 'Čavčić'). Born in 1482 or 1483 of a citizen merchant family, the young Vetranović joined the Benedictine order, taking the religious name of Mavro (or Maurus). He studied with some distinction at Monte Cassino, then returned to the Ragusan monastery on Mljet. For some reason he was sent into exile by the Ragusan Senate two years later, but the sentence was remitted and Mavro came back to spend the rest of his days on the territory of Dubrovnik. He became for a time the first head of the Mljet Congregation of Benedictine houses. But he later escaped his administrative chores and went to live as a virtual hermit between

1531 and 1541, on the little island of Sveti Andrija – a psychologically and physically gruelling experience on which he reflected in his poem *Remeta* ('The Hermit'). He then returned to spend his last years on the mainland at the monastery of St James at Višnjica, where he died in 1576.[27]

It has been well said that 'lament was Dum Mavro's most characteristic expression'.[28] But it is also true that, quite apart from the human shortcomings that are the usual stuff of ascetic criticism, the political situation of Christian Dalmatia was much to be lamented. Vetranović's poetry thus echoed many of the themes of Marko Marulić. In his *Pjesanca Latinom* ('Poem to the Latins') he deplored the way in which the struggle between France and the Habsburgs for Italy had divided the Christian great powers, so undermining effective resistance against the Turks. Similarly, in his *Tužba grada Budima* ('Complaint of the City of Buda') he depicted the Hungarian city as abandoned by the Habsburgs to its fate of Turkish domination. But Vetranović would not have been Ragusan if he had failed to add a distinctive patriotic flavour to his groaning. Thus, not entirely fairly, it was the Venetians who came in for the heaviest criticism for failing to resist the onslaught of the Ottoman Empire. Venice was castigated as a mud heap inhabited by cowards. The piratical inhabitants of nearby Perast – Venetian subjects – were given equally short shrift. By contrast, in his poem *Galiun* ('The Galleon') the Ragusan navy was proudly described as queen of all the ships that sailed the sea and depicted as being under the captaincy of St Blaise. Vetranović also wrote quantities of religious poetry – some of it, like his *Pjesanca šturku* ('Poem to a Cricket'), a reproach to a cricket who fails to sing the praises of Mary as dawn breaks, of great delicacy. He cooed in love poetry, thundered in denunciations of vice, sneered at human (particularly female) vanity.[29]

During his long literary career Vetranović also wrote plays, notably *Orfeo* (an account of the myth of Orpheus and the Underworld), and eclogues. Presumably, this was what gave rise to the slander circulated by gossips in Dubrovnik that Marin Držić's first (pastoral) play, *Tirena*, had been plagiarised from the work of Vetranović. It was in order to refute this rumour that the latter wrote his poem *Pjesanca Marinu Držiću u pomoć* ('Poem in aid of Marin Držić').

Marin Držić

For many reasons, not all of them equally admirable, Marin Držić is nowadays without doubt the most highly regarded and popular of the literary figures of old Dubrovnik.[30] After passing into oblivion for some four centuries, Držić's plays began to be performed once more in the 1930s in the first Yugoslavia.

But it was only after the creation of the second, communist, Yugoslavia after the Second World War that Držić's appeal to the regime – as a kind of proto-socialist conveniently capable of dwarfing the hitherto greater reputation of the aristocratic, 'conservative', Catholic Ivan Gundulić – resulted in earnest exploration of his work. Evidence of Držić's (already described) somewhat puerile conspiracy against the Ragusan authorities improved his socialist credentials still further.

By the end of his life in Italy, Marin Držić was probably not only embittered but unbalanced. And it is certainly true that as a comic writer with a sharp eye for plebeian cunning and popular wisdom he may sometimes have unsettled the more pompous of Dubrovnik's patricians – certainly, he had enemies.[31] But it is clear enough from the facts known about him that Držić's main artistic purpose was simply to entertain and that his main professional purpose was to pay his debts – a character, in fact, not unknown in artistic circles.

The Držić family had, it seems, originated in Kotor. They had at one time been regarded as patrician but had sunk into the ranks of the Ragusan citizenry by the end of the fourteenth century. Marin was born about 1508. The family had acquired rights of succession to the churches of the Domino in Dubrovnik and of St Peter on Koločep, so it was necessary that one of each generation be a priest. Thus Marin was early on marked out for holy orders. His father and brothers were merchants, but not, in the end, very successful ones: their business collapsed in 1538. In these straits, Marin first took up the post of organist at the cathedral but then received a scholarship from the Senate to go and study at the university of Siena. This was the turning point in his literary career. He may, in fact, already have written some of the love poems he later published; but it seems certain that contact with Latin and Italian drama during his six or so years stay in Siena made him into a playwright.

Marin Držić was clearly already something of a personality. In 1541 he was elected by his colleagues as rector of the student house. In 1542 he was punished for taking part in the production of a play which, being staged at night, had broken the city's curfew rules. Back in Dubrovnik, the Držić family's fortunes again collapsed: the firm went bankrupt once more, and definitively, in 1544. Marin's brother, the painter Vlaho, had to return from Venice to try to pay off the debts. Marin, himself, at the end of 1545, joined the retinue of the Austrian nobleman Christoph von Rogendorf as his secretary and travelled with his new master to Vienna and then, acting as *dragoman*, on to Constantinople. There he incurred the Ragusan government's suspicion through his contact with the Bučinčić brothers and was smartly summoned back to explain himself. Only now at the age of forty, one suspects with financial rather than spiritual interests uppermost, he was ordained first a deacon and then a priest.[32]

It was also at this time that he began to write and produce his plays. In fact, they were all, it seems, written between 1548 and 1558 – during which period he was also struggling to pay off his debts by, for instance, taking up employment as clerk in the state salt office.[33] The order in which the plays appeared is disputed, but it seems to have been much as follows:

Tirena (a pastoral play) in 1549
Novela od Stanca ('The Joke of Stanac' – a one-act comedy) in 1550
Pomet (a comedy, now lost) in 1553
Venera i Adon ('Venus and Adonis' – a pastoral play) in 1551
Skup ('The Miser' – a comedy of which the end is missing) in 1554
Džuho Krpeta (a pastoral play of which only fragments remain) in 1555
Dundo Maroje ('Uncle Maroje' – a comedy of which the end is missing) in 1551
Plakir (sometimes also known as *Grižula* – a pastoral play of which a few lines only are missing) in 1556
Hekuba (a translation of an Italian version of the tragedy of Euripides) in 1558

Nothing is known for certain about the dates of production of *Mande* (a comedy of which the beginning is missing), *Arkulin* (also a comedy missing the first part) and *Pjerin* (another comedy of which only a fragment remains).[34]

Although Marin Držić was a highly gifted and genuinely original playwright, his creative work was also influenced by and in some cases closely modelled upon that of others. His pastoral plays, for example, were not the first to appear in Dubrovnik; indeed, pastoral scenes peopled by the requisite shepherds, nymphs and cupids were performed from the first half of the fifteenth century.[35] But, probably influenced by the plays he encountered in Siena (the so-called *dramma rusticale*), Držić introduced into his own pastoral plays 'real', comic, sympathetic, rustic shepherds alongside the stereotypically cultivated models inherited from classical tradition. As a result, within the pastoral framework something fresh and original emerged.

The same willingness to turn traditional models to new creative purposes is evident in the case of Držić's comedies. The basis of all Renaissance comedies was the rediscovered works of Plautus. But Plautus's (and sometimes Terence's) characters were then adapted and combined with themes from

Boccaccio and other medieval writers, and finally a 'realistic' element from everyday life was added. Furthermore, whereas the Romans wrote their comedies in verse, the Italian comic playwrights wrote in a popular prose, laced with jocular obscenity. Plautus's comedies were probably introduced to Dubrovnik by Ilija Crijević who, as has been noted, was for ten years (1510–1520) rector of the Dubrovnik school. Weight is lent to this hypothetical connection by the fact that in the prologue to *Skup* (itself based on Plautus's play *The Pot of Gold*) the Satyr says that the story is 'stolen from some book older than age – from Plautus'.[36]

But Držić was no more a mere imitator of classical models in his comedies than in his pastoral plays. Whereas Plautus wrote in verse, Držić wrote all but one of his comedies – the exception is *Novela od Stanca* – in prose. (The Ragusan playwright occasionally uses verse within these plays, but only for some special effect.) Most obviously, he set all but two of his comedies this time the exceptions are *Dundo Maroje*, which takes place in Rome, and *Mande* which takes place in Kotor – in his own native Dubrovnik. The types and often the individual characters have classical counterparts, but Držić treats them in distinct and original ways. These elements can be illustrated by his comedy, *Skup*.

The plot, based on Plautus, is about a miser determined to keep hidden a pot of gold that is secreted in his kitchen hearth. Skup is also trying to find a suitably rich husband for his daughter, Andrijana, so as to avoid providing her with a dowry. She, however, is in love with the young Kamilo. The latter's interfering mother, unaware of her son's amorous preoccupation and believing that her own brother should find a wife to provide an heir, persuades him to ask the miser for Andrijana's hand. Skup agrees but, pleading poverty, says that he cannot provide a dowry. This, though, does not deter Andrijana's elderly would-be suitor, who is already rich and who is only concerned that his future wife behave properly and be duly deferential to his wishes. Kamilo and Andrijana are appalled to learn what has been arranged. Kamilo, at the suggestion of his cunning servant, now pretends to be gravely ill and retires to bed. When the servants of Andrijana's intended arrive at Skup's house to begin preparing the banquet for the wedding, the miser believes that they have really come to steal his gold and insultingly drives them away. On hearing of Skup's behaviour, their master decides to call off the wedding altogether. Kamilo's servant, meanwhile, hears Skup talking to himself about his plans to hide his treasure in a church, and proceeds to steal it. The miser has lost his treasure – and also lost his daughter, for Kamilo now tells him that he has secretly married Andrijana. Kamilo's servant returns the miser's gold. At this point –

just before an obviously happy ending – Držić's play abruptly ends, its last lines having been lost.

The humour comes first of all from the aptly named characters. The miser's cook is called Variva – 'Stewpot' – though she never actually does any cooking because the miser will not allow anyone near the hearth where his pot of gold is hidden. Andrijana's elderly, rich suitor is called Zlatni kum – 'Golden Godfather'. The latter's maidservant is called Gruba – 'Ugly' or 'Coarse' – a name she bewails. She is indeed coarse, though perhaps not ugly, as she shows when discussing with Variva the fate of those like Andrijana forced to marry old men. (See below.)

Držić provides, in a soliloquy by Skup, a psychologically compelling description of the anguish of avarice. The miser cannot think about anything but his gold which robs him of his peace of mind, turning everything in life upside down. In the end he concludes: 'What a calamity is gold! Love is not love, gold is love.'[37] But in fact almost everyone in the play is either selfish and dishonest or else like Dobre ('Good Woman'), Kamilo's mother, a busybody, or like Kamilo an ineffectual romantic who has to rely on the advice of an unscrupulous servant. No single group in Dubrovnik emerges from Držić's comedy unscathed, yet none appears either as without its merits. Thus Dobre scorns young brides who join their mother-in-laws' households only to

> … sleep till noon, and when they wake two maids are not enough to corset them and dress them. They're hardly dressed for dinner, they fidget with their hair, twist the curls round their fingers before the mirror… paint their faces, and do not get to church but as mass finishes… Work! – Hold their hands in their muffs, stroll from window to window winding their ball of silk…[38]

But this is only one side of the age-old mother-in-law/daughter-in-law conflict, for Držić has the Satyr in the introduction to the play give an equally biting and amusing account of the problems caused by ill-tempered, bossy mothers-in-law. Similarly, the views of the younger generation are expressed by another character, who answers Dobre's criticisms of young wives directly by saying that he does not expect his wife to rise at dawn just to work like a drudge but prefers to have her in bed with him in the mornings.

Skup is characterised by the use of comic irony at various levels. Much of the fun is had by ambiguity of meaning which leads to misunderstanding – for example, the miser imagines on separate occasions that Variva, Zlatni kum and

27. Detail of Lovro Dobričević's Virgin and Child, St Julian the Hospitaller (1465)

Previous page
26. Detail of Lovro Dobričević's Virgin and Child, St Anthony of Padua (1465)

28. Vicko Lovrin: St Michael and other Saints (1509)

Following page
29. Detail of Nikola Božidarević's Blessed Virgin with Saints, St Blaise and St Paul (early sixteenth century)

NICOLO
RAGVSEO
PINSE

MARCO D BIAGIO
DE NAVE FECCE FARE
QUESTO ALTARE

32. Detail of Nikola Božidarević's *Sacra Conversazione* (1517)

Previous pages
30. Detail of Nikola Božidarević's *Sacra Conversazione*, St Julian the Hospitaller and St James (1513)
31. Nikola Božidarević: The Annunciation (1513)

Kamilo know about his treasure, when they are actually talking about something else entirely.[39]

Although *Skup* is set in Dubrovnik, this circumstance is less important to the plot than it is in some of the other plays. Držić's works, like many other Ragusan literary productions, generally contain some patriotic praise of the Republic. *Tirena*, probably his first play, was perhaps for that very reason, when the playwright was less than confident of his reception, particularly flattering on the subject. It thus depicts in its introductory scene – consisting of a conversation between two peasant Vlachs looking down from the hills – a Dubrovnik which is peaceful and well-governed. The more intelligent of them, Vučeta, exclaims:

> Where there is peace, there is God.
> And life is just, where there is justice and reason.

Dubrovnik, he explains, is a place that the traveller can visit without fearing that he will be robbed of his possessions. It is full of beautiful women elegantly dressed. The other amusingly bumpkin-like Vlach, Obrad, replies that never was such beauty seen even among country maids. Vučeta then remarks:

> Do you see this city and its nobles?
> Their good name is nowadays praised throughout the world.
> The lords of the East of Ottoman stock, by God's grace,
> Are exceedingly gracious to them;
> And there in the West the powerful lords
> Now love them too – may God remain merciful to them;
> They have no quarrels with anybody in the world,
> Their ships sail by every wind.[40]

Tirena, being a pastoral play, is not, of course, actually set within the walls of the city but is depicted as occurring in some rural area nearby. By contrast, *Novela od Stanca* is closely dependent on the physical features of Dubrovnik. It takes place in the streets by night at carnival time. Two young bucks and their friends, dressed as nymphs, play a cruel trick on the gullible Hercegovinian Vlach yokel, Stanac. He has brought his goat, oil and cheese to sell in Dubrovnik but, finding nowhere to lodge, has to spend the night by the side of Onofrio's Great Fountain, where the prank takes place. Persuaded that if he drinks the water offered by these 'nymphs' he will become young and handsome, he later falls asleep; then his tormentors tie him up, cut off his beard, and take his goods – though leaving the money to pay for them. Old Stanac now wakes up and angrily realises what has happened.[41]

Hercegovinian Vlachs (who are to be understood in these plays simply as peasants, without any racial allusion) are not the only local figures of fun in Držić's plays. A special place in his roll call of buffoonery is reserved for the *Kotorani*. The inhabitants of Kotor were ideally placed to be the butt of Ragusan humour. They were physically and culturally very close to Dubrovnik. But they were also centuries-old rivals and, most important, they were ruled by Venice. The *Kotorani* in Držić's plays take both major and minor roles. But they are classically cuckolds, almost always greedy and dishonest, and they are usually to be found interjecting phrases in Italian – which Držić then translates, sometimes loosely, for the benefit of his Croatian-speaking audience in Dubrovnik. So Pasimaha, Zlatni kum's servant in *Skup*, is shown purchasing huge quantities of food in the market and can be heard exclaiming '*Santo nostro di Cattaro*!'[42] The saint in question is, of course, Kotor's patron, St Tryphon (Sveti Tripun). Most of Držić's *Kotorani* are called by some variant on that name – Tripe, Tripče or Tripčeta. The whole of the comedy *Mande* is set in Kotor. The eponymous central figure is the wife of the drunkard Tripče and the complicated plot consists of Kotoran wives and husbands playing tricks on one another. A rather more subtle treatment of the Kotoran joke is offered by a scene in *Dundo Maroje*. Here Maroje, far away from his hometown of Dubrovnik, is delighted to meet the Kotoran Tripčeta speaking his own language – though Tripčeta's lines are, of course, liberally laced with the statutory Italianisms. Maroje's servant Bokčilo is, in any case, less delighted and when Tripčeta declares that he is from Kotor replies: 'Oh, may God help you!' At which, doubtless, the Ragusans rolled in the aisles.[43]

Držić's characters are, as with the *Kotorani*, frequently and deliberately 'localised' by their speech. So little is known independently from the (possibly unrepresentative) literary sources, about the everyday language of Ragusans that it is difficult to make firm distinctions. But traces of the speech from Dubrovnik's hinterland alongside that of the Dubrovnik's own everyday speech have been analysed by scholars. More evident to the general reader is Držić's use to humorous effect of popular riddles, jokes and proverbial sayings in the mouths of his less educated characters.[44] A case in point is the suggestive observation of Gruba to Variva in *Skup*, which, like other such examples, is in verse:

> Remember the maid's prayer to her mother:
> Give me not an old husband, dearest mother mine,

For the old ones leave us hungry,
Though they may have gold in plenty,
While just a look from a young husband fills us to the full.[45]

The production of plays in Dubrovnik was strictly controlled by the government, which was always in the last resort more interested in public order and morals than in entertainment and culture. Generally speaking, plays could only be performed at carnival time – though not infrequently carnival performances, too, were banned. An exception could be made for wedding festivities.[46] Even when plays were performed in someone's house, permission had first to be obtained from the authorities and it would only be given if the work was deemed respectable. The authorities were also anxious to guard against the practice – evident from a somewhat later date, but doubtless occurring in Držić's day too – of depicting one's enemies in the guise of some ridiculous or hateful 'fictional' character.[47]

The place for public performances was traditionally outside, *prid dvorom* – that is, 'in front of the [Rector's] Palace'. *Tirena* was certainly first performed there, because we know from the introduction to the second performance (which was at a wedding) that its first showing was rained off.[48] *Dundo Maroje* may have been performed in the Ragusan Great Council Chamber, though this is disputed. Otherwise, weddings seem to have been the occasion for the performances of most of the plays.[49] Those performances *prid dvorom* had the full benefit of location in the architecturally dramatic centre of Renaissance Dubrovnik. Apart from the seated audience, people from the tall housing blocks around about would have been able to enjoy the fun from their open windows. But whether in public or private performances the contrived scenery was simple, usually a street corner and a house or two – though it seems likely that for *Novela od Stanca* a mock-up of the Great Fountain and the steps around it were built.[50]

Hardly less important than scenery in providing a sense of place to the performance would have been the fact that the actors themselves would often have been well known to most of those present. There was certainly no stigma attached to this amateur acting. The distinguished Ragusan philosopher Nikola Gučetić recalled in later life that as a young man he had acted in one of Držić's plays during the playwright's lifetime.[51] Detailed information about the companies of actors who performed Ragusan plays is only available for the period after Držić's death. Some of it comes from the account given by Stjepan Gradić of the life of his friend, the playwright Junije Palmotić (1605–1657), in which Gradić describes how companies of noble and citizen youths (men only) were formed – among other things – in order to put on these plays.[52] Of the companies which performed Držić's plays, it is known that there was the Pomet company, which put on (the now-lost) *Pomet*, *Dundo Maroje* and perhaps other works; there was the company *od Bidzara* which performed *Hekuba*; there was the company called *Garzarija* which played *Mande*; most famous of all, it seems, in view of the playwright's playfully laudatory remarks in the introduction to *Skup*, were the *Njarnjasi*, described by Držić as the 'chief of all companies'.[53]

Marin Držić has rightly been called 'the greatest playwright in the old Croatian Renaissance theatre, the best that any of the nations of Yugoslavia has ever produced and a significant dramatist by international standards'. Indeed, a comparison with Shakespeare's comic work is not too far-fetched.[54] Any modern analysis of the literary history of Dubrovnik runs the risk, however, of attributing a greater importance to Držić's genius than the contemporary circumstances of Dubrovnik would warrant. It is worth recalling that whatever the playwright may privately have thought, he considered that it was his Petrarchan poetry and pastoral plays rather than his comedies which most redounded to his public reputation. That, presumably, is why the former were published in Držić's own lifetime (in 1551) but the latter were generally not, and were consequently wholly or partly lost. (*Novela od Stanca* was, though, published with the poems, and with *Tirena* and *Venera i Adon*; consequently, alone among the comic pieces, it comes down to us intact).[55]

Latinists and Scholars

A still more important qualifying consideration is that – as noted above – the Renaissance Croatian literature of Dubrovnik and Dalmatia existed alongside a large output of Humanist Latin literature, which was at least as highly esteemed by contemporaries. Moreover, the latter's flourishing from the late fifteenth to early nineteenth centuries is a constant reminder of the extent to which Ragusans and Dalmatians were an integrated part of the Latin Mediterranean world.[56]

Dubrovnik's most distinguished early humanist author, Ilija Crijević, was initially educated in his hometown, then sent briefly to study in Ferrara – returning when the latter fell to Venice – before being sent to Rome by the Ragusan ambassador to the Vatican, Ilija's uncle. In the Eternal City he learned rhetoric and poetry, and fell entirely under the influence of the humanist scholar Pomponio Leto: he joined the latter's Academy and received the honour of being crowned as 'poet laureate'.[57] In 1487 Ilija Crijević returned to

Dubrovnik. In 1491 he married, but soon quarrelled with his wife's family and was sentenced to six months' imprisonment for insulting his mother-in-law. Crijević was, in truth, probably a bit too sophisticated for Dubrovnik and probably also knew it. He tried in vain to find teaching posts or librarianships in Buda, but failed. He had to settle instead for the posts first of Castellan of Ston and then – after a brief spell as Rector of Dubrovnik's school – as castellan of the even more isolated fortress of Soko in Konavle.[58] There he was, as has been noted, again in trouble – this time for bringing women into the castle by night. He was also twice town advocate. The last ten years of his life seem to have brought some peace and fulfilment. In 1510 he was again appointed Rector of the school and kept the post till his death ten years later. After the death of his wife, he was ordained priest. During the ups and downs of this largely frustrating and turbulent life, Ilija Crijević found solace in a prodigious output of Latin epigrams, poems (240 have been preserved) and letters. But his love for Roman cultivation in no way diminished his Ragusan patriotism, as his unfinished poem *De Epidauro* testifies.[59]

Other Ragusan Latinists followed Ilija Crijević's example. Jakov Bunić (1469–1534) was a diplomat and merchant, pursuing very much the standard career of the Ragusan ruling class and equally typically combining it with literature – though of a more serious kind than the run-of-the-mill patrician poetaster. Bunić published his allegorical poem *De Raptu Cerberi* in Rome at the end of the century and then won still greater acclaim in influential Catholic circles with his *De Vita et Gestis Christi* (published in Rome in 1526).[60] His Ragusan contemporary Damjan Benessa (1477–1539) wrote poems and epigrams, as well as his devotional *De Morte Christi,* in the manner of Bunić.[61]

Latin was not, though, simply the language of elegant or devout verse. It was, above all, traditionally the language of internationally recognised scholarship. Thus it was in Latin that the first serious historical work by a Ragusan was written. Ludovik Crijević Tuberon (1458–1527) – a distant cousin of Ilija – studied in Paris and distinguished himself as a classicist and historian, acquiring the name *Tubero* from his fellow academicians. He returned to Dubrovnik and, having abandoned his plans to marry a member of the wealthy and well-connected Đurđević family, in 1484 he joined the Benedictine order. The next eighteen years were spent living in the monastery on Sveti Andrija, which had been founded by the Crijević family. Crijević Tuberon then became Abbot (and soon sole inhabitant) of the monastery of St James at Višnjica. During these years in the cloister he wrote an eleven-volume history of his times that included a section (the fifth volume) on his native Dubrovnik: the latter was later published separately. Ludovik Crijević Tuberon dedicated his work to his friend and patron Grgur Frankopan, the Croatian-born archbishop of Kalocsa in Hungary, who first urged him to embark on the project and who doubtless provided him with a good deal of useful information for it. The work itself was notable not just for its humanistic mastery of language and learned allusions: it was also a serious historical account of the turbulent period from the death of Matthias Corvinus in 1490 to the election of Hadrian VI in 1522, and as such constituted an important step forward in European historiography.[62]

Latin was also pre-eminently, of course, the language of theology, which the relatively stable political circumstances of Dubrovnik allowed non-Ragusans to come and write about in peace. Juraj Dragišić (known in humanist circles as *Georgius Benignus Argentinensis Salvatius*) was born in about 1450 in Srebrenica, where he entered the Franciscans. On the fall of Bosnia to the Turks in 1463, he fled – probably via Dubrovnik – to Zadar, and then went on to study first in Ferrara, then in Bologna. At the end of 1469 he went to Rome and fell in with the Platonist circle of philosophers which gathered around the immensely influential Cardinal Bessarion.[63] Juraj Dragišić indeed distinguished himself now and later as a philosopher and theologian. He was accordingly sent to complete his studies at Paris and Oxford, where he immersed himself in, among other things, Oriental languages. Dragišić was then appointed professor at Urbino and acted as tutor to the son of the duke. Later, he went on to lecture in Florence. There he became a close associate of the controversial and doctrinally suspect Platonist Marsilio Ficino and again acted as tutor – this time to the sons of his new patron, Lorenzo de' Medici.[64] In Florence, however, Juraj Dragišić became involved in a bitter quarrel with his superiors and had to flee into exile. It was thus that he found his way back to Dubrovnik. On his arrival, as he records, he had envisaged spending a period of total inactivity, as if stranded somewhere in darkest Africa. But in fact, under the benevolent and tolerant protection of the Ragusan authorities, he passed five of the most productive years of his life (1496–1500). The first work he wrote in Dubrovnik – published in Florence in 1497 – was a bold if politically imprudent defence of the holy revolutionary of Florence, Girolamo Savonarola, who was actually burnt at the stake a month after Dragišić's text appeared.[65] The scholar's second and more learned work owed its genesis directly to Dubrovnik, for its consisted of a theological treatise on angels (*De Natura Caelestium Spirituum quos Angelos Vocamus*), written in the form of nine dialogues engaging young members of thirty-three great Ragusan families. Its publication in Florence in 1499 was subsidised by a grant of 30 ducats from the Ragusan Senate. A third work, published in the same year, consisted of a funeral oration on the death of the Ragusan nobleman Junije Đurđević, whose son was one of Dragišić's favourite students. In 1500, after the death of the Franciscan general who was his prime adversary, Dragišić returned again, and this time permanently, to Italy. He took part in the Fifth Lateran Council (1512–1517) and continued his controversial public career, defending the arguments of the Orientalist Johannes Reuchlin.[66] Juraj Dragišić died, probably in Barletta, in 1520. Damjan Benessa, in his eulogistic epigram in honour of Dragišić, proudly noted that his (adopted) fellow Ragusan's memory was revered in the most important cities of Italy.[67]

As has been observed, not just theology and philosophy but also the natural sciences were studied in the religious houses of medieval Dubrovnik – and Latin was, of course, the medium for scholars' conclusions. Ivan Gazul (c. 1400–1465) was of Albanian extraction and may or may not have been born in Dubrovnik, but he certainly considered himself a Ragusan. He was also one of the most internationally distinguished astrologer-astronomers of his day. His most influential work was *De Directionibus* (1438), greatly admired by fellow scholars. The Republic shrewdly exploited Gazul's reputation, contacts and education by employing his services on important diplomatic missions. On coming to the throne, the Emperor Matthias Corvinus in 1458 summoned Gazul to Hungary, almost certainly to fulfil the post of court astrologer. But Ivan Gazul – despite the urging of the Ragusan Senate – refused the Emperor's request. Gazul died in Dubrovnik in 1465 and was described on the occasion of the registration of his will as 'doctor of arts, and most distinguished astronomer'.[68]

Lay scholars, whose importance increased with the secular impulses of the Renaissance, were more likely to use Italian for their treatises. This was, for example, the case of Nikola Nalješković (before 1510–1587). After an early career blighted by the debts which he ran up in his unsuccessful business ventures, and by the disappearance of his betrothed into a convent, he temporarily restored his fortunes working for the state in various capacities. But study, writing and discussion were his true consolations. Nalješković was an ardent, even slavish, adherent of Aristotle in his theories about philosophy, mathematics, and astronomy. His main work is the *Dialogo sopra la sfera del mondo* – a treatise in the form of five dialogues commenting upon the medieval scholar John Sacrobosco's writings about the universe.[69] The Ragusan Senate paid for the cost of publication in Venice in 1579, and rewarded the author with a silver dish bearing the arms of Dubrovnik. Another Ragusan contemporary of Nalješković similarly evinced his scholarly prowess as a mathematician and natural scientist. Most of the works written by Miho

Monaldi (1540–1592) have been lost. But his *Irene overo della bellezza*, published in Venice in 1599, reveals that he was a gifted follower of the approaches of Pythagoras and Plato.[70]

Probably most significant, however, was the influential Ragusan polymath Nikola Vitov Gučetić (1549–1610). Born into one of the greatest noble houses, Gučetić spent some time in Rome before returning to Dubrovnik to marry Mara Gundulić, daughter of another powerful patrician. He was heavily involved in commerce and finance and in the management of his property – he had a large town house near the Domino and a villa at Trsteno, which he called 'Arcadia'. But he was also a serious (neo-Platonist) philosopher of international distinction. Thus he was a member of the literary academy of Perugia, and was awarded a doctorate in 1601 by Pope Clement VIII. He wrote treatises on beauty (*Dialogo della bellezza*), love (*Dialogo d'amore*), and managing the family household (*Governo della famiglia*).

Nikola Gučetić was also a theologian with a taste and gift for polemic. He wrote three books of commentaries on the psalms. The first was dedicated to Pope Sixtus V (1585–1590), and in his introduction Gučetić proudly describes Dubrovnik's deep and proven loyalty to Catholicism and the papacy. This set the scene for a ferocious attack upon Martin Luther's 'wicked ambition and Satanic doctrine' and upon his followers' pride, stubbornness and deceit. In all three books – the last two dedicated to Cardinal (Saint) Robert Bellarmine – Gučetić skilfully and energetically contested what he considered the crucial Protestant errors regarding penance, predestination and temptation.[71] As a reward for his efforts, he received a doctorate from Rome. Nikola Gučetić also delivered a course of theological lectures in Dubrovnik cathedral. His intellectual prowess was lauded by the Jewish poet Didachus Pyrrhus and by the historians Serafino Razzi and Mavro Orbini. Gučetić accumulated a large library which eventually, in 1670, found its way into the safekeeping of the Jesuits.[72]

Literature after Mavro Vetranović and Marin Držić

Croatian literature in Dubrovnik immediately after the death of Marin Držić in 1567 and of Mavro Vetranović in 1576 went through a period of rather uninspired consolidation, though not, it must be said, of sterility. The already-mentioned mathematician, Nikola Nalješković, is perhaps more notable for the cultivated circle around him than for his own creative literary achievements. Yet nor were the latter negligible, for Nalješković wrote seven plays and a quantity of Petrarchan poetry. Nalješković was also a scientist and astronomer.[73]

Nalješković's contemporary Antun Bratosaljić Sasin (1520–1594) is best known for an enthusiastic – even far-fetched – evocation of the prowess of the Ragusan navy in his poem *Mrnarica* ('Navy').[74] The poet portrays the ruler of Messina standing at his window, seeking to know whose is the great fleet he sees before him. His servants hurry to reassure him that the ships are not those of hostile Moors or Turks but rather of friendly Dubrovnik. And they add:

> Their sailors are like lions,
> They're brave and matchless,
> Hot tempered, quick and handsome,
> And true-believing Christians as well.
> ... St Blaise is their captain,
> It is he who rules this navy, famous throughout the world
> From East to West.

Bratosaljić Sasin then describes the Ragusan navy's ferocity in its battles with the infidel, and concludes:

> ...This is the same fleet
> Which can justly be called
> The mistress and queen
> Of all the navies of the world.
> And fortunate is he
> And most great his honour
> Who spends his life faithfully
> Beneath the flag of Dubrovnik.

The final line – *Pod bandijerom Dubrovnika* – sounds like a defiant refutation of the slur that Ragusans, as devious opportunists, sailed under *Sette bandiere* ('Seven flags').[75]

Other contemporaries contributed to Dubrovnik's large literary output. Of these, Dominko Zlatarić (1558–1613) has been esteemed more highly for his translations than his poetry. Another writer, Horacije Mažibradić (1566–1641), spent his years in Konavle surrounded by his wife and thirteen children – he received a grant from the Senate to help him out with the cost of raising and keeping them. When not otherwise engaged, he wrote quantities of verse, letters and epigrams.[76]

Ivan Gundulić

Little, though, suggested that as Dubrovnik entered the seventeenth century one of its sons was about to generate some of the finest poetry ever produced in the Slavic world. Ivan (Djivo) Gundulić (1589–1638) was the eldest son of one of the most powerful patrician families of Dubrovnik. Not much is known of his early life. He may or may not have received an education from Jesuits, though he certainly had close family contacts with them. He married at the age of thirty and had three sons and two daughters. One son, Frano, entered the Austrian army and died a Field Marshal in 1700. The other, Šiško, was, like his father, a writer and playwright. Ivan Gundulić died in 1638, probably of pleurisy. His early writings, not all of which have been preserved, were, it seems, pastoral plays with the usual intertwining of classical mythology and love scenes.

In the introduction to his translation of the seven penitential psalms in 1620, Gundulić signalled his rejection of his earlier works of 'vanity and frivolity' and vowed to be henceforth a 'Christian poet who knows, believes in and confesses God, from Whom, by Whom and in Whom all good things come...'[77] Quite what is to be made of this remains uncertain, despite much scholarly debate. There is no evidence that Gundulić had led an immoral life from which 'repentance' was required. And his pastoral play *Dubravka* (1628), which for all its moralising cannot be considered a 'Christian' work, was still to come. So perhaps Gundulić's resolution should best be understood as a passing if intense phase in the poet's growing spiritual, psychological and artistic maturity.[78]

Gundulić's reputation rests on three works, each of which is revealing both about his own mentality and about the circumstances of early Baroque Ragusan society. *Suze sina razmetnoga* ('Tears of the Prodigal Son') was published in Venice in 1622. It followed a tradition established in the Italy of the second half of the sixteenth century of poetical depictions of 'tears' of repentance, like those of St Peter (after his threefold denial of Christ) and St Mary Magdalene (after her life of sexual immorality). In Italy this type of poetry was known as a *pianto*, in Croatian *plač* ('lament'). But *Suze sina razmetnoga* is also a strikingly original work of moving religious piety and poetic delicacy. It may be autobiographical, while deliberately echoing St Augustine's *Confessions*.[79]

Six years later appeared *Dubravka*. This pastoral play is also of a type well-known in Dubrovnik, though its choruses reflect the increasing use of music and dancing in Ragusan dramatic productions at this time. Gundulić himself had written a number of such pastoral pieces in his earlier period. The characters lack the wit and originality of Držić's. But the poetry itself is of an unprecedented finesse and, most interesting and important, powerful political and social messages were subtly developed alongside the main plot. The latter is, it seems, deliberately pushed into the background: the main events are even retailed to the audience at second hand. The action takes place in the Grove (*Dubrava*, that is, an idealised Dubrovnik) on that day in the year when the most beautiful nymph is wed to the most handsome man at a special, joyful feast under the benevolent gaze of the (pagan) gods. However, in an unheard-of outrage, on this occasion corruption enters to disrupt the pristine order. As a result of bribery, the eponymous nymph, Dubravka, is not in fact adjudged to her lover, the handsome shepherd Miljenko, but rather to the rich and ugly shepherd Grdan ('Monstrous'). At the last moment, however, a miracle takes place and the judges and populace realise the horror of what is contemplated. Dubravka and Miljenko are then wed amid great rejoicing and general festivity.

Marxist literary criticism has seen in the tale of Grdan and Miljenko an allegory of the struggle between the rich commoner class and that of the patricians – the latter, of course, not being permitted to marry commoners.[80] But although there may be present some undertones of this latent tension, they certainly do not constitute the main theme. More important are the dominant ideas of unity and order upon which the Ragusan Republic placed such importance and which the poet may well have felt were threatened by avarice and social change.[81] The theme is also taken up in the play in an episode where a satyr abandons his satyress and tries to pursue a nymph, only to learn the hard but requisite lesson of his unnatural and so disorderly obsession. Life in the Grove, it is clear, is an evocation of the Golden Age, of lost innocence. True, it has become for a tragic moment corrupted by the love of gold. The fact remains, however, that it is clearly still an infinitely better place to live than elsewhere on the Dalmatian coast where, as a visiting fisherman complains, only oppression and violence are to be found (i.e. under Venetian rule). A love of liberty rather than a love of gold is the vocation urged upon his fellow Ragusans by Gundulić in his stirring final chorus:

O lijepa, o draga, o slatka slobodo
dar u kom sva blaga višnji nam bog je do,
uzroče istini od naše sve slave,
uresu jedini od sve Dubrave,
sva srebra, sva zlata, svi ljudski životi
ne mogu bit plata tvoj čistoj ljepoti!

Oh beautiful, dear, sweet Freedom,
The gift in which the god above hath given us all blessings,
Oh true cause of all our glory,
Only adornment of this Grove,
All silver, all gold, all men's lives
Could not purchase thy pure beauty![82]

Gundulić's last and greatest achievement was his epic poem *Osman*. It was inspired by the *Gerusalemme liberata* of Torquato Tasso (1544–1595); indeed, Gundulić had originally planned a Croatian translation of that immensely influential work, of which he completed just one canto. But the battle between Polish and Turkish forces at Chocim and the subsequent murder in Constantinople of the Ottoman sultan Osman II (1621–1622) caused the poet fundamentally to revise his intentions. Although the influence of Tasso is still evident – some of Gundulić's characters and several scenes closely echo Tasso's, and *Osman* like *Gerusalemme liberata* was to have twenty cantos – the Ragusan poet rejected the master's doctrine by choosing contemporary events, not those of the distant past, as his subject. Moreover, he did so with political and religious as well as just artistic considerations in mind. *Osman* is to be seen as in the tradition of Croatian poetic protests against Ottoman domination. It is also, and perhaps more significantly from the wider historical perspective, an expression of an early and very particular kind of pan-Slavism.

The Croats, including the Ragusans, were by the early seventeenth century already fully conscious of belonging to the Slavic race. Thus the Ragusan Benedictine Mavro Orbini (mid-sixteenth century-1611), had written during Gundulić's lifetime (in 1601) his *Il Regno degli Slavi* ('The Kingdom of the Slavs'), giving an account of the history of the Slavic peoples. He, in turn, was only continuing a theme addressed in 1525 by the Dominican Vinko Pribojević, from Hvar, in a famous lecture on the same subject. Gundulić clearly shared the view that Dubrovnik and Dalmatia were part of a wider entity which broadly covered the territories of what would be called in later times the Southern Slavs:

In the mouth of the fierce Dragon,
And under the claws of the ferocious Lion,
Surrounding thee from both sides,
Still is found the state of the Slavs'.[83]

Gundulić was not only aware of his Slavic identity: he was also proud of it. Thus *Osman* includes a sympathetic account of Serbian history and summarises several of the traditional (probably both Serbian and Croatian) heroic songs called *bugaršti*ce.[84] Gundulić was especially proud of his own language and wrote a glowing public letter of praise in honour of Grand Duke Ferdinand II of Tuscany for his decision to learn Croatian.[85] But the troublesome fact was that most of the Slavs were schismatics, rejecting papal authority. Gundulić, as a Catholic, and one most probably influenced by the Jesuit Counter-Reformation vision, had to find a Catholic rather than Orthodox Slavic hero who would unify the Slavs under the banner of the true faith to achieve their liberty. Thus he turned to Poland and its Crown Prince Wladyslaw, the accredited victor of the (in fact inconclusive) Battle of Chocim. For his own poetic and political purposes Gundulić both magnified Wladyslaw's role and exaggerated the significance of the military encounter itself. But this was not simply a personal whim or wishful thinking. Chocim occurred at a time when the Ottoman Empire was indeed evidently beginning to decay. Moreover, a tradition had it that the Empire would fall 1,000 years after the death of Muhammad (d. 632). Gundulić's portrayal of the battle's significance was potentially all the more persuasive because he had access to very detailed accounts of what took place in both Poland and Constantinople. Indeed, he may have enjoyed the added benefit of what his own relations in Ancona told him, for Wladyslaw stayed with them when he was in Italy.

The story of *Osman* takes place after the Turkish defeat on the battlefield. The Sultan laments the corruption which has so badly weakened the Ottoman armies and decides to go East to raise a new army in order to supplant the corrupt Janissaries on whom he and his predecessors have had to rely. Meanwhile, Osman sends one emissary to make peace with the Poles and another to find him a wife among the free-born Slavs. The Janissaries, however, get wind of what is planned and rise in revolt. Osman refuses to hand over to them his hated Grand Vizier and is then tortured and killed in humiliating circumstances. (There are also various sub plots.)

Osman is portrayed quite sympathetically. His attempts to restore the Empire are honest, but they are also hopeless. The Empire is so morally polluted and imbued with iniquitous practices – such as the Ottoman custom of fratricide – that to fail to apply them, as does Osman in sparing the brother who will later supplant him, is in such a context more imprudent than noble. Moreover, in ignoring the role of providence in human affairs – portrayed as the recurring *motif* of the 'wheel of fortune' – the young sultan suffers fatally from pride. Yet, for all that, Osman is flesh and blood, while Wladyslaw and the several heroines of the epic – plucked evidently from Tasso – are by contrast mere poetic cardboard.

Gundulić's wider (and highly conservative) political philosophy shows through in his sympathetic understanding of the problems faced by rulers and the lack of understanding they in turn receive from the ruled:

> For Kings, there is no sweet and easy life,
> As the common people think,
> They are ever taken up with anxieties
> And have not even a short hour of peace.
> They have to watch through the nocturnal darkness
> For those who sleep,
> To care for the care-free
> And to think and labour for the idle.[86]

It used to be thought that the missing two cantos of *Osman* were destroyed by the Ragusan government because they would have so infuriated the Turks. But what the other eighteen cantos of the epic already contained about the Empire's corruption and about the Prophet was surely embarrassing enough. The Ragusan authorities' unease about the poet's undiplomatic language about the Empire may, on the other hand, explain why *Osman* was not printed until the nineteenth century, even though the large number of extant manuscript copies testifies to its popularity among Ragusans themselves. In such matters Dubrovnik was nothing if not prudent.[87]

After Gundulić

Ivan Gundulić's death in 1638 can, in retrospect, be seen to mark the close of the great age of Ragusan literature. But at the time it would not have seemed like that. Ivan Bunić Vučić (1592–1658), for example, continued for another twenty years to write his pastoral and religious poems, with a lasting influence on later Ragusan writers.[88] It was, though, the playwright Junije Palmotić who probably made most impression upon his Ragusan contemporaries. Palmotić was in many respects in the mould of Gundulić. He was from a patrician family, Counter-Reformation-minded, conservative, patriotic. His melodramas were generally based upon classical models, though *Pavlimir* draws for its plot upon the chronicle of the Priest of Dioclea, and in *Kolombo* ('Columbus') the audience discovered, doubtless to its delight, that the crew of the great discoverer's ship were Ragusans. Palmotić's plays included singing and ballet, and the scenery was probably much more elaborate than that to which Ragusan audiences were accustomed. The pieces were very popular at the time, and were highly regarded by the Illyrianists for mainly ideological reasons. Modern critics, though, have found them less appealing.[89]

Perhaps the chief importance in Ragusan literary history of lesser writers like Palmotić is what they show about the mentality of the society in which they worked. And the most striking feature of that mentality is surely its robust self-confidence, not to say pride. In *Pavlimir*, Palmotić praises Dubrovnik thus:

> Hvar, Šibenik, and flat Zadar,
> Kotor, Trogir and brave Split
> Will always hold your glorious beauty
> At the highest worth.
> You shall be the brilliant crown
> Of all the Dalmatian cities
> And all the waters of the Adriatic
> Will serve and honour you.[90]

But it was not only the rest of Dalmatia but the whole of Europe from which the Ragusans of the day expected honour. After all, was not Dubrovnik part of that Croatian bulwark which protected Italy itself? So the Ragusan Vladislav Menčetić (1618–1666) in his *Trublja slovinska* ('The Slav Trumpet') proclaimed:

> Italy would have long since
> Sunk beneath the waves,
> Had Croatian shores
> Not broken the force of the Ottoman sea.[91]

II. *Art and Music*

The Background to Dubrovnik's School of Painting

The depredations of time upon the artistic heritage of Dubrovnik have been even greater than upon the literary. An episcopal visitation of 1573 recorded 150 polyptychs on the altars of Dubrovnik's churches. Less than a tenth of these works now exist.[92] But enough remains to establish both the quality and character of what has been lost.

Dubrovnik's greatest painters were all heavily dependent for their training and insights upon Italian, above all Venetian, achievement. Moreover, in speaking (as it is, with common-sense qualifications, permissible to do) of a 'Dubrovnik School' of painting, it is important always to recall that several of its greatest members were Ragusan by adoption rather than birth. Yet the fact remains that in late medieval and Renaissance Dubrovnik, through the interplay between the genius of individual painters and the continuity provided by the teams who worked in these men's *ateliers*, a distinctive artistic tradition was born, flourished and eventually died – and one whose achievements are on a par with many of the finest works of Italy.

What has been called the 'prehistory' of the Dubrovnik school of painting, from the eleventh to the end of the fourteenth centuries, essentially consisted of religious painting by Slavs and Venetians in a largely Byzantine style. The greatest masterpiece of this period is undoubtedly the painted crucifix with Our Lady and St John, which hangs in the Dominican Church in Dubrovnik. It is now firmly attributed to the great Venetian master Paolo Veneziano.[93] The work was commissioned in the will of Šimun Restić in 1348. It seems to have been made by Paolo in 1352 when he was in Dubrovnik, though it was only actually placed in the church in 1358 as a votive against the plague then ravaging the city.[94]

As the century wore on, there was an increase in the demand for secular painted artefacts like weapons, shields, belts and chests. This coincided with two further developments, of which Paolo Veneziano's appearance had been a forerunner – first, requirements to embellish the ecclesiastical buildings constructed or extended at this time and, secondly, the established policy of the Ragusan government of inviting foreign painters to the city and providing them with salaries and commissions. By the second decade of the fifteenth century the results were evident. So, for example, the famous Blaž Jurjev lived and worked on Ragusan territory from 1421 to 1427.[95] He was initially paid 30 *hyperperi* by the authorities towards the cost of his house and workshop opposite the Franciscans on Placa. But the sums increased as the government became ever more pleased with his work, which was in a severely traditional Venetian style which he had certainly learned in the workshops of that city. His two surviving works on the territory of the former Ragusan Republic are the Crucifixion painted for the Franciscan church of St Nicholas at Ston and the picture of Madonna and Child at the Dubrovnik church of St George (*Sveti Đurađ*) on Boninovo.[96]

Blaž Jurjev was not the only foreigner working in Dubrovnik at the time. Antonio di Jacopo from Lucca was employed by the Ragusan government between 1423 and 1428 to paint (with a team of six Ragusans) a series of murals in the cathedral. He stayed on in Dubrovnik. Ill and poor, he was provided with 10 *hyperperi* by the government in 1434 and probably died shortly thereafter. Similarly, Lorenzo di Michele from Florence was employed by the government in 1433 to paint the Small Council Chamber and then three years later was taken permanently into the service of the Ragusan state. The Florentine, like the Luccan, seems to have stayed on in Dubrovnik and died there.[97]

Even before native Dubrovnik painters appear as distinct figures in the historical record, one of the first characteristics of Dubrovnik's art is already evident – namely, the temperamental conservatism of its patrons. Blaž Jurjev's paintings were closely based on Venetian models. Neither Antonio di Jacopo nor Lorenzo di Michele brought, it seems, any trace of Tuscan early Renaissance influence. They were evidently instructed to imitate rather than innovate.[98] This determination by Ragusan patrons – public and private – to ensure that the artist carried out precisely his instructions based on specified models continued. Although it may on occasion have cramped originality, and it certainly discouraged adventure, it did mean that Ragusan art was firmly anchored in Ragusan society. And this was surely healthy.

The First Major Ragusan Painters

Ivan Ugrinović was born in Dubrovnik, almost certainly trained in Venice and was already working back in the Ragusan Republic in 1428. Although it was in sacred art that he excelled, he also painted chests, flags, rooms and beds in private houses, gilded statues and embellished the metal figures which struck the hour on Dubrovnik's clock tower. Sometimes he worked in co-operation with other artists and craftsmen, as with the woodcarver Radoslav Vukić on a number of projects between 1438 and 1457. Among his most important secular works were his painting of a room in the palace of Sandalj Hranić in 1427–28, of the doors and the surrounds of the palace given by Dubrovnik to Radoslav Pavolović in 1428, and of the hall of the Ragusan Great Council between 1430 and 1433. Such work was performed in azure – much prized and made from copper carbonates from Bosnia – and in gold (often in the form of stars) and in other colours.[99]

Ugrinović also painted for clients in Bosnia and Korčula. His main commissions, though, were for altarpieces, icons and murals. Only one example of his work remains – the altar polyptych of St Anthony Abbot on the island of Koločep.[100] It was commissioned by the parish priest and two inhabitants of the island and was to be based upon the model of a polyptych in the monastery of St Clare in Dubrovnik. It was completed in 1434 or 1435. The style, strongly resembling that of Paolo Veneziano, is a mixture of Byzantine and Gothic. Ugrinović's work was prolific, so it evidently suited and thus is an indicator of the taste of his Ragusan contemporaries.[101]

Ugrinović died in 1461 and his son Stjepan Zornelić, with his co-workers, continued the workshop. But Ugrinović's most eminent successor was his younger contemporary, Matko Junčić. The youngest son of a painter in the service of the Republic, Matko was apprenticed in a Venetian workshop before moving to Kotor, where his brother Nikola was then serving as a priest. In 1446, when Nikola was appointed rector of Dubrovnik's school, Matko went with him. Perhaps initially at least because of Nikola's connections, Matko Junčić's painting were almost all carried out for clerics and ecclesiastical foundations. He had begun to work with the great Lovro Dobričević during his time in Kotor and continued occasional collaboration with him and with Ivan Ugrinović in Dubrovnik.

Matko Junčić painted a large number of altar pictures for the churches of Dubrovnik: St Nicholas in Prijeko, St Peter the Great, St Mary *od Kaštela*, the chapel of St Jerome in the Dubrovnik Franciscan church and the Franciscans at Rijeka Dubrovačka all received his paintings, and he was working on others for the Domino and the cathedral at the time of his death. But all that now remains of his work is the altar painting for Our Lady *od Šunja* on Lopud. It was commissioned by the guilds of Lopud and was to be of the same quality as that which the artist had painted for the church of St Peter the Great a little earlier. The painting – a polyptych with figures on a gold background in a Venetian Gothic style with fewer Byzantine elements than are found in Ugrinović – was completed in 1452. Matko Junčić died just two years later.[102]

It was at about this time that a new style which represented a break with that of Paolo Veneziano started to leave its mark on Ragusan painting. Originating in Venice at the end of the fourteenth and the beginning of the fifteenth centuries, this fully-formed, pure High Gothic style, which would in due course pave the way for the Renaissance, is evident in a number of anonymous polyptychs, icons, frescoes, murals and miniatures in Dubrovnik. The gradual acceptance by Ragusan patrons of these trends made possible the triumphant success of one of Dubrovnik's greatest artists, Lovro Dobričević.[103]

Lovro Dobričević

The Dobričević family hailed from Kotor, where Lovro was born in about 1420. He subsequently went to serve his apprenticeship in Venice and practised his art there at the same time as the influential Venetian master and leading figure in the new cosmopolitan Gothic, Michele Giambono, from whom we may assume that he received instruction.[104] (They witnessed a will together in 1444.) Four years later, Lovro Dobričević returned to Kotor and opened a workshop. It was there that Lovro made the acquaintance of Matko Junčić. The two of them collaborated in 1448 on the polyptych for the high altar of the Dominican church in Dubrovnik: Matko was responsible for the wood carving and Lovro the painted saints. (The altarpiece is now in the Dominican sacristy). The centre panel is a somewhat stiff depiction of the Baptism of Christ. The side panels show some of the Dubrovnik patrons' favourite saints – St Michael, St Nicholas, St Blaise and St Stephen, who wears a magnificently embroidered red and gold Dalmatic. A tender Madonna and Child, flanked by more saints, are in the panels above. The approach throughout is emphatically symmetrical: for example, a pensive, fresh-faced St Michael on one flank balances St Stephen, similarly portrayed, on the other. On the immediate left of the Baptism is the bearded bishop St Nicholas, while on the immediate right is another bearded bishop, St Blaise. Each has his hand raised in blessing.

In 1455 Lovro Dobričević was commissioned by the Đurđević family to paint an altarpiece for the Dubrovnik Franciscans. Only one panel of this polyptych, depicting a rather forbidding St Blaise with Dubrovnik in his left hand, has been preserved. In 1456 he painted a Madonna and Child for the church of Our Lady *od Škrpjela* at Perast. Throughout this period Dobričević was still based in Kotor. But in 1457 he finally moved to Dubrovnik and set up a large workshop in which his wife also occasionally assisted. The *atelier* was soon deluged with commissions.

Lovro Dobričević painted for the church of St Peter the Great and the monastery of St Clare in Dubrovnik. In 1461 he painted a polyptych for the Franciscans of Slano and another for the Franciscans of Bosnia. At about this time he received into his workshop Božidar Vlatković, the father of the great Nikola Božidarević.

In 1465 or 1466 Dobričević began working to fulfill a commission from four Ragusan patricians for the high altar of the church of Our Lady at Danče. This work is undoubtedly one of the finest, most delicate and most evocative ever to be painted by a member (albeit by adoption) of the 'School of

Dubrovnik'. Elements of the Renaissance are visible, in particular the subtle dynamism of the treatment of the subject, the individualisation of facial expression, the free application of colour and markedly less use of gold than, for example, in the artist's earlier polyptych for the Dubrovnik Dominicans. The influence of the work of the Vivarini brothers of Murano has also been detected.[105] The centre of the polyptych is a depiction of the Madonna and Child against a dark blue and orange background. Below the Blessed Virgin two delicately painted angels play, respectively, a harp and a portable organ. The childlike, dreamy, elegant figure of St Julian the Hospitaller – a patron saint of travellers and thus naturally a favourite for the eternally peripatetic traders of Dubrovnik – is perhaps the most memorable feature of the painting.

From now until his death Dobričević and his workshop must have been very fully employed. In 1469 he completed an altar painting for the church of Our Lady at Rožat in Rijeka Dubrovačka. Between 1470 and 1473 he collaborated with Stjepan Zornelić on a large altar painting for the newly constructed church of St Sebastian in Dubrovnik. Between 1473 and 1477 he worked initially with Zornelić and later Vlatković on a painting of the Nativity for the church of St Peter the Great. He also collaborated with Vlatković on the upper part of the altarpiece of the church of St Blaise and other projects until his death in 1478.

Lovro Dobričević's influence depended not just on his personal genius and skill. He was also crucial in introducing into the artistic experience of Dubrovnik both the highest achievements of Gothic and the early elements of Renaissance sensibility. Moreover, the size of his workshop and the extent of his collaboration with other artists helped diffuse his insights and techniques. It undoubtedly helped too that he was succeeded by two painter sons, one of whom was exceedingly gifted.[106]

Vicko Lovrin

Marin Lovrin, Lovro Dobričević's elder son, learned his trade in his father's workshop before opening his own off Placa in *Široka ulica* ('Broad Street') in 1486. He operated from there for some years, collaborating with Stjepan Zornelić on a polyptych for the Dubrovnik Dominicans. But he fell into financial straits and returned to his father's hometown of Kotor. Only in 1497, when his younger brother Vicko returned from his studies in the workshops of Italy, did the two move back to Dubrovnik. Vicko had, it seems, absorbed when in Italy the influence of the Venetian Bartolomeo Vivarini and other masters and was clearly now a more skilled artist than Marin. Initially, though, the two opened a joint workshop, which dealt in both painting and woodwork. Their collaboration continued for almost a decade until, in 1506, Vicko set up on his own. Only now was he really successful, becoming *gestaldus* of the Dubrovnik guild of painters.

In 1508 Vicko Lovrin completed an altar painting for the chapel of St Bartholomew in the women's monastery of St Mark's in Dubrovnik. In 1509 he painted a triptych for the Ragusan citizen Vlaho Radošalić for the altar of St Michael in the Franciscan church at Cavtat, where it remains. The centre panel portrays a vigorous St Michael resplendent in elaborate golden armour. This, his only surviving work, is sufficient to show that he inherited much, though perhaps not all, of his father's genius, and followed faithfully in the tradition Lovro had established. Vicko Lovrin died in either 1517 or 1518.[107]

Nikola Božidarević

Oddly enough, the true identity of Dubrovnik's most famous painter was only discovered some four centuries after his death.[108] He signed himself only twice on his preserved paintings – as *Nicolaus Rhagusinus* and *Nicolo Raguseo* – respectively, in an inscription under the left arm of St Gabriel in his Annunciation painted for Marko Kolendić in 1513 and on the foot of the throne of the Madonna in the altar painting for Our Lady's church at Danče in 1517.[109]

Nikola Božidarević – for such was the mysterious Nicholas 'the Ragusan' – perhaps turned out to be the very greatest of Dubrovnik's painters partly because his skill was shaped over such a long period. His career can, indeed, be seen as an extension of that of his father, Božidar Vlatković. The latter had left his family home near Slano in about 1462 to join as a mere workman the Dubrovnik *atelier* of the successful Ragusan painter Vukac Rajanović. The following year he was apprenticed to Lovro Dobričević for whom he was probably working in Kotor when his son Nikola was born. By 1470 Vlatković had made such strides that he was able to open his own workshop in Dubrovnik.[110]

Nikola Božidarević doubtless learned much in his early years under his father's tuition. But on 2 September 1476 he was apprenticed to the Ragusan painter Petar Ognjanović, who promised to house, feed and teach him, and at the end of his apprenticeship to give him 10 *hyperperi*, a cloak and the tools of his trade. Božidarević then apparently had second thoughts, for on 6 January 1477 the contract was annulled by mutual agreement so that he could go to Venice. Not until 1491 does the painter reappear in Ragusan records.[111]

What happened to Vlatković in the intervening period is fairly clear: particularly after the death of Lovro Dobričević in 1478, he was regarded as one of Dubrovnik's leading painters and flourished accordingly. More obscure, and more intriguing, however, is what his son Nikola was doing – and where – during those seventeen years. Scholars have suggested that he worked with the masters of Murano, and he was evidently strongly influenced by the Venetian painters, the brothers Carlo and Vittorio Crivelli and Carpaccio.[112] It has been convincingly argued that he knew the frescoes of Perugino and Pinturicchio in Rome.[113] But such conclusions are ultimately based on study of Božidarević's four extant works rather than on direct evidence from Italy.[114]

After Nikola Božidarević's return to Dubrovnik, he and his father worked jointly on a number of important commissions (though each also worked individually). In 1494 the two painted a large polyptych for the Gradić family intended for the Dubrovnik Dominican church. The following year Božidarević was commissioned to paint the high altar of the Franciscan church in Slano. Also independently, he worked on a *pietà* and an altar picture for the cathedral. However, the earliest extant work of Božidarević – the triptych for the Bundić family chapel in the Dominican church in Dubrovnik – is, as already observed, almost certainly the result of collaboration with his father. Completed soon after 1500, it shows the influence both of Renaissance Venice and of the masters of Ancona. A strong similarity with the work of Carlo Crivelli and his students has also been detected. The painting is marked by its symmetry, which, as has been noted, appears to have been particularly prized by Ragusan patrons. On each side are two heavily bearded, mitre-wearing saints (St Blaise and St Augustine) standing beside two shaven-headed saints (St Paul and St Thomas Aquinas). The Madonna and Child are the focus of the central panel. Below the Virgin (echoing the Book of the Apocalypse 12:1) is an upturned crescent moon. Characteristically of Božidarević, it is the painter's treatment of detail that is most appealing. St Blaise holds in his hands a model of early sixteenth-century Dubrovnik, which remains the best indication of how the city looked at the time. The harbour, securely protected by chains and breakwater, is full of ships. Figures on foot and horseback bustle around Revelin and the Ploče gate. The painting itself can be dated by observation of the exact stage of reconstruction of the Great Arsenal.[115]

During the first decade of the sixteenth century Vlatković worked much less, while his son received a series of important independent commissions. In 1501 Nikola Božidarević was responsible for the upper part of the altarpiece in the Dubrovnik Franciscan church. In 1504 he painted a big triptych for the cathedral, in 1508 another tryptych there dedicated to St Nicholas and in 1510 another painting, and a large painting of St Jerome dressed as a cardinal, for the Rector's Palace.

Nikola was by now at the head of a flourishing workshop and had to rely heavily on collaborators to help him fulfil the increasing number of major commissions. His second extant work is the altar picture for the Dominican church in Lopud, painted in 1513. It was commissioned by the Lopud sea-captain Marko Kolendić. He is shown on the far right panel of the predella, kneeling by the side of Our Lord, Our Lady and St Nicholas, all of whom are waiting for the Lopud Dominicans, rowing a small boat, to reach the shore. Kolendić's carack, proudly riding in the bay of Lopud, appears in the centre of the predella. The main body of the painting is given over to the Annunciation. The idealised landscape behind the Virgin and the Angel Gabriel has far greater depth than could be found in any earlier Dubrovnik painting. Equally interesting, and innovative, are other elements which betoken Renaissance thinking, namely the depiction on the predella of scenes from the life of the Dominicans and of the realistic Lopud landscape behind the carack.

Very soon after completing this work, Božidarević received a commission from the Đurđević family for the chapter house of the Dubrovnik Dominicans. It was executed by early in 1514. For this painting Božidarević abandoned the traditional form of polyptych in favour of the fully developed and very popular Renaissance composition known as the *Sacra Conversazione*. The work is notable for its rhythmic flow and interaction between the holy figures – particularly St Julian the Hospitaller and St James, who stand on the left of the Madonna and Child. A diminutive portrait of the kneeling donor, Orsat Đurđević, appears on the far right, at the feet of St Matthew who is himself standing alongside St Dominic. Above the main panel within a triangular gable the dead Christ lies in the arms of His Mother, surrounded by other saints. The predella has been lost.

While still working on the Durdević painting, Božidarević received a commission from a Lopud cobbler of the same name for a triptych intended for Our Lady *od Špilica*, the Franciscan church on the island. For its execution he therefore appears to have had to rely on his numerous assistants. This has been blamed for weaknesses in the execution. Accordingly, the painting is not now attributed to Nikola Božidarević personally.

Three years later in 1517, shortly before his death, Nikola Božidarević completed the last of his four preserved works – the altar painting in the form of a triptych for Our Lady's church at Danče. This work, too, has been criticised for its reversion to a more traditional approach, after the innovative spirit evident in the earlier *Sacra Conversazione*. In particular, attention is drawn to the 'conservative' use of the triptych form and the liberal application of gold, held to be a 'Gothic' feature. But a painter, even one as distinguished as Božidarević at this the height of his fame, has ultimately to meet his patron's wishes. In any case, it is difficult from an aesthetic rather than academically critical viewpoint to do other than wonder at the painting's balance, delicacy and gentle piety. The centre panel depicts the Madonna and Child. The Holy Infant is holding wheat and grapes, an allusion to the eucharist, while blessing the infant St John the Baptist. Inquisitive cherubs peep around the back of Our Lady's throne. On the left panel stands Pope St Gregory the Great, holding a crucifix in his left hand and blessing with his right. The right panel depicts the encounter of the mounted St Martin of Tours with a near-naked beggar, who from his halo is clearly, in fact, Christ. The image of the beggar's face is reflected in St Martin's sword, with which the Saint is cutting his cloak. The Virgin Mother, St Gregory and St Martin are clothed with magnificently rich, tactile garments – St Gregory's cope with its miniatures of saints and holy scenes is particularly striking. Above the Madonna and Child, a lunette depicts the crucified Christ surrounded by women saints. Below, the central panel of the predella portrays St George in the act of slaying the dragon, surrounded by skulls, while the side panels show the papal coronation of St Gregory and the episcopal consecration of St Martin.

Nikola Božidarević died towards the end of 1517, while still working on a large polyptych for Dubrovnik's cathedral. He was by then a rich man and left 300 gold ducats and a large collection of medals. He had never married, perhaps remaining personally if not artistically dependent on his father who survived him. Božidarević's true personality is indecipherable from his paintings, which are characteristically lyrical, sentimental, and uncannily dreamlike. It is, though, reassuring to know that the master was capable of high spirits even in middle age, and that in the best Ragusan style he was imprisoned for three months for singing rude songs and making a disturbance at carnival time in 1509.[116]

Mihajlo Hamzić

The third outstanding painter in early sixteenth-century Dubrovnik – alongside Nikola Božidarević and Vicko Lovrin, and probably somewhere between the two in skill – was Mihajlo Hamzić. Mihajlo's father Hans was from Cologne and had come into the service of the Republic as its bombardier at Ston, in charge of the construction and maintenance of that town's cannons. Mihajlo's mother was the daughter of Ston's blacksmith. There were three sons and a daughter: Mihajlo was the second son. In the first years of the new century he very likely went to study in the workshop of the great Paduan painter Andrea Mantegna, whose influence on Mihajlo's late work is clear.[117] Mantegna died in 1506, and the young painter returned to Dubrovnik two years later. His reputation probably preceded him, because soon afterwards he was commissioned to paint a picture depicting the Baptism of Our Lord – to be hung in the Rector's Palace. Mantegna's influence is detectable in the grim and craggy landscape. There is none of the symmetry which Ragusan patrons usually liked, and which Božidarević offered, and apart from the halos there is little use of gold. The austere effect created by the cold light which irradiates the scene and by the emaciated figures of Christ and St John the Baptist is softened only a little by greener hills in the distance and the depiction of a stag in the valley on the left.

Whether by bad luck or poor judgement, Mihajlo Hamzić's career – measured in financial as opposed to creative terms – was not a success. He was always either short of, or at least greedy for, money. Alongside the income from his activities as a painter, he also drew a salary as clerk of the Ragusan customs. Early on, he became involved in a dispute with the Dubrovnik painters' guild: possibly this discouraged him subsequently from committing all his energies to painting. Yet he received a series of important commissions. In 1512 he was contracted to paint a tryptych for the Lukarević family altar in the Dubrovnik Dominican church. This painting is in a markedly different style from the Baptism and in a form much more accessible to Ragusan patrons.

Most obviously, whereas the Baptism was a free composition with no regard for symmetry, the Lukarević commission was for a triptych with saints on each side panel balancing each other. At the centre is a cold, dignified St Nicholas wearing a resplendent golden chasuble. The saints on either side are less formal and forbidding – on the left St John the Baptist stands close to St Stephen, on the right St Mark presents his gospel while St Mary Magdalene holds out her jar of precious ointment. St Stephen, like the central figure of St Nicholas, stares straight out of the canvas; the other saints, with half-closed eyelids, appear engrossed in contemplation. The marked differences between this second preserved Hamzić painting and the early Baptism in the Rector's palace strongly suggest that it was a joint work with the Venetian master Pietro di Giovanni, who was working with Hamzić at this time.

Mihajlo Hamzić was, indeed, by now collaborating extensively with a number of other artists and relying heavily upon his workshop to fulfil commissions, because he himself was increasingly involved in commerce. His brother Jakov, who had begun his professional life as a tailor, had graduated to participation in the lucrative but risky cloth trade, and Mihajlo was his partner. In 1514 the business fell into a crisis. The brothers were soon insolvent. Jakov stayed in Italy and Mihajlo, too, had to flee Dubrovnik. The painter was temporarily allowed back to try to arrange settlement with his creditors. Painting was now his only livelihood, and he was able to contribute to the current restoration of the cathedral. But he died, young and still in debt, in 1518.[118]

Later Painters

Simply because of its size, Dubrovnik was only ever able to accommodate a few first-class painters: the number of commissions would not have supported more. The danger of this was, of course, that if those painters died without suitably talented heirs or successors already trained in their workshops the future of Ragusan painting would immediately be threatened. This is what happened, for Vicko Lovrin, Nikola Božidarević and Mihajlo Hamzić all died in 1517 or 1518. It was, therefore, to foreigners – above all Italians – that Dubrovnik's patrons now increasingly looked to execute their commissions.

In a certain sense there is nothing unusual, let alone lamentable, in this. The Italian artists concerned were closely connected with and able continuators of the now dead Ragusan masters, bringing indeed some fresh elements to the paintings adorning the Republic's churches, civic buildings and private houses.[119]

Pietro di Giovanni, who had earlier collaborated with Mihajlo Hamzić, had been strongly influenced by the work of the great Venetian painter Giovanni Bellini.[120] Pietro spent so much of his life in Dubrovnik that he eventually became a Ragusan, joining the confraternity of the *Lazarini*. After Hamzić's death he founded his own independent workshop and was much in demand both as a painter and sculptor. Five of his works have been preserved, covering the period to 1555: they are a polytptych for the high altar of the Franciscan church on Lopud, a triptych for the church of Our Lady *od Napuča* on the same island, a *Sancta Conversazione* for the church of St Andrew at Pile, a miniature on the Statute of the Fraternity of St Lazarus and the painted ceiling of the Rector's Palace. Towards the end of his life Pietro fell on hard times and had to earn his living as a woodcarver in Ston.[121]

In 1526 the Ragusan government also invited two more Italian painters, Pier-Antonio Palmerini from Urbino and Giacomo di Marco from Florence, to come to Dubrovnik. They were taken into state service and provided with an *atelier* in a house belonging to the Clares near the church of the Domino. They probably stayed in Dubrovnik till 1530. In the summer of 1527 Pier-Antonio Palmerini was commissioned to paint a large altar picture of the Ascension of Christ for the newly built votive church of the Holy Saviour (*Sveti Spas*) on Placa, near the Franciscans. It was hung in 1530 and though the painting has received mixed reviews from modern critics, it clearly pleased the Ragusan authorities enormously, for the artist was rewarded with the substantial sum of 150 gold ducats. Palmerini was then commissioned by Luka Bunić to paint a large altarpiece for the sacristy of the Dubrovnik Franciscans.[122]

Italian painters were not the only masters to fill the requirements of Ragusan patrons at this time. Flemish masters also worked there. But all these newcomers had to adapt their style to satisfy the conservative tastes of Ragusan patrons, who had never altogether lost their desire for the retention of High Gothic elements, in particular their delight in triptychs and polyptychs.

Indeed, the career of the last notable Ragusan painter of the period, Frano Matijin, fully illustrates the degree to which artists had to adapt their styles to suit their customers. Born in the last decade of the fifteenth century and himself the son of a painter, Frano accompanied his father and other Ragusans to practise their crafts in southern Italy. He then returned to join the workshop of Vicko Lovrin. His earliest paintings were in the traditional Ragusan manner; but in the face of Italian and Flemish competition he turned instead to a mock-Byzantine, Italo-Cretan style. This had become – and long remained – extremely popular with those Ragusans who preferred its austere simplicity to the extravagance of fully developed Italian Renaissance painting. His commissions were, accordingly, for relatively modest works – a triptych for the church of St Stephen at Rijeka Dubrovačka, a depiction of the Life of St Anthony of Padua for the Franciscan friary at Rožat, a painting of the martyrdom of St Vincent for the Dubrovnik Dominicans and a votive picture for the little church of the *Sigurata* ('Transfiguration') also in Dubrovnik.[123] But Frano Matijin could still not make a living. Several times he had to flee Dubrovnik because of his debts. In 1548 he ended his days living the life of a peasant on Lopud.[124]

Dubrovnik continued to produce some competent local painters, and the Ragusan government continued to provide them with modest subsidies and assistance. Among the art forms which flourished throughout the life of the Republic and beyond were the votive pictures and engravings of ships whose captains and crews celebrated their deliverance in this way. These were for the most part, though, of human rather than aesthetic significance. The church of

Our Lady of Mercy (*Gospa od milosrđa*) was the traditional focus of this kind of devotion in Dubrovnik.[125] In truth, from the mid-sixteenth century on – in fact until the period of the Croatian national movement and the work of Vlaho Bukovac in the nineteenth century – Dubrovnik's artistic achievements were extremely limited. By the time of Frano Matijin's death in 1548 the 'Dubrovnik School' of painting had clearly already ceased to exist.[126]

Music and Musicians

Ragusan musical achievement cannot seriously be compared with Ragusan literary and artistic accomplishments. Not until the eighteenth century did Dubrovnik produce a first-rate (if still little-known) composer, in Luko Sorkočević (1734–1789).[127] On the other hand, music was an important, integral part of the cultural, social and, indeed, political life of Dubrovnik. The Ragusan government certainly thought so. It has, indeed, been estimated that in the course of the fifteenth and sixteenth centuries more than 150 musicians were employed out of state funds to satisfy the requirements of the Rector's chapel, the cathedral and the church of St Blaise.

The government made considerable efforts to recruit the best, though it usually retained musicians initially on a year's contract so as to judge their worth before taking them on as permanent state employees. These state musicians were kept busy with a large number of public functions, some more elevated in tone than others. They would play their instruments when the Rector left his palace in procession. They played at church services. They summoned the Councils by the sound of the trumpet. Trumpeters played at the solemn proclamation of decrees, when delinquents were denounced and when the condemned were executed.

It was, however, on religious feast days that the skills of Dubrovnik's state musicians were most likely to be fully stretched. By decree of the Senate the musicians were obliged to play at least one composition after solemn vespers before the high altar of the church of St Blaise and at the end of high mass before the altars of Dubrovnik's other churches.[128]

The Feast of St Blaise was the high point of the musical as well as the social, religious and political year. Evliya Çelebi, when he witnessed the celebration of the Feast in 1664, observed how the people in procession clapped their hands, a portable organ was played, trumpets sounded and drums beat, and how large numbers of priests chanted the litanies with melodic voices. The secular dancing was also accompanied by music.[129] In fact, so important was the event in Dubrovnik's musical calendar that the government had long been accustomed to recruit the cream of outside musicians to join its own for these splendid occasions.[130]

The portable organ of the sort described by Evliya Çelebi (and painted by Lovro Dobričević in his altar painting at Danče) had long ago been replaced within Dubrovnik's churches by the great fixed organs. In the fourteenth century the organ acquired pedals and more manuals and in the Baroque period the development continued. The first known cathedral organ in Dubrovnik was ordered in 1384. But in 1543 a splendid new replacement was built in Venice on the Ragusan Senate's instructions and placed in the cathedral. The present organ lofts in Dubrovnik's cathedral, in St Blaise and in the Franciscan church are the most monumental in the region and reflect a civic pride in these great instruments that survived the destruction wrought by the 1667 earthquake.[131]

While the most important centres for religious music were the principal churches of the religious orders, it was the Rector's chapel that provided the secular focus for excellence. The Ragusan state took great trouble in recruiting the chapel's directors of music from among the most highly reputed European candidates. It achieved particular success with the Courtois family, originally from France but soon with large international experience and connections. Lambert Courtois, who had previously been working in Verona, arrived in Dubrovnik in the company of a Flemish musician in 1551 or 1552. He acquired great renown as director of the Rector's music and was even employed by the Republic on a delicate mission to France in connection with the legacy of one of Dubrovnik's doctors. The discriminating archbishop Beccadelli described Lambert Courtois in 1556 as 'an excellent musician, not only in Dubrovnik but also in Italy'. In 1570 Lambert left the Republic's service, but his son Henri had taken his place by 1573 and went on to serve for many years. Lambert's grandson, also called Lambert, who first appears in the records in 1629, also grew old in a position which seems to have almost become his family's by right of inheritance.[132]

Music was enjoyed, it seems, by Ragusans of all types and classes. Nikola Gučetić, who was heavily influenced in these as in other matters by Greek philosophical speculations, thought that music was very important to a good education. He believed children should be able to sing, dance and play instruments – in the case of patrician children that meant stringed instruments, notably the viola, lute or harpsichord.[133] But a heartier kind of musical fare was likely to be available in the streets of Dubrovnik. Marriage processions were, of course, regularly accompanied by music. It was, though, during the carnival that all kinds of performance were most appreciated by the populace, if not always by the censorious authorities. Apart from the use of ballet and choral accompaniments, which from the early seventeenth century seem to have played an increasing role, groups of singers and players would at this time go through the streets entertaining and, if they felt so inclined, insulting onlookers.

Even more traditional was the accompanied singing of the Christmas carols known as *kolede* or *kolende*. First mentioned in the 1272 Statute of Dubrovnik, these carols appear as an ancient Croatian custom throughout coastal Dalmatia, and Dubrovnik was rich in them. The singing was alternately solo and harmony, and the soloist would be expected to improvise both in text and tune. The singers (*koledari*) would visit the houses of Dubrovnik and wish the householders a happy Christmas, expecting to receive a small gift. If they did not, the carols could quickly take a sarcastic turn.[134]

Music was equally important in the life of country folk. Diversis records how trumpeters from the villages in the surrounding countryside played a traditional part in the noisy processions which were held in Dubrovnik on the Feast of St Blaise.[135] Local musicians from Konavle were also employed to play at theatrical productions in the city. Apart from drums and flutes, the *Konavljani* almost certainly played those two highly traditional Croatian stringed instruments, the *gusla* and the *tambura*. In the villages of Konavle, the musicians would play at funerals, christenings, weddings and other religious celebrations. They would also accompany the distinctive folk dances and songs of the district.[136] Such simple traditions, alongside its sophisticated literature and its sometimes sublime painting, gave the Ragusan Republic a specific cultural identity that also helped preserve an underlying sense of social and, indeed, political cohesion.

TWELVE

The Construction of Dubrovnik: Settlement and Urban Planning, Fortification and Defence, Public and Private Building in the Ragusan Republic (c. 1272–1667)

I. Within the City of Dubrovnik

Expansion

The precise pace and direction of the expansion of the original Dubrovnik are not easy to determine. In light of new evidence suggesting that the area called 'the field' (*campus*, *campo*, *polje*) – broadly the centre of today's walled city – was potentially suitable for cultivation and habitation from the earliest date, it is no longer possible to accept the idea of expansion in clear, determined steps from an early settlement on the cliffs above the Adriatic towards the lower slopes of Mount Srđ.[1] What actually seems to have occurred is that zones which had been settled in some fashion from antiquity became more heavily so; that the Ragusan authorities subsequently imposed their ideas of urban planning upon them; and that later still – and over a more extended period than the Ragusan chroniclers suggest – these settlements were brought within the final configuration of the city walls.

The core of early Dubrovnik was constituted by the two first *sexteria* of Kaštio and St Peter. But from ancient times the harbour and the shore facing it must also have been settled and protected in some fashion. The area to the south was then laid out for settlement. The asymmetrical arrangement and twisting street pattern of this, the third, *sexterium* of Pustijerna, bears witness to the fact of its primitive, organic growth. It was probably enclosed by walls in the ninth century.

Beyond these three *sexteria* lay the area of the 'new' town, called the *burgus* or *borgo* of St Blaise. How early and how densely this large area was settled – and by whom – is not at all clear from the sources. It was only fully surrounded by walls at the end of the thirteenth century, though the process was many years in gestation and may have passed through several stages. Stefan Uroš I's attack on the town in 1253 was apparently intended to prevent the inclusion of the *borgo* within Dubrovnik's fortifications. Contrary to the assertion of the chronicler Rastić, the Serb ruler probably succeeded in this objective; for the Dubrovnik Statute of 1272, in prescribing the arrangement of this area, makes no mention of any existing town walls.[2]

The Statute is also important because it gives the first clear evidence of Ragusan town planning and the spirit behind it. The latter can be summed up as one of common sense, according to which public and private interests were carefully balanced to achieve an overall civic harmony. The forty-five chapters of the Statute's fifth book, supplemented by other provisions elsewhere, contain a series of well-thought-out regulations to cope with problems of fire, sanitation, structural collapse and, in particular, disputes between neighbours. The responsibility for upkeep of the streets was divided between the residents on either side (one third each), while the central third was the responsibility of the commune. In order to prevent people building outwards into the space above the street and so turning it into something resembling a tunnel – a constant risk in medieval towns – it was ordered that there be sufficient room for a woman to walk along, carrying a water jar on her head. Balconies and windows could be constructed by householders as they wished, but they could not be built facing straight out onto someone else's. It was not permitted to build a new floor onto one's house that jutted out over the roof of a neighbour. People who built up against party walls had to make a payment (to be assessed by trustworthy men) to the person living on the other side of the wall. When it was decided to replace wooden party walls with stone ones, both sides would share the cost. No one could alter his roof so that water flowed from it onto someone else's house. Houses made of straw – an obvious fire risk – were not allowed to be built within the town at all.

The *borgo* – which constituted the future *sexteria* of St Mary and of St Blaise – was originally arranged in large, fairly regular blocks. The owners of these substantial complexes were the great Ragusan patrician families, who lived there with their households. Only with the penetration of new streets, as the provisions of the Statute were implemented, were these blocks broken up into individual units.[3] The Statute prescribed the exact route and width of these streets. There was an evident attempt to improve the town's ambience and appearance in this area. So overhanging steps, which narrowed and darkened streets, were prohibited. Sanitation was improved too, by requiring that in the *borgo* sesspits be cleaned out every ten years. Three town officials were appointed annually to exercise planning control: no one was to build a house without their prior agreement.[4]

Whatever early progress was made on the construction of walls intended to join the *borgo* with the original old town turned out to be in vain. In spite of the Statute's provisions against fire risks, a terrible conflagration broke out on the night of 16 August 1296, in which the whole of the new and most of the old town were destroyed.

The expense of rebuilding was certainly considerable. But the fire did provide an opportunity to plan (or re-plan) in a still more rational manner and to establish solid and uniform defences for the whole settled area. In particular, the network of streets in the new *sexterium* of St Nicholas *del Campo* or Prijcki, which would constitute the northernmost part of the finally walled town, stretching from Placa to the north wall, was now laid out in great detail. The street known as Prijeko was to provide the area's main west-east axis. Prijeko would run from the church of St Nicholas to the west wall and was to be eighteen feet wide. At right-angles to it other streets running north-south were built. All these were wider than those in the older sections of the town. They were constructed on land owned by the commune, which allowed the whole area to be given a severely uniform pattern. Each house was to be eighteen feet wide and separated from the next by a sewerage channel. These houses were built on a common pattern, with a wine cellar or workshop on the ground floor and living accommodation above. All alike and constructed in facing rows, they represented an important development in Dubrovnik's approach to planning its built environment. Indeed, the formula would in due course be introduced to part of Pustijerna, the area around the sixteenth-century *Rupe* grain store, and elsewhere in the Republic.[5]

The enclosure within the walls of what is nowadays regarded as the 'old town' of Dubrovnik at the end of the thirteenth century marked the end of one stage in the life of the commune. The process of defining those settled areas which were crucial to Dubrovnik's survival and central to its identity had been accomplished. The decision during the fourteenth century to concentrate on fortifying ever more heavily the walls encircling the city effectively meant that it would never be practical to contemplate extending it – for example, to include the economically important industrial suburb that grew up in Pile in the following century. The result, upon which every generation of visitors remarked, was that Dubrovnik remained small – not just as a state, but as a city. How many people lived within that city's narrow confines is, though, far from easy to judge.

The oldest surviving list of inhabitants of the Republic, which is from 1673–1674, is of little help because it contains no separate figure for the city itself. For their part, the chroniclers, Ragusan diplomats and outside observers variously advance totals for city dwellers, in the years before the calamitous earthquake of 1667, of 30,000 or more. But these figures must be greatly exaggerated. The latest scientifically based attempt to reach conclusions about the numbers dwelling within the city at different periods principally relies on comparison with population densities in other Dalmatian urban communities. Such comparison suggests much more modest figures – about 2,000 inhabitants at the time of the 1272 Statute, rising to some 3,500 at the end of the century, when the new settlement of St Nicholas on the lower slopes of Srđ was included. In the mid-fourteenth century the population may have fallen to 2,500, largely as a result of the Black Death, before rising to about 3,500 once more. From the mid-fifteenth century the growth of the new, predominantly industrial suburbs of Pile and Ploče, and the increased activity in Gruž, suggests a rise in population to some 6,000 in the city and 500 outside it. Then from about the mid-sixteenth century numbers stagnated and started to decline until the catastrophic losses of the Great Earthquake of 1667.[6]

The Fortification of Dubrovnik

Visitors to the city immediately noted its great defensive strength. Georges Lengherand, a pilgrim from Mons, in 1485 remarked that Dubrovnik was 'one of the most beautiful cities [he had] seen, and also the best fortified'.[7] The following year another visiting pilgrim, Konrad von Grünemberg from Konstanz, confirmed the judgement:

> Dubrovnik is so immensely fortified a city that there is no other like it anywhere in the world: it has strong bastions, towers, two deep moats and between them baileys with strong walls and battlements, everything constructed in ashlar stone.[8]

The walls of Dubrovnik had, in fact, been greatly strengthened in the course of the fourteenth century, when fifteen square towers were placed along them facing both towards the hinterland and the harbour.[9] In particular, a sharply increased concern with security is evident from the period of the Hungarian-Venetian wars. Thus, in 1346, the authorities resolved to build a stone tower on the pier known in Dubrovnik as the Muo and to close the harbour by means of a chain hung between it and the tower of St Luke. In 1350 the Muo was further strengthened, and a ditch dug in front of the Pile Gate. The first mention of firearms in Dubrovnik comes from the following year, and understanding of the enormous destructive potential of gunpowder undoubtedly explains the building work that ensued, in particular the erection of substantial bulwarks to protect the city walls against bombardier fire.[10]

With the departure of the last Venetian count in 1358, the threat from the sea – where the Venetians' ability to strike was considerable, even after the loss of Dalmatia – became even greater. Attention was, therefore, given to ensuring that all unnecessary openings in the walls facing the harbour were sealed. The Venetian danger during the latter's war with Genoa and Hungary (the War of Chioggia) prompted in 1378 the destruction of private towers and churches near Dubrovnik's walls which might be used by an enemy. In 1387 and 1398 builders and building material employed on the construction of the new church of St Blaise were urgently diverted for use on the city defences.[11]

It was in the fifteenth and sixteenth centuries, however, that Dubrovnik's fortifications achieved their full development and, indeed, acquired more or less their current appearance. In 1430, faced with war against Dubrovnik's incorrigible enemy Radoslav Pavlović, the Senate issued a series of detailed provisions about the defence of the territories of the Republic. It was added that construction work in the city was to be carried out *non tanto per la belleza, quanto la forteza* ('not so much for beauty as for strength').[12] In fact, of course, the fortifications turned out to be as aesthetically satisfying as they were massively effective, and this was in spite of the speed at which some of them were erected.

News of the fall of Constantinople in 1453 appears to have prompted Dubrovnik to build a long stretch of wall – 22 metres high and 4 metres thick – between the Ploče Gate and the Minčeta Tower in just two and a half years. The War of the First Holy League (1537–1540) provided the occasion for the construction of Revelin and the St John's Fortresses. The War of the Second Holy League (the War of Cyprus: 1570–1573) led to the building of the tower of St Margaret.[13]

The excellence of the design of the array of fortifications around Dubrovnik bears witness both to the Ragusan government's shrewd assessments of the city's defensive requirements and to the genius of the architect-engineers who were employed to meet them. Perhaps the most impressive of the city fortifications is the (already mentioned) Minčeta Tower. The first – square – tower was built at the northwest corner of the walls as early as 1319. In 1455 it was decided to reconstruct it as a round tower, but the work had to be suspended because of an outbreak of plague. Then in 1461, as the Turks began their sweep through Bosnia, it was decided to employ the great Florentine architect Michelozzo Michelozzi for Dubrovnik's military and civil engineering purposes.[14] That May the Senators agreed to go ahead with the rebuilding of Minčeta according to a wooden model which Michelozzi had presented to them. Large quantities of stone and other building material were urgently required. In order to make use of all available manpower to transport it, it was decreed that anyone coming to the city from the directions of Gruž or Ploče was to bring a stone – large or small according to his stature – for use on the tower. Special lookouts were posted to ensure compliance.

Relations between the Senate and Michelozzi always seem to have been somewhat difficult, and in time they grew worse. The patrician rulers of Dubrovnik were inclined to both caution and to stinginess, as well as having a high regard for their own wisdom. For his part, the great architect was doubtless infuriated at being second-guessed and countermanded. Michelozzi's proposals for the building of the future Bokar Tower (which guards the southwest corner of the city and looks out to the Lovrijenac Fortress) were initially rejected by the Senate, though they were later accepted. The Senators even discussed docking his pay for what they considered the excessive amount of time he had spent away from his work, though they decided against it.

In 1463 Michelozzi's proposal to strengthen the Puncijela Tower (halfway between Bokar and the Pile Gate) was accepted. A still more important decision was that to build two Revelins – one at the Pile and one at the Ploče Gate, though for some reason the former project was stillborn.[15] In order to provide stone for the fulfilment of Michelozzi's plans, the hedges in the gardens and vineyards surrounding Dubrovnik were torn down. So, too, were the big dyeing factory on Pile and several churches outside the walls, though this was mainly for security purposes.

For the work to strengthen the wall running along the north of the city up against Srđ, two other architects – Bernardino of Parma (who had been employed to remodel the harbour) and Pavao the Goldsmith (who is better known as a master maker of medals and collaborator of Donatello) – were also asked to submit proposals, though Michelozzi's prevailed.[16] The breaking point with Michelozzi finally came not over military but civil architecture. On 5 May 1464, the Senate refused even to consider his plans for the rebuilding of the Rector's Palace. The Florentine master now seems to have flounced out of the city.

The pressing danger posed by the Turks and the fact that so many projects, not least the Minčeta Tower, were incomplete ensured that the Ragusan Senate dared not delay finding a replacement. And so by 5 June, Juraj Dalmatinac – not just an architect but also the finest Dalmatian sculptor of his day – had taken Michelozzi's place.[17] Juraj's relations with the Ragusan Senate were evidently a good deal smoother than his predecessor's. His first project was to submit plans for the rebuilding of the St Catherine's Tower, the third square tower along the northern wall stretching from Minčeta to Ploče. These were duly accepted. So, too, were his proposals for the continuation of the building of Minčeta. These substantially modified the earlier proposals of Michelozzi. The result was a tower that was slightly more than semi-circular, higher than originally planned and crowned with battlements. This was the structure that Evliya Çelebi, some two centuries later, would wonderingly compare with the Babylonian Tower of the Holy Testament, renowned in Muslim tradition.[18]

Juraj Dalmatinac's attention was also focused on the Lovrijenac Fortress. The origin of this fortification is obscure, though local legend associated it with an attempt by Venice to seize the position in the eleventh century. In any case, it is difficult to imagine circumstances in which this strategically vital site would not have been important to the defences of Dubrovnik. A fortification certainly existed there from the early fourteenth century. It was substantially strengthened in 1418, and further improvements made between 1421 and 1424 in face of the threat from Radoslav Pavlović. Juraj Dalmatinac's work now turned Lovrijenac into a well-nigh impregnable fortress. The walls on the north and west sides were ordered to be built more than twenty cubits (10.24 metres) thick, or thicker if necessary – in fact, the final thickness of the west wall was a full 12 metres. The wall facing the city was much less sturdy, only 60 centimetres thick – perhaps in calculation that if the fortress ever did fall into enemy hands the wall could be easily breached by Dubrovnik's cannons firing from Bokar.[19]

Juraj Dalmatinac seems to have left Dubrovnik's service in 1465, perhaps to escape the plague. He was succeeded as the state's architect-engineer by the Dubrovnik-born Paskoje Miličević, who would serve the Republic with legendary fidelity for 51 years.

Protection and Construction of the Harbour

Miličević was responsible, among a large number of other projects, for conceiving and executing a further stage in the lengthy process of developing, protecting and fortifying the city harbour. The eve of the 1667 earthquake would find it comprehensively defended by a series of fortifications of differing age and strength but which together were formidably effective. On the northern side were situated the Fortress of St Luke with its bastion and the Tower of St Dominic, and at the northeast the massive fortress of Revelin protecting the Ploče Gate. On the southern flank of the harbour lay the almost equally massive Fortress of St John. Between St John and St Luke lay (from south to north) the Rector's Tower, the Punishment Tower and the Fishmarket Tower. Behind the Rector's Palace and facing straight out onto the southeast facing harbour was the Great Arsenal. A little further to the north lay the Small Arsenal (on the site of today's Harbourmaster's Office). The breakwater which also faces southeast protected ships moored in the harbour from waves and swell, and from the end of the breakwater a chain ran to the foot of St John's Fortress to seal off the entrance against intruders.[20] Two gates led through the walls to the harbour – to the south, the Gate *od Ponte* and to the north, the Fishmarket Gate – before each of which was a quay of the same name. Of these various features, the four most important to the harbour's security were the Arsenals, the breakwater, the Fortress of St John and Revelin.

The origins of Dubrovnik's Great Arsenal are obscure. It is described in the chronicles as existing in eighth century. The fact that a primitive drawing of galleys has been discovered on a pillar from the recently excavated remains of the Byzantine cathedral suggests that some kind of arsenal existed in the eleventh century at least. It is natural to assume that the Great Arsenal of Venice exerted an influence in the development of its Ragusan equivalent once Dubrovnik came under Venetian control in 1205. The first clear evidence, though, only comes from much later, in the Statute of 1272.[21] In the course of the fourteenth century the Great Arsenal acquired its traditional form – as replicated in the eastern facade of what constitutes today's *Gradska kavana* ('Town Café'). In 1345 the Arsenal, with its four interconnecting spaces for four vessels, was fortified and enclosed. In 1386 and 1387 arches were built through which Dubrovnik's warships were launched. The arches were widened over the years in order to accommodate larger vessels. Initially, these openings were closed off by parallel beams. But with further widening this method of protection was deemed insufficient. So at the end of the fifteenth century the archways were lightly walled up. Whenever a vessel was launched or hauled back into the Arsenal, these walls had to be knocked down and then rebuilt. In 1525 the Arsenal was extended out towards the sea, so as to accommodate the larger warship known as *bastarda* which was then under construction.[22]

The complex must have been a hive of activity. The vessels of Dubrovnik's war fleet were built, laid up and repaired there. From the fourteenth to the sixteenth centuries these warships were as large and effective (if not, of course, as numerous) as any of their day; indeed, the Dubrovnik Great Arsenal was the most important on the shores of the Eastern Adriatic. From the mid-fourteenth century it was under the supervision of a 'Rector', and from the fifteenth an 'Admiral'. The latter had his lodgings on the first floor of the Arsenal, next to the Council Chamber.

In 1409 it was decided to supplement these facilities by building what came to be known as the Small Arsenal. Originally, it consisted of just one unit with space for a single brigantine, but spaces for two further vessels were added in 1412. The southernmost of these units was enlarged in 1574 so that a *galijica* could be built within it.[23]

The breakwater protecting Dubrovnik's harbour was a considerable feat of design and engineering, for which Paskoje Miličević was responsible. From the mid-fourteenth century the Ragusans had been keen to enlarge the area of Dubrovnik's sheltered anchorage. So in 1347 it was decided to place an improvised breakwater consisting of large stones off Pustijerna (a little to the west of today's Porporela harbour defence, built by the Austrians in the nineteenth century). But as the harbour became ever more crowded and cramped, something more ambitious had to be envisaged. In 1484 Paskoje Miličević's plans for a new breakwater were accepted. It is not clear whether two separate structures were built and later joined (as had evidently taken place by the time of Božidarević's portrayal of the harbour soon after 1500) or, as has recently been suggested, whether the breakwater was from the start built by Miličević as a single entity. What is quite evident, though, is his skill of conception and execution. The breakwater faced directly southeast against the incoming waves. The main southern entry to the harbour was to be some 40 metres wide – space enough for even the broadest-beamed, deep-draught vessel to pass easily, but not so wide as to admit any severe swell. The northern entry was narrower and shallower and posed problems which would later need to be addressed. The blocks below the water were laid without mortar. Those above were connected with iron ties and embedded in lime and clay. In order to give this mortar time to dry, the section above the waterline was protected by means of a wooded box, *cassetta,* or in Dubrovnik *kašeta.* From this derived the breakwater's name, *Kaše.* The engineer refused payment for his services but was prevailed upon to accept a gift of twelve ducats' worth of silver plate. The fact that Kaše has survived successive earthquakes, and even the bombardment of the harbour by the Yugoslav army, is testimony to the quality of his work.[24]

The breakwater was extended towards Ploče in 1514, which must have further reduced the already limited room for ships to enter the harbour by this northern channel. Indeed, the arrangement offered the worst of both worlds, because while this entry was inconvenient for large merchant vessels it might still offer a way for enemy ships to break into the harbour and thence through to the city itself. Consequently, in 1617, Dubrovnik's engineer Mihajlo Hranjac recommended the placing of large stones across the northern channel to seal it off completely. This was only actually done in 1631, at a time when the Venetian threat was again at its height. It effectively completed the harbour's protection.[25]

By then the southern flank of the harbour had also been secured. The Muo, built on the stony outcrop facing northeast from the tip of Pustijerna, was in all probability from the earliest times the site of some kind of defences. A tower belonging to the Gundulić family was constructed there, which was rebuilt of stone and lime at the city's expense in 1346. The foundations of this tower were later protected with a bastion. A connecting wall and gate were built to link the Gundulić Tower to the city. By the start of the sixteenth century the tower consisted of a large rectangular structure, based upon a circular bulwark to which was connected a stout chain. The tower was crowned with battlements and a sloping roof. (In Božidarević's picture in the Bunić chapel of the Dubrovnik Dominicans, St Blaise grasps it firmly in his right hand.) Soon afterwards this structure, by now widely called the tower of St John after a little church nearby, was fundamentally remodelled by Paskoje Miličević. A new semi-circular tower was created with a five-sided bastion in front of it. Then between 1552 and 1557, the whole complex was brought within a single walled structure, which was thenceforward known as the Fortress of St John on the Pier (*Tvrđava Svetog Ivana na Mulu*). The Fortress retained its late sixteenth-century appearance until after the fall of the Republic.[26]

The northeastern approach to the harbour was guarded by Revelin, whose construction was decided upon by the Senate in 1463. It was erected as a sort of island in the city moat in front of the Ploče Gate, connected by bridges with the city approaches and with the city itself. At first, a number of houses and even vegetable gardens were built on the platform of the fortress. But these were later swept away when it was paved. The present massive structure, however, is mainly the work of the sixteenth century. Fearful of Venetian attack during the War of the First Holy League, Dubrovnik sought the advice of the famous civil engineer Antonio Ferramolino from Bergamo, who arrived in the town through the good offices of Andrea Doria, Spain's Genoese admiral. At the end of 1538 the Senate accepted Ferramolino's proposals. Having spent four months in the city, he returned by Ragusan ship to Sicily, leaving behind him a very favourable reputation – all the more favourable, doubtless, because he refused any payment for his services, though he was prevailed upon to accept 200 ducats' worth of silverware and a horse.[27] The work on Revelin took eleven years to complete. Further alterations were made in the seventeenth century and a few more in the eighteenth, but the present structure is fundamentally that designed by Ferramolino. The solidity of Revelin's construction proved vital when in the immediate aftermath of the 1667 earthquake it served as headquarters for the emergency government of the Republic.[28]

Artillery

The work to strengthen and remodel Dubrovnik's fortifications, which was such a prominent – at times almost obsessive – preoccupation of the Ragusan authorities from the mid-fourteenth to the mid-sixteenth centuries was in large part a reflection of the deadly importance of firearms. As early as 1351 Dubrovnik commissioned its first cannon and by the time of the War of Chioggia (1378–1381), the city had acquired a large store of them. In the 1380s and 1390s Dubrovnik despatched its guns on several occasions to protect Ston.

The city artillery also quickly became an important element in Ragusan diplomacy. During Sandalj Hranić's wars with Radoslav Pavlović, Dubrovnik lent its ally two of the large cannons known as bombards. Indeed, the Ragusans promised Sandalj that should he attack Klobuk (which Dubrovnik wanted for itself) they would send bombards and a force of bombardiers to help him. But Radoslav had his own artillery, and in 1420 the Ragusans found themselves having to repair the fortress of Soko in Konavle which his guns had heavily damaged.

During Dubrovnik's battles with the Herceg, artillery assumed still greater significance. In the early years, Dubrovnik allowed him to repair his guns and acquire gunpowder in the city. But the danger posed by hostile artillery was brought sharply home when Dubrovnik found itself threatened by the Herceg's bombards in September 1451. The Ragusans must also have become acutely aware of the role of Ottoman cannons in the fall of Constantinople in 1453.[29]

Not surprisingly, given these circumstances, Dubrovnik was determined to remain at the forefront of European developments to maintain and upgrade artillery. From 1410 the city had its own foundry. Initially, its cannons were forged from iron components but later cast from bronze for greater strength.

The best foreign experts were sought out to perform this work. Italian, French and German masters of the Ragusan foundry came and went. But a new era in the design, casting and use of artillery opened with the arrival of Master Ivan Krstitelj (John the Baptist) from the island of Rab in October 1504. He brought his own equipment with him and installed it in his workshop on top of the new Revelin. He was paid eight ducats a month and a bonus according to the quantity of metal he cast. As his reputation grew, he began receiving orders from Italian princes, though the Republic closely supervised his activities and expected to have first call on his time. By the time of his death in 1540, Dubrovnik was as well provided with its own artillery as with effective defences against that of its enemies.[30]

The master of the foundry was also expected to act as the Republic's chief bombardier with charge of the city's cannons distributed around the different fortresses, towers and walls. Dubrovnik retained a small group of professional artillery men. But the authorities also considered that some of the civilian population should be conversant with firearms. Accordingly, bi-monthly shooting competitions were organised. In 1655 the chief bombardier of the day, Antonio Vanini, proposed that an artillery school be instituted, and this was agreed. The object was to provide a resource of young men with adequate training to assist the core of professionals in times of crisis, or to join their ranks if a vacancy arose.[31]

Garrisons and Military Service

Dubrovnik relied upon both foreign professionals and local conscripts for its defence. From the days when it was subject to Hungarian suzerainty until the fall of the Ragusan Republic it retained a regular force of Hungarian soldiers known as *barabanti*.[32] It often also recruited Italian mercenaries. Sometimes experienced Italian captains were employed to command Dubrovnik's soldiers, such as the Apulian *condottiere* who was made commander of the Republic's pikemen in the crisis of 1463.[33]

But all Ragusan citizens, patrician and commoner alike, were in principle subject to the obligation to fight for their country. Diversis gives a full description of the system:

> The names of all the nobles and commoners under 60 years of age are written down on pieces of paper. Those who have passed their sixtieth year are exempt by law from guard duty. The pieces of paper bearing the names of the older guards are in one bag and those of the younger ones in

> another. (I now discuss the nobility). So each month for the protection of the city three older nobles and six younger ones, who must be at least thirty, are chosen as commanders of the guard with the duties of watching over the city by day and night and of closing and opening the gates. Each night one of the three older nobles and two of the six younger ones is on duty [i.e. there is a rota every three days]. To these are added a number of commoners who are chosen by lot. One of those three nobles [i.e. who serve on a particular day], with some of the commoners, guards the Rector's Palace. The other two with the rest of the commoners inspect and patrol the city and Placa and check the guards on the walls, and if they come across anyone asleep on guard duty they reprimand him and place him in prison in irons.[34]

As Diversis implies, there was a separate permanent force guarding the walls. This practice is evident from the mid-fourteenth century. For example, in view of the threat from Venice, in March 1346 the numbers of commanders of the guard were increased to five and of guards to forty; the latter had to maintain watch at ten prescribed places around the walls.[35] By October 1366, the number of guards had increased to 81, who were to secure the walls at twenty-nine specified positions.[36]

Other features of the city's security mentioned by Diversis are the gatekeepers who reported on all arrivals to the noble officers called *cazamorti*, whose main task it was to keep out those who might have infectious diseases; the three lookouts on Mount Srđ stationed at the church of that name, who signalled Dubrovnik if they saw ships approaching, indicating how many there were; the young nobles and commoners who guarded the Lovrijenac Fortress; and the system of registering the names of islanders, from whose ranks oarsmen and the best crossbowmen were recruited – while Ragusan country-dwellers provided the most skilful swordsmen.[37]

Civic Buildings

Within the well-defended walls of Dubrovnik from the fourteenth century onwards, an elegant little city was constructed. Dubrovnik's buildings – public and private, secular and ecclesiastical – drew on the same fund of skills and materials and to a large extent reflected the same overall values and conception. As has been noted, the cathedral, church of St Blaise and Franciscan and Dominican friaries and churches were all subsidised and scrutinised by the government, and all were closely involved in Dubrovnik's civic life. This was true, too, of other churches. For example, the church of the Holy Saviour (*Sveti Spas*) which stands next to the Franciscans in Placa was built as a votive by the population in response to the serious earthquake of 1520 and according to the design of the architect Petar Andrijić. Its facade is the first full expression of the Renaissance style in Dubrovnik's built environment and it remains – largely untouched by the later earthquake – as one of the most exquisite of the city's churches.[38]

As the chroniclers bear witness, a special significance was accorded to certain secular constructions which placed them in a quite distinct category. Perhaps the most symbolically significant of these was Dubrovnik's earliest, and for years only, secular public monument – Orlando's Column. As noted earlier, the Ragusan chroniclers associated the erection of the Column (which depicts a knight in armour with drawn sword) with the aid given by the legendary hero Roland to Dubrovnik during an onslaught by the Saracens; but this is clearly myth. Such monuments erected in Imperial towns traditionally signified civic pride and demonstrated independence. There are only four – including that in Dubrovnik – outside Germany, and it has been persuasively argued that Dubrovnik's Column may have been erected during the Emperor Sigismund's stay in the city after his defeat at the battle of Nicopolis in 1396. In this case it would have represented a gesture of loyalty to the beleaguered monarch as well as an assertion of autonomy. A new Column was built in 1418, which was ordered to be an exact replica of its predecessor. The Dubrovnik cubit was measured by the length of the knight's forearm. At his side, Dubrovnik's heralds proclaimed decrees and other public announcements. At his feet, the bodies of traitors would be displayed. Above his head, the standard of Dubrovnik flew. In fact, Orlando's Column remained the symbol of Dubrovnik's freedom until the Republic was abolished by order of Napoleon in 1808.[39]

Only a little less symbolically important, and certainly ranking first among Dubrovnik's civic buildings, was the Rector's Palace.[40] A castle originally stood on the site; indeed, given the central importance of the harbour to the whole settlement, the place was probably fortified from the earliest times. By the mid-fourteenth century, however, the building was referred to as a 'palace', already housing the Count and his administration. At the end of the century towers, two wings and a courtyard are mentioned. The traditional requirement to keep the city's weapons under the Count's and his Council's direct control was probably responsible for the fact that large quantities of gunpowder were kept in the palace. This proved catastrophic. On the night of 10 August 1435, the ammunition supply ignited and destroyed most of the structure along with several adjoining towers.[41]

Nothing dismayed, however, the government ordered the construction of a true Palace worthy of the dignity and prosperity of the Republic. The chronicler Nikola Ranjina enthused mightily over the decision:

> In the year of Our Lord 1435 in Ragusa was begun to be built from the very foundations the stupendous, magnificent, superb palace over the square on the seashore, worthy of any great prince, for the dwelling place of the rulers of the city of Dubrovnik.[42]

The architect Onofrio della Cava was asked to design and build the new palace.[43] Diversis, who was present in Dubrovnik at this time, gives a full description of the work that now ensued. Onofrio's plans involved the building of an arcade the length of the western facade of the palace. Its vaulted roof rested on five tall, thick pillars of fine stone brought from Korčula, with two half-pillars at each end against the palace's northern and southern towers. The capitals of these pillars were richly carved by Pietro di Martino from Milan and local stonemasons, who worked alongside Onofrio. The capitals, the corbels of the loggia vaults and the main portal frame all show clear traces of Renaissance influence. Several parts of the palace depict scenes of deep allegorical significance for Dubrovnik and its government. Particularly notable are the portrayal on the loggia's capitals of Esculapius, the mythical physician who was thought to have lived in Epidaurus (which, of course, was confused with Epidaurum/Cavtat), and the depiction of the Judgement of Solomon, symbolic of the justice administered by the Ragusan patriciate. The theme of good government was reinforced within the atrium of the palace, where allegories of Wisdom, Justice and Harmony reminded the Councillors, judges and officials of their duties. The figure of Justice at the top of the staircase which leads to the court room is accompanied by an inscription which reads: *Iussi suma mei sua vos cuicumque tueri* ('My highest duty is to protect your right').

Onofrio's plans for the new palace were extensive and practical as well as merely decorative. Diversis notes that they included halls for the Great and Small Councils and the Senate; a courtroom; residential quarters for the Rector; rooms for clerks for the Slavic Chancery and for the heralds and guards; a prison; and a torture chamber. There was also an armoury where weapons and powder were stored.[44] This, unfortunately, once more proved disastrous. On the evening of 8 August 1463, a fire broke out, and again the gunpowder in the palace armoury exploded. Seventeen noblemen, four noble ladies and 104 commoners died in the conflagration. The palace itself was devastated, particularly the southern part. As noted earlier, Michelozzi submitted plans for the palace's reconstruction which were, however rejected, and other builders were entrusted with the work. The top storey of the building was never rebuilt but the arches and decoration of the loggia were remodelled in Renaissance style; so too were the windows on the western and southern facades. The palace was damaged in the earthquakes of 1520 and 1667. After the latter, the windows on the southern facade were remodelled in Baroque style, as was the staircase within the atrium. The fact that despite all these vicissitudes the Rector's Palace retains its fundamental harmony of styles and unity of form demonstrates Dubrovnik's enduring satisfaction with Onofrio della Cava's original conception.

Onofrio had not, in fact, arrived in Dubrovnik to rebuild the Rector's Palace, but rather in order to apply his engineering skills to the construction of an aqueduct. Again, Diversis was well-informed about the whole business. By the early fifteenth century the traditional means of supplying Dubrovnik with water were plainly inadequate to meet the needs of a growing population and increasing industrial activity. More large cisterns to collect the rain had been constructed in the course of the fourteenth century; for example, in 1388 one was built by the Franciscan church and the following year another by the Dominicans. The wells inside the city were by now only producing brackish water. Ships plying up the coast during the summer months to take on barrels of water from the springs near Mlini (in Župa) were an expensive and inefficient way to try to make up the deficit. On the suggestion of the Ragusan merchant Jakov Kotruljević, Onofrio della Cava and another master, Andreucci di Bulbito from Apulia, were summoned to Dubrovnik. The Senate appointed two nobles to oversee the execution of the plans which Onofrio proposed. Some faint-hearts thought the project was impossible, and so the Senate insisted that Onofrio and his colleague would themselves have to meet the large costs in that event.

The aqueduct originally carried water from the main spring at Šumet in the place called Vrelo (meaning 'spring') – water from two other Šumet springs also flowed into it – along 11,700 metres of channel to the main city reservoir. It relied on gravity, even though the incline was small – just 20 metres from beginning to end. Seventy litres per second could flow along it. Over subsequent years more springs were tapped to increase the water supply. More reservoirs were also built: in 1501 the sites of the salt warehouses near the churches of St Nicholas and St Stephen within the city walls were converted for use as reservoirs.

The public distribution points for water were, however, the city's fountains. The main one was that still known as Onofrio's Great Fountain in front of the convent of the Clares near the Pile Gate. It was originally splendidly embellished and only acquired its present, somewhat austere appearance when it was damaged by the Great Earthquake. Water from the reservoir at St Nicholas flowed through lead pipes to Onofrio's Small Fountain, which supplied the marketplace then in the main square; to the so-called Jews' Fountain, by the gate of the Arsenal; and to the later fountains on the Fishmarket Quay and in the Rector's Palace.

It was Onofrio himself who first suggested that the water from the aqueduct be used for industrial purposes. Dubrovnik needed it to drive flour mills and, increasingly, for the process of cloth manufacture. Accordingly, a separate branch of the aqueduct brought water to the washing and rolling works at Pile. At one time there were fourteen mills along its course. The temptation to drain off water for livestock, irrigation or the washing of wool was so great that in 1443 it was decreed that anyone breaking into or choking the flow of the aqueduct should lose his right hand.

By bringing large supplies of excellent water to a city which had so small a local supply of it, Onofrio not only transformed the living conditions of the inhabitants but also allowed the growth of a cloth industry upon which several thousand Ragusans and immigrants depended for their livelihood. But aqueducts are, of course, extremely vulnerable. Dubrovnik's was badly damaged by the 1667 earthquake and in 1806 it was sealed by the Montenegrins.[45]

Even greater than its requirement for external supplies of water was Dubrovnik's dependence upon imports of food – which then had to be stored under the right conditions. The first mention in the town records of the grain warehouse called *Fontik* is from the late thirteenth century. It had two floors and was situated on the south side of the Arsenal. Diversis describes how it also served as a wholesale market for grain and vegetables.[46] In the course of the fifteenth century Fontik gradually became less important, and part of it was taken over to house the Ragusan chancery office. From 1445 another grain warehouse was operating on the site of the northeastern section of today's Sponza Palace. But Fontik had never in any case been large enough to store all the grain required by Dubrovnik. Thus in 1410 dry wells called *rupe* ('holes') had been built in Kaštio – the highest and thus driest part of the city – beneath the convents of St Andrew and St Mark. Altogether there were over thirty *rupe*, with a capacity of some 16,000 *stara*.[47] In 1548 the government decided upon the construction of a new *rupe* building. The project, which was entrusted to a master builder from Apulia, was only completed in 1590. This massive new *rupe* had three storeys, and in the basement were dug fifteen silos, up to 9 metres into the rock. Some 1,500 tonnes of grain could be stored there.[48]

The Ragusan authorities had a clear interest in the storage, handling and sale of other commodities too, and made similar provisions about them. The location of each salt warehouse (*slanica*) was especially important to a government which depended upon salt for a substantial part of its revenues. In the fourteenth century seven of these warehouses were arranged alongside the walls between St Nicholas and the little church of St James on Peline. Other salt warehouses were constructed at the site of the fortress of St John, at Revelin and elsewhere.[49] The towers and fortifications around the harbour were also used as temporary stores of victuals of various kinds. Thus the fortress of St John was used to house salt and millet, the Fishmarket Tower held salt and corn and the Tower of St Luke stored millet.[50]

The most important – and certainly the most elegant – of Dubrovnik's civic buildings having an economic significance was, however, the Sponza Palace (also known as the *Dogana*, 'Customs'). Today's palace, built according to the design of Paskoje Miličević between 1516 and 1520 stands on a site previously occupied by several distinct buildings and indeed a street, which was incorporated into the structure to become its atrium. Diversis describes how the location looked in about 1440, and incidentally explains the two different names applied to the later building:

> By the Arsenal, or more exactly by the apartment of its custodian called the Admiral, is the place for weighing and measuring all goods that are sold in bulk. By this building which is called the Gabela or Dogana [i.e. Customs House] runs a wide street… This is near another place which all the merchants call the Sponza where the value is assessed of goods which are taken out of the city in bales. People in olden times built this spacious building and provided it with a cistern, rooms and loggias at a distance from the nearest buildings to serve as a hostel for those visiting the city.[51]

Paskoje Miličević's Sponza was constructed in the transitional Gothic-Renaissance style so characteristic of Dubrovnik before the baroque rebuilding in the aftermath of the earthquake. It was used as both a warehouse (the function of the original Sponza) and a Customs House (the function of the first *Dogana*). It also incorporated the mint and the armoury – which was thus finally moved out of the Rector's Palace complex. In later centuries it would serve to house a school and accommodate Dubrovnik's own learned academy.

The portico at street level was created by the Andrijić brothers, stonemasons from Korčula, and others. A medallion in relief depicting the monogram of Christ accompanied by two angels was executed by the French sculptor Bertrandus Gallicus.[52] The religious theme was also evident in that the separate storage units within the warehouse are distinguished by the names of different saints. The requirement for rigorous honesty – on pain of eternal as well as temporal sanctions – in dealings which took place in the Sponza was crisply encapsulated in the inscription on the archway into the atrium: *Fallere nostra vetant et falli pondera; meque pondero cum merces ponderat ipse deus* ('Our weights neither deceive nor are deceived. When I weigh merchandise, God also weighs me').[53]

Private Palaces

The town houses or 'palaces' of the patrician and rich commoner families in Dubrovnik were symbols of civic status as well as places in which to live and do business. Although there were significant differences according to taste, wealth and period, the most striking feature of these palaces is their similarity. This reflected the fact that they were often modelled on each other and incorporated stylistic features borrowed from public buildings such as the Rector's Palace. The uniform simplicity of both Ragusan palaces and country villas was ridiculed by the Venetians in the ditty:

> *Quatro stanze,*
> *Un salon,*
> *z'e la casa*
> *d'un Schiavon.*
>
> Four rooms,
> One Drawing room,
> That's the house
> Of a Slav.[54]

In actual fact, specific physical circumstances affected particular architectural solutions. Within the severe constraints of space within the city walls, owners and architects had to use all their ingenuity. Notably, they had to expand upwards, and so the typical Dubrovnik palace had three or four floors. This had the added benefit of allowing the principal floor on which the owner lived and entertained – the *piano nobile* – to be placed high above the noise and smells of the street and to catch some sun. The most prized positions were at the corners of streets, which offered the benefit of two facades suitable for embellishment and for more windows to introduce light into an otherwise gloomy interior.

Most of the Gothic palaces – like the splendid house built in the 1420s for Sandalj Hranić – have either disappeared or been remodelled. Duke Sandalj's palace had at least two floors, with an open facade and a balcony. On the first floor were three windows with pointed ('Gothic') arches and on the second, between two similar windows, one large window in four sections. Inside it was richly furnished and elaborately painted. The palace of the Isusović-Braichi families situated on Prijeko, probably built in the 1470s, provides an impression of late Gothic Dubrovnik – narrow, built on a corner site, with traditional two-sectioned and four-sectioned arched windows on the third and fourth floors respectively. The external carved decoration shows the influence of Juraj Dalmatinac and his followers.[55]

The classic and favourite style of architecture – as of painting – in Dubrovnik was transitional Gothic-Renaissance. Renaissance influences were visible notably in greater simplicity of external ornamentation, an increased concern with symmetry and wider square windows replacing the traditional pointed arch. The basic layout of palaces, however, remained unchanged. The main entrance would usually be through a profiled doorway with pillars bearing a tympanum. It would probably be placed off-centre, because it led to the staircase which itself was at the side. The ground floor would accommodate warehouses or workshops which had their own separate entrance – wide enough to bring in bulky wares. A small square window with an iron grille across it would open into the warehouse. Other larger windows – with pointed arches, or rectangular according to style and period – opened out from the first and second floors. On entering through the main doorway, one would find oneself in an atrium containing a cistern or well with carved surrounds, and near it against the wall a basin by the side of carved stone shelves for pots and other utensils.

One could then expect to climb a vaulted stone staircase with balustrade up to the first floor. (In the fifteenth century, staircases were within the palace walls, but during the course of the sixteenth century they were often built outside – above the space which separated one palace from its neighbour – so as to save space.) On the first and second floors (and others if the palace was a large one) the layout of rooms very much followed that mocked by the Venetians. Thus on each floor there would be a large central hall with two smaller rooms leading off it at each side. The first floor would probably house the kitchen in one of the smaller rooms. The main hall – the *saloča*, as it was called in Dubrovnik – would most likely be on the second floor or above. Against one wall would be found elaborately carved stone shelves and a stone basin (called *pilo* in Dubrovnik) in which to wash one's hands. Against the other, a low stone fireplace would provide warmth for the family and their guests as they sat down in slightly chilly splendour to talk and dine.[56]

The sixteenth century saw the erection of new palaces, reflecting both the wealth of Ragusan society and the ever stronger influence of the Italian Renaissance. In 1546 the lawyer-diplomat Frano Gundulić commissioned an architect from Ancona to build him the palace which – though it lost its top floor at the time of the 1667 earthquake – still stands in *Božidarevićeva ulica* ('Božidarević street'). It has been suggested that the model may have been one or more of the *palazzi* in which Gundulić spent his years in Rome.[57]

One of the finest palaces of Dubrovnik was built between 1549 and 1553 by the wealthy citizen-merchant, Tomo Stjepović Skočibuha. It is in *Restićeva ulica* (Restić street) in Pustijerna, and was erected where had once stood the palace of the patrician Niko Đurđević. For Skočibuha the erection of a palace in such a position was a statement that he had indeed 'arrived'. The characteristics of the palace reinforced the message. It was notably taller than the palaces of his patrician neighbours. On the ground floor was a small atrium with finely carved well, basin and staircase. The first floor was quite low, but the height of the second and third floors are emphasised by taller Renaissance-style windows. The *saloča* on the third floor is the finest of any palace in Dubrovnik. The palace's facade was entrusted to Master Antonio from Ancona, who was then acting as the Republic's engineer and bombardier. It bears the classical Renaissance embellishments with which Antonio would have been familiar from the architecture of Italy, particularly of Venice.[58]

II. Outside the City of Dubrovnik

Ston, Cavtat, Tumba, Ljuta, Molunat

The great majority of the Ragusan Republic's population lived outside the city and its immediate surrounds. In 1673–1674 (the date of the first reasonably complete register) some 20,000 of a population of just over 24,000 probably did so.[59] But from the very beginning of the period of the Ragusan state's expansion, with the acquisition of Ston and the Pelješac peninsula in the early 1330s, Dubrovnik demonstrated that it intended to impose its own pattern of life upon all those who inhabited its territory. Solutions to problems which had been reached within the city walls or in Astarea were thus applied to more or less parallel cases elsewhere. This is perhaps most clearly evident in Ston which still, in spite of the passage of time, damage from earthquakes and burden of economic decay, appears as an exquisite miniature of Dubrovnik.

Ston, in fact, quickly became a complex of three settlements: Veliki Ston, Mali Ston and Broce. The economic rationale of all three was, of course, the exploitation of salt. Immediately upon acquiring the territory, the Ragusan Great Council decided that the territory of both Veliki and Mali Ston should be divided up for settlement. At each, 150 houses were to be built. Each house was to be (as in Dubrovnik's Prijeko) eighteen feet wide. They were to be inhabited by people summoned from Astarea and the islands.

Already the first of what would be the massive fortifications of Ston was now being built – the long wall between Veliki and Mali Ston protecting the peninsula from the side of the isthmus and the hostile hinterland beyond. Soon further decisions were made to provide more comprehensive protection. Walls were accordingly built to the west. In 1347 the decision was made to construct the first of Ston's three great fortresses, that of Koruna above Mali Ston. In 1347 special superintendents of works were appointed to oversee the building. In 1349 Dubrovnik founded the third settlement of the complex, at Broce. Its purpose was also defensive – to guard the channel to the saltworks. The existing inhabitants were moved out and compensated with other property, while thirty men from outside Ston were summoned to take up free residence there. The following year a dozen more families were sought from Apulia to increase the numbers. The inhabitants of Broce were expected to defend the place and perform specific duties assigned to them by the count of Ston, while earning their living as farmers and fishermen.

By now the basic organisation of Ston was in place. Veliki Ston was the administrative, ecclesiastical and industrial centre (for the salt works). Mali Ston was the increasingly important centre for the storage and transport of salt. Broce was a community of frontiersmen with military obligations.

Veliki Ston soon expanded to the west, but its eastern side was still underpopulated. Accordingly, in 1370, it was decided to summon thirty families from outside Ston to come and build there thirty new houses, arranged in three blocks and along four streets. They received the land for nothing, but the houses could not be sold and should pass to their descendants. The government was also worried about the numbers present to defend Mali Ston. So, for example, when war broke out between Venice and Genoa in 1378 the

Ragusan authorities ordered the nobles of Ston to go to Mali Ston and not to leave it on pain of a fine of 1,000 *hyperperi*.[60]

Mention has already been made of the Koruna fortress. On top of the hill above Ston called Podvizd stood the fortress of the same name, strengthened at the end of the fifteenth century. Along the walls of the whole complex were erected ten round and thirty-one square towers. The strongest single fortress, however, was that known as Veliki Kaštio (the 'Great Castle'). Discussions had been underway about its construction from as early as 1347. But only in the mid-1380s did work begin on building a rectangular fortress with four square corner-towers and surrounded by a ditch. By 1393 it was complete. In the late fifteenth century the fortress was significantly remodelled and strengthened by Paskoje Miličević, who added a further bulwark, a semi-circular tower and two turrets. Veliki Kaštio, strategically placed between Veliki Ston and the salt works, thus constituted the core of Ston's fortifications. Like much of the rest of the defences, it was again updated during the sixteenth and early seventeenth centuries.[61] It is not surprising that Ston's fortifications evolved in style and pace alongside Dubrovnik's, since all of the principal Ragusan engineer-architects worked on them – Michelozzi, Juraj Dalmatinac, Onofrio della Cava and, of course, Paskoje Miličević.

In their civic buildings Veliki and Mali Ston were equally faithful reflections of the city of Dubrovnik from which they conceptually sprang. Each Ston had its own main street called Placa. The Placa of Veliki Ston remained throughout its history the main communal centre around which the town's public buildings clustered – notably the Count's Palace, a tall, imposing Gothic-Renaissance Chancery, and a fine late-Renaissance episcopal palace with adjoining garden (the only one then permitted within the walls of Veliki Ston). Veliki Ston's Placa was paved in the sixteenth century, and in 1581 drinking water was brought by aqueduct to a fountain at the end of the street. As in (pre-earthquake) Dubrovnik, the more important private houses on Veliki Ston's Placa had loggias.[62] Again like Dubrovnik, Veliki Ston had its own equivalent of Orlando's Pillar, fishmarket, *Rupe*, town clock and even its own *luža* or *sjenica* ('shady place'), where the better sort of people could sit, chat and while away the time. Finally, of course, Veliki Ston had its own church of St Blaise.

Mali Ston was a more determinedly businesslike community. It had not been so elaborately planned as Veliki Ston. Placa was the only significant street, and in the course of the fifteenth and sixteenth centuries it actually became less significant as a focal centre than the harbour. Here the likeness to Dubrovnik's harbour was equally obvious. In the mid-fifteenth century three arsenals were built, parallelling the Small Arsenal constructed at this time by the side of the

Fishmarket Pier in Dubrovnik. In Mali Ston's arsenals the locally based warships were repaired and maintained. There was also a shipyard in which other vessels were constructed. In 1491 Paskoje Miličević built a breakwater (a smaller version of Kaše), and twenty years later the round Toljevac Tower to secure the entrance to Mali Ston's harbour as he had Dubrovnik's. Salt to be loaded onto vessels bound for the Neretva was from 1581 stored in a large salt warehouse (*slanica*) there. The harbour complex was under the control of a captain who lived in a strongly fortified house facing out onto it.[63]

None of the other towns and settlements constructed or reconstructed by Dubrovnik was anything near as economically important or as developed as Ston, but all in different ways reflected the same organising mentality. In each case, security was the prime consideration, and this was reflected in the government's plans for defence and habitation. The oldest was, arguably, at Tumba (now Brgat Gornji) above Dubrovnik in Župa Dubrovačka, where as early as 1326, 50 Ragusans mounted guard, their wages paid by the local vineyard owners. But it was only in 1441, when the place was chosen as the seat of Župa's count, that – as in Broce a century earlier – it was decided to build a street with twenty-five houses along it in which families whose menfolk acted as the count's guards were accommodated.[64]

Other similar foundations aimed at defending vulnerable locations were made on Pelješac – Ledenići, Boljenovići, Zaradeže, Županje Selo, Potomje and Orebići. But most important were those in Konavle, namely Cavtat and Molunat. The last two sites had much in common. Each was a small peninsula, which could thus be both more or less sealed off with walls, ditches and towers from the hinterland, and protected from the sea by Dubrovnik's warships. Each was therefore well suited to serve as a haven to which the inhabitants of Konavle could flee in times of danger – Cavtat serving this function in the northwest and Molunat in the southeast.[65]

Cavtat was, however, also a functioning (if vulnerable) little town which in the later years of the Republic acquired a certain maritime prosperity, while Molunat was a far more modest foundation which, once it had ceased to serve its original purpose, simply became a fishing village. Both were divided up into plots and then settled in the 1460s, as Dubrovnik's earlier tenuous hold on Konavle was strengthened.[66] But whereas the Ragusan patriciate built houses on their land in Cavtat and spent part of the year there, Molunat was not permanently settled in this way. Both Cavtat and Molunat were intended to have buildings for the count and his chancellor and a Franciscan church, but these only actually appeared in Cavtat. What finally led to the depopulation of

Molunat in the seventeenth century was its vulnerability to attack from the sea during this period of acute disorder in the region.[67]

Villas

Over the last two centuries of the Ragusan Republic, Cavtat – unlike Molunat – became a favoured site for villas. But long before then, Diversis had remarked enthusiastically upon the summer residences built in the neighbourhood of Dubrovnik:

> Outside the town there are exceptional houses of wonderful beauty, great value and ample magnificence, which would be an adornment to any nice Italian town, even one in Tuscany.[68]

There is no doubt that the concept of the villa as a rural seat for leisurely living is classical, with its roots in the philosophical writings of Pliny, Tacitus and Seneca and the architectural theories of Vitruvius – all revived, mediated and developed by Italian Renaissance experience and speculation, notably through the work of Leon Battista Alberti.[69] The development of large numbers of fine Gothic-, Renaissance- and Baroque-style villas on the territory of the Ragusan Republic – some 300 or so – bears eloquent witness to the integration of Dubrovnik within the Mediterranean European world. Although with a similar degree of conservatism to that shown in its painting, Dubrovnik's rural architecture reflected trends emanating from the Italian master architects. But it is probably equally illuminating to consider Ragusan villas as developing out of the way of life that itself developed in the Republic. Thus, as was noted earlier, Beno Kotruljević regarded the possession of a house in the country – ideally two, one for farming and another for leisure – as almost a necessity for the busy, prosperous Dubrovnik merchant.[70]

The earliest rural residences built by Ragusan patricians were primarily constructed with an eye to security. Indeed, they were likely to be referred to as 'towers' or 'castles' – like that tower built by Luka Bunić at the mouth of Rijeka Dubrovačka in 1343 or the fortified house (*castrum*) built by Marin Junije Menčetić on Mount Srđ in 1350. Naturally, the further away a house was from the safety of the city walls the greater the emphasis would be on its defences. Most of these fortified dwellings have since been destroyed or reconstructed. An exception is the tall, strong Gothic-style fifteenth century fortified villa at Orašac called Arapovo-Morovo, where, as tradition has it, in 1512 the exiled Florentine *gonfaloniere* Piero Soderini took temporary refuge.[71]

Residences on the islands remained vulnerable longest because of the continuing danger of attack by pirates. Not that preoccupation with security need have resulted in austerity: at Suđurad on Šipan the Skočibuha family combined space and splendour with the erection of high walls with parapets and towers to which the family and their servants and tenants could repair in time of danger. Tomo Skočibuha's house and its tower were built between 1529 and 1546. But after 1542, when he moved to Dubrovnik, the residence served as his 'villa' in the sense that he used it when he could escape there from business in the city. His son Vice began to build his own villa by the side of Tomo's on the site of the old Suđurad shipyard in 1563. It is probably the best-preserved villa on Ragusan territory and consists of almost all the possible elements of such a complex – stone boathouse (known in Dubrovnik as *orsan*, derived from 'arsenal'); terrace; chapel on the terrace; roofed pavilion (in Dubrovnik *pavijun*) situated at the end of the terrace; mill; cistern; drawbridge and fortified gateway; separate large and small gardens. On the ground floor, the *saloča* has the classic stone fireplace, cabinet and wash basin. Above it on the first floor, the main hall has a choir loft (known as *balatur*) from which musicians would entertain Vice's guests, and a fine carved ceiling.[72]

Serafino Razzi, who greatly admired Vice Skočibuha as much for his virtues as his taste, decribed both Vice's and Tomo's houses as 'fine palaces with delightful gardens', which was evidently no more than the truth. Razzi mentions 'another [palace] of royal magnificence between Dubrovnik and Gruž' also built by Vice Skočibuha.[73] This villa, which is situated above Boninovo, was constructed between 1574 and 1588 on an Italian model by an unknown architect. The house is protected from prying eyes by being entirely surrounded by a high wall, but a loggia on the first floor and a raised garden terrace allowed those within a fine view out over the Adriatic.[74]

The Ragusans invested great care in choosing the location of their country houses. Apart from security – which became less of a problem, on the mainland at least, as the sixteenth century progressed – communications were probably the most consistently important consideration. With its jagged coastline, narrow shore, mountainous hinterland and numerous islands, the most convenient means of transport over any distance in the Republic was by boat. This helps explain why the great majority of villas were either very near or even faced directly onto the water. Some locations were ruled out for other reasons. Konavle, beyond Cavtat, was too distant and vulnerable, as to a lesser extent was Pelješac, to see the building of villas for more than local residents. On both Lastovo and Mljet, mainlanders were prevented by law from building or buying property. But elsewhere villas clustered in suitable spots – on Šipan,

Lopud and Koločep; at coves and inlets such as Trsteno, Orašac and Zaton; all along the shores of the harbour of Gruž and of Rijeka Dubrovačka; on Lapad and on the slopes of Kono; some further inland in Šumet and Župa; a number scattered along the coast of Župa bay with the chain finishing up at Cavtat.[75]

The style in which most Ragusan villas were built was a mixture of Gothic and Renaissance, though the mix was subject to many variations. For example, the Getaldić villa in Suđurađ built in 1516 combines side-by-side Renaissance features – horizontal emphasis of the design, the decoration of facades, the symmetrical arrangement and shape of windows – with Gothic ones, notably the arrangement of the garden. Similarly, the villa of Petar Sorkočević on Lapad, which has many Renaissance features, also has classic Gothic-style windows.

Rare are 'pure' Renaissance-style villas, such as that of Archbishop Lodovico Beccadelli in the middle of Šipansko Polje – and it is significant that the rebuilding in 1557 in Renaissance style of this archiepiscopal summer residence was undertaken by one of the most enlightened and scholarly Italians of his day. Beccadelli had a new one-storey wing built on to the old house, facing out onto the countryside of the Polje – an arrangement quite common in Tuscany from the fifteenth century, but unknown in Dubrovnik. In fact, the break from the simple arrangement of a single wing, with *saloča* and hall and four smaller rooms off each, was altogether revolutionary.[76] Beccadelli's villa was deliberately intended to be a centre of cultivated living in the Italian Renaissance style. Thus the archbishop's friend, the priest Bellegrino Brocardo, painted mural portraits of classical and contemporary figures, while visiting Italians helped create a kind of informal learned academy during Beccadelli's years in Dubrovnik. It should be added, however, that the influence which he had on his Ragusan environment was reciprocated, as Beccadelli demonstrates in a sonnet written on the eve of his departure which contains the lines:

> ... and with a burning heart
> I embrace you Dubrovnik, my beloved spouse,
> Model of Illyria and her highest merit.[77]

Beccadelli loved his house on Šipan. He wrote his *Life of Petrarch* there, in whose dedication he refers to 'the delightful leisure I enjoy in this sweet island of Šipan, where without any distractions I pass these dog days, delighting in a lovely view of land and sea.'[78]

Native Ragusans felt similarly. Their villas reflected a particular view of life, a distinct set of values. Perhaps because they were otherwise so often involved in sordid finance and commerce, conducted in the stuffy, smelly confines of the city, they expressed their attachment to the countryside, and above all the seaside, with special passion and eloquence.

This is shown in carved inscriptions. Renaissance Dalmatia was, in general, fascinated by them. Marko Marulić carefully deciphered and transcribed for posterity the late Roman inscriptions of Salona.[79] His contemporary Petar Hektorović, like Marulić a devout Catholic and humanist, had carved no fewer than twenty inscriptions, most religious, around his fortified villa known as Tvrdalj at Stari Grad on the island of Hvar.[80]

The tone of the Ragusan inscriptions is more secular and Horatian. Thus, at the entrance to the beautifully situated garden of the Saraka villa at Ploče:

Este procul livor, lites, ambitio, curae
Antra, hortos, scopulos pax colit atque quies.

Stay far away envy, quarrels, ambition and worries.
In peace and quiet he cultivates plants, gardens and cliffs.[81]

At the Gradić villa on Lapad is an inscription with much the same sense:

Errat, felices qui credit vivere in urbe
Huc veniat locus hic gaudia vera dabit.

He is mistaken who believes that they are happy who live in the city.
Let him come here – this place will give true joy.[82]

On completion of his villa at Trsteno, Ivan Marinov Gučetić had placed an inscription on its facade which encapsulates his approach to his villa. This went beyond the mere expression of delight at the beauty of the place and is an admonition to those who would visit in future years to remember that they are admiring nurture as well as nature:

Domus Io. Got.
Vicinis laudor sed aquis et sospite celo
Plus placeoet cultu splendidoris heri
Haec tibi sunt hominum vestigia certa viator
Ars ubi naturam perfecit apta rudem
MDII

The House of Ivan Gučetić.
I am admired for the nearby water and the smiling sky,
But more pleasing should be the cultivation of beauty in the past.
Here, O visitor, are the clear marks left by men,
Where art has brought rude nature to perfection.
1502[83]

In fact, Ivan Gučetić had particularly good reason to be proud of his achievement, which was unique in several respects. First, it was in 1494 a brave decision to decide to build a villa at Trsteno on the coast of Primorje. The district was still only sparsely settled, little cultivated and exposed to attacks from the sea, while there were as yet no land links with Dubrovnik itself. Secondly – and this is presumably the circumstance to which the inscription refers – enormous effort had to be expended upon preparing the land for building and the cultivation of the gardens which, from their size, can be seen to have had considerable significance right from the beginning.[84] Large numbers of terraces were built, underpinned with stone supports, and the house itself was erected on one of these terraces – the others being used for cultivation. Thirdly, the villa complex was evidently placed where it was, away from any other habitation and 50 metres above the sea, because supreme importance was ascribed to the vista – although a view was always, and increasingly, important to Renaissance Ragusan villa builders it does not elsewhere seem to have been such a dominant consideration. Fourth, the proximity of natural springs (to which the inscription refers) allowed Trsteno to sustain a much greater variety of trees, shrubs and plants than most other Ragusan villas, where water was usually scarce and even the fullest use of cisterns could not on occasion avoid the effects of drought. Finally, it is now clear from investigation of the demands made by Gučetić from his stonemasons that the design of much of his (now totally reconstructed) villa was strongly influenced by Renaissance architectural thinking at a period when this was unknown elsewhere in the Ragusan countryside.[85]

More typical of the mixture of Gothic and Renaissance styles that Ragusans enjoyed is the (already mentioned) villa of Petar Sorkočević (1472–1535) at Lapad.[86] Of the five known Sorkočević family villas in the area it is the finest and the best preserved. Petar decided to build his house on the Lapad shore facing onto the bay of Gruž. It was a popular, if conventional, location. Already in Diversis's time the shores of Gruž were (as he put it) 'adorned with many fertile vineyards, magnificent palaces and wonderful gardens'.[87] Since then the emphasis upon leisure rather than agriculture, villas rather than farms, had grown and continued to grow. Serafino Razzi, writing a century and a half after Diversis, omitted mention of vineyards but described Gruž as 'a very lovely and delightful sea coast, replete with gardens and palaces'.[88] Indeed, working around the shore from Petar Sorkočević's villa one would have encountered villas belonging to the Gradić, Bundić, Gundulić and Natali families. The shoreline of Rijeka Dubrovačka continued the chain.[89]

Petar Sorkočević's villa was constructed in the local style, not from a foreign model. It was a one-storey house, built on a wooded outcrop, surrounded by gardens inside a wall, set in a park. A terrace was laid out on top of the boathouse, which faced directly onto the harbour. At one end the terrace gave direct access to the *saloča*, at the other was a *pavijun*. A loggia on the ground floor led out to a salt-water fishpond. Alongside carved impressions of the Sorkočević family crest on doorways, fireplaces, the chapel and the capitals of the loggia are also to be found Petar's own initials, 'P. S.'. The exact date of building is unclear, but it was well underway in the second decade of the sixteenth century.[90]

It was almost certainly to Petar Sorkočević's villa that two visiting Venetians on their way to Kotor referred in 1553 – some twenty years after Petar's death – when they described how they spent the night 'in the brilliant palace of one of the Dubrovnik nobles'. It was situated on a hill by the side of the sea, and had a 'very pleasant park full of myrtle, jasmine, laurel' and other shrubs. There were also 'two carved fountains of completely drinkable water which made the park more beautiful and which served the palace. Right next to them [was] a fishpond into which the sea [entered] beneath the walls, which form a square around it'.

The Venetian visitors found the delights of Petar Sorkočević's villa, set in its gardens and park, all the more remarkable because they well understood the difficulty of the natural conditions. Thus they wrote:

> There are a number of luxuriously built houses and they are all adorned with fountains, parks and very fine loggias, which must be praised all the more in that they are situated on dry and infertile land, since all this hilly area is so harsh and rocky that the fertile soil which is there is brought from other places and far away areas like Apulia, where the Ragusan ships on their return from voyages load up with good soil and transport it onto their land.[91]

As these Venetians observed, enormous effort was invested in overcoming natural obstacles in order to create beautuful gardens to match the villas they encompassed. Similarly, Nikola Gučetić recalled how he and his workmen had broken up rocks and brought in new soil in order to create a garden full of fruit trees, productive vines and beautiful sweet-smelling flowering plants for his villa in Župa Dubrovačka.[92]

Probably because it was difficult on the dry Ragusan soil to grow large numbers of attractive trees, shrubs and border plants, Ragusan gardens made greater use than their Italian equivalents of architectural devices – terraces, low walls along the sides of the sternly geometrically arranged paths, and above all the pergola (in Dubrovnik known as *odrina*). The origins of the pergola were strictly practical – a means of growing a large number of grapes in a limited space close to the house. But from the fifteenth century, when the uprights began to consist of carved stone pillars rather than wood, pergolas assumed increasing aesthetic importance. These pillars were typically slender, of hexagonal or of rounded section, with a hollow for the wooden crossbar at the top, decorated with carved leaves and capitals. In the winter, bare and deprived of foliage, these pergolas looked somewhat forlorn; but in the summer and autumn, when the villa was most regularly in use, they offered both shade and bunches of grapes to those who walked beneath them.[93] (With the onset of Baroque influence the occasional statue appears – like the two 'unfinished' sculptures at the entrance of the end-of-the-sixteenth century Crijević-Pucić villa at the foot of Gradac outside the Pile Gate; but these are not typical of Dubrovnik.)[94]

The villa and garden had an emphatically social function. Life in them would have become tedious had the owners and their families not been able to invite their friends. The poet Dinko Ranjina (1536–1607) expressed the point simply in the inscription he had carved on his villa at Vrućica on Pelješac: *ad usum suum amicorumque commodum erexit* ('He built it fit for his own use and that of his friends'). Moreover, he was as good as his word, summoning his friend and fellow poet Maroje Mažibradić to come to join him, in the lines:

> Come now and spend a little time with me
> In this my sweet house built on the water's edge.[95]

Ranjina spent most of the last part of his life at Vrućica surrounded by his literary circle.[96] Similarly, his contemporary Nikola Gučetić gathered around him at Trsteno a group of learned friends, and indeed set his philosophical works there.[97]

When they were not sitting in their gardens, Ragusans liked to make boat trips either to fish, hunt or picnic on one of the islands. Although there are few written accounts of such visits – there is no Ragusan equivalent of Petar Hektorović – the importance attached to such things is evidenced in a letter of 1695 from the poet Ignjat Đurđević, urging a friend to join him on Šipan, where he was serving as count, and mentioning the beauties of nature, the fishing and the opportunity for boat trips to Koločep, Trsteno and Mljet.[98] But the most telling testimony to the Ragusan villa owner's enjoyment of the sea is the ubiquity and architectural significance of the *orsan* – whose position often determined the arrangement of the rest of the villa complex and whose robustness was such that they withstood the 1667 earthquake a good deal better than the other buildings of urban and rural Dubrovnik. Unfortunately, like the villas to which they were attached, many an *orsan* has since fallen prey to insensitive road schemes, socialist housing and a mindset unsympathetic to the cultivated, patrician lifestyle of the Ragusan Republic.[99]

THIRTEEN

Death and Resurrection: The Great Earthquake and its Aftermath (1667–1669)

Seismic Conditions

Dubrovnik and southern Dalmatia are subject to seismic conditions that are both dangerous and complicated, with the complication adding to the danger. The region's coastal strip has been sinking over the centuries, but not equally or in the same direction, because the Dinaric blocks in the hinterland are moving independently. Moreover, Dubrovnik and its neighbours are also subject to the impact of the movement of Adriatic blocks from the sea. The result is that phases of strong and destructive seismic activity are followed by phases of stability, in patterns that are difficult to interpret, let alone predict.[1]

The first recorded earthquakes in and around Dubrovnik are of the fifteenth century, though there is, of course, no reason to assume that records here fully reflect reality. Certainly, however, from 1430 there begins a century of frequent tremors, including eleven serious earthquakes.[2] For example, the Anonymous chronicler mentions an earthquake on 28 October 1496, memorable perhaps because it was on a day when the Great Council had met to elect a new Rector. The following year there was another which apparently destroyed 'many houses'.[3] Clearly, though, the earthquake at eleven o'clock in the morning of 17 May 1520 was of a quite different order and is described by the Anonymous chronicler as 'not an earthquake but God's punishment'.[4] The human losses were fairly light: about twenty people were killed and a number injured. But the structural damage was much more severe both inside and outside the city. Moreover, tremors continued for twenty months. Razzi records the miracle that some Ragusans standing just outside the Ploče Gate looked up to see Mount Srđ ready to fall on them, had not Our Lady and St

Blaise held it up. The citizens of Dubrovnik were sufficiently awed and grateful to build the previously mentioned church of the Holy Saviour (*Sveti Spas*) near the Franciscans on Placa as a votive. It was dedicated to the Ascension, the day on which the earthquake had struck, and on that Feast each year a special procession was held.[5] Dubrovnik experienced another earthquake in 1530, but for the rest of the sixteenth and early seventeenth centuries it was Kotor and its surrounds that suffered most from seismic activity. In the 1630s there were again several quite serious earthquakes affecting either Dubrovnik, Kotor or both.[6] But none of these unpleasant events could possibly have prepared the Ragusans for what was to happen next.

The First Impact

Contemporary accounts of the Great Earthquake are remarkably similar, although naturally the predicaments and subsequent experiences of those who survived to tell of them were different. It was somewhat after eight o' clock in the morning of the Wednesday of Holy Week, 6 April 1667. A gentle southerly breeze was blowing. Most of the patriciate were gathered in front of the Rector's Palace waiting for the Rector and his colleagues to finish mass. Many Ragusans, particularly pious Ragusan ladies, were at their devotions. Back at home their servants were cooking the traditional Dubrovnik sweetmeats and other dishes over kitchen fires.

Suddenly there was a deep rumbling, and a violent blow rocked the city. It lasted, according to a Franciscan who was saying mass at the time, no longer than required to say the phrase *passio domini nostri Jesu Christi secundum* ('the passion of Our Lord Jesus Christ according to...'). A large part of the city collapsed. Rocks poured down from Mount Srđ. A thick cloud of dust rose, spreading a pall of darkness over the ruins. The ground shook and large crevasses opened up, swallowing completely some modest dwellings in the suburbs. The city walls swayed before falling back into position. The wells emptied of water, only to be refilled with thick yellow mud, which in turn drained away, leaving them quite dry. From out over the Adriatic there arose a roaring sound similar to continuous cannon fire. The sea withdrew from the harbour entirely and the ships moored there smashed their hulls on the now-exposed rock bed. Several times the tide returned and withdrew again. Flames, which doubtless spread from the kitchen fires, now leapt from house to house, carried by a sudden strong and un-seasonal *maestral*. Soon the whole city was

33. Nikola Božidarević: Blessed Virgin with Saints (1517)

35. Detail of Mihajlo Hamzić (and Pietro di Giovanni): St Nicholas and other Saints, showing St John the Baptist, St Stephen and St Nicholas (1512)

Previous page
34. Detail of Nikola Božidarević's Blessed Virgin with Saints, St Martin and the beggar (1517)

36. Detail of Frano Matijin's Virgin and Child (1534)

S. NICCOLA

38. Votive Painting of Ragusan brigantine (nineteenth century)

39. Detail of Nikola Božidarević's Annunciation (1513): the donor Marko Kolendić's ship at anchor in Lopud harbour

Previous page
37. Votive painting of Ragusan ketch (1779)

40. The Coat of Arms of the Ragusan Republic

41. The Minčeta Tower

burning. This fire claimed the lives of many who had survived the earthquake but lay buried or stunned in the rubble.[7]

The catastrophe was so unexpected and so total that for a while it resulted in a fundamental social breakdown. The traditional patrician leaders of the Republic were dead, disabled or absent – having fled the scene. And from an account given by a Ragusan canon of the situation in the immediate aftermath it is easy to see why:

> The city was as it were buried in stones and rubble from the houses, which removed everyone's hope of ever being able to make them habitable. One could smell the odour of corpses and the unbearable stench of burning which gave many people head-aches. Nor did people want to commit themselves anew to a place where they had lost their friends and relations and had barely escaped with their lives and where they could still feel earth tremors.[8]

Into this void moved the often embittered and now opportunistic and predatory members of the poorest classes, servants, labourers and outsiders from the hinterland – people with little or no respect for Ragusan law, and at this juncture deprived of any fear of infringing it. Only with great difficulty would order be restored by those few patricians who found the courage to uphold the institutions of the state in this time of crisis – a time when Dubrovnik was also extremely vulnerable to external dangers.

The Earthquake as Experienced by Visiting Foreigners

When Joris Croock, the new Dutch ambassador to Constantinople, and Jacob van Dam, the new ambassador to Smyrna, were appointed in 1666, they judged that they and their parties and possessions would be most secure if they travelled together, and this they accordingly did. They left on 16 September but, having been delayed by an outbreak of plague in Germany, they did not arrive in Venice until mid-December. There they experienced more difficulties, both diplomatic – Venice was at war with the Porte – and personal – Joris Croock's wife was pregnant. So it was 28 March 1667 before they left aboard ship, and that vessel was bound for Dubrovnik, not Constantinople, because the political situation still made the direct sea route impossible. After a pleasant and uneventful journey they arrived at Gruž on 2 April.

Van Dam, who wrote an account of his experiences in the form of an official report to his government and in a pamphlet whose contents became widely known, observes that the Dutchmen were very well received in Dubrovnik. The Ragusan Senate gave them numerous presents and many distinguished visitors paid their respects at the house which had been made over for their use.[9] Another member of the party was a Frenchman called Harden, who later in Venice wrote down his own account of the earthquake in a letter to a French banker friend. While the Dutch dignitaries stayed in one house, the forty others in the group were found separate accommodation in the city. Harden notes that the fateful Wednesday had been appointed by the Ragusans for a public banquet in Croock's honour, 'but God decreed otherwise'.

Harden was still in bed when the earthquake struck. Only the fortunate position of a fallen beam prevented his being crushed by a wall. After a time he managed to pull free his legs, but he was still enclosed by rubble. He found that he could speak quite easily to another Frenchman buried beside him, and did so for two days and nights until his companion died. Harden could also hear servants trapped elsewhere in what remained of the building. His own servant was among them, and on the third day Harden heard him cry out that he could not stand it any longer because he was dying of thirst and that he wanted another servant to kill him. (They had kept alive thus far only by drinking their own urine.) Harden shouted back that he would be better off dying in an attempt to save his master and, urging him on, was finally rewarded by learning that the man had managed to escape. The servant described to Harden the scenes of devastation he found around him, where two or three houses had collapsed on top of one another. There was no one around to help, but eventually the servant found some Franciscans sheltering in the remains of their friary. He offered them money to help pull Harden out and they sent back three Slavs with him. The rescuers proved, however, to be more interested in gain than charity. Once they had broken through to Harden, they demanded money to set him free. Learning that he had none, they said in a surly fashion that they would leave. Harden then remembered that he was wearing a ring with two diamonds and passed it out to them through a hole. The Slavs then dug away the rubble and finally dragged him out. However, they refused to stop and dig out the other bodies, because they were anxious to go and rob the corpses of the wealthy.

Harden and his servant now set off naked through the ruins towards the harbour. As they went, they could hear the cries of the dying, concealed beneath the rubble. Bodies were strewn along their route, but it was otherwise quite clear, since all the walls and buildings towards the port had been flattened. In the harbour they saw only the wrecked hulls of ships, and so they set off again towards the city outskirts. That area too was abandoned, but they came across a nobleman who gave them some wine and advised them to head towards the Dominican friary at Gruž where they would be able to obtain something to eat. They slept that night outside in a garden for fear of the aftershocks of the earthquake, which indeed continued for a week. The next day a Theatine father took care of them and provided them with clothes and food. They now learned that the Dutch had embarked on a small ship bound for Venice, and they hurried to join them. A week later a favourable wind allowed them all to sail away to safety.[10]

The Dutch who sailed with Harden back to Venice were a much-diminished group. Joris Croock, his wife and others of his party were dead. Van Dam was alive but had had a narrow escape. He had been thrown out of bed by the earthquake and managed to push aside the rubble to get out onto the terrace. His calls to Croock were unanswered, and as the aftershocks began he leapt into the street. Croock's major-domo was alive but buried in the rubble. Showing the same rapacity as that witnessed by Harden, 'rescuers' robbed the major-domo of his money and then left him for dead, and the man who finally pulled him out was only prepared to do so after he had been given the last two gold buttons on the Dutchman's sleeves. The real prize, however, was the rich gifts that Croock had been carrying with him for the Sultan – fine quality cloth, silverware and 100,000 gold pieces. Part of this treasure was stolen, but Van Dam successfully engaged some men from Cavtat to save the rest. He also eventually managed to have the bodies of Croock, his family and household recovered and given a proper burial. As befitted a well-born Dutch Calvinist, Van Dam's experiences in his necessity confirmed him in his approval of the behaviour of the Ragusan nobility, who helped him recover Dutch property, and his disapproval of the Ragusan clergy, two of whom ignored the fate of one of his friends. Van Dam concluded that the earthquake was a visitation of divine wrath upon a tyrannical and ungodly Republic.[11]

The Earthquake as Experienced by the Clergy

Naturally, the clergy of that Republic viewed matters rather differently. The Franciscan friar Vido Andrijašević, in an account of his experience in a letter to a Ragusan friend in Ancona which was published there, confirms the impression of a city proccupied with its preparations for the great Easter triduum. Confessions were being heard. In Dubrovnik's monastery churches numerous pious Ragusan ladies were gathered for mass on that Wednesday of Holy Week. According to Fra Vido only a tenth of the clergy survived the disaster, though that certainly exaggerates the losses. Doubtless, the fact that the devastation occurred at such a moment magnified in the minds of priests and worshippers alike its apocalyptic significance.[12]

The archbishop of Dubrovnik, Pedro de Torres, hailing from a Spanish family settled in southern Italy, also provided the information for a description of the earthquake similarly published in Ancona. At the moment of the first terrible shock the archbishop was in the chapel of his palace attending a mass celebrated by his chaplain, the priest-poet Vlaho Skvadrović.[13] The archbishop seems to have shown both remarkable agility and an instinct for self-preservation. Feeling the episcopal palace rock like a ship on an ocean swell, he rushed out of the anteroom and towards the main hall, where he narrowly escaped being crushed by a falling block which crashed down filling the place with a thick cloud of dust. Although he injured his foot in the rubble, he and his entourage found their way outside safely. The archbishop and some of his companions ran through the marketplace in front of the cathedral, which had been utterly destroyed. Everywhere there were dead bodies as well as injured, some buried alive beneath the ruins. He and his priests gave absolution to many. In a touching scene one of the Republic's Senators, only half of whose body was above the rubble, made his confession to a priest and in gratitude made him his heir with his dying breath. The archbishop was by now sheltering beneath the remains of the *luža*, and a steadily increasing number of his flock joined him there. But deciding that the spot was still unsafe, he set out towards the *Lazzaretti* at Ploče. Like Harden and his servant, he soon discovered that this was a mistake; moreover, they were afraid that the gunpowder in the nearby towers might explode. So De Torres and his party went instead to Gruž. The archbishop then embarked on a ship in the company of most of the city's surviving nuns and after a difficult journey arrived in Ancona .[14]

The Earthquake as Experienced by the Poorest Classes

The sources probably give a somewhat misleading account of the impact of the earthquake on the poorest classes of Dubrovnik. Undoubtedly, their suffering would have been no less than that of the rich and powerful, and of course their losses in absolute terms would have been greater. The fact remains, however, that the disaster certainly provided those who chose to take advantage of them with real, if usually fleeting, opportunities for material gain from the resulting chaos. All the accounts emphasise the pillaging of the city which then occurred. For example, Fra Vido Andrijašević describes how a large number of Morlachs (Vlachs) who had accompanied caravans from the Ottoman Empire were joined by inhabitants of the Republic in plundering whatever lay in the ruins – gold, silver, jewels and even the relics from the cathedral treasury – with no one to stop them.[15]

Detailed evidence of the crime and disorder which now occurred comes from the court proceedings brought against offenders, once legality and stability were restored – though because these relate only to subjects of the Ragusan state, not foreigners, they understate the scale of the crisis. Servants figure prominently in the accounts of criminal behaviour. They knew, of course, where valuables were stored and they were in many cases joined by their family and friends in looting them. So a servant girl of the merchant Mato Matkov brought half the members of her village in Rijeka Dubrovačka to join her in looting the contents of his house and three shops of goods worth several thousand ducats. Another serving girl robbed her dead master Damjan Pucić. She and her brother stored their ill-gotten gains in the *Lazzaretti*, where they were later discovered: among the booty were twenty-two silver spoons, thirty-one silver forks, six gold signet rings, two gold and pearl rings, four golden signet rings mounted with precious stones, nine silver rings and three gold buttons.

Wealthy Ragusans who were absent at the time of the earthquake returned to discover that their possessions had been robbed. It could take some time to find who was responsible and bring him, her, or them, to justice. A number of these crimes were probably opportunistic rather than calculated. For example, some men from Konavle claimed that they had come to Dubrovnik with the honourable intention of helping those buried in the ruins but, finding such rich pickings, they had gathered together all the booty they could find and returned home with it. Similarly, it must have been vanity as much as greed which prompted one servant girl to loot from her dead master's house all his jewellery and then wear it as if she were a fine lady. She thus incriminated herself – as did serfs who walked around wearing the rich jackets belonging to a merchant.

Clearly, the behaviour of the plunderers towards the injured was particularly shocking – it certainly shocked Van Dam and Harden, who witnessed it. There are other cases, too, of people being robbed of their jewellery and money while lying injured in the ruins. Nor were the robbers particularly discriminating. Anything usable was worth stealing. Miho Crijević, for instance, had three houses in the area of Rijeka Dubrovačka. When he returned to them he found simply bare walls. The local peasants had taken away not just the contents and furnishings but even roof beams and tiles to use for their own houses.[16]

The Earthquake as Experienced by the Patriciate

Most of those patricians who were not away from Dubrovnik on business were at the time of the earthquake gathering outside the Rector's Palace. Frano Bobaljević, however, as he explained in the account contained in his letters to his cousin Marko Basiljević in Venice, had gone into the church of Our Lady of the Rosary situated nearby, and it was here that he experienced the first shock.[17] Bobaljević ran outside into Placa and sought shelter under the Bell Tower. From here he could see that the city was in ruins. He crossed himself and went off to see what had happened to his own family. He discovered that his house had been totally destroyed. Where just half an hour previously he had left his mother, wife and children, he now found no one. He called out, but there was no answer. Overwhelmed by the calamity, he entered the Franciscan church to pray. Only the next day were he and others able to pull out his daughter Ružica, his son Damjan, and the governess Marija. All the rest of his family were dead: his mother, wife, seven of his children, a cousin, a brother-in-law. Marko Basiljević's mother was also pulled out of the rubble. She was alive but had severe cuts about the head.

To judge from his letters – in Italian but bursting into Croatian when the emotion becomes uncontrollable – Frano Bobaljević's mind was somewhat unhinged by the experience. He and what remained of his family spent ten days sleeping under canvas at Pile on the bare earth. Like others of his class, he had seen much of the property that had escaped the earthquake and fire plundered by bands of robbers. Indeed, his financial losses appear to have become something of an obsession. From his house in Dubrovnik he retrieved only two carpets and two medallions. Everything else was gone. He worried ceaselessly about money owed him which would not now be repaid. He later moved his family to a house outside the city. From there, on 3 May, he wrote to ask his cousin to send him from Venice five or six chests with locks and keys in which he might place whatever he could retrieve of his stolen possessions. With order starting to be restored, he wanted to move back to somewhere nearer the ruined city in order to find out what those taking charge of the emergency were doing – he had a very low view of their general competence and honesty. He also wanted to make preparations for the grape harvest on his lands. But Marko Basiljević's mother was still too ill to be moved, and she begged him not to leave her. At one point in the letter Bobaljević observes that he writes with tears in his eyes, and cries out, 'Oh God! Oh God! Oh God!' The memories kept flooding back. Only in January 1668 did he learn that his little daughter Anica had still been alive in the rubble crying for water when the others had been pulled out, but that they had kept this from him at the time.[18]

The account of another patrician, Nikolica Bunić, though less psychologically revealing, is more informative about events than that of Frano Bobaljević; indeed, Bunić himself – evidently a man of cool judgement and great mental resources – played a leading part in the measures taken in the wake of the disaster. Having survived the first shock, Nikolica had returned to the house which his father had built near the church of St Blaise only to find it in ruins. His family, though, seem to have survived the disaster, because he took them to Gruž and found accommodation for them on board a ship. The discomfort this entailed decided him after three days to take them out to Ston. So on Easter Sunday they heard mass at ten o'clock on the shore by the side of the church of the Holy Cross and then sailed to Lopud. Here they met up with a vessel carrying another patrician family and had breakfast together before going on to Slano. They passed an uncomfortable night there aboard a ship which was loaded with hard tack from Venice, before taking a boat to Ston, where they arrived at seven o'clock in the evening. They were greeted by the count of Ston who, after the destruction of his own palace, was lodging with a priest. They themselves were lodged in the bishop of Ston's palace while the boat was sent back to bring from Gruž those of their belongings that had not been stolen. Bunić's family stayed two months in Ston, but the following day he himself sailed back via Koločep to Dubrovnik, where the core of the Republic's leadership was re-forming.[19]

Losses and Destruction

The scale of the task the survivors faced was formidable – perhaps still more so because the information they had in the immediate aftermath of the earthquake was even more imperfect than that available to later historians. There were and are widely differing estimates of the loss of life. The archbishop of Dubrovnik, for example, writing from Koločep immediately afterwards, believed that 14,000 people had been killed. In the same vein, the nobles comprising the interim government of Dubrovnik claimed that 'most' of the nobility and common people had died. Indeed, they instructed their ambassadors to the Porte to tell the Turks that less than a third of the inhabitants had survived, and repeated the same claim in a letter seeking assistance from Louis XIV.[20] Outsiders, too, arrived at very different figures. Van Dam, for example, thought that 5,000 had died and only 500 survived.[21] The Venetian *Provveditore generale*, Catarino Cornaro, reported back to his government that though the Ragusans were keen to minimise their losses, even they could not put them at less than 4,000.[22]

In fact, all these figures are exaggerated. The one figure in which one may place confidence is that for the number of adult patricians killed. Thirty-eight members of the nobility died in the destruction of the Rector's Palace, but others died elsewhere or later of their injuries, making a total of 57.[23] We also know that on the eve of the earthquake there were 177 members of the Great Council. Assuming that the losses endured by the nobility were similar proportionately to those suffered by the populace at large – they may actually have been rather higher because of the concentration of nobles in and outside the Rector's Palace – and assuming that on the eve of the earthquake there were about 6,000 inhabitants living within the city walls and in the suburbs, it seems likely that some 2,000 people were killed altogether in Dubrovnik. This figure must, of course, be increased, perhaps by up to another 1,000, to take in the rest of the Republic.[24]

All witnesses confirm the scale of the physical damage to the city. So does the list of major buildings which were partially or totally destroyed in the catastrophe. The Rector's Palace was severely damaged. The octagonal columns of its upper portico, its southern facade and above all its east wing facing the harbour, which had accommodated the Rector's apartments, were all destroyed. The roofs of the Arsenal collapsed and the building was turned over temporarily for use as a store for materials required for reconstruction.[25] By contrast, the destruction of Dubrovnik's magnificent Gothic cathedral was total. The nearby and contemporaneous Baptistery survived, but it was damaged and henceforth no longer used. A large number of other churches either disappeared or were integrated into other structures. These include the parish church of St Barbara, home to the woodcarvers' guild; the church of St Fosca; the church of St James, on whose site was built today's church of St Joseph; the churches of the Holy Cross and of St Lucy, whose sites were later taken over by the Jesuits; the church of St Martin, owned by the women's monastery of St Andrew, which was also destroyed; the church of St Nicholas of Tolentino with its hospice; the church of St Peter Klubučić, sometimes called St Peter the Less (*Mali*), with its hospice; the women's monastery of St

Mark (sometimes known as St Bartholomew) all of whose nuns died in the earthquake; the women's monastery of St Michael the Archangel at the foot of today's steps up to the Jesuits; and the women's monastery of St Thomas in Pustijerna. The church of the Three Martyrs of Kotor was destroyed, though later rebuilt.[26]

But it is also worth remarking upon those important structures which survived reasonably intact. This applies to the friaries and churches of the Dubrovnik Dominicans and Franciscans (though the Fransiscans had to erect a new bell tower, and their wonderful library was lost to the fire), to the church of St Blaise (whose damage was soon repaired) and to the church of the Holy Saviour (which does not seem to have suffered at all). The Sponza Palace also withstood the earthquake remarkably well.

Although the walls of one of the city's fortresses were seen by observers to open up and close again as the earthquake struck, Dubrovnik's fortifications as a whole were not severely damaged.[27] This would prove crucial to the state's survival in two respects: first, it was decisive in persuading the Turks that Dubrovnik was not about to fall to their Venetian enemies, and that therefore pre-emptive Ottoman action was unnecessary; secondly, it was in the Revelin fortress that the remnants of the city's patriciate gathered in order to restore control after the earthquake.

The damage done to the private houses of Dubrovnik is more difficult to gauge. This is partly because extensive use was made in reconstruction of materials found among the ruins. Moreover, the old plan of the city was largely retained. The eyewitness accounts suggest, however, that the destruction of both palaces and other more modest dwellings was enormous – writing to the pope immediately after the catastrophe, the Ragusan authorities said that not a single house was habitable.[28]

Outside Dubrovnik but within the frontiers of the Republic, Ston suffered – both private houses and the salt works.[29] Many of its public buildings were severely damaged and later rebuilt in Baroque style.[30] The shock of the earthquake was experienced also much further away from its epicentre. Buildings were damaged in Split, Šibenik, Zadar, Trebinje and Mostar. But after Dubrovnik the most severely affected towns were along the coast of what is now Montenegro. At Herceg-Novi most of the houses were damaged, though the fortifications stood firm. Perast was largely destroyed. At Budva only a few houses remained standing. It was in Kotor that the impact appears to have been most dramatic, though only 150 people were killed. The cathedral lost its facade and both bell towers. The Venetian governor's palace was destroyed, and the governor pulled half-dead from the rubble. As in

Dubrovnik, great crevasses opened up and the wells ran dry. Most memorable for the population, however, was a tidal wave which filled the whole of the market square with water.[31]

The Restoration of Order

The earthquake constituted a fundamental test of the moral resources of the ruling Ragusan patriciate, and not all of the patricians passed it. A number of nobles used the chaos in order to rob the treasury, the customs and other state moneys, and then fled by ship. Others, however, gathered round the venerable and experienced Senator Luka Zamanja and two members of the Basiljević family sheltering in the *Lazzaretti*, and began to make preparations to save what remained of the Republic.

On 11 April this group issued the first decrees of the emergency government. They forbade anyone to leave the city; all were to remain within the area from St James in Višnjica to Gruž. They resolved to maintain a force of 300 soldiers to defend the city. They appointed an interim government of ten patricians – Luka Zamanja, Andrija Basiljević, Marin Bundić, Đuro Đurdević, Sigismund Gradić, Đuro Getaldić, Šimun Menčetić, Djore Palmotić, Luka Franov Bunić and (the somewhat unstable) Frano Bobaljević. Six captains were also appointed, each of whom had charge of 50 soldiers. Amid the continuing disorder it was upon the shoulders of these half-dozen that the most crucial responsibilities rested. Among the captains, and indeed among the ranks of those in the interim government of which he was not at first formally a member, the most powerful figure was Marin Kaboga.[32] As Frano Bobaljević put it in a letter to his cousin: 'Lord Marin Kaboga is now *Generalissimo,* and by God he works like a dog! The whole government depends on him.'[33]

Kaboga was the kind of man who is as well-equipped for a crisis as he is ill-suited for ordinary times. He had performed good service to the Republic in resisting the *hajduk*s a few years earlier. But he was considered a rogue by his fellow patricians. On 26 July 1662 the Small Council debated and condemned his bad behaviour. Nikola Sorkočević, who had been one of Kaboga's accusers, had the misfortune to run into him outside the Rector's Palace. Kaboga stabbed him there, and then fled into the garden of the Franciscan friary, claiming sanctuary. Sorkočević later died of his wounds. The Ragusan Senate was determined to avenge this outrage. Claiming that the crime was an act of treason against which sanctuary had no force, the authorities sent their officers into the friary, where Kaboga was found hiding in the well, and he was taken off to prison. The dispute which this use of *force majeure* provoked with the church was only settled when the pope agreed that the secular authorities could try the miscreant in exchange for their promising that he would not be executed. Kaboga was instead sentenced to life imprisonment. He had just petitioned for clemency when the earthquake occurred. Almost overnight, he was transformed from Public Enemy Number One into the Saviour of the State.[34]

While Kaboga and his colleagues worked to restore order, the spirits of the interim government were raised by the arrival on 13 April of another robust patriot, Nikolica Bunić.[35] On 15 April he and other patricians went to the Sponza and rescued the rest of the money stored there, bringing it back to Revelin and placing it in a chest for which Luka Zamanja kept the key. Bunić stayed in the fortress, accompanied by Nikola Basiljević. They spent an uneasy night because an un-seasonal *bura* was blowing the still raging fire towards them, and both in Revelin and the nearby Tower of St Luke were stored large quantities of gunpowder. But they prayed the rosary, and in due course the wind direction duly changed. The following morning the powder was moved well out of reach of stray sparks.

On Sunday 17 April it was learned that the Venetian *Provveditore generale*, Catarino Cornaro, had arrived at the harbour of Suđurađ on Šipan. Nikolica Bunić, as the most senior figure available, was sent with another colleague to meet him. There was an unpleasantly choppy sea and they were glad to board Cornaro's vessel, which they encountered as it was sailing to Gruž. Cornaro appeared amiable enough, but both he and Bunić were suspicious of the other's motives. Bunić was anxious to stress the need for Cornaro to stay away from Dubrovnik for fear of alarming the Turks, but he also mistrusted Venice's own intentions. For his part, Cornaro was convinced that Dubrovnik's ambassadors were anxious to conceal the scale of the disaster. In truth, the Ragusans probably had little to fear immediately from this quarter: Cornaro was most concerned to reach Venetian Kotor as quickly as possible to estimate the damage done and minimize the risk of an Ottoman attempt to seize the town.[36] By the time Cornaro sent back a further despatch about the state of affairs in Dubrovnik on 2 May, he was able to report that though the city itself was deserted, the remaining Ragusans had based themselves in Revelin, summoned up their resolve and were busy restoring order.[37]

This, indeed, was no less than the truth. On 20 April the interim government had decided to appoint officers to carry out a range of vital tasks such as taking charge of the finances, watching over the customs and providing for public health.[38] Then, on 23 April, a gathering of over forty nobles and wealthy commoners met in Revelin to establish a broader-based government. Twelve 'governors' of the Republic were elected. For the first time in the Republic's history the commoners present were allowed to vote and five of them were candidates, though none was successful.[39] In practice, the Twelve consisted of the earlier ten in the emergency government with the addition of Nikolica Bunić and Marin Kaboga. The group sternly renewed the prohibition against leaving the territory of the Republic.[40] On 28 April it was decreed that those who had stolen the state's funds must return them within eight days if they were still on Ragusan soil, and within two months if they had fled abroad, or be proclaimed traitors and have their property confiscated.[41] When Catarino Cornaro again reported to his government on 9 May he was able to note the degree of self-confidence which the leading Ragusans expressed in Dubrovnik's future and their determination never to yield up their liberty.[42]

By the following month the traditional structure of Dubrovnik's government was once again evident. From 3 June the Senate was making decisions and issuing decrees.[43] On 10 June the first properly constituted Ragusan Great Council since the earthquake was convened.[44] This was of both symbolic and practical importance. Although the Council met in Revelin, not in the still-ruined Rector's Palace, its functioning renewed the established means of giving authority on behalf of the patriciate to the decisions of government.

The final stage of the process of re-establishing full governmental legitimacy would only come much later. Right from the immediate aftermath of the earthquake the interim government of Dubrovnik had been sending out diplomatic letters in the name of the Rector and Councillors of the Republic.[45] But no Rector was in fact elected. One of the administrators of the Republic appointed on 23 April would take his turn each week to act as chairman of that body. Perhaps a similar arrangement then continued once the Senate began to function once again, for according to the priest Brnja Đurđević, writing to Stjepan Gradić in Rome, it was only in May that the first Rector after the earthquake was elected, the Rector's quarters in the Palace having at last been put in order.[46]

Foreign Threats

Long before this, however, the government of the Ragusan Republic had been conducting a shrewd and vigorous foreign policy under conditions of extreme danger. It is unclear what Venice's real attitude towards Dubrovnik was at this time. Its underlying thrust seems to have been opportunism shrouded beneath a not-very-convincing humanitarian concern. In the aftermath of the earthquake a large number of Venetian patricians were apparently in favour of Dubrovnik's patriciate uniting with theirs, which in practice would have meant Dubrovnik's becoming subordinate to Venice.[47] Venice also had its supporters in Dubrovnik: Frano Bobaljević was one. But as Cornaro found when he revisited the city, with the passing of time the Ragusan patriciate's self-confidence, resolution and optimism only grew, as did their determination not allow him or any other Venetians inside the city.[48] Dubrovnik's able ambassador to Venice, Miho Sorkočević-Bobaljević, seems, however, to have suffered a classic diplomat's *déformation professionnelle* in this matter. As late as 16 December 1669 he wrote a despatch suggesting that the only way to avoid a reopening of Split after the end of the War of Crete was to agree a union between the Ragusan and Venetian Republics, about which he had been holding lengthy private discussions. The Ragusan government immediately responded with a vigorous rejection.[49]

Venice's approach to Dubrovnik was certainly heavily influenced by the latter's place in the Serenissima's relations with the Ottoman Empire. The Venetians were worried that the earthquake might give the Turks opportunities to seize either Dubrovnik or Kotor. But they were also desperate to see trade reopened and flowing through one or more Venetian ports rather than Dubrovnik, which had been enjoying since 1645 something of a monopoly. Even while hostilities continued, Venice was seeking to have at least one port opened, and Dubrovnik's misfortunes provided it with a splendid opportunity to convince the Porte that the Serenissima's old rival was no longer capable of handling the trade. The Ragusans were fully cognisant of this. For example, on 21 July the government wrote to Sorkočević-Bobaljević that it had learned that Cornaro had suggested to the Venetian Senate that it should tacitly license the *hajduks* to intercept Turkish caravans on their way to Dubrovnik in order to demonstrate the latter's insecurity.[50]

Trying to ensure that Split, Durrës and Gabela on the Neretva remained closed was a continuous objective of Ragusan diplomacy in Constantinople during the War of Crete. The latest twist in the negotiations at the time of the earthquake was the Venetian proposal – how serious it is difficult to judge – to exchange Kotor for the opening of an emporium on the Neretva. But even before the earthquake other still more dangerous issues had arisen.

Dubrovnik had fallen afoul both of the merchants of Sarajevo and of the Bosnian *pasha*. The underlying motive for their hostility was envy. Bosnian merchants resented the wealth which Dubrovnik enjoyed largely as a result of its privileged relationship with the Ottoman Empire. Two of these merchants, whose goods had been robbed by *hajduk*s at the Ragusan-Ottoman frontier in 1664, alleged that Dubrovnik was in league with the despoilers and demanded recompense. Bosnian merchants also claimed that Dubrovnik had illegally increased the tariffs levied on merchants using the city as an *entrepôt* when Split was closed after 1645.

Unfortunately for Dubrovnik, these issues were still unresolved at the time of the earthquake. More unfortunately still, it was not just the hostility of the Empire's merchants but also of the Empire's high officials that the Republic had to face. It was natural enough that the Bosnian *pasha*, whose interests were closely linked to those of the merchants of Sarajevo, should be a problem. But it was in Constantinople that the greater danger lurked. In the absence of the Ottoman Grand Vizier, Ahmed Kŏprülü, who was supervising the last stages of the War of Crete, all power was wielded by his deputy or *Kaymakam* Kara Mustafa, a grasping bully with none of the shrewdness that moderated the avarice of most other Ottoman officials.[51]

These difficult circumstances – in which Dubrovnik found itself faced by Venetian diplomatic plotting, Turkish blackmail and raids across its territory conducted by both *pandur*s (loosely obedient to the Turks) and *hajduk*s (still more loosely allied with the Venetians) – continued for some years after the earthquake. But it was their coincidence with that natural catastrophe which posed such a grave threat to the Republic's survival and which so alarmed Dubrovnik's interim government gathered in Revelin.

The day after the earthquake the Turkish commanders in Herceg-Novi sent messengers to Dubrovnik asking about its state and offering condolences.[52] But it was the movements of the *pasha* of Bosnia which were more important, and these were worrying. On 15 April Dubrovnik's ambassador in Sarajevo, Marin Gučetić, reported that the *pasha* was about to go south with his army, allegedly to Herceg-Novi but really, according to some sources, with the intention of extorting money from Dubrovnik.[53] Publicly, though, his intentions were of the best. In letters sent via two Vlach messengers the *pasha* expressed his desire to help, but as Catarino Cornaro noted in his despatch to Venice, these Vlachs were also spies able to provide him with full information about the damage done to the stricken city.[54] Before the *pasha* left Sarajevo Marin Gučetić had a lengthy conversation with him about Dubrovnik. The ambassador continued to discourage the *pasha*'s insistent offers to come to protect (in other words occupy) the city with his forces. He also did what he could to counter the demands of the merchants of Sarajevo that Gabela be opened to allow a resumption of trade with Venice.[55]

But the focus of the Ragusan administrators' attention was now no longer mainly the Bosnian *pasha* but Kara Mustafa, and the stakes were accordingly higher. The Ragusan *poklisari* only seem to have learned of the earthquake in early May from Dubrovnik's first letters sent to the *pasha*, which the latter somewhat belatedly forwarded to the *Kaymakam*.[56] Adrianople, the alarmed *poklisari* reported, was awash with speculation about the huge sums of money waiting to be seized by the Turks in a Dubrovnik that was ruined and desolate.[57] At the end of May, the government instructed the *poklisari* to concentrate their efforts upon reducing the *harač*, which was becoming due.[58] In fact, Dubrovnik's rulers were none too confident of the abilities of their ambassadors to the Porte at this stage and decided, much to the patrician diplomats' distaste, to send a Ragusan merchant from Belgrade to expedite the delicate business in that hostile court.[59]

In truth, neither the business with the *Kaymakam* in Adrianople nor that with the Bosnian *pasha* in Herceg-Novi was proceeding satisfactorily. Dubrovnik's enemies among the merchants of Sarajevo and the people of Herceg-Novi had lodged complaints with the *pasha*, which Marin Gučetić tried in vain to refute; he was thrown into prison for his pains. The complaints were relayed to Adrianople.[60] Moreover, the *Kaymakam* had perceived a further opportunity for extortion. Distorting for his own purposes the traditional relationship between Dubrovnik and the Porte, Kara Mustafa demanded in July 300 bags full of ducats which he claimed were due to the Sultan as Dubrovnik's sovereign for the property of Ragusans who had died without heirs as a result of the earthquake. The *poklisari* were to be held hostage until the sum was paid, though they managed to stay out of prison.[61] Their spirits sank further the longer they were detained and the more threatening and insistent Turkish demands became. By mid-August, plague was raging in Adrianople – it had already killed the Polish ambassador.[62] At the same time Marin Gučetić was reporting from Herceg-Novi that he, too, was again being threatened with imprisonment by an enraged Bosnian *pasha*, who was suffering from an acute case of humiliation as a result of his defeats at the hands of the *hajduks*. Still more alarming for Dubrovnik was doubtless Gučetić's report that the *pasha* was threatening to turn the Republic into an Ottoman *sandžak* unless the Porte's financial demands were fully met. As the *pasha* brutally put it: 'these [Ragusan] infidels aren't worthy of the Sultan's compassion but rather his sword'.[63]

Faced with these dangers, there was very little that the Ragusan Republic could expect from outside assistance, as it quickly learned. In the immediate aftermath of the earthquake, the interim government had sent desperate letters to the Western powers informing them of what had occurred and begging for help. By and large, these initiatives met with disappointing results. Europe was, not unusually but no less inconveniently, at war, which provided a reason and an excuse for the powers to do nothing. For example, the Ragusan authorities wrote to Louis XIV of France on 26 April to ask for money and arms to enable it to defend itself.[64] A special envoy was subsequently despatched via Rome to press Dubrovnik's cause with the Sun King. Dubrovnik's own Stjepan Gradić also helped bring Pope Clement IX's influence to bear upon France to try to ensure the mission's success. But in spite of all the high hopes it failed. On 12 January 1668 Louis wrote to Dubrovnik regretfully informing its government that the requirements of war prevented his complying with the requests which the Ragusan ambassador had conveyed to him.[65] Partly because of Gradić's efforts and partly because of the traditional sympathy between the Holy See and Dubrovnik, the pope was more forthcoming. But apart from exerting a degree of moral pressure on the Venetians not to mount a coup against Dubrovnik, there was little that the Vatican could do to afford it protection.

Dubrovnik's fundamental difficulty with the Turks at this juncture flowed from forces at work within the Ottoman state itself. The Empire was undergoing its own internal and external crises, and Dubrovnik was caught up in them. Both Kara Mustafa's inordinate demands and the security considerations that contributed to them resulted from the Empire's weakness, not strength. Accordingly, if Dubrovnik could stave off a break in relations for long enough, the Empire would have more than it to worry about. The immediate requirement, though, was to survive the last stages of the War of Crete which *pandur*s, *hajduk*s and increasing numbers of the Republic's own citizens, especially in Konavle, were fighting out on Ragusan territory. Dubrovnik accordingly demanded that its ambassadors hold firm, whatever the cost.

Two new, more experienced and effective *poklisari*, Jaketa Palmotić and Nikolica Bunić, were despatched to the Porte in September with the *harač*. Their instructions were to seek the diminution of the tribute, suspension of the demand for 300 bags of ducats and an end to talk of reopening Durrës and the Neretva to Venetian trade – either of which (as the *poklisari* were to stress) would greatly reduce the amount that the Porte could hope to gain from Dubrovnik.[66] In fact, largely through the diplomatic virtuosity of Palmotić, Dubrovnik eventually escaped the clearly outrageous demand of money in lieu of the estates of its dead citizens.[67] Their successors, Antun Rastić and Orsat Sorkočević, were empowered by Dubrovnik to offer large bribes to win over Kara Mustafa to the Republic's interests in the matter of Durrës.[68] But the envoys found it difficult to gain a hearing because the whole Ottoman court was constantly on the move following the Sultan on his obsessive hunting expeditions.[69]

By March 1669 the Ragusan government had caught wind of peace negotiations between the Porte and Venice. Dubrovnik instructed its ambassadors to see that its interests were not jeopardised by the terms.[70] They managed to ensure that Durrës remained closed while the last stages of the War of Crete dragged on. But it was beyond even the most skilful Ragusan diplomacy to affect the peace treaty between the Ottoman Empire and Venice, which was signed on 6 September that year. The one great benefit to Dubrovnik of the return to peace was the prospect of an end to the anarchy generated by *hajduk* raids supported by Venice. The disadvantages, however, probably outweighed this; for Venice, though deprived of Crete, held on to the substantial gains it had made in Dalmatia, and a strong Venetian presence there was bound to threaten Dubrovnik's independence. Of more direct concern was the imminent reopening of Split, Dubrovnik's great commercial competitor. Moreover, the end of the war by no means implied a final reckoning of accounts with Kara Mustafa.

Reconstruction

The same combination of determination and ingenuity which were shown by the Ragusan patriciate in the restoration of orderly government and the defence of the Republic's independence was also demonstrated in the process of reconstruction. This began almost immediately order returned. Three nobles were appointed to supervise 62 workmen clearing rubble out of the city streets.[71] Three more nobles were placed in charge of repairs to the city walls – thankfully, only lightly damaged.[72] Work to restore the church of St Blaise, which had to take the place of the destroyed cathedral until the latter was rebuilt, was also quickly and vigorously undertaken. Three hundred and sixty separate payments ranging from just one to more than 400 *hyperperi* were made out of the city treasury for various tasks of repair and reconstruction.[73]

In undertaking the city's restoration, the government was invaluably assisted by Stjepan Gradić in Rome. Gradić's career marked him out as a brilliant, and also in many ways typical Ragusan of his age. Born of one of the oldest and most prestigious patrician families, he was a (probably rather worldly) cleric, diplomat, scholar, internationalist and patriot. He had received a bursary from the Ragusan Republic to study in Rome. But he owed his promotion in the Vatican as much to his social as to his intellectual accomplishments. His uncle, canon Petar Benessa, afforded him protection and made him his heir. Gradić managed to become friends with several cardinals, including two future popes – Alexander VII (1655–1667) and Innocent XII (1691–1700). By the time of the earthquake he was deputy keeper of the Vatican Library. He was the leading Croat ('Illyrian') in the Vatican, and on four occasions he served as president of the Croatian Fraternity of St Jerome. He had already performed useful diplomatic services for Dubrovnik in a range of matters – including the resolution of commercial quarrels with Ancona (in the papal states), overcoming the difficulties about setting up the Jesuits' *collegium*, countering allegations by the rebels of Lastovo, making Dubrovnik's case against its recalcitrant archbishop, and – perhaps most importantly – ensuring that the Republic was not drawn into the anti-Ottoman schemes of Alexander VII.[74]

On 10 April the interim government of Dubrovnik wrote to Alexander VII and also to Stjepan Gradić about the destruction of the city. But Gradić had learned of the catastrophe before the letter ever arrived. Heartbroken, he walked by the side of the Tiber on that spring evening with another Dalmatian expatriate, his friend Ivan Lučić, the historian from Trogir, both of them bursting into uncontrollable sobbing as they reflected on what had happened.[75] From his first letter of encouragement and advice written back to Dubrovnik, Gradić worked tirelessly for the rebuilding of the city and the restoration of the Republic. It is, though, easy to imagine that those who received his exhortations and criticisms must have been heartily irritated by them. Gradić's starting point always seemed to be that everything in Italy was done better and that the provincials back home must copy it. The Ragusans were thus advised to use Italian-style carts to carry stones and rubble, to build Italian-style houses for the poor and to institute an Italian-style state bank. They should modernise their attitudes and institutions, widening the ranks of the patriciate, encouraging immigrants to settle and abandoning Erastian tendencies towards the Church. They were to practise what today would be called import substitution – ensuring that anything that could usefully be grown or produced by Ragusans in Ragusa was so. Some proposals were far-sighted but excessively ambitious – like that to open up a channel between Mali and Veliki Ston, which has proved too much for even modern governments.[76]

Gradić's main practical contributions lay in the realm of finance and technical expertise. It was largely thanks to his endeavours that Dubrovnik was enabled by the pope to liquidate or borrow on its investments in Roman and Neapolitan banks. These holdings, whether in the name of the Ragusan Republic or of its fraternities, were intended for strictly charitable purposes. But the need to rebuild the city after such a disaster was clearly consonant with that objective. Dubrovnik similarly sought permission to draw on a subsidy granted earlier to its archbishop, which should be used for the rebuilding of the cathedral. It also wanted to be able to liquidate for its own purposes the investments of private individuals who had died without heirs and whose property accordingly reverted to the state. Dubrovnik's requests were granted, and large sums were accordingly raised – including 71,665 *scudi* in three tranches from advances on interest due from the state's investments in Rome between 1669 and 1673.[77]

Gradić also sought architects and other experts to help with rebuilding the city. Between the summer of 1667, when the civil and military engineer Giulio Ceruti arrived in Dubrovnik, and the summer of 1680 when the architect Pier Antonio Bazzi departed, a series of Italians were recruited by Gradić and Dubrovnik's Cardinal-protector Giulio Barberini to help with the reconstruction. Ceruti is credited with designing and building the house which would serve as the model for the new baroque houses along Placa, with their distinctive shops *na koljeno* (literally 'onto the knee', conveying the shape of the entrance). Not all the Italians' suggestions were accepted, and Bazzi claimed that he had not been fully paid – circumstances which greatly irritated Cardinal Barberini. But their role in Dubrovnik's recreation as a Baroque Italian-style city was undoubtedly decisive.[78]

Gradić's own single greatest contribution to the rebuilding is to be seen in the Baroque cathedral for which he obtained much of the money and also found the architect, Andrea Buffalini of Urbino, whose sketches were in 1671 accepted by the parsimonious Ragusan Senate. The execution of the work was entrusted to other Italians and the structure was finished, long after Gradić's death, in 1713. Gradić's role is recalled by the marble plaque that was placed by a grateful Senate on the cathedral facade.[79]

The opening of the new cathedral was a great occasion, marking in a certain sense Dubrovnik's recovery from the traumas of its earthquake. An anonymous letter of the time provides a description. A procession, consisting of the archbishop bearing the Blessed Sacrament and the canons and other clergy bearing relics of St Blaise, was joined by the Rector and 100 or so patricians. Accompanied by a squad of uniformed soldiers and bombardiers, it made its way through the 'whole people' who had turned out for the spectacle. When the archbishop reached the great door of the cathedral, the canons, to applause from the populace, intoned the *Te Deum*; all the bells of the city chimed; firecrackers exploded along Placa; cannons fired off salutes – five shots apiece – from every fortress. Then the Ragusans themselves crammed into the church to attend a Solemn Mass with 'great devotion and joy, seeing after so many years their cathedral rise again even more beautiful'.[80]

The Baroque city above which towered the new cathedral dome was, as has been noted, laid out very much along the lines of that which had perished in the Great Earthquake and fire. Some minor streets were destroyed and the resulting space taken over for private use. The greatest changes occurred in the area around the Jesuit church and college, where some streets disappeared entirely and various sites were used for the new structures. *Gundulićeva poljana* (Gundulić Square), the site of today's market, was created on what had before the earthquake been a densely inhabited settlement. The somewhat altered location of the cathedral similarly resulted in the creation of a new square. In the southern part of the town some open spaces were now to be found where the destroyed women's monasteries had stood. In general, the new Dubrovnik was more airy and less cramped, and it seems likely that it contained about 150 fewer houses.[81] In spite of what has been lost – above all, in spite of the loss of the old cathedral – the new Baroque Dubrovnik retained much of its historic appearance as well as gaining – above all, in the Jesuit complex – some fine buildings. Stjepan Gradić apparently never returned to his native city to admire what had been achieved; but anyone looking at the city as it is today must feel that the hope expressed in Gradić's first letter to Dubrovnik after the disaster – that like 'an ancient olive tree' whose branches were cut down, it should send forth new shoots from its trunk and grow once more – was indeed accomplished.[82]

FOURTEEN

Sunset Years: Political, Economic, Social and Cultural Life (1669–1792)

Diplomatic Manoeuvrings

The end of the War of Crete in 1669 did not bring an end to Dubrovnik's troubles. The reopening of Venetian Split diverted Dubrovnik's commerce, particularly once Split's *lazzaretto* was restored in 1671. Venice itself remained hostile and regarded with unconcealed delight Dubrovnik's economic difficulties, which its agents believed would eventually lead to the loss of Ragusan independence.[1] The depredations of anti-Turkish fighters from eastern Hercegovina continued to disrupt Ottoman trade, and the resulting disorder spilled over into Konavle. And most serious of all, once that unpredictable extortionist Kara Mustafa became Grand Vizier in October 1676, Dubrovnik had to embark upon a new, exhausting strategy to defend its interests.

The excuse for the new Grand Vizier's demands was, as previously, the complaints of a vociferous group of Bosnian Muslim merchants about the levies they had been forced to pay at Dubrovnik over the previous thirty years. Having heard their complaints, Kara Mustafa demanded compensation amounting to the substantial sum of 350,000 ducats. In Constantinople the Republic's *poklisari*, Marin Kaboga and Đuro Buća, put up a vigorous resistance – so vigorous indeed that in March 1678 the Grand Vizier lost patience and had them both thrown into prison. He also ordered that the port of Dubrovnik be closed and the frontiers sealed until a truly enormous fine of more than three million ducats was handed over. The *pasha* of Bosnia was then entrusted with carrying out these instructions.

Dubrovnik responded by hurriedly despatching an embassy to the *pasha*. The chosen envoys, Marin Gučetić and Nikolica Bunić, were both able and experienced, but they found the *pasha* unmovable and they, too, were incarcerated. The *pasha* was now summoned to join Kara Mustafa in a campaign against the Russians and his forces moved off towards the Danube, taking the envoys with them. The Turks were now claiming that the imprisoned *poklisari* in Constantinople had agreed to pay the smaller amount of 200,000 ducats, and the *pasha* refused to negotiate further until the sum was paid. Gučetić and Bunić were accordingly thrown into a dungeon in Silistria where the army was assembling. Here Nikolica Bunić died of the plague on 16 August 1678, to be venerated until the end of the Republic for his sacrifice.[2]

By the time a new envoy, Sekondo Gučetić, entered into discussion with Kara Mustafa later that year, the latter was in a mood to compromise, the Turkish forces having been trounced by the Russians in Ukraine. The Grand Vizier accepted a personal bribe of 60,000 ducats, and in exchange reduced his official demand to another 60,000 ducats to be paid in two instalments. He also ended the blockade of Dubrovnik. In March 1679 the three remaining envoys were released from jail – though not before a violent and unseemly quarrel between the irascible Kaboga and Gučetić.

The renewed experience of dealing with Ottoman tyrannical behaviour at the hands of Kara Mustafa left a deep imprint on Dubrovnik. As in the previous century, the patriciate was in any case split in its sympathies between those who believed that good relations with the Ottoman Empire afforded Dubrovnik stability, protection and prosperity and must therefore be retained at all cost, and another group who urged the pursuit of a strategy hostile to the Turks and co-operative towards the Christian powers (notably Austria). The combination of Kara Mustafa's extortion and the Ottoman Empire's evident military weakness – illustrated dramatically by the defeat of the Turks outside Vienna on 12 September 1683 – now sharply swung the argument within the patriciate in favour of the anti-Turkish faction.[3]

Dubrovnik accordingly reverted to its old policy of the late fifteenth and early sixteenth centuries, trying to keep a foot in both Ottoman and Western camps. Thus it continued to protest its loyalty to the Porte, but it also entered into secret negotiations with Vienna. Rafo Vladislav Gučetić was despatched as special envoy to the Habsburg Emperor Leopold I in order to open discussion about the terms on which Dubrovnik might renew its submission to him in his ancient (and still notional) capacity as 'King of Hungary'.

There was, however another equally pressing – and equally traditional – consideration behind this approach, namely fear of Venice. The Venetian Republic had not immediately joined the new Holy League of Austria and Poland against the Ottoman Empire. Like Dubrovnik's, its ruling class was divided between an anti-Ottoman faction and those who thought that a profitable peace with the Porte was preferable to a commercially disruptive war. But Venice eventually did join the League, on 5 March 1684. From this point on it was doubly important that Dubrovnik intervene in Vienna to prevent Venice's seizing the opportunity to throttle Ragusan trade and destroy Ragusan independence.

Still, in its dealings with Venice as with the Ottoman Empire, Dubrovnik was fully aware that timing was everything. It was important that the Venetians learn that Dubrovnik now enjoyed Austrian protection, but not until that protection was a physical reality – otherwise Venice might be tempted to launch a sudden coup against its intended victim. After lengthy negotiations in Vienna, and thanks to the good offices of the anti-Venetian Spanish ambassador Carlo Emmanuele d'Este, Marquis of Borgomanero, the Ragusans agreed on 20 August 1684 to renew their allegiance to the Habsburg Emperor. They would pay, as they had in earlier times, a tribute to him of 500 ducats (or ongars). But this would only commence once the Emperor had regained control of the Balkan hinterland, or in the somewhat vaguer language of the undertaking, 'when the Turkish power and violence will be removed from these areas'.

Dubrovnik's enthusiasm for the Habsburg cause increased along with Austrian successes in battle. On 2 September 1686, Buda fell to much rejoicing in Catholic Christendom. Although not yet bound to do so, Dubrovnik now began secretly to pay its annual tribute to Vienna. At the same time, however, it continued to provide discreet assistance to the Turkish garrison besieged in Herceg-Novi. Having failed to send the annual *harač* to the Porte in 1684, Dubrovnik now resumed these payments for 1685 and 1686. To add to the diplomatic mare's nest, all this time the Venetians were still unaware that Dubrovnik was in fact under Austrian protection; only in January 1687 was this fact communicated to them, and then only because Dubrovnik had become more afraid of Venetian plots than of Ottoman wrath.

What was, in fact, to become the 'Long War' (1683–1699) was now looking as if it might be rather short and end in total victory for the Holy League. The fall of Herceg-Novi in October 1687 was followed by that of Belgrade in September of the following year. For its part, the Ragusan government was now almost exclusively preoccupied with Venice. Dubrovnik's diplomatic energies were concentrated on trying to ensure that the fall of Ottoman Hercegovina benefited the Habsburg Emperor rather than the Venetians. In this matter, Dubrovnik, indeed, proved more royalist than the king. Its ambassador in Vienna found it difficult to persuade the court that urgent action was required to assert the Emperor's claims. Undaunted, Dubrovnik made vigorous efforts to use its contacts with the Hercegovinian clan leaders to ensure that they declared for Leopold rather than Venice. This was by no means easy. Venetian forces had been pressing into Hercegovina via Ston since the summer of 1687. Their seizure of Herceg-Novi opened up the opportunity for a pincer movement against the Turks, which also allowed them to begin sealing off Dubrovnik from its hinterland. Venetian ships now blockaded the city from the sea, in spite of Dubrovnik's and Leopold's protests. A new blow to Ragusan interests came on 10 October 1688 when France declared war against Austria, thus further distracting the Emperor from his interests in the Balkans.

At last, on 19 December, Leopold issued letters patent by which he took all the inhabitants of Hercegovina under his protection. At the same time, he guaranteed their enjoyment of their old privileges, including freedom of religion. This last was in response to Venetian black propaganda which maintained that the mainly Orthodox Hercegovinians could expect to be forcibly converted to Catholicism. Under further Ragusan pressure, Leopold declared on 11 June 1689 that his armies would take Hercegovina by force. Austrian troops now re-entered Serbia. Initially, they were successful and broke through to take Sofia and Skopje. But that winter the fortunes of war dramatically altered. During 1690, Turkish forces pressed back the Austrians and on 8 October they retook Belgrade.

These developments left Dubrovnik once more in a perilous position. Its Austrian patron was in no position to offer protection. Its relations with the Porte had broken down. As the prospect of peace negotiations loomed, it was clear that the Republic had no powerful friends to defend its interests and, in Venice, it faced a victorious enemy which had every intention of incorporating it within Venice's regained Dalmatian dominions. In the summer of 1694 Venetian forces, supported by the *hajduks*, renewed their drive against what was left of Turkish Hercegovina with the evident intention of isolating Dubrovnik entirely from the Ottoman dominions. Čitluk, Gabela, Zažablje, Trebinje, Popovo polje and Klobuk all fell. Dubrovnik was now cut off completely.[4]

Dubrovnik desperately needed peace, but could not afford it on the proposed basis of retention by all sides of the territory they currently possessed – the principle of *uti possidetis*. For its own commercial and thus political survival it had to ensure that it was adjacent to Turkish, not Venetian, territory. It could probably hope to secure the support of Vienna in this goal. But it would first be necessary to re-establish good relations with the Porte. Dubrovnik's opportunistic transfer of allegiance from Constantinople to

Vienna had incurred considerable resentment among Ottoman officials. Luckily, however, Kara Mustafa was now dead, and in February 1695 there acceded a new Sultan, Mustafa II. Dubrovnik's offers to renew payment of the *harač*, as well as compensation for the years since 1686, were well-received. It was agreed that 42,500 thalers should be paid in lieu of all that was due.

The war dragged on desultorily, with successes and reverses for each side. Eventually, serious negotiations began at the end of 1698 at Srijemski Karlovci (Carlowitz). Dubrovnik was not itself a participant, and the main powers were preoccupied with many other matters. But Ragusan diplomacy worked vigorously and effectively in both Vienna and Constantinople. Under Dubrovnik's prompting, both the Austrian and Ottoman delegations became increasingly exasperated at Venetian obduracy about the territorial division of Dalmatia and Hercegovina and eventually resolved to impose their own terms. On 26 January 1699 all the parties except Venice reached agreement. Article IX of the treaty noted:

> The territory and districts of the government of Dubrovnik will form the continuation of the territories and districts of [the Ottoman] Empire, every obstacle being removed which would impede the continuation of the lands of the said government with the lands of the same Empire.

This provision was precisely what Dubrovnik required – hardly surprisingly, since it was in large part what Ragusan diplomacy had been pressing on Constantinople. But it would require time and effort before the treaty was fully implemented.

Throughout 1699 and 1700, the Venetians refused to withdraw from their positions. They justified their obduracy by claiming a right to hold onto 'forts' which were not covered by the territorial provision of the treaty. Venice also kept up its blockade of Dubrovnik by sea. But the Serenissima was interested in trade not just territory, and in order to keep goods flowing to its Dalmatian ports it was finally prepared to compromise. So on 14 February 1701 the Venetians and Turks eventually agreed a frontier. Venice now withdrew its forces from southern Hercegovina, thus allowing renewed contact between Dubrovnik and the Empire, and it also ended the blockade.

Dubrovnik could then re-establish the precise terms of its tributary status with the Porte. It formally withdrew allegiance from the Habsburg Emperor, explaining to Vienna that the Austrians had failed to fulfil the conditions on which it had been offered. After lengthy negotiation with the Porte, it was established that henceforth Dubrovnik would pay the *harač* at its old rate of

12,500 ducats (or ongars) but only once every three years; in 1707 Sultan Ahmed III (1703–1730) duly issued a *ferman* to that effect.[5]

Dubrovnik's defence of its interests during the period of the Long Turkish War demonstrated diplomatic skill of the highest order: it certainly suggests no decline in Ragusan political sinuosity and tenacity. A specific example of this singleness of purpose – which has, indeed, left its mark on today's maps showing the frontiers between Croatia and Bosnia – is the way in which Dubrovnik ensured the creation by the treaty of Srijemci Karlovci of Turkish 'buffer zones'. In the northwest at Klek (in today's Neum enclave of Bosnia-Hercegovina) and in the southeast at Sutorina (now in Montenegro) were two little strips of territory separating Ragusan from Venetian land. Both were the object of Dubrovnik's diligent and resourceful diplomacy, as well as careful local manipulation. Indeed, the Republic actually allowed, perhaps encouraged, the Ottoman Empire to usurp a crucial stretch of its own territory at Gornji Klek, in order to make the Turkish-held corridor wider and more secure.

These strategically crucial provisions were subsequently endangered as a result of Ottoman defeat at the hands of Austria and Venice in the Turkish War of 1715–1718. At the peace negotiations at Požarevac (Passarowitz) the Porte yielded extensive territories in Central Europe and the northern Balkans. But Dubrovnik strained every muscle to ensure that Constantinople resisted accepting the gains which Venice had once again made in southern Hercegovina, including Klek and Sutorina.

Again, Dubrovnik was not initially a party to the negotiations. But this time it was able to send Luko Kiriko, its shrewd resident ambassador to the Porte, to act as translator (of Turkish) for the English ambassador Sir Robert Sutton who, with his Dutch counterpart, served as mediator between the parties. Kiriko's role soon exceeded that of a mere *dragoman*. At the seventh conference he was summoned in his own right to represent the Ragusan Republic's interest. Kiriko's efforts won over the Austrians and the mediators to Ottoman and Ragusan demands. Venice was yet again diplomatically isolated and had to agree to a return to the *status quo ante* as regards Dubrovnik's links with the Empire, including the return to the Porte of Klek and Sutorina.[6]

New Threats for Old

Despite these setbacks, Venice had good reason to be satisfied. By the Peace of Požarevac (1718) it gained much of what it had sought during the previous century. It secured its territorial position on the coast of the Eastern Adriatic; its *entrepôt* of Split was again a prosperous competitor to Dubrovnik; and other Venetian-controlled ports such as Herceg-Novi and Makarska were handling much of the salt trade with the Ottoman hinterland that had once been Dubrovnik's effective monopoly. Yet, as the eighteenth century progressed, it also became clear that the great days of the Serenissima were definitively over. Britain, France and then Russia intruded into the Eastern Mediterranean. And although the traditional enmity with the Ottoman Empire abated, Venice faced a new challenge from a resurgent Austria intent on advancing as an economic power, notably through the development of its ports of Trieste and Rijeka.

Such pressures seem to have made the Venetians even more touchy about Dubrovnik. The days when Venice could hope to seize its old foe had passed. But resentment, born of growing impotence, led to unpleasant incidents. For example, in 1751 two corsair vessels from Tripoli seized a ship from Venetian Herceg-Novi and then took refuge from Venetian galleys in Dubrovnik's harbour. Loyal to the Porte, and careful of their own interests in North Africa, the Ragusans refused to yield up the culprits. Venice's galleys opened fire on the corsairs, who replied in kind and were supported by Dubrovnik's own cannons. Only the following year was the incident resolved, through an agreement brokered by the Ottoman Empire whereby the Ragusans paid half the value of the vessel from Herceg-Novi and the corsairs were permitted to sail away.

The success of the Porte's intervention on this occasion may have convinced Dubrovnik that the time had come to try to resolve the long-standing dispute with Venice regarding the latter's rights in its 'Gulf'. The days when this was a major issue had passed, but it remained an irritant. Whenever Dubrovnik found itself at odds with Venice, the Venetians would support their case with demands for back payments of dues owed in respect of its ancient rights. Venetian subjects also exploited the Serenissima's nebulous but extensive claims in order to fish in Ragusan waters and to cut down Ragusan timber on Mljet. After lengthy negotiations conducted under the aegis of the Ottoman Empire, agreement was finally reached between the two sides at Travnik (in Bosnia) on 16 July 1754. It was essentially symbolic. In recognition of Venetian rights, in place of any dues and in apparent imitation of the system whereby the Ragusans paid the Porte its *harač*, Dubrovnik would send two envoys to Venice every three years with a tribute of a pure silver jug worth thirty Venetian ducats. In exchange, the Venetians would not fell Dubrovnik's timber or do any other harm to its land, nor would they interfere with Ragusan fishing and coral collection.[7]

Dubrovnik's main difficulties from then on until the end of its life as an independent republic no longer, in fact, stemmed from Venice but rather from France. France was a prickly and aggressive force with which the Ragusans had built up little understanding during previous contacts. The French government was influenced by the interests of its great port of Marseilles, which was envious of Ragusan commerce. France also enjoyed unparalleled influence with the Porte, due to years of persistent diplomacy and, indeed, of military co-operation. The fact that at the end of the century contact with France also involved the risk of contagion from liberal and potentially revolutionary ideas would make it even more of a problem for the Ragusan patriciate.

In the early eighteenth century, two French mercantile houses, acting under the influence of the French government, established their offices in Dubrovnik. But it was during the Seven Years' War (1756–1763), which pitted Britain against France, that the Ragusan Republic began to have to take a close interest in its relations with Paris. The war itself provided rich commercial pickings for neutral Dubrovnik. But it also brought the unwelcome presence of the first French-born consul or agent, André-Alexandre Le Maire in 1757. Dubrovnik much preferred to deal with Ragusan-born consuls of foreign powers, for all the reasons that Le Maire now demonstrated. There ensued a series of disputes, mainly regarding his diplomatic standing and the ceremonial treatment he was to be afforded. The underlying problem for Dubrovnik was that of fitting within traditional diplomatic forms the reality of a mighty power dealing with a politically insignificant one. But neither was the French government much clearer about the policy it would adopt. On the one hand, it wanted to maximise its influence and trade in Dubrovnik. On the other, it was resentful of the privileged position which Dubrovnik enjoyed in its dealings with the Ottoman Empire and in particular with the rulers of North Africa. Le Maire heartily disliked the Ragusans – whom he considered 'subtle, cunning, suspicious [and] attentive to all that can hurt or profit them' – while they for their part plotted through their special envoy in Paris, the Franciscan Frano Sorkočević-Bobaljević, to have Le Maire recalled, eventually successfully in 1764.[8]

Le Maire's departure was something of a Ragusan diplomatic triumph; but the benefits were short-lived, for his successor, François-Auguste Le Prévôt, was not a great improvement. A long dispute ensued about how Le Prévôt was to be received as diplomatic representative, whether (as he demanded) by the Rector, thus recognising him as the agent of a major foreign power, or by the Small Council (as Dubrovnik insisted), thus recognising him simply as a foreign consul with commensurate privileges. This time Dubrovnik's manoeuvrings to have the obstreperous ambassador recalled were unsuccessful. He received the full support of Paris, including the despatch of two French warships to Gruž harbour followed by a dressing down of the Rector by a French admiral. A compromise was agreed. But Dubrovnik still held out against the most dangerous French demand, which revealed what underlay the tension – namely the proposition that all foreigners in Dubrovnik could place themselves under the King of France's protection. Behind what appears a somewhat exaggerated attachment to form, the Ragusan government was determined to guard at all costs against acknowledging the right of foreign powers to intervene in its internal affairs. It understood that this could only end with the loss of its independence.

Le Prévôt died in 1771 and was succeeded by the most influential of the French agents under the Ragusan Republic, René-Charles Bruère, Seigneur des Rivaux. Bruère was even more personally hostile to Dubrovnik than his predecessors. Indeed, he seems to have held the aristocratic Republic to which he came in such deep contempt that it is possible that he was a covert Revolutionary long before the Revolution. According to Bruère, Dubrovnik was 'an obscure hole governed by odious, proud aristocrats', while the 'Ragusan nation [entertained] an invincible repugnance for all foreigners'.[9] Bruère, supported by the merchants of Marseilles and in line with the instincts of his predecessors, saw trade in the Levant as consisting of a zero-sum game in which Dubrovnik's gain was France's loss. He accordingly suggested that France seek the revocation of the *ferman*s issued over the years by the Porte in Dubrovnik's favour. But the French Government, probably wisely, considered this unrealistic. The two-way trade between France and Dubrovnik was, moreover, increasingly important in its own right. The result of this approach was a new commercial treaty in 1776 between France and the Ragusan Republic which both established the terms on which the French could conduct their affairs and regularised Bruère's position as *chargé d'affaires* appointed by letters from the king of France.[10]

France was always in a position to bully Dubrovnik, and the uncertainty surrounding the status of its first three French-born representatives encouraged this tendency. But at least France was a long-standing ally of Dubrovnik's protector, the Ottoman Empire. Moreover, there were no occasions of religious tension between France and the Ragusan Republic.

Dealing with Russia was to prove a very different matter. While the Russians stayed conveniently distant, Dubrovnik had regarded them quite warmly. The early pan-Slavism evident in the writings of, for example, Mavro Orbini, Alexandar Komulović and Ivan Gundulić, disposed Ragusans even to take a certain pride in Russian political successes. Dubrovnik had, therefore, expressed its delight when two of its sons entered the service of Peter the Great. The Ragusans similarly waxed enthusiastic about the Tsar's victory over his old enemy Charles XII of Sweden at Poltava in 1709 and sent congratulations. Peter was, they gushed, the 'greatest glory of our race'. But the situation became more delicate when Charles took refuge with the Turks and successfully urged them to wage war against Russia. Fortunately for Dubrovnik, it had a friend at the Tsar's court in the form of the Hercegovinian Sava Vladislavić who was able to explain why they could not provide assistance against the Porte. Some years later, when they received an embarrassing request from the Tsar to have an Orthodox church built in the city, their friend Vladislavić again intervened on their behalf.[11]

The Republic's relations with Russia under Catherine the Great during the Russo-Turkish War (1769–1774) were more problematic. Dubrovnik learned early on that the Russians were planning a maritime campaign against the Porte and against Dubrovnik as its subject. Ships were to be acquired covertly in different ports under different pretexts so as to put this project into effect. With Dubrovnik's approval – later disavowed – the Ragusan consul in Genoa had one of these vessels destroyed by the authorities. The Russian purchaser was compensated, but Dubrovnik's action was much resented and held against it in St Petersburg. What Dubrovnik did not know was that the Russian Baltic fleet had also been ordered to sail to the Mediterranean. It arrived in February 1770 and made its base at Leghorn (Livorno). The Ragusan Republic made every effort to maintain its neutrality. But Ragusan ships kept on turning up in the most compromising situations – at sea battles at Corinth, at Navarino and then, worst of all, at Nauplion, where at the end of May two Ragusan ships carrying Turkish munitions were directly engaged.

Dubrovnik was, in fact, in an impossible position. It found itself under remorseless pressure from the Turks to transport Ottoman troops, and it occasionally complied. At the same time, it was subject to a barrage of complaints – true, false or merely exaggerated – from the Russians. In these circumstances, Dubrovnik decided to send embassies to the Russian representative Count Alexey Orlov at Leghorn and to the Empress Catherine in St Petersburg to justify its actions.

Of these missions the more important was that to Russia. Two envoys, Marin Franov Tudisić and Frano Savinov Ranjina, travelled by way of Vienna in order to solicit the help of the Empress Maria Theresa. She promised support but explained that Austro-Russian relations were not good enough for her to assist in any practical fashion. Tudisić now fell ill and Ranjina had to set off alone. He first journeyed to Prussia and obtained an audience with Frederick the Great in Berlin, who also received him favourably. But it was already clear that the matter could only be resolved in St Petersburg. Ranjina arrived there on 22 November 1771 and stayed until after the signing of the Russo-Turkish Peace of Kuchuk Kainarji (Turkish: Kücük Kainarca) of 21 July 1774. He then returned via Berlin and Vienna to agree final terms with Orlov in Pisa in early 1775. In the course of this diplomatic odyssey Ranjina encountered a great deal of ill-will, particularly stemming from Orlov, whose occasional presence and regular reports repeatedly stirred up trouble for Dubrovnik at the Imperial court.

The outstanding differences between Dubrovnik and the Russians were in the end mainly resolved by the terms of a declaration issued in the name of the Empress Catherine on 20 June 1775. Accompanying it was a letter from Count Orlov sharply critical of Dubrovnik's actions during the conflict. Both were given to the newspapers, for which they were indeed designed. Dubrovnik promised strict neutrality in any future wars involving Russia. It undertook to welcome a Russian consul enjoying all the privileges enjoyed by the consuls of other great powers. It even allowed the consul to have his own chapel of the Orthodox rite where he, his family and other Russian subjects – but by implication no one else – could worship.

The limitations surrounding this final provision were the result of a vigorous diplomatic resistance put up by Ranjina against Russian pressure. Dubrovnik had stressed that it was unnecessary to have a self-standing Orthodox church established there, as there were only between twelve and fifteen Orthodox families in the Republic. In any case, there were Orthodox churches for them to attend on nearby Venetian and Ottoman soil. Erecting an Orthodox church on Ragusan territory would, it was argued, result in an influx of Orthodox subjects of Venice and the Ottoman Empire, which would lead to the loss of Dubrovnik's independence.

The Treaty of Kuchuk Kainarji was of fundamental importance in European affairs because it established Russia's right of navigation through the Bosphorus and into the Mediterranean. But it was navigation in the reverse direction that interested the Ragusan Republic. Dubrovnik's merchant fleet had been badly damaged by Russian depredations during the war. Some 50 Ragusan ships had been seized, and most of them sold. Dubrovnik had hoped for a formal agreement whereby its vessels gained safe passage when sailing in the Black Sea, but for the moment it had to rely on Orlov's oral assurances.[12]

In fact, the Ragusan experience of dealing with the Russians was in many ways indicative of the future. Over the centuries, Dubrovnik had honed its diplomatic skills in contacts with the Ottoman Empire. It had, as a result, achieved an extraordinary insight into the Turkish mind and tastes. It sent the Sultan and his court gifts of cloth, watches, writing paper, sugar, sweetmeats, wine, rose-petal liqueur (*rozolin*), cinnamon water (*vodica*), almonds, rose-hips and limes. It had established friendly relations with a succession of local Ottoman officials, whom it invited to the theatre and even on occasion showed around the cathedral to the strains of dance music played on the organ. But the days when pandering to the Ottomans constituted the core of diplomacy had passed.[13] Dubrovnik's old protector was now too weak to defend itself, let alone its rich but politically insignificant tributary. The Ragusans had come face to face with the brutal exercise of power by a giant state over which they had no hold and into whose psyche they could not penetrate.

Economic Vagaries

Dubrovnik's fortunes were so closely involved with those of the Porte that the increasing disorder and decay which affected that once mighty empire were bound also to affect Ragusan prosperity. Serbia's conditions rapidly deteriorated and Dubrovnik's colonies there were almost completely abandoned – only Novi Pazar remained of some importance. Dubrovnik's Balkan trade was now concentrated on adjoining regions, Montenegro, southeast Bosnia and Hercegovina. It was mostly bulky stuff of rather low value, such as wax, wool, iron, pelts and cordovan.

Moreover, while the Balkan trade as a whole suffered, Dubrovnik's share of it was also reduced. This was partly because of the (already mentioned) increase in the number of Bosnian Muslims who built up important mercantile houses in Sarajevo and elsewhere. But as the eighteenth century progressed, competition from a resurgent Austria also became increasingly important. German traders purchased goods in Hungary, Wallachia and northern Bulgaria and transported them along the Danube and then via Trieste and Rijeka to Western Europe. Dubrovnik also faced greater competition along the Adriatic coast. Older small ports, like Makarska, Herceg-Novi, Budva, Bar and Ulcinj, were developed, while Split continued to benefit from the natural advantages it enjoyed over Dubrovnik.[14]

Foreigners who came to Dubrovnik saw the effects of this economic decline and commented upon it. At the end of the century Bruère reported back to his masters in Paris:

> There exists no art nor science in Ragusa. The commercial buildings are well enough built there, but nothing else of what are called manufactures. Even the most common brooms for using in bedrooms and streets come from Alexandria and Italy.[15]

He was biased, of course, but nonetheless probably right about the brooms.

Yet this is only part of the picture. Although the Ragusan Republic remained in a state of relative economic decline – which is only another way of saying that other powers were in a superior position to exploit broader economic changes – its period of absolute decline had probably come to an end before the middle of the eighteenth century. As always, it adapted. So, as the Balkans became less commercially important, the Republic concentrated its efforts on maritime trade across the Mediterranean.[16] This was reflected in an increase in the number of Ragusan consuls – including the new posts of consuls-general and vice-consuls – in Mediterranean ports. And within the Mediterranean the emphasis broadly shifted from the Ponent to the Levant.[17]

North Africa also became of greater importance to Dubrovnik. The Republic had the advantage over other commercial competitors that the Sultan's *fermans* in its favour were recognised by Tripoli, Tunis and Algiers (which were under Turkish suzerainty), and in practice by Morocco (which was an effectively independent state). Some 60 Ragusan ships dealt in the transport along the coast of slaves, Muslim pilgrims on the *hajj* to Mecca, corn and timber for shipbuilding. The business was risky – incidents concerning the treatment of pilgrims provoked the wrath of the Sultan of Morocco on several occasions. But the Ragusans were past masters at dealing with Oriental tantrums, and the North African trade continued to be extremely valuable to the Republic.[18]

As in previous centuries, Dubrovnik was able to put its somewhat precarious neutrality to good effect in wars that did not directly involve the Ottoman Empire. Thus while its merchant fleet suffered severely in the Russo-Turkish War of 1769–1774, its trade benefited substantially from the great wars between France and Britain – the War of Austrian Succession (1741–1748), the Seven Years' War (1756–1753), the War of American Independence (1775–1783) and the wars of the French Revolution (1793–1806). In these periods foreigners were keen to hire Ragusan ships which sailed under a neutral flag, and the Ragusans sensibly raised their freight charges to take advantage of the fact.

There was, in fact, a general turnaround in Dubrovnik's maritime as in its other economic fortunes from the 1740s. Having spent the first three decades of the century selling their ships, Ragusans now began to expand their fleet by purchasing ships from foreigners. Ragusan ships also began sailing again in large numbers beyond the Adriatic.[19]

The Ragusan government did what it could throughout the period to encourage shipping. Being Ragusan, the government's interest principally took a bureaucratic form. In order to ensure more systematic regulation, the various decrees relating to shipping were in 1745 brought together in one manuscript volume, the *Regolamento della Repubblica di Ragusa per la navigazione nazionale* (Croatian: *Pomorski pravilnik*). Each Ragusan vessel, it was decreed, must have on board a copy of this volume – something which became easier once it was printed in 1784 and again in 1794. A committee of five Senators presided over the enforcement of these regulations in the *Officio alla sopraintendenze della navigazione* (Croatian: *Pomorski ured*) or 'Maritime Office'. On their return home, Dubrovnik's captains had to present at the Maritime Office all the receipts for payment of the prescribed fees issued by the different Ragusan consuls with whom they had dealt. Originally, it was required that all members of a Ragusan ship's crew be Ragusans. This was modified in 1748 to allow a third of the crew to be foreigners. But in order to ensure strict financial and administrative control, the ship's clerk must always be a Ragusan.[20]

The late eighteenth century saw a further revival of Ragusan shipping. Dubrovnik's maritime business benefited from a recovery of Balkan output – notably cotton, maize, grain, dyes, wine, oil and currants. In exchange, the Ragusans brought back manufactured European goods and goods from the American colonies. Probably still more important was the opening up of commerce with the Black Sea, where Ragusan vessels sailed ever more frequently during the last quarter of the century. Russian timber, furs, honey, hemp, tar, linen, flax and above all wheat were shipped by Dubrovnik to Italian ports.[21]

The resurgence of shipping led also to a revival of Ragusan shipbuilding. Vessels were still built at Gruž, even in the last days of the Republic.[22] But Ragusan owners also commissioned ships to be built on Korčula and in the ports of the Northern Adriatic.[23]

Within the frontiers of the Republic, there was some diversification to the benefit of previously less favoured areas. Cavtat, for example, became home to a prosperous community of sea-captains. But it was probably the Pelješac peninsula which flourished most markedly under the new conditions. With the exception of Ston, the communities of Pelješac appear to have been relatively unscathed by the 1667 earthquake. In Trstenica (the area of western Pelješac), sea-captains often stemming from the poorest labouring families established themselves as a kind of minor aristocracy. The most successful maritime families lived at Orebići, where they built themselves sturdy houses which still evoke their prosperity and self-confidence.[24]

The shipping businesses of Pelješac, like those of the Republic as a whole, had endured a difficult period in the early years of the eighteenth century. Many ships were sold to Venetians, and only five remained in commission. Better times returned, thanks largely to the opportunities provided by the War of Austrian Succession, when neutral Ragusan ships were much sought after by merchants fearful of having their vessels and cargoes seized by the warring British and French. In 1742 twelve Pelješac vessels were operating; the following year there were three more. In 1746 and 1747, seventeen ships from Pelješac were plying their trade. The period from now till the end of the century – with the exception of the ruinous episode of the Russo-Turkish War – was marked by ever-increasing maritime prosperity for the region. Moreover, the *Pelješčani* were in most cases the exclusive owners of their vessels, as well as being part owners of others. The Golden Age of Pelješac shipping was between 1780 to about 1800. Its ships sailed throughout the Mediterranean, carrying corn from Constantinople and the ports of Greece and in the last years of the century were heavily involved in the Black Sea trade.[25]

Political Affairs

The contradictory patterns which characterise the economic life of eighteenth-century Dubrovnik also find echoes in political life. The Ragusan polity rested, as always, upon the Ragusian patriciate. That patriciate had struggled heroically in the wake of the Great Earthquake to rescue and preserve the Republic. But the unity achieved at this time did not persist. It is true that by and large the Ragusan polity remained less faction-ridden and fissiparous than that of Venice. Yet in the last two centuries of Dubrovnik's independent existence there was a decided trend to oligarchy, which – taken alongside patrician demographic decline – reduced the resilience of the state.

This trend took two forms. The first, and less damaging, was institutional. The existing primacy of the Senate was strongly reinforced at the expense of the wider patrician body, the Great Council. By the eighteenth century only death, in practice, resulted in a change of membership of the Senate. Moreover, the Senatorial group gained an iron grip on promotion to the other most politically important offices of the Republic. Indeed, selection of those who were to fulfil these offices was from 1747 made by lot. This was because there were now more than enough major posts to be filled by a limited group of powerful patricians.[26]

The more damaging aspect of oligarchy was the degree to which it favoured a particular factional group. The origins of this 'schism' within the nobility are, as has been noted, traceable to the factional lineups of the 'Great Conspiracy' of the early seventeenth century. The result over time, through an almost complete end to intermarriage between the two factions, was the emergence of a group of families which monopolised power. (These families were later described as *salamankezi* and their opponents *sorbonezi*, but the groupings long preceded the nomenclature – see below.) Families which were not part of the former group, no matter how great their historic prestige, had little or no hope of preferment. Thus the great *casata* of Gundulić was relegated to political impotence when, after the poet Ivan's death, it fell decisively into the *sorbonezi* camp.[27]

It was blood which determined whether a young man was summoned into the ranks of the Great Council to take his share of political power, and so naturally enough it was blood which was at the centre of the struggles which now ensued. The seventeenth century had seen a relaxation followed by a marked reinforcement of the rules governing admission to the patriciate. Ten new families were, however admitted into the nobility – the Boždari, Sorkočević-Bobaljevići, Natali, Zlatarići, Klašići, Primojevići, Serrature, Đurđević-Bernardi, Paoli, and Vodopići.[28] Most of them died out; only three – the Boždari, Natali and Zlatarići – survived until the end of the Republic. These new families were regarded as of inferior status to those of the old nobility, and for many years they were denied the most senior and prestigious positions. Thus they first entered the Senate in 1783, and the first Rector drawn from their ranks was only elected in 1786.

As has been noted, however, the distinction between the old and new noble families was not the only source of division within the patriciate. There were the political enmities of an earlier century which, long after the original points at issue had been forgotten, had been given the irrevocable seal of heredity. There were also other, more subtle, distinctions of lineage. The 'pollution' of the pure blood of the old nobility occurred in a variety of ways. For a very short period – 1666–1682 – Ragusan nobles had been permitted to marry the daughters of wealthy citizens, as long as those citizens had not engaged in manual work. There were also some permitted instances of Ragusan patricians marrying the daughters of patrician families from towns outside Dalmatia. When the offspring of any of these unions – as well as those resulting from marriages between members of the old nobility and girls from the new noble houses – were taken into account, the number of nobles who had excluded themselves or their successors from the highest class of patricians was much larger. It also grew cumulatively. Analysis of the membership of the Great Council from 1700 to 1808 reveals an almost continuous worsening of the ratio to the disadvantage of the highest class. In 1700 the latter were numerically stronger by a factor of five; in the 1740s it was by a factor of four; in the 1760s, by two; and from 1796 on they were actually a minority.[29]

By the last decades of the eighteenth century, the two groups were commonly (and humorously) known as *salamankezi* – referring to the old university of León – and *sorbonezi* – referring to the university of Paris.[30] The terms clearly have political overtones, the pure-blooded nobility being associated with reactionary Spain and the more miscegenated being associated with liberal and incipiently revolutionary France. But the distinction always remained fundamentally one of birth.

In fact, even the criterion of purity of blood began to look increasingly unconvincing as a measure of social standing. Numbered among the *sorbonezi* were, in due course, to be found some of the greatest family names of Dubrovnik – not just Gundulić but also Kaboga, Bunić, Crijević, Menčetić, Zamanja, Getaldić and Saraka. And, of course, once the taboo against marriage outside the ranks of those of pure blood was diminished, the process accelerated.

Such divisions, alongside the already mentioned trend towards exclusive oligarchy, weakened the patriciate in a number of ways. For example, they reduced further the already depleted resources of talent and experience on which to draw when filling the highest offices of state. It is likely, though not certain, that they also diminished the patriciate's solidarity when it faced the final and fatal challenge to the Republic's existence. But, that said, it is also easy to exaggerate their importance.

More significant for the life of the Republic than the exclusion of the *sorbonezi* from supreme power was the exclusion of the leading citizen families from power altogether. There is no evidence, it is true, that this created any deep resentment. Writing in the last years of the Republic, Appendini described the citizen class as living partly like nobles (*more nobilium*) and partly in commerce.[31] That was doubtless a very satisfactory balance for them. They enjoyed wealth, cultivated living and a large measure of respect, all without the distractions of high office. But it also meant that the burdens of political decision-making rested on too few – and increasingly feeble – patrician shoulders.

Again, one should not exaggerate. The Ragusan patriciate constituted a smaller proportion of the total Ragusan population as the eighteenth century progressed – 19 per cent in mid-century and 14 per cent in 1799. But it still remained substantially larger than was the case, *mutatis mutandis*, in Venice.[32] There was, though, a debilitating consciousness of demographic decline. The prescribed legal quorum for the Senate had time and again to be reduced 'temporarily', only for the reduction to be renewed.[33] A note of something like desperation appears in 1801: 'Considering the important public affairs that can occur in the coming months and that there are a large number of Senators in their seventies and others are ill', the quorum would again be reduced to twenty one.[34]

The final qualification which must be made to the picture of the Ragusan Republic as a 'victim... of its own conservatism' is that the rift which did indeed gravely weaken the state in the eighteenth century was much more a classic factional squabble than the result of broader social tension.[35] It was sharp but quite short, lasting from the end of 1762 to early 1763. A group of the old nobility – seven brothers of the Sorkočević-Debo family and families related to them – attempted to create a still narrower oligarchy. This was vigorously resisted by a coalition of both old and new nobility. Outside influences were also present, though outsiders probably overstated their importance. According to the French agent Le Maire, it was all about pro- and anti-French factions, with a ruthless patrician, Sabin Pucić, at the head of the anti-French Sorkočević-Debo party.

The resistance to the latter's power gathered around a traditional programme of restricting the influence of any single family in the institutions of the Republic – evident proof that this was the real root of the matter. But the oligarchists would not give way. Bitter conflict paralysed the government and spilled over into violence in the streets, where heavily armed bands of nobles confronted each other under the disinterested gaze of the citizens. For four months there was no effective government at all – the Great Council did not meet from 25 October 1762 to 28 February 1763. Eventually, a compromise was agreed as part of the Sorkočević-Debo faction – faced with the threat by their opponents to elect a Rector and officers with or without a quorum – accepted constitutional changes to limit the possibilities of narrow oligarchy. The most important of these required that only three members of the same family (three brothers, or a father and two sons) could vote in the Senate. In those special cases where the requirement was for a qualified majority – two thirds, three quarters or seven eighths – only two members of a single family could vote. These changes resulted in a return to traditional party allegiance based principally on the issue of 'blood'.[36]

Social Conditions

The population of the Ragusan Republic was in decline throughout the seventeenth century. It stood at about 26,000 in 1673.[37] But it had grown to over 30,000 once again by 1815, with the turning point probably occurring in the mid-eighteenth century.[38] (In Konavle, the population increase started in the 1730s.)[39] The precise reasons for this demographic turnaround are no clearer for Dubrovnik than for the rest of the Mediterranean world. But it seems to have impressed even sceptical French observers. Thus Le Maire in 1766 thought that the Republic's population stood at 60,000 – a significant exaggeration.[40] Such renewed population growth was a most obvious proof of deeper vitality.

Outside the diminished ranks of the patriciate, the impression is of a class of wealthy citizens which was expanding and consolidating. Some of them, as Appendini explains, held important office – the most important that a commoner could fill was that of Chancellor or Great Secretary of the Republic. Like Ragusan patricians, citizen office-holders were expected, whenever they went out before lunch, to wear large loose wigs and long black coats. At other times, they could be found wearing luxurious and elegant French-style clothes, with the addition of magnificent fur coats and hats to keep out the *bura*.[41]

Leaving aside politics, Ragusan society, being one in which talent and money were highly valued, was notably open to talent – even for those living far outside the city walls. One recent study has detected, for example, twelve *Konavljani* among the ranks of the best-known citizens in the second half of the eighteenth century. Of these, Petar Baletin left his community of Štravca in Konavle to trade in the Levant. There he learned Turkish, and on several occasions served as the Republic's *dragoman*. In 1679 he distinguished himself by his courage in dealing with Kara Mustafa and was rewarded by the Senate with an estate in Župa and 500 ducats for the dowry of one of his daughters. In 1675 he became a member of the *Lazarini*. His son Miho and his grandson Petar were both accepted in 1726 into the *Antunini*. Until his death in 1767, Petar (the younger) was clerk of the salt office. He was buried in the family tomb in the Dubrovnik Franciscan church.[42]

Another *Konavljanin* who made good was Antun Hidža from the community of Komaji. He was a mere serf when he made his way to the city of Dubrovnik in 1748. His abilities were swiftly exploited. Just three years later, the Republic used him as an envoy to Bosnia. He became a successful merchant and entered the *Lazarini* in 1752. His son Đuro studied medicine in Bologna, served as Dubrovnik's city doctor and joined the *Lazarini* in 1771. Đuro's main claim to fame, however, is as a poet and translator.[43]

A third variant is provided by the career of Nikola Ivanov Kosovac from the community of Kuna Konavoska. Nikola left home in 1755 and went to sea, serving as 'ship's boy' (*Mali*, or 'Little One'). Twenty years later he was captain of his own vessel. After a successful career as a merchant, he settled on Lopud in 1788. The following year the Republic appointed him its consul in Genoa and he was accepted into the *Lazarini*. In 1808 he died, and on his death – as on the deaths of Petar Baletin and Đuro Hidža – his line expired.[44]

As in any cohesive aristocratic state, all the people who mattered in the Ragusan Republic aped the aristocracy. Thus, in the eighteenth century important citizen families started to adopt hereditary (though heraldically unauthorised) coats-of-arms.[45] Enlightened foreign observers found it all rather contemptible. In 1805, before the entry of French troops into the city, two French emissaries spent some months there. One of them, Charles de Pouqueville, could not conceal his scorn for the 'bizarre utopia of Ragusa', where 'the pride of the masters passed into the spirit of their clients, their valets and their serfs, who copied in grotesque fashion the absurdities of their patrons.'[46]

Pouqueville's remarks about 'valets and serfs' applied to some, though not all, of the poorest classes. Traditional bonds linked Ragusan country folk to the Ragusan nobility. Appendini describes how boys and girls from poor families would be brought up by patricians. The boys would be sent to sea where, if they were lucky and talented, they could eventually earn their fortunes as sea-captains. Girls would be taken into service as maids (known as *čupe* or *čupavice*), provided with food, clothing and a small annual wage, and after ten years receive a lump sum in the form of a dowry. A special celebration called *sprava* would then take place, after which the young woman would return to marry and settle down in her village.[47]

This idyllic picture was not, however, universally valid. The late eighteenth century saw a polarisation within the peasant class. Some peasants acquired full ownership of the land they worked and others took it on perpetual leases – a concealed form of purchase. In principle, it was still forbidden for peasants in Pelješac, Primorje and Konavle to own land. But they found means to evade the regulations. In reaction to this, the prohibition was repeated in a law of 26 June 1777. This tacitly accepted the sales which had occurred. But it stated that only those who lived within the walls or in the suburbs of Dubrovnik could henceforth acquire land in those regions. Richer peasants were not, however, to be stopped: they came to live in the city, acquired land back home and then left it to their families. Another group of peasant families who improved their prospects during these years were those living in or near flourishing maritime communities like Cavtat and Pelješac and those on Koločep, Lopud and Šipan. These could hope to increase their income from fishing or in connection with the flourishing maritime trade.

On the other hand, for peasants who had fallen into serfdom and lacked the means or the opportunity to rise out of it, conditions were becoming harder. Serfdom, in its (still limited) Ragusan form, had become fully developed by the eighteenth century. The serf's obligation to work for his lord – known in Dubrovnik as *služba* ('service') – seems in Konavle to have increased from 75 days in 1713 to over 90 days by the end of the century; the authorities set 90 days as the maximum by a law of 1800. During this period the serf received his food from the lord; but, of course, in the meantime he could not work on the land he tilled on his own behalf. Serfdom never acquired two of its most hated features elsewhere, for in Dubrovnik the serf was neither legally bound to the soil nor was he justiciable in the court of his lord. It was probably, therefore, economic conditions and the level of income which these sustained that mattered most to the Ragusan peasantry. A growing population and increasing prosperity in theory meant more economic opportunities. Landlords were keen to exploit these by increasing the burden on their peasants – just as peasants were keen to exploit them, too, by increasing their output. This was a recipe for tension and, indeed, as would be evidenced in the Konavle Revolt of 1799–1800, for conflict.[48]

It is doubtless significant that Konavle was to be the scene of the only major peasants' revolt that the Ragusan Republic had to face. Here in the borderlands with the Ottoman Empire, Hercegovina and Montenegro, political and criminal disorder undermined social and economic stability. The frontiers between the Republic and the Empire were patrolled by Ottoman *pandur*s and *klančari* – irregular soldiers, usually Vlachs, who largely lived by plunder and by exacting a due called *klančarina* on Ragusan traffic. The Republic viewed their behaviour with mixed feelings, as did its subjects, for one of the duties of *pandur*s and *klančari* was to protect both Konavle and Hercegovina from Montenegrin raiders.

The Ragusan authorities were ingenious in finding ways of securing the frontier region. They organised village guards from the local population and appointed the Republic's own captains to serve in vulnerable spots like the village of Mrcine, where the captain was known as the *harambaša*. They paid spies in Boka and other areas to find out what robber bands were planning. With the authority of the Porte, they then recruited communities of Vlachs to resist the Montenegrins.

These measures had some success. But the main trouble was that the Vlachs were not reliable, shifting their loyalties according to political circumstances and material opportunities. Nor could Ragusan subjects in the area be trusted always to support the authorities. Many of them supplemented their income by smuggling salt and collaborating with the Montenegrins. And although the *Konavljani* had plenty of firearms, it was not always clear against whom they would be used. As a result, the government was careful about sending too much gunpowder out from Dubrovnik, for fear it might fall into the wrong hands.

On balance, however, the *Konavljani* lost more as victims than they ever gained as occasional predators. In periods of severe disorder they even lost their lives. But they were more likely to lose their cattle. Towards the end of the eighteenth century, there was rustling on a huge scale. It has been estimated that between 1793 and 1800 over 4,000 head of livestock were stolen, that is, about a third of all those pastured in Konavle. Resistance was usually futile. In 1800 the Vlachs who were pillaging Duba shouted at those *Konavljani* minded to defend their property: 'We'll tie you up and sell you!' Order in the region had altogether broken down.[49]

It is, however, important not to equate the criminal disorder on the Ragusan frontier with a breakdown of judicial order elsewhere in the Republic. Eighteenth-century Ragusan society as a whole was probably somewhat less criminal than in the previous century. Certainly the number of homicides fell, though Konavle stood out against the trend.

The system of dealing with criminals remained very much as it had been in earlier times. A shortage of patricians now meant that there were occasional problems in finding a quorum of judges to sit in the Republic's criminal court. But in any case, the main burden in the court fell on the patrician judges' professional advisers, the chancellors, who were well-versed in the Republic's law and often highly experienced, serving long terms of office.[50] Local courts, too, seem to have functioned very much as in earlier periods.[51]

The punishments administered were also similar. As in earlier years, Dubrovnik made significantly more use of imprisonment as a sentence than was common elsewhere. But Ragusans whose business took them beyond Pile might still see a murderer's corpse hanging on the gibbet at Danče. Nearly 100 executions were carried out in eighteenth-century Dubrovnik. In some particularly heinous cases the body was subject to mutilation by quartering, with sections displayed on Danče, at the criminal's house and in other conspicuous locations.[52] Even in the last days of the Republic, the law was not mocked.

By the eighteenth century, Dubrovnik was well past its political, economic and cultural zenith. But this does not mean that it was a mere backwater. Far from it. That discerning travel writer Alberto Fortis (1741–1803), for example, was greatly impressed by Dubrovnik, which he visited on three occasions. Fortis thought that Ragusan society outshone in its sophistication that of the rest of Dalmatia, and he noted with particular approval Dubrovnik's merchant fleet, agriculture, education and legal system.[53]

Eighteenth-century Ragusan society was, indeed, sufficiently open to outside influences to be ever more affected by the fads and fashions of contemporary Europe. This latter trend was evident in adoption of French styles of dress and mannerisms, and it provoked the wrath of such crotchety Ragusan conservatives as the poet Djono Rastić (son of the historian). Of the elegant cravats which young Ragusan dandies wrapped around their throats, he exclaimed:

> They will suffocate themselves! Take them to the doctor's!

And of their other affectations:

> Who pierced his pert ear with a golden ring? That in olden times was the sign of slaves, whom merchants displayed for sale. Men! It is the mark of slavery!

Rastić was particularly scathing about the obsession for visiting Paris in search of superficial social polish:

> Once someone has had a peep at Paris and has smeared his boot with the muddy water of the Seine, it is as if he had absorbed like a child's sponge the customs of that frivolous people, had created for himself a ridiculous spine, and had determined to introduce into his own language foreign words and sounds of barbarous origin. Fashion has demanded that the elegant young man should walk with a stoop. The young Ragusan, when he returns home, imitates these high and mighty personages in each movement of his bemused body, in his conversation, in his manner, and in his mother tongue larded with some rare French expression. And the rich young lady

> who departs with her husband on a visit [to Paris] returns with fashionable fabrics in her trunk – and unsatisfied desires in her head.[54]

On the other hand, Dubrovnik's age-old habits and customs were still strong when it came to traditional occasions for celebration. The festivities of the triduum of St Blaise, for example, were as noisy as ever, and even more dangerous as a result of a lethal combination of alcohol and ubiquitous fire-arms. The traditional Ragusan marriage customs, as described in former years by Diversis, had been largely superseded in Dubrovnik itself by others imported from Italy. But the old ways could still be found in the countryside, especially in Konavle. The traditional funeral rites were also maintained.

All the young nobles of less than eighteen years of age were expected, as in the past, to enroll in societies. The purpose of these bodies was essentially somewhat stylised entertainment. Notably, they were responsible for bringing a big green branch into the city every evening between Holy Saturday and 1 May to be contended for and then burnt as a focus for merry-making accompanied by the letting off of fireworks. Similarly, on other Vigils and Feast Days bonfires were lit and traditional Croatian songs sung in the streets.

Appendini observed that Ragusan cuisine also retained something of the old alongside the new. Traditionally, Ragusans preferred their food to be quite simply prepared; for example, they liked their meat boiled or roasted without added exotica. Half a century earlier that hyper-critical and fastidious Frenchman, Le Maire, had found it all too gross:

> The cooking of food for the Ragusans demands no apprenticeship. All the variety of their dishes, whether rich or poor, consists of either boiling, roasting or frying. They do not even distinguish the qualities of the meat to which such preparations are applied. Thus one will serve alternately a fried chicken, a boiled partridge, and a roast leg of beef. All the dishes…are extremely badly prepared…The bread which one buys there is detestable.[55]

Ragusan popular wisdom, on the other hand, had it that such gastronomic simplicity, along with the healthy climate, was responsible for the Ragusans' famed longevity. Modern tastes had, in any case, been making headway by the end of the Republic, and greater benefit was derived from the excellent local products available – oysters from Slano, fruit tarts and delicious cheeses. The local *malvazija* was much appreciated, as was Muscat from Lastovo.[56]

Culture

Dubrovnik was, by the eighteenth century, no longer a major cultural centre. But Ragusan society retained a certain polish, sustained a degree of intellectual life and generated two figures of true international importance.

The lesser known of these is the composer Luko Sorkočević (1734–1789). Dubrovnik had, of course, a long musical tradition. But it was mainly ecclesiastical. Luko Sorkočević worked outside that tradition and drew his inspiration from the trends and tastes of secular Europe. Coming from one of the most venerable and powerful familes of Dubrovnik, it was natural that he should be sent abroad on diplomatic missions. He thus represented the Republic in negotiations with France in 1776 and Austria in 1781–1782. Such foreign travels brought him into contact with Haydn, Gluck and other musical celebrities of the age. When Sorkočević was in Vienna, Haydn brought him the scripts of his most recent compositions.

Luko Sorkočević wrote eight symphonies, two overtures and a number of choral works. In the last part of his life the original talent seems to have dried up, though he continued to perform his own and others' compositions. In 1789, afflicted by both mental and physical illness, he committed suicide by throwing himself out the third-floor window of the Sorkočević palace, near the cathedral.[57]

Better known is Luko Sorkočević's contemporary, the scientific polymath Ruđer Bošković (1711–1787). Bošković was educated by the Jesuits in Dubrovnik, decided to join the order and was sent to continue his studies in Rome. This was, in fact, decisive for his career, for had he stayed in Dubrovnik he could not have learned the mathematics and physics in which he was destined to excel. Bošković became ever more fascinated by the theories of Isaac Newton. He was also increasingly preoccupied with astronomy. In 1758 he published in Vienna his principal work, *Philosophiae naturalis theoria.* Two years later he arrived in London, and was admitted as a member of the Royal Society. His interests took him variously to Constantinople and Milan, where he became administrator of the astronomical observatory. Already more scholar than priest, the disbanding of the Jesuits in 1773 nonetheless left him uncertain of his future. He contemplated returning to Dubrovnik but was persuaded instead to go to Paris, where he joined the government service, became director of optics (i.e. telescopes and binoculars) for the French navy, and adopted French citizenship.

Bošković never returned home to Dubrovnik, but neither did he forget his roots. He corresponded regularly with his devout and learned sister Anica.[58] He also intervened with his friend the king of Poland to try to influence the Russians to respect the neutrality of the Ragusan Republic. His letter reveals his affection:

> My homeland is facing extinction, my old mother is all-a-tremble at the thought of a hail storm of bombs about to fall on her head, a general consternation is felt in the letters I am receiving from my native city.

Bošković was proud of his Dalmatian identity. When he was in Vienna in 1757 he saw through his telescope companies of Croatian soldiers marching to serve on the battlefields of the Seven Years' War. He immediately rode out to see them and wish them 'Godspeed!' in Croatian. And when he was mistakenly referred to as 'an Italian mathematician' he indignantly responded in a note appended to his *Voyage astronomique et géographique* that 'our author is a Dalmatian from Dubrovnik, and not an Italian'.[59]

Of course, Dubrovnik was not populated by Ruđer Boškovićs. Such people needed to break out of the Ragusan cocoon if they were to take flight. But it was Dubrovnik that bred them and prepared them to move with ease in European circles. This was only possible because Dubrovnik itself still valued cultivation of the intellect.

Appendini, who had served as Dubrovnik's schoolmaster for ten years when he wrote, was much impressed by the character and brains of his young charges. He considered the Ragusans naturally gifted: if they were determined to pursue any branch of literature they were sure to succeed in it as well as any other nation. And, he added:

> Most remarkable is the fire and vivacity of their temperament, their natural eloquence and the witty conceits with which they conduct familiar conversation.[60]

Those Ragusans of a literary bent could display their talents in the learned societies or 'academies' which modestly flourished in the city. Such bodies had begun to sprout up along the Adriatic coast – in the Istrian towns, in Zadar, Split and Dubrovnik – from the last decade of the seventeenth century. Their inspiration was the Roman academy *degli Arcadi* whose ideal was a return to 'Arcadian' classical purity of expression in place of the florid style often referred to as Baroque. In about 1690 Dubrovnik saw the foundation of the Academy of Learned Idlers (*Accademia degli oziosi eruditi*, *Akademija učenih ispraznih*). Its achievements were limited and its activity sporadic, but it lasted longer than any of the other Dalmatian academies – till the 1730s. Moreover, it numbered some writers of real talent among its membership. It was the natural forum for the reading of formal poetry on set-piece occasions: the first public event was arranged in 1695 in honour of the *poklisari* who had re-established relations with the Porte at that difficult juncture. Four years later the Academy received rooms for its use in the Sponza Palace. Its first collection of poetry was published in Venice in 1702.

Two quarrels disturbed the ordinarily serene life of the Academy. The first reflected a serious cultural issue which would influence Croatian history for many years to come – the relative importance to be given to different languages. Two of the Academy's members – the poets Dživo Bunić and Ivo Natali Aletin – provided the occasion for the dispute by proposing an alteration of its name, removing the word 'Learned', and other rule changes. But what caused strongest disagreement was the order of precedence to be given in the Academy's transactions to the languages used – Latin, Italian and Croatian. The Italian Benedictine Lodovico Moreno argued unsuccessfully for his native Italian. In this he was vigorously opposed by Junije Rastić, who said that Croatian (or Slavic – *slovinski*) should have precedence, because it was used by 'half the world', including Russia.

The second dispute was rather less elevated: it concerned the Academy's premises. The academicians complained to the Ragusan Senate that the rooms set aside for them were in fact largely used by the nobility to play cards. The Senate at first forbade this, and ordered that the key be kept by the Chancellor of the Republic and only made available to the President of the Academy. But the government later relented and, to the distress of the more fastidious academicians, card playing was resumed.

The Dubrovnik Academy's life became ever more fitful. But intellectual activity found new outlets. There grew up other 'particular' academies of poets, in part as a reaction to the closer links which the majority of the Learned Idlers seem to have wanted to develop with Italy in general and Rome in particular.[61]

The Dubrovnik academies were more important for the often talented individuals within their ranks than for their achievements as institutions. And even when the institutions themselves faded into obscurity Dubrovnik continued to produce – and to attract – men of letters.

An interesting example was the Korčulan poet Petar Kanavelović (1637–1719). Although born of a patrician family from that Venetian-ruled island, Kanavelović was an unashamed Ragusophile. He spent spent much of his time in Dubrovnik. Both his wives came from Dubrovnik. He spied for Dubrovnik, reporting back on what the Venetians were planning. He would have moved to Dubrovnik permanently, but the Ragusan authorities thought that his current status was more useful to them. He was much influenced by Ivan Gundulić and *Osman*. His poetry was thus largely patriotic and heroic.[62]

Kanavelović's somewhat younger contemporary, Ignjat Đurđević (1657–1737), was the last of the great Ragusan poets. His father was one of those who had joined the patrician class after the Great Earthquake. Ignjat was, it seems, a dissolute young man: he was rumoured to have had carnal relations with all the women of Šipan, married and unmarried, during his term as count there. But he was a complex personality. During his stay on the island he was also engaged in writing a poem on that favourite Ragusan subject, the repentance of St Mary Magdalene (*Uzdasi Mandaljene pokornice*, 'Sighs of the Repentant Magdalene'). At the end of 1697 he departed to Rome on the pretence of having some of his work published – perhaps in actual fact because of an amorous rejection – and joined the Society of Jesus. But he found that the life of a Jesuit did not suit him. So in 1706 he joined the Benedictines and went to live at the little monastery of St James in Višnjica. Just four years later, he was expelled by the Republic because of his role in uniting the Dubrovnik Benedictine Congregation with the Benedictine mother house of Monte Cassino. After the intervention of the Vatican, however, he was allowed back to St James and settled down to his true vocation – writing poetry and history. He was also a leading figure in the Academy and served for one year as its president. Đurđević was much influenced by the great Ragusan literary figures of the past and, like them managed – somewhat incongruously to the modern taste – to combine writing religious, sensual and comic verse. Also like them, he saw no contradiction between using different languages for different purposes, being both an accomplished Latinist and a devotee of his own native tongue. Perhaps his most important achievement was the rendering of the psalms in Croatian.

Ignjat Đurđević was a better poet than he was historian. But he engaged in painstaking research into Dubrovnik's past and invested great efforts in unearthing all that he could about the lives and work of Ragusan men of letters. The trouble was that he was too much a patriot to be very objective. In 1730 he published in Venice his *Ricerche Anticritiche*, arguing for the veracity of the ancient Ragusan tradition to the effect that the 'Melita' on which St Paul landed was not Malta but rather the Ragusan island of Mljet. This opinion provoked the wrath of the Maltese and the Knights of the Order, but Đurđevic replied in his turn with great ferocity. Ignjat Đurđević also argued that St Jerome not only knew Croatian, but had actually translated the scriptures into that language.[63]

The career of Djono Rastić (1755–1814), whose father the historian was Đurđević's contemporary, provides a vignette of intellectual life during the last years of the Republic and indeed its aftermath. He was educated by the Jesuits in Dubrovnik and duly joined the Great Council. On his father's death he went to Italy with two of his uncles on the Ragusan equivalent of the 'Grand Tour', returning to Dubrovnik to continue his studies. At the age of twenty he married into the patrician Zamanja family, and while his wife took all the practical decisions he henceforth concentrated on his books. He became an expert on Roman law, though he was never taught it, and he was also a master of Italian rhetoric. His attitude to life, literature, leisure and politics was very much that of earlier generations of Ragusan scholars: all these things were enjoyed in a cultivated, balanced and complementary fashion. Rastić also inherited their love of the countryside, and whenever he could he went to his estates in Rijeka Dubrovačka, Konavle and on Mljet, all of which figured in his poems. It was at his villa at the place still called Đonovina in Rijeka Dubrovačka that he started to learn Greek, in which he became so proficient that he translated many classical Greek texts into (the more accessible) Latin. In turning to the study of English he embarked on an arguably still more taxing challenge. He seems to have been intrigued by all that he discovered about that faraway country whose books soon filled his shelves, and he developed great admiration for the British system of government. In the time that remained, and when he was not reading books on history and theology, Rastić fulfilled his obligations as a patrician, joining the Senate in 1792 and serving as Rector on five occasions.

In later years, Djono Rastić began to build a new house for himself in the suburbs of Dubrovnik, where he intended to concentrate on his literary pursuits. But he aborted the project when the area was burnt down by the Montenegrins, and with the final fall of the Republic he gave up on public life and the city altogether. Retiring to his estates, he spent the rest of his days with his family, friends and books. Unlike most of Dubrovnik's writers, whose appearances and characters are rather obscure, we know thanks to Appendini that he was a man of medium stature, physically frail, short-sighted, with a high forehead and protruding nose. His forbidding appearance concealed a sharp wit which was evident in his amusing conversation. His historical importance is greater than his achievements would suggest, because he quintessentially represents the last of the old Ragusan *literati*.[64]

As in the case of Rastić, the intellectual tone of Dubrovnik was more often than not severely conservative. Examples of this are the concentration of Ragusan scholars both on composition in Latin and on the translation of already well-known works into Croatian. The *Konavljanin* Đuro Hidža (1752–1833), already mentioned in another context, was a specialist in both fields. He was a doctor, but his friends claimed that he knew and cared a great deal more about poetry than medicine.[65] Ragusan Jesuits, spending most of their careers in Italy, were also prominent latinists. The two outstanding examples are Raimund Kunić (1719–1794), who translated Homer's *Iliad* into Latin, and Brnja Zamanja (1735–1820) whose Horatian-style epistles portrayed the scenes and personalities he had encountered in the course of his extraordinarily long life.[66]

But not everything in Dubrovnik's cultural life at this time smacked of clericalism and the classics. Appendini notes, for example, the Ragusan enthusiasm for the theatre. Some years after the ruin of the Great Arsenal as a result of the 1667 earthquake, a theatre was erected on the site. By 1682 Ragusan amateur dramatics groups were already performing there. Groups of players from Italy, recruited by a standing committee of nobles, would also perform there. If they gave satisfaction, the players might then be asked to stay on for some months; in 1784 the Senate allowed one company to give forty performances. Not just patricians, but commoners and even unaccompanied women were to be found in the audience. The city theatre remained in operation until it was burnt down in 1817.[67]

Theatre-going in Dubrovnik was often a rumbustious business. When seats proved scarce for a popular production, tempers rose and blows were exchanged. The authorities accordingly intervened to try to enforce some decorum. Thus in 1748 the Small Council decreed that the first five rows in the theatre should be reserved for nobles aged forty-five or over. Behind them would sit younger patricians and members of the *Antunini* and *Lazarini*, and then behind them everyone else. It was forbidden to reserve places for late-comers; but of course people did, with handkerchiefs and scarves draped over the seats. More disruption could be expected from noisy servants, who were accustomed to wait just outside while the performance was under way. The Small Council instructed the city guard to be on hand to take away those servants who misbehaved and to give them a sound thrashing.[68]

Some Croatian comedies continued to be written and performed. Many Italian plays were also presented. But probably the main influence was French. Ragusans were exceedingly keen to learn that language. Ignjat Đurđević, echoing Rastić, complained: 'The French language rules here and whoever knows it, albeit superficially, considers himself the first man in the world.' But it was in translations that French plays were largely performed. The comedies of Molière were shown earlier in Dubrovnik than elsewhere in the Slavic world and seem to have taken the place by storm.[69]

Franco-Ragusan influence was not, however, all one-way. Dubrovnik retained the ability to seduce those who made an effort to appreciate it. Such was the case of the poet and playwright known alternatively as Marko Bruerović or Marc Bruère (1765–1823), the son of that harsh critic of Dubrovnik, the French consul. Marko came to the city as a child in 1772 and was educated by the Piarist fathers (who succeeded the Jesuits as Dubrovnik's schoolmasters). From them he learned Latin and Italian, but it was in Croatian that he preferred to speak and mainly wrote. He was friendly with all the writers and intellectuals of the Dubrovnik of his day. His first wife was a Bosnian Croat whom he met when he was serving as a French consular official in Travnik. His second was the Dubrovnik girl who acted as his servant. Eventually, after years working as his father's assistant, he became a naturalised citizen of Dubrovnik and organised some of the last masquerades for the Republic's annual carnival.[70]

The school, the academy and the theatre were, clearly, important focuses for Ragusan cultural life. But so was the church. The Jesuits (until the order's dissolution in 1773), Piarists, Franciscans and Dominicans, with their libraries, were vital sources of learning and centres of study. For example, the Dominican Saro Crijević (Cerva) [1681–1759] was at this time preparing his compendious history of the Ragusan church. The Jesuit Ivan-Marija Matijašević (Mattei) [1714–1791] had embarked upon a lifetime's work of collecting and transcribing documents relating to Dubrovnik's past. The Franciscan Sebastijan Slade (Dolci) [1699–1777], was writing his biographies of eminent Ragusan writers. Nor was erudition cultivated only within the city's religious houses. Matijašević records a mission he undertook to the island of Koločep in 1752. The parish itself was a mere 200 souls, most of whom earned their living by netting sardines. But in this simple setting he found in charge a priest who had himself translated into Croatian an Italian devotional classic and whose fine library was full of books on theology and catechetics.[71]

Also well-stocked with books were the private libraries of many of the great patrician families of Dubrovnik. The library of Marija Đurđević Bunić, most of which she acquired herself in the second half of the eighteenth century, reveals a woman (and a family) of cosmopolitan tastes and obvious sophistication. Greek and Roman classics, theology, science, Italian poetry, French philosophy and English novels all found places on her shelves.[72]

As in earlier centuries, the great majority of such books were imported. But from 1782 there was a printing shop at work in Dubrovnik. The Venetian

Carlo Antonio Occhi was appointed 'Printer of the Ragusan Republic' and provided with a loan of 500 ducats to be repaid over fifteen years, during which he was accorded an exclusive privilege. Two censors were appointed by the authorities to ensure that no dangerous works were published. This, though, was hardly likely, and Occhi seems to have concentrated on verse by well-known authors. Nor did his successors ruffle doctrinal feathers. Their business was, after all, heavily dependent upon state commissions.[73]

Ripples of Revolution

Eighteenth-century Dubrovnik was, in truth, still largely unmoved by the philosophical and political thinking of the Enlightenment. Most of its patriciate were determined to keep it that way. Foreign newspapers with offensive liberal opinions did, though, find their way to the Republic. The Senate itself might on occasion subscribe to journals like the *Leiden Gazette* in order to supply it with news of world events. Other journals arrived in the city through the consuls of foreign powers. In 1776 the government decided that newspapers emanating from Tuscany – considered a hotbed of unsettling ideas – might only be read in the Secretary of the Republic's office, unless special permission was given by the Small Council.

But one should not exaggerate the extent of controls. Those who wished to obtain forbidden material could do so. Thus the library of Tomo Basiljević, Dubrovnik's most prominent advocate of liberal thinking, contained many works by suspect authors of the French Enlightenment including Voltaire, Montesquieu and Rousseau.[74]

It was external events that began to crystallise liberal ideas into impulses for political change in the minds of some Ragusans. But Tomo Basiljević was unusual in regarding the American Revolution as a social and political upheaval with far-reaching implications for the existing order. The patriciate as a whole was more interested in seeking from it commercial advantages without incurring too many risks. The Republic's ambassador in Paris, Francesco Favi, kept it well-informed about what was happening. The government also employed the services of Ruđer Bošković, who made use of his acquaintance with the American representative Benjamin Franklin to cross-question him over dinner in Paris.[75] Both Favi and Bošković were strongly sympathetic to the new Republic. But while the Ragusan government was anxious to establish good relations with the fledgling United States so as to benefit from the trade to be done, it was also fearful of antagonising the British. Only after much hesitation, and when Favi was able to assure it that a peace treaty was all but signed, did he receive permission to make formal contact with Franklin, which he did in early July 1783.[76]

The French Revolution would evoke echoes of a far more disturbing kind in Dubrovnik (as elsewhere in Europe) than did the revolt of the American colonies. In neither case was it the blows against royal government as such that mattered to the Ragusan authorities: after all, theirs was an ancient Republic whose public ideology was symbolised by the very word *Libertas*. Rather, the French Revolutionary spirit was threatening because it was democratic (and only the patriciate ruled in Dubrovnik) and because it was anti-religious (and Dubrovnik was a Catholic state).

Yet it is not clear that much if any of this was initially grasped by the Ragusan government. It received detailed reports of events in France from Favi. But until the outbreak of the first great Revolutionary war in 1792 Dubrovnik had little reason to be alarmed for its own security. There was not even a change in the French representation to the Republic, for the aristocratic Bruère would continue in office under the new as under the *ancien régime*.

Thus, in the last years of the eighteenth century, Dubrovnik flourished economically; it enjoyed a large degree of social peace; its patricians ruled in very much the manner they had always done, barring the occasional factional squabble.

And it was quite unprepared for the fate that was about to overtake it.

FIFTEEN

The Fall of the Ragusan Republic: The Background to and Circumstances of the Abolition of the Republic in 1808

External Pressures

The abolition of the French monarchy and the declaration of a French Republic in 1792 was duly noted in Dubrovnik. According to the official French newspaper, *Le Moniteur*, the erection of the new French coat of arms over his residence by France's long-serving (and time-serving) representative, Bruère, was greeted with public demonstrations of support. But the source is obviously suspect. For its part, the Ragusan government – as Austria's agent reported back to Vienna – was scrupulous in avoiding commitment either to France or to its enemies, including Austria.[1]

How much intellectual and political ferment already lay beneath the surface of the Ragusan state? The influence of all things French was clearly considerable among at least a section of the patriciate. But from how far back one should begin to date the origins of later 'revolutionary' thinking, it is difficult to tell. In any case, only when Dubrovnik's own security was at stake did the Ragusan government become seriously alarmed about the contagion of French ideas.

On 13 May 1797, the Ragusan agent in Vienna, Sebastiano di Ayala, reported back to his government the abolition of the Venetian Republic, noting that this would be to the benefit of Austria.[2] And indeed, by terms secretly agreed at Leoben the previous month Venetian Istria and Dalmatia were transferred to Austrian rule. During the summer, Austrian troops proceeded to occupy Dalmatia, including Kotor, although the ultimate destination of that strategically crucial base was still undecided. Austria was thus transformed in the eyes of Dubrovnik from being a distant and usually benevolent power into the Republic's neighbour, only separated from its territory by the two Ottoman buffer zones of Klek and Sutorina. The Ragusan government immediately sent its congratulations to Vienna. The Emperor Francis II responded warmly and promised to protect the little republic. But the Emperor also warned Ayala that the Senate should look to the state's security, because ill-disposed individuals informed by wrong principles were plotting against it. The Austrian minister Count Thugut elaborated on this allegation, explaining to Ayala that the Austrians had intercepted letters from Ragusan 'Jacobins' intended for their counterparts in Venice. However, neither now nor later was the Austrian minister prepared to hand over the letters, nor indeed to provide concrete proof of their existence. When Ayala's report – written in code and despatched by special courier and then ship from Rijeka – reached Dubrovnik, it provoked alarm and dismay. While declaring a day of public rejoicing and prescribing solemn exposition of the Blessed Sacrament in gratitude for Austria's protection, the Senate also resolved to keep totally silent about the rest of the message. A special envoy was sent back to Vienna to learn more. But before his return, on the evening of 19 October a large French fleet under the command of Rear Admiral Paul-François Brueys arrived and moored in the Koločep channel. The French were graciously received and proved themselves a model of amiability. Indeed, their convivial mingling with the local inhabitants stirred up more rumours of plots and persuaded the Senate, after the fleet's departure, to institute a commission to inquire into Jacobin influences in the Republic.

The commission, consisting of three conservative-minded Francophobes, continued its investigations from 31 October 1797 till 15 March 1798. It was then suspended and not reconvened. Its investigations were not very productive. They unearthed the names of various individuals of minor significance who, it was thought, had fraternised too enthusiastically with the French. More significantly, the commission named three powerful French supporters among the leading patricians – Tomo Basiljević, Antun Sorkočevic and Niko Luko Pucić – all of whose sympathies were undoubtedly already well-known. The most serious charges were those levelled against the Republic's undersecretary of state, Maro Martellini, who had to resign his position. But no one was condemned for treason.[3] The main effect of the commission was to sharpen divisions between the 'French' party and its opponents. The planned proscription of the Francophiles would also provide a useful propaganda weapon for the French in 1808.

Within months of the suspension of the anti-Jacobin commission's work, Dubrovnik found itself faced with a further, this time highly unpleasant manifestation of French power. The treaty of Campo Formio on 17 October 1797 had largely confirmed the terms agreed at Leoben, though it was now stated that Austria should gain Boka Kotorska. The treaty also granted France the Ionian islands, and General Comeyras was despatched as commissioner to take control of them. But Paris did not provide him with sufficient funds, and so the new commissioner, hearing well-founded rumours of Dubrovnik's current prosperity, sent Captain Briche with a frigate to demand a loan. Briche's tactics were brutal. He bluntly threatened that unless the Ragusan government lent him one million *livres tournoises* within twenty-four hours he would bombard the city, seize its fortresses and institute a revolutionary government. While the Ragusan authorities tried to stave off this disaster, Comeyras himself arrived in the city. It was finally agreed that the Republic would lend 300,000 Turkish *grossi* at 4 per cent interest. Comeyras received immediately a sum of 200,000 dinars in cash. Only a very small amount of this money would ever, in fact, be repaid.[4]

In order to appreciate the effect of this and later demands it is necessary to consider the financial resources and economic vulnerabilities of the Ragusan Republic in what would turn out to be the last decade of its existence. Maritime trade was still flourishing as a result of the Republic's neutrality at a time when one by one the Italian ports were falling into the hands of the French. The accounts of the ancient due called *arboraticum* suggest that at the beginning of 1806 there were 277 Ragusan long- and short-haul vessels with a total capacity of 25,512 *carri*. In the course of 1806 twenty-six of these ships were lost, having mostly been seized or destroyed by the Russians.[5] These figures illustrate the extent, but also the fragility, of the trade.

Other figures, drawn up by one of the former secretaries of the Republic, Baro Bettera, for the Austrian general Teodor Milutinović in 1815, intended to give an account of circumstances at the end of the Republic, illustrate a further vulnerability. During all this period Dubrovnik was running a large trade deficit. It exported little that was of value to foreigners apart from oil, wine, brandy and salted sardines. But it had to import corn, rice, meat, coal and luxury goods. In the last years of the Republic this deficit grew to the substantial sum of 1,385,750 piasters. The trade deficit was, though, more than covered by income from shipping and from funds invested in banks in Rome, Vienna, Venice and Naples. Total income from maritime trade – that is, shipping profits, dues levied by the state and wages paid to crews – apparently amounted to 3,615,500 piasters. Total income from bank deposits came to 252,613 piasters, which was a little more than that required to cover all state expenses of 226,818 piasters. Of course, the period covered by Bettera's calculations was exceptional. Dubrovnik was now able to add to its traditional markets that of France, as its ships loaded their holds with corn from the Black Sea ports in order to supply the population of Marseilles and elsewhere. The maritime business had, in fact, probably never enjoyed such prosperity. But the conditions for it could not – and would not – last. What Bettera's memorandum reveals is that Dubrovnik was now almost entirely economically and financially dependent upon respect for its rights by foreign powers. If its merchant fleet was systematically attacked, its economy would collapse. If its funds invested abroad were raided, its government would sooner or later be paralysed.[6]

Such was the state of affairs when Comeyras demanded and obtained his loan. Dubrovnik could not afford to risk antagonising the French because of their firepower. Yet at the same time it was desperate to preserve its neutrality, for fear of British action against its ships. And all the while, despite the Republic's current general prosperity, there was precious little leeway available within the public finances to accommodate sudden demands of the sort that were now being made.

The Konavle Revolt

In fact, Dubrovnik's public finances faced a double blow. Not only did they have to withstand extortion by the French: the Austrians, who were equally pressed for cash to pay for their war efforts, also seized 30 per cent of the Ragusan Republic's investments in Venice.

As Bettera himself emphasised, government imposts in Dubrovnik were low and those that there were fell predominantly on the wealthy rather than on the peasantry. The tax on food was not high, and affected urban, not rural, dwellers. Thus there was no land tax or tithe.[7] The fact that peasants were not really used to government exactions at all may, indeed, have made them more recalcitrant now. And, of course, as was noted earlier, many of them were under strong pressure to increase the labour they owed to their landlords, which meant that they were most unwilling to pay more to the state.

But the Ragusan government now decided that more money must urgently be raised. The pope's permission was sought, and received, for the dissolution of the (now empty) monastery on Lokrum and the island's sale to some Ragusan citizens. This, though, was not nearly sufficient: taxes had to be increased. A new tax of 2 percent was, therefore, levied on the worth of shareholdings in ships. The tax on land sales was increased to 6 per cent.

Import dues rose sharply from 50 to 400 per cent. These measures affected the better-off, but the peasantry was also expected to share the burden. So 12 *pari* were levied on each olive tree, another 12 per head of livestock and 10 per barrel of wine produced. Most vexing of all, the whole adult population was now required to buy salt – which was, of course, a state monopoly – at a much higher price than usual. Everyone over fourteen was thus compelled to purchase it at the rate of 20 *dinarići* a bushel (*uborak*): those dwelling in the city or suburbs had to buy half a bushel a year, and rural dwellers a third of a bushel.

As was customary on such occasions, the count of Konavle at the end of June or the beginning of July 1799 summoned a *zbor* to which he announced the new measures. There was immediate uproar. The peasants now held their own assembly at which some 800 of them swore to combine in order to resist the new imposts: anyone who failed to honour this oath could expect to see his house burnt down. There were five ringleaders, coming from different villages in the district, and their influence was sufficient to ensure that all attempts by the local gentry to quieten tempers were in vain.

The Ragusan government felt too weak to put down the revolt alone, so while strengthening its local garrisons it also sought to bring to bear outside pressures on the insurgents. It wrote to the Austrian commander at Boka Kotorska, General Brady, asking him to despatch his troops so as to intimidate the *Konavljani* into submission, and to cut off all links between them and the inhabitants of Boka. It even asked him – probably insincerely – to send 150 soldiers to be lodged on Lokrum or at Gruž for Dubrovnik's defence. The government also wrote to inform the Austrian commander at Zadar, Brady's superior General Rukavina. In fact, little help could be expected from the Austrians in the crisis. Some of the leading figures in the Austrian camp were keen to achieve complete domination of the Dalmatian coast down to Boka, which would involve the abolition and absorption of the Ragusan Republic. Brady himself was fairly clearly of this opinion. He therefore responded coolly to Dubrovnik's request, noting that he could not move his troops without orders from his superiors. Such scruples did not, however, prevent his later receiving a delegation of *Konavljani*, the shrewdness and sophistication of whose subsequent arguments suggest that Brady or his advisers may indeed have helped assemble them.

The *Konavljani* claimed in their written petition to Vienna that they had been well-treated until about 50 years earlier. But since then the rule of their lords had become intolerable, the exactions growing, the harvests yielding less. Now they were faced with the salt due. The peasants declared that they were being maltreated because 'they would not follow the nobility in the paths of Jacobinism' and wanted to live instead under the Habsburg Emperor's authority. The last of these assertions was subtly persuasive, for Vienna, of course, knew all about the alleged 'Jacobin plot' in Dubrovnik of 1797. A further colour of credibility was doubtless also provided by the general revolt of the devout and discontented Catholic Dalmatian peasantry against French exactions and doctrinal deviations in the same year.[8]

How far Brady would have gone it is impossible to know. General Rukavina's attitude in Zadar was not very reassuring for Dubrovnik either: he seemed more inclined to mediate than to see the rebellion suppressed. But in any case Dubrovnik had never placed much faith in the Austrians; indeed, Ragusan tactics were possibly intended to ensure that at least they knew exactly what Brady and his colleagues intended.[9]

But as in previous centuries – and as would be increasingly the case in the last years of its existence – the Ragusan Republic looked, above all, to the Ottoman Empire to protect its integrity. Immediately after the outbreak of revolt, the Ragusan government had sought the help of the Porte. It also asked the *pasha* of Bosnia to instruct his commander in Trebinje to send his troops to the border so as to cut off all contact between the *Konavljani* and Turkish subjects. The *pasha* was far more helpful that Brady. He despatched 500 soldiers to the frontier to await the Senate's instructions and promised a further 1,600 if needed. In its justification, Dubrovnik claimed to the Porte that the *Konavljani* were prosperous, and 'riches never grow under tyranny'. Indeed, they enjoyed such a measure of freedom from oppressive burdens that this had been to the detriment of their masters. The peasantry had, in truth, become rich, soft and obstreperous. And as for the salt tax, the system had only been introduced to stop smuggling.

Dubrovnik's frustration with the attitude of Vienna and in particular of Brady led to the Ragusan ambassador in Constantinople, Federigo Kiriko – almost certainly with the full approval of the Ragusan government – launching a strong verbal attack on Austria, claiming that it intended to seize the Republic for itself. This so outraged the Reis Effendi, effectively the Ottoman Foreign Minister, that he demanded from the Austrian agent a written guarantee of the Dubrovnik's integrity. At the same time, Kiriko spread rumours around the Ottoman court that General Brady had already begun to move against the Republic. Although these tactics roused the fury of the Austrian Emperor – which Dubrovnik's apologies, excuses and insincere rebukes of Kiriko were hard-put to appease – they achieved their goal. Austria was not prepared at this delicate stage to face outright conflict with the Porte. And above all,

Dubrovnik had gained time to browbeat and lure the *Konavljani* back into submission.

The Ragusan government had responded to the revolt by ordering the confiscation of all assets owned by the rebels. All the inhabitants of the Republic were to make public declaration of any such assets to the state treasurers so that this measure could take effect. As early as mid-July, a first group of thirty *Konavljani* had come to the monastery of St James in Višnjica to hold talks with the Ragusan authorities. At the end of the month a further delegation arrived there to seek mercy. The Ragusan Senate agreed, but only if the ringleaders were handed over or, if this was impossible, their names given. While the *Konavljani* living in the west and in the mountains areas were prepared to yield, those from Vitaljina and the east remained recalcitrant, continuing to seek Austrian intervention.

In the end, even the die-hards understood that there was no point in holding out. On 15 January Ragusan forces accordingly began to move back into Konavle. The five ringleaders had by now fled the Republic. They had been sentenced to death *in absentia* or, if they could not be found, to the destruction of their property, expulsion of their families and symbolic execution – their effigies to be hung on gibbets erected in the midst of their ruined houses. This picturesque sentence was, however, only carried out in two of the five cases. Yet if punishment was limited, so too was reform. The forced purchase of salt had already been suspended at the start of the revolt, and the measure was not renewed. On 29 March 1800 the government also acted to regulate the quantity and terms of service on the lord's estate. The maximum was set at 90 days and the amount of food and drink to be given to the peasant employed on such labour was specified. The authorities saw no need to go further.[10]

The Occupation of Dubrovnik

As the new century began, the Ragusan Republic seemed in some respects reasonably placed to survive well enough during it. Konavle had been brought back under control – though admittedly, in this vulnerable frontier zone that concept was only relative. Relations with Austria, albeit soured by Dubrovnik's accusations, were more or less stabilised. Diplomatic contacts with Russia (conducted with the Russian representative in Constantinople) were also commercially fruitful. The Ragusan ambassador Kiriko, assisted by another Ragusan, Miho Božović (officially Prussia's representative to the Porte), and in conjunction with the Ragusan *poklisari*, negotiated with the Russians and Turks the terms under which Dubrovnik's ships and merchants could trade in the Black Sea. This commerce was accordingly placed on a sound footing and prospered greatly.

Russia's own representative in Dubrovnik from 1802 was somewhat more troublesome, though more nuisance than real danger. Charles Fonton, a Frenchman by birth – and thus possibly a Catholic, a Freemason, an agnostic or an atheist, but not Russian Orthodox – took up cudgels against Dubrovnik's long-standing exclusion of Orthodox churches from the Republic.[11] Although Fonton as consul was allowed his own Orthodox chapel, the Ragusan government was only prepared to allow an Orthodox priest to come to the city twice a year and not stay more than a week at a time. Fonton contrasted this discrimination with the freedom of religion that the Jews enjoyed in Dubrovnik, and indeed that which the Ragusans themselves enjoyed in Russia – also, more ominously, with the commercial concessions that the Russians had given for the Ragusan Black Sea trade. But not even these implied threats could move the Ragusan authorities much in this matter. In 1804 it was finally agreed that the Orthodox priest could come back to Dubrovnik from where he had been expelled; the Russian crest would be placed above the gates of the consul's chapel, thus emphasising Russian protection; if an Orthodox believer died in Dubrovnik, an Orthodox priest could enter the city to accompany the body to burial; but the priest could not chant the liturgy over the body until he was outside the gates, and he was not allowed to enter the Dubrovnik hospital, which was considered a Catholic institution.[12] There is no evidence that this very traditional dispute had an effect on subsequent Russian attitudes during Dubrovnik's final agony. Indeed, after the squabble was resolved Fonton seems to have fallen under the Republic's charm, and became a committed if not very effective advocate of its interests.

During this period, Dubrovnik's contacts with the French were limited and distant. Napoleon Bonaparte, for his part, was heavily involved in his Egyptian venture. The destruction of the French fleet by Nelson at Aboukir Bay had left him isolated; the first news he had from Europe arrived after eight months – on a Ragusan ship. Back in France and soon First Consul, Bonaparte's attention was focused on domestic politics and diplomacy. When he proclaimed himself Emperor of the French on 18 May 1804, Dubrovnik sent an ingratiating message of congratulations, which was politely acknowledged.[13]

Having destroyed the armies of the coalition which had assembled against him, Napoleon imposed terms on Austria by the Peace of Bratislava (Pressburg) of 26 December 1805. (Russia remained obdurate.) The Austrians now ceded formerly Venetian Istria, Dalmatia and Kotor to France, or more precisely to the 'Kingdom of Italy' of which Napoleon's stepson Eugène de Beauharnais, was Viceroy. Again, Dubrovnik sent a congratulatory message. This may even have been sincere, since a large number of Ragusan patricians were now strongly Francophile – at least if the Austrian secret agent's report to his government is to be believed.[14] But there is no reason to think that even the Francophiles were at this stage any less keen than their critics to preserve Ragusan independence.

Unfortunately, events now started to conspire against that. The French armies were extremely slow to take possession of their new territory. The task was entrusted to Generals Lauriston and Molitor.[15] While Lauriston was placed in overall command of French forces in Dalmatia, it was Molitor's role to move down the coast and receive from the Austrian authorities all the territories which the peace of Bratislava had specified. But this proved complicated. The French did not know the terrain or the population, and one by one the deadlines set for taking possession of key centres were missed. Kotor was due to be handed over on 28 February 1806. But Molitor was still on that date at Split. In the absence of French forces, and thanks to the incompetence – or more probably malice – of the Austrian authorities, Kotor was instead yielded on 6 March by General Ghislieri to the Russian fleet and to Russia's Montenegrin allies under the command of the Orthodox bishop of Montenegro, Petar Petrović Njegoš.

Dubrovnik viewed these developments with alarm. From early February the Ragusan government had been aware that Molitor would seek permission to cross its territory in order to occupy Kotor. The Senators debated for three whole days on the necessary response. Although extra measures were taken in order to secure the city's defences, there was clearly no hope of resisting a French force determined to have its way. The issue, therefore, was how to facilitate the passage of French troops with as little risk as possible to the Republic. Dubrovnik had always gone to great diplomatic lengths to avoid the entry of foreign forces into the city.[16] There was all the more reason to adhere to this rule now: Dubrovnik knew full well what had happened to Venice in 1797 – and even if, unlike the Serenissima, the Ragusan Republic survived formally intact, it would at the least have forfeited its neutrality in the eyes of the Russians and British, who could combine to destroy its commerce.[17] The only questions outstanding were, therefore, who should be despatched to Molitor as the Republic's envoys and what should be the precise terms of their brief.

Eventually, Senators Djivo Basiljević and Marojica Zlatarić departed on their mission. It was envisaged that once Molitor had agreed that his troops could be transported by sea, sufficient ships would gather at Ston to take them to Cavtat. At dawn on 8 March the envoys' ship sighted Molitor's fleet riding off the island of Brač, and duly boarded his vessel. The French general, who presumably already knew what had happened in Kotor, assured them that he had been given instructions to respect and protect the Ragusan Republic's independence. The following day he received a self-serving exculpatory account from Ghislieri of why he had handed the place over to the Russians. Perhaps this brought home to Molitor the urgency of pressing on as quickly as possible, for at their next audience with him at Makarska the Ragusan envoys heard from his lips that he was indeed resolved to move to Dubrovnik and quarter his army there to await further instructions. When they protested that the roads were poor and that there was insufficient food or water he appeared to relent: if Dubrovnik could raise a loan for him of 300,000 francs he would not enter the city, though he would not say this publicly at present. It was, of course, extortion; but the envoys had to relay the message to the Senate, which on 13 March duly agreed the loan.

Unknown to Basiljević and Zlatarić, however, the Ragusan Senate had been faced in their absence with a crisis from the opposite quarter. On Tuesday 4 March, Solemn Benediction of the Blessed Sacrament in the church of St Blaise was attended by the Rector and the Small Council in petition for the success of the mission to Molitor. The same day they learned from the count of Konavle, Sigismund Sorkočević, that the Russian commissioner at Kotor, Stefan Sankowski, had informed him that having heard that French troops were about to enter the Republic, Sankowski was sending a force of Russian and Montenegrin soldiers onto Ragusan territory and now demanded provisions for them. The Senate immediately reconvened. The Russian consul, Fonton, was summoned from his sickbed to hear Sorkočević's account but protested that he knew nothing of the matter – which was certainly true, because he, Sankowski and the Russian Admiral Senyavin all seem to have been following different orders from St Petersburg. Sorkočević was sent back to Sankowski to explain that the Republic was at this moment seeking to prevent French forces from entering its territory – a point to be reinforced by an offer of a bribe, which the Senate emphasised should be made 'delicately'.

There was not, though, much delicacy in the response. Sankowski made five demands. First, Dubrovnik must inform the Russians within forty-eight hours how many French were in Dalmatia and where they were positioned. Second, provisions gathered for the French must instead be sent to Cavtat. Third,

Senators must no longer speak favourably of the French. Fourth, ships assembled to transport French troops must be dispersed. Finally, the Republic must commit itself to strict neutrality. Dubrovnik accepted all five demands and despatched further bribes. In fact, the Russians and Montenegrins had other things on their minds that day: on 6 March they took control of Kotor.[18]

For the present, Dubrovnik was spared further threats. The French continued to press Austria to honour its agreement to hand over Kotor, which it was now, of course, unable to do. And both the French and the Russians and Montenegrins waited for the other side to violate Ragusan neutrality, so providing an excuse for intervention. But as spring wore into summer, it was Napoleon who began to lose patience. On 6 May he wrote to Prince Eugène:

> My Son:
>
> With a view to occupying the whole territory of the Ragusan Republic, you will order General Lauriston to move with the Fifteenth and Twenty-Fifth Infantry Regiments of the Line with a company of French and Italian artillerymen and as much artillery as we can give him, to occupy the city of Dubrovnik and its territory. He will leave in place the existing government, while disarming the citizens and taking all measures necessary for security. I have convincing proof of how that Republic is behaving towards our enemies, and because of the infringement of its neutrality it must be considered in a state of war… I do not need to tell you that the success of this expedition depends upon secrecy.[19]

It was left to the Emperor's ever-ingenious Foreign Minister, Charles-Maurice de Talleyrand, to elaborate a justification of this decision.[20] Writing on 23 May to the Seigneur de Raymond, the newly appointed (but not yet installed) French consul for Dubrovnik, Talleyrand explained:

> Before receiving the latest information, His Majesty was in two minds as to whether to occupy Dubrovnik, although he had the right to protect his own territory and to help a weak state resist attack by the Russians. But seeing that Dubrovnik has made an agreement with them, His Majesty had to avenge the offence inflicted on him. Dubrovnik, by negotiating with the Russians, has demonstrated that it does not consider itself bound by any link of vassalage with, or even any recognition of, the Ottoman Porte. The question of the relations between these two states, of which I spoke to you in earlier instructions, is resolved. An independent Dubrovnik has to bear

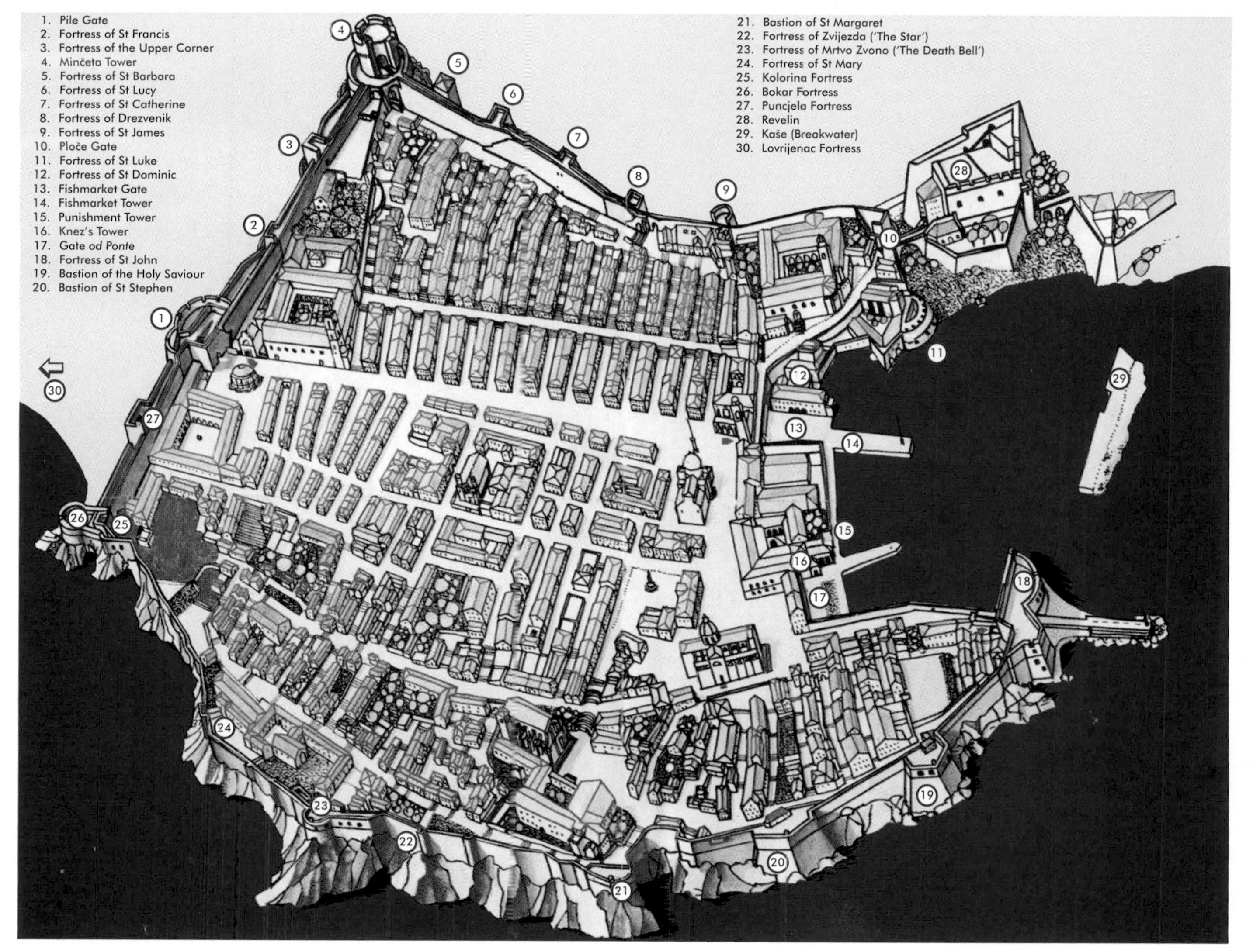
1. Pile Gate
2. Fortress of St Francis
3. Fortress of the Upper Corner
4. Minčeta Tower
5. Fortress of St Barbara
6. Fortress of St Lucy
7. Fortress of St Catherine
8. Fortress of Drezvenik
9. Fortress of St James
10. Ploče Gate
11. Fortress of St Luke
12. Fortress of St Dominic
13. Fishmarket Gate
14. Fishmarket Tower
15. Punishment Tower
16. Knez's Tower
17. Gate od Ponte
18. Fortress of St John
19. Bastion of the Holy Saviour
20. Bastion of St Stephen
21. Bastion of St Margaret
22. Fortress of Zvijezda ('The Star')
23. Fortress of Mrtvo Zvono ('The Death Bell')
24. Fortress of St Mary
25. Kolorina Fortress
26. Bokar Fortress
27. Puncjela Fortress
28. Revelin
29. Kaše (Breakwater)
30. Lovrijenac Fortress

42. The Principal Fortifications of Dubrovnik

43. Detail of Statue of St Blaise, showing Dubrovnik (probably mid-fifteenth century)

44. Depiction of Dubrovnik in Konrad von Grünemberg's account of his pilgrimage (1486)

45. Detail of Nikola Božidarević's Blessed Virgin with Saints, showing Dubrovnik (early sixteenth century)

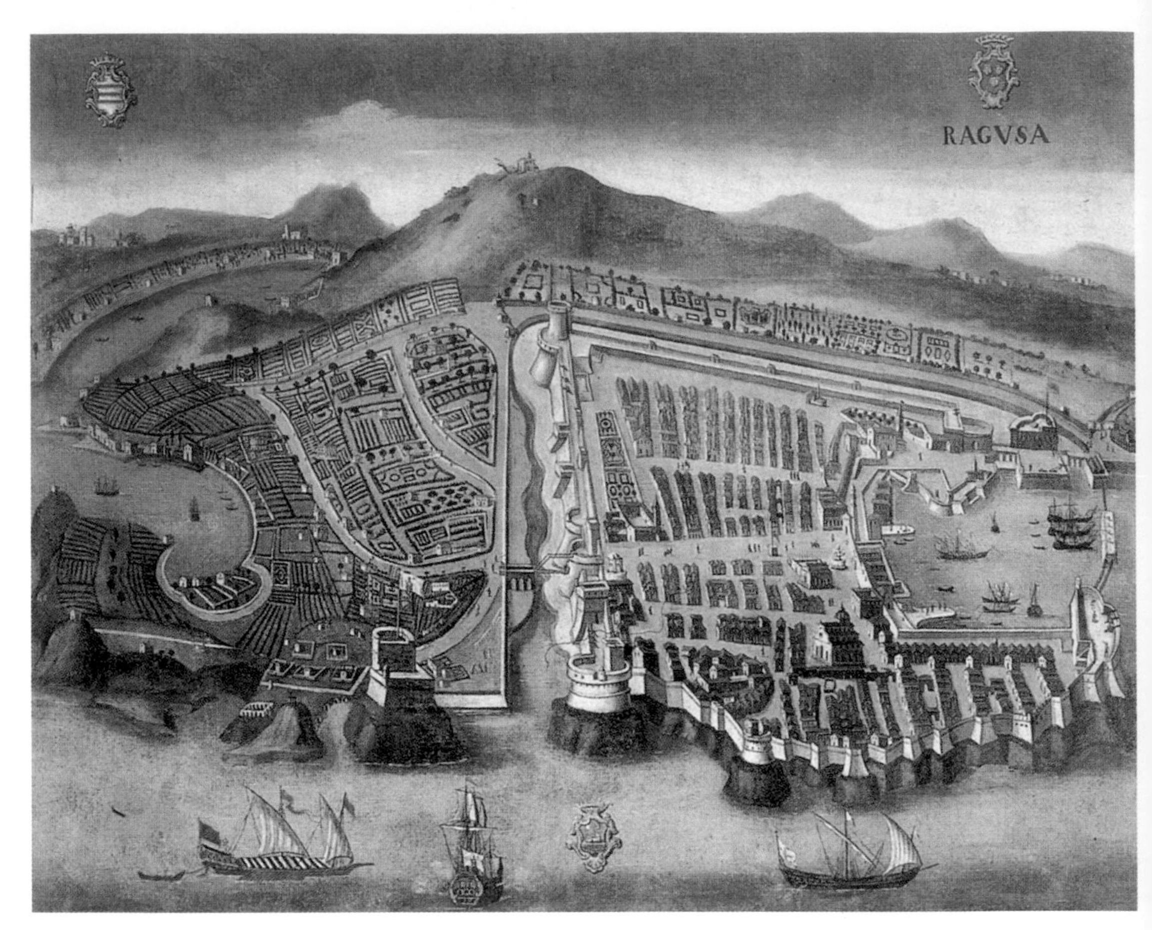

46. Painting of Dubrovnik by Giovanni Batista Fabri (1736), showing the city and its suburbs as they were before the Great Earthquake of 1667

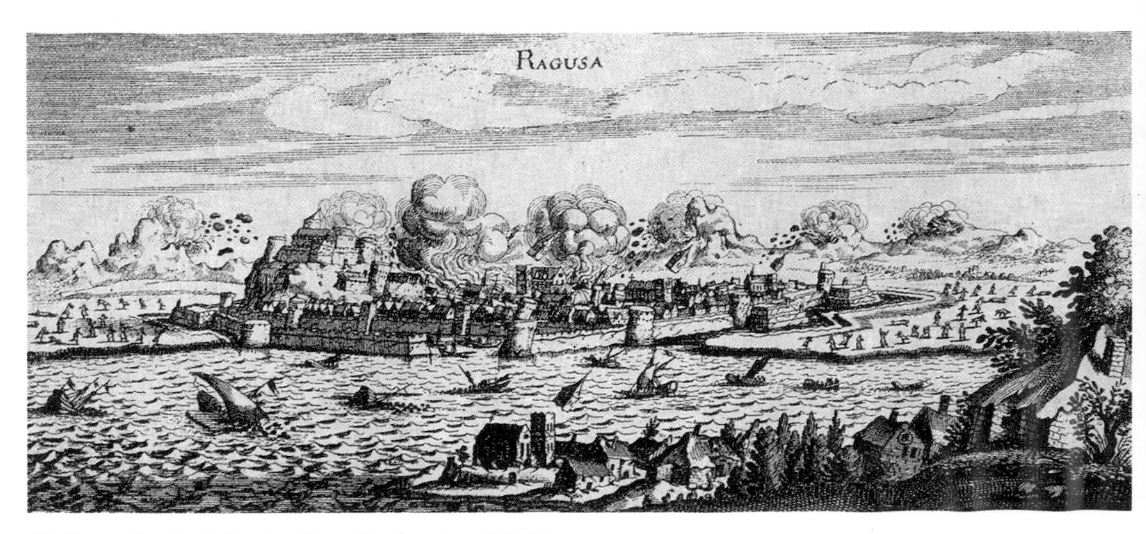

47. Engraving depicting the Great Earthquake of 1667

48. Reliquary of (the head of) St Blaise (eleventh/twelfth century)

49. Statue of St Blaise (probably mid-fifteenth century)

50. Lorenzo Vitelleschi's depiction of Veliki Ston (1827)

51. Ruined Zvekovica, in Konavle (February 1992)

52. Burning house in Dubrovnik's *Široka ulica* (6 December 1991)

> the responsibility for its actions. It alone has determined its fate and has drawn the weapon of His Majesty upon itself.
>
> Dubrovnik has had a thousand years of existence. Such a long history can leave behind it many memories, but control by His Majesty can bestow greater security and greater hope. The situation in Europe has changed. Most of the weaker states have fallen. Dubrovnik, isolated between the great powers, could not find any more the old means of holding on to its territory and commerce.[21]

All that remained was to see that the deed was done.

On 23 May – the same day that Talleyrand gave his instructions to Raymond – Lauriston set off with 15,000 men from Makarska bound for an unsuspecting Dubrovnik. The twenty-sixth of May was Pentecost Sunday, and so a special feast day celebrated with due pomp in Dubrovnik's cathedral. At half past twelve there arrived a messenger sent by the chancellor of Slano, just fifteen miles up the coast. The message he carried was devastating. A force of French soldiers was even now hastening to Dubrovnik, taking the difficult mountainous rather than the obvious sea route, doubtless for reasons both of surprise and security. The Small Council and the Senate were immediately convened. The Russian agent, Fonton, was also informed. The Senators found it difficult to believe the information they had received: why had not the count of Ston, who must have known of any such expedition, not informed them earlier? (In fact, on reaching and seizing Ston, Lauriston had forbidden the Ragusan count on pain of death to convey any news to Dubrovnik.) For several hours the senators debated what should be done. Eventually, two envoys were sent to the commander of the Russian warship moored off Daksa in order to try to stave of violence from that quarter, while two of the leading senators were sent on the vital mission to Lauriston.

The choice of envoys to the French commander fell on Tomo Basiljević, probably the most erudite and enthusiastic of the Francophile party in the Senate, and on Karlo Natali, another well-educated and experienced diplomat. At half past four the two envoys arrived at Gruž, where they learned what had happened at Ston and sent a report back to the Senate. They then hurried on in search of Lauriston. At half past eight they arrived at Orašac and discovered that Lauriston was not now far away. They pressed on through the night and eventually found the French camped at the mountain village of Osojnik.

General Lauriston was far from pleased to see them, knowing that he had now lost the advantage of surprise. But in any case there was nothing that anyone could do stop him. Keeping Natali with him, Lauriston sent Basiljević ahead to demand that the Ragusan government prepare sufficient shipping to take him and his men across Rijeka Dubrovačka to the city. The government had no option but to comply. And so it was that at half past nine on the morning of 27 May Lauriston, accompanied by 800 French troops, crossed the river and marched his men up to the Pile Gate.

Here he was met by two senators. He told them that he needed to refresh his army before going on to Kotor; his other instructions he could only convey to the government in person. The senators then invited him into the city. Accompanied by the old French consul Bruère, whose replacement had still not arrived, Lauriston was received in audience by the Rector and the Small Council. He informed them that he had received a command from his Emperor to occupy all the fortifications of the Republic, while respecting its freedom and independence. This, he explained, was a security measure. With all the other ports of the Adriatic coast sealed fast against English and Russian vessels, Dubrovnik could not alone remain open.

It was effectively an ultimatum, and there was only one possible response. The keys of the city fortresses were duly handed over. The gates were flung open. And Colonel Testa, at the head of 800 French troops, entered and occupied Dubrovnik.[22]

Under Siege

The following morning a proclamation was posted from Napoleon, signed by Lauriston and printed in French, Italian and Croatian ('Illyrian') overnight by the Republic's official printer. It accused the Republic of having demonstrated its hostility to France, which had required the despatch of French forces to the city. It promised that when the Russians had withdrawn from the region the independence of the Republic would be respected. It appointed Bruère Imperial Commissioner in Dubrovnik. Lauriston soon demonstrated what in practice this state of affairs involved. Brushing aside the protest of the Turkish *emin*, he set about reorganising the administration so as to place it on a war footing and ensure French military control. He also demanded a huge 'contribution' of one million francs, which the Republic was quite unable to pay.

The Russian representative, Fonton, now withdrew. But the Austrian agent, Giovanni Timoni, an Italian from the Levant who had arrived the previous year and who like Fonton became a sympathetic friend of Dubrovnik, remained as a shrewd and well-informed observer of developing events. Timoni described the forced loan as spelling death for the Ragusans, and thought that its size demonstrated that the French entertained greatly exaggerated ideas of Dubrovnik's wealth, considering it a 'little Paris'.

For their part, the Senators sought a diminution of the sum and at least partial postponement, while taking measures to liquidate state-owned bonds held in foreign banks. The officials of the Republic's mint were instructed to draw up a register of all the silver plate in Dubrovnik's churches and that held by the Jewish community, with a view to its being turned into Ragusan ducats to pay the French 'loan'. At the same time, provision was made to convert most of the city's monasteries into makeshift barracks for French troops, whose number was steadily increasing as the rest of Lauriston's force arrived. Soldiers and military equipment were also accommodated in deconsecrated churches and other public buildings. Officers were lodged in the houses of private individuals. On Lauriston's orders, the *collegium* was turned into a military hospital.[23]

The likelihood that this last facility would be put to good use was, indeed, growing by the day. Knowing that the Russians and Montenegrins were already entering Konavle, Lauriston sent a force of 450 French soldiers by ship to Cavtat. Leaving 100 of these to guard the town, he ordered the rest to confront the enemy. The first bloody but indecisive skirmish between the French and Montenegrins took place on 30 May at Zvekovica. While the Russians attempted an unsuccessful landing at Rijeka Dubrovačka, in which the whole Russian force of 160 men was killed, the Montenegrins set about pillaging Konavle. In Cavtat the French resisted another Russian attack; but, greatly outnumbered, they and most of the population withdrew on the night of 3–4 June to a line between Obod and Mlini. Cavtat was now plundered by the enemy. An eyewitness recorded how the Russians proceeded to plunder 'not just money, silver and the furnishings they found in the houses, but stripped everything, even breaking off the iron from the doors and windows, so that hardly the roofs and walls were left intact, and some storeys lost their bricks.'[24] This pattern was to be repeated – and perfected – by the Montenegrins in the ensuing weeks.

The French soldiers now withdrew further and dug in at Mlini, Srebreno and in the hills of Župa Dubrovačka as far as Brgat. On 8 June the Montenegrins, having done their worst in Konavle, descended upon Župa. On 12 June they were forced back by the French. But they were then given cover by the Russian warships blockading the city and continued to plunder and burn down the houses they found in their path – and not just in Župa but also in the

Dubrovnik suburbs of Kono and Pile. They proceeded to seize the heights of Mount Srđ and the ridge above the monastery of St James in Višnjica.

Panic now broke out among the Ragusan population living outside the walls of Dubrovnik. More than 4,000 people abandoned their homes and sought safety in the city.

On 17 June there was a fierce battle at Brgat in which the outnumbered French force was totally defeated by the Russians and Montenegrins. Appendini, who kept a war diary during these weeks, decribed the Montenegrin tactics. They were unbeatable in skirmishing amid rocks. Wearing white, blending into the pale stone background of the karst, they were all but invisible. In Dubrovnik people used to say that they 'flew' from crag to crag and that 'no animal had their agility'. The French were unable to respond and 'the war was reduced to a quail shoot'.[25]

Around 450 Frenchmen were killed, among whom was their commander General Delgorgue. The Montenegrins cut off his head, stuck it on a pole, and triumphantly paraded it three times around the local church. Colonel Testa fled with the rest of the defeated army back to Dubrovnik. By now people were flooding into the city. When the gates were closed at nine o'clock that night the crowds seeking entry were so large that women and children were crushed to death and others fell off the drawbridge into the moat. The siege now began in earnest.

The French garrison was hard-pressed. Lauriston had arrived with too few men and too little artillery. Some of the citizens from Konavle, Župa Dubrovačka and Brgat were enrolled to fight, but they proved more an encumbrance than a help. Nor did the Dubrovnik arsenal offer much of use to the defenders, since the artillery it contained was somewhat antiquated, having been donated to the Republic by the Spanish in the seventeenth century.

Within the city were crammed 15,000 civilians and about 1,000 French troops. During the twenty days of siege, which was conducted from both land and sea, the inhabitants were not short of grain, though lack of access to the mills meant that flour itself was scarce. The Montenegrins cut off the aqueduct, but reactivation of old wells and the digging of new ones meant that there was enough (albeit brackish) water to drink. The French authorities required a declaration by every household of its provisions so as to enforce rationing if necessary.

The main problem was that there were simply too many people to accommodate within Dubrovnik – some three times the usual population. Lauriston therefore ordered the *Konavljani* to leave the city and return to their homes. The bishop of Montenegro had actually issued a proclamation inviting them back and promising liberation from servitude and that their lands would be held rent-free for the next ten years. But the pledge was worthless. As the *Konavljani* arrived at St James, the Montenegrins demanded money from them, and when the refugees were unable to pay, sent them back to Dubrovnik. (Some *Konavljani*, though, managed to return home by way of Ottoman territory.)

For all the material discomforts, it was probably the psychological effects of the siege that were most severe. The Montenegrins proved expert in techniques of intimidation. The bishop of Montenegro thus made his appearance before his troops in full view of the defenders. He was carried on a litter with a parasol held over his head to keep off the sun, and his arrival was greeted by loud cheering from the Montenegrins and imprecations against the 'French lepers' (as they called them) sheltering behind the city walls.

The role of the bishop had indeed been crucial throughout. It was through his efforts that the Montenegrins and the other Orthodox Vlachs and Hercegovinians had been fired up with zeal against the French and Ragusans – the Catholic enemy. Appendini notes that the struggle had been declared a 'Holy War' and that the Montenegrins and their allies had pledged to take their campaign as far as Zagreb.[26]

Fear was also instilled into the hearts of the besieged by the brutality practised upon those who fell into the enemy's hands. While the Russians took prisoners, the Montenegrins did not. The French tried to persuade the Russian commanders to enforce observance by their allies of the laws of war. When this failed, a more direct approach was adopted. Three Montenegrins discovered looting in Pile were beheaded: their corpses were thrown into the ditch and their heads into the Adriatic.

Another source of terror was the firing of Russian and Montenegrin cannons down into the city from Mount Srđ. An estimated 1,800 to 3,000 projectiles rained upon the inhabitants in the course of the siege. Most of the houses within the walls and in the suburbs were hit a number of times by different sorts of balls and shot. About 60 people were killed. When the shelling was heaviest, the inhabitants of the city sought refuge in churches, warehouses and cellars – though as a result of the 1667 earthquake the number of cellars was actually rather small.

Finally, both the regular residents of the city and the refugees accommodated there could see from the walls enough of the devastating destruction of property to imagine what must be happening elsewhere. Attempts by the French to drive off the predators were generally unsuccessful.

Indeed, these sorties were blamed by the Ragusans for provoking still more destruction. Thus on the night of 1 July a detachment of French soldiers guided by Ragusan scouts moved out of the Pile Gate to Gruž and then up into the hills where the enemy was encamped. They engaged them, but were then surrounded and forced to escape, leaving three of their number dead and with others wounded. In revenge, the Russians and Montenegrins set fire to the finest villas they could find in the area: between forty and sixty were burnt down.

On the evening of 2 July there was a great storm which discouraged military operations, but when it ended at about eight o'clock hordes of Montenegrins descended, intent on destroying those houses which had escaped their attentions previously. Fires sprang up in thirty of the finest houses in Pile. A vigorous resistance, though, was mounted by a force of 100 or so local inhabitants, who had remained in the district of St George (*Sveti Đurađ*) and were well-provided with weapons. A strong *maestral* blew the flames from house to house, and thick smoke rose over the city. Seeing this, the Russian and Montenegrin guards on top of Mount Srđ cheered loudly. The smoke also, however, had the effect of drawing the attention of French to what was occurring. Two companies of French soldiers were accordingly sent out from the city to help the men of Pile in their struggle with the Montenegrin arsonists. A fierce battle ensued, and the Montenegrins eventually withdrew.[27]

On 5 July there was more shelling from near the little church on Mount Srđ, and the inhabitants of Dubrovnik ran for shelter. But the next day the firing stopped and it was not long before rumours started to circulate that the guns had been withdrawn and that only a few of the enemy remained at their posts. Then there was further, even better news – that French reinforcements were approaching. And this was indeed the truth. General Molitor had left Makarska for Dubrovnik with a force of 1,500 men on 3 July, arriving the following day at Slano.

Many Ragusans regarded their deliverance as nothing less than a miracle. The Saturday before the good news arrived had seen the celebration of the Feast of the Transfer of the (relic of) the Arm of St Blaise accompanied by many prayers for an end to the agony of the city. Accordingly, the streets of Dubrovnik now rang with joyful shouts of 'Long Live St Blaise!' and 'Long Live the Three Martyrs of Kotor!'[28]

Molitor was well informed about the Russian and Montenegrin positions and decided to attack them at the rear. So he took, as Lauriston had, the route to Osojnik, and then entered Ottoman Hercegovina before advancing on Brgat. Defeating and putting to flight the Montenegrin forces he encountered, he sent a message to Lauriston which greatly exaggerated the size of his army.

This, as he had intended, fell into enemy hands and had the desired effect of spreading panic among them. With the assistance of an Ottoman force under the command of the governor of Hutovo in Hercegovina, Molitor now drove back the Russian army, which withdrew all the way to Sutorina.

Molitor's arrival ended the siege, but not the destruction. The Russians landed men from their warships who proceeded to burn Zaton, Trsteno and Orašac. At Gruž on the evening of 6 July the Russians and Montenegrins burnt down the remaining houses and the ships laid up in the shipyard. The fires were still raging the following day. Those inhabitants of Gruž who could not get to Dubrovnik had to be saved by the Russians themselves, who took them to the islands. The bishop of Montenegro and his men were also evacuated by a Russian ship, as he and his allies started to engage in bitter mutual recriminations.

Only now, in fact, did the full extent of the damage suffered throughout the territories of the Ragusan Republic become evident. This was later estimated as amounting in total to 8,827,525 ducats. Six hundred and sixty-six houses – almost 10 per cent of all the houses in the Republic – were destroyed. The greatest damage was sustained in Pile, where 134 houses – almost half – were burnt down. Župa Dubrovačka also suffered severely. There 188 houses, or almost a quarter, were burnt. Two hundred and thirty-five houses – a quarter – were destroyed in Konavle.[29] The *Konavljani* had suffered over a longer period than anyone else, because they had already been subject to the marauding and pillaging of their Vlach and Montenegrin neighbours.[30] Some communities lying near the Montenegrin border were utterly devastated. Thus in the village of Vodovađa almost 90 per cent of the homes were burnt. Obod, adjoining Cavtat, was also virtually levelled. The destruction of documents during the Montenegrin incursion and occupation makes it impossible to be precise, but it is likely that between 500 and 600 *Konavljani* were killed.

As the Ragusans returned to their abandoned villas and farm houses, they were confronted with an extraordinary sight. Appendini records the impression:

> The houses were first stripped [by the Montenegrins]. All sorts of linen, kitchen appliances and good quality furnishings were taken away. Doors, windows and all other movable property which contained any pieces of iron were broken up and scattered throughout each floor and in each room and corner of the house. Mattresses were emptied and the straw they contained was spread in different places and put in the middle of the pieces of broken furniture. Thus everything was arranged for the fire, so that it should not

> attack one place only but that all the rest should burn too, as indeed happened. Of the houses that were burnt only the four main walls remained.

Nor did the Montenegrins restrict their attentions to the houses' interiors, as was evident wherever fire had not obscured most traces of their handiwork:

> In every well a ladder was let down in order to find treasure. Any rock or piece of wood in the gardens was moved in search of treasure. Wherever they saw recently disturbed earth they dug for treasure. Altars were destroyed, and at the top of the stairs where the beams rested on the walls they dug and demolished in quest of treasure. In the churches where people were buried they opened the tombs, dug up the bodies and took away any iron. They took down the crucifixes in order to steal the three nails [from Christ's hands and feet].[31]

The Last Days of the Republic

The inhabitants of Dubrovnik had tried to avoid the French entering their city, not least because it was bound to provoke the Russians and their allies. But all that they had since experienced must have convinced them that given a choice, oppressive French rule was better than being abandoned to the anarchic violence of the Russians and Montenegrins. And since that broad preference for orderly relations with the European West rather than disorderly dangers from the Orthodox Slavs of the hinterland had been a central element of much of Dubrovnik's history, the choice of the moment was probably also supported by a deeper instinct.

Another important and more contemporary influence was the presence in Dubrovnik of individuals and groups who were extremely sympathetic to the French for reasons of political orientation. It is difficult to estimate how strong was the influence of these people. Equally, it is unclear whether and when they acted as direct agents for the replacement of the Republic's aristocratic government by French rule. French agents may have overestimated both their numbers and political commitment.

The evidence of the experienced and well-connected Austrian representative, Giuseppi Timoni, during his stay in the city between 1805 and 1809 is probably more reliable. According to Timoni, the core of the movement was the 'Citizen's Club'. It had some 60 members and apparently kept the French well-informed about discussions and intrigues by the Ragusan government. Timoni mentions a wider group of French sympathisers, consisting of twelve patricians, three secular priests, a Dominican, all the Jews and most of the city employees. More broadly, public opinion was affected by the needs and circumstances of the moment, rather than ideological preconceptions. In 1805, when he arrived, Timoni found the people well-off and quite pro-Austrian. As the likelihood increased of a French military occupation of the city there was no evident increase in Francophilia; the main worry was about the consequences for Dubrovnik's shipping from the English fleet if the Republic lost its neutrality. The events of the siege aroused considerable hatred of the Russians and sympathy for the French, whose successes were warmly applauded. But as the end of the Republic approached, Ragusan antipathy to France grew in line with the increasingly onerous demands made upon the populace by the forces of occupation.[32] According to Marmont in his subsequent letter of explanation to Napoleon, this hostility was manifested by shouted insults in the street and even by the firing of shots at French soldiers.[33]

French policy from the time of the despatch of Lauriston with his force was more concerned with practicalities than with form. Napoleon wanted effective control of the whole Dalmatian coastline in order to defeat his enemies, and gaining a grip on Dubrovnik was part of that. It goes without saying that he and his agents had no respect for the institutions of the Ragusan Republic. The French appear to have expected that once the Republic had fallen under their control, the Ragusan patriciate would at some point voluntarily abdicate in their favour – as had happened at Venice in 1797. In this, however, they were to be disappointed.

On 9 June, the Ragusan Senate resolved to complain to France about the sorry state of Dubrovnik as it emerged from the agony of the siege and three days later letters to this effect were sent to Napoleon and to the Viceroy of Italy. On 2 August the latter replied, promising compensation for the damage done during the siege, but making no mention of withdrawal of French troops. Dubrovnik reactivated its diplomacy, re-establishing links with the Austrians, Russians and – increasingly important as the months passed by – the Porte. But clearly the focus for diplomatic activity to preserve the Republic and protect its interests had to be Paris.

Accordingly, after lengthy debates, the Senate on 11 December entrusted its defence to Antun Sorkočević, a sophisticated patrician Francophile and the son of the late composer, already residing in the French capital. (Sorkočević was supported in his endeavours by the Republic's earlier representative, the Ragusan citizen Damjan Bračević.)[34]

Sorkočević was later, we learn from a biased Austrian source, suspected by the other patricians of having betrayed them and the Republic. In 1815 he was described as being of stocky build, about forty years old, well-educated, a bachelor who could have been the greatest man of letters of Dubrovnik were it nor for his laziness. He had a very rich library and spoke perfect Croatian, Latin, Italian and French. He was extremely rich, but in France – where he spent most of the remainder of his life – he built up numerous debts. He lived with his sister, a nun, in deference to whom, the source alleged, he had not become a Freemason. He hated the Austrians 'like all the aristocrats [of Dubrovnik]', having first become Napoleon's mayor of Dubrovnik and later a fierce Republican (that is, a partisan of the Ragusan Republic's restoration).[35]

This account, for all its bile and for all that it was markedly influenced by events after the abolition of the Ragusan state, also inadvertently reveals why Sorkočević was so well-suited to put the Republic's case to the Imperial court in Paris. The Senate was clearly extremely grateful to him for his efforts, and he in turn pressed vigorously the various matters entrusted to him. He eventually managed to obtain audiences with both Talleyrand and Napoleon. But at no point could he get official accreditation as the Republic's ambassador. This fact turned out to be more significant than anything else about his mission, for it meant that the French, for all the outward courtesies, had no intention from at least the date of his appointment at the end of 1806 of respecting the sovereignty of the Ragusan state. That unpleasant truth, which only gradually dawned upon the Ragusan government, was also reflected in time in the words and actions of the agents of France.

The first priority for the French now, however, was that the whole area be cleared of the enemy. On 21 July 1806, Napoleon had written to the Viceroy instructing him to command General Marmont, then in Zadar, to take charge of a mission to occupy Kotor.[36] By the terms of an agreement made between French and Russian representatives in Paris on 20 July, the Russians had agreed to leave, abandoning their Montenegrin allies.[37] The agreement was due to be ratified by the Tsar by 15 August. Marmont arrived in Dubrovnik on 30 July before advancing into Konavle, from where he might swiftly occupy Kotor as the Russian forces withdrew.

But Tsar Alexander refused to ratify the peace terms. The Russians then attacked the positions which Marmont and his men had occupied on Prevlaka (adjoining Kotor), and the French on 26 September were forced to withdraw to Cavtat. Hearing that Russian reinforcements were on their way from Corfu, Marmont decided that the enemy had to be brought to an early engagement. After lengthy manoeuvres under cover of darkness and thick rain between 29

September and 1 October, the French totally defeated the opposing army of Russians, Montenegrins and Orthodox Hercegovinians at Debeli Brijeg. It was a bloody affair: 350 Russians and 400 Montenegrins were killed. Many others were wounded or captured. French losses were twenty-five dead and 130 injured. Marmont then withdrew to Sutorina, while the chastened but not broken Russian forces kept their hold on Kotor. The French were satisfied with the outcome. As Marmont reflected: 'I had attained my goal and shown the barbarian peoples my superiority over the Russians.'[38]

The next few months saw no significant change in the status of Dubrovnik. Marmont and Lauriston demanded loans and levies. For their part, the Ragusan authorities resisted where possible and continued their attempts to ensure that whenever a new general peace was agreed the full freedom of the Republic should be restored. In the meantime, the patricians were doubtless pleased to learn from the Austrian Emperor Francis I, writing on 7 June 1807, that the Republic's 'independence was fundamentally indisputable'. But even were these sentiments sincere, the fate of Dubrovnik did not yet depend on Vienna.[39]

Finally, France and Russia came to terms. On 25 June the French Emperor and the Russian Tsar met and two days later agreed the terms of the Treaty of Tilsit. This, among other things, regulated the French and Russian spheres of influence in Southeast Europe. Russia at last definitively agreed to give up Kotor. Although there was no specific mention of the Ragusan Republic, this omission itself implied that Dubrovnik was regarded as Napoleon's to do with as he pleased. That was certainly how the French understood it, and General Berthier accordingly wrote from Tilsit to General Marmont: 'Dubrovnik will definitively remain united with Dalmatia.' In Dubrovnik itself Lauriston ordered a fireworks display to celebrate news of the peace treaty.

The government of the Republic was not initially worried by the turn of events. When the Senate wrote to Sorkočević on 10 August, it was on the secondary matter of the freezing of its investments in Venice. The patriciate was also at this time fighting a vigorous battle against French exactions. Marmont's grand design of linking all of Dalmatia with a coastal road which would stretch through the territory of the Ragusan Republic involved the forced labour of hundreds of peasants, who showed their objections by absenteeism. The Ragusan patriciate took up their cause, and to General Lauriston's great annoyance demanded that the peasants be properly remunerated. Unlike Lauriston, who seems to have heartily disliked the patrician Republic in which he found himself, Marmont – as he would later demonstrate – had aristocratic pretensions and rather liked Dubrovnik and its people. But he was also sensitive if his dignity was offended, and it is probable that the Senate's obstruction of his ambitious plans to modernise the road network touched a nerve.

On 12 August Marmont arrived in Dubrovnik and received a deputation of Senators. Although there is some confusion about the context, it seems that he told them: '*Vous allez être des nôtres.*' ('You are going to be ours.') The Senators withdrew in consternation, rightly gauging they had just heard a declaration that the Ragusan Republic was about to be incorporated into French Dalmatia. The timing of Marmont's remark had probably been a slip. The following day he explained that he was merely predicting the future. But news of the exchange rapidly spread beyond the confines of the Ragusan Republic and fuelled speculation that was already rife in the Italian press.

Dubrovnik's efforts to apply the influence of the Ottoman Empire in order to preserve its independence also succeeded in provoking French anger. The French ambassador in Constantinople, General Sebastiani, wielded great influence and it was only natural that France should learn about Dubrovnik's dealings. Talleyrand's instructions to Sebastiani were brutally effective:

> If the Sublime Porte expresses its displeasure and reminds you that Dubrovnik is under the sovereignty of the Ottoman Empire, you will reply that those old relationships are at an end, that the annexation of Dubrovnik to the Kingdom of Italy has been a matter of fact for some years [*sic*] and that this new measure does not change the existing order.[40]

The 'measure' of abolishing the Republic was in fact already taking place outside the frontiers of the state. Sebastiani demanded that Kiriko, the Ragusan agent in Constantinople, transfer his office to Sebastiani's control, hand over his archives and order the replacement of the Ragusan flag on Ragusan ships with that of the Kingdom of Italy. Kiriko supinely complied with all this. He was roundly criticised in early November by the Ragusan Senate for doing so. But the pressure was building relentlessly. On the night of 18–19 November in Leghorn, the Ragusan consul took down the Ragusan coat of arms, told Ragusan ship captains to fly the flag of the Kingdom of Italy, and announced that Dubrovnik had been annexed.

In Dubrovnik itself, Marmont did not yet give formal notice of the end of the Republic, but his demands became ever more arbitrary. On 1 October he imposed a levy of 300 sailors to be raised from the Ragusan population to serve on French ships. The Ragusan government protested that this would infringe the state's neutrality. Marmont listened to the protest but demanded that the requirement be met. The Senate tried to put on a brave face. Ever conscious of the importance of symbols, it stressed to Kiriko in Constantinople:

> The government of our Republic has not ceased to carry out its functions and our flag of St Blaise flies daily from its standard in the Public Square.

But others were less convinced. Local tradition has it that when the Ragusan envoy Miho Messi arrived in Paris to inform Antun Sorkočević about the situation of the Republic, Sorkočević remarked: 'The Republic! Hasn't the Devil done away with it?'[41] For all that, he continued to try to influence the French government. Similarly, when Dubrovnik learned that Napoleon was in Italy, the leading patrician Djivo Natali went to Milan at his own expense to try to gain an audience with him. He did manage to see Prince Eugène, and was assured by the (doubtless uninterested) Viceroy that Dubrovnik's position was unchanged.

At the beginning of December, Dubrovnik reverted to its old stratagem of seeking the intervention of the Porte. The patriciate must have known the risks, but it was by now desperate as power ebbed away daily from the Republic. Unfortunately, Karlo Natali's mission stood no chance of success, so completely was the Porte now under Napoleon's and his agent Sebastiani's influence. Natali's complaints about French attempts to take control of Dubrovnik at the expense of the Ottoman Empire made no headway. Nor were Ragusan envoys to the *pasha* of Bosnia and the *aga* of Mostar any more successful. Worse still, everything was relayed to the French. The account sent by the French consul in Bosnia to Marmont who was in Zadar about the (alleged) imprecations of one of the envoys at the expense of France must have been particularly damning.[42]

A further significant step towards the abolition of the Republic was made on 21 December when Lauriston, acting on Marmont's orders, told the Ragusan government that all Ragusan ships henceforth required the patent of the Kingdom of Italy, which meant that they must fly its rather than the Republic's flag. The government refused to accede to this, pleading both the consequences at the hands of English warships and the ancient relationship of Dubrovnik with the Ottoman Empire. Lauriston threatened that if the declaration was not made by the Ragusans then the French would make it themselves. But the Senate still resisted, and eventually on 26 December Lauriston issued the proclamation in French, Italian and Croatian. This was Lauriston's last public act, since he was about to be replaced by General Clauzel. But he had secretly given still more devastating instructions.

The next day Colonel Godart informed the Senate that Lauriston had ordered that the flag of St Blaise should no longer fly on Placa and that the commander of the guard had been told to give effect to this. The Ragusan government protested vigorously in a letter to General Marmont. On 28 December Godart confirmed that he intended to adhere strictly to the letter of Lauriston's order. For some days no flag at all flew over Orlando's Column. Then on 6 January, the tricolour of the Kingdom of Italy was unfurled.

The previous day the Senate, unbowed, again refused the demand for 300 sailors. It sent letters of protest to Clauzel copied to Marmont. It also prepared to send a letter of protest with one of their number, Djivo Kaboga, to Napoleon. But they were out of time. On 24 January Marmont arrived in Dubrovnik and at once forbade Kaboga to leave. The government still continued to function. On 29 January the Senate sent a despatch to Constantinople, hoping to rouse the Porte. But this also was far too late.

Marmont, who had made a brief visit to Kotor, arrived back in Dubrovnik on 31 January. He was by now totally exasperated by the Ragusan patriciate's refusal to follow the course of genteel suicide that the Venetian patriciate had accepted almost ten years earlier. Knowing that in this he was merely anticipating his Emperor's and Talleyrand's long-conceived intentions, Marmont gave the order which the Ragusan patricians dreaded.

At about two o'clock that afternoon Colonel Delort arrived with a company of soldiers at the Rector's Palace. He entered the Senate and read out a prepared speech. It is worth quoting in full, because it reflects in tone and substance the scornful arrogance that characterised the dealings of the new order, represented by Napoleonic France, with the old, represented by the ancient patrician Republic of Ragusa:

> My Lords:
>
> His Excellency the General-in-Chief [Marmont] announced to you six months ago that the lot of your Republic had changed and that the Empire through circumstances provoked by the irrevocable decrees of destiny was going to absorb it into the Kingdom of Italy. He had then the right to appoint on the spot an administration; but he left you all the functions that you had exercised. He did not want to cause you difficulties; he did not want to submit you to the demands of a provisional government, before you were able to enjoy the benefits of a final government. His solicitude for you, for the citizens, for all the inhabitants of Dubrovnik, went further. He knew that in a state where a small number has long enjoyed the authority and the privileges, and the majority had only duties and obligations – he

knew, I say – that in such a state there are passions to be extinguished, many ills to be rectified, many humiliations to be forgotten, many hearts to conquer. Interpreting the paternal feelings of the Emperor Napoleon, he wanted to give you the time to achieve all these objectives.

But, My Lords, you paid more attention to vague noises aroused by madness, perhaps by wickedness, which played upon your credulity, than to the communications which you received. You have suspected traps, where you should only have seen a delicate attention to your interests.

Having recalled the conduct of the General-in-Chief towards you, I will present before your eyes your own conduct.

From the moment when your lot was known, your conduct, which until then had been prudent and passive, became disordered and turbulent. Remember the lists proscribing those whom you thought were adherents of the French system; your intemperate resistance to allowing to be hoisted within your walls the flag of your new sovereign; the public and private threats made against merchant shipping, if it dared to take the colours of the Emperor Napoleon; the almost criminal approaches of the Senate to the *pasha* of Bosnia, approaches which were accompanied in order to give them effect by money and by letters whose expressions, although obscure, were no less evidently injurious to the French nation.

If to these grave wrongs, My Lords, I add that you have sought to excite the fanaticism of the people by means of all that men consider most sacred – religion, ordering processions, the erection of altars, pilgrimages for the salvation of the Republic and of the Rector of the Republic which you knew with complete confidence no longer existed – then you will look into your conscience, My Lords. You will agree that it has gone too far, and that it is time to make an end.

For all these reasons, and also in order to prevent the greatest misfortunes whose consequences would be personally fatal for you, the General-in-Chief orders me to communicate to you this decree.

Delort then proclaimed on behalf of Marmont the end of the Republic:

Article 1: The Government and the Senate of Dubrovnik are dissolved.
Article 2: The civil and criminal tribunals which exist at present are dissolved.
Article 3: M. Bruère, consul of France, will for the moment and provisionally be charged with the administration of the territory.

Article 4: The administrations of the different parts of the States [*sic*] of Dubrovnik will be provisionally as they are today.
Article 5: Civil justice will be administered until new orders by a tribunal composed of Masters Nicolò di Nicolò Pozza, Giacomo Natali, Pietro Stulli, Antonio Chersa, and in the name of His Majesty, the Emperor of the French, King of Italy, but according to the customs of Dubrovnik.

Criminal justice will be administered by the same tribunal, which will co-opt three people with [law] degrees.

It was hardly necessary to add, but Delort did so:

As a result, My Lords, the Republic of Dubrovnik and its government are dissolved and the new administration is installed.

Yet Marmont had a further message that he wanted the Senators to hear, and so Delort, his mouthpiece, continued:

Before you depart, My Lords, I shall leave you a final proof of the interest which the General-in-Chief entertains towards you, by offering you some reflections which when elaborated by your own judgement cannot be other than useful for you.

You are going to live under the laws of a sovereign who knows no rival, whom not even the most ingenious jealousy would dare to compare to another, who positioned between the centuries which have passed and those that are to come will henceforth be, for both past and future generations, the man against whom genius and all manner of glory will be measured. Amid immense states, amid vast ideas, at the most delicate moment in the execution of the most bold and most complex project, his eye passes over all his provinces and rests on each of his subjects. His active solicitude balances their interests and establishes them. As the price of this solicitude, as the price of the happiness he provides for all, he asks for an unfailing but noble loyalty, a boundless but unostentatious devotion.

You have long governed. You will long maintain over individuals the influence which has been given you over the masses by an authority consecrated by the centuries. Use this influence to make them appreciate the benefits of the new government, to bind by heart and by sentiment all people to your new sovereign. Finally, My Lords, be yourselves good, loyal and faithful subjects of his Majesty the Emperor and King Napoleon, and

> henceforth as members of a great and glorious family you will have as equals and as leaders only those whom their high destiny has born for it.[43]

At the end of this rodomontade there was a period of silence. Then Djivo Kaboga, so recently empowered to put Dubrovnik's case to the Emperor-King whose decision the Senators now knew, stood up. He spoke briefly. This, he said, was not the time or place for justifications; his conscience was clear; and he could answer for the loyalty of his colleagues. The Senate would obey the will of God manifested by the will of the Emperor. Kaboga asked for a written copy of the speech and the decree, but there was none at present available. The Senators waited and eventually received the decree, but not the text of the speech. Soldiers then entered and took control of all the offices of the Republic, locking the doors and placing seals upon them. The Senators left quietly.

Marmont duly won, on 18 February, Napoleon's full approval for his action. On 1 March he was rewarded with the title *Duc de Raguse*.[44]

Ragusan Shadows: Episodes and Themes From the Later History of Dubrovnik

I. The Attempted Restoration of the Republic (1808–1815)

French Rule

There is no evidence to suggest that the French were initially concerned about the risk of a movement aimed at the restoration of the Ragusan Republic. For his part, Marmont seems genuinely to have fallen in love with the Dubrovnik he encountered. In his *Memoirs* he reflected fondly on 'that little country [*petit pays,* i.e. Ragusa] which enjoyed the greatest happiness, whose inhabitants are of such sweet disposition, are so industrious and intelligent – an oasis of civilisation amid barbarism'.[1] As *Duc de Raguse*, he in any case was keen to make something of his new title, and to this end he endeavoured with considerable success to ingratiate himself with the population. Many in Dubrovnik soon looked to Marmont as a powerful patron and protector. The city celebrated his arrival from Dalmatia with a special performance by the Dubrovnik literary academy organised by the Piarist fathers. On 24 May he, in turn, held a splendid ball for more than 300 guests.

Marmont also sought to establish himself as a promoter of local culture and showed some flair in doing so. Thus he became patron of the *lycée* which was set up in the old monastery of St Catherine, where Appendini – formerly head of the Ragusan *collegium* – became Rector. The school catered for boys from Dubrovnik and Kotor and, unlike at its equivalent in Zadar, at least some of the teaching was in Croatian. Marmont played an important role in the publication of Appendini's Croatian grammar (*Gramatica della lingua illirica*), and he supported the publication of the third and most important part of Joakim

Stulli's Croatian-Latin-Italian dictionary. (Both these scholarly initiatives would play a significant part in later linguistic and national developments.) In response to popular tastes, Marmont also established a new theatre in the hall of the old Ragusan Great Council. This doubtless annoyed some of the nobility, but it also provided extra entertainment for the citizens: since notices recording the great Emperor's military triumphs were also posted there, the place served a useful propagandist function as well.[2]

The achievements of the French administration in Dalmatia have been highly praised.[3] Dubrovnik was fortunate enough to have an extremely able civil administrator appointed to it in the form of Giovanni Domenico Garagnin, who also enjoyed Marmont's complete trust.[4] The administration of the city was now divided from that of the rest of the region – which now included Boka Kotorska and Korčula. New administrative and judicial structures were created, though most of the old laws applied. Special commissions were set up. The collection of statistics proceeded apace. Under the French the first state elementary schools were founded – in Dubrovnik, Cavtat, Ston and Orebići. The prosperous Jewish community was finally permitted to enjoy all the benefits enjoyed by Christians as citizens, property owners and traders. The Orthodox were similarly treated as equals in all respects with Catholics. An Orthodox church functioned at Posat, just outside the city walls. The secularisation of large amounts of Catholic church property, especially that belonging to the now-abolished women's orders, the introduction of civil marriages and the prohibition (allegedly for health reasons) of entombments within churches more or less completed the rearrangement of old Ragusa's affairs in the light of French ideas of liberal modernisation.[5]

The Strains of War

It is an ultimately unanswerable question whether the new order could have won and kept the loyalties of the local inhabitants if it had not been for the impact of war. But in one sense, of course, the hypothesis is flawed: it was for military reasons, after all, that Napoleon and his agents had determined on taking control of Dubrovnik in the first place. Correspondingly, among the arguments most frequently advanced by the representatives of the Ragusan Republic for the French government to respect its sovereignty was that the consequences of failing to do so would be economically devastating. The old Ragusans were quickly proved right: rarely can the wealth of a city have been so rapidly destroyed as that of Dubrovnik in the years that followed French occupation.

France had no ability to defend its subjects by sea. So once Dubrovnik's claim to neutrality was undone, its maritime commerce was hopelessly vulnerable to British and Russian depredations. During the years of French rule, the contraction of Dubrovnik's merchant fleet was catastrophic – from 277 ships at the start of that period to a total of forty-nine, of which eleven were laid up, at the end of it. Of the rest, thirty-eight previously Ragusan vessels henceforth sailed under different flags – twenty-three under the English, twelve under the Russian and three under the French.[6] This was, of course, a huge blow to all classes in Dubrovnik. Whatever satisfaction citizens, craftsmen, labourers, Jews and the scattering of Orthodox in and around the city may have felt as a result of the political changes which the French regime wrought, these can hardly have compensated for the enormous economic dislocation. That dislocation was also exacerbated by the raising of burdensome compulsory or semi-compulsory loans, which generally went un-repaid.

The French were bound to be blamed for the resulting hardship. Nor in all probability can it have helped their administrative experiment that the control exercised by a distant administration became tighter – with the creation in 1809 of the 'Illyrian provinces' – just as the real military situation was about to worsen dramatically. From early 1810, the problems resulting from the British blockade became more intense. Garagnin was forced to control the price of basic victuals. He sought money from Paris for the major public works to which the French government had committed him, but he received nothing. So in June 1810 new taxes were imposed. A land tax and a poll tax produced great discontent when they began to be collected the following year. A house tax was then imposed within the city. Typical of the way in which rhetoric and reality had grown altogether out of kilter was the proclamation by the French authorities of Dubrovnik as a free port – when almost all legitimate trade in and out of it was impossible.[7]

At the same time, the growth of illegitimate trade – smuggling – undermined French control still further. The island of Vis was seized by the British fleet, and by 1810 it had become all but impossible for the French authorities to prevent the seafaring population of coastal Dalmatia from slipping away to Vis in search of luxuries such as coffee, tea, cutlery, tableware and even Havana cigars.[8]

The French, from Napoleon downwards, seem on the whole to have been quite sympathetic to the inhabitants of Dubrovnik – a view which may have been accentuated by growing experience of the peoples of the Balkan hinterland and their Russian backers. In 1811, the Emperor in a 'Note on Ragusa' addressed to General Clarke stressed that the inhabitants of Dubrovnik 'must be befriended even before we think of what advantage we can gain from them'.[9] But it was still the military significance of the place that mattered most. Thus major works were begun to construct fortifications on Mount Srđ (Fort Impérial), Nuncijata, Žarkovica (Fort Delgorgue) and the islands of Daksa and Lokrum (Fort Royal). The greatest of these was the first. The Fort Impérial, perched where the little church of St Sergius had once stood, was completed in 1812, and from it that October the roar of cannons first thundered over the city to celebrate Napoleon's entry into Moscow.

All the heavy work was done by local conscript labour. Peasants were brought in from the countryside; stone was obtained and shipped – when possible – from the famous quarries of Korčula. The population of Dalmatia was also forced to work on the great Napoleonic road – today's *Jadranska magistrala* – that still constitutes the main artery between the Dalmatian coastal towns. Years later, Marmont would boast:

> These works gained me great popularity... The Dalmatians said and reported, in their language full of images: 'The Austrians for eight years have made and discussed plans of routes instead of executing them: Marmont mounted his horse to see they were carried out, and when he got down again they were finished.'[10]

But he seems to have been guilty of a large amount of wishful thinking, certainly in assessing Ragusan reactions. The section approaching Dubrovnik only began to be constructed in 1811, when French control was already slipping. The peasants of Pelješac, Primorje and Korčula were repeatedly drafted, and repeatedly fled the work. Finally, in April 1812 the French *indentant* issued a general order of conscription for public works which brought the discontent to a climax. And all the while, the military conscription of the peasantry, which had provoked the last quarrel between the old patrician government and the French, bore ever harder on the population.

It might have been expected that the Catholic priesthood would have constituted an important element of the growing resistance to French rule. Perhaps in private it did. But publicly at least, the church in Dubrovnik was generally prepared to collaborate. The archbishop, the aged Nikola Ban, became overnight an enthusiastic, indeed grovelling, supporter of French control and the cult of the Emperor Napoleon. On 8 October 1810 when the clergy of Dubrovnik were ordered to take an oath of loyalty, only sixteen out of 69 refused, and a majority of those changed their minds when unpleasant consequences threatened. A (probably small) number of clergy were also committed adherents of French Revolutionary ideology. In any case, the blows inflicted against the church by the French – confiscation of property, abolition of the women's orders, dissolution of the ancient Raguan fraternities including the *Antunini* and *Lazarini* and the fraternity of St Peter which supported poor priests – all left the clergy's power and self-confidence temporarily shattered.[11]

Yet religion did eventually combine with social, economic and political elements to fan the flames of resentment which the French in the last two years of their rule in Dubrovnik managed to kindle. The one-time liberators were now seen as plunderers and oppressors; the reformers had dismantled not just the old inequalities but also the traditional limits and safeguards. This painful disillusionment inspired bitterness and nostalgia for the old order among, for example, people like the poet Đuro Hidža, who wrote:

> It's more than seven years
> That the state of Dubrovnik
> Has groaned under the yoke of the French robbers.
> They broke down churches and altars.
> They destroyed all our laws.
> They cast our bones from our family graves,
> And they sold our ancient saints.
> They drove out all the peasants by force,
> Hungry, poor, barefoot and languishing,
> To build level roads across the karst
> So as to take away their plunder more easily.[12]

The leadership of any anti-French movement was bound to fall to what remained of the old Ragusan patriciate. But the Ragusan nobility no longer had the resources necessary to retake power on their own. The wealth of the patricians like that of the more prominent citizens had been decimated by the collapse in maritime trade. The nobility still had its estates, of course, and the French regime resisted demands to overthrow the rights of landlords in the name of abolishing 'serfdom'. But the peasantry became increasingly recalcitrant and levying rents and labour thus became accordingly more difficult. Probably most serious were the effects of a French decree of 1811 which abolished the institution of the family trust. The latter had for centuries been used as a device to entail upon the oldest male heir succession to the family inheritance. In the dire financial circumstances faced by patricians at this time, the abolition of these trusts allowed rapid wholesale alienation of lands until the Austrians, in a measure designed to appease the Dubrovnik nobility, revoked the measure in 1817. Moreover, alongside, the diminution in patrician wealth went rapid demographic decline – the result of emigration, loss of nobility through marriage, poverty leading to lack of heirs, and perhaps some deeper understanding that the rationale of the old governing class had been lost.[13]

The Revolt

Dubrovnik's revolt against the French could never have succeeded – indeed it could hardly have occurred – without external assistance. Similarly, its fate and that of the broader attempt to restore the Republic were eventually determined by outside forces.

From early 1812, Dalmatian Croat soldiers serving under the French flag were deserting in increasing numbers, and most French troops were withdrawn from Dubrovnik altogether at the end of that year. In February 1813 the British occupied Pelješac and the neighbouring islands. Finally, on 18 June they seized Šipan and made Jero Natali its governor in the name of the old Republic. Later Koločep, Lopud and Mljet were also placed under Natali's administration. The flag of St Blaise would fly over these islands from 1813 until the summer of 1815, and other nobles hostile to the French – and later the Austrians – rallied around it. Natali was much more than a mere British appointee. He exercised real control over the Elaphites and lobbied hard with his British contacts, to whom he provided much useful information, for the restoration of the Republic. Jero Natali's brothers, Djivo and Karlo, remained in Dubrovnik for a time plotting. They were eventually arrested, then released, and fled to Šipan.

Among the other noble insurgents, the Bunić family was also prominent. From the end of 1811 Miho Bunić was permanently resident in Vienna waiting for an opportunity to put the case for the restoration of the Republic at the peace conference which would follow Napoleon's final defeat – whenever that occurred. Miho's sons, Pjerko and Frano, were both actively involved in advancing the same cause at home. Frano Bunić, acting in concert with the British, worked on the resentments of the peasants of Konavle. The (false) rumour that the Montenegrins were approaching, supplemented by the provision of a liberal supply of strong drink, sufficed to encourage the peasants to take up arms, and these were then turned against the French. The advancing *Konavljani* were later joined by the peasants of Župa Dubrovačka, and so the substantial but undisciplined force moved gradually toward Dubrovnik.

The other leader of the Dubrovnik rebels, Vlaho Kaboga, has gone down in local tradition as a young egotist who betrayed the Republic. This may be justified, but he also retrospectively served as a useful scapegoat – for the truth is that nothing that Kaboga or his colleagues did could alter Dubrovnik's destiny, once the British and Austrian governments had decided upon it.

When the British seized Cavtat they appointed Vlaho Kaboga its provisional governor. Captain William Hoste, the local commander, though he emphasised that he had no instructions about the matter of the future of the Republic, said that he was prepared to recognise and salute the flag of St Blaise. This was accordingly raised amid loud applause and volleys of rifle fire. Kaboga then took up residence in Gruž, in the villa belonging to Antun Sorkočević. With the encouragement of his British sponsor, Captain Lowen, Kaboga now grandiloquently titled himself 'Governor General of the Land Forces of the Republic'. His headquarters were the target of a fierce French assault which was, however, beaten back.

On 18 January 1814 a meeting of the nobility was held in a villa at Mokošica to establish what should now be done. The Natali and Bunić families and their supporters were keen to press ahead directly with proclaiming the Republic. But a larger group headed by Kaboga, and enjoying the crucial backing of the British, were unwilling to press the issue at this stage. (Kaboga was perhaps also already working with the Austrians.) Instead, the meeting made a number of resolutions. Miho Bunić in Vienna was thus entrusted with the mission of seeking from the victorious allies restoration of the Republic. Vlaho Kaboga was to continue as Governor General. That faithful Ragusan, Miho Božović in Constantinople, was urged to occupy himself with the Porte. The following day a specially appointed commission visited the local Austrian commander, General Milutinović, to tell him – perhaps a little naively – of the nobility's decisions.[14]

In any case, events were overtaking them. The siege was pressed on land by the lightly armed peasant troops under the command of Kaboga and other patricians, and from the sea by the British who, however, had no intention of allowing their cannons to be used by their 'allies'. After further heavy bombardment, General Montrichard agreed on 27 January to go to Gruž to agree the city's capitulation. In his absence and without knowing of his mission, insurgents within the city disarmed the French guards, disabled their artillery and, amid great rejoicing, hoisted the flag of St Blaise to its proper place above Orlando's Column. This symbolic support for the Republic was probably not in any case shared by the mayor and the governing elite. It is also likely that even middle-class Republican enthusiasts would have been reluctant to open the gates to the unruly local insurgents at the Ploče Gate under the command of Djivo Natali who were now loudly demanding entry. So, instead, the city authorities waited until the Austrians and British approached and then gave them entry instead, while Vlaho Kaboga dismissed the rebel army – thus removing the last weapon that might possibly have been used to try to restore the Republic.

For two more days the flag of St Blaise flew over Placa. But on 29 January General Milutinović ordered that it be taken down. The mayor refused, saying that he lacked the authority since it had been raised by the people. So the next day the Austrian General ordered one of his soldiers to carry out the task. Henceforth the Austrian and British flags, and later just the Austrian flag, flew on Placa.

This was not, however, quite the end of the attempts to restore the Republic. The hard core of the nobility would not yield easily. Miho Bunić tried to fulfil his diplomatic mission in Vienna. But it was hopeless. He was unable to gain contact with Prince Metternich, who was in Paris, and had to address his observations to his assistant Josip von Hudelist.[15] But Metternich had already on 23 November 1813 written to Hudelist, telling him not to worry about Dubrovnik because the British had promised during talks in Saxony that they would not support the demands of the Ragusan insurgents. And this was no more than the truth. Whatever sympathy local British commanders felt for the demands of their Ragusan allies, London had firmly decided to support Vienna. Consequently, Miho Bunić's mission was a pathetic failure. Eventually, he was expelled by the police from the Austrian capital as an undesirable and, after issuing a protestation at Trieste, sadly returned to Dubrovnik.

As events now demonstrated, most of the nobility in Dubrovnik did not, however, initially accept Austrian rule. The government demanded that a delegation from Dalmatia, including representatives from Dubrovnik, should pledge loyalty to the Emperor in Vienna. The Austrian governor, General Tomašević, ordered the new intendant – none other than Vlaho Kaboga – to instruct the mayor of Dubrovnik and his fellow councillors to deal with the matter. Although a majority of the council was prepared to comply, one of the patricians present, Niko Pucić-Sorkočević, mounted a determined resistance. And when this failed, he fled to Šipan. At the session of the council held on 1 September 1814, his protest was read out. Still more significant was the arrival of another memorandum of protest signed by forty-nine nobles which recalled the circumstances of the previous meeting of the 'Great Council' of January and emphasised the temporary character of Austrian rule.

On hearing what had happened, a furious General Milutinović hurried back from Kotor and ordered severe measures to be taken against the signatories. They were ordered to be exiled and their property was confiscated. Eighteen fled to Šipan; the rest were forced to submit. Meanwhile, the Austrians organised a loyalist counter-protest signed by 100 citizens of Dubrovnik. Satisfied with the results of his measures, in mid-December Milutinović withdrew the penalties.

The only territory that now remained under the authority of the old Republic was the Elaphite Islands, where Jero Natali, surrounded by a number of recalcitrants, remained in control thanks to the British. But Austria could not allow this alternative focus of loyalty to survive for long. Vienna repeatedly pressed London to have the islands handed over to its representatives. Eventually, the British Foreign Minister, Lord Castlereagh, agreed to comply with Metternich's request.[16] On 30 June 1815 the British thus instructed Jero Natali to hand over the islands, and he did so on 13 July. For the last time the flag of St Blaise was lowered. The corpse of the Republic had given its last noticeable twitch.[17]

II. Stagnation and Enforced Amnesia Under Austrian Rule (1814–1918)

Economic Decline

Seen through the spectacles of South Slav nationalism, Austrian rule over Dalmatia had little to be said for it. Its great merit lay in fact in what it prevented and what came later, namely ideological strife and violent disorder, and this benefit was only appreciated in retrospect. Dubrovnik, which unlike the other cities of the Dalmatian coast had enjoyed a long history of both political independence and economic prosperity, was doubly ill-served within the Habsburg Empire, for it now enjoyed neither.

The territories of the old Ragusan Republic were joined with Korčula to become a subordinate administrative unit (*Circolo, Kreis, Okrug* consisting of six *Preture*) within Austrian Dalmatia – itself an autonomous region, governed for most of the time by military personnel. The Dalmatian seat of government was Zadar and the official language was Italian. Along with Zadar and Split, Dubrovnik was still one of three main cities of the region. Within the *Circolo di Ragusa* Dubrovnik enjoyed the status of being an administrative centre. But it lost its political significance and it had also, of course, lost through the destruction of its maritime fleet its main source of wealth.

The first quarter-century was, in any case, a time of depression in the region as a whole, and its immediate consequences were worsened by a sharp population growth. In the 1840s, however, there began something of a revival of agriculture, particularly the production of wine and oil. Dubrovnik was at the forefront of this.

From the 1850s and 1860s there was also a revival of shipping and shipbuilding in the Dubrovnik area which continued into the late 1870s. The captains of Pelješac were among the most prominent beneficiaries. But hopes were eventually unfulfilled. The increase in competition from steam and the fact that the maritime investors of Dubrovnik had committed so much of their limited capital to the construction of large sailing vessels squeezed the new maritime prosperity. By the late 1860s Austrian Lloyd, based in Trieste, enjoying state subsidies and privileges, was overwhelmingly dominant in steam. The first long-haul Dubrovnik steamship only sailed in 1891.

The Austrians throughout pursued a crude mercantilist policy which offered little opportunity for less influential or less capitalised enterprises and locations. They were intent on developing Trieste and Rijeka as the Empire's main ports and gave them free-port status. Dubrovnik's requests for such status were refused, and so much potential trade bypassed the city. Even after the Austrian annexation of Bosnia-Hercegovina in 1878, which many in Dubrovnik hoped would re-establish that ancient and vital link with the Balkan hinterland to the city's advantage, the flow of goods was still largely directed to Rijeka.

Communications were another problem. Both Trieste (from 1857) and Rijeka (from 1873) had good rail links with the markets of Central Europe; by contrast, Dubrovnik did not until 1901 even gain a rail link via Gruž to the hinterland.[18] As for roads, the Napoleonic *magistrala* was finally extended all the way to Dubrovnik under the Austrians; but it later fell into some disrepair. The sea route was always cheaper and quicker.

Austrian rule thus became associated with economic stagnation. In fact, the main contribution which the Austrians made to Dubrovnik's economic prospects was probably their shrewd instinct for a good health- and holiday-resort. The magnificent and luxurious Hotel Imperial was opened in Pile in 1897 with capital found by Austrian Lloyd, by a group of society doctors, and by numerous individual *Dubrovčani* shareholders.[19]

The Austrians also became associated with burdensome taxation. This was not so initially. In order to win over local opinion, and in recognition of the dire legacy of French rule, the Austrians remitted the house tax and exempted Dubrovnik from the tithe (which applied in regions previously ruled by Venice). There was no conscription on the population of Dubrovnik until 1880. But taxes were increased again well before then. The year 1840 saw the reintroduction of the house tax, and in 1841 the introduction of the tithe, which was later increased and paid as an annual lump sum. In 1844 dues on crafts were levied, and four years later increased. These were particularly damaging to Dubrovnik's domestic economy.[20]

Memories and Monuments

Vienna and its representatives viewed Dubrovnik without much sympathetic imagination. They were not rootedly hostile, just cautious and otherwise occupied, and they did not intend to invest much time or money in the place. One should not, though, fall into the trap of echoing the sometimes exaggerated criticisms of the regime that were subsequently nourished by Yugoslav propaganda. For example, the work of Lorenzo Vitelleschi in Dubrovnik as state civil engineer and architect between 1816 and 1831 was both conscientious and effective. He had not only to deal with the damage caused by the French and the Montenegrins but also with the consequences of repeated earthquakes.

Vitelleschi's attitudes conveyed by the commentary to his beautifully illustrated *Notizie storiche e statistiche del Circolo di Ragusa* (1827) probably reflected those of the more enlightened elements of the Habsburg administration. He appreciated the scenery and, in particular, liked visiting the islands. But he had a low view of the abilities of many of the inhabitants and, as a relentless moderniser, he had little time for the legacy of the old Republic. He thought, for example, that the peasants of Konavle grossly mismanaged the water supply, so failing to take advantage of the opportunities for cultivation. Similarly, he considered that the salt pans of Ston needed completely re-modelling, even concluding that all those centuries earlier they had, in fact, been constructed in the wrong place. Modern hydraulic engineering, though, could help solve both problems.[21]

The Austrian authorities were in their own terms generally benevolent. But equally, having experienced numerous irritations and inconveniences in trying to wrest the territory from the Ragusan insurgents, they were determined to repress any hankerings after the Republic. Thus if the occasion presented itself to extinguish an evocative symbol of the Ragusan past, it was not to be missed.

So when Orlando's Column was blown down in a storm in 1825 it was not re-erected for over 50 years. In 1830 the ancient medieval baptistry by the side of the cathedral was blown up by the army.[22] Soon afterwards, the old Dubrovnik cannons and some of the medieval church bells were melted down. In 1853 the medieval Fishmarket Tower was demolished. In 1864 the same fate befell the old City Hall (earlier Council Chambers). Part of the Arsenal was demolished and the rest turned into an army bakery. The fortress of St John was transformed into a barracks. Meanwhile, most of the Dubrovnik archives were taken to Vienna, only to return to the city after the First World War.

The Austrians, Catholic as their sympathies might be, continued the ban introduced by the French on public celebration of the Feast of St Blaise. When they later allowed it again in 1836, the procession was held with a large police presence. More generally, the Austrian authorities had decided as early as 1815, during the Congress of Vienna, that for financial and political reasons they intended to reduce the number of Dalmatian archbishoprics and bishoprics. The Dubrovnik archbishopric was one of those to be abolished. After several years of relentless pressure, the pope agreed with the plans. The old Ragusan government had taken so much administrative and financial responsibility for the church that the end of the Republic had, in any case, left the archdiocese with insufficient funds. Moreover, the behaviour of the last Ragusan archbishopric in so openly collaborating with the atheistic French had probably diminished the enthusiasm of the rest of the clergy to defend the institution. So there was no public opposition when the archbishopric of Dubrovnik was first left vacant for fifteen years and then reduced to a bishopric. The see of Ston – originally suppressed by the French in 1807 – was also now formally abolished with papal approval. In such ways the institutional landscape of old Ragusa was incrementally but also fundamentally changed.[23]

On 24 May 1818, the Emperor Francis I, visiting Dalmatia, arrived in Dubrovnik where he stayed until 1 June. Local tradition has it that, in contrast to the efforts made by the municipality to flatter their distinguished guest – including the erection of an improvised triumphal arch on Pile – Niko Pucić greeted the Emperor in the name of the nobility with a certain coldness, emphasising that it was not 'fear or hope, but loyalty and upbringing' which brought them before their sovereign. For his part, the Emperor, as his diary reveals, was certainly a great deal more interested in Dubrovnik's military value than its historic past.[24]

In actual fact, Austrian officials were more skilful in dealing with Dubrovnik's past and the patricians who embodied and championed it than the stolid reflections of the Emperor would suggest. Sticks and carrots were both employed. Members of the old Ragusan nobility, often desperately in need of money, looked successfully to the authorities to provide them with pensions, offices and military commands. Deprived of their position as hereditary rulers of the aristocratic Republic, most of the Dubrovnik patrician families also petitioned successfully to have their noble status recognised by the Austrian heraldic commission in Zadar.

Those nobles who did not avail themselves of such benefits were regarded by the authorities with suspicion and subjected to close surveillance. Within the city, Fra Inocent Čulić acted as chief informer. His reports must generally have been reassuring. The population, he said, 'do not like Austria'. But they were no threat. The nobles he considered 'lacking in intellect and in land', and he characterised the *Dubrovčani* as a whole as 'ignorant and poor, but peaceful'.

Police surveillance also extended to those few irreconcilables who continued to plot the restoration of the Republic. The most eccentric and courageous of these was Vito Bettera – of a distinguished citizen family under the Republic, and whose cousin Baro would become a servant of the Austrian state. In 1816, having fled to England, Vito Bettera published his first pamphlet attacking the Habsburgs. While in London, his actions were the subject of detailed reports by the Austrian ambassador and of requests for his expulsion by the Austrian government. He left for the Continent two years later. In 1824 he was arrested in Amsterdam and sent off to Vienna, where he spent six years in prison awaiting trial. He was then banished to Ukraine, imprisoned again, and died there in 1841. By now, in any case, most of the other prominent pro-Ragusan exiles were also dead. Only Antun Sorkočević lived on until 1840 in Paris, his enthusiasm for the old order – whose last representative he had been – steadily increasing as the years went by and as the practical possibilities of restoring it faded.

It was not just the exiles but also the nobility who stayed behind in Dubrovnik who were now dying out. Although the last trace of the nobility's traditional rights as landlords to the 'service' of their peasants was only extinguished in 1876, the nobles' wealth and numbers had already declined catastrophically before that date. From the time of the French occupation to the 1830s, six noble families died out altogether.[25] And the process continued.

Yet some sense of their past gave the offspring of the old patrician families, and even the non-patrician familes, of Dubrovnik a mysterious and occasionally irritating sense of their own worth. As one Austrian travel writer noted in 1850:

> ... [T]oday, more than thirty years after their fall and impoverishment, we see how these nobles prance along like horses, convinced that they possess a high and inherited culture which is the gift of their families... Even the little people and the craftsmen live in the conviction that they are something greater and special, because they are *Dubrovčani*.[26]

Their fellow countrymen sometimes say the same today. Amnesia, for all Austrian and later efforts, has clearly been less than complete.

III. Issues of Identity – Dubrovnik and the Croatian and Serbian National Movements (c. 1830–c. 1890)

The 1830s and 1840s saw a ferment of ideas, debate and polemic about national identity in the Slavic Balkans, whose echoes are still evident. Dubrovnik played a unique and distinctive, if necessarily secondary, role in these intellectual movements, one which was in large measure based upon the legacy of Ragusan Republic.

Although Croatian and Serbian thinkers differed about nearly everything else, they shared at this time the prevailing – partially false and certainly simplistic – view that language was the essential and determining element in national identity. Because not all those who considered themselves Croats or Serbs spoke the same dialect, and because the frontiers between dialects did not coincide with national consciousness, scholars of linguistics were under powerful pressures to reach politically useful conclusions. This work was not merely analytical, it was also normative. Those involved sought to prove that people who considered themselves Serbs or Croats were 'really', because of their speech, something else; and at the same time they strove to achieve the maximum linguistic uniformity among the groups which they intended to integrate or assimilate. Naturally enough it was the written, not spoken, language which was crucial as an expression of public identity. Consequently, orthography was more important than pronunciation, and what would appear to anyone outside the region – and some within it – to be an inordinate amount of time and energy was spent then and since on details of spelling.

In these matters, Dubrovnik's traditional outlook was both more practical and at a certain level more sophisticated. The great Ragusan writers used a subtly changing mixture of čakavian and štokavian dialects, with the latter in its ijekavian form finally predominating.[27] This poetic willingness to adapt and absorb had its counterpart in the fact that Ragusan writers were often strongly conscious of their links with the wider Slavic world. They felt, as has been noted, particularly close ties with other Dalmatians. They sometimes described the language they wrote as Croatian – never Serbian – but they were as likely to call it Slavic or Illyrian. Yet there is no point in trying to read into these expressions later, anachronistic concepts of nationality. The focus of the Dubrovnik writers' patriotism and the core of their identity was, in short, Dubrovnik.

For Ragusans, the determining ideology of their state was not linguistic but religious. The Republic's identity, underlying the institutional framework of the Republic, was Roman Catholic. Until its last days this conviction was manifested in what today seems a pettifogging and imprudent determination to keep the Orthodox population and their priests down and if possible out. Nothing, except perhaps its own survival, seemed more important to the Republic's ruling class, and there is no evidence that outside the group of Francophile liberals this perception would have been challenged.

This fact explains the otherwise somewhat baffling paradox of Dubrovnik's role in the nineteenth century nationalist movements. On the one hand, Dubrovnik's literary legacy and the linguistic structures built by the reformers upon it placed the city at the very heart of the attempt to develop and express an 'Illyrian' – in practice a Croatian – identity. On the other hand, although some *Dubrovčani* played a part in that enterprise, and although as the years went by more and more of them shared the patriotic desire for Croatian unification, there was also a distinctive, recurring ambiguity about 'national' identity – even to the extent of the promotion by some intellectuals of a 'Serbo-Catholic' identity.

The reasons why Ljudevit Gaj (1809–1872) and the Illyrian Movement (1835–1858) decided that the Dubrovnik ijekavian štokavian dialect was the only possible basis for a Croatian literary language, which the Illyrians hoped would also embrace the Serbs and other South Slavs, have already been mentioned.[28] It was not a very difficult decision, considering that (in the words of Ivo Banac): 'By the turn of the eighteenth century, in the twilight of Ragusan independence, Dubrovnik's Baroque classics were the rage of Zagreb.'[29] Gaj and his Zagreb friends, though Kajkavians, were therefore deeply aware of the importance of the Ragusan literary heritage. Some opponents accused them of 'dancing after Dubrovnik'.[30] And it is true that Gaj was entranced with the city – which he had described many years earlier as the 'Illyrian Parnassus' – when he visited it for twenty-five days in the company of the poet Ivan Mažuranić in 1841. The printing in Zagreb in 1844 of Ivan Gundulić's *Osman*, with Mažuranić contributing the missing cantos, caused a sensation which extended far beyond intellectual circles.

Gundulić became, as it were, the secular patron saint of the whole Illyrian movement. The veneration accorded his memory was boundless. In the course of fifteen years his verses were used on no fewer than 83 occasions in the changing motto on the masthead of Gaj's weekly literary journal *Danica* (*Morning Star*).[31]

Moreover, in Dubrovnik itself there was great enthusiasm now as in the past for the Croatian language. Stulli's and Appendini's volumes testified uncontestably to that.[32] The sentiment was expressed pithily in verse by Antun Kaznačić (1784–1874), one of Gaj's collaborators in Dubrovnik:

Rodni jezik ko ne ljubi
Narodnosti pravo gubi.

Whoever does not love his language
Loses the right to nationhood.[33]

The older generation of Dubrovnik writers were, it is true, less enamoured of the Illyrians' attempts to create a common orthography based on the use of diacritic signs – as, for example, in Czech.[34] But the younger Dubrovnik *literati* later embraced the full package of Illyrian reforms and goals. Indeed, *Dubrovčani* came to provide more collaborators with Gaj than their other Dalmatian equivalents.

While the Illyrian Movement flourished, the underlying tensions and contradictions in Dubrovnik as elsewhere went largely unnoticed. From the years 1848 and 1849, all this changed. These two years saw the overthrow of the old Austrian Absolutism and the departure of Prince Metternich, its essential genius. They saw the upsurge in demands for the unification of Dalmatia with the banate of Croatia (enthusiasm for which Dubrovnik fully shared). They saw the appointment of the popular Colonel Josip Jelačić (1801–1859) as *Ban* of Croatia and his emergence at the head of Croat armies in the role of saviour of the Habsburgs from Hungary's rebellion. And finally, they saw the betrayal of hopes for equal treatment of the Slavs in general and the Croats in particular within the Empire with the return of a new Absolutism.[35]

Illyrianism had always in one sense been based on an illusion, one that would recur repeatedly in different times and forms in Yugoslavia. This was that the search for unity among the South Slavs, as a whole, was ultimately compatible with the aspirations and ambitions of the Serb nation. From before 1836, when Ljudevit Gaj published the seminal article in *Danica* that can be said to have launched the Illyrianist programme, another brilliant linguist with his own programme – the Serb Vuk Stefanović Karadžić (1787–1864) – had been pointing in a quite different direction.

Karadžić had indeed spent five months in Dubrovnik in 1834–1835. Like Gaj, he too settled on the form of speech he found there as the norm. But this was not in deference to Dubrovnik but rather because the same variant was spoken in eastern (ethnically Serb) Hercegovina and because it was Karadžić's radical aim to establish a new simplified language, alphabet and orthography based on popular rather than traditional church Slavic which would then serve as the Serbs' national language.[36] For Karadžić, as for later propagandists, the fact that Dubrovnik and Kotor were the only non-Orthodox regions where the ijekavian variant of štokavian was traditionally spoken provided a useful proof that the *Dubrovčani* were 'really' Serbs. Actually, Karadžić and his successors were prepared to go much further in their assimilationist expansionism. The view, with its all-too-recognisable overtones, that most of the South Slavs were mistaken about their 'true' identity was summarised in the slogan: *Srbi svi i svuda* ('Serbs, all and everywhere').[37]

The breakdown of Illyrianism, the fracturing of the South Slav national movement and the increased influence of Serb nationalism and of Serbia proper – all had an especially disorientating impact in Dubrovnik. Vuk Karadžić's attempt to achieve a linguistic rather than religious basis for Serb identity was strongly contested in Serbia by the Serbian Orthodox Church. But the thesis provided an excellent opportunity to dislodge Dubrovnik from the rest of Croatia, because it meant that the irredeemably Catholic *Dubrovčani* might still be persuaded to adopt a Serbian identity. The 'Serb-Catholic' circle in Dubrovnik composed a variety of very different individuals and interests. The Serbian Orthodox priest in Dubrovnik, Đurde Nikolajević (1807–1896) was a particularly powerful influence. Nikolajević was the first important proponent of the argument, subsequently repeated with varying degrees of sophistication into modern times, that Ragusan literary culture was Serbian. A spurious but impressive demonstration of the 'Serbian-ness' (*Srpstvo*) of Dubrovnik was also provided by the publication, at his instigation, of 'Serbian Documents' (*Srpski spomenici*) – actually Cyrillic documents, which might or might not be 'Serbian'.

Nikolajević was a talented and effective propagandist, but being an Orthodox priest he was hardly an advertisement for the notion that it was language, not Orthodox faith, that defined Serb nationhood. His collaborator Matija Ban (1818–1903) was, by contrast, born into a poor Catholic family from Petrovo Selo near Gruž, and though his Catholicism seems to have been nominal he was at least clearly not Orthodox. Ban's activities involved acting as an energetic secret agent of Serbia as well as intellectual advocate for the doctrine of a Serbian Dubrovnik. A congenital liar and fantasist, it is difficult to know how much of his writings reflected personal belief and how much personal self-interest. But Ban's position appears to have been more flexible and pragmatic than that of the Serbian cultural leaders. He never, for example, rejected Illyrianism as such, and he was even prepared to avoid the 'Serb' label for Dubrovnik, if and when tactics required. But in the last resort his Greater Serbian sentiments were clear enough. As he expressed them at a commemorative session of the Serbian Royal Academy on the occasion of what was then thought to be Gundulić's tricentennial: 'The past to Dubrovnik, the future to Belgrade!'[38]

The most interesting of the leaders of the Serb-Catholic circle was certainly Medo (otherwise known as Orsat) Pucić (1821–1882). As a practising Catholic, social conservative and the scion of a great Ragusan patrician house, Pucić embodies the link between the old Republic and the later ambiguity about national identity. His opinions, which graduated through wholehearted commitment to Illyrianism, were decisively influenced by his acquaintanceship when studying in Padua in 1841 with the Slovak philologist Jan Kollár. The latter's view that the proper name for the South Slavs was 'Serbs', not 'Illyrians', was adopted by Pucić in a verse he wrote at this time:

Mladi Srbi bud'mo mi
Bra'a jedne misli svi
Misli sloge, misli slave,
Misli ljubve bratske prave,
U nas gleda narod sav !

Young Serbs let us be
Brothers of one idea all,
Idea of unity, idea of glory,
Idea of true fraternal love,
All the people are watching us![39]

The Serb-Catholics of Dubrovnik acquired significant political importance some while after the first flowering of the ideology itself. With the Austrian annexation of Bosnia and Hercegovina in 1878 the hostility between Croatian and Serbian nationalism became much sharper. Between 1890 and 1899 a coalition between the Serb-Catholic group and the pro-Italian Party was in control of Dubrovnik's civil administration. It waged a vigorous campaign against the unification of Dalmatia with Croatia and disputed the Croatian character of Dubrovnik. The young Frano Supilo (1870–1917) – the future member of the Yugoslav Committee – from 1891 was the most active proponent of the contrary viewpoint of Croatian nationalism through his newspaper *Crvena Hrvatska* (*Red Croatia*).[40] He and his colleagues achieved a large measure of success, but it was only in the inter-war period that the Serb Catholic movement completely failed, as Croats everywhere rallied against the oppressive policies of the regime in Belgrade.

In 1929, after the assassination of the Croatian Peasant Party Leader Stjepan Radić and the imposition of King Alexander's centralising dictatorship, Croatia was systematically divided up into historically meaningless and thus more controllable administrative units. Dubrovnik thus found itself included within the Zetska *banovina* which included Dalmatia from the Neretva to the Bojana, Montenegro, eastern Hercegovina, western Kosovo and the Sandžak. The capital of the *banovina* was Cetinje in Montenegro. Not surprisingly, only the most committed Serbophiles could consider this anything other than humiliating for Dubrovnik.

IV. History, Historicism and the Last Siege (1991–1992)

In the autumn of 1991 Dubrovnik suddenly acquired a new image, that of a war zone. As commentators attempted to piece together the circumstances under which an internationally venerated cultural centre was being attacked from air, land and sea, attempts were made to connect contemporary events with past history. Most of these endeavours were merely embarrassing. Some, however, were more harmful in that they persuaded powerful figures like the present US Secretary of State, Colin Powell, that what were at work were 'ancient hatreds' operating in a 'thousand-year-old hornet's nest'.[41] Such misunderstandings masked the reality of aggression and the need to respond to it.

Yet the distortions and abuses of history which characterised the polemics of this time are themselves of historical interest, and nowhere more than in Dubrovnik. Of course, in a certain sense the earlier image of the city as a haven of peace, harmony and culture was itself a fabrication. As these pages have noted, the Ragusan Republic's security was always fragile. Two years before its fall it suffered the most severe depredations by the Russians and Montenegrins. Life under Austria was stagnant rather than tranquil. And from the late nineteenth century Dubrovnik experienced, like the rest of Dalmatia, the tensions of nationalism. Above all, the Second World War and its aftermath saw events which subsequent generations tried hard to forget as they strove to make liberal culture and the annual Dubrovnik Festival the distinctive marks of their city. Thus more was spoken about Dubrovnik's (real if limited) traditional tolerance of the Jews in the days of the Republic than of the more recent persecution of the Jews under the fascist Ustaša regime from the spring of 1941.[42] And until the fall of communism there was no open discussion of the bloody settling of old scores by the Partisans when they entered Dubrovnik. A plaque now marks the spot on the idyllic little island of Daksa where between 25 and 27 October 1944 forty-four men, including four priests, were summarily executed.[43]

On the other hand, the counterpart of modern Dubrovnik's propensity for a certain amount of selective amnesia about its past was an atmosphere of pragmatism and tolerance in the present. On the eve of the attack by units of the Yugoslav Army, the results of the 1991 census showed that of the inhabitants of Dubrovnik 82 per cent considered themselves Croat, 6.7 per cent Serb, 4 per cent Muslim and 1.7 per cent Yugoslav. Dubrovnik was thus overwhelmingly Croat. But Croatian national consciousness was an established fact rather than a programme. Serbs (and indeed Muslims) were fully part of the Dubrovnik urban community and treated as such.

This, however, was not how Serbs in Belgrade and elsewhere saw matters. In one sense, it is understandable that perceptions had grown so out of touch with reality. As already noted, there persisted for a number of years in some influential quarters in Dubrovnik an ambiguous attitude towards national identity. Even after this ambiguity had been dissipated by the process of national polarisation in the late nineteenth and early twentieth centuries, a cultural programme which stressed the 'Serbian-ness' (*srpstvo*) of Dubrovnik was sponsored from Belgrade. The fact that this ideological programme was espoused by some of the finest historians of Dubrovnik such as Jorjo Tadić and Miroslav Pantić, whose works have been frequently cited in these pages, endowed it with an intellectual respectability which would otherwise have been lacking. Generally speaking, the programme proceeded through assumption rather than assertion. Only rarely did it come out into the open – as, for example, in a polemical exchange about whether Ragusan literature was 'Serb', which filled the pages of the Belgrade Communist journal *Borba* in 1967.[44]

By 1991 the argument that Dubrovnik should be understood as having a Serb identity had been lost in all but the most intransigent Greater Serbian intellectual circles. But it was precisely these circles which from the mid-1980s had been gaining power in Belgrade. Thus, in combination with crude propaganda about the rise of a new Croatian Ustaša intent on renewed massacres of Serb minorities, a somewhat less crude but equally unrealistic attempt to justify Serbian policy towards Dubrovnik was made on the basis of the latter's 'true' identity. This produced a flurry of quasi-academic tracts. For example, in 1992 there appeared in Belgrade a short volume entitled *Srpstvo Dubrovnika* ('The Serbian-ness of Dubrovnik') by Jeremija Mitrović which asserted:

> Many historical sources, indications of Dubrovnik writers and historians, of objective Croatian, Serbian and foreign histories, force the conclusion that

> Dubrovnik developed in a Serbian popular milieu, that its territory expanded thanks to the benevolence of Serb rulers and renewed itself nationally for the most part with Serb immigrants from far and near. The language of its Slavicised inhabitants and the language of its writers was fundamentally the language of the Hercegovinians, and many of the customs, traditions and costumes were Hercegovinian also.

Mitrović continued:

> With the undertaking of the Serbs aimed at the defeat of the Greater Croatian attack on Serb territory, Dubrovnik will save itself from Greater Croatian shackles.[45]

In the same vein, and making more explicit the promise hidden in that last phrase, a pamphlet in English of the same year, entitled *Short History of Dubrovnik* by Prvoslav Ralić, stated:

> The idea of the Republic of Dubrovnik is a living one. Its advocates today are not the Serbs, but rather the Croats of Dubrovnik. Opposing the re-founding of the Republic of Dubrovnik are the Ustashi elements in Croatia and in Dubrovnik… Serbia and Serbs do not ask Dubrovnik to follow their policy. They support the policy of the people of Dubrovnik themselves.[46]

The offer of an autonomous existence for Dubrovnik as a province of Serbia or perhaps of a Serb-dominated rump Yugoslavia was seriously (which is not necessarily to say sincerely) meant. At the end of October 1991 – when the JNA (Yugoslav Army) action against Dubrovnik was well underway – Hrvoje Kačić, who would later become the Croatian Government's chief adviser on the delimitation of frontiers, visited Belgrade and was summoned to a meeting at JNA headquarters. Here he was received by General Pujić, who offered to stop the shelling if his terms were accepted. Dubrovnik, said the General, was being offered a high degree of autonomy within the Yugoslav Federation. It could, he envisaged, became a great financial centre, a focus for foreign investment, enjoying the status of a free port. Naturally, Kačić was unimpressed.[47]

The tempting of Dubrovnik never had any real prospect of success. But as the shells rained down on its citizens and cultural heritage, attitudes hardened against any accommodation with Belgrade. Intellectuals played a prominent role in the resistance of the city, which was all the more necessary because of the very limited military resources available to its defenders. For their part, various public figures in Croatia and abroad proved extremely efficient at communicating Dubrovnik's plight to the outside world. The symbolic breaking of the maritime blockade by the last president of Federal Yugoslavia (and current president of Croatia), Stipe Mesić, and a group of returning refugees on board the ferry *Slavija* at the end of October 1991 was another blow to the credibility of the JNA's campaign.[48]

Compared with the sufferings inflicted at the time on Vukovar and other Croatian towns, those of Dubrovnik were limited. Yet they were real enough, and it is difficult to convey through bare statistics the impact of events on the terrified and isolated population. Attacks on Konavle began sporadically in the second half of September 1991. They were justified by historically spurious claims by Montenegro to the strategically crucial Prevlaka peninsula and by equally spurious allegations that JNA units had been fired upon by Croatian forces. (On 20 September Pero Poljanić, Dubrovnik's mayor, was informed by the JNA commander in Boka that JNA troops were under continuous fire from the bell tower of the church at Brgat; the mayor observed that this was unlikely, since the Brgat church did not have a bell tower.)[49]

Refugees were, therefore, already flooding in Dubrovnik when the city itself was first attacked on 1 October. Water and electricity supplies were targeted and this combined with the blockade, which interrupted the flow of food, medicine and fuel, increased the psychological pressure on the besieged. (Dubrovnik would go thirty-eight days without electricity.) The old city itself was shelled on 23 and 28 October, again between 6 and 13 November, and most seriously of all on 6 December. Not till 10 April 1992 did Croatian forces begin to retake the occupied territory. By 26 May the whole of the territory of Dubrovnik was in Croatian hands. But JNA forces based at Čilipi airport and paramilitaries in the north continued to fire sporadically on the city during the summer of 1992. Indeed, the attacks of the paramilitaries from Hercegovina on Konavle and Primorje were only finally silenced by the Croatian Army's 'Operation Storm' in August 1995.

Two hundred and twenty-one people lost their lives as a result of these attacks – 92 civilians and 129 members of the Croatian security forces. Paradoxically, one of the first victims of a war launched allegedly to 'protect' the Dubrovnik Serb minority was the Serb poet Milan Miličić. The devastation inflicted by the attacks on Dubrovnik and the surrounding countryside was enormous. Among historic monuments severely damaged were Placa, the Franciscan friary (especially the library), the Dominican friary, the Cathedral, the church of St Blaise, the Sigurata church, the monastery on Lokrum, the Rector's Palace, the *Rupe* and numerous palaces (some completely burnt out). But the often disproportionate focus on the old city's treasures in fact understates the scale of the damage as a whole. Dubrovnik's economic heart was torn out. Its tourist industry was destroyed. The main hotels – the Imperial, the Excelsior, the Belvedere and others – were badly damaged. Of 335 vessels in the marina, 154 were sunk; fourteen of the larger vessels were stolen and taken off to Montenegro. Modern cultural institutions were also targeted. Twenty-five thousand books were destroyed when the JNA shelled the Inter-University Centre. The headquarters of the Dubrovnik Festival was gutted.

Outside the city the destruction was even worse. Buses, lorries and cars were stolen *en masse*. Power plants, shops, garages, farms and private houses were looted. The patterns of devastation remind one of those of 1806 and suggest similar motives. Whether by design or for convenience, Slobodan Milošević and his colleagues in Belgrade chose to rely heavily on Montenegrin reservists in the early stages of the assault. Following the traditions of their forefathers, the Montenegrins went to work with a will. Konavle suffered terribly. Nine hundred and eighty houses there were either severely damaged or destroyed. Forty per cent of the houses in Cavtat, 42 per cent of those in Gruda and 45 per cent of those in Čilipi fell into this category. By contrast, the houses in Vitaljina, right on the border with Montenegro, were largely undamaged – the population had been taken by surprise and bundled out of their homes without a serious struggle.[50] The regions of Župa Dubrovačka, Rijeka Dubrovačka and Primorje also suffered heavy losses to property; in Primorje the great arboretum at Trsteno was badly damaged.

More than ten years on, the restoration is so great that it is difficult for visitors to conceive of the scale of what occurred. Most of the hotels are functioning again, the houses rebuilt, and the monuments – with the exception of the occasional boarded-up palace – largely restored. History is what it should be – a source of entertainment and of income, not a justification for violence and plunder. At last the sentiment of the inscription carved on the city's Ploče Gate, at which the figure of St Blaise keeps watch, seems less wistful aspiration, more confident prediction:

Este procul, saevi,
Nullum haec per saecula Martem castra timent,
Sancti quae fovet aura senis.

Keep away, men of violence.
For centuries war has not affrighted this fortress
Cherished by the spirit of the aged Saint.

APPENDIX ONE

A Note on Dubrovnik's 'Independence'

Concepts such as 'independence' or 'sovereignty' when applied to the state of Ragusa inevitably run the risk of oversimplification and anachronism. Throughout almost its whole existence the Ragusan Republic was paying tribute to a superior authority to which it recognised, however grudgingly, that it owed some measure of allegiance. On occasion, the Ragusans would indeed magnify this subordination for their own diplomatic and security requirements: thus from the Porte they were not above demanding protection as its 'subjects'. Certainly, this is what their status was in Ottoman eyes, and in a number of respects it reflected political and economic reality. In the words of the distinguished Turkish historian Halil Inalcik:

> [T]he Republic was one of the most significant components of what we call the Ottoman Empire, or more precisely the Ottoman Commonwealth, to the success of which Turks and Balkan peoples contributed collectively.[1]

On the other hand, this is not the whole story. The Ragusans were clearly intent on ensuring the minimum outside interference in their affairs and maximum diplomatic freedom in dealings with foreign powers. Through their negotiations with Louis of Hungary in 1358–1359 they secured so much control over their destiny that it is right to describe what they achieved as a 'kind of independence'. This they maintained, albeit within a quite different institutional and ideological framework, once they began paying *harač* to the Ottoman Empire. At least by the seventeenth century, as witnessed by the writings of Jakov Lukarević and Ivan Gundulić, a fuller and more self-confident expression of the aristocratic Republic's 'freedom' is also evident.

Judged according to current modern criteria for 'independence', the Ragusan Republic can broadly be so described.[2] An expert in international law has, in particular, drawn attention to the Republic's exercise of sole legislative and judicial authority over its own territory, and to its powers to grant asylum, decide on its defences, carry on diplomacy (including the recognition of other states), and conduct foreign trade.[3]

APPENDIX TWO

A Note on Money, Weights and Measures[1]

Money

Dubrovnik used a variety of coins and units of account. But the main ones, including those referred to in this book, were:

1 *hyperperus* = 12 *denarii grossi* (or just *grossi*) = 40 *miliarenses* = 120 *follari* (or *minca*).
1 *soldo* (*solad*) = 1/6 *grosso.*
1 *scudo* (*škuda*) = 36 *grossi.*
1 ducat = 40 *grossi* (*dinarići*).
1 (Ottoman) piaster or *grosso* = 40 *pari.*

Dry Weights

1 *libra ad pondus subtile* – the 'thin' pound used for gold, silver and pearls.
1 *libra ad pondus grossum* – the 'fat' pound used for other goods.
1 *starium* (*star* or *modius*) = 6 *cupelli* – used for grain. Estimates of the equivalent metric weight of a *starium* vary from 64.5 kg. to 71.5 kg.
1 *carro* – used for capacity of a ship's hold. Equivalent to just under 20 hectolitres of grain.
1 *modius* – used for salt. Estimates of the equivalent metric weight are 42 to 43 kg.
1 bushel (*cupellus*, *uborak*) – used for salt, grain etc. Estimates of the metric weight are about 10.7 to 11.9 kg.

Fluid Weights

1 *quinquum parvum* (*vjedro* or 'bucket') – used for wine sold in taverns. Equivalent to 19.2 litres.
1 *quinquum grossum* (*veliko vjedro* or 'big bucket') – used for wine sold wholesale. Equivalent to 21.9 litres.
1 *starium* – used for oil. Equivalent to 9.5 litres.

Measures of Length and Area

1 ell (*lakat*, *braccio*, *cubitus*). Equivalent to 0.55 metres.

1 fathom (*passus*, *sežanj*). Equivalent to 2.048 metres (or six feet).
1 *zlatica* (*solad*). Equivalent to 167.7 square metres.

Chronology[1]

6th–mid-7th C. AD	Expansion of pre-existing settlement in Dubrovnik as a result of collapse of Epidaurum (Cavtat)
7th–8th C.	Building of Byzantine basilica, Dubrovnik's first cathedral
8th–9th C.	Dubrovnik is ruled by a Byzantine pro-consul and later *strategos* based in Zadar
c. 878	Emperor Basil I authorises the Dalmatian towns, including Dubrovnik, to pay tribute to the Slavic rulers of the hinterland
9th C.	Dubrovnik is subject to raids by the Saracens
c. 992	Tsar Samuilo of Macedonia-Bulgaria burns the town
996–999	Institution of the Dubrovnik archbishopric
998 or 1000	Expedition of Doge Pietro II Orseolo and first temporary submission of Dubrovnik to Venetian rule
1022	Bull of Benedict VIII, the oldest original document in the Dubrovnik archives
c. 1050	Abolition of the Ragusan archbishopric
1081–1085	Dubrovnik is briefly under Norman rule, before returning to Byzantine allegiance
1120	Restoration of the Ragusan archbishopric
1125–1145	Dubrovnik is under Venetian rule
1148	Dubrovnik's trade agreement with Molfetta, the first of many with Italian and Dalmatian towns
1171	Dubrovnik again seized briefly by Venice
1180s	First military clashes with Stefan Nemanja, ruler of Serbia
1186–1192	Dubrovnik accepts Norman overlordship as a means of resisting both Serbia and Venice, before returning to Byzantine allegiance
1189	Commercial treaty with *Ban* Kulin of Bosnia
1190	Institution of the Franchise (immunity) of St Blaise

1205	Dubrovnik is seized by a Venetian fleet and brought under a century and a half of Venetian control
1225	Arrival of the Dominicans
1231	Temporary expulsion of the Venetian count from Dubrovnik
1232	Imposition by Venice of political and commercial conditions on Dubrovnik
1235	Arrival of the Franciscans
1235–1236	The 'Bosnian Crusade'
1251	Temporary expulsion of the Venetian count, who returned the following year
1252	Attack on the town by Stefan Uroš I of Serbia
1252	The archbishop of Dubrovnik finally loses jurisdiction over Bosnia
1265	Renewed war with Serbia
1268	Peace treaty with Serbia and start of payment of tribute (St Demetrius's Revenue) by Dubrovnik
before 1272	Dubrovnik gains control of the island of Lastovo
1272	Promulgation of the Statute of Dubrovnik
1275	War with Serbia
1277	Promulgation of the Dubrovnik Customs Statute
1301	War with Serbia's new ruler, Stefan Uroš II Milutin
1301	Dubrovnik establishes control of the island of Mljet
1317	Start of the construction of the Franciscan friary (today's *Mala braća*) within the City walls
1333	Acquisition by Dubrovnik, from Stefan Uroš IV Dušan of Serbia, of Ston and Pelješac and the beginning of its division and colonisation
1335	Revolt by the inhabitants of Ston and Pelješac
1344	Final allocation of land on Pelješac
1345	The proclamation of the Statute of Mljet
1348	The Black Death
1350	Visit of Tsar Dušan and his family to Dubrovnik
1357	Acquisition by Dubrovnik, from Stefan Uroš V of Serbia, of the heights of Župa, divided and settled in the 1360s.
1358	End of Venetian rule in Dubrovnik; establishment of Hungarian suzerainty and Dubrovnik's effective independence
1360	Death of Archbishop Ilija Saraka
1367	Visit of *Ban* (later King) Tvrtko of Bosnia to Dubrovnik
1371	Battle of Marica; Serb magnates start to become Ottoman tributaries
1373	Dubrovnik receives permission from Gregory IX to trade *ad partes Saracenorum*

1378	Treaty between Dubrovnik and Tvrtko: Dubrovnik acquires commercial privileges, while paying Tvrtko the St Demetrius's Revenue
1378–1381	The War of Chioggia
1389	Battle of Kosovo; Serb defeat; murder of Sultan Murad I
before 1396	Dubrovnik enters into negotiations with the Ottoman Empire
1397	Institution on Mljet of what was probably the first quarantine detention station (*lazzaretto*) in Europe
1399	Acquisition by Dubrovnik, from King Ostoja of Bosnia, of the Slansko Primorje (Petrovo Selo to Ston)
1400	Discovery of plot to overthrow the Ragusan government
1403–1404	War between Dubrovnik and King Ostoja, who was then overthrown
1413	Grant of the islands of Brač, Hvar and Korčula to Dubrovnik by King Sigismund of Hungary
1416	Brač, Hvar and Korčula definitively lost by Dubrovnik
1416	Dubrovnik outlaws the slave trade
1419	Acquisition by Dubrovnik from Sandalj Hranić of the eastern part of Konavle
1423	Beginning of division and colonisation of eastern Konavle
1426	Acquisition from Radoslav Pavlović of western Konavle (including Cavtat and Obod)
1427	Beginning of division and colonisation of western Konavle
1430	Dubrovnik obtains commercial privileges from the Ottoman Sultan
1430–1433	War between Dubrovnik and Radoslav Pavlović
1431–1432	Foundation of the Dubrovnik confraternity of the *Antunini*
1433	Dubrovnik receives permission from the Council of Basel, subsequently confirmed by successive popes, to trade with the Muslim world
1435	Construction of a new Rector's Palace according to designs of Onofrio della Cava
1436–1438	Construction by Onofrio of the aqueduct and city fountains
1440	Institution of the *Specchio del Maggior Consiglio*
1442	Dubrovnik begins to pay tribute (*harač*) to the Sultan, receiving highly favourable trading concessions
1444	Battle of Varna; crushing defeat of Hungary; death in battle of King Vladislav I
1451–1454	War between Dubrovnik and Stjepan Vukčić Kosača, the Herceg
1459	Fall of the fortress of Smederevo to the Turks; Serbia ceases to exist

1461–1463	Reconstruction of the Minčeta Tower according to plans of Michelozzo Michelozzi and Juraj Dalmatinac
1462–1464	Construction of the Bokar Fortress according to plans of Michelozzi
1463	Fall of Bosnia to the Turks; execution of the last king of Bosnia, Stjepan Tomašević, in Jajce
1463	Fire followed by reconstruction of the Rector's Palace
1469	The annual *harač* payment by Dubrovnik to the Sultan is raised from 1,500 to 5,000 ducats a year
1471	Dubrovnik's *harač* is set at 9,000 ducats and 10,000 for future years
1476	Over and above the *harač*, Dubrovnik has to pay a further 2,500 ducats tax (*đumruk/gümrük*) in lieu of customs
1480	The *harač* raised by a further 2,500 ducats, though not in fact levied because of death of Mehmed II; total payment reduced again to 12,500 by his successor Bayezid II
1484–1485	Construction of Dubrovnik's breakwater (*Kaše*) according to plans of Paskoje Miličević
1516–1520	Construction of the Sponza Palace (*Dogana*) according to plans of Miličević
1518	Increases in dues levied by the Ottoman Empire on Ragusan merchandise
1520	Major earthquake strikes Dubrovnik
1521	Consolidation on favourable terms of Dubrovnik's commercial relations with the Empire by agreement with the new Sultan, Suleyman 'the Magnificent'
1525	Opening of the new state shipyard at Gruž
1526	Battle of Mohacs; crushing defeat of Hungary by the Turks; death of King Louis II of Hungary in battle
1531	Foundation of the Dubrovnik confraternity of the *Lazarini*
1538–1539	Reconstruction of Revelin (Fortress) according to plans of Antonio Ferramolino
1538–1540	The [First] War of the Holy League
1541–1590	Construction of the *Rupe* (state grain silos)
1541	Fall of Buda to Ottoman forces
1552–1557	Reconstruction of the Fortress of St John (Sveti Ivan)
1570–1573	The War of Cyprus (The Second War of the Holy League)
1570–1571	*Uskok* raids on Ragusan territory
1571	Turkish defeat at the battle of Lepanto
1588	Three Ragusan vessels lost in the defeat of the Spanish Armada
1590	Opening of the *entrepôt* of Split as a rival to Dubrovnik
1593–1606	The First Long Turkish War
1602–1606	Lastovo in rebellion, with Venetian support, against Dubrovnik

1610–1612	The 'Great Conspiracy'
1627	Building begins of the *Lazzaretti* at Ploče
1630–1631	Venetian incursions on Lokrum
1645	Fall of the fortress of Klis to (anti-Ottoman) *hajduks*
1645	Closure of the Split *entrepôt*
1645–1669	The War of Crete
1667	The Great Earthquake
1683–1699	The Second Long Turkish War
1699	Peace of Srijemci Karlovci (Carlowitz)
1715–1718	War between Austria/Venice and the Ottoman Empire
1718	Peace of Požarevac (Passarowitz)
1754	Settlement at Travnik between Dubrovnik and Venice
1757	Arrival of first French consul/agent in Dubrovnik
1769–1774	Russo-Turkish War
1774	Russo-Turkish Peace of Kuchuk Kainarji
1776	Trade Agreement between Dubrovnik and France
1797	Abolition of the Venetian Republic
1797	Treaty of Campo Formio
1799–1800	Konavle Revolt
1806	Entry of French troops into Dubrovnik – Siege by Russians and Montenegrins
1808	Abolition of the Ragusan Republic
1809	Dubrovnik incorporated into the French 'Illyrian Provinces'
1813–1814	Revolt by the Ragusan patriciate against French rule
1813–1815	English occupation of the Elaphite Islands and Cavtat
1815	Congress of Vienna: Dubrovnik recognised as part of Habsburg Dalmatia
1818	Visit of Emperor Francis I to Dubrovnik
1828	Papal Bull *Locum Beati Petri* proclaims abolition of the Dubrovnik archbishopric (given effect in 1830)
1835–1858	The Illyrian Movement
1841	Ljudevit Gaj's visit to Dubrovnik
1844	Ivan Gundulić's *Osman* printed in Zagreb
1848–1849	Crisis in the Habsburg Empire
1880	The 'Dubrovnik', the city's first steamship, arrives in Dubrovnik harbour
1891	Frano Supilo begins to publish *Crvena Hrvatska* in Dubrovnik
1892	Formation of the Dubrovnik Steamship Navigation Company (*Dubrovačka Parobrodarska Plovidba u Dubrovniku*)
1897	Opening of the Hotel Imperial
1914–1918	First World War
1918	Proclamation of the Kingdom of the Serbs, Croats and Slovenes (the first Yugoslavia)

1928	Assassination of Stjepan Radić and other Croat leaders in the National Assembly in Belgrade
1934	Assassination of King Alexander of Yugoslavia in Marseilles
1939–1945	Second World War
1941	Proclamation of the Independent State of Croatia (NDH) by the Ustaša leadership in Zagreb
1944	Entry of Partisan forces into Dubrovnik
1990	Proclamation of the independent Republic of Croatia
1991–1992	Dubrovnik under siege from Serb-Montenegrin JNA forces
1995	Dubrovnik finally secured from attacks as a result of Croatian Army's Operation 'Storm' (*Oluja*)
2000–2003	Tourism restored to approaching pre-1991 level

Notes

Acknowledgments

1. 'Izvještaj', 41.

A Note on Names

1. It appears that from late medieval times the great Ragusan families were more likely to use the Italian version of their names, while commoners increasingly used the Slavic version of theirs. But the pursuit of uniformity and simplicity seemed to me more important than to try to catch these shifting nuances.
2. The Natali family, who played such a prominent role in the last years of the Republic and in attempts at its restoration, never (as far as I know) used a Slavic version of their name.

Preface

1. Rebecca West, *Black Lamb and Grey Falcon*, i (London, 1942), 238–239.
2. The only other recent account in English of the Ragusan Republic – F. W. Carter, *Dubrovnik (Ragusa): a Classic City State* (London, 1972) – though valuable as a pioneering study and providing interesting insights into the economy, has a number of deficiencies: see the review by Bariša Krekić, *Slavic Review*, 33/2 (1974), 386–387. Krekić has himself written an excellent short account of the medieval period, *Dubrovnik: A City Between East and West* (Norman, Oklahoma, 1972). By far the best account in Croatian is the monumental and indispensable work of Vinko Foretić, *Povijest Dubrovnika do 1808.*, 2 vols (Zagreb, 1980), on which I have drawn frequently, as will be apparent from the references.
3. 'Izvještaj gosp. La [*sic*] Maire, francuzkoga konsula u Koronu o Dubrovačkoj Republici', *JAZU Starine*, xiii (1881), 40.
4. F. M. Appendini, *Notizie istorico-critiche sulle antichità, storia e letteratura de' Ragusei*, i (Dubrovnik, 1802), 157.
5. Although this book in its 'Postscript' also covers briefly some themes from modern Dubrovnik's history, it concentrates upon the history of the Ragusan Republic, which ends in 1808.

Chapter One

1. A. Ničetić, *Povijest dubrovačke luke* (Dubrovnik, 1996), pp. 23, 43–44. Ničetić's study offers a fundamental reassessment of the early history of Dubrovnik. Above all, he shows that since over 2,000 years the level of the Adriatic rose by 2 metres and the level of the land fell by 1 metre, many of the assertions confidently made by earlier historians – e.g. that the first harbour was Kolorina, or that today's Placa was originally a swampy river dividing the 'island'

of Ragusa from the lowest slopes of Mount Srđ – must be false (*Ibid.*, pp. 14–23.)

2. For this early warning system and other means taken to protect the town see p. 298–299.
3. C. Jireček, *Die Bedeutung von Ragusa in der Handelsgeschichte des Mittelalters. Die feierliche Sitzung der kaiserlichen Akademie der Wissenschaften am 31. Mai 1893* (Vienna, 1893), pp. 128–9.
4. *Ibid.*, p.138.
5. For evidence of continuity of settlement in Dubrovnik, see p. 28.
6. J. Fine, *The Early Medieval Balkans: a Critical Survey from the Sixth to the late Twelfth Century* (University of Michigan Press, 1991), pp. 9–12.
7. I. Goldstein, *Hrvatski rani srednji vijek* (Zagreb, 1995), pp. 50–51.
8. G. Novak, 'Povijest Dubrovnika od najstarijih vremena do početka vii. stoljeća (do prepasti Epidauruma)', *Anali*, 10–11 (1966), 3–11; M. Suić, *Antički grad na istočnom Jadranu* (Zagreb, 1976), p. 10.
9. Goldstein, *op. cit.*, p.51.
10. Novak, 'Povijest Dubrovnika', p.12.
11. *Ibid.*, pp. 24, 31.
12. See p. 301.
13. Novak, 'Povijest Dubrovnika', pp. 50, 52.
14. Suić, *op. cit.*, pp. 116 117.
15. *Chronica Ragusina Junii Restii (ab origine urbis usque ad annum 1451), item Joannis Gundulae (1451–1484)*, ed. S. Nodilo, Monumenta spectantia historiam Slavorum meridionalium, 14. Scriptores, II (Zagreb, 1883), p. 15.
16. J. Lučić, 'Dubrovčani na jadranskom prostoru od vii. stoljeća do godine 1205', *Dubrovačke teme* (Zagreb, 1991), 5.
17. Constantine Porphyrogenitus, *De Administrando Imperio*, ed. G. Moravcsik, trans. R. Jenkins [Magyar-Görög Tanulmányok, 29] (Budapest, 1949), p. 135.
18. V. Košćak, 'Epidaurum – Ragusium – Laus – Dubrovnik', *Anali*, 27 (1989), 7–39. The argument that Epidaurum was destroyed by an earthquake, probably in the fourth century, rests principally on 1) the lack of archeological evidence at the site (Cavtat); 2) the mention of a tidal wave at Epidaurum in St Jerome's account of the miracles of St Hilarion; 3) the known incidence of earthquakes in the region. Also at one time adduced to support this theory was the alleged discovery of the remains of a 'city' in the sea off Cavtat. Subsequent investigation has, however, shown that the 'city in the sea' does not actually exist at all (Ničetić, *op. cit.*, p. 108 note 1). Against the 'natural catastrophe' theory of the end of Epidaurum, must be set the strong evidence offered by the chronicles and the tradition they represent that Epidaurum was finally destroyed by barbarians. This does not, of course, rule out the possibility that a severe earthquake did occur at some point, after which the town was rebuilt.
19. Constantine Porphyrogenitus, *De Administrando*, pp. 142–3.
20. Fine, *Early Medieval Balkans*, pp. 49–59.
21. N. Budak, *Prva stoljeća Hrvatske* (Zagreb, 1994), p. 12.
22. Budak, *op. cit.*, pp.13 14.
23. The relevant passages are: *Miletii Versus*, ed. A.K. Matas, Biblioteka za povijest dalmatinsku, part 1 (Dubrovnik, 1882), pp. 9–12; *Letopis popa dukljanina*, ed. F. Šišić (Belgrade, 1928), pp. 313–21; Thomas Archidiaconus, *Historia Salonitana,* ed. F. Rački, Monumenta spectantia historiam Slavorum meridionalium, 26. Scriptores, III (Zagreb, 1894), p. 30; *Annales Ragusini anonymi, item Nicolai de Ragnina*, ed. S. Nodilo, Monumenta spectantia historiam Slavorum meridionalium, 14. Scriptores, I (Zagreb, 1883), pp.3–4 for the 'Anonymous' and pp. 168–76 for Ranjina; Serafino Razzi, *La Storia di Ragusa,* ed. G. Gelcich (Dubrovnik, 1903), pp.13–16; *Chronica Ragusina Junii Restii,* ed. Nodilo, pp.16–17.
24. *Miletii Versus*, ed. A. K. Matas, Biblioteka za povijest dalmatinsku, part 1 (Dubrovnik, 1882), pp. 9–12; *Letopis popa dukljanina*, ed. F. Šišić (Belgrade, 1928), p. 320; V. Foretić, *Povijest Dubrovnika do 1808.*, i (Zagreb, 1980), 33.
25. J. Lučić, 'Povijest Dubrovnika od vii. stoljeća do godine 1205.', *Anali*, 13–14 (1976), 12. The Anonymous chronicler directly refers to Spilan and Gradac but places their population's

move to Dubrovnik in 691 (*Annales Ragusini anonymi*, ed. Nodilo, p.7).
26. Ničetić, *op. cit.*, pp. 75–76.
27. Ž. Rapanić, 'Archaeological Explorations in Dubrovnik after the Earthquake', *The Restoration of Dubrovnik 1979–89*, ed. B. Letunić (Zagreb, 1990), p. 343.
28. See p. 221 and note 3.
29. Goldstein, *op. cit.,* pp. 65–68; J. Stošić, 'Research finds and display problems connected with the area below the Cathedral and Bunićeva Poljana', in *The Restoration of Dubrovnik 1979–89*, ed. B. Letunić (Zagreb, 1990), 326–335.
30. L. Beritić, *Utvrđenja grada Dubrovnika* (Zagreb, 1955), p.19; Foretić, *Povijest Dubrovnika do 1808.*, i, 32; V. Putanec, 'Naziv *Labusedum* iz 11. stoljeća za grad Dubrovnik', *Rasprave zavoda za hrvatski jezik*, xix (1993), 289–302.
31. Lučić, 'Povijest Dubrovnika', 11.
32. Cf. Lučić, 'Povijest Dubrovnika', 14.
33. Ničetić, *op. cit.*, p. 28. For the later expansion of Dubrovnik see pp. 287–290.
34. Some historians favour a later date, but the greater likelihood is surely that of continuity. Cf. S. Krasić [and] S. Razzi, *Povijest dubrovačke metropolije i dubrovačkih nadbiskupa (x-xvi. stoljeća)* (Dubrovnik, 1999), p. 18.
35. Novak, 'Povijest Dubrovnika', 46–47; Lučić, 'Povijest Dubrovnika', 66. For the early history of the archbishopric see pp. 40–43.
36. *Annales Ragusini anonymi*, ed. Nodilo, pp.4, 173; Razzi, *Storia di Ragusa,* ed. Gelcich, pp.18–19.
37. For the cult of St Blaise see pp. 237–240.
38. *Annales Ragusini anonymi*, ed. Nodilo, pp. 147–63, 181–186; Razzi, *Storia di Ragusa,* ed. Gelcich, p. 5; *Chronica Ragusina Junii Restii*, ed. Nodilo, p.1.
39. *Annales Ragusini anonymi,* ed. Nodilo, p. 8. The Vlachs, transhumant shepherds, were probably the descendants of the Romanised pre-Slavic population of the Balkans. In later centuries, though, the term would be used in Dubrovnik simply to mean 'peasant' and later still Eastern Orthodox Christians.
40. *Ibid.,* pp.8–9.
41. Lučić, 'Povijest Dubrovnika', 35–44.
42. Constantine Porphyrogenitus, *De Administrando*, p. 147.
43. Lučić, 'Povijest Dubrovnika', 47–49.

Chapter Two

1. Lučić, 'Dubrovčani', 7–13; Goldstein, *op. cit.,* p. 203.
2. *Annales Ragusini anonymi*, ed. Nodilo, pp. 8, 11.
3. Lučić, 'Dubrovčani', p. 14.
4. *Ibid.*, pp. 14–16; Fine, *Early Medieval Balkans*, pp. 251–7; Goldstein, *op. cit.*, pp. 139–50.
5. Constantine Porphyrogenitus, *De Administrando*, p. 147.
6. *Letopis popa dukljanina*, ed. F. Šišić, (Belgrade, 1928) p. 333. In due course, it should be added, Dubrovnik reached a satisfactory relationship with Samuilo, at least in ecclesiastical matters: see below.
7. F. Lane, *Venice : a Maritime Republic* (Baltimore, 1973), pp. 24–26.
8. *Chronica Ragusina Junii Restii*, ed. Nodilo, pp. 38–39.
9. Lučić, 'Dubrovčani', 21–25; Goldstein, *op. cit.*, 339–343; F. W. Carter, *Dubrovnik (Ragusa): a Classic City-State* (London, 1972), pp. 58–60.
10. *Annales Ragusini anonymi*, ed. Nodilo, pp. 20–24, 199–201 (Ranjina); Razzi, *Storia di Ragusa*, ed. Gelcich, pp. 35–38.
11. See pp. 237–238.
12. Lučić, 'Dubrovčani', pp. 29–30.
13. D. Mack Smith, *Medieval Sicily: 800–1713 [A History of Sicily, i]* (New York, 1968), pp. 13–16.
14. Fine, *Early Medieval Balkans*, pp.281–2; Foretić, *Povijest Dubrovnika do 1808.*, i, 27.
15. Foretić, *Povijest Dubrovnika do 1808.*, i, 29.
16. *Annales Ragusini anonymi*, ed. Nodilo, p. 29. The *Annali storani* version lists the names of the Venetian Counts, *ibid.*, pp. 30–31, which itself suggests that the account is based on fact.

Foretić argues persuasively for Ranjina's date, 1125 (*Povijest Dubrovnika do 1808.*, i, 331–2, footnote 34).

17. Foretić, *Povijest Dubrovnika do 1808.*, i, 31; Lučić, 'Dubrovčani', 40.
18. Fine, *The Late Medieval Balkans: a Critical Study from the Late Twelfth Century to the Ottoman Conquest* (University of Michigan Press, 1994), pp. 7–8.
19. See p. 42.
20. Foretić, *Povijest Dubrovnika do 1808.*, i, 45.
21. See also pp. 50–51.
22. Foretić, *Povijest Dubrovnika do 1808.*, i, 46; *Liber statutorum civitatis Ragusii compositus anno 1272 cum legibus aetate posteriore insertis atque cum summariis, adnotationibus et scholiis a veteribus iuris consultis ragusinis additis*, ed. V. Bogišić and C. Jireček, Monumenta historico-juridica Slavorum meridionalium, 9 (Zagreb, 1904), book III, chapters l-lvi, pp. 76–80. See also p. 124.
23. Lučić 'Političke i kulturne prilike', 52–53. On the count and the Ragusan commune's government see pp. 39–40.
24. Lučić 'Političke i kulturne prilike', 56–59. See plate 2.
25. Foretić, *Povijest Dubrovnika do 1808.*, i, 47. See plate 3.
26. Gojslav Kročov 1192, Lukar 1195–97, Dobrol or Dobroslav 1199–1201.
27. *Ibid.*, pp. 52–3; Lučić, 'Političke i kulturne prilike', 68–9; Lučić, 'Povijest Dubrovnika', 123–124.
28. There were, however, also important differences. In Italy 'communes' were generally ruled by officials called 'consuls'. Italian communes were bound together by a public oath. They generally received their autonomy from the pope or bishops, rather than acquiring it by degrees from the secular (Imperial) power. None of these conditions applied in Dubrovnik or the rest of Dalmatia (Z. Janeković-Römer, *Okvir slobode: Dubrovačka vlastela između srednjovjekovlja i humanizma*, HAZU, Prilozi povijesti stanovništva i okolice Dubrovnika, book 8 (Dubrovnik, 1999), pp. 56–58).
29. D. Waley, *The Italian City-Republics* (London, 1969), pp. 22, 56, 58, 218–238. On the Ragusan 'tyrant' Damjan Juda, see p. 45.
30. Whereas Dubrovnik had from its inception been Christian, the Slavs – who became its neighbours – had first to be converted. The most intensive period of conversion was probably in the second half of the ninth century (Goldstein, *op. cit.*, p. 236).
31. Lučić, 'Dubrovčani', 20.
32. Krasić-Razzi, *Povijest dubrovačke metropolije*, pp. 22–25; I. Puljić, 'Uspostava dubrovačke metropolije', *Tisuću godina dubrovačke (nad)biskupije: Zbornik radova znanstvenoga skupa u povodu tisuće godina uspostave dubrovačke (nad)biskupije/metropolije (998.-1998.)*, ed. Ž. Puljić and N. A. Ančić (Dubrovnik, 2001), 15–56. See plate 1.
33. Lučić, 'Povijest Dubrovnika', 66–71.
34. Krasić-Razzi, *Povijest dubrovačke metropolije*, pp. 26–31.
35. *Chronica Ragusina Junii Restii*, ed. Nodilo, p. 52.
36. *Chronica Ragusina Junii Restii*, ed Nodilo, p. 63.
37. Fine, *Late Medieval Balkans*, pp. 18, 43–48, 143.
38. Lučić, 'Povijest Dubrovnika', 73.
39. *Copioso ristretto degli annali di Ragusa di Pietro Luccari, gentilhuomo di Ragusa* (Dubrovnik, 1790), p. 289. For archbishop Bernardo see p. 221.
40. Lane, *op. cit.*, pp. 36–43; Fine, *Late Medieval Balkans*, pp.60–63.
41. *Annales Ragusini anonymi*, ed. Nodilo, pp. 33–34; *Chronica Ragusina Junii Restii*, ed. Nodilo, pp. 70–73. The once disputed existence of Damjan Juda and the true date of his conspiracy – stated by Rastić, but not the other Ragusan chroniclers – have been established by Foretić, *Povijest Dubrovnika do 1808.*, i, 57–59.

Chapter Three

1. Foretić, *Povijest Dubrovnika do 1808.*, i, 59–60.
2. *Chronica Ragusina Junii Restii*, ed. Nodilo, pp. 79–80.
3. For the *hyperperus*, see Appendix 2: A Note on Money, Weights and Measures.

4. For this and other measures of capacity, see Appendix 2.
5. *Dubrovačka akta i povelje*, ed. J. Radonić, 1/1, SKA Zbornik za istoriju, jezik i književnost, Section III, book 2 (1934), no. xviii, pp. 21–25; *Chronica Ragusina Junii Restii*, ed. Nodilo, pp. 80–82; Foretić, *Povijest Dubrovnika do 1808.*, i, 60–62.
6. Lane, *op. cit.*, pp. 57–64.
7. Foretić, *Povijest Dubrovnika do 1808.*, i, 60 ; *Dubrovačka akta i povelje*, ed. Radonić, i, no. xviii, p. 24.
8. Foretić, *Povijest Dubrovnika do 1808.*, i, 62–65.
9. Fine, *Late Medieval Balkans*, pp. 199–201.
10. *Chronica Ragusina Junii Restii*, ed. Nodilo, pp. 90–92.
11. See also pp. 5, 152.
12. Foretić, *Povijest Dubrovnika do 1808.*, i, 88–89.
13. *Chronica Ragusina Junii Restii*, pp.75, 98.
14. K. Vojnović, 'Crkva i država u Dubrovačkoj Republici', *Rad*, 119 (1894), 40. See also pp. 168, 224.
15. Fine, *Late Medieval Balkans*, p. 139.
16. J. Fine, *The Bosnian Church: a New Interpretation. A Study of the Bosnian Church and its Place in State and Society from the 13th to the 15th Centuries* (New York, 1975), pp. 115–123. By dualism – as for example held by the Bulgarian Bogomils and French Cathars and Albigensians – is meant the belief that God (the force of Good) made the heavens but Satan (the equally powerful force of Evil) the world, that flesh and matter are inherently evil and that the life of perfection has no need of the sacraments but rather of abstention from material things and from carnal activity.
17. *Ibid.*, pp. 134–149.
18. Philippus de Diversis de Quartigianis de Lucca, *Situs Aedificiorum, Politiae et Laudabilium Consuetudinum Inclytae Civitatis Ragusii*, ed. V Brunelli (Zadar, 1882), p. 123.
19. Perhaps it was under the nominal authority of the Hungarian kings. In 1221 it was, in any case, subject to the *knez* of the island of Krk.
20. *Knjiga o uredbama i običajima skupštine i občine otoka Lastova*, ed. F. Radić, Monumenta historico-juridica Slavorum meridionalium, 8 (Zagreb, 1901), p. 1; J. Lučić, 'Prošlost otoka Lastova u doba Dubrovačke Republike', in *Lastovski statut* ed. V. Rismondo *et al.* (Split, 1994), 25–30; Foretić, *Povijest Dubrovnika do 1808.*, i, 85, 88.
21. Razzi, *Storia di Ragusa*, ed. Gelcich, p. 224.
22. *Copioso ristretto delli annali di Ragusa di Pietro Luccari, gentiluomo di Ragusa* (Dubrovnik, 1790), p. 50.
23. Lučić, 'Prošlost otoka Lastova', 35–36.
24. Marsilio Zorzi was also briefly count of Mljet but never managed to entrench his or his family's position there.
25. Foretić, *Povijest Dubrovnika do 1808.*, i, 88–89.
26. I. Ostojić, *Benediktinci u Hrvatskoj*, ii (Split, 1964), 443, 448.
27. Razzi, *Storia di Ragusa*, ed. Gelcich, pp. 228–229. For Ignjat Đurđević's later espousal of this view see p. 368. It has most recently been championed – at least as a possibility on the basis of prevailing tides and winds – by A. Ničetić, 'O nekim navigacijskim aspektima plovidbe svetoga Pavla od Krete do Melite', *Anali*, 38 (2000), 305–370.
28. Razzi, *Storia di Ragusa*, ed. Gelcich, p. 227; Lukarević, *Copioso ristretto*, p. 31.
29. Foretić, *Povijest Dubrovnika do 1808.*, i, 99.
30. Fine, *Late Medieval Balkans*, p. 266.
31. Foretić, *Povijest Dubrovnika do 1808.*, i, 91.
32. *Ibid.*, p. 92.
33. *Annales Ragusini anonymi*, ed. Nodilo, p. 51.
34. J. Lučić, 'Najstarija zemljišna knjiga u Hrvatskoj – dubrovački zemljišnik diobe zemlje u Stonu i Pelješcu iz god. 1336', *Dubrovačke teme* (Zagreb, 1991), 104–151. For the colonisation of Primorje and Konavle see pp. 69, 75–76.
35. J. Tadić, *Promet putnika u starom Dubrovniku* (Dubrovnik, 1939), pp. 42–45.

36. *Annales Ragusini anonymi*, ed. Nodilo, pp. 39 (the Anonymous) and pp. 328–329 (Ranjina).
37. Foretić, *Povijest Dubrovnika do 1808.*, i, 93.
38. DAD, 12/4, Libro rosso, fos 1r-8v. Further cadastral surveys in Župa continued well into the following century, comprising the folios in this substantial volume up to fo 57r.
39. Fine, *Late Medieval Balkans*, pp. 339–340.
40. *Libri Reformationum*, ed. F. Rački, i, Monumenta spectantia historiam Slavorum meridionalium, 10 (Zagreb, 1879), 115.
41. *Ibid.*, p. 183.
42. D. Gruber, 'Borba Ludovika I. s Mlečanima za Dalmaciju (1348–1358)', *Rad*, 152 (Zagreb, 1903), 87–157.
43. *Chronica Ragusina Junii Restii*, ed. Nodilo, pp. 134–135.
44. *Ibid.*, pp. 136–137; Foretić, *Povijest Dubrovnika do 1808.*, i, 77–80.

Chapter Four

1. On the question of Dubrovnik's 'independence' see Appendix 1.
2. Foretić, *Povijest Dubrovnika do 1808.*, i, 18; Lučić, 'Dubrovčani', 7.
3. Foretić, *Povijest Dubrovnika do 1808.*, i, 132.
4. Z. Janeković-Römer, 'Priznanje krune Sv. Stjepana – izazov dubrovačke diplomacije', *Međunarodni simpozij: diplomacija Dubrovačke Republike. Zbornik diplomatske akademije* (Zagreb, 1998), 293–296.
5. For the full career of Marin Gučetić, see M. Medini, *Dubrovnik Gučetića* (Belgrade, 1953), pp. 1–131.
6. *Dubrovačka akta i povelje*, ed. Radonić, 1/1, no. xlix, pp. 86–90; no. l, pp. 90–98; no. lii, pp.99–100; Foretić, *Povijest Dubrovnika do 1808.*, i, 133–134.
7. *Dubrovačka akta i povelje*, ed. Radonić, i, no. xlvii, pp.84–5. Foretić, however, corrects the date : *Povijest Dubrovnika do 1808.*, i, 345, footnote 9. See also p. 130.
8. *Pisma i uputstva Dubrovačke Republike*, ed. J. Tadić, i, SKA Zbornik za istoriju, jezik i književnost, Section III, book 4 (Belgrade, 1935), no. x, pp.10–11.
9. Foretić, *Povijest Dubrovnika do 1808.*, i, 158.
10. *Ibid.*, 157–158. See also plate 5.
11. There was never any lack of particular disputes between the two maritime powers: for example, in May 1362 Venice complained indignantly to the Hungarian king about a Ragusan attack on one of their convoys (*Listine ob odnošajih između južnoga slavenstva i Mletačke Republike*, ed. Š. Ljubić, i, Monumenta spectantia historiam Slavorum meridionalium, i (Zagreb, 1868), no. lxxxiii, pp. 46–48). But for all that, relations between the Venetians and Ragusans were not seriously interrupted between 1358 and 1378.
12. B. Krekić, 'Le rôle de Dubrovnik (Raguse) dans la navigation des *mudae* vénitiennes au xive siècle', *Dubrovnik: a Mediterranean Urban Society, 1300–1600* (Aldershot, 1997), 250–252.
13. Catholic, commercial, maritime Kotor retained close links with its more powerful and successful neighbour. But both because of its vulnerability to seizure by Dubrovnik's enemies and its aspirations to rivalry, in particular as regards the sale of salt, Kotor was frequently the object of Ragusan machinations and occasionally violence. When a Venetian fleet arrived in Kotor and seized the town, Dubrovnik received its political refugees. Dubrovnik also sent agents and sought, though unsuccessfully, to foment a revolt there.
14. B. Krekić, 'Dubrovnik (Ragusa) and the War of Tenedos/Chioggia (1378–1381)', *Dubrovnik, Italy and the Balkans in the Late Middle Ages* (London, 1980), 1–25.
15. *Pisma i uputstva Dubrovačke Republike*, ed. Tadić, i, no. i, p. 1.
16. L. Beritić, 'Stonske utvrde', *Anali*, 3 (1954), 321–324 For a fuller description of the fortifications of Ston see pp. 308–310.
17. Beritić, *Utvrđenja grada Dubrovnika*, pp. 26–29.
18. Fine, *Late Medieval Balkans*, pp. 395–398; S. Ćirković, *Istorija srednjovekovne bosanske države* (Belgrade, 1964), p. 70.
19. *Dubrovačka akta i povelje*, ed. Radonić, i, no. lxvi, pp. 118–119.
20. Ćirković, *Istorija srednjovekovne bosanske države*, pp. 185–186; F. Šišić, *Vojvoda Hrvoje Vukčić*

Hrvatinić i njegovo doba (1350–1416.) (Zagreb, 1902), pp. 132–134.
21. J. Lučić, 'Stjecanje, dioba i borba za očuvanje dubrovačkog primorja (1399–1405)', *Arhivski vjesnik*, xi-xii (1968–1969), 121–130.
22. Foretić, *Povijest Dubrovnika do 1808.*, i, 169–172.
23. *Annales Ragusini anonymi*, ed. Nodilo, p. 242.
24. V. Foretić, 'Vjekovne veze Dubrovnika i Korčule', *Dubrovnik,* 8/4 (1965), 18–54.
25. *Dubrovačka akta i povelje*, ed. Radonić, i, no. c, pp. 213–215.
26. Fine, *Late Medieval Balkans*, pp. 465–468; F. Šišić, *Vojvoda Hrvoje Vukčić Hrvatinić i njegovo doba (1350–1416.)* (Zagreb, 1902), pp. 225–235.
27. *Dubrovačka akta i povelje*, ed. Radonić, i, no. civ, pp. 221–223.
28. *Ibid.*, no. cii, pp. 235–236; no. ciii, pp. 237–238; no. civ, pp. 238–239; no. cvii, pp. 242–243; no. cix, p. 245; no. cxx, pp. 246.
29. V. Foretić, *Otok Korčula u srednjem vijeku do g. 1420* (Zagreb, 1940), pp. 195–209.
30. The succession of rulers in Cavtat and the neighbouring district of Obod during the fourteenth century is obscure. But it seems likely that the place had been lost by Dubrovnik, albeit briefly, at the start of the fourteenth century to the Serbian King Stefan Uroš II Milutin, and that it had then returned to Ragusan control, before slipping away again – this time to the local magnate, Pavle Radenović in 1391. The rest of Konavle, by contrast, had been outside the control of Dubrovnik since Byzantine times and, whatever Ragusan chroniclers and diplomats might assert, any historical or political connection with 'Old Ragusa' was therefore exiguous (N. Kapetanić and N. Vekarić, *Stanovništvo Konavala*, i, HAZU Prilozi povijesti stanovništva Dubrovnika i okolice, book 7 [Dubrovnik, 1998], 12–28).
31. R. Grujić, 'Konavli pod raznim gospodarima od xii. do xv. veka', *Spomenik SKA,* lxvi (1926), 17–18, 38–43; Kapetanić and Vekarić, *Stanovništvo Konavala,* i, 33–45.
32. Ćirković, *Istorija srednjovekovne bosanske države*, pp. 171–172, 185.
33. Diversis, *Situs Aedificiorum*, ed. Brunelli, p. 123.
34. For Sandalj this was by no means an extraordinary arrangement. He was a large and regular investor of funds in Dubrovnik over twenty years (1413–1433) (E. Kurtović, 'Motivi Sandaljeve prodaje Konavala dubrovčanima', *Anali*, 38 (2000), 110 and 119, table.)
35. Grujić, 'Konavli pod raznim gospodarima', 20–38; Kapetanić and Vekarić, *Stanovništvo Konavala,* i, 28–33.
36. The Serbian word for priest is *pop*.
37. Grujić, 'Konavli pod raznim gospodarima', 52–66, 118; Kapetanić and Vekarić, *Stanovništvo Konavala,* i, 59–62.
38. Foretić, *Povijest Dubrovnika do 1808.*, i, 196–300 For Dubrovnik's dealings with the Porte on the matter see pp. 79–80.
39. See p. 346.

Chapter Five

1. H. Inalcik, *The Ottoman Empire : the Classical Age 1300–1600*, translated by N. Itzkowitz and C. Imber (London, 1973), pp. 6–13.
2. For a discussion of the different versions of Murad's death, see Noel Malcolm, *Kosovo: A Short History* (London, 1998), pp. 68–72.
3. Fine, *Late Medieval Balkans*, pp. 379, 406, 408–414; Malcolm, *op. cit.*, pp. 81–82.
4. N. Vekarić, 'Opsade Dubrovnika i broj stanovnika', *Dubrovnik*, New Series, 4/2 (1993), 240.
5. *Annales Ragusini anonymi*, ed. Nodilo, p. 241.
6. For Ragusan trade in the Balkan hinterland see pp. 152–160.
7. Diversis, *Situs Aedificiorum*, ed. Brunelli, p. 122.
8. I. Božić, *Dubrovnik i Turska u xiv. i xv. veku* (Belgrade, 1952), pp. 8–55.
9. *Ibid.*, pp. 56–60.
10. *Dubrovačka akta i povelje*, ed. Radonić, i, no. clxiii, pp. 340–343. See plate 6.
11. N. Biegman, *The Turco-Ragusan Relationship according to the Firmans of Murad III (1575–1595) extant in the State Archives of Dubrovnik* (The Hague, 1967), pp. 16, 29–32.
12. Fine, *Late Medieval Balkans*, pp. 530–531.

13. As early as 7 March 1385, however, the Great Council of Dubrovnik had referred to *nostra res publica ragusina*. B. Krekić, 'Developed Autonomy: the Patricians in Dubrovnik and Dalmatian Cities', *Dubrovnik: a Mediterranean Urban Society, 1300–1600* (Aldershot, 1997), p. 211, footnote 71.
14. The *kadi*, though in theory an official applying religious law to the faithful, was in practice largely responsible in the Ottoman Empire for administering the secular Sultan-made laws, contained in the codes called *kanuns*, binding on Muslims and non-Muslims alike.
15. Foretić, *Povijest Dubrovnika do 1808.*, i, 203–211.
16. Knowledge, however, will have to await further research by those with the relevant linguistic and paleographical skills in the Ottoman archives.
17. Božić, *op. cit.*, pp. 98–103; Fine, *Late Medieval Balkans*, pp. 548–551; Inalcik, *Ottoman Empire: the Classical Age*, pp. 20–21.
18. B. Krekić, 'Dubrovnik's Participation in the War against the Ottomans in 1443 and 1444', *Dubrovnik, Italy and the Balkans in the Later Middle Ages* (London, 1980), 11.
19. S. Ćirković, *Herceg Stefan Vukčić-Kosača i njegovo doba* (Belgrade, 1964), pp. 269–277.
20. Cf. Foretić, *Povijest Dubrovnika do 1808.*, i, 217.
21. Ćirković, *Herceg Stefan*, p. 106.
22. *Ibid.*, pp.15–47, 100–102, 112 – 113.
23. Foretić, *Povijest Dubrovnika do 1808.*, i, 163–165. Although it may smack of artificiality, for simplicity's sake I refer to the place as 'Novi' in the period before the Herceg and by its modern name of 'Herceg-Novi' later.
24. Ćirković, *Herceg Stefan*, pp. 121–128; Foretić, *Povijest Dubrovnika do 1808.*, i, 217–220.
25. Ćirković, *Herceg Stefan*, pp. 153–172.
26. Foretić, *Povijest Dubrovnika do 1808.*, i, 222–226.
27. Inalcik, *Ottoman Empire : the Classical Age*, pp. 26–27.
28. Božić, *op. cit.*, pp.138–156.
29. Fine, *Late Medieval Balkans*, pp. 581–585.
30. Božić, *op. cit.*, pp.160–161, 164–165, 177–183, 196–199; Foretić, *Povijest Dubrovnika do 1808.*, i, 233–234; Lukarević, *Copioso ristretto*, p. 186.
31. Božić, *op. cit.*, pp. 185–192.
32. Actually, the term comes to the Turkish from the Latin *commercium* via its Byzantine equivalent. I owe this information to Noel Malcolm.
33. The combined payment of the original *harač* and *đumruk* was now simply called *harač* without any differentiation.
34. *Annales Ragusini anonymi*, ed. Nodilo, p. 64.
35. *Chronica Ragusina Julii Restii*, ed. Nodilo, p. 366. There is no archival evidence to support the account, but in the light of the adoption of the same tactic by the Herceg of handing undefendable strongholds to the Hungarians it should not be dismissed as entirely fictitious.
36. Jakov Bunić's son later converted to Islam (B. Bojović, *Raguse et l'empire ottoman [1430–1520]. Les actes impériaux ottomans en vieux-serbe de Murad II à Sélim 1er* [Paris, 1998], pp. 113–117).
37. In 1482 Sultan Bayezid asked Dubrovnik to let him have any news about Đem's movements and to capture him if he appeared on Ragusan soil. See plate 7.
38. Inalcik, *Ottoman Empire : the Classical Age*, pp. 30–33.
39. T. Popović, *Turska i Dubrovnik u xvi. veku* (Belgrade, 1973), pp. 18–20, 55, 64.
40. *Ibid.*, pp. 22, 406 note 19, 407.
41. *Ibid.*, p. 90.
42. *Ibid.*, pp. 93–98.
43. *Ibid.*, pp. 117–128.
44. Buda itself fell to the Turks in 1541.

Chapter Six

1. *Dubrovačka akta i povelje*, ed. Radonić, 2/1, no. ci, pp. 224–225; no. cii, pp. 225–226; no. ciii, pp. 227–228; no. cv, pp. 229–230; no. cxxx, pp. 286–287; no. cxlvi, pp. 348–349; no. cxlviii, pp. 359–361; no. cxlix, pp. 361–362.

2. *Ibid.*, no. cliii, pp. 373–375.
3. Foretić, *Povijest Dubrovnika do 1808.*, ii, 19–33.
4. For these plans see pp. 150–151.
5. See also p. 161.
6. R. Knecht, *Francis I* (Cambridge, 1982), pp. 217–218.
7. J. Tadić, *Španija i Dubrovnik u xvi. veku* (Belgrade, 1932), p. 45 and footnote.
8. *Ibid.*, p. 58.
9. *Ibid.*, p. 115.
10. Foretić, *Povijest Dubrovnika do 1808.*, ii, 64–65.
11. V. Kostić, 'Ragusa and the Spanish Armada', *Dubrovnik's Relations with England : a Symposium, April 1978*, ed. R. Filipović and M. Partridge (University of Zagreb, 1977), 48–57.
12. Foretić, *Povijest Dubrovnika do 1808.*, ii, 66–70. For further discussion of Dubrovnik's maritime trading families see pp. 194–195.
13. M. Deanović, *Anciens contacts entre la France et Raguse*, Bibliothèque de l'institut français de Zagreb, iii (Zagreb, 1950), pp. 10–11.
14. Popović, *op. cit.*, p. 155.
15. *Ibid.*, p. 239.
16. R. Samardžić, *Veliki vek Dubrovnika* (Belgrade, 1962), pp. 36, 45, 103.
17. On the Slavic Chancery see p. 140.
18. B. Krizman, *O dubrovačkoj diplomaciji* (Zagreb, 1951), pp. 115–126.
19. Popović, *op. cit.*, p. 93.
20. *Ibid.*, pp. 126–127.
21. Foretić, *Povijest Dubrovnika do 1808.*, ii, 73.
22. Specifically, the practice contained in the *Cerimoniale* reflects the instructions given to the *poklisari* of 1708, Frano Gundulić and Đuro Gučetić, when the mission was despatched for the 'first time after the [Austro-Turkish] war' (DAD, Leges et Instructiones, 21/1, no. 8, Cerimoniale, fos 1r-11v.) For what follows: N. Lonza, 'O dubrovačkom diplomatskom ceremonialu', *Međunarodni simpozij: Diplomacija Dubrovačke Republike. Zbornik diplomatske akademije* (Zagreb, 1996), 169–175. From 1676 the Ragusan Republic employed a full time official to oversee ceremonial. The Ragusan *Cerimoniale* is also heavily influenced by Florentine and, naturally, Venetian equivalents.
23. Z. Zlatar, *Our Kingdom Come: the Counter-Reformation, the Republic of Dubrovnik, and the Liberation of the Balkan Slavs* (Boulder, 1992), pp.90–93; B. Krizman, *Diplomati i konzuli u starom Dubrovniku* (Zagreb, 1957), pp. 45–50, 110. For an example of such code see plate 8.
24. The Hercegović family's goodwill was worth soliciting. For example, in 1568 the *poklisari* were instructed to bring a 'special' provision to them so that they would wield their influence on the Republic's behalf (*Dubrovačka akta i povelje*, ed. Radonić, SKA Zbornik za istoriju, jezik i književnost srpskog naroda, Section III, book 8 [1938], 2/2, no. lxviii, p. 171).
25. For discussion of the *uskok*s see p. 114.
26. Popović, *op. cit.*, pp. 350–361; Biegman, *op. cit.*, 61–63.
27. Inalcik, *Ottoman Empire: the Classical Age*, p.41; *idem*, 'Lepanto in the Ottoman Documents', *The Ottoman Empire: Conquest, Organisation and Economy. Collected Studies* (London, 1978), 191.
28. For the Counter-Reformation enthusiasts and propagandists see pp. 235–237.
29. J. Tadić, *Dubrovački portreti* (Belgrade, 1948), pp. 24–52.
30. Tadić, *Španija i Dubrovnik*, pp. 60–62.
31. Popović, *op. cit.*, pp. 185–186.
32. Tadić, *Španija i Dubrovnik*, pp. 63–65.
33. *Ibid.*, pp. 71–73.
34. For Dubrovnik's trade at this time see p. 171.
35. Tadić, *Dubrovački portreti*, pp. 234–280. For Frano Gundulić's fate see p. 150.
36. *Depeschen des Francesco Gondola, Gesandten der Republik Ragusa bei Pius V. und Gregor XIII. (1570–1573)*, ed. L. Voinovich, Archiv für österreichische Geschichte, 98. Band (Vienna, 1909), pp. 545–645; Tadić, *Španija i Dubrovnik u xvi. veku*, pp. 104–117.
37. *Lettres d'information de la république de Raguse (xviie siècle)*, ed. I. Dujev, *Godišnjak na sofijskija*

universitet istoriko-filologičeski fakultet, book 33/10 (Sofia, 1937), 1–72; I. Dujčev, 'A propos de l'historiographie de Dubrovnik', (Recueil des travaux à l'hommage du professeur Radovan Samardžić), *Balcanica*, xiii-xiv (1982–1983), 97–103.

38. This confusion certainly affected Dubrovnik, which called local raiders from Boka Kotorska '*uskoks*' – and not unreasonably. See below.
39. DAD, Lamenti politici, 11/7, fos I, 1r-2v, 75r, 77r, 79r-v, 83r-v, 85r-v.
40. *Ibid.*, fo 15r-v.
41. *Ibid.*, fos 29r-v, 33r.
42. *Ibid.*, fo 11r-v.
43. *Ibid.*, fo 27r-v.
44. *Ibid.*, fos 17r-20r.
45. C. W. Bracewell, *The Uskoks of Senj: Piracy, Banditry, and Holy War in the Sixteenth Century Adriatic* (Ithaca, 1992), pp. 3–5, 11–12, 135, 165–166, 202–203; Foretić, *Povijest Dubrovnika do 1808.*, ii, 61–63.
46. Bracewell, *op. cit.*, p. 166, note 40; Popović, *op. cit.*, p. 271.
47. Popović, *op. cit.*, pp. 365–366.
48. For the opening of Split and its impact see pp. 172–173.
49. G. E. Rothenburg, 'Christian Insurrections in Turkish Dalmatia 1580–96', *The Slavonic and East European Review*, 40 (1961), 136–147.
50. Foretić, *Povijest Dubrovnika do 1808.*, ii, 74; Samardžić, *Veliki vek*, p. 51.
51. For the intrigues and intriguers see pp. 150–151.
52. Foretić, *Povijest Dubrovnika do 1808.*, ii, 80–84; Samardžić, *Veliki vek*, pp. 14–46; Lučić, 'Prošlost otoka Lastova', 61–70.
53. Foretić, *Povijest Dubrovnika do 1808.*, ii, 87.
54. Samardžić, *Veliki vek*, pp. 82–83.
55. *Ibid.*, pp. 84–87.
56. For quarantine in Dubrovnik see pp. 167–169.
57. Foretić, *Povijest Dubrovnika do 1808.*, ii, 95–102; Samardžić, *Veliki vek*, pp. 89–110.
58. Samardžić, *Veliki vek*, pp.117–144.
59. See chapter 13.
60. Tadić, *Promet Putnika*, p. 271.

Chapter Seven

1. B. Stulli, 'O 'knjizi statuta grada Dubrovnika' iz god. 1272', *Dubrovnik*, 1–2/15 (1972), 17–26.
2. On the 'franchise of St Blaise' see p. 238.
3. *Liber Omnium Reformationum Civitatis Ragusii,* ed. A. Solovjev, Dubrovački zakoni i uredbe. Monumenta historico-juridica, 1. Zbornik za istoriju, jezik i književnost srpskog naroda, section III, book 6, pp. i-v; *Liber Statutorum*, ed. Bogišić and Jireček, book I, page 2.
4. *Liber Statutorum*, ed. Bogišić and Jireček, pp. xv-xxiii and book II, chapter 1, pp. 24–55.
5. *Ibid.*, book III, chapter 50, p. 76.
6. *Ibid.*, book VIII, chapter 18, p. 202.
7. *Liber Omnium Reformationum*, ed. Solovjev, pp. iv-v.
8. *Knjiga odredaba dubrovačke carinarnice 1277 (Liber Statutorum Doane Ragusii MCCLXXVII.),* ed. and trans. J. Lučić (Dubrovnik, 1989).
9. The results of his notarial work in the Dubrovnik chancery have been published: *Spisi dubrovačke kancelarije*, i, *Zapisi notara Tomazina de Savere (1278–1282.)*, ed. G. Čremošnik, Monumenta historica Ragusina, I (Zagreb, 1951).
10. *Ibid.*, pp. vi, ix.
11. *Liber Statutorum*, ed. Bogišić and Jireček, pp. vii-xiv, xxviii-xxxiv.
12. Such luminaries as the Ragusan intellectual Nikola Vitov Gučetić, and the historians Jakov Lukarević and Junije Rastić all drew attention to the numerous similarities between Venice and Dubrovnik. Less flatteringly, a visiting Frenchman in the sixteenth century thought that the Ragusans imitated the Venetians 'like monkeys' (Z. Janeković-Römer, *Okvir slobode: Dubrovačka vlastela između srednjovjekovlja i humanizma*, HAZU, Prilozi povijesti stanovništva

i okolice Dubrovnika, book 8 [Dubrovnik, 1999], p. 15).

13. *Liber Statutorum*, ed. Bogišić and Jireček, book I, chapter 5, p.7; chapter 6, pp. 7–8; chapter 8, p. 8; chapter 10, p. 9; chapter 11, p. 9; chapter 12, p. 10; chapter 13, p. 11; chapter 14, p. 11; chapter 17, pp. 12–13; chapter 18, pp. 13–14; chapter 21, pp. 14–15; *Libri Reformationum,* i, 34.
14. *Liber Statutorum*, ed. Bogišić and Jireček, book I, chapter 9, p. 8; chapter 10, p. 9.
15. 'Dubrovačka Republika', in *Enciklopedija Jugoslavije* (Zagreb, 1984), p. 612. This authoritative but anonymous article is the work of Bernard Stulli.
16. *Libri Reformationum*, i, 117.
17. *Ibid.*, pp. 179–181.
18. *Libri Reformationum*, ii, 119.
19. *Ibid.*, p. 282.
20. *Libri Reformationum*, i, 177.
21. *Libri Reformationum*, ii, 212.
22. *Ibid.*, p. 163.
23. *Ibid.*, p. 282.
24. *Libri Reformationum*, i, 12–14.
25. *Ibid.*, p. 74.
26. *Libri Reformationum*, ii, 25, 208.
27. See also p. 129.
28. Cf. R-H. Bautier, *The Economic Development of Medieval Europe* (London, 1971), pp. 227–228; P. S. Lewis, *Later Medieval France – the Polity* (London, 1968), pp. 245–254.
29. Lane, *op. cit.*, pp. 112–114.
30. Foretić, *Povijest Dubrovnika do 1808.*, i, 122. In Dubrovnik, from the earliest times to the fall of the Republic, the age of nobles for this purpose was calculated from the date of conception rather than of birth.
31. *Libri Reformationum*, v, 349.
32. For further discussion of the Ragusan patriciate see pp. 185–191.
33. On the question of the Ragusan Republic's 'independence' see Appendix 1.
34. *Libri Reformationum*, ii, 247.
35. *Ibid.*, 208–209, 257.
36. Medini, *Dubrovnik Gučetića*, p. 67.
37. Janeković-Römer, *Okvir slobode*, p. 35.
38. G. Čremošnik, 'Dubrovački pečati srednjega vijeka', *Anali*, 4–5 (1956), 31–3; *Dubrovačka akta i povelje*, ed. Radonić, 1/2, no. cclxiii, pp. 598–599.
39. *Ibid.*, no. cclxii, pp. 596–598.
40. *Ibid.*, no. cclxiv, pp. 600–601.
41. Razzi, *Storia di Ragusa*, ed. Gelcich, p. 68 note 1, and p.127. See plate 40.
42. A. Vučetić, *Sveti Vlaho u Dubrovniku* (Dubrovnik, 1924), pp. 5, 9. The soldiers were, of course, likely to be Italians.
43. *Dubrovačka akta i povelje*, ed. Radonić, 1/2, no. cclxv, pp. 601–602; no. ccciv, pp.675–676. Dubrovnik did not in fact mint gold coins. For the Ragusan coinage see pp. 173–175.
44. Diversis, *Situs Aedificiorum*, ed. Brunelli. p. 57.
45. Ivan Gundulić, *Dubravka*, translated by E. Goy in *BC Review,* 9/3 (October, 1976), pp. 22–23. For further discussion of *Dubravka* and the poet's other works see pp. 226–270.
46. Diversis, *Situs Aedificiorum*, ed. Brunelli, p. 58.
47. Lukarević, *Copioso ristretto*, p. 257.
48. *Ibid.*, p. 265; Janeković-Römer, *Okvir slobode*, pp. 127–131. Cerimoniale, fos 83r-94r. These provisions for the (necessarily) rare event of a death of a Rector in office were indeed implemented. On Shrove Tuesday 1662 the Rector dropped dead amid the celebrations. Consequently, it was established that in such cases the Carnival would be cancelled. Another such death occurred in June 1798. *Ibid.*, fos 88r, 92r-94r.
49. Zlatar, *Our Kingdom Come*, pp. 43–44.
50. Lukarević, *Copioso ristretto*, pp. 264–265; Zlatar, *Our Kingdom Come*, p. 42.

51. B. Krekić, 'Influence politique et pouvoir économique à Dubrovnik (Raguse) du xiiie au xvie siècle', *Dubrovnik: a Mediterranean Urban Society, 1300–1600* (Aldershot, 1997), 256. On demographic change and its consequences for the patriciate see pp. 190–191.
52. Zlatar, *Our Kingdom Come*, pp. 40–41; Lukarević, *Copioso ristretto*, pp. 260–262.
53. Janeković-Römer, *Okvir slobode*, p. 101.
54. *Ibid.*, pp. 106–108. On Ragusan factionalism and the problems it caused see pp. 151, 356–359. Zlatar's study, *Our Kingdom Come: the Counter Reformation, the Republic of Dubrovnik, and the Liberation of the Balkan Slavs* (Boulder, 1992), is the best examination of this phenomenon. On the unscrupulous behaviour of Venetian patrician politicians, see D. Queller, *The Venetian Patriciate – Reality versus Myth* (Urbana and Chicago, 1986).
55. B. Krekić, 'The Attitude of Fifteenth Century Ragusans towards Literacy', *Dubrovnik: a Mediterranean Urban Society, 1300–1600* (Aldershot, 1997), 229.
56. DAD, Leges et Instuctiones, 21/1, no. 1, Specchio del Maggior Consiglio, fo Ir.
57. *Ibid.*, fos 382r *et seq.*
58. This was also the day on which the Rector for January was appointed – other Rectors being chosen at the relevant session, the month before they held office – and when the elections for most of the other important offices of the Republic took place.
59. Janeković-Römer, *Okvir slobode*, p. 103.
60. The fullest and most authoritative account of the electoral process is that given by Nella Lonza in 'Izborni postupak Dubrovačke republike', *Anali*, 38 (2000), 9–52.
61. The process of direct election – applying to the Republic's external offices (*de foris*) – was known as *scrutinium* (*Ibid.*, 24). See below.
62. Cf. Lane, *op. cit.*, p. 110.
63. From the mid-fifteenth century the Great Council had its own building by the side of the Rector's Palace and connected with it. This Council Hall was pulled down in the nineteenth century (Lonza, 'Izborni postupak', 14).
64. These proceedings were somewhat simplified from the seventeenth century as the number of Councillors fell, but as far as possible the outward forms of the past were retained (*Ibid.*, 23–24).
65. *Ibid.*, 25.
66. Lukarević, *Copioso ristretto*, pp. 257–260. The electoral procedure was taken immensely seriously. On one occasion when, on inspection of the contents of the electoral urn, it was discovered that some mischievous councillor had dropped a playing die into it in place of a regular ballot the miscreant was threatened, if found, with loss of his right hand and of his nobility (Janeković-Römer, *Okvir slobode*, p. 110).
67. Lukarević, *Copioso ristretto*, pp, 265–267.
68. *Ibid.*, pp. 273–274.
69. *Ibid.*, pp. 271–272, 279–282. On the hospices and hospital see pp. 213–214.
70. *Ibid.*, pp. 272–273, 276, 278, 282–283; Lane, *op. cit.*, pp. 98–104.
71. Recent analysis of the career paths of Ragusan office-holders has even led one scholar to conclude that, 'there is no single road or path up through the offices' (D. Rheubottom, *Age, Marriage, and Politics in Fifteenth Century Ragusa* [Oxford, 2000], p. 158).
72. Lukarević, *Copioso ristretto*, pp. 282–283; Janeković-Römer, *Okvir slobode*, pp. 117–119.
73. Diversis, *Situs aedificiorum*, ed. Brunelli, pp. 75–76; G. Čremošnik, 'Postanak i razvoj srpske ili hrvatske kancelarije u Dubrovniku', *Anali*, 1 (1952), 75–79.
74. Lukarević, *Copioso ristretto*, pp. 285–286; *Enciklopedija Jugoslavije*, p. 613.
75. By the time of the fall of the Republic the number of Župa's *kaznačine* had increased to eleven.
76. For the *kapituli* of Mljet, see pp. 144–145.
77. J. Lučić, 'Uprava u Župi Dubrovačkoj', *Zbornik Župe Dubrovačke*, 1 (1985), 100–124.
78. A. Marinović, 'Lopudska universitas (pravni položaj otoka Lopuda u Dubrovačkoj Republici)', *Anali*, 3 (1954), 181–235; J. Lučić, 'Pučki zborovi na Lopudu i Koločepu od 17. do 19. stoljeća', *Zbornik Dubrovačkog Primorja i otoka*, 2 (1988), 41–47.
79. *Libri Reformationum*, i, 141.

80. *Ibid.*, p. 155; *Libri Reformationum*, ii, 86–87.
81. *Stonske odredbe izdate g. 1333–1406 (Ordines Stagni editi annis 1333–1406),* ed. Solovjev, article II, nos. 9 and 12, p. 362.
82. On the salt industry and the wine trade see respectively pp. 153–154 and pp. 183–184.
83. Z. Šundrica, 'Stonski rat u xiv stoljeću (1333–1399.)', *Pelješki zbornik*, 2 (1980), 81–82.
84. *Libri Reformationum*, i, 193.
85. Cf. *Ibid.*, p.240. In August 1346 the Senate debated what to do with three villains, once banished but now reported to be at large again on Pelješac: the only disagreement was about the savagery of the mutilation to be inflicted as punishment.
86. *Stonske odredbe,* ed. Solovjev, article II, no. 1, p. 360; no. 2, p. 361; no. 7, p. 361; no. 8, p. 362; no. 14, p. 362.
87. K. Bagoje, 'Knežev dvor u Pridvorju', *Konavle u prošlosti, sadašnjosti i budućnosti*, 1 (1998), 279–293.
88. Grujić, *Konavli pod raznim gospodarima*, pp. 82–97; Z. Šundrica, 'Dubrovačka vlastela i konavoski knezovi', *Konavoski zbornik*, 1 (1982), 44–53; Janeković-Römer, *Okvir slobode*, pp. 148–149, 150.
89. For the abbey of Mlet see pp. 231–232. For society on Mljet see pp. 217–218.
90. J. Lučić, 'Pučki zborovi na Mljetu', *Zbornik otoka Mljeta*, 1 (1989), 185–189.
91. Lučić, 'Prošlost otoka Lastova', 37, 48.
92. C. Fisković, 'Lastovski spomenici', *Prilozi povijesti umjetnosti u Dalmaciji*, xvi (1966), 91–135.
93. Gundulić, *Dubravka*, trans. Goy, p. 5.
94. *Liber Statutorum*, ed. Bogišić and Jireček, book VI, chapter 1, pp. 124–125; chapter 3, p. 125; chapter 4, p. 127; chapter 5, pp.127–128; chapter 6, p. 128; chapter 8, p. 128; chapter 10, p. 129; chapter 14, p. 130.
95. *Ibid.*, book VI, chapter xii, p. 129.
96. *Libri Reformationum*, i, 209.
97. *Liber Omnium Reformationum*, ed. Solovjev, pagina VII, capitulum x, p. 46; pagina XVII, capitulum iii, pp. 99–100; pagina XVII, capitulum v, pp. 100–101; *Libri Reformationum*, i, 201.
98. Diversis, *Situs Aedificiorum*, ed. Brunelli, p. 130.
99. DAD, Lamenti politici, 11/3, fo 184v.
100. *Ibid.*, fo 195v.
101. Lamenti politici, 11/4, fo 11r.
102. *Ibid.*, fo 3r.
103. Razzi, *Storia di Ragusa*, ed. Gelcich, pp. 191–192.
104. Lamenti politici, 11/4, fo 22r.
105. Tadić, *Dubrovački portreti*, pp. 162–1948; J. Dayre, *Dubrovačke studije* (Zagreb, 1938), pp. 24–38.
106. Samardžić, *Veliki vek*, pp. 54–57. For the remainder of Stijepo Đurđević's career see below.
107. *Annales Ragusini anonymi*, ed. Nodilo, pp. 86–87, 242–246; Razzi, *Storia di Ragusa*, ed. Gelcich, pp. 86–87.
108. *Liber Omnium Reformationum*, ed. Solovjev, pagina XXIII, capitulum iv, p. 131.
109. *Annales Ragusini anonymi*, ed. Nodilo, pp. 99–101, 278–280; *Chronica Ragusina Junii Restii*, ed. Nodilo, pp. 437–439.
110. Mavro Orbini, b. mid-sixteenth century, d. 1610, 1611 or 1614 (possibly executed as a conspirator); abbot of monastery of Sv. Mihovil on Šipan; later abbot of monastery of Sv. Marija on Mljet (Zlatar, *Our Kingdom Come*, pp. 361–363).
111. Zlatar, *Our Kingdom Come*, pp. 171–175.
112. *Ibid.*, 269–324; Samardžić, *Veliki vek*, pp. 63–66. For the longer term effects of the 'Great Conspiracy' on the cohesion of the patriciate see pp. 356–359.

Chapter Eight

1. Foretić, *Povijest Dubrovnika do 1808.*, i, 47.
2. M. Dinić, 'Dubrovački tributi – Mogoriš, Svetodimitarski i Konavoski dohodak, Provižun braće Vlatkovića', Glas SKA, 168 (1935), 203–239; Foretić, *Povijest Dubrovnika do 1808.*, i, 46, 84–88.

3. See pp. 50–51.
4. Jireček, *Die Bedeutung von Ragusa*, 148.
5. *Libri Reformationum*, ii, 136.
6. S. Ćirković, 'Ragusa e il suo retroterra nel Medio Evo', *Ragusa e il Mediterraneo: ruolo e funzioni di una repubblica marinara tra medioevo ed età moderna. Atti del convegno internationale di studi, Bari, 21–22 ottobre 1988*, ed. A. Di Vittorio (Bari, 1990), 20.
7. *Enciklopedija Jugoslavije*, p. 624.
8. See p. 67 and note 13, pp. 89–92.
9. Jireček, *Die Bedeutung von Ragusa*, p. 144.
10. Biegman, *op. cit.*, pp. 155–163.
11. *Enciklopedija Jugoslavije*, p. 625.
12. The names of both Srebrenica and Olovo reflect their production: in Croatian *srebro* is silver and *olovo* lead.
13. Jireček, *Die Bedeutung von Ragusa*, pp.144–153; *idem*, *Die Handelsstrassen und Bergwerke von Serbien und Bosnien während des Mittelalters*, Abhandlungen der königlichen bömischen Gesellschaft der Wissenschaften vom Jahre 1879 und 1880, vi. Folge, 10. Band (Prague, 1881), 42–62; Carter, *op. cit.*, 225–321; S. Ćirković and D. Kovačević-Kojić, 'L'Economie naturelle et la production marchande aux xiiie-xive siècles dans les régions actuelles de la Yougoslavie', Recueil des travaux à l'hommage du professeur Radovan Samardžić, *Balcanica*, xiii-xiv (1982–1983), 50; D. Kovačević-Kojić, 'Il commercio raguseo di terraferma nel Medio Evo', *Ragusa e il Mediterraneo,* ed. Di Vittorio, 70; S. Ćirković, 'The Production of Gold, Silver and Copper in the Central Parts of the Balkans from the 13th to the 16th Century', Precious Metals in the Age of Expansion. Papers of the XIVth International Congress of the Historical Sciences, ed. H. Kellenbenz. *Beiträger zur Wirtschaftsgeschichte*, Band 2 (Stuttgart, 1981), 42–48; M. Dinić, *Za istoriju rudarstva u srednjevekovnoj Srbiji i Bosni*, part 1, SKA Posebna izdanja, 240 (1955), pp. 92–97.
14. Ćirković and Kovačević-Kojić, 'L'Economie naturelle', 50–51; B. Krekić, 'Italian Creditors in Dubrovnik (Ragusa) and the Balkan Trade, Thirteenth through Fifteenth Centuries', *Dubrovnik, Italy and the Balkans in the Later Middle Ages* (London, 1980), 250–252.
15. Jireček, *Die Handelsstrassen und Bergwerke*, pp. 45–46.
16. For the Ragusan coinage and goldsmiths see pp. 173–175, 177–178.
17. Ćirković, 'The Production of Gold, Silver and Copper in the Central Parts of the Balkans', 54–60.
18. Carter, *op. cit.*, pp. 248–256.
19. B. Krekić, *Dubrovnik (Raguse) et le Levant au moyen âge.* Documents et recherches sur l'économie des pays byzantins, islamiques et slaves et leurs relations commerciales au moyen âge, v (Paris, 1961), pp. 109–110.
20. *Knjiga odredaba dubrovačke carinarnice*, ed. Lučić, articles xi-xii, pp. 18–21.
21. V. Vinaver, 'Trgovina bosanskim robljem tokom xiv veka u Dubrovniku', *Anali*, 2 (1953), 132.
22. B. Krekić, 'L'Abolition de l'esclavage à Dubrovnik (Raguse) au xve siècle: mythe ou réalité?', *Dubrovnik: a Mediterranean Urban Society, 1300–1600* (Aldershot, 1997), 309–317.
23. H. Inalcik, *An Economic and Social History of the Ottoman Empire* (Cambridge, 1994), pp. 257–262. On the Ragusan cloth industry see pp. 180–182.
24. *Ibid.*, pp. 265–266.
25. S. Dimitrijević, *Dubrovački karavani u južnoj Srbiji u xvii. veku*, SAN Posebna izdanja, 304 (1958), pp. 2–80.
26. Jireček, *Die Handelsstrassen und Bergwerke*, pp. 46–47.
27. Popović, *op. cit.*, pp. 245–247.
28. I. Mitić, *Konzuli i konzularna služba starog Dubrovnika* (Dubrovnik, 1973), pp. 31–33.
29. Zlatar, *Our Kingdom Come*, pp. 91, 120–122.
30. *Libri Reformationum*, i, 2–4, 10, 31, 39, 40, 66–67, 70, 75–76, 101; D. Dinić-Knežević, 'Trgovina žitom u Dubrovniku u xiv veku', *Godišnjak filozofskog fakulteta u Novom Sadu*, x (1967), 80–81.

31. B. Krekić, 'Four Florentine Commercial Companies in Dubrovnik (Ragusa) in the First Half of the Fourteenth Century', *Dubrovnik, Italy and the Balkans in the Late Middle Ages* (London, 1980), 40.
32. Diversis, *Situs Aedificiorum*, p. 82.
33. Lukarević, *Copioso ristretto*, p. 280.
34. L. Beritić, 'Ubikacija nestalih gradjevinskih spomenika u Dubrovnik', part 1, *Prilozi povijesti umjetnosti u Dalmaciji*, x (1956), 43–44; *The Restoration of Dubrovnik 1979–89*, ed. B. Letunić (Zagreb, 1990), p. 133.
35. Tadić, *Španija i Dubrovnik*, p. 19; M. Spremić, *Dubrovnik i Aragonci 1442–1495* (Belgrade, [1971]), pp. 7–27, 128–148.
36. *Annales Ragusini anonymi*, ed. Nodilo, pp. 90–91.
37. Biegman, *op. cit.*, pp. 109–111.
38. M. Aymard, *Venise, Raguse et le commerce du blé pendant la seconde moitié du xvie siècle. Ecole pratique des hautes études – VIe section. Centre des recherches historiques. Ports-Routes-Trafics*, xx (Paris, 1966), p. 119.
39. *Liber Statutorum*, ed. Bogišić, book 7, chapter iii, pp. 152–153; chapter xi, pp. 155–156; chapter xiii, p. 156; B. Krekić, 'Ragusa (Dubrovnik) e il mare: aspetti e problemi (xiv-xvi secolo)', *Dubrovnik: a Mediterranean Urban Society, 1300–1600* (Aldershot, 1997), 139–141.
40. *Liber Statutorum*, ed. Bogišić, book 7, chapter ii, pp. 151–152; Foretić, *Povijest Dubrovnika do 1808.*, i, 127.
41. The real differences, beyond those of terminology, between many of the known types of Ragusan ships are not always very clear from the sources. But they are examined in the detailed survey by J. Luetić, *Pomorci i jedrenjaci Republike Dubrovačke* (Zagreb, 1984), pp. 199 (carack), 201–205 (*grippo*), 217–226 (galleon), 227–229 (*nava*), 231–232 (*marsiliana*), 233–234 (berton), 235 (frigate), 237–241 (*ormanica* – warship), 243–244 (frigatoon), 245 (*šajka*), 247 (*pink*), 249 (*šionica*), 241–253 (*patache*), 255–256 (*urque*), 257–258 (tartan), 277–286 (*filjuga* – warship), 287–292 (polacre), 293–296 (brig).
42. J. Tadić, 'Le Port de Raguse et sa flotte au xvie siècle', *Le Navire et l'économie maritime du moyen-âge au xviiie siècle principalement en Méditerranée – Travaux du deuxième colloque international d'histoire maritime tenu, les 17 et 18 mai 1957, à l'Académie de Marine*, 14–16; *idem*, 'O pomorstvu Dubrovnika u xvi i xvii veku', *Dubrovačko Pomorstvo: u spomen sto godina nautičke škole u Dubrovniku* (Dubrovnik, 1952), 179–181; S. Vekarić, 'Dubrovačka trgovačka flota 1599 godine', *Anali*, 3 (1954), 430.
43. F. Braudel, *The Mediterranean and the Mediterranean World in the Age of Philip II*, trans. S. Reynolds, i (London, 1972), 602–636.
44. Tadić, 'O pomorstvu Dobrovnika', p. 181.
45. J. Luetić, *Brodovlje Dubrovačke Republike xvii stoljeća* (Dubrovnik, 1964), p. 39, 44.
46. Tadić, 'O pomorstvu Dubrovnika', p. 171
47. I. Voje, *Kreditna trgovina u srednjovjekomnom Dubrovniku*, Akademija nauka i umjetnosti Bosne i Hercegovine, Djela, 49 (Sarajevo, 1976), pp. 105–107.
48. J. Tadić, 'Pomorsko osiguranje u Dubrovniku xvi stoljeća', *Zbornik iz dubrovačke prošlosti Milanu Rešetaru o 70–oj godišnjici života*, ed. V. Ćović *et al.* (Dubrovnik, 1931), 109–112; A. and B. Tenenti, *Il prezzo del rischio. L'assicurazione mediterranea vista da Ragusa: 1563–1591* (Venice, 1985), pp. 176, 186–206.
49. Mitić, *Konzulati*, pp. 40–42.
50. *Ibid.*, pp. 43–44; Foretić, *Povijest Dubrovnika do 1808.*, ii, 92–94. A Ragusan consul re-appeared in Alexandria in the seventeenth century.
51. Mitić, *Konzulati*, pp. 45–48.
52. *Ibid.*, pp. 53–54. For the later history of the Ragusan consular service see p. 353.
53. Foretić, *Povijest Dubrovnika do 1808.*, ii, 95.
54. See p. 211.
55. M. Grmek, 'Le Concept d'infection dans l'antiquité et au moyen âge, les anciennes mesures sociales contre les maladies contagieuses et la fondation de la première quarantaine à Dubrovnik (1377)', *Rad*, 384 (1980), 38–53.

56. V. Bazala, 'Pomorski Lazareti u starom Dubrovniku', *Dubrovačko Pomorstvo: u spomen sto godina nautičke škole u Dubrovniku*, ed. J. Luetić *et al.* (Dubrovnik, 1952), 296–306; Evlija Čelebija, *Putopis. Odlomci o jugoslovenskim zemljama*, trans. and ed. H. Šabanović (Sarajevo, 1957), ii, 191–192.
57. V. Kostić, *Dubrovnik i Engleska 1300–1650,* SAN Posebna izdanja, 488 (1975), pp. 7–8, 97–148, 233–237. For an account of life in this expatriate community, see pp. 197–198.
58. Foretić, *Povijest Dubrovnika do 1808.*, ii, 44–45.
59. For the history of the port and its defences see pp. 293–297.
60. Popović, *op. cit.*, p. 64.
61. Carter, *op. cit.* p. 396 and his Table on p. 397.
62. Popović, *op. cit.*, 260–261, 302–305; Carter, *op. cit.* pp. 396–297. For Dubrovnik's Jewish community see pp. 192–201.
63. R. Paci, 'La concorrenza Ragusa-Spalato tra fine Cinquecento e primo Seicento', *Ragusa e il Mediterraneo,* ed. Di Vittorio, 185–188; Inalcik, *Economic and Social History*, pp. 267–268.
64. Samardžić, *Veliki vek*, p. 67.
65. Paci, 'La concorrenza', 194.
66. Foretić, *Povijest Dubrovnika do 1808.*, pp. 111–112.
67. B. Mimica, *Numizmatička povijest Dubrovnika* (Rijeka, [1996]), pp. 50–52.
68. *Ibid.*, pp. 329–331.
69. M. Rešetar, *Dubrovačka numizmatika*, i, SKA Posebna izdanja, 48 (1924), pp. 29–70 and table.
70. Krekić, 'Italian Creditors in Dubrovnik (Ragusa) and the Balkan Trade, Thirteenth through Fifteenth Centuries', *Dubrovnik, Italy and the Balkans in the Late Middle Ages* (London, 1980), 252; V. Vinaver, *Pregled istorije novca u jogoslovenskim zemljama (xvi-xviii vek)* (Belgrade, 1970), 113–114, 232, 234–237, 351–354.
71. Mimica, *op. cit.*, pp. 332–338.
72. Voje, *Kreditna trgovina*, pp. 12–13, 39–41, 90–91, 105–107, 169–186.
73. *Enciklopedija Jugoslavije*, p. 616. For the Kosača legacy see pp. 88, 94–95, 108–110.
74. Voje, *Kreditna trgovina*, p. 170.
75. Lukarević, *Copioso ristretto*, p. 271.
76. In 1575 the Ragusan government imposed a 20 per cent tax on the interest received by private individuals on their funds invested in foreign banks. Data exist for the periods 1575–1577, 1583–1588, 1601, 1621, 1700–1724 and 1789–1790. There was a large increase in the number of *rentiers* at the end of the sixteenth/early seventeenth centuries, possibly reflecting a growth in wealth among the most important commoner families. A sharp reduction in the total amount invested in the first quarter of the eighteenth century compared with 1621 almost certainly reflects the economic damage wrought by the earthquake and ensuing crises (A. Di Vittorio, 'Gli investimenti finanziari ragusei in Italia tra XVI e XVIII secolo', *Tra mare e terra. Aspetti economici e finanziari della Repubblica di Ragusa in età moderna* (Bari, 2001), 37–78).
77. S. Krasić, *Stjepan Gradić (1613–1683). Život i djelo* (Zagreb, 1987), pp. 158–159.
78. Diversis, *Situs Aedificiorum*, ed. Brunelli, p. 78.
79. See pp. 191–193, 242–243.
80. D. Roller, *Dubrovački zanati u xv. i xvi. stoljeću.* Građa za gospodarsku povijest Hrvatske, 2 (Zagreb, 1951), pp. 1–3.
81. *Ibid.*, p. 157.
82. *Bratovštine i obrtne korporacije u Republici Dubrovačkoj od xiii. do konca xviii. vijeka,* ii. *Dubrovačke obrtne korporacije (cehovi)*, ed. K. Vojnović. Monumenta historico-juridica Slavorum meridionalium, vii (Zagreb, 1899), pp. xv-xviii, xxii-xxvi.
83. The Ragusans, like the modern Croatians, made no distinction corresponding to the English terms 'goldsmith' and 'silversmith'. Ragusan 'goldsmiths' were in fact largely working in silver.
84. C. Fisković, 'Dubrovački zlatari od xiii. do xvii. stoljeća', *Starohrvatska prosvjeta*, series iii, vol. 1, (1941), 150. In jewellery, filigree became a particular speciality and the tradition still continues.

85. I. Lentić, *Dubrovački zlatari* (Zagreb, 1984), p. 13.
86. *Ibid.*, pp. 14, 16; *idem*, 'Zlatarstvo', *Zlatno doba Dubrovnika XV. i XVI. stoljeće* [Exhibition Catalogue: Zagreb and Dubrovnik, 1987.], 229.
87. *Ibid.*, 230–233; *idem*, *Dubrovački zlatari*, pp. 8, 19, 33; Fisković, 'Dubrovački zlatari', 171–175. See plates 48 and 49.
88. C. Fisković, *Prvi poznati dubrovački graditelji* (Dubrovnik, 1955), p. 85.
89. For painters see pp. 271–284.
90. Tadić, 'O pomorstvu', 166–170; *idem*, 'Le Port de Raguse', 11–13.
91. G. Novak, 'Vunena industrija u Dubrovniku do sredine xvi stoljeća', *Zbornik iz dubrovačke prošlosti Milanu Rešetaru o 70–oj godišnjici života*, ed. V. Ćorović *et al.* (Dubrovnik, 1931), 99; Roller, *Dubrovački zanati*, p. 3.
92. Cf. *Annales Ragusini anonymi*, ed. Nodilo, p. 55; Diversis, *Situs Aedificiorum*, ed. Brunelli, pp. 113–114; Lukarević, *Copioso ristretto*, p. 270.
93. Roller, *Dubrovački zanati*, pp. 6–7, 44–46; D. Dinić-Knežević, 'Petar Pantela – Trgovac i suknar u Dubrovniku', *Godišnjak filozofskog fakulteta u Novom Sadu*, xiii/1 (1970), 87–114, 137–140.
94. *Annales Ragusini anonymi*, ed. Nodilo, p. 95; Roller, *Dubrovački zanati*, pp.3, 9–11.
95. Roller, *Dubrovački zanati*, pp. 6, 82.
96. *Ibid.*, pp. 2, 14–21, 51–82.
97. Spremić, *op. cit.*, p. 149.
98. Diversis, *Situs Aedificiorum*, ed. Brunelli, p. 132.
99. M. Blagojević, 'L'agricoltura nell'economia ragusea del Medioevo', *Ragusa e il Mediterraneo*, ed. Di Vittorio, 34–35.
100. *Ibid.*, 39–40.
101. D. Dinić-Knežević, 'Trgovina vinom u Dubrovniku u xiv. veku', *Godišnjak filozofskog fakulteta u Novom Sadu*, ix (1966), 39–85.
102. *Stonske odredbe*, ed. Solovjev, article I, no. 2, p. 357; nos. 4–5, p. 358; no. 5, p. 359; no.6. p. 360; *Libri Reformationum*, i, 180–181.

Chapter Nine

1. Lukarević, *Copioso ristretto*, p. 257.
2. Diversis, *Situs Aedificiorum*, ed. Brunelli, p. 56.
3. *Ibid.*, p. 124.
4. Janeković-Römer, *Okvir slobode*, pp. 42–27; Krasić, *Stjepan Gradić, Život i djelo*, p. 3; *Annales Ragusini anonymi*, ed. Nodilo, p. 222.
5. I. Mahnken, *Dubrovački patricijat u xiv veku*, SAN Posebna izdanja, 340 (1960), 8–9.
6. A. Soloviev, 'Le Patriciat de Raguse au xve siècle, *Zbornik iz dubrovačke prošlosti Milanu Rešetaru o 70–oj godišnjici života*, ed. V. Ćorović *et al.* (Dubrovnik, 1931), 64–65.
7. Krekić, 'Influence politique', 246.
8. *Liber Viridis*, ed. V. Nedeljković, SAN Zbornik za istoriju, jezik i književnost srpskig naroda, section III, book xxiii (1984), cap.188, p. 145; cap. 459, p. 402; *Liber Croceus*, ed. V. Nedeljković, SAN Zbornik za istoriju, jezik i književnost srpskig naroda, section III, book xxiv, cap. 86, pp. 94–111.
9. Krekić, 'Influence politique', 245–247.
10. *Liber Croceus*, ed. Nedeljković, cap.18, pp. 21–22. It is probable that the decision to 'close' the patriciate in 1462 was in part the result of demographic over-confidence resulting from the recent and unsustainable increase in the patrician birth-rate.
11. *Ibid.*, cap. 178, pp. 194–195.
12. Foretić, *Povijest Dubrovnika do 1808.*, i, 282.
13. Krekić, 'Developed Autonomy', 188–195.
14. The gloomy assertions contained in D. Pavlović, 'O krizi vlasteostog staleža u Dubrovniku', SAN Zbornik radova, book 17 (1952), 27–38 are shown to be unfounded by Zlatar in 'The 'Crisis' of the Patriciate in Early Seventeenth Century Dubrovnik: A Reappraisal', *Balcanica*, vi (1975), 111–131.

15. Zlatar, *Our Kingdom Come*, p. 132.
16. G. Novak, *Prošlost Dalmacije*, i (Zagreb, 1944), 207–211.
17. G. Novak, 'Nobiles, populus i cives – komuna i universitas u Splitu 1525.-1707.', *Rad*, 286 (1952), 5–22.
18. Janeković-Römer, *Okvir slobode*, pp. 66–67, 104. This judgement must be qualified, however, by evidence from recent research that the polarisation between two sharply opposed parties within the Ragusan nobility preceded by several decades the entry of the new families. See p. 356.
19. Tadić, *Dubrovački portreti*, pp. 111–125. For Marin Držić as poet and playwright see pp. 252–260.
20. Moreover, the effects of 'caste' upon the birthrate must have been magnified by what has been described as a 'schism' between the two main factions of the nobility, which would become qualified in later years by the names 'salamankezi' and 'sorbonezi'. Stjepan Ćosić and Nenad Vekarić have discovered that between 1667 and 1808 93.5 per cent of marriages were contracted within the same group (S. Ćosić and N. Vekarić, 'Raskol dubrovačkog patricijata', *Anali*, 39 [2001], 343).
21. Zlatar, *Our Kingdom Come*, pp. 40, 47.
22. *Liber Croceus*, ed. Nedeljković, cap. 315, pp. 374–375.
23. *Ibid.*, cap.314, pp. 373–374.
24. *Ibid.*, cap. 321, p. 379.
25. *Ibid.*, cap. 323, pp. 380–383.
26. *Ibid.*, cap. 323, p. 380–381.
27. *Ibid.*, cap. 325, p. 382.
28. *Ibid.*, cap. 326, pp. 382–383.
29. *Ibid.*, cap. 328, p. 384. For the debate about degrees of consanguinity see p. 205.
30. Janeković-Römer, *Okvir slobode*, p. 339.
31. DAD, Matrikula antunina, fos 1r-15r.
32. Masses were said in the different churches associated with the confraternity – The Holy Saviour (once opposite the Rector's Palace), St Peter the Great (which gave its name to that *sexterium* of the old city), St Nicholas (still standing in the street called Prijeko) and, of course, St Anthony (which stood on Ploče). For religious confraternities and their functions more generally see pp. 242–243.
33. Matrikula antunina, 16r-32r, 93r-101r. See plate 9.
34. DAD, Fratrie, 22/1, no.15, Matrikula lazarina, fo 1r. See plates 10 and 11.
35. The church stood on the site occupied now by the Hotel Excelsior.
36. All the brothers of the confraternity were obliged to pay into its coffers a prescribed due on whatever they imported from or exported to the Levant (Matrikula lazarina, fo 4v).
37. *Bratovštine i obrtne korporacije*, ii, ed. Vojnović, pp. xi-xii, xxix-xxxii, 99. The *Antunini* and *Lazarini* have not been much investigated: but see Stjepan Ćosić, 'Dubrovački plemički i građanski rodovi konavoskog podrijetla', *Konavle u prošlosti, sadašnjosti i budućnosti*, 1 (1998), 62–63.
38. Tadić, *Dubrovački portreti*, pp. 13–15.
39. *Ibid.*, pp. 284–314.
40. Skočibuha means 'jumping flea'. The nickname presumably reflected upon Tomo's ability to escape trouble on the high seas but perhaps, too, his mental agility.
41. The term 'palace' for houses of this sort leaves something to be desired, since essentially we are talking about substantial town houses. But there is no easy alternative translation for *palača* or *palazzo*.
42. *Ibid.*, pp. 199–230. For Vice Skočibuha's building projects see p. 312.
43. Also from Lopud was another distinguished sea captain and diplomat, Vice Bune (born in 1559), who spent much of his career in the service of Spain – though always standing ready to assist the interests of Dubrovnik. He died in Naples (in 1612) where he had been acting as Ragusan consul. His body was brought back for burial on Lopud. See J. Luetić, 'Pomorac i diplomat Vice Bune', *Anali*, 1/1 (1952), 255–267 and Foretić, *Povijest Dubrovnika do 1808.*,

ii, 70.

44. *Ibid.*, pp. 126–161.
45. Beno Kotruljević, *O trgovini i o savršenu trgovcu*, ed. R. Radičević and Ž. Muljačić, JAZU Djela znanosti Hrvatske, i (1985), pp. 6, 31, 40, 41, 65, 126; *Della Mercatura et del Mercante perfetto. Libri Quatro. Di M. Benedetto Cotrugli Raugeo. Scritti gia piu di anni cx. et hora dati in luce. Utilissimi ad ogni Mercante. Con Privilegio* (Venice, 1573 – New Impression: Zagreb, 1975), fos 2r-3v.
46. *Della Mercatura et del Mercante perfetto*, fo 24r.
47. *Ibid.*, fos 27r, 37r-38v.
48. *Ibid.*, fos 26v-28r.
49. *Ibid.*, fos 88r-90r.
50. *Ibid.*, fos 84r-87r.
51. See pp. 169–170.
52. Kostić, *Dubrovnik i Engleska 1300–1650*, pp. 182, 186.
53. *Ibid.*, pp. 209–212, 221–224, 262–298; *idem*, 'The Ragusan Colony in London in Shakespeare's Day', *Dubrovnik's Relations with England: a Symposium, April 1978*, ed. R. Filipović and M. Partridge (Zagreb, 1977), 261–273.
54. B. Stulli, *Židovi u Dubrovniku* (Zagreb, 1989), pp. 17–18; *Annales Ragusini anonymi*, ed. Nodilo, (Ranjina) p. 227.
55. B. Krekić, 'The Role of the Jews in Dubrovnik (Thirteenth-Sixteenth Centuries)', *Dubrovnik, Italy and the Balkans in the Later Middle Ages* (London, 1980), 261–262.
56. B. Stulli, *Židovi u Dubrovniku* (Zagreb, 1989), p. 19; J. Tadić, *Jevrei u Dubrovniku do polovine xvii stoljeća* (Sarajevo, 1937), pp. 108–115.
57. Stulli, *Židovi*, pp. 19–22.
58. *Ibid.*, pp. 27–37; Tadić, *Jevrei*, pp. 119–134.
59. Tadić, *Jevrei*, pp. 276–297; Stulli, *Židovi*, 25–26.
60. Serbophile historians have discerned the omnipresent influence of the Slavic *zadruga* (community or co-operative). But the latest research suggests that community of property, which was at the heart of the *zadruga*, finds no counterpart in Dubrovnik where, although administration of property might be, and often was shared, property rights themselves resided in individuals (Mahnken, *op. cit.*, pp. 16–17; cf J. Lučić review of Mahnken in *Historijski zbornik*, xvii (1964), 393–411 and, definitively, Z. Janeković-Römer, *Rod i grad. Dubrovačka obitelj od xiii do xv stoljeće*, HAZU Prilozi povijesti stanovništva Dubrovnika i okolice, book 4 (Dubrovnik, 1994), pp. 15, 27–28).
61. Janeković-Römer, *Rod i grad.*, pp.19–20, 29–30.
62. *Ibid.*, pp. 14, 83.
63. *Ibid.*, pp. 23–26.
64. *Ibid.*, pp. 27–36.
65. Kapetanić and Vekarić, *Stanovništvo Konavala*, i, 102, 338.
66. Diversis, *Situs Aedificiorum*, ed. Brunelli, pp. 126–128.
67. *Liber Viridis*, ed., Nedeljković, cap. 160, pp. 133–134.
68. *Ibid.*, cap. 371, pp. 325–329.
69. *Liber Croceus*, ed. Nedeljković, cap. 2, p. 4.
70. *Ibid.*, cap. 185, pp. 200–201.
71. Janeković-Römer, *Rod i grad.*, pp. 63, 78, 80–81; Diversis, *Situs Aedificiorum*, ed. Brunelli, p. 123.
72. *Della Mercatura et del Mercante perfetto*, fo 94v.
73. Diversis, *Situs Aedificiorum*, ed. Brunelli, p. 125.
74. *Liber Viridis*, ed. Nedeljković, cap. 478, pp. 418–419.
75. *Liber Croceus*, ed. Nedeljković, cap. 2, p. 4.
76. Janeković-Römer, *Rod i grad.*, p. 44.
77. *Liber Viridis*, ed. Nedeljković, cap. 237, pp.186–187.
78. S. Krivošić, *Stanovništvo Dubrovnika i demografske promjene u prošlosti*, HAZU Prilozi povijesti stanovništva Dubrovnika i okolice, book 1 (Dubrovnik, 1990), pp. 105–121 and appendix 1.
79. Janeković-Römer, *Rod i grad.*, pp. 130–131.

80. D. Dinić-Knežević, *Položaj žena u Dubrovniku u xiii i xiv veku*, SAN Posebna izdanja, 469 (1974), pp. 48–54.
81. Janeković-Römer, *Rod i grad.*, p. 133.
82. *Liber Viridis*, ed. Nedeljković, cap. 479, pp. 419–420.
83. Diversis, *Situs Aedificiorum*, ed. Brunelli, p. 92.
84. Lukarević, *Copioso ristretto*, p. 254.
85. Diversis, *Situs Aedificiorum*, ed. Brunelli, pp. 92–23; P. Skok, 'Iz dubrovačkog vokabulara', *Zbornik iz dubrovačke prošlosti Milanu Rešetaru o 70–oj godišnjici života*, ed. V. Ćorović *et al.*, (Dubrovnik, 1931), 429–433.
86. For Ragusan love poetry see pp. 250–251.
87. Tadić, *Dubrovački portreti*, p. 197.
88. Deanović, *Anciens contacts*, p. 12.
89. Tadić, *Dubrovački portreti*, p.269.
90. V. Kojaković, *Dubrovnik u privatnom životu* (Dubrovnik, 1933), p. 25.
91. M. Franičević, F. Švelec and R. Bogišić, *Od Renesanse do Prosvjetitelstva, Povijest hrvatske književnosti*, iii (Zagreb, n. d.), 162.
92. Tadić, *Dubrovački portreti*, pp. 316–348.
93. *Liber Statutorum*, ed. Bogišić, book 6, chapter xliii, p. 140; chapter xliv, p. 140; chapter xlv, p. 141; chapter xlvii, pp. 141–142.
94. *Liber Omnium Reformationum*, ed. Solovjev, pagina xiv, cap. 1, pp. 75–76.
95. *Libri Reformationum*, i, pp. 205, 207–208, 216 (1346).
96. Janeković-Römer, *Rod i grad.*, pp. 122–124. For the treatment of servants in later years see p. 360.
97. Diversis, *Situs Aedificiorum*, ed. Brunelli, p. 16.
98. Krivošić, *op. cit.* p. 92.
99. For contemporary, competing theories about infection and contagion see Grmek, *op. cit.* pp. 23–27.
100. *Liber Statutorum*, ed. Bogišić, book 5, chapter iv, pp. 111–112.
101. *Ibid.*, book 8, chapter lvii, pp. 192–200.
102. *The Restoration of Dubrovnik 1979–89*, ed. B. Letunić (Zagreb, 1990), pp. 240–211. For more details on the layout of Dubrovnik's streets see pp. 288–289.
103. *Prilozi za istoriju zdravstvene kulture starog Dubrovnika*, ed. R. Jeremić and J. Tadić, i (Belgrade, 1938), 52, 54.
104. *Libri Reformationum*, i, 171.
105. *Ibid*,. 10–11.
106. *Prilozi za istoriju zdravstvene kulture*, ed. Jeremić and Tadić, ii (Belgrade, 1939), 7, 137–139; B. Krekić, *Dubrovnik in the 14th and 15th Centuries: A City between East and West* (Norman, Oklahoma, 1972), pp. 91–92.
107. *Prilozi za istoriju zdravstvene kulture*, ed. Jeremić and Tadić, ii, 147–161.
108. *Chronica Ragusina Junii Restii*, ed. Nodilo, p. 101.
109. *Libri Reformationum*, ii, 11, 18.
110. *Ibid.*, 20; *Annales Ragusini Anonymi*, ed. Nodilo, pp. 39, 227–228; Grmek, *op. cit.*, pp. 38–40.
111. On religious life after the Black Death see p. 238.
112. *Libri Reformationum*, ii, 30.
113. *Libri Reformationum*, ii, 102, 106, 117.
114. *Ibid.*, 118.
115. *Annales Ragusini Anonymi*, ed. Nodilo, pp.230, 233–235, 248–249, 261, 280–282; *Prilozi za istoriju zdravstvene kulture*, ed. Jeremić and Tadić, i, 65–111 – for a list all the epidemics known to have struck Dubrovnik from the earliest times till the fall of the Republic.
116. Diversis, *Situs Aedificiorum*, ed. Brunelli, p. 17.
117. *Liber Viridis*, ed. Nedeljković, cap. 319, pp. 261–268.
118. *Ibid.*, 116–119.
119. Krivošić, *op. cit.*, pp. 88–89.
120. *Prilozi za istoriju zdravstvene kulture*, ed. Jeremić and Tadić, ii, 174–175; B. Krekić, 'Images of

Urban Life: Contributions to the Study of daily Life in Dubrovnik at the Time of Humanism and the Renaissance', *Dubrovnik: a Mediterranean Urban Society, 1300–1600* (Aldershot, 1997), 6–7.

121. Janeković-Römer, *Rod i grad.*, pp.116–119.
122. *Liber Viridis*, ed. Nedeljković, cap. 252, p. 198.
123. *Ibid.*, pp.198–201; Krekić, 'Images of Urban Life', 18–20.
124. *Prilozi za istoriju zdravstvene kulture*, ed. Jeremić and Tadić, ii, 175–177. Only in 1888 did Dubrovnik's general hospital move to a site on Boninovo (today's Old Hospital).
125. For the urban crafts see pp. 176–182.
126. See pp. 180–182.
127. J. Lučić, 'Iz prošlosti Župe Dubrovačke (do polovice xiv stoljeća)', *Zbornik Župe Dubrovačke*, 1 (1985), 97–98; *idem*, 'Pučki zborovi na Mljetu', 196. The name 'Kupari' (meaning 'tiles') bears witness to the importance of this factory, manned by labourers from Župa and supplied with wood for its furnaces by peasants from Mljet.
128. *Liber Croceus*, ed. Nedeljković, cap. 42, p. 41.
129. For state policy towards the cultivation of vines and grain see pp. 182–184.
130. D. Roller, *Agrarno-proizvodni odnosi na području Dubrovnika od xiii. do xv. stoljeća*, Građa za gospodarsku povijest Hrvatske, 5 (Zagreb, 1955), pp. 54–58, 66, 77–78, 89, 91, 98–103.
131. Roller, *Agrarno-proizvodni odnosi*, pp. 108–127, 265.
132. *Ibid.*, 204–224.
133. Z. Šundrica, 'Stonski rat u xiv stoljeću (1333–1399.)', *Pelješki zbornik*, 2 (1980), 130.
134. See pp. 308–310.
135. Roller, *Agrarno-proizvodni odnosi*, pp. 224–235.
136. J. Lučić, 'Gospodarsko-društveni odnosi u Stojkovićevo vrijeme (1392–1442)', *Historijski zbornik*, 38/1 (1985), 111.
137. Roller, *Agrarno-proizvodni odnosi*, pp. 165–173.
138. *Ibid.*, 159–165.
139. Petar Hektorović, 'Fishing and Fishermen's Conversation', translated by E. Goy, *BC Review*, 15 (January, 1979), pp. 13–48. Hektorović specifically mentions, among other sorts of fish, dentex, bogue, gilthead, wrasse, black bream, red mullet, scorpion fish and sea urchins.
140. Lučić, 'Pučki zborovi na Lopudu i Koločepu', 47.
141. Š. Županović, *Ribarstvo Dalmacije u 18. stoljeću* (Split, 1993), 174–177, 191.
142. For culture see chapter 11, and for religious life chapter 10.

Chapter Ten

1. B. Krizman, 'Mémoire Bara Bettere austrijskom generalu T. Milutinoviću o Dubrovačkoj Republici iz 1815. godine', *Anali*, 1/1 (1952), 434.
2. See pp. 40–43, 51–53.
3. Stošić, 'Research Finds', 327–329. For a different and, to my mind, unpersuasive view: Ž. Peković, 'Développement de l'ensemble de la cathédrale de Dubrovnik', *Hortus Artium Medievalium*, i (1995), 162–165.
4. J. Lučić, 'The Earliest Contacts between Dubrovnik and England', *Dubrovnik's Relations with England: A Symposium, April 1976* (Zagreb, 1977), ed. R. Filipović and M. Partridge, 9–29.
5. Stošić, 'Research Finds', 329.
6. See plates 43 and 45.
7. The value of Diversis's work in illuminating the buildings of old Dubrovnik is assessed by I. Fisković, 'Djelo Filipa de Diversisa kao izvor poznavanja umjetnosti i kulture Dubrovnika', *Dubrovnik*, 30 1–3 (1987), 232–249.
8. Diversis, *Situs Aedificiorum*, ed. Brunelli, pp. 29–30. See plate 48.
9. Saraka was from a great Ragusan patrician family. But he did not owe his elevation to this fact – indeed, it may be that being a local patrician already weighed against one's chances of becoming archbishop of Dubrovnik. He was a learned member of the household of Cardinal Colonna in Avignon at the time of his appointment by the pope. The canons of Dubrovnik had already chosen another candidate, the serving bishop of Ulcinj, and their election had

to be over-ridden (Krasić-Razzi, *Povijest dubrovačke metropolije*, p. 121 and note 364; [S. Cerva/Crijević], Sacra Metropolis Ragusina, i/1, 273–274).

10. *Annales Ragusini anonymi*, ed. Nodilo, p. 233.
11. *Liber Viridis*, ed. Nedeljković, cap. 129, pp. 94–95.
12. The first Ragusan-born archbishop appointed was in 1722 (Lukarević, *Copioso ristretto*, p. 291).
13. Vojnović, 'Crkva i država', i, 40–43.
14. A. Gulin, 'Srednjovjekovni dubrovački kaptol: utemeljenje, ustroj i djelatnost', *Tisuću godina dubrovačke (nad)biskupije*, ed. Puljić and Ančić, 175–196.
15. *Liber Viridis*, ed. Nedeljković, cap. 338, p. 286.
16. Zlatar, *Our Kingdom Come*, pp. 153–155.
17. J. Sopta, 'Reformacija i Tridentinski sabor u Dubrovniku', *Tisuću godina dubrovačke (nad)biskupije*, ed. Puljić and Ančić, 379–395.
18. *Ibid.*, 384–385.
19. Zlatar, *Our Kingdom Come*, pp. 160–161.
20. Consecrated 13 March 1521 and died 27 June 1543 (Krasić-Razzi, *Povijest dubrovačke metropolije,* p. 133). For Trivulzio's misdeeds see p.111.
21. *Ibid.*, p. 134.
22. Sacra Metropolis Ragusina, i/3, 360–361.
23. For Beccadelli's circle see p. 313.
24. J. Torbarina, *Italian Influence on the Poets of the Ragusan Republic* (London, 1931), pp. 41–52.
25. Krasić-Razzi, *Povijest dubrovačke metropolije*, pp. 141–144.
26. [G.-M. Mattei/Matijašević] Zibaldone, memorie storiche su Ragusa raccolte dal. P.Gian-Maria Mattei, iii, 117–120.
27. Krasić-Razzi, *Povijest dubrovačke metropolije*, pp. 144–146.
28. *Ibid.*, p. 147.
29. *Ibid.*, pp. 52–54. In a Satire against the Ragusan patriciate Kaboga wrote: 'Do not usurp the name of Noble, You who live by deceit and duplicity...That's not a Gentleman, it's a sluggard' (Zibaldone, iii, 717).
30. Krasić-Razzi, *Povijest dubrovačke metropolije*, pp. 151–152.
31. *Ibid.*, pp. 153–165; Zibaldone, ii, 281–322; Zlatar, *Our Kingdom Come*, pp. 163–172.
32. Ostojić, *Benediktinci u Hrvatskoj*, ii, 417–418, 420–425.
33. For this settlement see pp. 217–218.
34. Ostojić, *Benediktinci u Hrvatskoj*, ii, 437–448.
35. Lukarević, *Copioso ristretto*, p. 60.
36. S. Krasić, 'Dubrovnik i dominikanci', *Dubrovački horizonti*, 2/5 (Spring 1970), pp. 57–60.
37. C. Fisković, *Prvi poznati dubrovački graditelji* (Dubrovnik, 1955), pp. 107–114. See plate 18.
38. Diversis, *Situs Aedificiorum*, ed. Brunelli, p. 35.
39. A. Matanić, 'Franjevački Dubrovnik u svom povijesnom presjeku', *Samostan Male braće u Dubrovniku*, ed. J. Turčinović (Zagreb, 1985), 31.
40. The conventuals followed the 'mitigated' Franciscan rule. But during the fifteenth century there was increasing pressure from both friars and lay rulers for a return to the more rigorous 'primitive' observance. Despite his interest in ecclesiastical matters, the chronicler Ranjina probably here exaggerates the suddenness of the shift from conventuals to observants – he says that from this point on there were only observant friars in the Ragusan Republic. Conventuals seem to have continued for almost a century to live in some predominantly observant friaries – hence they could give spiritual direction to the Dubrovnik nuns: see below (*Ibid.,* 32; *Annales Ragusini anonymi,* ed. Nodilo, 251).
41. Razzi, *Storia di Ragusa*, ed. Gelcich, p. 119.
42. A. Marinović, 'Dubrovačka legislacija glede prosjačkih redova', *Samostan male braće u Dubrovniku*, ed. J. Turčinović (Zagreb, 1985), 40.
43. Krasić-Razzi, *Povijest dubrovačke metropolije*, p. 131.
44. *Liber Viridis*, ed. Nedeljković, cap. 80, p. 50.
45. *Ibid.*, cap. 178, p. 130.
46. *Ibid.*, cap. 209, p. 160.

47. *Libri Reformationum*, i, 73.
48. Diversis, *Situs Aedificiorum*, ed. Brunelli, p. 103.
49. Bobadilla continued to entertain the friendliest relations with Dubrovnik. For example, on 18 January 1570 he wrote to the government from Messina to say that he prayed constantly for the Republic 'knowing the necessity, because you find yourselves between a Dragon and a Lion'. He promised to use his influence with the Viceroy of Sicily if they should wish it (Zibaldone, i, 13).
50. M. Vanino, *Isusovci i hrvatski narod*, i (Zagreb, 1969), 9–30.
51. Vanino, *op. cit.*, ii, 3–5.
52. Zlatar, *Our Kingdom Come*, 205–218.
53. *Ibid.*, 228–232. The three principal variants of Croatian – *čakavski*, *štokavski* and *kajkavski* (kajkavian) – all gain their names from the regional name for 'what', i.e, *ča*, *što* and *kaj*. For further discussion of the impact of the Ragusan dialect upon literary and modern standard Croatian see pp. 416–418.
54. The full text has been printed as: *Autobiografija Bartola Kašića*, Građe za povijest književnosti Hrvatske, xv (1940).
55. For this early school and the later *collegium* see pp. 246–247.
56. Vanino, *op. cit.*, ii, 5–27.
57. Diversis, *Situs Aedificiorum*, ed. Brunelli, p. 92.
58. Tadić, *Promet putnika*, pp. 195, 197.
59. Krasić-Razzi, *Povijest dubrovačke metropolije*, pp. 74–75.
60. Razzi, *Storia di Ragusa*, ed. Gelcich, p. 242.
61. Vanino, *op. cit.*, ii, 15–18.
62. Beritić, *Utvrđenja grada Dubrovnika*, pp. 16–17; *idem*, 'Ubikacija', part 1, 67. For a contrary view, see Ž. Peković, 'Développement de l'ensemble de la cathédrale de Dubrovnik', *Hortus Artium Medievalium*, i (1995), 162–163.
63. *Chronica Ragusina Junii Restii*, ed. Nodilo, p. 41. The arrival of this and other prestigious relics in Dubrovnik at this time, when the Ragusan-born Vitalis was archbishop (1022–1047), was doubtless intended to bolster the fragile status of the Dubrovnik metropolitanate. St Blaise, in particular, served as a more than sufficient rival to neighbouring Kotor's holy patron, St Tryphon (Sveti Tripun), martyred in about 250 in the reign of Decius (J. Belamarić, 'Sveti Vlaho i dubrovačka obitelj svetaca zaštitnika', *Dubrovnik*, New Series, 5–5 (1994), 29–39). See plate 48.
64. *Annales Ragusini anonymi*, ed. Nodilo, p. 227.
65. *Ibid.*, pp. 39, 228.
66. *Libri Reformationum*, ii, 11, 13, 15.
67. *Ibid.*, 87–88.
68. Diversis, *Situs Aedificiorum*, ed. Brunelli, pp. 34, 46–47. The Church of St Blaise was damaged in the 1667 earthquake but was repaired. It burned down on the night of 24 May 1706 and was then rebuilt in Baroque style by the Venetian architect Marino Gropelli and reopened in 1715.
69. *Ibid.*, pp. 93–96; Razzi, *Storia di Ragusa*, ed. Gelcich, pp.196–198; F. M. Appendini, *Notizie istorico-critiche sulle antichita, storia e letteratura de' Ragusei*, i (Dubrovnik, 1802), 177–180. These sources are usefully summarised and integrated by Vučetić, *op. cit.*, pp. 30–53. Equally interesting are the observations of the Turkish travel writer, Evliya Çelebi. As a Muslim, his understanding of the symbolism was somewhat shaky – thus he confused the reliquary bust of St Blaise with a depiction of Our Lord. But he was enormously impressed by the sight of a great procession of clergy from whose smoking thuribles 'the smell of ambergris, honey, rosemary and hyacinth [*sic*] intoxicated the whole world' (Evlija Čelebija, *Putopis*, ii, 195–197).
70. Diversis, *Situs Aedificiorum*, ed. Brunelli, p. 95.
71. Appendini, *Notizie*, i, 179.
72. See pp. 192–193.
73. Razzi, *Storia di Ragusa*, ed. Gelcich, p. 254.
74. Cerimoniale, fo 3v.

75. Janeković-Römer, *Okvir slobode,* pp. 374–377.
76. It was also, of course, intended to demonstrate the Ragusans' wisdom in contrast to the short-sightedness of the *Kotorani* and their Venetian masters.
77. Razzi, *Storia di Ragusa*, ed. Gelcich, pp. 57–59.
78. Beritić, 'Ubikacija', part 1, 58–59. The site was sold to Mato Nikola Sorkočević with papal permission on condition that an altar was erected in the Cathedral in honour of The Three Martyrs of Kotor. This was done. Not surprisingly in an age of ecumenism, the cult is not now officially encouraged and the altar itself, although adorned with a painting depicting the three *Kotorani*, is today overshadowed by a statue promoting devotion to the Sacred Heart.
79. F. M. Appendini, *Ratovanje oko Dubrovnika godine 1806*, ed. P. Kolendić and J. Nagy (Dubrovnik, 1906), p. 21.
80. *Annales Ragusini anonymi*, p. 53. See p. 149.
81. *Liber Viridis*, ed. Nedeljković, cap. 154, p. 108.
82. *Ibid.*, cap. 307, p. 254.
83. *Ibid.*, cap. 139, p. 100.
84. *Ibid.*, cap.177, pp. 129–130; *Liber Croceus*, ed. Nedeljković, cap. 226, p. 244.
85. *Liber Viridis*, ed. Nedeljković, cap. 364, p. 320.
86. Diversis, *Situs Aedificiorum*, ed. Brunelli, pp. 23, 34.
87. Vanino, *op. cit.*, ii, 21.
88. *Annales Ragusini anonymi*, ed. Nodilo, p. 228.
89. Ž. Dadić, 'Mavro Vetranović kao astrolog', *Egzaktne znanosti hrvatskoga srednovjekovlja* (Zagreb, 1991), 174–176.
90. *Annales Ragusini anonymi*, ed. Nodilo, p. 94.
91. *Bratovštine*, i, ed. Vojnović, pp. i-xxi, 1–7.
92. Indeed, over the centuries the churches of Dubrovnik accumulated a huge collection of such relics. Among the most prized was what was alleged to be the garment in which the baby Jesus was presented to Simeon in the Temple (Luke, 2, v. 25–25). It was borne in solemn procession on the Feast of St Simeon (8 October). It was kept in the convent of that name until the nuns were discovered to have been clipping off pieces to give to important people. In 1380 the secular authorities, fearing it seems that the whole thing might disappear to Zadar to please Queen Elisabeth of Hungary, intervened and entrusted the prestigious relic to the safekeeping of the Dubrovnik cathedral (Razzi, *Storia di Ragusa*, ed. Gelcich, pp. 34–35; Belamarić 'Sveti Vlaho i dubrovačka obitelj svetaca zaštitnika', 33). An inventory drawn up in the eighteenth century listed 162 relics in the cathedral alone, with many more possessed by the Dubrovnik Dominicans and Franciscans, the nuns of St Clare and others (Zibaldone, i, 219–237).
93. Lukarević, *Copioso ristretto*, p. 194.

Chapter Eleven

1. Diversis, *Situs Aedificiorum*, ed. Brunelli, pp. 44–45.
2. For Ilija Crijević see pp. 260–261.
3. Torbarina, *Italian Influence*, pp. 19–25, 39–41.
4. Diversis, *Situs Aedificiorum*, ed. Brunelli, p. 103.
5. F. Šanjek, 'The Studies of Exact and Natural Sciences in the History of the Dubrovnik Dominicans', *Dubrovnik Annals*, 1 (1997), 13–14. Apart from his assistance to Dubrovnik at the Council of Basel (which he opened on behalf of the papal legate in 1433), Stay also seems to have tried to gain trade concessions for his compatriots while he was in Constantinople, also on high ecclesiastical business. He died in 1443 (Božić, *op. cit.*, pp. 59, 226).
6. Šanjek, 'Studies of Exact and Natural Sciences', 18–22.
7. M. Brlek, *Rukopisi knjižnice male braće u Dubrovniku*, i (Zagreb, 1952), 10–12.
8. Vanino, *op. cit.*, i, 15, 27; *idem*, ii, 13–15, 36–76.
9. M. Franičević, *Povijest hrvatske renesansne književnosti* (Zagreb, 1983), p. 225. As Franičević observes, 'Croatian Renaissance literature is an inseparable part of that Europe' (*Ibid.*, p. 7).
10. *Liber Viridis*, ed. Nedeljković, p. xvi.

11. Diversis, *Situs Aedificiorum*, ed. Brunelli, p. 70.
12. B. Krekić, 'On the Latino-Slavic Cultural Symbiosis in Late Medieval and Renaissance Dalmatia and Dubrovnik', *Dubrovnik : a Mediterranean Urban Society, 1300–1600* (Aldershot, 1997), 322–326.
13. Examples quoted in Mahnken, *op. cit.*, pp. 55–56.
14. Vanino, *op. cit.*, ii, 15–16.
15. The earliest evidence comes from inscriptions, of which an account is given in B. Fučić, *Croatian Glagolitic Epigraphy* (London, 1999). The process was long and complex. It continued through different scripts, with Cyrillic (principally the western version known as *bosančica*) and, increasingly, Latin taking over from Glagolitic (M. Moguš, *A History of the Croatian Language: Towards a Common Standard* (Zagreb, 1995), pp. 13–33). Evidence of Glagolitic penetration into Konavle in the eleventh/twelfth centuries comes from a recently discovered inscription at Soko (B. Fučić and N. Kapetanić, 'A Glagolitic Inscription in Konavle', *Dubrovnik Annals*, 3 (1999), 7–11).
16. The latter terms derive from the three possible different pronunciations of the old Church Slavonic letter *jatь* as – *i*, – *ije* or – *e*.
17. Moguš, *op. cit.*, p. 61; Franičević, *Povijest hrvatske renesansne književnosti,* pp. 132–148. For a concise account of the development of Croatian as a literary language, see B. Franolić, *An Historical Survey of Literary Croatian* (Paris, 1984).
18. I. Banac, *Main Trends in the Croatian Language Question* (Zagreb, 1990), p. 31.
19. I. Banac, 'Ministration and Desecration: the Place of Dubrovnik in Modern Croat National Ideology and Political Culture', *Nation and Ideology. Essays in Honor of Wayne S. Vucinich*, ed. I. Banac, J. G. Ackerman and R. Szporluk (Boulder: new York, 1981), 152–158. See also pp. 416–417.
20. Franičević, *Povijest hrvatske renesansne književnosti*, pp. 271, 336; F. Švelec, *Komički teatar Marina Držića* (Zagreb, 1968), pp. 10–14.
21. Franičević, *Povijest hrvatske renesansne književnosti*, p. 215; A. Kadić, 'Marulić and Držić: the Opposite Poles of the Croatian Renaisance', *The Tradition of Freedom in Croatian Literature* (Bloomington, 1983), 21–24. In what seems likely to become, when it is complete, the standard history of Croatian literature, Slobodan Prosperov Novak calls Marulić's *Molitva* 'the most patriotic Croatian poem of the Renaissance' and adds: 'It is not a prayer, it is the cry of those who are dying of fear, and when it is a prayer, it is less directed to God and Our Lady, more to the deaf ears of Europe' (S. P. Novak, *Povijest hrvatske književnosti*, ii (Zagreb, 1997), 183).
22. Franičević, *Povijest hrvatske renesansne književnosti*, p. 8.
23. Notably, the eight-lined poem known as the *strambotta* or *rispetta* (M. Kombol, *Povijest hrvatske književnosti do preporoda* (Zagreb, 1961), pp. 95–96).
24. T. Butler, *Monumenta Serbocroatica: A Bilingual Anthology of Serbian and Croatian Texts from the 12th to the 19th Century* (Ann Arbor: Michigan, 1980), pp. 184–185.
25. Novak, *Povijest hrvatske književnosti*, ii, 153.
26. S. P. Franičević, Švelec and Bogišić, *Povijest hrvatske književnosti*, iii, 56–57.
27. *Ibid.*, 347–348.
28. The remark is of Ivo Banac in his 'Political Themes in the Poetry of Mavro Vetranović', *American Benedictine Review*, 36/1 (1985), 33. (Uniquely in Dubrovnik, a Benedictine monk is referred to as *Dum*). Slobodan Prosperov Novak calls Vetranović the 'poet of pain' (S. P. Novak, *Povijest hrvatske književnosti*, ii, 248).
29. Banac, 'Political Themes', 34–40; *Pjesanca šturku* is reproduced and translated in Butler, *Monumenta Serbocroatica*, pp. 190–193.
30. It is, though, worth noting that most of Držić's plays are still not available in English translations.
31. Marin Držić's last work, the political tragedy *Hekuba*, was at first prohibited from being performed because the Ragusan authorities considered that it might disturb the populace (S. P. Novak, *Povijest hrvatske književnosti*, ii, 409).
32. Franičević, Švelec and Bogišić, *Povijest hrvatske književnosti*, iii, 124; Tadić, *Dubrovački portreti*,

pp. 91–105; Švelec, *Komički teatar Marin Držića*, pp. 52–53.
33. Švelec, *Komički teatar Marin Držića*, p. 55.
34. *Ibid.*, pp. 11, 21.
35. R. Bogišić, 'Pastorala Marina Držića', *O hrvatskim starim pjesnicima* (Zabreb, 1968), 188.
36. Držić, *Skup*, PSHK, 6 (1964), p. 140; translation from Marin Držić, *The Miser*, trans. S. Bičanić (Zagreb, 1968), p. 10.
37. Držić, *Skup*, PSHK, 6, p. 145, translation from Bičanić, *op. cit.*, p. 16.
38. Držić, *Skup*, PSHK, p. 162, translation from Bičanić, *op. cit.* pp. 32–33.
39. R. Reed, 'Satirical Devices in Marin Držić's Play 'The Miser'', *Slavic and East European Journal*, 21/3 (Autumn, 1977), 366–377.
40. Držić, *Tirena*, PSHK, 6, pp. 63–65.
41. There is an excellent translation with introduction of *Novela od Stanca* by E. Goy, 'The Dream of Stanac', *BC Review*, 17, December 1980, 3–17.
42. Držić, *Skup*, *PSHK*, 6, p. 159.
43. Butler, *op. cit.*, pp. 244–245.
44. Švelec, *Komički teatar Marina Držića*, pp. 33, 303–306.
45. Držić, *Skup*, *PSHK*, 6, p. 142; translation from Bičanić, *op. cit.*, p. 13.
46. An exception was also apparently made for the performance of *Plakir* in May 1556 (Švelec, *Komički teatar Marina Držića*, p. 24).
47. *Ibid.*, pp. 23, 38.
48. M. Rešetar, 'Kako su pretstavljene Držićeve drame', *Marin Držić 1508–1958*, ed. M. Pantić (Belgrade, 1958), 348.
49. The experts disagree. Cf. V. Javarek, 'Marin Držić: A Ragusan Playwright', *The Slavonic and East European Review*, 37/38 (December, 1958), 147, and Rešetar, 'Kako su pretstavljene Držićeve drame', 348.
50. C. Fisković, 'Pozornice Držićevih igara', *Baština starih hrvatskih pisaca* (Split, 1971), 308–329.
51. Švelec, *Komički teatar Marina Držića*, p. 26. On Nikola Gučetić see p. 264.
52. PSHK, *Hrvatski latinisti*, ii (1970), 114–121.
53. Franičević, Švelec and Bogišić, *Povijest hrvatske književnosti*, iii, 127; *Skup*, PSHK, 6 (1964), p. 139.
54. J. Torbarina, 'A Croat Forerunner of Shakespeare: In Commemoration of the 400th Anniversary of the Death of Marin Držić (1508–1567)', *Studia Romanica et Anglica Zagrabiensia*, 24 (December 1967), 6–11.
55. R. Bogišić, 'Marin Držić – Petrarkist', *O hrvatskim starim pjesnicima* (Zagreb, 1968), 157–167.
56. The point is well-made of Croatian literature as a whole by Branko Franolić: '[U]p to the mid-nineteenth century, Croatian authors had written more works in Latin than in Croat' (*Idem*, *Works of Croatian Latinists Recorded in the British Library General Catalogue* [London, 1997], p. 30).
57. Pomponio Leto b. 1426 and d. 1497.
58. Crijević opens his poem *De Epidauro* with an evocative description of the landscape around the Soko fortress (PSHK, *Hrvatski latinisti*, i (1969), 448–452).
59. Franičević, *Povijest hrvatske renesansne književnosti*, pp. 310–314; Franičević, Švelec and Bogišić, *Povijest hrvatske književnosti*, iii, 60–61.
60. PSHK, *Hrvatski latinisti*, i (1969), 462–489, 490–513.
61. Franičević, *Povijest hrvatske renesansne književnosti*, pp. 314–318; Franičević, Švelec and Bogišić, *Povijest hrvatske književnosti*, iii, 61.
62. Franičević, *Povijest hrvatske renesansne književnosti*, pp. 305–310; V. Rezar, 'Dubrovački humanistički historiograf Ludovik Crijević Tuberon', *Anali*, 37 (1999), 47–94.
63. Cardinal Bessarion (b. about 1403 and d. 1472) was one of those Greek clergy who attended the Council of Florence (1439), which agreed a short-lived union between the Western and Eastern Churches. He remained in Italy and became a patron and focus for neo-Platonist and other Humanist study.
64. Marsilio Ficino b. 1443 and d. 1499.
65. Girolamo Savonarola, Dominican, b. 1452 and d. (burnt as a heretic) 1498.

66. Johannes Reuchlin b. 1455 and d. 1522.
67. I. Martinović, 'Humanist, filozof, i teolog Juraj Dragišić', *Dubrovnik*, New Series, 6/4 (1995), 213–230; PSHK, *Hrvatski latinisti*, i, 540–541.
68. Ž. Dadić, 'Astrološki rad Gjina Gazullija u Dubrovniku u 15. stoljeću', *Egzaktne znanosti hrvatskoga srednjovjekovlja* (Zagreb, 1991), 121–130.
69. John Sacrobosco (i.e. Hollywood, Yorks.), thirteenth century astrologer-astronomer.
70. Ž. Dadić, 'Mathematical Views in Sixteenth Century Dubrovnik', *Dubrovnik Annals*, 1 (1997), 25–30.
71. L. Šifler-Premec, *Nikola Gučetić* (Zagreb, 1977), pp. 49–55. Cardinal Bellarmine b. 1542 and d. 1621.
72. M. Pantić, 'Gučetić, Nikola Vidov', *Leksikon pisaca Jugoslavije*, ii (Belgrade, 1979), 326–327.
73. Franičević, *Povijest hrvatske renesansne književnosti*, pp. 424–438.
74. *Ibid.*, 510–520.
75. Butler, *op. cit.*, pp. 202–207.
76. Franičević, *Povijest hrvatske renesansne književnosti*, pp. 653–674.
77. *Djela Ǵiva Frana Gundulića*, SPH, ix (1938), p. 330.
78. See for different interpretations of Gundulić's 'conversion', Franičević, Švelec and Bogišić, *Povijest hrvatske književnosti*, iii, 200 and Z. Zlatar, *The Slavic Epic: Gundulić's Osman* (New York, 1995), p. 66 .
79. Franičević, Švelec and Bogišić, *Povijest hrvatske književnosti*, iii, 197–201; Zlatar, *Slavic Epic*, pp. 44–73.
80. J. Ravlić, 'Odraz domaće stvarnosti u dubrovačkoj književnosti: Ivan Gundulić i njegova Dubravka', *Anali*, 6/7 (1956), 323–354.
81. Cf. Zlatar, *Slavic Epic*, pp. 95–108.
82. *Dubravka*, PSHK, 12/1 (1964), p. 149. The translation is from Gundulić, 'Dubravka', introd. and trans. Goy, 23. This thought is also conveyed in the inscription on the Lovrijenac fortress: *Non bene pro toto libertas venditur auro* – 'it is not right to trade liberty for all the gold in the world'.
83. *Osman*, PSHK,12/2 (1964), p. 106; trans. Zlatar, *Slavic Epic*, p. 248. The Dragon represents the diabolical power of Islam, the Lion the oppressive force of Venice. Investigation of this idea is the central (though by no means the only) theme of Zlatar's seminal study of *Osman*.
84. The first recorded *bugarštica* is that contained in Petar Hektorović's *Ribanje i ribarsko prigovaranje*, written in 1556, first published in Venice in 1568 (*Djela Petra Hektorovića*, SPH, xxxix (1986), pp. 37–77).
85. *Ferdinandu drugome od Toskane*, PSHK, 12/1, pp. 153–161.
86. *Osman*, PSHK,12/2 (1964), p. 238; the translation is from Ivan Gundulić, *Osman*, trans. E. Goy (Zagreb, 1991), p. 241.
87. *Ibid.*, pp. xviii-xix.
88. Franičević, Švelec and Bogišić, *Povijest hrvatske književnosti*, iii, 211–222.
89. *Ibid.*, 223–229; Bogišić, 'Junije Palmotić', *O hrvatskim starim pjesnicima*, 327–344; '... Palmotić owed his celebrity... more to his tendencies than to his poetic qualities' (Kombol, *op. cit.*, p. 261); 'Palmotić, without doubt, had a very significant role in the Dubrovnik theatre of his time... However, the literary worth of his dramas is modest' (Franičević, Švelec and Bogišić, *Povijest hrvatske književnosti*, iii, 227).
90. *Djela Gjora Palmotića*, SPH, xii/1, p. 110.
91. Franičević, Švelec and Bogišić, *Povijest hrvatske književnosti*, iii, 232.
92. Cited by J. Belamarić, 'Nikola Božidarević', *Prilozi povijesti umjetnosti u Dalmaciji*, 34 (1996), 122.
93. Paolo Veneziano b. about 1300 and d. 1362. See plate 21.
94. G. Gamulin, *The Painted Crucifixes in Croatia* (Zagreb, 1983), pp. 31–32.
95. Although sometimes called *Trogiranin*, Blaž was in fact born in Lapac near Jajce in Bosnia. His first recorded, and fully mature, work is of 1412. He died in 1450.
96. K. Prijatelj, *Slikar Blaž Jurjev* (Zagreb, 1965), 5, 11, 26–27, 36, 43; V. Đurić, *Dubrovačka slikarska škola*, SAN Posebna izdanja, 363 (1963), 11–34; C. Fisković, 'Neobjavljeno djelo

Blaža Jurjeva u Stonu', *Prilozi povijesti umjetnosti u Dalmaciji*, 13 (1961), 114–132. The Ston crucifix was probably influenced by Paolo Veneziano's masterpiece in Dubrovnik's Dominican church (Gamulin, *op. cit.*, p. 43).

97. Đurić, *op. cit.*, pp. 35–36.
98. V. Marković, 'Slikarstvo', *Zlatno doba Dubrovnika*, 171–172.
99. The use of azure is first mentioned in Dubrovnik in 1345 (A. Deanović, 'Marginalije o modrome pigmentu u Dubrovačkom slikarstvu', *Prilozi povijesti umjetnosti u Dalmaciji*, 13 (1961), 248–265).
100. Ugrinović also illuminated the opening of the Statute of Dubrovnik in the 1430s (A. Badurina, 'Iluminirani rukopisi', *Zlatno doba Dubrovnika*, 221).
101. Đurić, *op. cit.*, pp. 38–48; Marković, 'Slikarstvo', 347–348.
102. Đurić, *op. cit.*, pp. 48–61; Marković, 'Slikarstvo', 348. See plate 22.
103. Đurić, *op. cit.*, 63–70.
104. Michele Giambono, Venetian painter, active 1420 to 1462.
105. Antonio and Bartolommeo Vivarini from Murano worked in Venice from 1440 to the early years of the sixteenth century.
106. Đurić, *op. cit.*, pp 70–84 ; Marković, 'Slikarstvo', 349; K. Prijatelj, *Dubrovačko slikarstvo xv-xvi stoljeća* (Zagreb, n. d.), pp. 18–20; K. Prijatelj, *Dalmatian Painting of the 15th and 16th Centuries* (Zagreb, 1983), pp. 22–24. See plates 23, 25–27.
107. Đurić, *op. cit.*, pp. 108–113; Marković, 'Slikarstvo', 350; Prijatelj, *Dubrovačko slikarstvo*, pp. 21–22. See plate 28.
108. The successful detective was the director of the Dubrovnik archives, Karlo Kovač, in 1917.
109. Belamarić, 'Nikola Božidarević', 121.
110. Đurić, *op. cit.*, pp. 116–117.
111. *Građa o slikarskoj školi u Dubrovniku xiii-xvi veku*, ed. J. Tadić, i: 1284–1499 (Belgrade, 1952), no. 569, pp. 270–271; no. 674, pp. 326–327.
112. Carlo Crivelli (b. 1430/5 and d. 1493/5) and Vittorio Crivelli (b. 1440/5 and d. 1500/02). Vittore Carpacio (b. 1445/6 and d. 1525/6).
113. Marković, 'Slikarstvo', 351–352. Pietro Vanucci Perugino b. 1446 and d. 1523. Bernardo di Betto Pinturichio b. 1454 and d. 1513.
114. Đurić, *op. cit.*, p. 118; Belamarić, 'Nikola Božidarević', 121, 123. As with the other great Dubrovnik masters, it is necessary to recall how much of Božidarević's work has perished. Seventeen works are known from the archival sources, but only these four remain. Among the masterpieces lost must be included a number of triptychs painted for the old Dubrovnik cathedral, which were doubtless destroyed by the earthquake and fire of 1667.
115. Ničetić, *op. cit.* p. 140. See plates 29 and 45.
116. Đurić, *op. cit.*, pp. 119–143; Belamarić,' Nikola Božidarević', 121–140; Marković, 'Slikarstvo', 352; Prijatelj, *Dalmatian Painting*, pp. 30–32. See plates 30–34, 39.
117. Andrea Mantegna b. 1431 and d. 1506.
118. Đurić, *op. cit.*, pp. 143–157; Marković, 'Slikarstvo', 351; Prijatelj, *Dubrovačko slikarstvo*, pp. 26–28. See plates 24 and 35.
119. In fact, rather little is known about the paintings contained in private houses. Portrait painting (a typically 'Renaissance' development) was probably only in fashion much later. The murals painted in Lodovico Beccadelli's villa on Šipan by his friend and chaplain Pellegrino Brocardo were an exception (Marković, 'Slikarstvo', 170). By contrast, religious paintings are common in the inventories of Ragusan houses from the end of the fifteenth to the start of the seventeenth centuries (E. Portolan, 'Prilog o unutrašnjoj opremi renensansne kuće u Dubrovniku', *Likovna kultura 15. i 16. stoljeća. Znanstveni skup uz izložbu 'Zlatno doba Dubrovnika'* (Zagreb, 1991), 267–270).
120. Giovanni Bellini b. about 1429 and d. 1516.
121. Đurić, *op. cit.*, pp. 183–195; Marković, 'Slikarstvo', 353.
122. Đurić, *op. cit.*, pp. 165–169; Marković, 'Slikarstvo', 354 – 355.
123. The little church of the Sigurata gained its name from a popular misreading of its official dedication, perhaps through a broken or worn inscription: *tranSfIGURATio*. See plate 36.

124. Đurić, *op. cit.*, pp. 195–217; Marković,'Slikarstvo', 174, 359.
125. C. Fisković, 'Dubrovački brodovi na zavjetnim slikama u muzejskom prostoru u Zagrebu', *Likovna kultura Dubrovnika 15. i 16. stoljeća. Znanstveni skup uz izložbu 'Zlatno doba Dubrovnika'* (Zagreb, 1991), 239–241; A. Kišić, 'Pomorska ikonografija u likovnoj kulturi Dubrovnika 15. i 16. stoljeća', *idem*, 242–249. See plates 37 and 38.
126. K. Prijatelj, 'Slikari xvii i xviii stoljeća u Dubrovniku', *Starohrvatska prosvjeta,* Third Series, i (1949), 250–278.
127. For Luko Sorkočević see p. 365.
128. M. Demović, 'Veze glazbenika i slikara u renesansnom Dubrovniku', *Likovna kultura 15. i 16. stoljeća. Znanstveni skup uz izložbu 'Zlatno doba Dubrovnika'* (Zagreb, 1991), 261.
129. Evlija Čelebija, *Putopis*, ii, 195.
130. M. Demović, *Glazba i glazbenici u Dubrovačkoj Republici od početka xi. do polovine xvii. stoljeća* (Zagreb, 1981), p. 14.
131. Demović, 'Veze glazbenika', 261.
132. Demović, *Glazba i glazbenici*, pp. 107–112.
133. *Ibid.*, pp. 26–27.
134. *Ibid.*, p. 18.
135. Diversis, *Situs Aedificiorum*, ed. Brunelli, pp. 94–95.
136. M. Demović, 'Glazbeni folklor Konavala', *Konavle u prošlosti, sadašnjosti i budućnosti*, 2 (1999), 155–263.

Chapter Twelve

1. See p. 29.
2. *Chronica Ragusina Julii Restii*, ed. Nodilo, p. 90; Beritić, *Utvrđenja grada Dubrovnika*, pp. 10–20.
3. M. Planić-Lončarić, *Planirana izgradnja na području Dubrovačke Republike*, Studije i monografije, Institut za povijest umjetnosti, book 1 (Zagreb, 1980), pp. 18–20.
4. *Liber Statutorum*, ed. Bogišić and Jireček, book V, chapters i, pp. 110–111; ii, p. 111; iii, p. 111; iv, pp. 111–112; v, p. 112; vi, p. 112; viii, p. 112; xvi, p. 114; xix, p. 115; xli, pp. 122–123; xlii, pp. 123–124; xliii, p. 124; xliv, p. 124; book VI, chapter lvii, p. 145.
5. Planić-Lončarić, *Planirana izgradnja*, pp. 26–28.
6. These ingeniously argued but ultimately still speculative figures are from Krivošić, *op. cit.*, pp. 13–14, 50–51. For the total number of inhabitants of the Republic outside Dubrovnik, see p. 307.
7. Tadić, *Promet putnika*, pp. 188.
8. E. Pivčević, 'Konrad von Grünemberg's Visit to Croatian Coastal Towns in 1486', *BC Review*, 17 (December 1980), 36. See plate 44.
9. L. Beritić, *The City Walls of Dubrovnik* (Dubrovnik, 1989), p. 7.
10. Beritić, *Utvrđenja grada Dubrovnika*, pp. 23–25.
11. *Ibid.*, pp. 26–33.
12. *Ibid.*, p. 51.
13. Beritić, *City Walls*, p. 8. For Dubrovnik fortifications, see plate 42.
14. Michelozzo di Bartolomeo Michelozzi (1396–1472) is best known for his design of the Medici Palace in Florence.
15. A 'revelin' is classically a fortification jutting out from, but connected with, the walls in order to guard a place of potential vulnerability, such as a gate.
16. Pavao, known as *Paulus de Ragusa* (1420 – c. 1479), minted many medals of which four have been preserved, three depicting Alfonso V King of Naples and one his marshal Federigo Montefeltre. Pavao was even summoned by Sultan Mehmed II to his cultivated court, where like other Westerners such as Bellini, he found patronage (Fisković, 'Dubrovački zlatari', 171–174).
17. Beritić, *Utvrđenja grada Dubrovnika*, pp. 84–93. Juraj Dalmatinac is perhaps best known for his masterpiece, Šibenik cathedral. Among his sculptures *The Flagellation of Christ*, at the altar of St Anastasia in the cathedral at Split, is highly regarded. The only sculpture in Dubrovnik which has convincingly been attributed to him is that of St Blaise, which probably once

stood over the gateway to the harbour and which is now in the chapel of the villa built by Petar Sorkočević at Gruž used by the HAZU Historical Institute (M. Montani, *Juraj Dalmatinac i njegov krug* (Zagreb, 1967), p. 9; C. Fisković, 'Neobavljeno djelo Jurja Dalmatinca u Dubrovniku', *Anali*, 1/1 (1952), 145–150).

18. Evlija Čelebija, *Putopis*, ii, 193. See plate 41.
19. Beritić, *City Walls*, pp. 39–43.
20. Before the building of the breakwater the chain ran across to St Luke's. From a mid-sixteenth century sketch it also appears that another chain may have run from the northern end of the breakwater to the slope at the foot of the Ploče Gate (Ničetić, *op. cit.*, p. 162).
21. Ničetić, *op. cit.*, pp. 129–133.
22. L. Beritić, 'Izgradnja i utvrđivanje gradske luke', *Dubrovačko pomorstvo: u spomenu sto godina nautičke škole u Dubrovniku* (Dubrovnik, 1952), ed. J. Luetić *et al.*, 286–287.
23. Ničetić, *op. cit.*, pp. 134–151.
24. *Ibid.*, pp. 157–168; *The Restoration of Dubrovnik 1979–1989* (Zagreb, 1990), ed. B. Letunić, pp. 23–24.
25. Ničetić, *op. cit.*, pp. 161–162.
26. Another storey and new windows were added in 1889 when the Austrians turned it into a barracks (Beritić, 'Izgradnja i utvrđivanje gradske luke', 288–289).
27. Razzi, *Storia di Ragusa*, ed. Gelcich, p. 142.
28. Beritić, *City Walls*, pp. 36–39. For artists' impressions of the harbour, see plates 19 and 45.
29. L. Beritić, *Dubrovačka artiljerija* (Belgrade, 1960), pp. 25–41; Ćirković, *Herceg Stefan*, p. 165; Inalcik, *The Ottoman Empire*, p. 23.
30. Beritić, *Dubrovačka artiljerija*, pp. 64–77.
31. *Ibid.*, pp. 133–154.
32. The precise identity of these *barabanti* remains rather obscure in spite of the work of Trpimir Macan (T. Macan, 'Dubrovački barabanti u xvi stoljeću', *Anali*, 8–9 (1962), 301–323).
33. Beritić, *Utvrđenja grada Dubrovnika*, p. 92.
34. Diversis, *Situs Aedificiorum*, ed. Brunelli, p. 77.
35. Beritić, *Utvrđenja grada Dubrovnika*, p. 23.
36. *Ibid.*, pp. 27–28.
37. Diversis, *Situs Aedificiorum*, ed. Brunelli, p. 79. Like recruitment of the city guard, registration of the islanders was also established well before Diversis's day. Thus in January 1351 the Great Council ordered that the names of all islanders and other seamen be enrolled, from which those chosen by lot would serve as oarsmen on the state war galley (*Libri Reformationum*, ii, 119).
38. The earliest signs of Renaissance conceptions in Dubrovnik's churches have been detected in the cloister of the Dominican friary (1456–1470), the semi-circular apse of the church of St Sebastian (*Sveti Sebastijan*) (1466), the chapel of the Annunciation (*Navještenje*) at the source of Rijeka Dubrovačka (1480) and the church of the convent of St Mary *od Kaštela* (about 1500) (A. Badurina, 'Sakralna arhitektura', *Zlatno doba Dubrovnika XV. i XVI. stoljeće* [Exhibition Catalogue: Zagreb and Dubrovnik, 1987], 111.)
39. Janeković-Römer, *Okvir slobode*, pp. 382–384.
40. By 'Rector's Palace' I also mean here and elsewhere the complex of public buildings, such as the council chambers, of which it was the core. See plates 13 and 14.
41. *The Restoration of Dubrovnik 1979–89*, ed. B. Letunić, p. 71; Diversis, *Situs Aedificiorum*, ed. Brunelli, p. 41.
42. *Annales Ragusini anonymi*, ed. Nodilo, p. 251.
43. Onofrio della Cava, Neapolitan architect and engineer, active in the second half of the fifteenth century. His life and work do not seem to have been much investigated.
44. Diversis, *Situs Aedificiorum*, ed. Brunelli, pp. 41–42.; I. Fisković, 'Kiparstvo', *Zlatno doba Dubrovnika XV. i XVI. stoljeće* [Exhibition Catalogue: Zagreb and Dubrovnik, 1987], 127–128; Janeković-Römer, *Okvir slobode*, pp. 385–387.
45. Diversis, *Situs Aedificiorum*, ed. Brunelli, pp. 47–49; L. Beritić, 'Dubrovački vodovod', *Anali*, 8–9 (1962), 99–108.

46. Diversis, *Situs Aedificiorum*, ed. Brunelli, p. 42.
47. Beritić, 'Ubikacija', part 1, 40–41, 43–45.
48. *The Restoration of Dubrovnik 1979–1989*, ed. B. Letunić (Zagreb, 1990), p. 133.
49. Beritić, 'Ubikacija', part 1, 46–48.
50. Ničetić, *op. cit.*, p. 123.
51. Diversis, *Situs Aedificiorum*, ed. Brunelli, pp. 42–43. See plates 15 and 16.
52. Fisković, 'Kiparstvo', 342–344.
53. *The Restoration of Dubrovnik 1979–1989*, ed. B. Letunić (Zagreb, 1990), p. 101.
54. Janeković-Römer, *Okvir slobode*, p. 341.
55. N. Grujić, 'Reprezentativna stambena arhitektura', *Zlatno doba Dubrovnika XV. i XVI. stoljeće* [Exhibition Catalogue: Zagreb and Dubrovnik, 1987], 69, 307.
56. I. Zdravković, *Dubrovački dvorci: analiza arhitekture i karakteristika stila*, (Belgrade, 1951), pp. 15–18.
57. Grujić, 'Reprezentativna stambema arhitektura', 309–310.
58. *Ibid.*, p. 310.
59. Krivošić, *op. cit.*, p. 21.
60. Planić-Lončarić, *Planirana izgradnja*, pp. 33–78; L. Beritić, 'Stonske utvrde', *Anali*, 3 (1954), 313–324.
61. Beritić, 'Stonske utvrde', 325; M. Planić-Lončarić, 'Ston u 15. i 16. stoljeću', *Likovna kultura Dubrovnika 15. i 16. stoljeća. Znanstveni skup uz izložbu 'Zlatno doba Dubrovnika'* (Zagreb, 1991), 39; *The Restoration of Dubrovnik 1979–1989*, ed. B. Letunić (Zagreb, 1990), p.285.
62. These Dubrovnik loggias are visible along Placa both in a detail of the painting of Our Lady with St Blaise and St Dominic by A.de Bellis in the Dominican friary museum and in the anonymous painting of Dubrovnik now in the Franciscan friary museum, which show the city on the eve of the Great Earthquake.
63. Planić-Lončarić, 'Ston u 15. i 16. stoljeću', 41–41; *idem*, *Planirana izgradnja*, pp. 63–64.
64. On the countship of Župa see p. 141.
65. Cavtat's six-metre-high walls and four small square towers were standing until the last years of the nineteenth century (L. Beritić, 'Utvrđenja i regulacioni plan Cavtata', *Anali*, 12 (1970), 191–203).
66. For the division and settlement of Konavle see pp.71–76.
67. Planić-Lončarić, *Planirana izgradnja*, pp. 101–114; *idem*, 'Organizacija prostora – urbanizam', *Zlatno doba Dubrovnika XV. i XVI. stoljeće* [Exhibition Catalogue: Zagreb and Dubrovnik, 1987], 33, 300.
68. Diversis, *Situs Aedificiorum*, ed. Brunelli, p. 21.
69. Marcus Vitruvius, Roman architect and engineer of the first century BC, author of the influential ten-volume work *De Architectura.* Leon Battista Alberti (1404–1472), Florentine architect. These and other influences are discussed by Nada Grujić in *Ladanjska arhitektura dubrovačkog područja* (Zagreb, 1991), pp. 38–39 and 'Dubrovačka ladanjska arhitektura 15. stoljeća i Gučetićev ljetnikovac u Trstenom', *Prilozi povijesti umjetnosti u Dalmaciji*, xxxiv (1994), 142–145. (The latter article is henceforth abbreviated to 'Gučetićev ljetnikovac').
70. See p. 197.
71. Grujić, 'Gučetićev ljetnikovac', 146–148.
72. N. Grujić, 'Ladanjsko-gospodarska arhitektura 15. i 16. stoljeća na otoku Šipan', *Zbornik dubrovačkog Primorja i otoka*, 2 (1988), 261; *idem*, 'Reprezentativna stambena arhitektura', *Zlatno doba Dubrovnika XV. i XVI. stoljeće* [Exhibition Catalogue: Zagreb and Dubrovnik, 1987], 98–99, 316–317.
73. Razzi, *Storia di Ragusa*, ed. Gelcich, pp. 230–231.
74. Grujić, 'Reprezentativna stambena arhitektura', 320–321.
75. The known locations of villas are shown on the map in Grujić, *Ladanjska arhitektura*, pp. 52–53.
76. *Ibid.*, pp. 121, 126, 130; Grujić, 'Reprezentativna arhitektura', 314–315, 317–318.
77. *... et con ardente core,*
    Ragusa abbraccio, mia diletta sposa,

Specchio d'Illiria et suo pregio maggiore
(Torbarina, *Italian influence*, p. 51).

78. *Ibid.*, p. 45.
79. Franičević, Švelec and Bogišić, *Povijest hrvatske književnosti*, iii, 32.
80. J. Belamarić, 'Kultura ladanja u renesansnoj Dalmaciji: slučaj Hektorovićeva Tvrdalja', *Prilozi povijesti umjetnosti u Dalmaciji*, xxxiv (1994), 176–188.
81. Grujić, *Ladanjska arhitektura*, p. 5.
82. *Ibid.*, p. 39.
83. On balance, I prefer this to the translations suggested by Nada Grujić (*Idem*, 'Gučetićev ljetnikovac', 154; *idem*, 'Reprezentativna arhitektura', 313.)
84. They are now, of course, the site of the fine arboretum at Trsteno, which however has in recent times suffered devastation by Serb forces in 1991 and the effects of forest fires in 1999.
85. Grujić, 'Gučetićev ljetnikovac', 151–167.
86. It is now home to the Dubrovnik Historical Institute. See plate 20.
87. Diversis, *Situs Aedificiorum*, ed. Brunelli, p. 23.
88. Razzi, *Istoria di Ragusa*, ed. Gelcich, p. 213. For the destruction wrought by the Montenegrins on this area in 1806 see below, pp. 391–392.
89. Zdravković, *op. cit.*, p. 47.
90. Grujić, 'Reprezentativna arhitektura', pp. 314–315; C. Fisković, *Kultura dubrovačkog ladanja (Sorkočevićev ljetnikovac na Lapadu)* (Split, 1966), pp. 6–10.
91. Fisković, *Kultura dubrovačkog ladanja*, p. 28.
92. *Ibid.*, p. 32.
93. B. Šišić, *Dubrovački renesansni vrt: nastajanje i oblikovna obilježja* (Dubrovnik, 1991), pp. 67–73.
94. Grujić, *Ladanjska arhitektura*, p. 136.
95. *Dođi k meni malo sad*
Na ovi dvor mili moj sazidan na vodi (*Ibid.*, p. 56).
96. Franičević, Švelec and Bogišić, *Povijest hrvatske književnosti*, iii, 143–145.
97. *Ibid.*, p. 162.
98. Fisković, *Kultura dubrovačkog ladanja*, p. 10.
99. Examples of this state vandalism are given by Nada Grujić in her essay 'Some Aspects of the Renovation of Dubrovnik Summer Residences', *The Restoration of Dubrovnik 1979–1989*, ed. B. Letunić (Zagreb, 1990), 346–363.

Chapter Thirteen

1. J. Mihailović, *Seizmički karakter i trusne katastrofe našeg južnog primorja*, SAN Posebna izdanja, 140 (1947), pp. 6–7.
2. *Ibid.*, p. 17.
3. *Annales Ragusini anonymi*, ed. Nodilo, p. 80.
4. *Ibid.*, pp. 98–99.
5. Razzi, *Storia di Ragusa*, ed. Gelcich, pp. 120–121.
6. Mihailović, *Seizmički karakter*, pp. 14–18.
7. Samardžić, *Veliki vek*, pp. 241–244. It has been estimated that the force of the earthquake was 10 degrees on the Mercalli (7–8 degrees on the Richter) Scale (*The Restoration of Dubrovnik 1979–1989* (Zagreb, 1990), ed. B. Letunić, p. 13).
8. Krasić, *Stjepan Gradić*, p. 143 note 116.
9. A. Bloed, M. Brinkman, A. P. van Goudever, W. Rongen, 'A Missing Link in the Relations between the Northern Countries and Ragusa: Dutch-Ragusan Relationships in the 17th and 18th Centuries', *Dubrovnik's Relations with England: a Symposium, April 1978*, ed. R. Filipović and M. Partridge (University of Zagreb, 1977), 280–285.
10. R. Samardžić, *Borba Dubrovnika za opstanak posle velikog zemljotresa 1667 godine. Arhivska građa (1667–1670)*, SAN Zbornik za istoriju, jezik i književnost srpskog naroda, section III, book xix (1960), no. 1, pp. 19–22.
11. Bloed, Brinkman, Van Goudever, Rongen, 'A Missing Link in the Relations between the

Northern Countries and Ragusa: Dutch-Ragusan Relationships in the 17th and 18th Centuries', 283–286; Samardžić, *Veliki vek*, pp.251–253.

12. Samardžić, *Borba Dubrovnika za opstanak*, no. 16, pp. 46–49.
13. Vlaho Skvadrović, from Koločep, had written shortly before the earthquake a romantic tale of two lovers, depicting a village and hill on his native island, entitled *Mačuš i Čavalica* (Franičević, Švelec and Bogišić, *Povijest hrvatske književnosti*, iii, 233–234).
14. Samardžić, *Veliki vek*, pp. 255–257.
15. Samardžić, *Borba Dubrovnika za opstanak*, no. 16, p. 47.
16. Samardžić, *Veliki vek*, pp. 265–271.
17. The building of the church of the Rosary began in 1594 but had still not been completed by 1611. The church was destroyed in a fire in 1642 and only repaired in 1659 (Badurina, 'Sakralna arhitektura', p. 330).
18. Samardžić, Veliki vek, pp. 260–263; Samardžić, *Borba Dubrovnika za opstanak*, no. 17, pp. 49–52, no. 23, pp. 60–62, no. 40, pp. 84–87, no. 43, pp. 89–91, no. 198, pp. 269–270.
19. Samardžić, *Borba Dubrovnika za opstanak*, no. 3, pp. 24–26.
20. Krivošić, *Stanivništvo Dubrovnika*, pp. 16–17.
21. Bloed, Brinkman, van Goudever, Rongen, 'A Missing Link', 282.
22. Samardžić, *Borba Dubrovnika za opstanak*, no. 18, p. 52.
23. *Ibid.*, no. 66, p. 121. When the Senate met in the shelter of Revelin on 3 June 1667, the first time after the earthquake, it was reported that 57 members of the Great Council had been killed. The minutes are in a different hand to those on the eve of the disaster, doubtless because the clerk had also died (DAD, Acta Consilii Rogatorum, 3/15 (1666–1667), fo 55r).
24. I assume that the losses outside the city would have been proportionately a good deal smaller, because the inhabitants were not so likely to be crushed or trapped by falling masonry and because only Dubrovnik seems to have endured a fire in which many perished.
25. Ničetić, *op. cit.*, p. 155.
26. Beritić, 'Ubikacija', part 1, 50–61, 70–79.
27. Samardžić, *Veliki vek*, p. 242.
28. Samardžić, *Borba Dubrovnika za opstanak*, no. 8, p. 37.
29. *Ibid.*, no. 30, p. 71.
30. Planić-Lončarić, *Planirana izgradnja*, p. 34.
31. Samardžić, *Veliki vek*, pp. 279–281.
32. Samardžić, *Borba Dubrovnika za opstanak*, no. 10, pp. 39–40.
33. *Ibid.*, no. 40, p. 86.
34. I. Mitić, 'Primjer pružanja crkvenog azila u dubrovačkom samostanu Male braće tijekom xvii stoljeća', *Samostan male braće Dubrovnika*, ed. J. Turčinović, 405–411.
35. For Bunić's later fate see p. 342.
36. Samardžić, *Borba Dubrovnika za opstanak*, no. 3, pp. 26–27, no. 18, p. 54; G. Novak, 'Dubrovački potres 1667 i mletci', *Anali* 12 (1970), 13.
37. Samardžić, *Borba Dubrovnika za opstanak*, no.39, pp. 83–84.
38. *Ibid.*, no. 20, pp. 55–57.
39. The terrible events of this period were, as far as possible, treated as marking a physical but not a constitutional break in the traditional order of things. Clearly, the decisions made could not be easily fitted into the established conventions. Probably for this reason, they were written separately in a short volume entitled 'Book of the Provisions and Decisions of 1667' (Acta Consilii Rogatorum, 3/15 (1667), '1667 Libro delli providimenti et terminazioni'). The nearest that the patriciate came to establishing a new constitutional order was at the meeting of 23 April. But no citizen ever again participated in the Republic's government. Moreover, the powers of the Twelve were in practice limited. Votes continued to be taken before the main decisions – and even some quite secondary ones, such as the sending of envoys. It was also stated that the laws of the Republic remained fully in force.
40. Samardžić, *Borba za opstanak.*, no. 26, pp. 65–66.
41. *Ibid.*, no. 35, p. 78.
42. *Ibid.*, no. 43, pp. 89–91.

43. Foretić, *Povijest Dubrovnika do 1808.*, ii, 139 .
44. Samardžić, *Borba Dubrovnika za opstanak*, no. 66, pp. 121–125.
45. Samardžić, *Borba Dubrovnika za opstanak*, no. 9, pp. 38–39.
46. *Ibid.*, no. 359, p. 441.
47. *Ibid.*, no. 38, pp. 82–82.
48. *Ibid.*, no. 55, pp. 105–108.
49. *Ibid.*, no. 417, pp. 503–504, no. 419, pp. 504–505.
50. *Ibid.*, no. 101, p. 168.
51. Foretić, *Povijest Dubrovnika do 1808.*, ii, 140–143; Z. Zlatar, *Between the Double Eagle and the Crescent: the Republic of Dubrovnik and the Origins of the Eastern Question* (Boulder, 1992), pp. 25, 105.
52. Samardžić, *Borba Dubrovnika za opstanak,* no. 7, p. 36.
53. *Ibid.*, no. 14, p. 45.
54. *Ibid.*, no. 18. p. 53.
55. *Ibid.*, no. 32, pp. 73–76.
56. *Ibid.*, no. 42, p. 88.
57. *Ibid.*, no. 50. pp. 100–101.
58. *Ibid.*, no. 60, p. 111.
59. *Ibid.*, no. 68, pp. 126–127.
60. *Ibid.*, no. 71, pp. 128–130, no. 73, pp. 133–135, no. 76, p. 141, no. 80, pp. 146–147.
61. *Ibid.*, no. 82, pp. 148–149, no. 84, pp. 150–151, no. 90, pp. 156–157.
62. *Ibid.*, no. 121, pp. 188–190.
63. *Ibid.*, no. 126, pp. 193–194.
64. *Ibid.*, no. 33, pp. 76–77.
65. *Ibid.*, no. 195, p. 267.
66. *Ibid.*, no. 138, pp. 203–208.
67. Samardžić, *Veliki vek*, pp. 338–375.
68. Samardžić, *Borba Dubrovnika za opstanak*, no. 335, pp. 414–415.
69. *Ibid.*, no. 338, pp. 419–420.
70. *Ibid.*, no. 350, p. 430.
71. DAD, Fabricae, 7/115.
72. Fabricae, 7/116.
73. Fabricae, 7/117, 'Libro della fabrica di S. Biagio 1667'.
74. Krasić, *Stjepan Gradić*, pp. 4–29, 35–95.
75. *Ibid.*, p. 111.
76. *Ibid.*, pp. 125–160.
77. *Ibid.*, pp. 173–175.
78. *Ibid.*, pp. 121–125.
79. *Ibid.*, pp. 177–182.
80. Cerimoniale, fos 230r-231v. See plate 17.
81. L. Beritić, *Urbanistički razvitak Dubrovnika* ([Zagreb], n. d.), p. 36.
82. Krasić, *Stjepan Gradić*, pp. 109–110.

Chapter Fourteen

1. Foretić, *Povijest Dubrovnika do 1808.*, ii, 148.
2. A plaque was erected to his memory that same year in the hall of the Great Council. It reads (in translation from the Latin): 'To Nikola Ivanov Bunić, Senator of exceptional prudence, who in very difficult times for the Republic willingly accepted a mission to the neighbouring viceroy of Bosnia and by him was sent by force to the Emperor of the Turks in Silistria, where having been kept for a long time in chains, he died, by which death and constancy of spirit he earned immortality from posterity. By the decision of the Senate this memorial was placed in his honour and in his memory. The Year 1678.'
3. Zlatar, *Between the Double Eagle and the Crescent*, pp. 105–128.
4. *Ibid.*, pp. 141–196; Foretić, *Povijest Dubrovnika do 1808.*, ii, 175–192.

5. Zlatar, *Between the Double Eagle and the Crescent*, pp. 196–211; Foretić, *Povijest Dubrovnika do 1808*, ii, 192–197.
6. S. Ćosić, 'Dubrovačka granica i područje Kleka (presjek jednog problema iz diplomatske povijesti)', *Međunarodni simpoziji: diplomacija Dubrovačke Republike. Zbornik diplomatske akademije* (Zagreb, 1998), 203–217. Ćosić's article surveys the history of the Klek enclave based on fascinating historical detective work. One fruit of the dispute between Croatia and Montenegro about the border area of Prevlaka has been detailed examination of the historic frontier by Stijepo Obad, Serđo Dokoza and Suzana Martinović in their excellent historical atlas of the area, *Južne granice Dalmacije od 15. stoljeća do danas* (Zadar, 1999).
7. Foretić, *Povijest Dubrovnika do 1808.*, ii, 210–211.
8. 'Izvještaj', 97.
9. L. de Voïnovitch, *La Monarchie française dans l'Adratique: Histoire des relations de la France avec la République de Raguse* (Paris, 1918), pp. 202–203, 211.
10. Foretić, *Povijest Dubrovnika do 1808.*, ii, 238, 248–250, 267–273.
11. *Ibid.*, 201–204.
12. *Ibid.*, 256–268.
13. V. Miović-Perić, *Na razmeđu: osmansko-dubrovačka granica (1667.-1806)* (Dubrovnik, 1997), p. 42.
14. Carter, *op. cit.*, pp. 409–427.
15. R. Warnier, 'Comment un consul de France décrit au directoire la civilisation ragusaine', *Zbornik iz dubrovačke prošlosti Milanu Rešetaru u 70–oj godišnjici života*, ed. V. Ćorović *et al.* (Dubrovnik, 1931), 162.
16. J. Luetić, *O pomorstvu Dubrovačke Republike u xviii stoljeću* (Dubrovnik, 1959), p. 16.
17. Mitić, *Konzulati*, p. 71.
18. B. Lukić, 'Diplomatski odnosi i sukob između Dubrovačke Republike i Maroka u xviii. stoljeću', *Anali*, 3 (1954), 545–558.
19. Luetić, *O pomorstvu Dubrovačke Republike u xviii stoljeću*, pp. 133–134.
20. Mitić, *Konzulati*, pp. 139–146.
21. Carter, *op. cit.*, pp. 433–441.
22. V. Ivančević, 'O brodogradnji u Dubrovniku potkraj Republike', *Anali*, 3 (1954), 559–579.
23. Foretić, *Povijest Dubrovnika do 1808.*, ii, 218.
24. S. Vekarić and N. Vekarić, 'Tri stoljeća pelješkog brodarstva', *Pelješki zbornik*, 4 (1987), 54–57.
25. S. Vekarić, 'Prilozi za povijest pelješkog pomorstva u xvii. i xviii. stoljeću', *Anali*, 3 (1954), 527–544.
26. Lonza, 'Izborni postupak', 46–50.
27. The continuity between the 'conspirator' families and the *salamankezi* and the effect of the polarisation upon office-holding have been demonstrated in the already mentioned seminal article by Ćosić and Vekarić, 'Raskol dubrovačkog patricijata', 305–379.
28. Unusually, the Vodopić family hailed from Konavle, but they had been trading in Dubrovnik since 1340, so were hardly *parvenus*, let alone bumpkins (Ćosić, 'Dubrovački plemički rodovi konavoskog podrijetla', 58).
29. Ž. Muljačić, 'O strankama u starom Dubrovniku', *Anali*, 6–7 (1959), 25–29.
30. The terms *salamankezi* and *sorbonezi* have been traced back to 1785 and 1781 respectively (*Ibid.*, 30).
31. Appendini, *Notizie istorico-critiche*, ii, 192.
32. Krivošić, *op. cit.*, p. 61. In Venice the patriciate consisted of 2.5 per cent of the population on the fall of the Venetian Republic in 1797.
33. *Liber Croceus*, ed. Nedeljković, cap. 381, pp. 433; cap. 400, p. 477; cap. 402. pp. 478–479; cap. 403, pp. 479–480.
34. *Ibid.*, cap. 458, pp. 545–546.
35. The phrase in quotation marks comes from H. Bjelovučić, *The Ragusan Republic, Victim of Napoleon and Its Own Conservatism* (Leiden, 1970).
36. *Ibid.*, 25–40; Foretić, *Povijest Dubrovnika do 1808.*, ii, 239–247.
37. N. Vekarić, 'Broj stanovnika Dubrovačke Republike u 15., 16., i 17. stoljeću', *Anali*, 29

(1991), 7–22.

38. Vekarić, 'Opsade Dubrovnika i broj stanovnika', 244.
39. Kapetanić and Vekarić, *Stanovništvo Konavala*, i, 108.
40. 'Izvještaj', 46.
41. Appendini, *Notizie istorico-critiche*, ii, 192.
42. Ćosić, 'Dubrovački plemički i građanski rodovi konavoskog podrijetla', 66, 73.
43. *Ibid.*, 70. For Đuro Hidža see pp. 370, 406.
44. *Ibid.*, 71.
45. *Ibid.*, 68.
46. Deanović, *Anciens contacts*, pp. 19–20.
47. Appendini, *Notizie istorico-critiche*, i, 97–198.
48. Foretić, *Povijest Dubrovnika do 1808.*, ii, 282–284. Foretić offers a more balanced view of the (limited) evidence regarding underlying economic conditions than the otherwise useful work of S. Antoljak, 'Konavoska buna u središtu jednog dijela Europske diplomacije (1799–1800)', *Rad*, 286 (1952), 107–108. On the Konavle Revolt see pp. 377–380.
49. Miović-Perić, *Na razmeđu*, pp. 28–35, 61–63, 212–241.
50. N. Lonza, *Pod plaštem pravde: kaznenopravni sustav Dubrovačke Republike u XVIII. stoljeću* (Dubrovnik, 1997), pp. 42–43, 50–51, 79–82, 105–114.
51. N. Vekarić, 'Sud janjinske kapitanije', *Anali*, 27 (1989), 133–148.
52. Lonza, *Pod plaštem pravde*, pp. 140–147.
53. Ž. Muljačić, 'Kako je A. Fortis pripremio za drugo francusko izdanje 'Puta u Dalmaciji' novo poglavlje o Dubrovniku', *Anali*, 17 (1979), 229–250.
54. J. Bersa, *Dubrovačke slike i prilike (1800–1880)* (Zagreb, 1941), pp.16–17.
55. 'Izvještaj', 87.
56. Appendini, *Notizie istorico-critiche*, i, 179–180, 194–199.
57. M. Demović, *Glazba i glazbenici u Dubrovačkoj Republici od polovine xvii. do prvog desetljeća xix. stoljeća* (Zagreb, 1989), pp. 179–192.
58. Her life and poetry are the subject of a study by Slavica Stojan, *Anica Bošković* (Dubrovnik, 1999).
59. Ž. Dadić, *Ruđer Bošković* (Zagreb, 1990), pp. 27, 31–34, 51–56; M. Korade, M. Aleksić and Jerko Matoš, *Isusovci i hrvatska kultura* (Zagreb, 1993), pp. 209–225.
60. Appendini, *Notizie istoricho-critiche*, i, 180.
61. Franičević, Švelec and Bogišić, *Povijest hrvatske književnosti*, iii, 272–275.
62. *Ibid.*, 276–279.
63. *Ibid.*, 283–291; Kombol, *op. cit.*, pp. 307–323; Appendini, *Notizie istorico-critiche*, ii, 20–21.
64. *De Vita et Scriptis Junii Antonii comitis de Restiis, patricii Ragusini, Commentariolum Francisci Mariae Appendini e scholis piis*, in *Junii Antonii comitis de Restiis, patricii Ragusini, Carmina* (Padua, 1816).
65. Franičević, Švelec and Bogišić, *Povijest hrvatske književnosti*, iii, 346–347.
66. Korade, Aleksić and Matoš, *Isusovci i hrvatska kultura* (Zagreb, 1993), pp. 231–239.
67. Appendini, *Notizie istorico-critiche*, i, 193; N. Beritić, 'Iz povijesti kazališne i glazbene umjetnosti u Dubrovniku', *Otkrića iz arhiva: iz književne i političke povijesti Dubrovnika i Dalmacije u 18. i 19. stoljeću* (Split, 2000), 7; M. Deanović, 'Talijanski teatar u Dubrovniku xviii vijeka', *Zbornik iz dubrovačke prošlosti Milanu Rešetaru o 70–oj godišnjici života*, ed. V. Ćorović *et al.* (Dubrovnik, 1931), pp. 289–355.
68. Beritić, 'Iz povijesti', 7–10.
69. Franičević, Švelec and Bogišić, *Povijest hrvatske književnosti*, iii, 350–355.
70. *Ibid.*, 348–349.
71. M. Deanović, 'Dnevnik M. Matijaševića', *Anali*, 1 (1952), 320–321.
72. S. Stojan, *U salonu Marije Giorgi Bona* (Dubrovnik, 1996), pp. 75–88.
73. M. Breyer, 'Prilozi povijesti dubrovačkog štamparstva', *Zbornik iz dubrovačke prošlosti Milanu Rešetaru o 70–oj godišnjici života*, ed. V. Ćorović *et al.* (Dubrovnik, 1931), 289–305.
74. D. Živojinović, *Američka Revolucija i Dubrovačka Republika, 1763–1790* (Belgrade, 1976), pp. 169–178.
75. I. Martinović, 'Rađanje 'Ujedinjene Amerike' – diplomatski izazov za Ruđera Boškovića',

Međunarodni simpoziji: diplomacija Dubrovačke Republike. Zbornik diplomatske akademije (Zagreb, 1998), 267–268.

76. L. Antić, 'Dubrovačka Republika i međunarodno priznanje Sjedinjenih Američkih Država', *Međunarodni simpoziji: diplomacija Dubrovačke Republike. Zbornik diplomatske akademije* (Zagreb, 1998), 259–264.

Chapter Fifteen

1. L. Vojnović, *Pad Dubrovnika*, i (Zagreb, 1808), 12–13.
2. As was typical in the eighteenth-century Ragusan diplomatic corps, Sebastiano had succeeded his uncle Francesco di Ayala as agent in Vienna.
3. Ž. Muljačić, 'Istraga protiv Jakobinaca 1797. god. u Dubrovniku', *Anali*, 2 (1953), 235–252.
4. Foretić, *Povijest Dubrovnika do 1808.*, ii, 334–336.
5. S. Vekarić, 'Podaci o dubrovačkim brodovima za vrijeme i nakon francuske okupacije', *Anali*, 2 (1953), 361; I. Rusko, 'Stanje dubrovačke trgovačke mornarice pred samu propast Dubrovačke Republike početkom xix. stoljeća', *Dubrovačko pomorstvo: u spomen sto godina nautičke škole u Dubrovniku* (Dubrovnik, 1952), ed. J. Luetić *et al.*, 205–222.
6. B. Krizman (trans.), ' Mémoire Bara Bettere austrijskom generalu T. Milutinoviću g. 1815', *Anali*, 1 (1952) 423–464; Bjelovučić, *op. cit.*, pp. 40–45.
7. Bjelovučić, *op. cit.*, p. 44.
8. P. Pisani, *La Dalmatie de 1797 à 1815*, i (Paris, 1893), 23–32.
9. For an illuminating (if not entirely persuasive) explanation of Ragusan diplomacy as aimed at the 'internationalisation' of the crisis, see I. Prlender, 'Internacionalizacija krize u praksi diplomatske službe Dubrovačke Republike u dva primjera', *Međunarodni simpozij: diplomacija Dubrovačke Republike. Zbornik diplomatske akademije* (Zagreb, 1998), 222–231.
10. Antoljak, *op. cit.*, 107–141; Foretić, *Povijest Dubrovnika do 1808.*, ii, 336–343; Bjelovučić, *op. cit.*, pp. 74–76.
11. Fonton's family originated in the Dauphiné but had joined the service of the Russian Empire (Pisani, *op. cit.*, i, 139).
12. Foretić, *Povijest Dubrovnika do 1808.*, ii, 434–435.
13. *Ibid.*, 439–440.
14. Foretić, *Povijest Dubrovnika do 1808.*, ii, 437.
15. Jacques (James) Law, marquis de Lauriston and Marshal of France b. 1768 and d.1826. Gabriel, comte de Molitor and Marshal of France b. 1770 and d. 1849.
16. The exception to this generalisation provided by Dubrovnik's request at the time of the Konavle Revolt for Austrian forces to come to Lokrum is more apparent than real. The Ragusans must have known that the Austrian commander, General Brady, had no authority to agree this. See p. 378.
17. For the circumstances of the Serenissima's suicide, see J. M. Thompson, *Napoleon Bonaparte* (Oxford, 1988), pp. 87–88.
18. Vojnović, *Pad Dubrovnika*, i, 66–124.
19. *Ibid.*, 165–167.
20. Charles-Maurice de Talleyrand-Périgord, formerly bishop of Autun, prince of Benevento, Foreign Minister to Napoleon (1799–1807), b. 1754 and d. 1838.
21. Vojnović, *Pad Dubrovnika*, ii, 175.
22. *Ibid.*, 176–189.
23. *Ibid.*, 190–198. The holes which the French dug into the low stone wall around the cloister of the Dominican friary to serve as make-shift horse troughs can still be seen.
24. V. Čučić, 'Rat u Konavlima 1806.', *Konavle u prošlosti, sadašnjosti i budućnosti*, 1 (Dubrovnik, 1998), 163.
25. F. M. Appendini, *Ratovanje oko Dubrovnika*, ed. P. Kolendić and J. Nagy (Dubrovnik, 1906), p. 7.
26. *Ibid.*, pp. 7–8.
27. *Ibid.*, pp. 17–19.
28. *Ibid.*, pp. 20–21.

29. Kapetanić and Vekarić, *Stanovništvo Konavala*, i, 110 and table 4 on p. 112.
30. V. Miović-Perić, 'Što je prethodilo katastrofi 1806.?' *Konavle u prošlosti, sadašnjosti i budućnosti*, 1 (Dubrovnik, 1998), 147–156.
31. Appendini, *Ratovanje oko Dubrovnika*, p. 23.
32. Bjelovučić, *op. cit.*, pp. 115–116, 177–178.
33. Vojnović, *Pad Dubrovnika*, ii, Appendix 4, p. 426.
34. Foretić, *Povijest Dubrovnika do 1808.*, ii, 449–451.
35. R. F. [Rudolf Maixner], 'La Traduction française de l' 'Osman'', *Annales de l'institut français de Zagreb*, 2/5–6 (1938), note 5, pp. 250–251.
36. Auguste Viesse de Marmont, Duc de Raguse and Marshal of France b. 1774 and d. 1852. Marmont's final betrayal of Napoleon did the disservice to Dubrovnik of introducing to the French language the word *ragusade*, 'treason'.
37. [Marshal Marmont] *Mémoires du duc de Raguse de 1792 à 1832*, iii/10 (Paris, 1857), 5.
38. *Ibid.*, iii/10, 9–19; Čučić, 'Rat u Konavlima 1806.', 67–8.
39. Bjelovučić, *op. cit.*, p. 114.
40. Foretić, *Povijest Dubrovnika do 1808.*, ii, 454–456.
41. *Ibid.*, 456–458.
42. Bjelovučić, *op. cit.*, pp. 117–118.
43. Vojnović, *Pad Dubrovnika*, ii, Appendix 3, pp. 420–423.
44. *Ibid.*, 79–98.

Postscript

1. Marmont, *op. cit.*, ii/9, 375.
2. Vojnović, *Pad Dubrovnika*, ii, 98–99; S. Ćosić, *Dubrovnik nakon pada Republike (1808.-1848.)* (Dubrovnik, 1999), pp. 60–61.
3. Cf. Pisani, *op. cit.*, i, 244–256.
4. Giovanni Domenico Garagnin b. 1761 and d. 1848. His family was from Trogir and strongly pro-French. He withdrew from public life in 1811 when Marmont left Dalmatia.
5. Ćosić, *Dubrovnik nakon pada Republike*, pp. 43–54, 66.
6. Vekarić, 'Podaci o dubrovačkim brodovima', 366–367; I. Rusko, 'Stanje dubrovačke trgovačke mornarice pred samu propast Dubrovačke Republike početkom xix. stoljeća', *Dubrovačko pomorstvo: u spomen sto godina nautičke škole u Dubrovniku* (Dubrovnik, 1952), ed. Luetić *et al.*, 205–222.
7. Ćosić, *Dubrovnik nakon pada Republike*, pp. 69, 80–82, 88.
8. Bjelovučić, *op. cit.*, p. 139.
9. Vojnović, *Pad Dubrovnika*, ii, 126. Henri (Henry) Clarke, Marshal of France, b. 1765 and d. 1818.
10. Marmont, *op. cit.*, iii/10, 45.
11. Vojnović, *Pad Dubrovnika*, ii, 111–116, 126–136; Ćosić, *Dubrovnik nakon pada Republike*, pp. 84, 91–95.
12. Quoted by Ćosić, *Dubrovnik nakon pada Republike*, p. 98.
13. *Ibid.*, pp. 56, 97, 206.
14. Vojnović, *Pad Dubrovnika*, ii, 147–188.
15. Clemens Fürst von Metternich b. 1773 and d. 1859, Austrian Minister of Foreign Affairs/Chancellor 1809–1848.
16. Viscount Robert Stuart Castlereagh b. 1769 and d. 1822, Marquis of Londonderry from 1821, Foreign Secretary 1812–1822.
17. Vojnović, *Pad Dubrovnika*, ii, 194–312; Ćosić, *Dubrovnik nakon pada Republike*, pp. 100–126.
18. I. Perić, *Dubrovačko pomorstvo u 19. i 20. stoljeću* (Zagreb, 1984), pp. 55–119, 206.
19. *Ibid.*, p.142.
20. Ćosić, *Dubrovnik nakon pada Republike*, pp. 180–184.
21. *Povijesne i statističke bilješke o Dubrovačkom okrugu prikupio okružni inženjer Lorenzo Vitelleschi, Dubrovnik, 1827 (Notizie storiche e statistiche del Circolo di Ragusa compilate dell'ingegnere circolare Lorenzo Vitelleschi, Ragusa, 1827)*, ed. V. Lupis (Dubrovnik, 2002), pp. 21–51 , 66–69,

142–161. See plate 50.

22. Vinicije Lupis observes that the ancient Baptistry, in a state of dilapidation, was no longer used. Baptisms now took place in a side chapel of the Cathedral. So the strong local tradition that the structure was removed to improve the view for an Austrian general can only be at best partly correct. But it is still difficult to acquit the Austrian authorities of cultural vandalism (*Ibid.*, pp. 47–48).
23. Ćosić, *Dubrovnik nakon pada Republike*, pp. 165–215–217; S. Kovačić, 'Dubrovačka metropolija tijekom višestoljetne krize, do ukidanja i preustroja dotadašnje nadbiskupije u sadašnju dubrovačku biskupiju u travnju 1803.', *Tisuću godina dubrovačke (nad)biskupije*, ed. Puljić and Anćić, 253–274.
24. Bersa. *op. cit.*, pp. 75–76; I. Pederin, 'Putni dnevnik Cara Franje I. o Dubrovniku (1818. godine)', *Anali*, 17 (1979), 431–464. The Emperor was not a born diarist. For example, his entry for 29 May reads: 'Nothing. In the evening there was a storm. I watched the storm, which was not as strong as the storm I saw in Leghorn' (*Ibid.*, 459).
25. Ćosić, *Dubrovnik nakon pada Republike*, pp. 158–162, 206–207.
26. Heinrich Stieglitz quoted in Ćosić, *Dubrovnik nakon pada Republike*, p. 204.
27. For these terms see p. 248 and note 16.
28. See p. 249 *et seq.*
29. Banac, 'Ministration and Desecration', 152.
30. Banac, 'Main Trends in the Croatian Language Question', 46.
31. Banac, 'Ministration and Desecration', 156.
32. See pp. 402–403.
33. Quoted in Ćosić, *Dubrovnik nakon pada Republike*, p. 313.
34. For an admirable account of this complicated matter, see Moguš, *op. cit.*, pp. 158–175.
35. For a lively account of these events, see Marcus Tanner, *Croatia: A Nation Forged in War* (New Haven and London: Yale, 1997), pp. 82–93.
36. Later in the century his decision would, in fact, be reversed, and the ekavian dialect of Belgrade and Novi Sad would become the basis of official Serbian.
37. Ivo Banac, 'Main Trends in the Croatian Language Question', 53–77, examines this thinking and its consequences. One should add that the ideologue of Croatian historic 'State Rights', Ante Starčević (1823–1896) embraced, *mutatis mutandis*, much the same approach. For a discussion of Starčević's aims, see Banac's magisterial *The National Question in Yugoslavia: Origins, History, Politics* (Ithaca and London: Cornell University Press), pp. 85, 106.
38. I. Banac, 'The Confessional 'Rule' and the Dubrovnik Exception: The Origins of the 'Serb-Catholic' Circle in Nineteenth Century Dalmatia', *Slavic Review*, 42/3 (Autumn 1983), 452–455; Banac, 'Ministration and Desecration', 163.
39. Quoted and translated by Banac, 'The Confessional 'Rule' and the Dubrovnik Exception: The Origins of the 'Serb-Catholic' Circle in Nineteenth Century Dalmatia', 455. This section is largely based upon Ivo Banac's subtle and illuminating article.
40. 'Red Croatia' echoes the expression used to describe Duklja in the chronicle of the Priest of Dioclea.
41. C. Powell with J. Persico, *A Soldier's Way: An Autobiography* (London, 1995), p. 291.
42. Only the fact that the Italians took over the administration of Dubrovnik in November 1941 prevented still worse persecution. But even so, under Nazi pressure the Dubrovnik Jews and the hundreds of other Jews who had fled to the city were interned in Kupari and Gruž and on Lopud, before being sent off to the island of Rab. Of the 87 Jews living in Dubrovnik before the War, twenty-seven were eventually victims of the Holocaust (Stulli, *Židovi*, pp. 83–90).
43. The full facts of this individual atrocity – one of many – were investigated by a conference organised in Dubrovnik in 1994 whose proceedings were published as *Crveni teror u Dubrovniku, listopad 1944*, Matica hrvatska Dubrovnik, Posebna izdanja, 13 (1994). The persecution of the church at this time was extremely severe in Dubrovnik as elsewhere. From the Dubrovnik diocese twenty-four priests were killed – among these the bishop of Dubrovnik, Josip Carević, tortured and then killed near Zagreb on 10 May 1945 (A. Franić,

Svećenici mučenici: svjedoci komunističkog progona (Dubrovnik, 1996).

44. V. Koščak, 'Polemika o propadnosti dubrovačke književnosti 1967. godine', Velikosrpska svojatanja Dubrovnika: Dubrovnik u ratu, *Dubrovnik*, New Series, 3/2–3 (1992), 462–474.
45. J. Mitrović, *Srpstvo Dubrovnika* (Belgrade, 1992), pp. 266, 280.
46. P. Ralić, *Short History of Dubrovnik* (Belgrade, 1992), p. 7.
47. H. Kačić, 'Razgovor pod slikom Josipa Broza', *Dubrovački horizonti*, 27/36 (1996), 152–156.
48. S. Mesić, *Kako je srušena Jugoslavija* (Zagreb, 1994), pp. 294–303.
49. For a full account of the dispute over Prevlaka, see T. Macan, *Rt Oštra u povijesti i politici* (Zagreb, 1998). The exchange between Poljanić and the commander of Boka is recounted by Feđa Šehović, *Dubrovački ratni dnevnik: Zla kob zaborava* (Zagreb, 1994), p. 8.
50. These figures are from *Kategorizacija ratnih šteta na stambenim objektima: Općina Konavle*, Komisija za popis i procjenu ratne štete u općini Dubrovnik (Dubrovnik, February 1993). See plates 51 and 52.

Appendix One

1. H. Inalcik, 'Dubrovnik i Otomansko Carstvo', *Međunarodni simpozij: diplomacija Dubrovačke Republike. Zbornik diplomatske akademije* (Zagreb, 1998), 116. This important paper was actually delivered in English and as such it is best read in the English version of the Diplomatic Academy collection: see Bibliography.
2. I. Mitić, *Dubrovačka država u međunarodnoj zajednici (od 1358. do 1815.)* (Zagreb, 1988), pp. 15–23.
3. Vladimir Ibler's Introduction to Mitić, *Dubrovačka država*, pp. 7–12; also Ibler's paper, 'Međunarodnopravni subjektivitet i vanjskopolitička nezavisnost Dubrovačke Republike', *Međunarodni simpozij: diplomacija Dubrovačke Republike. Zbornik diplomatske akademije* (Zagreb, 1998), 49–59.

Appendix Two

1. The contents of this note are based upon M. Rešetar, *Dubrovačka numizmatika*, i, SKA Posebna izdanja, 48 (1924), 67–68; *Liber Statutorum Doane Ragusii MCCLXXVII (Knjiga odredaba dubrovačke carinarnice 1277.)*, ed. J. Lučić (Dubrovnik, 1989), p. 9; B. Mimica, *Numizmatička povijest Dubrovnika* ([Rijeka], 1996), pp. 64–248; and H. Bjelovučić, *The Ragusan Republic: Victim of Napoleon and of Its Own Conservatism* (Leiden, 1970), p. 171.

Chronology

1. This chronology draws on that of Josip Lučić, in his *Dubrovačke teme* (Zagreb, 1991), pp. 512–570.

Bibliography

I list here only those sources which I found of direct use for the writing of this book and to which, therefore, specific reference is made in the footnotes. (A valuable bibliography of 'foreign' – i.e. not Yugoslav/Croatian/Serbian – works on Dubrovnik is to be found in *Anali*, 35 (1997), 195–239, compiled by Neven Budak.)

Manuscript Sources

Dubrovnik State Archive

Acta Consilii Minoris, 5/83 (1668–1671); 5/83 (1668–1671).

Fabricae, 7/115; 7/116; 7/117.

Lamenti politici, 11/3 (1441); 11/4 (1537–1544); 11/7 (1570).

Cathasticum, 12/4, Libro rosso.

Leges et instructiones, 21/1, no. 1, Specchio del Maggior Consiglio; 21/1, no. 8, Cerimoniale.

Fratrie, 22/1, no. 15, Matrikula lazarina; [no present catalogue reference] Matrikula antunina.

Dubrovnik Dominican Archive

[S. Cerva/Crijević] Sacra Metropolis Ragusina , i/1–5.

Dubrovnik Franciscan Archive

[G.-M. Mattei/Matijašević] Zibaldone, memorie storiche su Ragusa raccolte dal. P. Gian-Maria Mattei, 3 vols.

Published Primary Sources

Annales Ragusini anonymi, item Nicolai de Ragnina, ed. S. Nodilo, Monumenta spectantia historiam Slavorum meridionalium, 14. Scriptores, I (Zagreb, 1883).

Autobiografija Bartola Kašića, Građe za povijest književnosti Hrvatske, xv (1940).

Beno Kotruljević, *O trgovini i o savršenom trgovcu*, ed. R. Radičević and Ž. Muljačić, JAZU Djela znanosti Hrvatske, i (1985). (See also *Della Mercatura* below.)

Bojović, B., *Raguse et l'empire ottoman (1430–1520). Les actes impériaux ottomans en vieux-serbe de Murad II à Sélim 1er* (Paris, 1998).

Bratovštine i obrtne korporacije u Republici Dubrovačkoj od xiii. do konca xviii. vijeka, i. *Bratovštine dubrovačke*, ed. K. Vojnović, Monumenta historico-juridica Slavorum meridionalium, vii (Zagreb, 1899).

Bratovštine i obrtne korporacije u Republici Dubrovačkoj od xiii. do konca xviii. vijeka, ii. *Dubrovačke obrtne korporacije (cehovi)*, ed. K. Vojnović, Monumenta historico-juridica Slavorum meridionalium, vii (Zagreb, 1900).

Butler, T., *Monumenta Serbocroatica: A Bilingual Anthology of Serbian and Croatian Texts from the 12th to the 19th Century* (Ann Arbor: Michigan, 1980).

Chronica Ragusina Junii Restii (ab origine urbis usque ad annum 1451), item Joannis Gundulae (1451–1484), ed. S. Nodilo, Monumenta spectantia historiam Slavorum meridionalium, 14. Scriptores II (Zagreb, 1883).

Constantine Porphyrogenitus, *De Administrando Imperii*, ed. G. Moravcsik, trans. R. Jenkins [Magyar- Görög Tanulmányok, 29] (Budapest, 1949).

Copioso ristretto degli annali di Ragusa di Pietro Luccari, gentiluomo di Ragusa (Dubrovnik, 1790).

[Crijević, Ilija *et al.*] PSHK, Hrvatski latinisti, i (1969).

Della Mercatura et del Mercante perfetto. Libri Quatro. Di M. Benedetto Cotrugli Raugeo. Scritti gia piu di anni cx. et hora dati in luce. Utilissimi ad ogni Mercante. Con Privilegio (Venice, 1573 – New Impression: Zagreb, 1975).

Depeschen des Francesco Gondola, Gesandten der Republike Ragusa bei Pius V. und Gregor XIII. (1570–1573), ed. L. Voinovich, Archiv fur osterreichische Geschichte, 98. Band (Vienna, 1909).

Djela Ǵiva Frana Gundulića, SPH, ix (1938).

Djela Gjora Palmotića, SPH, xii/2 (1882).

Djela Petra Hektorovića, SPH, xxxix (1986).

Dubrovačka akta i povelje, 1/1 and 2/1, ed. J. Radonić, SKA Zbornik za istoriju, jezik i književnost srpskog naroda, Section III, book 2 (1934).

Idem, 2/2, ed. J. Radonić, SKA Zbornik za istoriju, jezik i književnost srpskog naroda, Section III, book 8 (1938).

Evlija Čelebija, *Putopis. Odlomci o jugoslovenskim zemljama*, trans. and ed. H. Šabanović 2 vols. (Sarajevo, 1957).

Građa o slikarskoj školi u Dubrovniku xiii-xvi veka, ed. J. Tadić, i: 1284–1499 (Belgrade, 1952).

Ivan Gundulić, 'Dubravka', trans. E. Goy, *BC Review*, 9/3 (October, 1976).

Ivan Gundulić, *Osman*, PSHK, 12/2 (1964).

Ivan Gundulić, *Osman*, trans. and introd. E. Goy (Zagreb, 1991).

Ivan Gundulić, *Suze sina razmetnoga, Dubravka, Ferdinandu drugome od Toskane*, PSHK, 12/1 (1964).

Krizman, B., 'Mémoire Bara Bettere austrijskom generalu T. Milutinoviću o Dubrovačkoj Republici iz 1815. godine', *Anali*, 1/1 (1952), 423–464.

Letopis popa dukljanina, ed. F. Šišić (Belgrade, 1928).

Lettres d'information de la république de Raguse (xviie siècle), ed. I. Dujčev, Godišnjak na sofijskija universitet istoričko-filologičeski fakultet, 33/10 (1937), 1–172.

Liber Croceus, ed. V. Nedeljković, SAN Zbornik za istoriju, jezik i književnost srpskog naroda, section III, book xxiv (1997).

Liber Omnium Reformationum Civitatis Ragusii, ed. A. Solovjev, Dubrovački zakoni i uredbe. Monumenta historico-juridica, 1. SKA Zbornik za istoriju, jezik i književnost srpskog naroda, section III, book 6 (1936).

Liber statutorum civitatis Ragusii compositus anno 1272 cum legibus aetate posteriore insertis atque cum summariis, adnotationibus et scholiis a veteribus iuris consultis Ragusinis additis, ed. V. Bogišić and C. Jireček, Monumenta historico-juridica Slavorum meridionalium, 9 (Zagreb, 1904).

Liber Statutorum Doane Ragusii MCCLXXVII. (Knjiga odredaba dubrovačke carinarnice 1277), ed. J. Lučić (Dubrovnik, 1989).

Liber Viridis, ed. V. Nedeljković, SAN Zbornik za istoriju, jezik i književnost srpskog naroda, section III, book xxiii (1984).

Libri Reformationum, ed. F. Rački, i, Monumenta spectantia historiam Slavorum meridionalium, 10 (Zagreb, 1879).

Idem, ii, Monumenta spectantia historiam Slavorum meridionalium, 13 (Zagreb, 1882).

Listine ob odnošajih između južnog slavenstva i Mletačke Republike, ed. Š. Ljubić, i, Monumenta spectantia historiam Slavorum meridionalium, 1 (Zagreb, 1868).

Lukarević, J. (See *Copioso ristretto*).

Knjiga o uredbama i običajima skupštine i občine otoka Lastova, ed. F. Radić, Monumenta historico-juridica Slavorum meridionalium, 8 (Zagreb, 1901).

Marin Držić, *Novela od Stanca, Tirena, Skup, Dundo Maroje*, PSHK, 6 (Zagreb, 1964).

Marin Držić, 'The Dream of Stanac (*Novela od Stanca*)', trans. E. Goy, *BC Review*, 17 (December, 1980), 3–17.

Marin Držić, *The Miser*, trans. S. Bičanić (Zagreb, 1968).

Miletii Versus, ed. A. K. Matas, Biblioteka za povijest dalmatinsku, part 1 (Dubrovnik, 1882).

Petar Hektorović, 'Fishing and Fishermen's Conversation', trans. E. Goy, *BC Review*, 15 (January, 1979).

Philippus de Diversis de Quartigianis de Lucca, *Situs Aedificiorum, Politiae et Laudabilium Consuetudinum Inclytae Civitatis Ragusii*, ed. V. Brunelli (Zadar, 1882).

Pisma opata Stjepana Gradića dubrovčanina senatu Republike Dubrovačke od godine 1667. do 1683., ed. Đ. Körbler, Monumenta spectantia historiam Slavorum meridionalium, 37 (Zagreb, 1915).

Pisma i uputstva Dubrovačke Republike, ed. J. Tadić, i, SKA Zbornik za istoriju, jezik i književnost srpskog naroda, Section III, book 4 (Belgrade, 1935).

Prilozi za istoriju zdravstvene kulture starog Dubrovnika, ed. R. Jeremić and J. Tadić, 2 vols. (Belgrade, 1938, 1939).

Serafino Razzi, *La Storia di Ragusa*, ed. G. Gelcich (Dubrovnik, 1903).

Spisi dubrovačke kancelarije, i. *Zapisi notara Tomazina de Savere (1278.–1282.)*, ed. G. Čremošnik, Monumenta historica Ragusina, I (Zagreb, 1951).

Stonske odredbe izdate g. 1333–1406 (Ordines Stagni editi annis 1333–1406), ed. A. Solovjev, Dubrovački zakoni i uredbe. Monumenta historico-juridica, 1. SKA Zbornik za istoriju, jezik i književnost srpskog naroda, section III, book 6 (1936).

Thomas Archidiaconus, *Historia Salonitana*, ed. F. Rački, Monumenta spectantia historiam Slavorum meridionalium, 26. Scriptores, III (Zagreb, 1894).

Secondary Sources

Antić, L., 'Dubrovačka Republika i međunarodno priznanje Sjedinjenih Američkih Država', *Međunarodni simpozij: diplomacija Dubrovačke Republike. Zbornik diplomatske akademije* (Zagreb, 1998), 259–264. (An English translation of the proceedings of this symposium has been published: *Diplomacy of the Republic of Dubrovnik*).

Antoljak, S., 'Konavoska buna u središtu jednog dijela Europske diplomacije (1799–1800)', *Rad*, 286, 107–141.

[Appendini, F. M.,] *De Vita et Scriptiis Junii Antonii comitis de Restiis, patricii Ragusini, Commentariorum Francisci Mariae Appendini e scholis piis* (in *Junii Antonii comitis de Restiis, patricii Ragusini, Carmina* (Padua, 1816)).

Appendini, F. M., *Notizie istorico-critiche sulle antichità, storia e letteratura de' Ragusei*, i (Dubrovnik, 1802).

Appendini, F. M., *Ratovanje oko Dubrovnika godine 1806*, ed. P. Kolendić and J. Nagy (Dubrovnik, 1906).

Aymard, M., *Venise, Raguse et le commerce du blé pendant la seconde moitié du xvie siècle. Ecole pratique des hautes études – VIe section. Centre de recherches historiques. Ports-Routes-Trafics*, xx (Paris, 1966).

Badurina, A., 'Iluminirani rukopisi', *Zlatno doba Dubrovnika XV. i XVI. stoljeće* [Exhibition Catalogue: Zagreb and Dubrovnik, 1987], 221–228, 364–367.

Badurina, A., 'Sakralna arhitektura', *Zlatno doba Dubrovnika XV. i XVI. stoljeće* [Exhibition Catalogue: Zagreb and Dubrovnik, 1987], 109–124, 324–330.

Bagoje, K., 'Knežev dvor u Pridvorju', *Konavle u prošlosti, sadašnjosti i budućnosti*, 1 (1998), 279–293.

Banac, I., *Main Trends in the Croatian Language Question* (Zagreb, 1990).

Banac, I., 'Ministration and Desecration: the Place of Dubrovnik in Modern Croat National Ideology and Political Culture', *Nation and Ideology. Essays in Honor of Wayne S. Vucinich*, ed. I. Banac, J. G. Ackerman and R. Szporluk, (Boulder: New York, 1981),149–175.

Banac, I., 'Political Themes in the Poetry of Mavro Vetranović', *American Benedictine Review*, 36/1 (1985), 23–43.

Banac, I., 'The Confessional "Rule" and the Dubrovnik Exception: The Origins of the "Serb-Catholic" Circle in Nineteenth Century Dalmatia', *Slavic Review*, 42/3 (Autumn 1983), 448–474.

Bautier, R-H., *The Economic Development of Mediaeval Europe* (London, 1971).

Bazala, V., 'Pomoski Lazareti u starom Dubrovniku', *Dubrovačko pomorstvo: u spomenu sto godina nautičke škole u Dubrovniku* (Dubrovnik, 1952), ed. J. Luetić *et al.*, 293–308.

Belamarić, J., 'Nikola Božidarević', *Prilozi povijesti umjetnosti u Dalmaciji*, xxxiv (1996), 121–140.

Belamarić, J., 'Kultura ladanja u renesansnoj Dalmaciji: slučaj Hektorovićeva Tvrdalja', *Prilozi povijesti umjetnosti u Dalmaciji*, xxxiv (1994), 169–192.

Belamarić, J., 'Sveti Vlaho i dubrovačka obitelj svetaca zaštitnika', *Dubrovnik*, New Series, 5/5 (1994), 29–29.

Beritić, L., *Dubrovačka artiljerija* (Belgrade, 1960).

Beritić, L., 'Dubrovački vodovod', *Anali*, 8–9 (1962), 99–116.

Beritić, L., 'Izgradnja i utvrđivanje gradske luke', *Dubrovačko pomorstvo: u spomenu sto godina nautičke škole u Dubrovniku* (Dubrovnik, 1952), ed. J. Luetić *et al.*, 285–292.

Beritić, L., 'Stonske utvrde', *Anali*, 3 (1954), 297–354.

Beritić, L., *The City Walls of Dubrovnik* (Dubrovnik, 1989).

Beritić, L., 'Ubikacija nestalih gradjevinskih spomenika u Dubrovniku', part 1, *Prilozi povijesti umjetnosti u Dalmaciji*, x (1956), 15–83.

Idem, part 2, *Prilozi povijesti umjetnosti u Dalmaciji*, xii (1960), 61–84.

Beritić, L., *Urbanistički razvitak Dubrovnika* ([Zagreb], n. d.).

Beritić, L., *Utvrđenja grada Dubrovnika* (Zagreb, 1955).

Beritić, L., 'Utvrđenja i regulacioni plan Cavtata', *Anali*, 12 (1970), 191–203.

Beritić, N., 'Iz povijesti kazališne i glazbene umjetnosti u Dubrovniku', *Otkrića iz arhiva: iz književne i političke povijesti Dubrovnika i Dalmacije u 18. i 19. stoljeću* (Split, 2000), 7–36.

Bersa, J., *Dubrovačke slike i prilike (1800–1880)* (Zagreb, 1941).

Biegman, N., *The Turco-Ragusan Relationship according to the Firmans of Murad III (1575–1595) extant in the State Archives of Dubrovnik* (The Hague, 1967).

Bjelovučić, H., *The Ragusan Republic, Victim of Napoleon and of Its Own Conservatism* (Leiden, 1970).

Blagojević, M., 'L'agricoltura nell'economia ragusea del Medioevo', *Ragusa e il Mediterraneo: ruolo e funzioni de una repubblica marinara tra medioevo ed età moderna.* Atti del convegno internationale di studi, Bari, 21–22 October 1988, ed. A. Di Vittorio (Bari, 1990), 27–44.

Bloed, A., Brinkman, M., van Goudever, A. P., and Rongen, W., 'A Missing Link in the Relations between the Northern Countries and Ragusa: Dutch-Ragusan Relationships in the 17th and 18th Centuries', *Dubrovnik's Relations with England: a Symposium, April 1978*, ed. R. Filipović and M. Partridge (University of Zagreb, 1977), 277–296.

Bogišić, R., 'Junije Palmotić', *O hrvatskim starim pjesnicima* (Zagreb, 1968), 327–344.

Bogišić, R. 'Marin Držić – Petrarkist', *O hrvatskim starim pjesnicima* (Zagreb, 1968), 157–167.

Bogišić, R. 'Pastorala Marina Držića', *O hrvatskim starim pjesnicima* (Zagreb, 1968), 187–219.

Božić, I., *Dubrovnik i Turska u xiv. i xv. veku* (Belgrade, 1952).

Bracewell, C. W., *The Uskoks of Senj: Piracy, Banditry, and Holy War in the Sixteenth Century Adriatic* (Ithaca, 1992).

Braudel, F., *The Mediterranean and the Mediterranean World in the Age of Philip II*, trans. S. Reynolds, i (London, 1972).

Breyer, M., 'Prilozi povijesti dubrovačkog štamparstva', *Zbornik iz dubrovačke prošlosti Milanu Rešetaru u 70-oj godišnjici života, ed. V. Ćorović et al.* (Dubrovnik, 1931), 339–347.

Brlek, M., *Rukopisi knjižnice male braće u Dubrovniku*, i (Zagreb, 1952).

Budak, N., *Prva stoljeća Hrvatske* (Zagreb, 1994).

Carter, F. W., *Dubrovnik (Ragusa): a Classic City State* (London, 1972).

Crveni teror u Dubrovniku, listopad 1944, Matica hrvatska Dubrovnik Posebna izdanja, 13 (1994).

Čremošnik, G., 'Dubrovački pečati srednjega vijeka', *Anali*, 4–5 (1956), 31–47.

Čremošnik, G., 'Postanak i razvoj srpske ili hrvatske kancelarije u Dubrovniku', *Anali*, i (1952), 73–84.

Čučić, V., 'Rat u Konavlima 1806.', *Konavle u prošlosti, sadašnjosti i budućnosti*, 1 (1998), 157–169.

Ćirković, S., *Istorija srednjovekovne bosanske države* (Belgrade, 1964).

Ćirković, S., *Herceg Stefan Vukčić-Kosača i njegovo doba* (Belgrade, 1964).

Ćirković, S., 'Ragusa e il suo retroterra nel Medio Evo', *Ragusa e il Mediterraneo: ruolo e funzioni de una repubblica marinara tra medioevo ed età moderna.* Atti del convegno internationale di studi, Bari, 21–22 October 1988, ed. A. Di Vittorio (Bari, 1990), 15–26.

Ćirković, S., 'The production of Gold, Silver and Copper in the Central Parts of the Balkans from the 13th to the 16th Century', Precious Metals in the Age of Expansion. Papers of the XIVth International Congress of the Historical Sciences, ed. H. Kellenbenz, *Beiträger zur Wirtschaftsgeschichte*, Band 2 (Stuttgart, 1981), 41–69.

Ćirković, S., and Kovačević-Kojić, D., 'L'Economie naturelle et la production marchande aux xiii xive siècles dans les régions actuelles de la Yougoslavie' (Recueil des travaux à l'hommage du professeur Radovan Samardžić), *Balcanica*, xiii-xiv (1982–1983), 45–56.

Ćosić, S., 'Dubrovačka granica i područje Kleka (presjek jednog problema iz diplomatske povijesti', *Međunarodni simpozij: diplomacija Dubrovačke Republike. Zbornik diplomatske akademije* (Zagreb), 203–217.

Ćosić, S., 'Dubrovački plemički i građanski rodovi konavoskog podrijetla', *Konavle u prošlosti, sadašnjosti i budućnosti*, 1 (1998), 47–75.

Ćosić, S., *Dubrovnik nakon pada Republike (1808.–1848.)* (Dubrovnik, 1999).

Ćosić, S., and Vekarić, N., 'Raskol dubrovačkog patricijata', *Anali*, 39 (2001), 305–379.

Dadić, Ž., 'Astrološki rad Gjina Gazullija u Dubrovniku u 15. stoljeću', *Egzaktne znanosti hrvatskoga srednjovjekovlja* (Zagreb, 1991), 121–130.

Dadić, Ž., 'Mathematical Views in Sixteenth Century Dubrovnik', *Dubrovnik Annals*, 1 (1997), 25–30.

Dadić, Ž., 'Mavro Vetranović kao astrolog', *Egzaktne znanosti hrvatskoga srednjovjekovlja* (Zagreb, 1991), 174–176.

Dadić, Ž., *Ruđer Bošković* (Zagreb, 1990).

Dayre, J., *Dubrovačke studije* (Zagreb, 1938).

Deanović, A., 'Marginalije o modrome pigmentu u dubrovačkom slikarstvu', *Prilozi povijesti umjetnosti u Dalmaciji*, xiii (1961), 248–265.

Deanović, M., *Anciens contacts entre la France et Raguse*, Biblioth čque de l'institut français de Zagreb, iii (Zagreb, 1950).
Deanović, M., 'Dnevnik M. Matijaševića', *Anali*, 1 (1952), 279–330.
Deanović, M., 'Talianski teatar u Dubrovniku xviii vijeka', *Zbornik iz dubrovačke prošlosti Milanu Rešetaru u 70-oj godišnjici života*, ed. V. Ćorović *et al.* (Dubrovnik, 1931), 289–305.
Demović, M., *Glazba i glazbenici u Dubrovačkoj Republici od početka xi. do polovine xvii. stoljeća* (Zagreb, 1981).
Demović, M., *Glazba i glazbenici u Dubrovačkoj Republici od polovine xvii. do prvog desetljeća xix. stoljeća* (Zagreb, 1989).
Demović, M., 'Glazbeni foklor Konavala', *Konavle u prošlosti, sadašnjosti i budućnosti*, 2 (1999), 155–263.
Demović, M., 'Veze glazbenika i slikara u renesansnom Dubrovniku', *Likovna kultura 15. i 16. stoljeća. Znanstveni skup uz izložbu 'Zlatno doba Dubrovnika'* (Zagreb, 1991), 260–267.
Dimitrijević, S., *Dubrovački karavani u južnoj Srbiji u xvii. veku*, SAN Posebna izdanja, 304 (1958), pp. 1–207
Dinić, M., 'Dubrovački tributi – Mogoriš, Svetodimitarski i Konavoski dohodak, Provižun braće Vlatkovića', *Glas SKA*, 168 (1935), 203–257.
Dinić, M., *Za istoriju rudarstva u srednjevekovnoj Srbiji i Bosni*, SAN Posebna izdanja, 240 (1955), pp. 1–109.
Dinić-Knežović, D., 'Petar Pantela – Trgovac i suknar u Dubrovniku', *Godišnjak filozofskog fakulteta u Novom Sadu*, xiii/1 (1970), 87–144.
Dinić-Knežović, D., *Položaj žena u Dubrovniku u xiii i xiv veku*, SAN Posebna izdanja, 469 (1974).
Dinić-Knežović, D., 'Trgovina žitom u Dubrovniku u xiv veku', *Godišnjak filozofskog fakulteta u Novom Sadu*, x (1967), 79–131.
Dinić-Knežović, D., 'Trgovina vinom u Dubrovniku u xiv veku', *Godišnjak filozofskog fakulteta u Novom Sadu*, ix (1966), 39–85.
Dujčev, I., 'A propos de l'historiographie de Dubrovnik' (Recueil des travaux à l'hommage du professeur Radovan Samardžić), *Balcanica*, xiii-xiv (1982–1983), 97–103.
Đurić, V., *Dubrovačka slikarska škola*, SAN Posebna izdanja, 363 (1963).
Fine, J., *The Bosnian Church: a New Interpretation. A Study of the Bosnian Church and its Place in State and Society from the 13th to the 15th Centuries* (New York, 1975).
Fine, J., *The Early Mediaeval Balkans: a Critical Survey from the Sixth to the Late Twelfth Century* (University of Michigan Press, 1991).
Fine, J., *The Late Mediaeval Balkans : a Critical Survey from the Late Twelfth Century to the Ottoman Conquest* (University of Michigan Press, 1994).
Fisković, C., 'Dubrovački brodovi na zavjetnim slikama u muzejskom prostoru u Zagrebu', *Likovna kultura 15. i 16. stoljeća. Znanstveni skup uz izložbu 'Zlatno doba Dubrovnika'* (Zagreb, 1991), 239–241.
Fisković, C., 'Dubrovački zlatari od xiii. do xvii. stoljeća', *Starohrvatska prosvjeta*, series iii, vol. 1 (1941), 143–249.
Fisković, C., *Kultura dubrovačkog ladanja (Sorkočevićev ljetnikovac na Lapadu)* (Split, 1966).

Fisković, C., 'Lastovski spomenici', *Prilozi povijesti umjetnosti u Dalmaciji*, xvi (1966), 5–152.
Fisković, C., 'Neobjavljeno djelo Blaža Jurjeva u Stonu', *Prilozi povijesti umjetnosti u Dalmaciji*, 13 (1961), 114–132.
Fisković, C., 'Neobjavljeno djelo Jurja Dalmatinca u Dubrovniku', *Anali*, 1/1 (1952), 145–150.
Fisković, C., 'Pozornice Držićevih igara', *Baština starih hrvatskih pisaca* (Split, 1971), 308–329.
Fisković, C., *Prvi poznati dubrovački graditelji* (Dubrovnik, 1955).
Fisković, I., 'Djelo Filipa Diversisa kao izvor poznavanja umjetnosti i kulture Dubrovnika', *Dubrovnik*, 30 1–3 (1987), 232–249.
Fisković, I., 'Kiparstvo', *Zlatno doba Dubrovnika XV. i XVI. stoljeće* [Exhibition Catalogue: Zagreb and Dubrovnik, 1897], 125–167, 331–346.
Foretić, V., *Otok Korčula u srednjem vijeku do g. 1420* (Zagreb, 1940).
Foretić, V., *Povijest Dubrovnika do 1808.*, 2 vols. (Zagreb, 1980).
Foretić, V., 'Vjekovne veze Dubrovnika i Korčule', *Dubrovnik*, 8/4 (1965), 18–54.
Franičević, M., *Povijest hrvatske renesansne književnosti* (Zagreb, 1983).
Franičević, M., Švelec, F., and Bogišić, R., *Od Renesanse do Prosvjetiteljstva. Povijest hrvatske književnosti*, iii (Zagreb, n. d.).
Franić, A., *Svećenici mučenici: svjedoci komunističkog progona* (Dubrovnik, 1996).
Franolić, B., *An Historical Survey of Literary Croatian* (Paris, 1984).
Franolić, B., *Works of Croatian Latinists Recorded in the British Library General Catalogue* (London, 1997).
Fučić, B., *Croatian Glagolitic Epigraphy* (London, 1999).
Fučić, B., and Kapetanić, N., 'A Glagolitic Inscription in Konavle', *Dubrovnik Annals*, 3 (1999), 7–11.
Gamulin, G., *The Painted Crucifixes in Croatia* (Zagreb, 1983).
Goldstein, I., *Hrvatski rani srednji vijek* (Zagreb, 1995).
Grmek, M., 'Le Concept d'infection dans l'antiquité et au moyen âge, les anciennes mesures sociales contre les maladies contagieuses et la fondation de la première quarantaine à Dubrovnik (1377)', *Rad*, 384 (1980), 1–55.
Gruber, D., 'Borba Ludovika I. s Mlečanima za Dalmaciju (1348–1358)', *Rad*, 152 (1903)
Grujić, N., 'Dubrovačka ladanjska arhitektura 15. stoljeća i Gučetićev ljetnikovac u Trstenom', *Prilozi povijesti umjetnosti u Dalmaciji*, xxxiv (1994), 141–167.
Grujić, N., *Ladanjska arhitektura dubrovačkog područja* (Zagreb, 1991).
Grujić, N., 'Ladanjsko-gospodarska arhitektura 15. i 16. stoljeća na otoku Šipan', *Zbornik dubrovačkog Primorja i otoka*, 2 (1988), 223–274.
Grujić, N., 'Reprezentativna stambena arhitektura', *Zlatno doba Dubrovnika XV. i XVI. stoljeće* [Exhibition Catalogue: Zagreb and Dubrovnik, 1987], 65–108, 307–323.
Grujić, N., 'Some Aspects of the Renovation of Dubrovnik Summer Residences', *The Restoration of Dubrovnik 1979–1989*, ed. B. Letunić (Zagreb, 1990), 346–363.
Grujić, R., 'Konavli pod raznim gospodarima od xii. do xv. veka', *Spomenik SKA*, lxvi (1926), 3–122.

Gulin, A., 'Srednjovjekovni dubrovački kaptol: utemeljenje, ustroj i djelatnost', *Tisuću godina dubrovačke (nad)biskupije: zbornik radova znanstvenoga skupa u povodu tisuće godina uspostava dubrovačke (nad)biskupije/metropolije (998.–1998.)*, ed. Ž. Puljić and N. A. Ančić (Dubrovnik, 2001), 175–196.

Ibler, V., 'Međunarodnopravni subjektivitet i vanjskopolitička nezavisnost Dubrovačke Republike', *Međunarodni simpozij: diplomacija Dubrovačke Republike. Zbornik diplomatske akademije* (Zagreb, 1998), 49–59.

Inalcik, H., *An Economic and Social History of the Ottoman Empire* (Cambridge, 1994).

Inalcik, H., 'Dubrovnik i Otomansko Carstvo', *Međunarodni simpozij: diplomacija Dubrovačke Republike. Zbornik diplomatske akademije* (Zagreb, 1998), 113–116.

Inalcik, H., 'Lepanto in the Ottoman Documents', *The Ottoman Empire: Conquest, Organisation and Economy. Collected Studies* (London 1978), 185–192.

Inalcik, H., *The Ottoman Empire : the Classical Age 1300–1600*, trans. N. Itzkowitz and C. Imber (London, 1973).

Ivančević, V., 'O brodogradnji u Dubrovniku potkraj Republike', *Anali*, 3 (1954), 559–579.

'Izvještaj gosp. La [*sic*] Maire, francuzkoga konsula u Koronu o Dubrovačkoj Republici', *JAZU Starine*, xiii (1881), 38–118.

Janeković-Römer, Z., *Okvir slobode: Dubrovačka vlastela između srednjovjekovlja i humanizma*, HAZU, Prilozi povijesti stanovništva i okolice Dubrovnika, book 8 (Dubrovnik, 1999).

Janeković-Römer, Z., 'Priznanje krune Sv. Stjepana – izazov dubrovačke diplomacije', *Međunarodni simpozij: diplomacija Dubrovačke Republike. Zbornik diplomatske akademije* (Zagreb, 1998), 293–301.

Janeković-Römer, Z., *Rod i grad. Dubrovačka obitelj od xiii do xv stoljeće.* HAZU Prilozi povijesti stanovništva Dubrovnika i okolice, book 4 (Dubrovnik, 1994).

Javarek, V., 'Marin Držić: A Ragusan Playwright', *The Slavonic and East European Review*, 37/38 (December, 1958), 141–159.

Jireček, C., *Die Bedeutung von Ragusa in der Handelsgeschichte des Mittelalters. Die feierliche Sitzung der kaiserlichen Akademie der Wissenschaften am 31. Mai 1893* (Vienna, 1893).

Jireček, C., *Die Handelsstrassen und Bergwerke von Serbien und Bosnien während des Mittelalters*, Abhandlungen der königlichen bömischen Gesellschaft der Wissenschaften vom Jahre 1879 und 1880, vi. Folge, 10. Band (Prague, 1881).

Kačić, H., 'Razgovor pod slikom Josipa Broza', *Dubrovački horizonti*, 27/36 (1996), 152–156.

Kadić, A., 'Marulić and Držić: the Opposite Poles of the Croatian Renaissance', *The Tradition of Freedom in Croatian Literature* (Bloomington, 1983), 19–33.

Kapetanić, N., and Vekarić, N., *Stanovništvo Konavala*, i, HAZU Prilozi povijesti stanovništva Dubrovnika i okolice, book 7 (Dubrovnik, 1998).

Kategorizacija ratnih šteta na stambenim objektima: Općina Konavle, Komisija za popis i procjenu ratne štete u općini Dubrovnik (Dubrovnik, February 1993).

Kisić, A., 'Pomorska ikonografija u likovnoj kulturi Dubrovnika 15. i 16. stoljeća', *Likovna kultura 15. i 16. stoljeća. Znanstveni skup uz izložbu 'Zlatno doba Dubrovnika'* (Zagreb, 1991), 242–249.

Knecht, R., *Francis I* (Cambridge, 1982).

Kojaković, V., *Dubrovnik u privatnom životu* (Dubrovnik, 1933).

Kombol, M., *Povijest hrvatske književnosti do preporoda* (Zagreb, 1961).
Korade, M., Aleksić, M., and Matoš, J., *Isusovci i hrvatska kultura* (Zagreb, 1993).
Kostić, V., *Dubrovnik i Engleska 1300–1650*, SAN Posebna izdanja, 488 (Belgrade, 1975).
Kostić, V., 'The Ragusan Colony in London in Shakespeare's Day', *Dubrovnik's Relations with England: a Symposium, April 1978*, ed. R. Filipović and M. Partridge (University of Zagreb, 1977), 261–273..
Kostić, V., 'Ragusa and the Spanish Armada', *Dubrovnik's Relations with England: a Symposium, April 1978*, ed. R. Filipović and M. Partridge (University of Zagreb, 1977), 47–61.
Košćak, V., 'Epidaurum – Ragusium – Laus – Dubrovnik', *Anali*, 27 (1989), 7–39.
Košćak, V., 'Polemika o pripadnosti dubrovačke književnosti 1967. godine', Velikosrpska svojatanja Dubrovnika: Dubrovnik u ratu, *Dubrovnik*, New Series, 3/2–3 (1992), 462–474.
Kovačić, S., 'Dubrovačka metropolija tijekom višestoljetne krize, do ukidanja i preustroja dotadašnje nadbiskipje u sadašnu dubrovačku biskupiju u travnu 1820.', *Tisuću godina dubrovačke (nad)biskupije: zbornik radova znanstvenoga skupa u povodu tisuće godina uspostava dubrovačke (nad)biskupije/metropolije (998.–1998.)*, ed. Ž. Puljić and N. A. Antić (Dubrovnik, 2001), 253–274.
Krasić, S., 'Dubrovnik i dominikanci', *Dubrovački horizonti*, 2/5 (Spring, 1970), 57–60.
Krasić, S., *Stjepan Gradić (1613–1683). Život i djelo* (Zagreb, 1987).
Krasić, B., and Razzi, S., *Povijest dubrovačke metropolije i dubrovačkih nadbiskupa (x.-xvi. stoljeća)* (Dubrovnik, 1999).
Krekić, B., 'Developed Autonomy: the Patricians in Dubrovnik and Dalmatian Cities', *Dubrovnik: a Mediterranean Urban Society, 1300–1600* (Aldershot, 1997), 185–215.
Krekić, B., *Dubrovnik: A City between East and West* (Norman, Oklahoma, 1972).
Krekić, B., 'Dubrovnik (Ragusa) and the War of Tenedos/Chioggia (1378–1381)', *Dubrovnik, Italy and the Balkans in the Late Middle Ages* (London, 1980), 1–34.
Krekić, B., *Dubrovnik (Raguse) et le Levant au moyen âge.* Documents et recherches sur l'économie des pays byzantins, islamiques et slaves et leurs relations commerciales au moyen âge, v (Paris, 1961).
Krekić, B., 'Four Florentine Commercial Companies in Dubrovnik (Ragusa) in the First Half of the Fourteenth Century', *Dubrovnik, Italy and the Balkans in the Late Middle Ages* (London, 1980), 25–41.
Krekić, B., 'Images of Urban Life: Contributions to the Study of daily Life in Dubrovnik at the Time of Humanism and the Renaissance', *Dubrovnik: a Mediterranean Urban Society, 1300–1600* (Aldershot, 1997), 1–38.
Krekić, B., 'Influence politique et pouvoir économique a Dubrovnik (Raguse) du xiiie au xvie siècle', *Dubrovnik: a Mediterranean Urban Society, 1300–1600* (Aldershot, 1997), 241–258.
Krekić, B., 'Italian Creditors in Dubrovnik (Ragusa) and the Balkan Trade, Thirteenth through 14th Centuries', *Dubrovnik, Italy and the Balkans in the Late Middle Ages* (London, 1980), 241–254.

Krekić, B., 'L'Abolition de l'esclavage à Dubrovnik (Raguse) au xve siècle: mythe ou réalité?', *Dubrovnik: a Mediterranean Urban Society, 1300–1600* (Aldershot, 1997), 309–317.

Krekić, B., 'Le rôle de Dubrovnik (Raguse) dans la navigation des *mudae* venitiennes au xive siècle', *Dubrovnik: a Mediterranean Urban Society, 1300–1600* (Aldershot, 1997), 247–254.

Krekić, B., 'On the Latino-Slavic Cultural Symbiosis in Late Mediaeval and Renaissance Dalmatia and Dubrovnik', *Dubrovnik: a Mediterranean Urban Society, 1300–1600* (Aldershot, 1997), 321–332.

Krekić, B., 'Ragusa (Dubrovnik) e il mare: aspetti e problemi (xiv-xvi secolo)', *Dubrovnik: a Mediterranean Urban Society, 1300–1600* (Aldershot, 1997), 131–151.

Krekić, B., [Review of F. W. Carter, *Dubrovnik (Ragusa): a Classic City State*], *Slavic Review*, 33/2 (1974), 386–387.

Krekić, B., 'The Attitude of Fifteenth Century Ragusans Towards Literacy', *Dubrovnik: a Mediterranean Urban Society, 1300–1600* (Aldershot, 1997), 225–232.

Krekić, B., 'The Role of the Jews in Dubrovnik (Thirteenth-Sixteenth Centuries)', *Dubrovnik, Italy and the Balkans in the Late Middle Ages* (London, 1980), 257–271.

Krivošić, S., *Stanovništvo Dubrovnika i demografske promjene u prošlosti*, HAZU Prilozi povijesti stanovništva Dubrovnika i okolice, book 1 (Dubrovnik, 1990).

Krizman, B., *Diplomati i konzuli u starom Dubrovniku* (Zagreb, 1957).

Krizman, B., *O dubrovačkoj diplomaciji* (Zagreb, 1951).

Kurtović, E., 'Motivi Sandaljeve prodaje Konavala dubrovčanima', *Anali*, 38 (2000), 103–120.

Lane, F., *Venice: a Maritime Republic* (Baltimore, 1973).

Lentić, I., *Dubrovački zlatari* (Zagreb, 1984).

Lentić, I., 'Zlatarstvo', *Zlatno doba Dubrovnika XV. i XVI. stoljeće* [Exhibition Catalogue: Zagreb and Dubrovnik, 1987], 229–270.

Letunić, B., ed., *The Restoration of Dubrovnik 1979–89* (Zagreb, 1990). (See also entries for separate articles.)

Lewis, P. S., *Later Mediaeval France – the Polity* (London, 1968).

Likovna kultura 15. i 16. stoljeća. Znanstveni skup uz izložbu 'Zlatno doba Dubrovnika' (Zagreb, 1991). (See also entries for separate articles).

Lonza, N., 'Izborni postupak Dubrovačke republike', *Anali*, 38 (2000), 9–52.

Lonza, N., 'O dubrovačkom diplomatskom ceremonialu', *Međunarodni simpozij: diplomacija Dubrovačke Republike. Zbornik diplomatske akademije* (Zagreb, 1998), 169–176.

Lonza, N., *Pod plaštem pravde: kaznenopravni sustav Dubrovačke Republike u XVIII. stoljeću* (Dubrovnik, 1997).

Lučić, J., [Review of I. Mahnken, *Dubrovački patricijat u xiv veku*] *Historijski zbornik*, xvii (1964), 393–411.

Lučić, J., 'Dubrovčani na jadranskom prostoru od vii. stoljeća do godine 1205.', *Dubrovačke teme* (Zagreb, 1991), 5–49.

Lučić, J., 'Gospodarsko-društveni odnosi u Stojkovićevo vrijeme (1392–1442)', *Historijski zbornik*, 38–1 (1985), 95–114.

Lučić, J., 'Iz prošlosti Župe Dubrovačke (do polovice xiv stoljeća)', *Zbornik Župe Dubrovačke*, 1 (1985), 87–99.

Lučić, J., 'Najstarija zemljišna knjiga u Hrvatskoj – dubrovački zemljišnik diobe zemlje u Stonu i Pelješcu iz god. 1336', *Dubrovačke teme* (Zagreb, 1991), 104–151.
Lučić, J., 'Političke i kulturne prilike u Dubrovniku na prijelazu xiii. u xiii. stoljeće', *Dubrovačke teme* (Zagreb, 1991), 50–79.
Lučić, J., 'Povijest Dubrovnika od vii. stoljeća do godine 1205.', *Anali*, 13–14 (1976), 7–139.
Lučić, J., 'Prošlost otoka Lastova u doba Dubrovačke Republike', *Lastovski statut*, ed. V. Rismondo *et al.* (Split, 1994), 7–111.
Lučić, J., 'Pučki zborovi na Lopudu i Koločepu od 17. do 19. stoljeća', *Zbornik Dubrovačkog Primorja i otoka*, 2 (1988), 41–63.
Lučić, J., 'Pučki zborovi na Mljetu', *Zbornik otoka Mljeta*, 1 (1989), 183–225.
Lučić, J., 'Stjecanje, dioba i borba za očuvanje dubrovačkog primorja (1399–1405)', *Arhivski vjesnik*, xi-xii (1968–1969), 99–201.
Lučić, J., 'Uprava u Župi Dubrovačkoj', *Zbornik Župe Dubrovačke*, 1 (1985), 100–124.
Luetić, J., *O pomorstvu Dubrovačke Republike u xviii stoljeću* (Dubrovnik, 1959).
Luetić, J., 'Pomorac i diplomat Vice Bune', *Anali*, 1/1 (1952), 255–267.
Luetić, J., *Brodovlje Dubrovačke Republike xvii stoljeća* (Dubrovnik, 1964).
Luetić, J., *Pomorci i jedrenjaci Republike Dubrovačke* (Zagreb, 1984).
Lukić, B., 'Diplomatski odnosi i sukob između Dubrovačke Republike i Maroka u xviii. stoljeću', *Anali*, 3 (1954), 545–558.
Macan, T., 'Dubrovački barabanti u xvi stoljeću', *Anali*, 8–9 (1962), 301–323.
Macan, T., *Rt Oštra u povijesti i politici* (Zagreb, 1998).
Mack Smith, D., *Mediaeval Sicily: 800–1713* [*A History of Sicily*, i] (New York, 1968).
Mahnken, I., *Dubrovački patricijat u xiv veku*, SAN Posebna izdanja, 340 (1960).
[Maixner, R.], 'La Traduction française del' 'Osman'', *Annales de l'institut français de Zagreb*, 2/5–6 (1938).
Malcolm, N., *Kosovo: A Short History* (London, 1998).
Marinović, A., 'Dubrovačka legislacija glede prosjačkih redova', *Samostan male braće u Dubrovniku*, ed. J. Turčinović (Zagreb, 1985), 34–71.
Marković, V., 'Slikarstvo', *Zlatno doba Dubrovnika XV. i XVI. stoljeće* [Exhibition Catalogue: Zagreb and Dubrovnik, 1987], 169–220 and 347–363.
[Marshal Marmont], *Mémoires du duc de Raguse de 1792 à 1832*, 6 vols. (Paris, 1857).
Martinović, I., 'Humanist, filozof, i teolog Juraj Dragišić', *Dubrovnik*, New Series, 6/4 (1995), 213–230.
Martinović, I., 'Rađanje 'Ujedinjene Amerike' – diplomatski izazov za Ruđera Boškovića', *Međunarodni simpozij: diplomacija Dubrovačke Republike. Zbornik diplomatske akademije* (Zagreb, 1998), 265–271.
Matanić, A., 'Franjevački Dubrovnik u svom povijesnom presjeku', *Samostan Male braće u Dubrovniku*, ed. J. Turčinović (Zagreb, 1985), 29–36.
Medini, M., *Dubrovnik Gučetića*, SAN Posebna izdanja, 210 (1953), 1–131.
Mesić, S., *Kako je srušena Jugoslavija* (Zagreb, 1994).
Mihailović, J., *Seizmički karakter i trusne katastrofe našeg južnog primorja*, SAN Posebna izdanja, 140 (1947).
Mimica, B., *Numizmatička povijest Dubrovnika* (Rijeka, [1996]).
Miović-Perić, V., *Na razmeđu: osmansko-dubrovačka granica (1667.–1806)* (Dubrovnik, 1997).

Miović-Perić, V., 'Što je prethodilo katastrofi 1806.?' *Konavle u prošlosti, sadašnjosti i budućnosti*, 1 (Dubrovnik, 1998), 147–156.
Mitić, I., *Dubrovačka država u međunarodnoj zajednici (od 1358. do 1815.)* (Zagreb, 1988).
Mitić, I., *Konzuli i konzularna služba starog Dubrovnika* (Dubrovnik, 1973).
Mitić, I., Primjer pružanja crkvenog azila u dubrovačkom samostanu Male braće tijekom xvii stoljeća', *Samostan Male braće Dubrovnika*, ed. J. Turčinović (Zagreb, 1985), 405–411.
Mitrović, J., *Srpstvo Dubrovnika* (Belgrade, 1992).
Moguš, M., *A History of the Croatian Language: Towards a Common Standard* (Zagreb, 1995).
Montani, M., *Juraj Dalmatinac i njegov krug* (Zagreb, 1967).
Muljačić, Ž., 'Istraga protiv Jakobinaca 1797. god. u Dubrovniku', *Anali*, 2 (1953), 235–252.
Muljačić, Ž., 'Kako je A. Fortis pripremao za drugo francusko izdanje 'Puta po Dalmaciji' novo poglavlje o Dubrovniku', *Anali*, 17 (1979), 229–250.
Muljačić, Ž., 'O strankama u starom Dubrovniku', *Anali*, 6–7 (1959), 25–40.
Ničetić, A., 'O nekim navigacijskim aspektima plovidbe svetoga Pavla od Krete do Melite', *Anali*, 38 (2000), 305–370.
Ničetić, A., *Povijest dubrovačke luke* (Dubrovnik, 1996).
Novak, G., 'Nobiles, populus i cives – komuna i universitas u Splitu 1525.–1707.', *Rad*, 286 (1952), 5–40.
Novak, G., 'Povijest Dubrovnika od najstarijih vremena do početka vii. stoljeća (do propasti Epidauruma)', *Anali*, 10–11 (1966), 3–84.
Novak, G., *Prošlost Dalmacije*, i (Zagreb, 1944).
Novak, G., 'Vunena industrija u Dubrovniku do sredine xvi stoljeća', *Zbornik iz dubrovačke prošlosti Milanu Rešetaru o 70-oj godišnjici života*, ed. V. Ćorović *et al.* (Dubrovnik, 1931), 99–107.
Obad, S., Dokoza, S., and Martinović, S., *Južne granice Dalmacije od 15. stoljeća do danas* (Zadar, 1999).
Ostojić, I., *Benediktinci u Hrvatskoj*, ii (Split, 1964).
Paci, R., 'La concorrenza Ragusa-Spalato tra fine Cinquecento e prime Seicento', *Ragusa e il Mediterraneo: ruolo e funzioni de una repubblica marinara tra medioevo ed età moderna.* Atti del convegno internationale di studi, Bari, 21–22 October 1988, ed. A. Di Vittorio (Bari, 1990), 185–196.
Pantić, M., 'Gučetić, Nikola Vidov', *Leksikon pisaca Jugoslavije*, ii (Belgrade, 1979), 326–327.
Pavlović, D.,'O krizi vlasteostog staleža u Dubrovniku', *SAN Zbornik radova*, book 17 (1952), 27–38.
Pederin, I., 'Putni dnevnik Cara Franje I. o Dubrovniku (1818. godine)' *Anali*, 17 (1979), 431–464.
Peković, Ž., 'Développement de l'ensemble de la cathédrale de Dubrovnik', *Hortus Artium Mediaevalium*, i (1995), 162–168.
Pisani, P., *La Dalmatie de 1797 à 1815*, 2 vols. (Paris, 1892).
Pivčević, E., 'Konrad von Grünemberg's Visit to Croatian Coastal Towns in 1486', *BC Review*, 17 (December 1980), 23–42.

Planić-Lončarić, M., 'Organizacija prostora – urbanizam', *Zlatno doba Dubrovnika XV. i XVI. stoljeće* [Exhibition Catalogue: Zagreb and Dubrovnik, 1987], 33–64, 289–306.

Planić-Lončarić, M., *Planirana izgradnja na području Dubrovačke Republike*, Studije i monografije, Institut za povijest umjetnosti, book 1 (Zagreb, 1980).

Planić-Lončarić, M., 'Ston u 15. i 16. stoljeću', *Likovna kultura Dubrovnika 15. i 16. stoljeća. Znanstveni skup uz izložbu 'Zlatno doba Dubrovnika'* (Zagreb, 1991), 39–45.

Popović, T., *Turska i Dubrovnik u xvi. veku* (Belgrade, 1973).

Portolan, E., 'Prilog o unutrašnjoj opremi renesansne kuće u Dubrovniku', *Likovna kultura 15. i 16. stoljeća. Znanstveni skup uz izložbu 'Zlatno doba Dubrovnika'* (Zagreb, 1991), 267–270.

Povijesne i statističke bilješke o Dubrovačkom okrugo prikupio okružni inženjer Lorenzo Vitelleschi, Dubrovnik, 1827 (Notizie storiche e statistiche del Circolo di Ragusa compilate dall' ingegnere Lorenzo Vitelleschi, Ragusa, 1827), ed. V. Lupis (Dubrovnik, 2002).

Powell, C., with Persico, J., *A Soldier's Way: An Autobiography* (London, 1995).

Prijatelj, K., *Dalmatian Painting of the 15th and 16th Centuries* (Zagreb, 1983).

Prijatelj, K., *Dubrovačko slikarstvo xv-xvi stoljeća* (Zagreb, n. d.).

Prijatelj, K., *Slikar Blaž Jurjev* (Zagreb, 1965).

Prijatelj, K., 'Slikari xvii i xviii stoljeća u Dubrovniku', *Starohrvatska prosvjeta*, Third Series, i (1949), 250–278.

Prlender, I., 'Internacionalizacija krize u praksi diplomatske službe Dubrovačke Republike u dva primjera', *Međunarodni simpozij: diplomacija Dubrovačke Republike. Zbornik diplomatske akademije* (Zagreb, 1998), 219–231.

Puljić, I., 'Uspostava dubrovačke metropolije', *Tisuću godina dubrovačke (nad)biskupije: zbornik radova znanstvenoga skupa u povodu tisuće godina uspostava dubrovačke (nad)biskupije/metropolije (998.–1998.)*, ed. Ž. Puljić and N. A. Antić (Dubrovnik, 2001), 15–56.

Putanec, V., 'Naziv Labusedum iz 11. stoljeća za grad Dubrovnik', *Rasprave zavoda za hrvatski jezik*, xix (1993), 289–302.

Queller, D., *The Venetian Patriciate – Reality versus Myth* (Urbana and Chicago, 1986).

Ralić, P., *Short History of Dubrovnik* (Belgrade, 1992).

Rapanić, Ž., 'Archaeological Explorations in Dubrovnik after the Earthquake', *The Restoration of Dubrovnik 1979–89*, ed. B. Letunić (Zagreb, 1990), 339–345.

Ravlić, J., 'Odraz domaće stvarnosti u dubrovačkoj književnosti: Ivan Gundulić i njegova Dubravka', *Anali* 6/7 (1956), 323–354.

Reed, R., 'Satirical Devices in Marin Držić's Play 'The Miser'', *Slavic and East European Journal*, 21/3 (Autumn, 1977), 366–377.

Rešetar, M., *Dubrovačka numizmatika*, i, SKA Posebna izdanja, 48 (1924).

Rešetar, M., *Dubrovačka numizmatika*, ii, SKA Posebna izdanja, 59 (1925).

Rešetar, M., 'Kako su pretstavljene Držićeve drame', *Marin Držić 1508–1958*, ed. H. Pantić (Belgrade, 1958), 347–358.

Rezar, V., 'Dubrovački humanistički historiograf Ludovik Crijević Tuberon', *Anali*, 37 (1999), 47–94.

Rheubottom, D., *Age, Marriage, and Politics in Fifteenth-Century Ragusa* (Oxford, 2000).

Roller, D., *Agrarno-proizvodni odnosi na području Dubrovnika od xiii. do xv. stoljeća*, Građa za gospodarsku povijest Hrvatske, 5 (Zabreb, 1952).

Roller, D., *Dubrovački zanati u xv. i xvi. stoljeću*. Građa za gospodarsku povijest Hrvatske, 2 (Zabreb, 1951).

Rothenburg, G. E., 'Christian Insurrections in Turkish Dalmatia 1580–96', *The Slavonic and East European Review*, 40 (1961), 136–147.

Rusko, I., 'Stanje dubrovačke trgovačke mornarice pred samu propast Dubrovačke Republike početkom xix. stoljeća', *Dubrovačko pomorstvo: u spomenu sto godina nautičke škole u Dubrovniku* (Dubrovnik, 1952), ed. J. Luetić *et al.*, 205–222.

Samardžić, R., *Borba Dubrovnika za opstanak posle velikog zemljotresa 1667 godine. Arhivska građa (1667–1670)*, SAN Zbornik za istoriju, jezik i književnost srpskog naroda, section III, book xix (1960).

Samardžić, R., *Veliki vek Dubrovnika* (Belgrade, 1962).

Skok, P., 'Iz dubrovačkog vokabulara', *Zbornik iz dubrovačke prošlosti Milanu Rešetaru o 70-oj godišnjici života*, ed. V. Ćorović *et al.* (Dubrovnik, 1931), 429–433.

Soloviev [*sic*], A., 'Le Patriciat de Raguse au xve siècle', *Zbornik iz dubrovačke prošlosti Milanu Rešetaru o 70-oj godišnjici života*, ed. V. Ćorović *et al.* (Dubrovnik, 1931), 59–66.

Sopta, J., 'Reformacija i Tridentinski sabor u Dubrovniku', *Tisuću godina dubrovačke (nad)biskupije: zbornik radova znanstvenoga skupa u povodu tisuće godina uspostava dubrovačke (nad)biskupije/metropolije (998.–1998.)*, ed. Ž. Puljić and N. A. Antić (Dubrovnik, 2001), 379–395.

Spremić, M., *Dubrovnik i Aragonci 1442–1495* (Belgrade, [1971]).

Stojan, S., *Anica Bošković* (Dubrovnik, 1999).

Stojan, S., *U salonu Marije Giorgi Bona* (Dubrovnik, 1996).

Stošić, J., 'Research Finds and display problems connected with the area below the Cathedral and Bunićeva Poljana', *The Restoration of Dubrovnik 1979–89*, ed. B. Letunić (Zagreb, 1990), 326–335.

[Stulli, B.], 'Dubrovačka Republika', *Enciklopedija Jugoslavije* (Zagreb, 1984), 607–652.

Stulli, B., 'O 'knjizi statuta grada Dubrovnika' iz god. 1272', *Dubrovnik*, 1–2/15 (1972), 17–26.

Stulli, B., *Židovi u Dubrovniku* (Zagreb, 1989).

Suić, M., *Antički grad na istočnom Jadranu* (Zagreb, 1976).

Šanjek, F., 'The Studies of Exact and Natural Sciences in the History of Dubrovnik', *Dubrovnik Annals*, 1 (1997), 9–24.

Šehović, F., *Dubrovački ratni dnevnik: Zla kob zaborava* (Zagreb, 1994).

Šifler-Premec, L., *Nikola Gučetić* (Zagreb, 1977).

Šišić, B., *Dubrovački renesansni vrt: nastajanje i oblikovanje obilježja* (Dubrovnik, 1991).

Šišić, F., *Vojvoda Hrvoje Vukčić Hrvatinić i njegovo doba* (1350–1416.) (Zagreb, 1902).

Šundrica, Z., 'Dubrovačka vlastela i konavoski knezovi', *Konavoski zbornik*, 1 (1982), 44–53.

Šundrica, Z., ' Stonski rat u xiv stoljeću (1333–1339)', *Pelješki zbornik*, 2 (1980), 73–190.

Švelec, F., *Komički teatar Marina Držića* (Zagreb, 1968).

Tadić, J., *Dubrovački portreti* (Belgrade, 1948).

Tadić, J., *Jevreji u Dubrovniku do polovine xvii stoljeća* (Sarajevo, 1937).

Tadić, J., 'Le Port de Raguse et sa flotte au xvie siècle', *Le Navire et l'économie maritime du moyen âge au xviiie siècle principalement en Méditerranée – Travaux du deuxième colloque international d'histoire maritime tenu, les 17 et 18 mai 1957, à l'Académie de Marine*, 9–26.

Tadić, J., 'O pomorstvu Dubrovnika u xvi i xvii veku', *Dubrovačko pomorstvo: u spomenu sto godina nautičke škole u Dubrovniku* (Dubrovnik, 1952), ed. J. Luetić *et al.*, 165–188.

Tadić, J., 'Pomorsko osiguranje u Dubrovniku xvi stoljeća', *Zbornik iz dubrovačke prošlosti Milanu Rešetaru o 70-oj godišnjici života*, ed. V. Ćorović *et al.* (Dubrovnik, 1931), 109–112.

Tadić, J., *Promet putnika u starom Dubrovniku* (Dubrovnik, 1939).

Tadić, J., *Španija i Dubrovnik u xvi. veku* (Belgrade, 1932).

Tanner, M., *Croatia: A Nation Forged in War* (New Haven and London: Yale, 1997).

Tenenti, A., and B., *Il prezzo del rischio. L'assicurazione mediterranea vista da Ragusa: 1563–1591* (Venice, 1985).

The Restoration of Dubrovnik 1979–89, ed. B. Letunić (Zagreb, 1990). (See also entries for separate articles).

Thompson, J. M., *Napoleon Bonaparte* (Oxford, 1988).

Torbarina, J., 'A Croat Forerunner of Shakespeare: In Commemoration of the 400th Anniversary of the Death of Marin Držić', *Studia Romanica et Anglica Zagrabiensia*, 24 (December 1967), 5–21.

Torbarina, J., *Italian Influence on the Poets of the Ragusan Republic* (London, 1931).

Vanino, M., *Isusovci i hrvatski narod*, 2 vols (Zagreb, 1969 and 1970).

Vekarić, N., 'Broj stanovnika Dubrovačke Republike u 15., 16., i 17. stoljeću', *Anali*, 29 (1991), 7–22.

Vekarić, N., 'Opsade Dubrovnika i broj stanovnika', *Dubrovnik*, 4/2 (1993), 240–244.

Vekarić, N., 'Sud janjinske kapitanije', *Anali*, 27 (1989), 133–147.

Vekarić, S., 'Podaci o dubrovačkim brodovima za vrijeme i nakon francuske okupacije', *Anali*, 2 (1953), 359–368.

Vekarić, S., 'Prilozi za povijest pelješkog pomorstva u xvii. i xviii. stoljeću', *Anali*, 3 (1954), 527–544.

Vekarić, S. and Vekarić, N., 'Tri stoljeća pelješkog brodarstva', *Pelješki zbornik*, 4 (1987).

Vinaver, V., 'Trgovina bosanskim robljem tokom xiv veka u Dubrovniku', *Anali*, 2 (1953), 125–147.

Vitelleschi, L., (See *Povijesne i statističke bilješke*).

Vittorio, A. Di, 'Gli investimenti finanziari ragusei in Italia tra XVI e XVIII secolo', in A. Di Vittorio, *Tra mare e terra. Aspetti economici e finanziari della Repobblica di Ragusa in età moderna* (Bari, 2001), 37–78.

Voïnovitch, L. de, *La Monarchie française dans l'Adriatique: Histoire des relations de la France avec la République de Raguse* (Paris, 1918).

Voje, I., *Kreditna trgovina u srednjovjekovnom Dubrovniku*, Akademija nauka i umjetnosti Bosne i Hercegovine, Djela, 49 (Sarajevo, 1976).

Vojnović, K., 'Crkva i država u Dubrovačkoj Republici', *Rad*, 119 (1894), 32–142.

Vojnović, L., *Pad Dubrovnika*, 2 vols. (Zagreb, 1908).

Vučetić, A., *Sveti Vlaho u Dubrovniku* (Dubrovnik, 1924).

Waley, D., *The Italian City-Republics* (London, 1969).

Warnier, R., 'Comment un consul de France décrit au directoire la civilisation ragusaine', *Zbornik iz dubrovačke prošlosti Milanu Rešetaru u 70-oj godišnjici života*, ed. V. Ćorović *et al.* (Dubrovnik, 1931), 157–164.

West, R., *Black Lamb and Grey Falcon*, 2 vols. (London, 1942).

Zdravković, I., *Dubrovački dvorci: analiza arhitekture i karakteristika stila* (Belgrade, 1951).

Zlatar, Z., *Between the Double Eagle and the Crescent: the Republic of Dubrovnik and the Origins of the Eastern Question* (Boulder, 1992).

Zlatar, Z., *Our Kingdom Come: the Counter-Reformation, the Republic of Dubrovnik, and the Liberation of the Balkan Slavs* (Boulder, 1992).

Zlatar, Z., 'The 'Crisis' of the Patriciate in Early Seventeenth Century Dubrovnik: A Reappraisal', *Balcanica*, VI (1975), 111–131.

Zlatar, Z., *The Slavic Epic: Gundulić's Osman* (New York, 1995).

Zlatno doba Dubrovnika XV. i XVI. stoljeće [Exhibition Catalogue: Zagreb and Dubrovnik, 1987]. (See also entries for separate articles).

Živojinović, D., *Američka Revolucija i Dubrovačka Republika, 1763–1790* (Belgrade, 1976).

Županović, Š., *Ribarstvo Dalmacije u 18. stoljeću* (Split, 1993).

Sources for Illustrations

Dubrovnik State Archive – plates 1–12, 19, 40
Dominican Friary, Dubrovnik – plates 21, 23, 29–32, 35, 39, 45
Church of St Blaise, Dubrovnik – plates 43, 49
Lopud Parish Museum – plate 22
Dubrovnik City Museum – plates 24, 46
Church of Our Lady at Danče, Dubrovnik – plates 25–27, 33–34
Franciscan Church, Cavtat – plate 28
Church of St Stephen at Sustjepan, Dubrovnik – plate 36
Church of Our Lady of Mercy, Dubrovnik – plates 37–38
Dubrovnik Cathedral Treasury – plate 48
Plate 52, photograph taken by the late Miro Kerner, is reproduced by kind permission of his family

Index

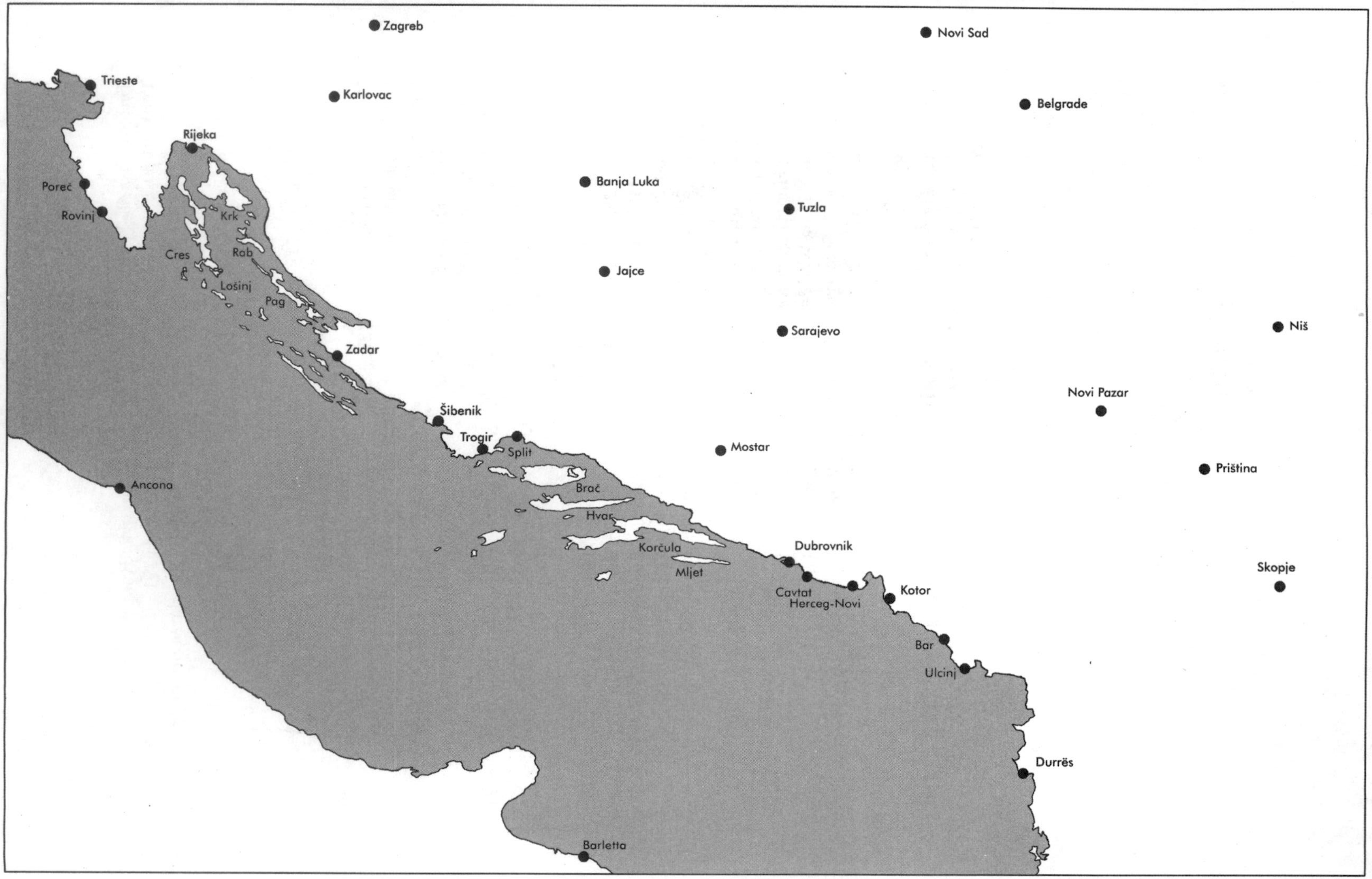

Dalmatia and South-East Europe